JEFFERSON IN POWER

THOMAS JEFFERSON
From the life mask by Browere

JEFFERSON
IN POWER

The
Death Struggle
of the
Federalists

CLAUDE G. BOWERS

with illustrations

SENTRY   EDITION

1967

HOUGHTON MIFFLIN COMPANY BOSTON
The Riverside Press Cambridge

PREFACE

THE eight dramatic years of Jefferson's two Administrations marked the consolidation of the triumph of democracy after the ten-year struggle I have described in 'Jefferson and Hamilton.' Since some distinguished historians have written bitterly partisan interpretations of this period, out of the fullness of their fierce hate of Jefferson, it can scarcely be amiss, or in bad taste, for one who is frankly partial to Jeffersonian principles and policies to tell the story of these two Administrations as he finds it written luminously in the record.

It was a lusty period, by no means so sedate as is the popular impression — a period of marching mobs, of rebellions more brazen than that of Shays, of backstairs gossip and back-room intrigues, of whispering campaigns and political assassinations. The fighting was continuous, always bitter, often brilliant, and by no means confined to the reasonably dignified polemics of politicians. Men of light and leading occasionally engaged in common tavern brawls, many deliberated in House and Senate with guns in their pockets, and statesmen crept from their homes and boarding-houses in the chilly dawn to face one another on 'the field of honor' at Bladensburg.

Again Hamilton, in the shining armor of his genius, rides right gallantly upon the scene. In some ways he has changed under the skies, so gray to him, of Jeffersonian domination. But that which will impress us most about him will be his pathetic isolation. We shall find him frequently at odds with the Federalist leaders, who will continue to pay him lip service while utterly ignoring his advice. He cannot share their treasonable attitude on the acquisition of Louisiana; he will not join them in their bitter battle against a new and necessary constitutional amendment. He will

stand four square against the secession movements to which the
most impressive portion of his party will give adherence. He will
refuse to join them in their conspiracy to raise Aaron Burr to
gubernatorial honors, and he will pay the penalty of his opposition
with his life.

Midway of our story, this Homeric figure will pass to history.

No Federalist ever after was to wear his mantle or to wield his
mighty sword. The most scintillating of the congressional leaders
of the party were as insects crawling on the earth, compared with
Jefferson. The real leadership of the Federalists passed to John
Marshall, a consummate, constant, and bitterly partisan politician, who fought with far-seeing cunning from behind the protecting shield of the Supreme Court.

These were, on the whole, eight remarkably brilliant years,
though the anti-Jefferson historians are careful to convey no such
impression. They were years of unprecedented prosperity. The
industrial life of the nation developed rapidly. The management
of the finances was brilliantly successful. There was a complete
absence of scandal in administration. The federal judiciary was
purged of the indecencies that were destroying faith in its im-
partiality, integrity, or justice, though the partisan historian has
smugly called this purgation an 'attack on the courts.' The
acquisition, without the shedding of a drop of blood, of an empire, from which many of the richest commonwealths of the
nation have been carved, was a memorable and immortal triumph.

And we shall follow, in a more sympathetic manner than has
been fashionable among the sword-rattlers of the ivory tower,
Jefferson's superb effort, in the utter collapse of all international
law, to find, in economic pressure, a civilized substitute for the
savagery of war.

Perhaps the really tragic note of this narrative comes from the
demoralization and degeneration of the brilliant Federalist Party
that for years had sparkled with the genius of Hamilton. Maddened by electoral rebukes, instead of seeking wisdom in the
warnings of Hamilton, it sought revenge alone. Defeated in this,
it invited chaos, and adopted the destruction of the Union as a
party policy. We shall have to follow its leaders to secret conferences with the enemies of the Republic, as they skirt, where

they do not cross, the boundary line of treason; and we shall see them slinking from the secret sessions of the Senate to betray their country to the envoys of unfriendly Powers. The anti-Jeffersonian historians have been much too tender with the Federalists of the days of their degeneracy and treason, partly, perhaps, because, in the damning of Jefferson, it has been found convenient to accept as truth the fallacies and falsehoods which wrought the ruin of the desperate and unscrupulous politicians who gave them currency. There is ineffable pathos in the death struggle of this once great party, and the story is offered as a warning to all succeeding political parties and politicians that public opinion cannot be defied with impunity.

I have sought to re-create, as flesh and blood, the characters of the drama, and such characters! — Jefferson and Hamilton, Marshall and Burr, Madison and Monroe, Randolph of Roanoke and Gouverneur Morris, Fisher Ames, Timothy Pickering, and Josiah Quincy. Never has the stage of American history been so crowded with the picturesque, the clever and profound.

And I have tried to paint in the social background of their political activities, and to present a picture of the crude but interesting country-town capital in the days when Jefferson sometimes received guests in carpet slippers. Perhaps some will think the amusements simple, as Bayard did, but it may not be without interest to many to find Humboldt rummaging among the papers on Jefferson's desk, Gilbert Stuart bewildered by the flock of pretty women in his crowded studio, Robert Fulton illustrating his torpedo in the waters of Rock Creek, Tom Moore scenting the card-tables with his exotic perfumes, Jerome Bonaparte and 'Glorious Betsy' feeding malicious gossip on juicy fare, Captain Pike gallantly posing as a bachelor for the delectation and deception of the ladies, and Mistress Merry 'exhibiting' at the Capitol. And if, by chance, we break in on Turreau, the French Minister, lashing his wife while his accomplished secretary plays wildly on the fife to drown her screams, we shall do no more than Washingtonians did in the days of Jefferson.

As in the writing of 'Jefferson and Hamilton,' I have resorted generously to that rich mine of history in the rough — the newspapers of the time.

To tell the truth, as it appears to me; to disclose the leaders on both sides of the struggle in disarray and covered with the sweat of conflict; to picture the actors off the stage and out of their full-dress uniforms; to make them men and not mere steel engravings; and to sweep away a part of the débris of political and historical propaganda — such is the purpose of this story of Plutarchian days.

CLAUDE G. BOWERS

MADRID, *February* 7, 1936

CONTENTS

ILLUSTRATIONS

JEFFERSON IN POWER

CHAPTER I

Mayfair in the Mud

I

IF YOUNG ladies and their contriving mothers in the days of Jefferson were not eager to journey to Washington for such official society as it had to offer, it was due, in part, to the hardships and dangers of travel. The roads leading to the little capital from any point of the compass were wretched beyond description. Jefferson faring forth to, and from, Virginia usually rode horseback to spare both his carriage and his body. The roads were streaks of mud, with innumerable ruts. Streams frequently were unbridged. The taverns along the way were abominations of dirt and poor accommodations. Through the correspondence of the statesmen of those days runs a constant current of self-commiseration over the miseries of these journeys. The majority went by coach. This was little better than a box mounted on springs, without doors or windows or any protection from the summer rains and the winter winds beyond leathern curtains that could be raised when the day was fair. Into this were crowded all sorts and conditions of both sexes. To the New-Englanders, the journey seemed interminable and intolerable. Timothy Pickering would leave his home in Salem and reach Hartford after four days of hard driving. Another day would find him in New Haven. Two days more, and he would reach New York. Thence, crossing the Hudson by ferry, he would proceed to Philadelphia, riding day and night through torrential rains, fording swollen streams whence the bridges had been washed away. Another day of riding, day and night, would find him in Baltimore. Thence, on to Washington, the roads were fit for the pencil of a Doré, the coach sinking into ruts that

seemingly were bottomless, and into mud up to the hubs. Not
infrequently the coach would be upset by the shying of the
horses in the moonlight to escape a miry slough.[1] To prevent an
upset the coachman, approaching a dangerous rut or gully,
would request the passengers to move 'first to the right side and
then to the left to prevent a catastrophe.'[2] While the robust
Pickering would make good time from New York by riding day
and night, Gouverneur Morris, more devoted to his comfort,
would go by easier stages and take eleven days.[3] Senator Samuel
Latham Mitchill, more impatient, would ride from New York
to Philadelphia without rest, sleeping in the cold coach, and
consoling himself at Francis Tavern by supping on partridge
and turtle.[4] Burr found the road from Baltimore persecution.
Once when descending a bad hill the harness broke, the horses
took fright, and had not one of them got his leg over the pole,
he wrote Theodosia, 'the poor world would have been deprived
of the heir-apparent to all its admiration and glory.[5] On another
occasion, returning from Annapolis to the capital over the same
road, he was lost to the Senate for a day 'by the swelling of the
waters of the Patusent.'[6] So dangerous were the roads from the
South that Senator Giles, en route, was thrown from his carriage
and crippled for life.[7] The wife of Josiah Quincy throughout her
life was to recall these journeys to Washington with horror.[8]

And as the bruised and unhappy traveler drove into the crude
town with its scattered houses, over mud roads, little better than
those of the country, the reward seemed scarcely worth the suffering in the coach and taverns. Despite the high-sounding name
of the Tiber, a tiny sandy stream with a boulder bottom, which
crossed Pennsylvania Avenue at Second Street, there was nothing
in the new capital to suggest imperial Rome. Could the visitor

[1] C. K. Upham, *Life of Timothy Pickering*, IV, 94–95; 101–02. (Cited hereafter as
Pickering.)

[2] Ann Carey Morris, *Diary and Letters of Gouverneur Morris*, II, 393–95.

[3] *Ibid.*

[4] Dr. Samuel L. Mitchill's 'Letters from Washington,' *Harper's Magazine*, April, 1879

[5] Matthew L. Davis, *Memoirs of Aaron Burr*, II, 241. (Cited hereafter as *Burr*.)

[6] Charles Francis Adams, *Memoir of John Quincy Adams*, I, 281. (Cited hereafter as
Adams, *Diary*.)

[7] *Pickering*, IV, 96.

[8] Edmund Quincy, *Life of Josiah Quincy*, 72. (Cited hereafter as *Quincy*.)

have looked down upon the town from a height, he would have noted, first, two buildings a mile apart on the Avenue. On the east, a large unfinished stone structure of promise — the Capitol; on the west, the President's Mansion. Around the former, fifteen or sixteen buildings were grouped, crudely built of wood, and most of these were boarding-houses of ten or twelve rooms. A washerwoman occupied one, and the rest were modest shops where a shoemaker, a tailor, a printer, a grocer, a stationery and dry-goods merchant plied their trade. Nothing rewarded the eye along the mile stretch of the Avenue but a muddy road with numberless ruts and puddles and an occasional brick or wooden building. In rainy weather this Avenue was all but impassable because of the yellow clinging mud, and in dry weather the wind swirled blinding dust in the passer's eyes.

About the President's Mansion were five or six brick houses seated in lonely isolation. Beyond, on the Avenue in the direction of Georgetown, were a few more pretentious brick houses, including a row which statesmen of distinction occupied. Such was Washington proper at the beginning of the Jefferson Administration, meager enough, and yet there had been an increase of sixty-five per cent in the number of houses since Adams had taken possession. Very soon Jefferson would disturb the masters of the purse-strings by spending something less than twelve thousand dollars on the improvement of the Avenue, including the planting of Lombardy trees.

Looking from the height toward Georgetown, a more promising prospect greeted the eye, something of charm and beauty in the narrow Old-World streets lined with trees, with a few brick mansions of excellent architecture, dreaming in their gardens.

The disgusted statesmen recalled with poignant pain all they had lost in leaving Philadelphia with its wealth and fashionable houses. Gouverneur Morris not unnaturally was crushed by the outlook. 'We only need more houses, cellars, kitchens, scholarly men, amiable women and a few other such trifles to possess a perfect city,' he wrote satirically.[1] Others were quite content, since the hunting was good within the city limits! The less

[1] Morris, *Diary*, II, 393–95.

fastidious Manasseh Cutler found 'the situation much more
delightful' than he had expected, since 'the ground in general is
elevated, mostly cleared and commands a pleasing prospect of
the Patomac River.'¹ Small as the town was, it had its problem
of poverty among workingmen, for employment was sporadic,
and during the intervals they found themselves dependent on
charity. Out on the wastes, they built rude huts for shelter,
or took possession of unfinished houses begun during the madness of speculation and now crumbling to ruin. Conspicuous
enough was the public whipping-post.

And yet, as we shall find, there was a society, much gaiety,
with beautiful, attractive and daring women and brilliant men.

II

Let us fancy ourselves a contemporary and fare forth on pleasure
bent to dinners, parties, balls, and on familiar calls at the homes
and boarding-houses of this Mayfair in the mud. Naturally
we turn first to the acknowledged leader of Washington society,
the Mrs. Bingham of the democratic régime, beginning a reign
which is to continue, with a brief interruption, for thirty years.
Dolly Madison, wife of the Secretary of State, has just moved
into the new house planned by Dr. Thornton on F Street between Thirteenth and Fourteenth,² conspicuous for its cupola
and for its wine section occupying half the cellar space.³ The
clever pretty little Quakeress, widowed as a girl, and wooed by
Aaron Burr in the Philadelphia days before he made the blunder
of introducing 'little Madison,' is in the full bloom of her charm.
Her irresistible appeal is in her zest for life, her spontaneous
response to gaiety in others. Physically pleasing, well-formed,
and with pretty features, she moves with easy grace. 'She
moves a goddess and she looks a queen,' exclaims one of her
contemporaries.⁴ 'She has a fine person and a most engaging
countenance which pleases not so much from mere symmetry
or complexion as from expression,' rhapsodizes one of the most
intellectual and sober of senators. 'Her smile, her conversation

¹ A. C. Clark, *Life and Letters of Dolly Madison*, 48.
² Present site of the Adams Building.   ³ *Life of Dolly Madison*, 46.
⁴ Margaret Bayard Smith, *First Forty Years of Washington Society*.

and her manners are so engaging that it is no wonder that such
a young widow with her fine blue eyes and large share of animation should be indeed a queen of hearts.'[1] 'Mrs. Madison,' says
Gouverneur Morris, a gallant and an expert in feminine charms,
'has a good disposition from which the shriveled condition of
the Secretary are the less to be wondered at.'[2] 'Mrs. Madison
is still pretty,' observes Burr, who had found in her one castle
that remained none the less attractive because it could not
be stormed, 'but oh that unfortunate propensity to snuff-taking.'[3]
We catch a glimpse of her driving back from Georgetown, a
bit troubled over her winnings at cards, and making a mental
resolution to abandon the vice — until tempted again — and
we shall see her frequently in our meanderings, a white silk
turban on her head, with large ostrich feathers hanging over
her face.[4] Since we shall prolong our sojourn in the city, we
shall see her often. Let us begin by going to dinner.

We enter the house with the cupola immediately to be impressed by the absence of stiff formality. We are in an atmosphere
of Virginia hospitality, and the ease and familiarity of the blithesome Dolly and the cordial Madison, who loses his solemnity
in the presence of women, relieve us of all restraint. All about
us we see one of the secrets of our hostess's social popularity —
a bevy of beautiful women and very young and pretty girls.
Here is Ann Payne, the charming sister, but recently married
in a brilliant ceremony to Richard D. Cutts; here the famous
beauty, Mrs. Van Ness, already celebrated for her charms as
Marcia Burnes; Ann Randolph; Harriet Stoddert, attractive
daughter of Adams's Secretary of the Navy and soon to marry
a Jeffersonian leader of the House — Dolly's lure to tired statesmen. And these, the most distinguished, we see about us. At
the table even Madison unbends and stoops to puns, bantering
the ladies. And such a dinner! The impressionable Cutler is
delighted. 'The round of beef of which the soup is made is
called Boulli. It had in the dish spices and something of the
sweet herb and Garlic kind, and a rich gravy,' he writes glow-

---

[1] Mitchill's Letters.   [2] Morris, *Diary*, II, 417.
[3] Burr to Theodosia, *Burr*, II, 242.
[4] Mrs. Smith; *Life of Dolly Madison*, 53.

ingly. 'We had a dish with what appeared to be Cabbage, much
boiled, then cut in long strings and somewhat mashed; in the
middle a large ham with the cabbage around. The Desert good;
much as usual except two dishes which appeared like Apple pie
in the form of a half of a musk melon, the flat side down, top
creased, and the color a dark brown.' ¹ An elaborate dinner,
with the best of imported vintages — costly service. The lofty
Mrs. Merry, wife of the British Minister, of whom we shall
hear much, is a bit critical. 'More like a harvest home supper
than the entertainment of a Secretary of State,' she complains.
But Dolly, unruffled and not impressed, replies that the 'profusion
so repugnant to foreign customs arises from the happy circumstance of abundance and prosperity in our country.' Yes, she
would not hesitate 'to sacrifice the delicacy of European taste
for the less elegant but more liberal fashion of Virginia.' ²

And liberal indeed is the entertainment in the house on F
Street. Madison, politically ambitious, does not neglect the
politicians of the capital, as the frequency of his stag dinners
testifies.³ 'A very good disposition,' smugly comments Gouverneur Morris when Dolly takes the wife of the ruined Robert Morris under her kindly wing.⁴ After the stag dinners, the ladies are
invited in for cards and the hostess presides over the loo tables
far into the night.⁵ Many are the card-parties at the Madisons',
and often receptions with men and women. 'Went with the
ladies to a party at Mr. Madison's,' writes Adams. 'There was a
company of about seventy persons.' Cards, gossip, flirtations —
and political discussions in corners. Does not the too serious
Adams draw his host from the congenial company of the ladies
to drag him into a full exposition of his navigation policy? ⁶
Thus the Madisons keep open house and it is seldom without
guests; and it is never dull.

III

Almost as popular is the salon of Mrs. Bayard Smith, wife of
the Jeffersonian editor of the *National Intelligencer*. A keenly

¹ Manasseh Cutler, *Life, Journal, and Correspondence*, II, 154.
² *Life of Dolly Madison*, 65.   ³ Adams, *Diary*, I, 416.
⁴ Morris, *Diary*, II, 417.   ⁵ Adams, *Diary*, I, 416.   ⁶ *Ibid.*, 408.

intelligent and pretty young woman, but recently married, she has both a social flair and a relish for politics. The kindliness of Jefferson had won her heart completely and for eight years he is to have a no more faithful champion. Her youth, charm, intelligence soon make her home a rallying-ground for the most interesting men, and literally she keeps open house without attempting pretentious entertaining. At her home on New Jersey Avenue near the Capitol one may always count on finding company, for morning calls are fashionable in the reign of Jefferson. Let us call.

There is Madame's favorite among women, Madame Louis André Pichon, young and winsome wife of the French Chargé d'Affaires, for long an almost inseparable companion.[1] The attractive wife of Bayard, the Federalist leader, is glancing over a manuscript of ominous length, a poem called 'Agitation' which Thomas Law, who dabbles in poetry and love, has sent to the hostess for her delectation. Mrs. Gallatin comes in to arrange for a shopping expedition on the morrow, and Mrs. Thomas Tingey, whose husband is in command at the Navy Yard, stops for a chat. She is a lively and cordial lady and has taken the young bride to her heart.[2] At the fireplace, Mrs. Smith is listening to Peter Pederson, the young Danish Chargé d'Affaires, who has the habit of appearing almost daily and lingering long.[3] Sometimes when conversational topics are exhausted on his prolonged sojourns, Mrs. Smith settles herself comfortably and makes him read to her.[4]

We make an evening call, and find much the same company, with a few congressmen added, the stiff and stately Van Cortlandt of New York among them. Here, too, is Dr. May, a young physician, clever in the planning of winter entertainments. 'Very merry over the successive dishes of fine oysters' they are, and Captain Tingey sings, accompanied by his wife and daughters.[5]

Dinners, dances, teas, card-parties thickly sprinkle the letters the lady writes, and Washington in the mud seems far from dull and dreary. But soon she has a more attractive rendezvous

[1] Mrs. Smith, 33.   [2] *Ibid.*, 2; 18.
[3] *Ibid.*, 56–57.   [4] *Ibid.*, 56.   [5] *Ibid.*, 18–19.

to offer, a country place called 'Sydney,' which, seated in the
midst of trees and flowers, becomes a center for political conversations.[1]

A typical scene there in springtime: A rumble of carriages
on the country road, and soon the passengers alight in front
of the door — Dolly Madison with her turban, and her distinguished spouse 'in one of his most sportive moods,' with
Dr. Thornton, the architect, and his wife. Madison teases the
ladies, Thornton philosophizes, and, with ceremony tabooed,
they sit and chatter on the benches under the trees, or swing in
the hammocks, or walk in the garden, until Mrs. Thornton's
curiosity leads her through the kitchen to the milk-house, when
all are summoned to wonder and admire. But often there are
more serious scenes beneath the trees when Gallatin, Madison,
and the Administration leaders of House and Senate go into a
huddle on the policies of state and party.[2]

Mayfair in the mud is gay from necessity. 'There is no alternative in this place between gay company and perfect solitude,' writes a lady of fashion.[3] 'I have often gone out with
the ague,' she writes, 'and sometimes with fever on me, so much
has habit done in reconciling one to this enemy. I know that
nothing will keep off the fit, and I may as well have it in one
place as another.'[4] But the houses of entertainment are all
too few, and society is confined to the homes of the Cabinet
members and a few rich residents, such as Marcia Van Ness
who has a mansion, the Thomas Laws and Charles J. Nourse
and the Georgetown gentry.

The Laws are an interesting couple and their nuptials had
delighted the heart of the master of Mount Vernon. He is a
nephew of Lord Ellenborough, and she a descendant of Lord
Baltimore. Their home becomes a social center and not a few
distinguished foreigners enjoy its hospitality.[5] But at this time,
only a few years after the promising beginning, shadows are
falling on the house. Law is a quiet man, dabbling in poetry,
and his pretty wife is said to think too highly of worldly pleas-

---

[1] It still stands on the grounds of the Catholic University.
[2] Mrs. Smith, 51.   [3] *Ibid.*, 45.   [4] *Ibid.*, 33.
[5] Ann Wharton, *Social Life of the Early Republic*, 67. (Hereafter cited as *Social Life.*)

ures.[1] Hers is the most gorgeous chariot of her time, and hers, to the outward seeming, the gayest of homes. Here gather many of the belles, and hither in pursuit come the young beaux, and some who have aged a bit without suspecting it. Burr lives with the Laws for a time and is content. 'We make a pleasant society here,' writes this fastidious gallant, 'so that one may get through the winter without ennui. I live at Mrs. Law's, not nominally, but in fact.' [2]

Out to the 'Highlands,' beyond Georgetown, across the road from 'Friendship,' Nourse frequently summons the statesmen to choice dinners. On one of his visits there Jefferson plants some shrubbery which thrives after a century. Pickering, his enemy, often sits about the board with leading Federalists.[3] However the personnel of the men guests may change, Marcia Van Ness is always present.

IV

The burden of sustaining the social end of the Administration falls on the Madisons, Gallatins, Smiths, and Dearborns of the Cabinet. The Gallatins have a house on M Street near Thirty-Second, and they give dinners and card-parties, and their friends come and go with the same informality as at the Madisons'. Daughter of Commodore Nicholson, with an established social position in New York, she had married Gallatin in her twenty-sixth year. Her early environment and contacts had fitted her as the wife of a politician. In her father's home she had been a friend of Burr, Clinton, and the Livingstons, and she had no love for Hamilton. Among her early friends, in his better days, was Thomas Paine. Gallatin has painted her portrait with an almost ungallant restraint. 'Her person,' he wrote a friend at the time of his marriage, 'is far less attractive than either her mind or her heart, and yet I do not wish her to have any other than that which she has got. . . . I can read in her face the expression of her soul; and as to her shape and size you know my taste. . . . She is possessed of the most gentle disposition. Her understanding is good; she is as well informed as most young ladies; she is perfectly

[1] Mrs. Smith, 2.
[2] Burr to Theodosia, *Burr*, ii, 172.   [3] *Social Life*, 88–89.

simple and unaffected; she loves me and she is a pretty good democrat.'[1] Mrs. Smith finds her 'extremely friendly.' She is in her thirty-fourth year when she assumes her duties in official society.

The Dearborns are generous in their entertaining — especially with their champagne. If taken in moderation, Madison observes at one of the Dearborn dinners, after a few bottles are consumed, 'champagne is most delightful,' but 'more than a few glasses always produces a headache the next morning.' 'Fine!' exclaims Granger, the Postmaster-General. 'This is the very time to try the experiment since tomorrow, being Sunday, we shall have time to recover from the effect.' The host agrees, and bottle after bottle is consumed, 'without, however,' comments a lady present, 'the least invasion of sobriety.'[2]

But it is in the home of Robert Smith, Secretary of the Navy, that the most elaborate entertainments are given — balls, dinners, cards, receptions. A wealthy man, he can afford it; a society man, he likes it.

Burr abandons his residence with the Laws to take a house on F Street, soon to become famous for its elegant stag dinners for the politicians. Soon the *Columbian Centinel* is announcing that 'the Vice President supports more the style of a gentleman here than any other of his sect. He is extremely unpopular among the Jacobins and I greatly mistake if he does not give "the greatest man in America" much discomfiture.'[3] Though on the verge of bankruptcy, he acquires a handsome chariot and lives like a grand seigneur. Handsome, brilliant, captivating to women and fascinating to men, he is the object of ceremonious attention. His unattached state makes him the more interesting, though his thoughts are on Mars rather than Venus. 'I had liked to have forgotten to say a word in reply to your inquiries of matrimony which must seem to indicate that I have no plan on the subject,' he writes Theodosia. 'Such is the fact. ... Yet I ought not to conceal that I have had a most amiable overture from a lady who is "always employed at something useful." ... If I should meet her and she should challenge me, I shall probably strike at once.'[4]

[1] Henry Adams, *Life of Albert Gallatin*, 99; 109.
[2] Mrs. Smith, 35.   [3] March 13, 1802.   [4] *Burr*, I, 151.

He fairly drips suavity with men he hopes to find useful. John Quincy Adams, walking to the Capitol, and taken into Burr's carriage, is much impressed when asked particularly about his father. 'He spoke of his social intimacy with him when he was senator,' Adams writes in his diary.[1] But when, a little later, Adams dines at Burr's with a company of politicians, he notes that Mr. Burr is a man of very insinuating manners and address.'[2] Distinguished foreigners are certain of an invitation to his board, and when nineteen-year-old Jerome Bonaparte appears in Washington he is given a breakfast 'à la Français at twelve o'clock.'[3] Burr is not the man to neglect the brother of Napoleon.

v

Most of the statesmen, shut up in dingy boarding-houses, are in no position to return their social obligations. They make a virtue of necessity and receive without giving. Though Washington has hotels, it does not appear that the politicians use them as living quarters. In the beginning of Jefferson's second Administration, Pontius D. Stelle removes from his cramped quarters on Capitol Square to the 'spacious hotel lately erected by Mr. Carroll near the Capitol,' and, making much of the 'hundred-foot front,' invites travelers to patronize his fifty-room hostelry.[4] Soon it becomes such a social center that it is the custom to leave letters at the bar 'to be called for.'[5] Meyer's Tavern, advertising twenty-six rooms and fireplaces, is situated on the Avenue near the center market, and the host is making much of the fact that 'the celebrated ridge spring is conveyed in places to the yard of this hotel, where it supplies the whole neighborhood with flowing cool water, to which the general health of this city has in a great measure been attributed.'[6] The Anchor Tavern, within view of Mason's Island on the river, features its beefsteak and oyster dinners, and boasts of 'a copious and elegant garden with rural walks where a despairing lover can meditate on the object of his

---

[1] Adams, *Diary*, i, 179.

[2] *Ibid.*, i, 288.   [3] *Ibid.*, ii, 250.

[4] *National Intelligencer*, November 13, 1805.

[5] *New York Evening Post*, December 23, 1805.

[6] *National Intelligencer*, November 27, 1805.

affections, and the man of pleasure can pass away many a dull
and tedious hour.'[1]

Even so, the statesmen are drawn to the boarding-houses, and
within the precincts of their crowded quarters they make a social
life of their own, though scarcely reminiscent of the golden days
in Philadelphia. The tables are turned. The more elaborate
entertaining is that of the Democrats. The dour John Quincy
Adams complains not at all of his lot in a boarding-house. He
rises at seven, works in his room until nine, breakfasts at ten,
and walks to the Capitol. The session over, he trudges back,
dines, and passes the evening quietly, unless invited out with the
ladies, and sups at ten. By eleven the lights are out. But, within
the four walls of the boarding-house, he is not without elevating
and profitable pleasures which he shares with his fellow boarders.
'Read part of a play this evening to the ladies — The Marriage
Promise. But it was so bad that I could not finish it.'[2] 'Read
to the ladies in the evening.'[3] 'Mr. and Mrs. Huger and Mr.
Purviance, member of Congress from N. C., passed the evening
with us' — recording a blue-ribbon evening.[4] 'Read also the
first act of Hamlet to the ladies ... later the Merry Wives of
Windsor.'[5] Such the merry routine of the Adams boarding-house.

The boarding-house of Pickering, Federalist leader in the
Senate, no less drab, is less given to cultural improvement.
Eleven members from New England take a house not far from the
Capitol 'with a landlord and landlady most obliging.'[6] They walk
to the Capitol, but 'the roads are good.' In another session sixteen
Federalists board together, 'and all agreeable.' Senator Tracy
is among them and gives a touch of gaiety to the life with daily
'sallies of his wit.'[7] Unhappily each session finds the mess broken
up, but always a few of the old crowd, with accessions from among
the Federalists, find a boarding-house that pleases. Once Pickering, with Hillhouse, has to board two miles from the Capitol
and walk the distance, though 'the road is very good.' Each has
a room to himself, but only Hillhouse and Pickering have fireplaces
to drive the chill away.[8]

[1] Washington Federalist, October 4, 1803.   [2] Adams, Diary, I, 271.
[3] Ibid., I, 274.   [4] Ibid., I, 280.   [5] Ibid., I, 290.
[6] Pickering, IV, 68.   [7] Ibid., IV, 95.   [8] Ibid., IV, 155.

The Reverend Manasseh Cutler, Federalist M.C., finds a boarding-house to his fancy. There is a pianoforte, and a daughter in the house who sings. 'The gentlemen generally spend a part of two or three evenings in a week in Mr. King's room where Miss Ann entertains us with delightful music.' But Sunday evenings offer the real treat for this Federalist group, for then Miss Ann 'plays psalm tunes,' in which her mother, who is a woman of great piety, always joins. The congressmen, 'extravagantly fond of music,' always join 'in the Psalms.' 'Old Hundred' and 'Canterbury' are the favorites. 'Miss Ann gave us some good music this evening, particularly "Wayward Traveller,"' Cutler writes with gusto.[1] It was a gentle society, for 'an unbecoming word is never uttered by one of them.'[2] Cutler, lamenting the lost feasts with his parishioners, occasionally steals away from the coarse food of the house to dine on canvasback duck at Gadsby's Tavern in Alexandria — despite the cost.[3] 'The first public house in America and equal to the best in Europe,' he proudly records.[4]

Such is the social life in the homes of most of the statesmen.

But when Josiah Quincy, Federalist leader in the House, reaches Washington, discovers the 'difficulties of keeping house,' and observes 'the discomfort and want of security from intrusion in a boarding-house,' he takes rooms in the home of Judge Cranch, where he is able to lord it over the other members of his party. He brings his coachman, horses and carriages, and finds accommodations for all on the premises. Very soon Mrs. Quincy is conducting a political salon, the more clever and important members of the party finding her rooms a haven of refuge from the torture of the boarding-houses. Here Pickering and Hillhouse with their group foregather and denounce the wicked contrivings of Jefferson, for Democrats are not welcome, and none appear. John Marshall, an ardent politician, though on the bench, is a frequent caller. But Mrs. Quincy, a beautiful woman with fine conversational powers, winning manners and pleasing person, who first had captivated her husband by the singing of the songs of Burns, would have made her home a delightful retreat had he

[1] Cutler, ii, 60.   [2] Ibid., ii, 51–53.
[3] Ibid., ii, 154.   [4] Ibid., ii, 55.

been dull and heavy.[1] He himself ascribes the popularity of his home at the Cranches' to the 'vivacity, intelligence and cultivated mind and manners' of his wife.[2]

But for the most part, the Federalists, who had gorged in the refined atmosphere of the Bingham mansion in the days of Federalist supremacy and arrogance, are reduced to the pathetic status of a working girl confined to one bedroom and forced to entertain her lover in the park. They are glad to accept invitations even from Jefferson for the sake of the French food and the fine wines, and many find their way over the wicked roads to Alexandria to dine on canvasback ducks at Gadsby's.

But they had one other resource — the homes of the members of the meager diplomatic corps.

VI

The diplomatic corps in the days of Jefferson is interesting, if not impressive. First, in point of service, is the Marquis de Casa Yrujo, representative of Charles IV of Spain. The handsome marquis, who looks out haughtily from the Stuart portrait, bears all the marks of a dandy keenly conscious of his charm. A delicate. sensitive, almost effeminate face it is. Here he has found a wife in the daughter of the Jeffersonian leader in Pennsylvania, and the dark hair and dreamy eyes of Sally McKean seemed to call for an Andalusian setting. The marquis is on intimate terms with Jefferson, making more than one visit to Monticello. Always garbed for instant attendance on the King at Aranjuez, even in this capital in the wilderness, he takes the air in a most elegant chariot, though the mud plays havoc with the trimmings. Unhappily, he all but commutes to Philadelphia, and Washington society sees less of the interesting couple than it would wish.

For quite a while Napoleon is represented by Louis André Pichon as Chargé d'Affaires, a clever and agreeable young man with a delightful wife, who dine out when they are not giving dinners. Peter Pederson, Chargé d'Affaires of Denmark, is a social animal who loves nothing better than conversation with a pretty woman, married and preferably young.

But soon British and French Ministers appear upon the scene

[1] *Quincy*, 56.   [2] *Ibid.*. 82.

to cause no end of trouble. Disillusionment and distress disturb Anthony Merry, the British Minister, who comes after a diplomatic sojourn in the stiff Spanish Court, bringing with him a wife who thinks, or thinks she thinks, in terms of Parisian salons. Rufus King had urged Merry's selection because favorably impressed by his simplicity and equitable disposition. But King did not know Mrs. Merry. The chroniclers of the time rather slight Mr. Merry to hurry on to descriptions of his more vivid, flamboyant, and articulate spouse. But one has left us a thumbnail sketch of the head of the house as 'a well-formed gentleman extremely easy and social.'[1] A battleship bears the couple to Norfolk, where, at considerable expense, Merry is forced to charter a boat to carry him to Alexandria. It is a six-day journey, battling against wind and tide, and at Alexandria they have to take a coachee to reach the capital. The weather is very cold and the frozen roads are rough. Mr. Merry has never been 'in one of these vehicles,' and his quiet astonishment and inward groanings arouse 'the mirth and risibilities' of his more robust and merry wife. The next disillusionment comes in the crude hotel. Mrs. Merry, in her most regal manner, summons the host to demand what they are to have for dinner. A bit ruffled at the lady's manner, the free-born American innkeeper slowly walks in silence to the fireplace, and, reclining his head upon his hand, gives her an impolite stare.

'Why, Mistress Merry, our custom is to give the best we have; but I keeps no schedule whatever. My house is full, but you shall have your dinner.' And so she did, but 'neither His Majesty's Minister nor Mistress Merry could eat a morsel that was served.'

But Mrs. Merry soon is immensely diverted by the droll ways of the Americans. 'We have alarmed Congress itself with the number of our servants and the immensity of our baggage,' she writes Tom Moore, the poet, who had accompanied them as far as Norfolk. 'Matters arise every instant that you would convert into amusement... Mr. Merry frets and every moment exclaims, "Why, it is a thousand times worse than the worst parts of Spain."' And the Capitol? 'Good Heavens, what profanation! Here is a creek too, a dirty arm of a river, which they

[1] Cutler, II, 163.

have dignified by calling it the Tiber.' And then, with a sigh, 'What patience one need have with ignorance and self-conceit.'[1] The Merrys make a speedy exit from the hotel of horrors, but, unable to find a residence of ample proportions, they lease two large brick houses on the south side of K Street between Twenty-Sixth and Twenty-Seventh. Even this is a disillusionment. 'Mere shells of houses,' he complains, 'with bare walls and without fixtures of any kind, even without a pump or well.' The fact that partridges could be shot from the front door fails to reconcile the unhappy man.[2]

But Mrs. Merry loses no time in making herself known. 'I shall exhibit at the Capitol,' she writes Tom Moore the day of her arrival. Nor are her exhibits to be confined to that dreadful spot. Soon she is the talk, if not the toast, of the town.

That she is no mean woman may be assumed from the descriptions and observations of her contemporaries. One describes her as 'a tall well-built woman, rather masculine, very free and affable in her manner, but easy without being graceful,' and as 'a woman of fine understanding . . . so entirely the talker and actor in all companies that her good husband . . . plain in appearance and called rather inferior in understanding . . . passes quite unnoticed.'[3] Aaron Burr finds her not unattractive and interesting — tribute enough from one so exacting in his taste. 'Mrs. Merry is tall, fair, fat — pas trop, however, no more than a desirable embonpoint. Much of grace and dignity, ease and sprightliness; full of intelligence. An Englishwoman who has lived much in Paris and has all that could be wished of the manners of both countries. An amiable and interesting companion.'[4] To satisfy a rake like Burr, and a Puritan like Cutler, should be the supreme test. And Cutler finds her 'a remarkably fine woman.' When first he meets her, 'she entered instantly into the most agreeable conversation which continued during the visit . . . easy and social as if we had been long acquainted.'[5]

But, on festive occasions, conservative ladies are prone to be a wee bit critical of her attire. Her first appearance is at a ball at

[1] Mrs. Merry to Moore, *Life of Dolly Madison*, 58–59.
[2] W. B. Bryan, *A History of the National Capital*, i, 574–75.   [3] Mrs. Smith, 46
[4] Burr to Theodosia, *Burr*, ii, 269.   [5] Cutler, ii, 163–64.

the Smiths', where her dress attracts 'great attention.' An observer finds it 'brilliant and fantastic, white satin with a long train, blue crêpe of the same length over it, and white crêpe drapery down to the knees and open at one side, so thickly covered with silver spangles that it appeared to be a brilliant silver tissue; a breadth of blue crêpe, about four inches long, and, in other words, a long shawl over her head, instead of over her shoulders and hanging to the floor, her hair bound tight to her head with a band like a drapery, with a diamond crescent before and a diamond comb behind, diamond earrings and necklace, displayed on a bare bosom.'[1]

The dinners at the Merrys' create as much of a sensation as her diamonds and crescents. Cutler is a bit awed by the display. 'Table superb,' he records in his diary, 'the plate in the center and in the last service, the knives, forks and spoons were gold. Six double-branched silver candlesticks with candles were lighted.' The serving of coffee in the drawing-room after dinner impressed the simple statesman much. Dinner follows dinner in rapid succession, the Federalist finding in the anti-Jeffersonian, anti-republican atmosphere a congenial lounging-place. The lady's malicious flings at the ruling party endear her to the enemies of the Administration. And she finds the American women amusing too. 'At Baltimore and Philadelphia,' solemnly records Cutler, 'when she went into a lady's apartment, she found nothing but toilets and dressing-tables — not a flower, not a dried specimen of any kind, not a book, but some foolish novels.'[2] Mrs. Merry is something of a bluestocking and holds for the cultivation of the mind. Even Cutler becomes a favorite because of their mutual interest in botany. 'She expresses her astonishment,' writes Cutler, 'at the want of taste in garden walks, etc., and that the ladies of this country have no relish for the most beautiful productions of nature.'[3] But we must not underestimate Mrs. Merry's mind. In her drawing-room, her petulant, unintelligent spouse soon is whispering with Federalist leaders about ways and means to destroy the American Union; and soon Aaron Burr will have him drawn into his plot to effect the separation of the Western States from the Union.

[1] Mrs. Smith, 46.   [2] Cutler, II, 190.   [3] Ibid.

Quite a different character is Napoleon's representative, General Turreau de Garambonville, whose not ungallant but checkered life has led him through a prison cell, where he was awaiting execution until the jailer's handsome daughter saved his life, to be rewarded with his name, if not his heart. He is a man of good ability, as his dispatches show, but his vanity and his ornate taste in uniforms touch the risibilities of the yokels of the capital. He establishes his Legation in the corner house of the Seven Buildings at Nineteenth Street and the Avenue, and begins to entertain. Inordinately vain and flamboyant, he dons full uniform, with a superabundance of gold lace that fairly drips from him, and makes his initial call on Jefferson. The impressionable Cutler, making a New Year's call at the White House, later meets him as he is leaving 'covered with lace almost from head to foot and very much powdered,' carrying his hat, though it is drizzling rain.[1] A few days later some members of Congress call upon him. Up one flight of stairs they are conducted into a large hall, where Turreau receives them and they find him disposed to be quite cordial, 'though he speaks but little English and converses through the interpretation of an Aide-de-Camp.'[2]

Declining to meet Merry, he is not so popular as the Britisher with the Federalists, and he is to cultivate the Administration more. He gives large dinners, inviting the members of the Cabinet and such Administration leaders as Giles, Logan, Nicholson, and Eppes.[3] Though women are invited, the conversation is largely political.

And Madame Turreau? Alas, the great man's gratitude is soon threadbare and there is not enough remaining to protect the sensibility of the lady from the worse than insults of her lord. Her culture, unhappily, is not so alluring as her body, and her training in the prison had not fitted her for the new rôle. Mrs. Smith thinks her an 'amiable, sensible woman,' but soon she is hearing sad things of Turreau — 'that he whips his wife and abuses her dreadfully.'[4] Gossip will give us the details a little later. But soon she is seen no more at social functions and the cynical, coldhearted Burr is writing Theodosia that 'Madame Turreau is supposed to be lost or captured.'[5]

[1] Cutler, II, 180.   [2] Ibid., II, 181–82.   [3] Adams, Diary, I, 343–44
[4] Mrs. Smith, 77.   [5] Burr, II, 288.

A little later when the Merrys happily are recalled to England by the unsympathetic Charles James Fox, Britain sends a more comfortable type of Minister in David Montagu Erskine, the eldest son of the brilliant Lord Erskine. He knows America, having served some years before in Philadelphia, where he had wooed and won the beautiful Frances Cadwallader. A man of ability and real promise, he had represented Plymouth in the Commons before his appointment as Minister. Cordial, sincerely friendly and conciliatory, Erskine becomes personally popular with both political sets. The Legation is famous for its dinners, for beautiful young women from Philadelphia, friends of the hostess, usually are guests, and one entertains the company by her 'performance on a tambourine.' [1]

VII

Such, impressionally, is the society of the time. Dinners, card-parties, teas, informal gatherings and squeezes — these are as much as most houses will permit. But young Dr. May, under the encouragement of the women, essays the rôle of Beau Nash and organizes an Assembly where all the élite of the town can dance at intervals. These, held at Stelle's Hotel,[2] are invariably crowded, and curiosity and malice feed greedily upon them. Official society turns out *en masse*, along with belles and beaux resident in Washington. One may well wonder from the chroniclers of the time whether the greater pleasure was in the dance or in sitting the dances through making malicious comments on the dancers.[3]

But the great sporting and social event of the year is the races when every house empties its inhabitants, and Congress finds it impossible to maintain a quorum. As early as 1803 there is a Washington Jockey Club, and the race-track, about four miles from the town, is the very center of racing interests in the country. This had come about through the influence of John Tayloe, who built and occupied the Octagon House. He had a passion for the sport and maintained a distinguished stable and raised blooded horses on his estate at 'Pentworth.'

A month before the races, they become the one topic of con-

¹ Adams, *Diary*, I, 448.
² *National Intelligencer*, December 9, 1805.   ³ Mrs. Smith, 18–19.

versation, and lovers of the horse flock from the four corners, making them a social event.[1] 'So keen was the relish for the sport,' Senator Mitchill writes, 'that there was a serious wish of a number of members of Congress that Congress adjourn for a few days.' [2] Even the staid John Quincy Adams packs his family into a carriage and hurries to the track at eleven in the morning lest he fail to find a good point of vantage at the track at two. 'I have never seen regular horse races before,' he writes in his diary.[3] The next year the rigid Puritan goes again, satisfying his conscience afterward with the notation: 'The races at length are finished and the Senate really met this day.' [4] An indignant member of the 'sovereign people,' writing to the *Columbian Centinel*, could 'not wholly approve of legislators sitting half an hour and then adjourning to countenance and view a horse race.' Bad enough for 'high-toned Federalists,' but 'rather odd' in 'money and time saving Democrats'! [5]

Let us look in upon the spectacle. Soon we reach the old field, the ground rising gently to the center. Around us is the track, a mile long and forty feet wide. In the center section of the grounds we find 'a prodigious number of booths' where refreshments are sold. On tables by these booths arrangements are made for the accommodation of the common people who view the races from the tops — laborers, farmers, boys and girls, blacks and whites. On the western side of the track these plain people do not venture, for this is sacred to fashion. Here are great numbers of 'elegant' carriages filled mostly with women fashionably gowned and keenly conscious of it. Not a few of the more daring women ride their own horses to the track and view the races mounted; and hundreds of men, excellently mounted, follow the races at close quarters around the track. Here is Dolly Madison in her turban, her cheeks glowing with excitement, surrounded by her set; there is Madame Yrujo in her showy chariot, her dark eyes dreamily surveying the scene; and yonder looms the emaciated form of a man with hectic eyes — John Randolph; beside him a heavy man with a red round face, eager for a bet — Senator Giles. And here,

[1] Mitchill's Letters, to his wife; *Life of Dolly Madison*, 56–57.
[2] Mitchill's Letters.   [3] Adams, *Diary*, I, 278.
[4] *Ibid.*, I, 318.   [5] November 30, 1803.

among the blacks and whites, the aristocrats and beggars, surrounded by his friends, is Thomas Jefferson, a kindling eye upon
the track.[1] This American Derby of the dawning days of the
nineteenth century quivers with excitement as sums, then vast,
are bet on the events, and one congressman loses seven hundred
dollars in an hour. And yet an orderly crowd. 'I saw very few
instances of intoxication,' writes Cutler, who is a bit disturbed by
the gambling.

But the races over, gambling does not cease, as both men and
women rush to the card-tables, available in almost every home,
and begin to play for money. The men, especially from the South
and West, fall to brag, which Sir Augustus Foster of the British
Legation thinks 'the most gambling of games.' The women fall to
loo, and when they are looed 'pronounce the word in the most
mincing manner.'[2] Wherever the ladies play, money passes between fair hands, for few play without stakes. 'What do you
think of my going to such an extent as to win two dollars at loo?'
asks Mrs. Smith. 'I confess I felt some mortification at putting
the money of Mrs. Madison and Mrs. Duval into my pocket.'[3]
And Dolly Madison is mortified as well, for frequently her losses
are so heavy that her conscience hurts.

It is not long until the country-town capital has a theater on the
Avenue close to the market-house where a stock company per-
forms zealously, if not with consummate art. One can sit in a
box seat for a dollar or in the pit for seventy-five cents, and pa-
trons can get tickets at McLaughlin's Tavern in Georgetown, at
the office of the *Washington Federalist*, or at Way's Printing Shop.
The doors are open at six and the performance begins at seven.
But alas, the names of the players are not preserved in the literature of the stage, and the names of the dramas are not alluring.
One season there is an offering of *She Would, and She Wouldn't*, a
comedy; *Raising the Wind*, a farce; *The Sailor's Daughter*, *The
Adopted Child*, *Adelmorn, or the Outlaw*, *The Lilliputian Hero*,
Child of Nature, and 'a celebrated play in five acts, as performed
with universal applause in the theaters of London, Philadelphia,
New York, Boston, Charleston, and Norfolk.'[4] Perhaps it is not

[1] Cutler, II, 141.   [2] *Life of Dolly Madison*, 54.   [3] Mrs. Smith, 38.
[4] *National Intelligencer*, September 3, October 7, October 4, November 6, 13, 16, 1805.

surprising that in the memoirs and letters of the times there are
few references to attendance on the play.

Even the amusement of shopping is denied the women, for the
shops are few and crude. Elisha Riggs is offering 'seasonable
goods'; Mrs. Oliver 'respectfully acquaints the ladies of Georgetown and the City of Washington that she has just received an
elegant assortment of embroidered and plain satin kid shoes.'
The ladies are cordially invited to purchase 'a genuine eye wash,
toothache drops and the sovereign ointment for the itch.' [1] Mrs.
Lytton, milliner, invites attention to her 'fashionable velvet
bonnets, black and white leghorn bonnets, chenille and pearl caps,
Egyptian turbans, ladies' extra kid and silk gloves, dress fans,
etc.' [2] But a large part of the press advertisements are of stray
cows, runaway slaves and slave auctions, where 'very likely negro
boys, all about twelve years old and accustomed to waiting,' can
be purchased at a sale.[3]

VIII

As against the amusements and frivolities of the times religion has hard sailing. There are no churches. The Treasury
sometimes serves as one, but both times John Quincy Adams goes,
forenoon and afternoon, there is no preacher. Better fortune can
be expected at the Hall of the House of Representatives, where
services are held almost every Sunday, the chaplain or some visiting minister in charge.[4] These services are little more than dress
rehearsals for the parties of the ensuing week. Men and women go
as to a social function, and the scene is more that of a ballroom
than of a place of worship, with the women whispering and titter-
ing at each other's malicious observations. The Marine Band
furnishes music, but Mrs. Smith thinks 'the music as little in
unison with devotional feeling as the place,' and when the band
tries to accompany the psalm singing, it completely fails, and soon
the attempt is abandoned — 'it was too ridiculous.' [5]

But if the religious tone of the young capital is low, it cannot be
charged to Jefferson. The Reverend Manasseh Cutler, Federalist

[1] *Washington Federalist*, August 13, 1802.
[2] *Ibid.*, December 10, 1802.   [3] *Ibid.*, December 29, 1802.
[4] Adams, *Diary* I, 265.   [5] *Life of Dolly Madison* 91.

M.C., is almost disappointed to note the regularity of the President's attendance. When John Leland, a Baptist minister and an ardent Jeffersonian, officiates at the first service, the preacher-politician attends and writhes as Leland preaches from the text, 'And behold a greater than Solomon is here.' 'Jefferson was present,' Cutler writes, 'and the allusion was intended and obliquely directed more to him than to the glorious Christ to whom the text refers.' [1] But as Sunday follows Sunday, with Jefferson always there, the political preacher is resentful. 'Such a garrage bawled with stunning voice, horrid tone, frightful grimaces, and extravagant gestures, I believe was never heard in a decent auditory before,' he writes of the Leland Sunday. 'Such an outrage on religion, the Sabbath and common decency, was extremely painful to every thinking person.' But he adds, in explanation, 'it answered the much wished for purpose of the Democrats to see religion exhibited in the most ridiculous manner.' [2]

But soon this tone is changed. 'Mr. Gant preached in the Hall. A very full assembly. Mr. Jefferson present.' [3] 'Attended worship at our Hall. Meeting very thin, but the President, his two daughters and a grandson attended, although a rainy day.' [4] Soon Cutler is writing of another minister in terms of admiration. 'On the third Sunday it was very rainy, but his [Jefferson's] ardent zeal brought him through the rain on horseback to the Hall.' And then, lest too much had been conceded to the devil, he adds: 'Although this is no kind of evidence of any regard for religion, it goes far to prove that the idea of bearing down and overturning our religious institutions, which I believe has been a favorite object, is now given up.' [5] It clearly is becoming irksome to record Jefferson's attendance at religious services, but there is no escape. 'Attended worship. . . . Jefferson at the Hall in the morning.' [6] 'Attended worship at the Capitol. . . . Mr. Jefferson and his secretary attended.' [7] One day, when an exiled Irish patriot and the brother of Robert Emmet attends, there again is Jefferson! 'The adulation offered to the President was disgusting,' adds the minister, resenting the patriot's tribute to the

[1] Cutler, ii, 69.   [2] Ibid., ii, 87.   [3] Ibid., ii, 72.
[4] Ibid., ii, 114.   [5] Ibid., ii, 118–19.   [6] Ibid., ii, 172.   [7] Ibid.

champion of liberty and human rights.[1] But the Federalist's
champions of God and morality are less attentive to religious
worship than Jefferson, and the meetings are neither impressive
nor devout.

IX

The sober-minded James A. Bayard, much given to levity,
finds Washington dull. 'I have written to you very seldom,' he
writes, 'in consequence of living in a place where very few occurrences take place worth communicating.'[2] Even so, numerous
occurrences are being communicated from the drawing-rooms and
boarding-houses. Had not the gaudy Turreau, the French Minister, been caught red-handed beating his wife? Was it not his
practice? To cover the screams of the lady, was it not his custom
to order his accomplished secretary, Count de Carbre, a talented
performer on the flute, to play like mad on these occasions? Had
not the entire neighborhood of the Seven Buildings where Turreau lived been aroused, despite the music, by the lady's cries of
fear and pain? And had not Dr. Thornton, the architect, burst in
upon the immunity of the Legation to discover the Minister
vigorously applying the whip to his cringing spouse, and stopped
the punishment? Had not Turreau indignantly protested, 'Dr.
Thornton, you do not know ze law of ze nation,' and had not the
infuriated Thornton replied with scorn, 'But I know the law of
humanity and justice and I mean to enforce it.' Mere gossip?
Had not Thornton, as justice of the peace, reduced his testimony
to a sworn statement and filed it away in legal form? No doubt of
it. And so the tongues wag for days and days, and Washington is
not dull.[3]

And then, there is Madame X, American wife of a foreigner,
beautifully formed and not selfish in concealment, whose frag-
mentary dress sets the country town on edge. Did she not drive
out in her 'splendid equipage' so scantily attired that the boys in
the streets gathered about the carriage to peek in? Did she not
appear at a party at the Robert Smiths' with so much revelation
of her charms as to 'throw the company into confusion and no one
dared to look at her except by stealth'? Did not crowds assemble

---

[1] Cutler, II, 174.   [2] Bayard Papers.   [3] Life of Dolly Madison, 78.

outside the windows to 'look at this beautiful little creature, for everyone allows that she is extremely beautiful'? Had not scores of gossips seen the dress she wore — 'the thinnest, scantiest of white crêpe without the least stiffening in it, made without a single plait in the skirt, the width at the bottom being made of gores . . . no sleeves . . . her back, her bosom, part of her waist uncovered, and the rest of her form visible'?

Thus runs the excited gossip as the ladies pick their way on foot or drive from house to house. Had not some of the women, including Mrs. Robert Smith, sent the lady word that 'if she wished to meet them she must promise to have more clothes on'? [1]

And how they gossip the winter the gallant Captain Zebulon M. Pike, fresh from the discovery of the peak that bears his name, lays siege, when he does not take by storm, the heart of many a young lady! Vain as a peacock, gay as a cavalier, and gorgeous in his uniform, this meteor of a season dazzles the girls and matrons at many a dance, captivates them, like Othello, at many a dinner, with the story of the dangers he has known. The card-tables buzz with speculation on whom his fancy may fall. And then the houses roar with laughter when the gossips speedily spread the news of the trifler's bold confession that he is married and has a daughter as old as many he had wooed. 'He has been masquerading here all winter and was a favorite beau among all the belles,' writes Mrs. Smith sadly.

And then young Tom Moore, bearing himself with the hauteur of a man who knows a lord, highly perfumed, and all the dandy, appears to beau about Mrs. Merry. His 'Irish Melodies' have not yet appeared, and to the women he is merely a handsome young foreigner with a tongue for blarney. A bit supercilious, society thinks him, but the Federalists readily forgive him his jeers at the raw capital and his sneers at Jefferson in Mrs. Merry's drawing-room. And he dances divinely, turns a phrase neatly, and his name is bandied about at many a card-table where ladies in 'mincing tones' say 'loo.'

And who can say that the town is dull where the gorgeous scintillating Theodosia, daughter of Aaron Burr, and but recently married to a South Carolinian, comes visiting her father? And

[1] Mrs. Smith, 46-47.

how the tongues clatter over the advanced views and unconventionality of the beautiful young woman! And how they chatter over the card-tables about the infatuation of young Meriwether Lewis, the brilliant and elegant young secretary of Jefferson! They dance together, dine together, and together they canter over the Virginia hills on horseback. And she a married woman! How the country town would have rocked had it then known that he had declared his passion, and the wise Theodosia, unshocked, had dismissed it as 'romantic idiocy' and remained his friend!

And what a tumult in the town when Tom Paine, whose pen in the fight for independence had been worth an army, appears in Washington and dines at the White House — but we must wait for the story of the sound and fury that greeted his return to the nation he had served so well.

x

But there is another visitor the ladies do not snub, who proves a godsend to the gossips. What could do more to set the peacock tail of society spreading than the sudden appearance of Jerome Bonaparte, brother of Napoleon? A mere boy he is, but nineteen years of age — but what a name! What though he be the brother of a hated tyrant, he smells of courts and kings — quite different from Paine. And so they flock about him. But alas, the beautiful eighteen-year-old daughter of a rich Baltimore merchant, Betsy Patterson, speedily wins him, and they return to Washington to be fêted and discussed. Burr finds her beautiful, and Monroe thinks her 'amiable, very handsome and perfectly innocent.' [1] But the malicious tongue of the jealous gossips has it that 'it was really the young man who was seduced.' [2] Pichon, French Chargé d'Affaires, gives a dinner for the bride and groom, but he is 'profoundly mortified at the marriage of Jerome,' and thinks it 'impossible the First Consul should put up with it.' To some of his guests he confides that Napoleon 'undoubtedly will break the marriage.' [3] Monsieur shrugs his shoulders — had he not given due warning to the young lady's parents? Disappointed belle and matron sympathize deeply with Pichon's distress, and glorious

---

[1] Monroe to Marbois, S. M. Hamilton, *The Writings of James Monroe*, IV, 140.
[2] Adams, *Diary*, I, 284.   [3] *Ibid.*, I, 284–85.

Betsy is raked over the live coals of malice about many a fireside and at many a card-table that winter.

Soon the controversy takes on the color of a feud. The Smiths of Maryland are the backbone of the Jeffersonian strength in that Commonwealth. In the Cabinet one is Secretary of the Navy; in the Senate, General Sam Smith is a tower of strength; and the wife of Senator Smith is the sister of Betsy Patterson's mother. Nicholson, of Maryland, leader in the House, is related by marriage, and soon the Federalists are hinting that the wicked Jeffersonians have arranged a sinister political alliance. John Quincy Adams, snooping about the cloakrooms, his ears wide open for private conversations, hears a 'curious conversation between S. Smith, Breckinridge, Armstrong, and Baldwin about "Smith's nephew, the first Consul's brother."' He hastens with the choice morsel to his diary, and gives it Godspeed on its journey among the card-tables. Yes, runs the gossip, 'they have such an inconceivable infatuation, they and the whole family of the Smiths, for the match, that make it they must.... Even the sound sense of Nicholson ... has not been proof against the ridiculous vanity.'[1] Soon the Federalists are chortling over the exaltation of the Smiths, sympathizing with Monsieur Pichon at American impertinence, and a social war is on. Betsy is a beautiful young girl; her father is an important merchant; the Smiths, related, are a family distinguished socially, politically, commercially, and on intimate terms with Jefferson, who sees the possibilities of a brutal humiliation of the young lady. He seeks to minimize the danger. He shows her marked atten-tion; Dolly Madison takes her under her ample wing; Monroe writes Marbois in Paris commending to his consideration the brother of Betsy, then en route with a letter from the father to Napoleon.[2] And the men and women of Federalism plan to snub the Jerome Bonapartes and the Smiths. Aaron Burr looks on with cynical amusement, too much a gentleman to join in the crucifixion of a girl. 'Jerome Bonaparte, wife, maids of honor, will be here to-morrow,' he writes Theodosia. 'There are various opinions about the expediency, policy, decency, propriety, and future prospects of this match. I adhere to Mrs. Caton.'[3] 'Mrs. Caton approves of

---

[1] Adams, *Diary*, I, 284-85.
[2] *Writings of Monroe*, IV, 140.   [3] *Burr*, II, 266.

the match and therefore A. B. does, for he greatly respects the opinions of Mrs. Caton.'[1] The appearance of Betsy strengthens the chivalrous impulse of Burr. 'She is a charming little woman; just the size and nearly the figure of Theodosia Burr Alston; by some thought a little like her; perhaps not so well in the shoulders; dresses with taste and simplicity (by some thought too free); has sense and spirit and sprightliness'[2] — so runs the comment to his daughter. And so grumbles the guerrilla war for the crushing of the spirit of a charming young girl. With tongues wagging over the teacups, dripping malice, with pens flashing over paper recording the gossip, with the town divided into two camps, Washington assuredly is not dull.

For always interesting men are sojourning for a season. Humboldt comes and lingers, held by his interest in Jefferson, and exhibits himself solemnly at parties; and curious eyes follow a strange young man, Robert Fulton, who has queer notions about boats and torpedoes and peddles them to Jefferson; and Joel Barlow, poet, philosopher, diplomat, friend of Jefferson and Madison, with a family of interesting girls, builds his mansion 'Kalorama,' where he entertains visiting literary friends and generously lends them out for parties.[3] It is with the Barlows that Fulton lives while trying to instruct Congress on the torpedo; and it is there that Jefferson, with some members, sees the inventor illustrate harpooning and the principles of torpedo attacks.[4]

But to the ladies, far more interesting than the dreams of Fulton are the studios of two distinguished artists who spend some years in the capital. Gilbert Stuart is in the first flush of his success, and while pretty women eagerly beg him to paint their portraits, few dream of the ultimate value of the pictures he may paint. In his studio on the Avenue near Sixteenth Street the women flock, to his annoyance. The demands upon his genius are appalling, for it has become the fashion to have a portrait by Stuart; and the women find him easy to sit to, for he has the art of so entertaining and amusing them that invariably they are painted at their best. 'Dear Mr. Stuart,' they say, 'I am afraid you will be very much tired; you really must rest when MY picture is done.' One season

[1] *Burr*, II, 266.   [2] *Ibid.*, II, 269.
[3] *Social Life*, 121.   [4] Bryan, I, 582.

during her absence, Dolly Madison is regaled by a woman correspondent. 'Stuart is all the rage,' she reads. 'He is almost worked to death and everyone afraid they will be the last to be finished.' [1] It is a procession of fashion that files into the studio on the Avenue — Dolly Madison in her turban and the 'great little Madison,' the stately Colonel John Tayloe of the Octagon and his pretty wife, the haughty handsome Yrujo and his dark dreamy-eyed spouse, and the lively Ann Payne, sister of Dolly, who was luckiest of all. For during her sitting she enters into an animated debate with Stuart as to which is the most expressive feature of the face. Stuart says the nose; the lady insists upon the eyes and mouth. Unable to outtalk the belle, the artist paints as the background of her portrait the shadowy profile of himself with an exaggerated nose, intending to remove it later. Delighted to have as the background of her portrait the silhouette of the artist she admires, she insists that it remain, and so the picture will descend to the future.[2]

While Stuart paints on the Avenue, the ladies also flock to the studio at the southwest corner of Fourteenth and F Streets where Saint-Mémin is doing exquisite miniatures; and both artists replenish the store of gossip at teas, dinners, and about the card-tables.

With painters like Stuart and Saint-Mémin, with poets like Moore and Barlow, with scientists like Humboldt, inventors like Fulton, soldiers of fortune like Pike, world figures like Bonaparte, Washington is far from dull, despite the inconvenience and mud.

Nor is the democratic court of Thomas Jefferson one bit less interesting or distinguished than the aristocratic courts of Washington and Adams. Now let us go to 'Court.'

[1] *Memoirs of Dolly Madison*, 15.   [2] *Social Life*, 143–44.

CHAPTER II

Jefferson's Democratic Court

I

NOTHING could have been less impressive than the White House when Jefferson finally abandoned his comfortable quarters at Conrad's to take possession. Despite the unfinished state of this structure, he spent less than two thousand dollars on the house, preferring to use as much as possible on the improvement of Pennsylvania Avenue. The walls of the East Room and the eastern parts of the house were still unplastered, and the East Room was not to be used during his tenure. There was not a single outhouse, necessary for proper housekeeping. The slate roof leaked, and three years were to pass before it was to be made proof against the weather. The grounds were rough and ugly, and visitors entering either of the principal entrances to the house ascended crude wooden steps. Jefferson wished to beautify the grounds with trees and shrubs, but Congress was adamant against an appropriation. It was four years before the post and rail fence was displaced by a low stone wall, which was not completed, however, until Jefferson was about to return to Monticello. The grounds at this time were leveled and made more sightly. When Meriwether Lewis returned from the historic Jeffersonian exploration in the great West, the grizzly bears he brought were turned loose on the grounds, and the Federalists laughed uproariously over 'Jefferson's bear garden.' In time, outhouses for meat, liquors, coal, and wood — a long range of one-story buildings — were constructed on the west side, and at the far end of the eastern range was built a temporary stable. But during the first four years Jefferson's horses were inconveniently kept at Fourteenth and G Streets, N.W.[1] The horses stabled were the four full-blooded bays he had acquired for his carriage, and his riding-horse. The bays cost sixteen hundred dollars, for he was exacting, and when they clattered through the streets and along the country roads of Georgetown they made a spirited and showy picture.[2]

When Jefferson took possession, the house itself was but sketchily furnished with articles used by Washington and Adams in Philadelphia. The chairs and sofas were worn and faded. The crimson damask furniture of the drawing-room had seen service throughout the Washington Administrations, and this was retained by Jefferson for sentimental reasons. This, however, was not enough for the much larger house, and the furniture Jefferson acquired to meet necessities was pathetically plain and unimpressive. However, his inventive genius led him to introduce some novelties of his own.

Wishing frequently to be undisturbed in important conversations at table, when he seldom had more than four guests at a time, he devised a plan to dispense with servants in the room. 'A set of circular shelves were so contrived in the wall,' says one familiar with the house in his day, 'that on touching a spring they turned into the room loaded with dishes placed on them by servants without the wall, and by the same process the removed dishes were conveyed out of the room.'[3] Downstairs, in a spacious room, he had his office, where he worked and held conferences with his Cabinet. This room he had arranged to suit his taste. In the center was a long table with drawers on each side. In some of the drawers he kept small garden implements with which he amused himself. Upon the walls were maps and charts, with books on shelves. Near the table was a large globe. In the recesses of the windows were flowers and plants that he himself tended. Suspended from the ceiling was a cage with a mocking-bird of which he was very fond. Often, when alone, he would open the cage and permit the bird to flit

---

[1] Bryan, I, 459; Mrs. Smith, 394.

[2] Sarah N. Randolph, *The Domestic Life of Thomas Jefferson*, 277. (Hereafter cited as *Domestic Life*.)

[3] Mrs. Smith, 307.

about from object to object, until, its curiosity satisfied, it lighted on his table and sang rapturously. Frequently when he went upstairs to his chamber to rest, the bird would hop up the steps behind him, and sit on his couch and sing as the master slept.[1]

II

To visualize the Jefferson of reality, one must brush aside the débris of partisan scurrility which has been taken with too much solemnity by historians of the anti-democratic school. Dandies like Yrujo, and pompous mediocrities like Anthony Merry, were never quite satisfied with his appearance. At one period he must have carried simplicity and comfort to excess. Sir Augustus Foster, a partisan of Mrs. Merry, painted a caricature of a man of worse than careless toilet, and Senator Plumer, when venomously opposed to Jefferson, described him as 'a tall raw-boned man ... dressed or rather undressed in an old brown coat, red waistcoat, old corduroy small-clothes much soiled, woolen hose and slippers without heels.' [2] The irate Merry thus found him, when making his first ceremonious call. Mrs. Margaret Bayard Smith, a woman of refinement, more inclined to aristocracy than democracy, can find in Foster's portrait nothing in which 'one who knew him can discover a trait of resemblance.' She, who saw him constantly and familiarly, concedes that his dress was 'plain, unstudied and sometimes old-fashioned in its form,' but she always found it 'of the finest material.' We may well prefer her testimony to that of Jefferson's notoriously embittered political enemies when she says that 'in his personal habits he was fastidiously neat.' She concluded that he 'despised the conventional and artificial usages of court and fashionable life,' but that 'his simplicity never degenerated into vulgarity, nor his affability into familiarity.' [3]

Senator Samuel Latham Mitchill, noted scholar of his day, associated with Columbia College, and capable of appraising character and capacity, found nothing in him to justify the libels

---

[1] Mrs. Smith, 384–85.
[2] William Plumer, Jr., *Life of William Plumer*, 242. (Hereafter cited as *Plumer*.)
[3] Mrs. Smith, 386.

of his foes. 'Tall in stature and rather spare in flesh,' he found him. 'His dress and manners were very plain; he is grave, or rather sedate, but without tincture of pomp, ostentation or pride,' and 'capable of relating humorous stories.' While the dandies were looking at his shoes, the more cultured Mitchill was glancing at his library in the White House. He found the French Encyclopedia in the original; the history of Tacitus, with the Latin text on one side and a translation into Spanish on the other, and 'one of the elegant copies of Plato which was printed a few years ago at Deuxponts.' He was as interested in the fact that Jefferson had been at Deuxponts and purchased copies of Plato and Aristophanes as Plumer was in his slippers. And he concluded that 'Jefferson is more deeply versed in human nature and human learning than almost the whole tribe of his opponents and revilers.' [1]

No one ever doubted his innate dignity, or questioned his intellectuality, or suspected him of pose. He was singularly free, socially, from the vulgarity of petty minds.

III

For the first time the White House was to be without a mistress. The wife, whose memory Jefferson revered, had long been dead, and his daughters had duties and inclinations in Virginia. To these he had been both a father and a mother. In Paris he had trudged from store to store on the Rue Saint-Honoré doing their shopping. He had summoned them to him there, and Mrs. John Adams had taken the younger and more winsome under her maternal care. In Monticello he had supervised their reading and made them his companions. Soon after his first inauguration, he was summoning them to his side. 'I have reason to suspect that both yourself and your sister will come here in the fall,' he wrote the younger. 'I hope it myself, and our society here is anxious for it. I promise them that one of you hereafter will pass the spring here, and the other the fall, saving your consent to it.' [2]

However, he had no illusions on Washington society. 'I have company enough,' he wrote his younger daughter, 'part of which

---

[1] Mitchill's Letters.   [2] *Domestic Life*, 278.

is very friendly, part well enough disposed, part secretly hostile, and a constant succession of strangers. But this only serves to get rid of life, not to enjoy it.'¹

The daughters came, though they spent little time in Washington, despite their husbands' attendance on Congress. Mary Eppes, the younger, with her auburn hair, was the more beautiful of the two, but her health was delicate, and she was timid among strangers and in crowds. 'Beautiful — simplicity and timidity personified when in company, but when alone with you of communicative and winning manners,' Mrs. Smith thought.² Jefferson tried to coax her more into society. 'I observe your reluctance at the idea . . . but for your own happiness must advise you to get the better of it,' he wrote her. 'I think I discover in you a willingness to withdraw from society more than is prudent.' Then, recalling the effect of the years of his own retirement after his wife's death, he added: 'I am certain you would be pleased with the state of society here, and after the first moments you would feel happy in having made the experiment. I am convinced our own happiness requires that we should continue to mix with the world, and to keep pace with it as it goes; and that every person who retires from free communication with it is severely punished afterwards by the state of mind into which he gets.'³

Martha Randolph, the older daughter, not so beautiful nor winsome, was well fitted for the duties of hostess. Mrs. Smith thought her 'rather homely, a delicate likeness of her father.' She had a keen intelligence, and sensibility and kindness were reflected in her countenance. Perfectly natural, with no affectations, frank and affectionate, and an excellent conversationalist, she could command respect in any gathering of men or women anywhere. As a young girl when in Paris with her father she had studied under the famous Madame Genlis, the mother of the lovely Pamela. 'You know her at once and feel perfectly at ease with her,' wrote one who knew her. 'Mrs. Randolph has that rare and charming egotism which can interest the listener in all one's concerns.'⁴ Though courteous and amiable, she was

---

¹ *Domestic Life*, 281.   ² Mrs. Smith, 34.
³ *Domestic Life*, 284.   ⁴ Mrs. Smith, 34.

to demonstrate her ability to put Mistress Merry in her place. But the demands of a large family requiring her presence in Virginia, her sojourns in the White House were all too rare.

In the absence of his daughters, Jefferson depended on Dolly Madison, who thus began her reign of more than thirty years, sixteen in the mansion of the Presidents. Constantly she was being summoned, sometimes with her sister Ann, to serve as hostess. 'Thomas Jefferson begs that either Mrs. Madison or Miss Payne will be so good as to dine with him today to take care of female friends expected,' runs one note. 'Thomas Jefferson presents his respectful thanks to Mrs. Madison for the trouble she has been so kind as to take on his behalf,' runs another.[1]

Very soon his marked partiality for the pretty Quakeress will involve him in a tempest in a teapot, as we shall see.

IV

Almost immediately, the democratic chieftain found himself embroiled with the ladies who loved and would have a court. He had determined to end all imitations of royalty and to make his a truly democratic court. 'It is said the President will have no levees during the session, which will be short,' wrote Cutler.[2] The mere thought seemed scarcely less than sacrilege to the ladies, accustomed to fare forth in their finery on these occasions during previous administrations. Instantly the spirit of rebellion swept the drawing-rooms and boarding-houses. The women would put a speedy end to such democratic foolishness! And so on the usual levee day they went forth in force to storm the White House. They were admitted to the public rooms, but the host was absent. He was cantering on horseback over the country roads toward Georgetown. Returning soon, and learning that he was inundated with company, he understood the implications of the visit. Not pausing to change his clothing, pretending to be delightfully surprised, he strode into the room, booted and spurred, his riding-suit covered with the red dust of the roads, and greeted his visitors with a disarming cordiality. Graceful and gracious, the pink of courtesy, bubbling with light talk and more serious conversation, he captivated and amazed

[1] L. B. Cutts, *Memoirs and Letters of Dolly Madison*, 29.   [2] Cutler, II, 46.

the women, who felt all the more intruders because of the friend-
liness of their reception. But they drew their skirts aside as he
moved among them with his dusty clothes. When satisfied they
had failed, they were ready to leave, but he insisted that they
remain longer, and accompanied them to the door with his most
winning smile.[1] This, however, was the last of the levees during
the eight-year reign of Thomas Jefferson.

Instead he kept open house, and anyone could see him at
any time of the day or evening. While the women were still
laughing over their defeat, the men were saying that Jefferson
was holding a perpetual levee — and so he almost was. No
President ever was to be more accessible to the public, none
more familiar by sight to the people of the capital. Every day
he took the air. Seldom, except when his daughters were with
him, was he seen driving behind the prancing bays, for he preferred, when alone, to go on horseback. A bold and fearless
rider, he might be seen almost any day between one and three,
even in a drizzle, astride 'Wildair,' cantering about the environs
of the town. Occasionally he would stop to chat with a farmer
or laborer or a child; not infrequently he made a short call at
some house in the country.

Hardly had the excitement over the abolishing of the levees
simmered down when he threw another bombshell into the
midst of the imitative society of the town. He issued his own
rules of etiquette, designed, in his mind, to give a more democratic tone to official society. These rules were predicated on
the theory that in official society no nation or people is bound
by the rules of another. Sir Augustus Foster of the British Legation was shocked almost into hysteria. 'Mr. Jefferson knew
too well what he was about,' he wrote. 'He had lived in good
society at Paris . . . where he had been admitted to the coteries
of Madame du Deffand, not to set a value on the decencies and
proprieties of life.' [2] But Sir Augustus evidently felt that nothing
not approved by Paris could possibly be decent, and that there
was no such thing as good society in America. Jefferson had
been sickened by the sycophancy and parroting of foreign cus-

---

[1] *Domestic Life*, 282; H. S. Randall, *Life of Thomas Jefferson*, II, 668.
[2] *Social Life*, 108.

toms, both in New York and Philadelphia. He would adopt rules in harmony with those unwritten but observed by American gentlemen, of whom he assumed the country could boast a few. And so — the rules.

First, foreign Ministers reaching the capital should pay the first visit to the members of the Cabinet, which the latter would return. The families of foreign Ministers should receive the first call from the families of the members of the Cabinet, 'as from all other residents, and as all strangers, foreign and domestic, do, from all the residents of the town.'

And then came the first shock. On the principle of personal and national equality, the Executive Government would consider every Minister 'as the representative of his nation, and equal to every other, without distinction of grade.' This bold assault on the most precious privilege of diplomats was greeted with groans.

Then followed a rule that would have caused consternation in the rarefied atmosphere of the Bingham mansion: 'No titles being admitted here, those of foreigners have no precedence.'

But the end was not yet.

'At any public ceremony to which the Government invites the presence of foreign Ministers and their families, no precedence or privilege will be given them, other than the provision of a convenient seat with any other strangers invited, and with the families of the National Ministers.'

Wicked as this was, there was something worse: for 'at dinners in public or private, and on all occasions of social intercourse, a perfect equality exists between the persons composing the company, whether foreign or domestic, titled or untitled, in or out of office.'

But there was still worse to follow: 'To give force to the principle of equality, or *pêle mêle*, and prevent the growth of precedence, the members of the Executive at their own houses will adhere to the ancient usage of their ancestors — gentlemen *en masse* giving place to ladies *en masse*.'

Then followed less provocative and revolutionary rules. The President would receive but not return calls, and the family of the President would receive the first call and return it.

Society gasped, and the more sensitive could scarcely look
the haughty and injured Yrujo in the eye; but this Minister,
thinking discretion the better part of valor, followed the rules
without protest until Mistress Merry appeared upon the scene
to create an international incident over how a diplomat's wife
should be taken in to dinner.

v

Mr. Merry had received a cruel shock on the occasion of his
initial call upon the President. The hour had been fixed, and
Madison was to accompany him to the White House. The
Minister appeared in his most impressive uniform, set for a
stately ceremonial. But when he reached the White House
Jefferson was not in the reception room into which he was conducted. In a moment, however, he appeared, and not in somber
black. He wore his usual clothes, and he was in heelless slippers,
since he preferred these for comfort. Could there be any doubt
that Jefferson had hurled an insult in the face of George III?
True, Jefferson received his envoy cordially, led him to a chair,
and conversed with him in the most friendly manner — but
the thing rankled. It was well enough, if Americans must be
vulgar, to base rules of society upon the prevalent usages of
gentlemen in America, but the diplomatic corps was sacrosanct,
and its members, not the head of the State, should be permitted
to lay down the law.

Jefferson was amused. He, better than most, knew the usages
of the courts, and among the courts of Europe he would have
conformed to them. He had no disposition to affront the super-
sensitive members of the corps, some depending wholly on the
precedence and pomp of arbitrary rules to lift them above the
most painful commonplace. Once, when a Danish diplomat
on friendly terms gently took him to task for receiving him
in slippers, and entered into a defense of the stiff formalities,
Jefferson smilingly told him a story. Once upon a time King
Ferdinand of Naples had complained bitterly to his Minister
Caraccioli of the boresomeness of court ceremonial, and asked
if he could not be relieved of such suffering. 'Ah,' said the
Minister, intent on illustrating the danger to so many in abandon-

ing ceremonial, 'your Majesty must remember that you, your-self, are but a ceremony.' [1]

But to Merry, who was hardly a ceremony, the memory of the reception wounded, and then came the unbearable blow, and soon the dreamy-eyed wife of Yrujo, a bit distraught, would be rushing into a drawing-room crying, 'Oh, this will mean war!' Jefferson had invited the Merrys, the Yrujos, the Pichons, the Madisons, the Gallatins, and some others to dinner. When it was announced, Jefferson, following the custom among American gentlemen at the time, offered his arm to Mrs. Madison, with whom he was talking. Merry, dumbfounded by what he considered an affront to his fair spouse, stood in indecision. Meanwhile, others were escorting the women nearest them into the dining-room, and finally the Merrys stood in solitary grandeur. At which Merry, in a rage, gave his arm to his wife, and followed. Even Madison had neglected her, preferring Mrs. Gallatin as a dinner companion.

But this did not entirely fill the irritated diplomat's cup of woe. Thinking to soothe his wounded spirit in the serene smile of Madame Yrujo, he was about to seat himself beside her when an uncouth congressman pushed in ahead and took the seat.[2] That night the Merrys left early, and soon their cries of indignation rang through the drawing-rooms and board-ing-houses. Instantly the town was in a turmoil. Many thought Jefferson had shown good taste in his selection; others agreed that he had as much right to make rules for official society as the King of England; and most of the women were incensed against Mrs. Merry, who was described privately by Jefferson as 'a virago who has already disturbed our harmony extremely.' The *Washington Federalist* pounced upon the silly incident as proof of the vulgarity of democracy, and accentuated the bitterness in social circles with sarcasms on the Administra-tion, 'making a burlesque of the facts,' as Pichon reported to Paris.[3]

Jefferson was amazed. Nothing was more remote from his

[1] F. W. Hirst, *Life and Times of Thomas Jefferson*, 385–86.
[2] Bryan, I, 577; Randall, III, 117; *Social Life*, 104.
[3] Allen Johnson, *Jefferson and His Colleagues*, 14.

thought than insulting either the King of England or his envoy, and as the gossips chattered at the card-tables, wishing to 'keep open for cordial civilities whatever channels the scruples of Mr. Merry might not have closed,' he asked Madison to inquire whether the infuriated diplomat and his virago of a wife would 'come and take a friendly and familiar dinner with him.' Madison made his inquiry through a Swedish diplomat, and was assured that the advance would not be repulsed. The invitation was sent, and Merry gluttonously grasped his opportunity. Madison soon was reading an amazing letter that Mrs. Merry must have inspired.

'It so happens that Mr. Merry has engaged some company to dine with him on that day,' ran the letter. 'Under other circumstances, however, he would have informed himself whether it is the usage, as is the case in most countries, for private engagements of every kind to give way to invitations from the chief magistrate of the United States, and if such were the usage he would not have failed to have alleged it as a just apology for not receiving the company he has invited. But after the communication which Mr. Merry had the honor to receive from Mr. Madison ... respecting the alteration which the President of the United States had thought proper should take place in the treatment to be observed by the Executive Government toward foreign Ministers, from those usages which had been established by his predecessors, and after the reply which Mr. Merry had the honor to make to that notice, stating that notwithstanding all his anxiety to cultivate the most intimate and cordial intercourse ... he could not take upon himself to acquiesce in that alteration on account of its serious nature, which he would therefore report to his own Government and wait for their instructions upon it, it is necessary that he should have the honor of observing to Mr. Madison that combining the terms of the invitation above mentioned with the circum- stances which have preceded it, Mr. Merry can only under- stand it to be addressed to him in his private capacity and not as His Britannic Majesty's Minister to the United States. Now, however anxious he may be, as he certainly is, to give effect to the claim above expressed of conciliating personally and privately the good opinion and esteem of Mr. Jefferson, he hopes that the latter will feel how improper it would be on his part to sacrifice to that desire the duty which he owes to his Sovereign, and consequently how impossible it is for him to lay aside the consideration of his public character. If Mr. Merry should be mistaken as to the meaning of Mr. Jefferson's note and it should prove that the invitation is designed for him in his public capacity, he trusts that Mr. Jefferson will feel equally, that it must be out of his power to accept it without receiving previously, through the channel of the Secretary of State, the necessary formal assurance of the President's determination to observe toward him those usages of distinction which have heretofore been shown by the Executive Government of the United States to persons who have been accredited to them as His Majesty's Ministers.'[1]

Disgusted by the solemnity of this state paper, Madison, after consulting with Jefferson, sent a curt reply:

'Mr. Madison presents his compliments to Mr. Merry. He has communicated to the President Mr. Merry's note of this morning and has the honor to remark to him that the President's invitation being in the style used by him in like cases had no reference to the points of form which will deprive him of the pleasure of Mr. Merry's company at dinner on Monday next.'[2]

This closed the chapter. Mr. Merry could not attend, and never thereafter did he appear at a social function at the White House. Meanwhile, encouraged by the Federalist leaders, who at this very time were conspiring with him against the Republic, he was zealously seeking to stir up the Government in London. Indifferent to Merry and his pretensions, Jefferson was concerned over the misrepresentations sent to the British Cabinet. Soon Madison was sending Monroe, in London, a complete explanation of the episode and advising the American envoy that 'to apply an antidote to this poison will require your vigilant and prudent attention.' He was convinced that 'the British Government will at once see the folly committed by its representative, especially in the last scene of the farce.'[3] Mean-

---

[1] Madison to Monroe, February 16, 1804, G. Hunt, *Writings of Madison*, VII, 118.
[2] *Ibid.*   [3] *Ibid.*

while Madison had written a full explanation to Baring, the London banker.[1]

Monroe was in no mood to sympathize with Merry. The latter had resented a general rule applying to all alike; Monroe had been denied courtesies commonly extended to others at the British court. Lord Hawkesbury had not been kind. At social functions Monroe had heard remarks on America that had disgusted him. In the Queen's drawing-room she had passed him without sign of recognition, though he ascribed the apparent slight to her age or a defect of vision. 'In all cases of the kind,' he wrote Madison, 'I have commanded myself, being resolved to make them subordinate to great objects, or, if ever noticed, to do so on a suitable occasion.'[2] Whether the Mrs. Merry incident was responsible he did not know, but Monroe constantly was affronted. Lady Hawkesbury had not returned Mrs. Monroe's call, and the Monroes, in consequence, had declined an invitation to dine with the Hawkesburys. At a previous dinner at the house of the Foreign Minister, Monroe had encountered no end of vulgarity. Referring, in conversation with the beautiful Lady Castlereagh, to the great number of equipages at the races in Charleston, the lady had asked, superciliously, what sort of equipages the Americans possessed. He assured her that they were such as he had seen in London. Whereupon Sir William Scott commented in a loud tone on an account of a grand fête at the Cape of Good Hope attended by the 'beauty, taste and fashion of Africa.' The table roared its approval of the delicate allusion, though Monroe, keeping his composure, noted that Lord Hawkesbury 'by his reserve did not appear to think that the remark was made on a suitable occasion.' Later, conversing with Lord Castlereagh and others, Monroe expressed astonishment that the most learned men in England appeared so uninformed on the rapid growth of the United States. 'They know as little of us as they do of the Cape of Good Hope,' he concluded gravely.

But the pin-pricks continued. At a Hawkesbury dinner the hostess was seen whispering to Lady Bristol, whose husband

[1] Madison to Monroe, February 16, 1804, *Writings of Madison*, VII, 118.
[2] Monroe to Madison, *Writings of Monroe*, IV, 148.

held no official position, and she took precedence of Mrs. Monroe. At all the diplomatic functions Monroe invariably was at the foot of the table, the Minister of Portugal lording it over him. Was all this a reaction to the Merry episode? Monroe did not know. Cobbett had ridiculed Merry's pretensions in his paper, and the other papers had merely quoted the ill-natured misrepresentations of the Federalist press.[1] Even the London drawing-rooms found the incident a choice morsel to roll under their tongues. Most who talked with Monroe agreed that the United States had a right to make its own official etiquette.[2] But Monroe could find no graceful opportunity to broach the subject to the Foreign Minister. He thought it incredible that the Government would interest itself in Merry's grievances, since it was 'invariably admitted that every government should regulate its own rights and ceremonies with the corps diplomatique as it thought fit.'[3] But two months later a friend told him he had been shown the Merry dispatches to the Foreign Office and that 'his communications to his government produced at the time much irritation.' However, it had been 'impossible to touch on this subject without asking an interview and difficult to act in it in that mode without lessening ourselves, unless Mr. M.'s recall was desired.'[4]

Meanwhile, the Federalists were getting their reports on the London reaction in letters from Christopher Gore to Rufus King. 'M.'s dispatches are truly of a sombre hue,' he wrote. 'The President's reception, the details of leading in to the dinner, etc., were as particularly recounted as the wounded pride of the lady or the injured dignity of the Minister could possibly require.'[5] More fortunate than Monroe, Gore was able to draw Hawkesbury into a conversation on the subject. The Foreign Minister was almost as somber as Napoleon when he sent Lord Whitworth on his travels. Gore expressed the hope to Hawkesbury 'that when Mr. M. saw that whatever course had been adopted was alike to all the foreign ministers,

---

[1] Monroe to Jefferson, *Writings of Monroe*, IV, 153.
[2] Monroe to Madison, *ibid.*, IV, 148.
[3] *Ibid.*, IV, 179.   [4] *Ibid.*, IV, 205.
[5] Gore to King, *Life and Correspondence of Rufus King*, V, 341.   (Hereafter cited as *King's Corr.*)

both himself and His Majesty's Government would not feel
in any way particular cause of dissatisfaction.' But Gore noted
that Hawkesbury was most concerned about 'the leading in to
dinner and seating at table.' 'In this silly business,' Gore wrote,
'they probably see here a disposition to affront England, and it
will, with others, increase the discontent with us.' [1]

Meanwhile, with diplomats choking the mails with lugubrious dispatches, Jefferson momentarily was doubtful of his
course, and soon Madison was appealing to Rufus King, familiar
with the usages of courts, for guidance. What was the custom
elsewhere? 'Our wish would be to unfetter social intercourse
as well as public business from ceremonious clogs,' he wrote,
'by substituting the pell mell; but this may be rendered difficult by the pretensions and expectations opposed to it.' [2]

In the end Jefferson stoutly held to his concept of a democratic court; but he was to fight, in forcing it, a more venomous
battle than that necessitated by the introduction of democracy
into government.

VI

But the chatter was not abated at the card-tables and in
the boarding-houses. In the midst of the mêlée, young Tom
Moore appeared from Bermuda to stay with the Merrys, and
soon he was parroting the indignation of Mrs. Merry and the
Federalists, to whose company she confined him. He had been
mortally offended at his presentation to Jefferson on receiving day. Though he had written poetry, his 'Irish Melodies'
were not yet published, and his literary renown had not yet
extended to the new world. Young, extravagantly vain of
his acceptance by peers and poets, the man Jefferson saw before him was a foppish youth exhaling perfume; and fixing
him with his cold first glance, he shook the poet's hand and
turned to others more important. Soon Moore was writing
home: 'I stopped at Washington with Mr. and Mrs. Merry
near a week; they have been treated with the most pointed
incivility by the present Democratic President, Mr. Jefferson;
and it is only the precarious situation of Great Britain which

[1] Gore to King, *King's Corr.* IV, 241–42.   [2] *Ibid.,* IV, 332–33.

could possibly induce it to overlook such indecent, though at the same time petty, hostility.' [1]

Soon he was lampooning Jefferson outrageously and writing his much-quoted verse:

> In fancy now beneath the twilight gloom
> Come, let me lead thee o'er this 'second Rome.'
> Where tribunes rule, where dusky Davi bow
> And what was Goose Creek once is Tiber now; —
> This embryo capital, where Fancy sees
> Squares in morasses, obelisks in trees;
> Which second-sighted seers even now adorn
> With shrines unbuilt, and heroes yet unborn.
> Though nought but woods, and Jefferson they see,
> Where streets should run, and sages ought to be.

Before many years, grown wiser with age, he was to apologize for these lampoons, ascribing them 'to the influence, the feelings and prejudices of those I chiefly consorted with; and certainly in no quarter was I so sure to find as decided hostility both to the men and principles then dominant throughout the Union as in the ranks of the angry Federalists.' Ten years later, when the 'Irish Melodies' appeared, Jefferson's daughter placed a copy in the hands of her father. Glancing at the title-page, he exclaimed, with a smile, 'Why, this is the little man who satirized me so.' Then, reading on, he added: 'Why, he is a poet after all.' And thereafter some of the songs of Moore were his favorites to the end.[2]

The American and Jeffersonian lampoons of Moore were the inspiration of Mrs. Merry and the Federalists.

But Mrs. Merry never gave up the fight, and she was to suffer another rebuff from Jefferson's daughter, Mrs. Randolph. When that lady appeared in Washington, she was astonished to receive a note from Mrs. Merry inquiring whether she were visiting the White House as the President's daughter or as the wife of a Virginia gentleman. In the former case, she would make the first call, but in the latter she would expect to receive it. Mrs. Randolph replied that she was visiting as the wife of a Virginia gentleman, and as such she expected the first

---

[1] Randall, III, 115.   [2] *Ibid.*, 117–18.

call, since in the code of etiquette drawn up by her father, all strangers in the capital should be called upon by the residents first.[1]

Mrs. Merry called.

VII

But no supercilious brows were raised over Jefferson's dinners, for neither under Washington nor Adams had the food been so perfectly prepared, the wines so choice, or the conversation so interesting. His French chef, who had served some of the first families in Europe and had followed him to America, soon became his best ally in conciliating political opponents. No predecessor had maintained such a cellar, the wines abundant and the very best. No one understood better the art of the dinner-table, and almost every day his table was surrounded by guests. The company usually was confined to fourteen, and the table was round 'to encourage general conversation.'[2] The personnel of the dinners, when Congress was in session, was drawn from official life with just a few outsiders; during the congressional recesses Jefferson drew his friends from Georgetown, Alexandria, and the surrounding country-houses. The extraordinary generosity of his hospitality shines forth in a typical invitation: 'Th. Jefferson requests the favor of Mr. and Mrs. Smith to dine with him on Tuesday next (26th) at half after three, and any friends who may be with them.'[3] Having abolished the levee he met the members of Congress at dinner, but he did not mix the political parties at these functions. All were either Federalists or Democrats. 'He ought to invite them without regard to their political sentiments,' grumbled Senator Plumer. 'The more men of good hearts associate, the better they think of each other, notwithstanding their differences of opinion.'[4] The Federalists eagerly went for the food and the wines, satisfying their conscience afterward by finding fault with the host in letters and diaries. Jefferson knew the undertone of society in Washington too well to undertake to mix the parties. He preferred to choose his guests for each dinner with a view to the congeniality of the

[1] *Social Life*, 114. [2] Mrs. Smith. 29; *Social Life*, 388.
[3] *Social Life*, 105. [4] *Plumer*, 245–46.

company. At one time he sat down to dinner with no one but the Federalists from Massachusetts and Connecticut, his most venomous foes. He knew how some would repay his hospitality. The elegant Gouverneur Morris, unable to find fault with the dinner, epicure that he was, emptied his spleen on the host. 'His constrained manner of reception showed his enmity,' he wrote, 'and his assiduous attentions demonstrate his fear.' [1] It was not easy always for Morris to understand the impulses of a gentleman. 'Although two clergymen were present, no blessing was asked,' growled Cutler in his throat. [2] 'I wish his French politics were as good as his French wines,' complained Plumer. [3]

None, however, complained of the dinners. 'Dined at the President's,' wrote Cutler. 'Rice soup, round of beef, turkey, mutton, ham, loin of veal, cutlets of mutton, fried eggs, fried beef, a pie called macaroni which appeared to be a rich brown crust . . . an Italian dish. Ice cream, very good, crust wholly dried crumbled into thin flakes; a dish somewhat like a pudding — inside white as cream or curd, very porous and light, covered with cream sauce . . . very fine. Many other jimcracks, a great variety of fruit, plenty of wines and good.' [4] Lemaire, purveyor of the household, complained bitterly that often he spent fifty dollars a day. The frugal French soul of Perit, the steward, was constantly stirred by this American extravagance.

If the food and wines were better than ever before, the conversation was far more interesting. 'You drink as you please and converse at your ease,' wrote the appreciative Mitchill. 'In this way every guest feels inclined to drink to the digestive or social point and no further.' [5] Under the host's skillful direction the conversation was general, and if he observed any guest silent, he would draw him out on some subject in which he was known to be interested; and if he noticed anyone neglected, he gave him special attention. [6] 'I had a good deal of conversation with the President,' wrote Adams. 'The French Minister, just arrived, had been this day first presented to him, and appears to have displeased him by the profusion of gold lace on his clothes. He says they must

---

[1] Morris, *Diary*, II, 418. [2] Cutler, II, 116.
[3] *Plumer*, 245. [4] Cutler, II, 71–72.
[5] Mitchill's Letters. [6] Mrs. Smith, 389.

get him down to a plain frock coat or the boys in the streets will run after him.'¹

After dinner that day Jefferson had delighted Adams by showing him a copy of Parrot's 'Natural History,' in French, 'very beautifully executed.'² At one of the dinners there was an exchange of repartee between Jefferson and the scholarly Mitchill. For a while Jefferson regaled his guests with a dissertation on wines, and he suggested that 'the Epicureans' philosophy was nearer to the truth than any other ancient system.' It had been misunderstood and misrepresented. He referred enthusiastically to the work of Gassendo upon it, lamenting that it had not been translated, since 'it is the only accurate account of it extant.' Adams reminded him of Lucretius. 'Only a part of it,' rejoined Jefferson — 'only the natural philosophy.' The moral philosophy could only be found in Gassendo. Mitchill veered the conversation with the suggestion that Fulton's steamboat was an invention of great importance. Yes, said Jefferson, 'and I think his torpedo a valuable invention too.' The talk shifted to chemistry, geography, natural philosophy, and Mitchill, who was a scientist, held forth on 'oils, gases, beasts, birds, petrifactions, incrustations, citing Humboldt, Lewis, Pike, and Barlow.' But inevitably at some time Jefferson brought the conversation to agriculture, of which he complained that he 'knew nothing.' But Madison did, he added — 'the best farmer in the world.' And so the conversation always ran on until night. 'A most agreeable dinner,' wrote Adams.³

Usually the most uncompromising of the Federalists who went to scoff or pout remained to praise, captivated by the entertainment. 'All decided Federalists,' wrote Cutler of one dinner. 'We enjoyed ourselves very well; were handsomely received and entertained.'⁴ At one of the dinners where only Federalists were guests, Jefferson's powers of captivation were put to the supreme test. Bayard and Griswold had not been invited, and the other guests decided to exhibit their polish with a pout. The table was constrained, the guests silent. Cutler, resenting this childish conduct, 'felt very disagreeable' himself. At length, knowing of

---

¹ Adams, *Diary*, I, 316.   ² *Ibid.*, I, 317.
³ Adams, *Diary*, I, 473.   ⁴ Cutler, II, 66.

Jefferson's interest in his travels, Cutler began to draw him out on his journeys in France, 'the qualities of different kinds of fruit, what their usual desserts were at table, their great varieties of dishes, etc.' But 'when the wine began to pass round the table a little more freely, all their tongues began to be in motion.' And so the guests lingered late as usual, 'spending the evening tolerably agreeably.' [1] The intellectuality and charm of Jefferson was deeply resented by the Federalists, who claimed a monopoly on culture, but try as they would, they could not resist the lure of his dinner-table conversation.

VIII

In discontinuing the levees, Jefferson did not abolish all receptions. Those of the nation's natal day and New Year's Day were observed, and the capacity of the White House was taxed on these occasions. On these days it was opened to the public *en masse*. The first of the receptions came on July 4, 1801, when the people of Washington and Georgetown flocked to the President's house. They found Jefferson in a room surrounded by the five Cherokee chiefs then visiting the capital. After a moment's conversation with Jefferson, they filed into the dining-room, where they found four large sideboards loaded with refreshments — cakes of various kinds, punch in silver urns, wine. Diplomats rubbed shoulders with grocers, Dolly Madison chatted familiarly with a clerk, Jefferson mingled promiscuously, having a word for everyone. Martial music in the street drew many to the windows, and the Marine Corps, headed by a band playing 'The President's March,' appeared. Out on the lawn they went through the military evolutions, then joined the merry crowds at the sideboards.[2]

The New Year's receptions were more fashionable occasions, belle and matron appearing in their gayest to receive the compliments of the beaux. Jefferson stood in the middle of the reception room to greet and exchange a word with each guest. At the first New Year's reception of Jefferson's régime the Federalists conferred soberly on whether they should attend, since the levee had been abandoned. They concluded to go, and they went in a group in carriages and were 'received with politeness, entertained

[1] Cutler, II, 132–33.   [2] Mrs. Smith, 30.

with cake and wine.' It was the very day Leland's Mammoth
Cheese had arrived, and Jefferson smilingly accompanied his
critics to the East Room to view 'this monument of human
weakness and folly.' [1]

At another New Year's reception, Cutler was delighted to find
conspicuously on the table a piece of wadding for bed-ticking of
American manufacture, which he had left on a previous visit.
The women, very curious, gathered about it and 'their fertile
imaginations suggested a great number of uses.' The company
broke up into small groups for 'promiscuous conversation,' some
standing, some sitting, Dolly Madison dominating the scene with
her smiles and her bonnet. [2]

Dinners, the best yet given by a President, state receptions,
no levees — Society soon became accustomed to the new rules of
conduct and accepted what it had no power to reject. In the
evenings the White House was reserved for the calls of close
friends; during the day anyone could get access to the President
in his study. Occasionally distinguished guests stayed at the
White House. These were more likely to be intellectuals than
politicians, and of these Humboldt was the most conspicuous.
He spent many hours a day with Jefferson discussing matters
remote from politics. Incidentally, he found nothing 'slovenly'
to comment on in Jefferson's attire. But he was much more
interested in his mind and may not have noticed. When on
entering a room unannounced, he found Jefferson on his back
on the floor playing with his grandchildren, he was not shocked.
'You have found me playing the fool, Baron,' said Jefferson,
laughing, 'but I am sure to you I need make no apology.' [3] And
there was no need.

One day, taking up a Federalist newspaper from the table in
Jefferson's study, and noting the falsity and scurrility of the
personal attack on his host, he asked, indignantly:

'Why are these libels allowed? Why is not this libelous journal
suppressed or its editor at least fined or imprisoned?'

Jefferson smiled happily.

'Put that paper in your pocket, Baron,' he said, 'and should
you hear the reality of our liberty, the freedom of the press

[1] Cutler, II, 54-55.   [2] *Ibid.*, 115.   [3] Mrs. Smith, 396.

questioned, show them this paper — *and tell them where you found it.*' [1]

Such was the tone and temper of Jefferson's democratic court; and such the social background of the bitter battles which now begin.

[1] Mrs. Smith, 397.

CHAPTER III

The Tables Turned

I

AT a complimentary dinner in honor of Oliver Wolcott on the eve of Jefferson's inauguration, Alexander Hamilton in the keynote speech of the occasion makes a bitterly malicious speech assailing his successful rival. The sweeping victory of the Democrats offers but scant hope of an early reaction, but Hamilton still is fighting. He will continue to fight until he dies.

Jefferson in these dawning days of his power is in more mellow mood. Determined to be a generous victor, he has sounded the note of conciliation in his inaugural address. He is ineffably happy over the triumph of his principles and the definitive acceptance of his political philosophy, and he looks back over the dark years of his defeats without malice. 'The tough sides of our argosy have been thoroughly tried,' he writes a friend of Revolutionary days. 'Her strength has stood the waves into which she was steered with the view to sink her. We shall now put her on her republican tack and she will show by the beauty of her motion the skill of the builders.' [1] Convinced that the minds of many had been poisoned through the misrepresentation of his purposes, he is infinitely happy in the thought that through administration he will rid these of their delusions. To his friend Barlow, the poet, he is writing that 'the recovery bids fair to complete and to obliterate the line of party division which has been so strongly drawn.' The Federalist leaders, he admits, will continue in their evil ways, 'but they stand at present almost without followers.' [2]

Thus, with Hamilton disgusted and embittered, it would have been difficult to find a more serene and contented creature than the Jefferson who sits at his desk in these spring days of 1801 scribbling

[1] To John Dickinson, *Writings of Jefferson*, x, 216. (P. L. Ford, ed.) [2] *Ibid.*, x, 222.

confidently to his followers. He believes ardently in democracy and in republican institutions, and he has seen the consummation of the second revolution without the shedding of a drop of blood. The people have moved with determination but restraint, and the peaceful transfer of the powers of government has moved him deeply. 'We can no longer say there is nothing new under the sun,' he writes Joseph Priestley. 'For this whole chapter in the history of man is new. The mighty wave of public opinion which has rolled over it is new. But the most pleasing novelty is its quietly subsiding over such an extent of surface to its true level again.' The fact is impressive, but more impressive to Jefferson is its significance. 'The order and good sense displayed in this recovery from delusion ... really bespeaks a strength of character in our nation which augurs well for the duration of the republic.' [1] The freedom of the press, the right peaceably to assemble, for which he had battled, had justified themselves. 'In every country where men are free to speak and think,' he writes, 'differences of opinion will arise ... but these differences, when permitted, as in this happy country, to purify themselves by free discussion, are but as passing clouds overspreading our land temporarily, and leaving her horizon more bright and serene.' [2]

The jarring note of the Wolcott dinner does not disturb his perfect serenity as he looks forward to the work ahead with complete confidence.

II

Despite the disgust of Hamilton, there was serenity enough in the hearts of Jefferson's enemies. The conciliatory tone of the inaugural address had gone far to soothe the wounded spirits of the dispossessed. Had he not said, 'We are all republicans, we are all federalists'? The Federalist leaders, exchanging letters in those spring days, were delighted with their own interpretation of the implication of the phrase. The repercussion in England was quite as pleasing. The same 'Porcupine' (Cobbett), who had lied so shamelessly in his Philadelphia paper in the interest of the Federalists, had caused a momentary fear of war in England by his misrepresentations in his paper there of the inaugural address. 'But

[1] *Writings of Jefferson*, x, 227.   [2] To Benjamin Waring, *ibid.*, x, 236.

these fears have vanished,' reported Rufus King, 'and the speech of Mr. Jefferson has been very generally well received.' [1]

England might well have been reassured when even George Cabot, brains of the Essex Junto, was encouraged. 'I have good reasons to believe that our new President is determined to keep clear of the war,' he wrote.[2] The stiff-necked aristocrat even was reassured on the important subject of patronage, and was writing Wolcott that 'our common people are yet not sensibly affected by anything done or threatened by Jefferson,' though he wrote proudly that he was dependent for information 'on our own sect exclusively.' [3] Jefferson had been in a month without a guillotine to mar the landscape. Even the jobholders were unmolested, and when Christopher Gore wrote from London warning against too intemperate attacks on Jefferson, Cabot demurred on the ground that these attacks had 'retarded the revolution which is begun,' since the Administration had been 'alarmed at the public indignation.' [4] So thoroughly satisfied were the Federalist leaders that their noisy abuse had cowed Jefferson that Timothy Pickering was quite positive that he would 'make no great strides from the old Administration and would look more to the Federalists than to the Jacobins for his support.' [5]

Hamilton aside, never had the Federalist leaders been so wrapped in a smug complacency as during the first weeks of the new régime. 'The strong opposition made by the Federalists to his election' had intimidated him, Theodore Sedgwick wrote Rufus King, and disposed him 'to conciliate and to soothe.' But 'this is disgusting beyond measure the leaders of his own party,' chortled the man from Stockbridge.[6] Most of his enemies were contemplating with glee the ruin of Jefferson because of his liberality toward his foes. One of them, surmising from the inaugural note of conciliation that he might be so 'prudent' as not to change the course of administration, was delighted with the thought that he would bring 'a hornets' nest of Jacobins about his ears . . . little insects he has been so long hatching.' [7] One of Hamilton's friends

---

[1] King to Troup, *King's Corr.*, III, 444.
[2] Henry Cabot Lodge, *Life and Letters of George Cabot*, 318. (Hereafter cited as *Cabot*.)
[3] *Ibid.*, 320.   [4] *Ibid.*, 324.
[5] Cutler, II, 44–45.   [6] *King's Corr.*, III, 456.   [7] Cutler, II, 44.

informed King that the address had had 'a wonderful lullaby effect,' and there no longer was fear of 'the serious mischiefs that have been foretold.' [1]

Meanwhile, Jefferson began to feel the breeze from the flapping of the hornets' wings. That robust partisan, Giles, was a bit disturbed. Of course he was 'highly gratified' with the tone of the address, finding 'the principles proposed... correct in themselves... and peculiarly adapted to the present state of public opinion.' But — and here he hurried to the real purpose of his letter — 'I am still of the opinion that the success of the Administration will depend very much upon the manner in which those principles are carried into effect.' Indeed, some of Jefferson's 'best and firmest friends already suggest apprehensions that the principle of moderation... although correct in itself, may, by too much indulgence, degenerate into feebleness and inefficiency.' In truth, 'a pretty general purgation of office has been one of the benefits expected by the friends of the new order of things.' Of course 'an indiscriminate privation of office for differences of politics' could not be expected, 'yet it is expected, and confidently expected, that obnoxious men will be ousted.' [2]

Almost as much disturbed was the equally partisan Monroe, who also was pleased with the principles of the inaugural address. 'It is sound and strong in principles' and 'still there are dangers in your way which it is necessary to shun.' There have been two parties; one had 'enjoyed the government for twelve years past and greatly abused the trust.' In putting the principles of the triumphant party into operation, Jefferson would have the support of the Democrats, and, Monroe assumed, of 'those who lately came over.' He realized that 'these new converts should be cherished, but it should be done with care so as not to wound the feelings of those who have deserved better of their country and of mankind.' To advance any of these converts 'would be impolitick, as it might lessen the confidence of the republicans in your administration.' Certainly favors should not be shown the members of the former Administration; and assuredly there would be a thorough investigation into all charges of irregularities and corruption.

---

[1] Troup to King, *King's Corr.*, III, 461.
[2] D. P. Anderson, *William Branch Giles*, 77. (Hereafter cited as *Giles*.)

Would not the uncovering of these things and the punishment of
the culprits 'contribute much to aid the republican cause and
separate forever these new converts from their ancient leaders'?
But Monroe did not wish to be misunderstood. No official in a
subaltern grade should be removed from office because of his
political belief, since this difference of opinion was 'a right in
which he ought to be protected,' and 'by retaining them in office
you will give a proof of toleration, moderation and forbearance.' [1]

Giles and Monroe had accurately surmised the interpretation of
weakness and fear which Cabot, Pickering, Sedgwick, and Troup
had read into the moderation of Jefferson's inaugural address.

Meanwhile, Jefferson was giving much thought to his own
course. With the announcement of his Cabinet he was to learn
what Federalism called moderation in a Democrat.

III

He set about the selection of his Cabinet with the utmost care.
Never for a moment had he wavered in the determination to give
the portfolio of State to Madison and that of the Treasury to Gallatin. He was eager to include Chancellor Livingston, but his approach with the portfolio of the Navy was repulsed. And one of
his regrets was that age precluded the inclusion of Samuel Adams.
To Jefferson, the venerable patriot whose devotion to republicanism and democracy had caused him to be 'avoided, insulted,
frowned on' by his neighbors in Boston was one of the high
priests of the new Americanism. 'How much I lament that time
has deprived me of your aid,' he wrote Adams in reply to Adams's
note of commendation on the address. 'It would have been a day
of glory which should have called you to the first office of the Administration. But give us your counsel, my friend, and give us
your blessing, and be assured that there exists not in the hearts of
man a more faithful esteem than mine for you, and that I shall
ever bear you in the most affectionate veneration and respect.' [2]

With Samuel Adams eliminated by age, it was inevitable that
Jefferson should turn to Madison to head the Cabinet. With no
one had he been so intimately identified in the organization and
consolidation of the party that had wrought the second revolution.

[1] *Writings of Monroe*, III, 268.   [2] *Writings of Jefferson*, x, 250.

JOHN BRECKINRIDGE

ALBERT GALLATIN

JAMES MADISON

JAMES MONROE

A personal intimacy had existed between these two Virginians for many years. He who had been the most useful and erudite member of the Constitutional Convention, and whose brilliant efforts as co-author of the *Federalist* and as the chief of the ratificationists in the Virginia Convention, was easily one of the foremost figures of his time. His familiarity with the literature of political science, his industry and loyalty, set him apart. His devotion to the Jeffersonian concept of the State had been abundantly tested.

Quite as inevitable was the choice of Gallatin. He alone among the Jeffersonians had shown himself capable of dealing intelligently with the financial system of Hamilton. His analysis and criticism had been penetrating enough to incur the bitter hostility of the Federalists. Where Hamilton sincerely believed that a national debt would tend to the centralization he sought, Gallatin thought a debt at least a necessary evil.[1] Jefferson had resented the studied secrecy and finesse of Hamilton's management and charged him with so phrasing his reports as to confuse the lay mind as to their meaning. Where Hamilton was contemptuous of the curiosity of Congress regarding financial matters, Gallatin was sure it was not without wisdom that the Constitution had made the House of Representatives the custodian of the public purse. Thus, no sooner had Hamilton retired to private life than Gallatin conceived and forced the creation of the Ways and Means Committee to supervise the operations of finance. For that departure from the Hamiltonian idea he was not easily forgiven.[2] His disdain for Hamilton's sinking fund, borrowed from Pitt, had aroused the wrath of the 'wise and the good,' but he stoutly insisted that, where there is no surplus, a sinking fund is both expensive and futile. With the instincts of a philosopher and teacher he had written his 'Sketch of the Finances of the United States,' to arouse a more general public interest in financial matters, and to furnish a textbook for his party which was sadly in need of education.[3]

At first contemptuous of this 'foreigner' who spoke English with an accent, and who boldly attacked the whiskey tax, the Federalists' hate increased with their fear as they noted the skill and caution with which he led his party. His positions were so sound as not easily to be refuted; his tone was so temperate as not

---

[1] Adams, *Gallatin*, 167–68.   [2] *Ibid.*, 172.   [3] *Ibid.*, 174.

reasonably to be resented, and his coolness and patience under attack infuriated his foes.

For the War Department, Jefferson turned to General Henry Dearborn, of New England, the most distinguished soldier, thus far, who had held this post. With the shot at Lexington, he had abandoned a comfortable medical practice to muster sixty volunteers and march them to Cambridge, where he was commissioned captain. At the head of his company he had marched across Charlestown Neck under the fierce fire of British ships to give battle at Bunker Hill. Here, with a musket in his hands, he had fought with the common soldiers. Learning of the hazardous expedition of Arnold against Quebec, he traded commands with another captain that he might share in the desperate enterprise. En route, he was stricken with fever and forced to take refuge in a wretched hut, and when a weeping soldier begged to remain with him to attend him, he sternly ordered him to march on. Just as the assault on Quebec was beginning, he appeared upon the scene, fought with grim determination against tremendous odds, and was captured. After months of imprisonment he was released on parole, and almost immediately he was again under fire at Ticonderoga. And now, in command of a corps reserved for desperate enterprise, he was ordered on the heights of Saratoga to take a battery of eight cannon that was playing on the American troops. Passing around the right flank of the enemy, and encountering unexpectedly a corps of infantry, he led a charge with the bayonet, swept the enemy aside, captured the cannon and their corps, and, still undiscovered by the main body of the foe, he charged it from the rear and forced its retreat. With Washington he suffered the horrors of Valley Forge, and such was his gallantry at the battle of Monmouth that it attracted the particular attention of the commander. And when the end came at Yorktown, this man who had fought at Bunker Hill was there! One of the first acts of President Washington was to make him Marshal of Maine. Later he had served two terms in Congress.

He was a cool, collected man of abundant common sense, kindly, frank, and loyal to his friends. Gallatin, no mean judge of men, admired and trusted him. 'A man of strong sense,' he wrote, 'with great practical information on all subjects connected with his department, and what is called a man of business. He is not, I believe, a scholar, but I think he will make the best Secretary of War we have ever had.' [1]

Jefferson was to find the portfolio of the Navy more difficult to place. His first choice was Livingston, who declined; and then General Sam Smith, who was dissuaded by his wife's distaste for Washington City. Finally the choice fell on Robert Smith, the General's brother, a wealthy business man of Baltimore with a flair for society. A commercial lawyer specializing in maritime law, son of a shipowner and owner of ships himself, he was as well qualified, by interest, as any of his predecessors. Though not brilliant, he had good ability, decision, and determination, as Gallatin was to find, and a capacity for hard work. No one ever questioned his integrity. He was a handsome man of commanding presence, dignified, uniformly courteous, socially accomplished, and soon he became popular with the Navy whose officers gave color to the elegant hospitality of his home.

Not content with one Cabinet member from New England, Jefferson, whose favorite political purpose was the ultimate redemption of that section, found his Attorney-General in Levi Lincoln, of Massachusetts. He, too, was a patriot of '76, and because of his faith in republicanism and democracy he was a disciple of Jefferson from the beginning. He had early attained distinction at the Worcester Bar, and forged to the front as a party leader. Among the active Jeffersonians of Massachusetts, none other quite approached him. His authorship of a number of strong political pamphlets in criticism of Federalist policies had made him the pet aversion of the Essex Junto. Gallatin found him 'a good lawyer, a fine scholar, a man of great discretion and sound judgement, and of the mildest and most amiable manners.' [2]

Though the Postmaster-General was not then of Cabinet rank, Jefferson, in appointing Gideon Granger, for the first time placed him on a footing with the actual members for the purposes of consultation. Again Jefferson had turned to New England, for Granger long had been one of the militant Jeffersonians of Connecticut. He was a good lawyer, a clever politician, an excellent business man, and a powerful pamphleteer.

[1] Adams, *Gallatin*, 276.   [2] *Ibid.*

Such was the Cabinet of Jefferson — by odds the most distinguished since the first Cabinet of Washington.

IV

But the Federalists were shocked. None of their sect had been retained in the Cabinet to betray Jefferson as Pickering had betrayed Adams, and that was convincing evidence of Jefferson's 'trickery.' And what could have been more offensive than the selection of three Democrats from New England? Surely there must be something sinister in a Cabinet with but one Southerner. Madison was bad enough, they thought, but Gallatin! That was intolerable. A mere 'foreigner'! screamed the Federalist scribes. And what an accent! So intemperate and indecent was the ridicule and denunciation of Albert Gallatin that he, fearing an adverse vote on his confirmation, persuaded Jefferson to withhold his appointment until the Senate had adjourned.

But, with the announcement of his appointment, the floodgates of billingsgate were opened. 'Gallatin is at length officially announced,' wrote Troup to Rufus King — 'an appointment by all virtuous and enlightened men amongst us considered as a violent outrage on the virtue and respectability of the country.' [1] Bayard was disgusted, though less shocked. 'Mons. Gallatin,' he wrote, 'is among the best of them.' [2] Outraged as was his peculiar sense of decency, Troup could still smile over the absurd. 'Some say,' he wrote, 'that Gallatin and Smith are ridding themselves of commercial concerns and other business in order to enter upon their offices in a short time hence in a freer and purer state.'

Troup had to laugh.

The scribes were shameless, and one Federalist paper did not hesitate to stoop to conquer. 'What shall we say of Albert Gallatin?' it asked. 'Shall we say that to save his life he was compelled to flee his country on account of the enormity of his crimes? Shall we say that the vagabond, having landed on our shores, ragged and lousy, took his course at Harvard University and offered himself as an instructor of the Italian Language, and when, by the charity of the benevolent students, his necessities were answered and his pockets filled with money, he took to his heels,

---

[1] *King's Corr.*, III, 454.   [2] *Bayard Papers.*

and fled into Virginia where he opened a school for instructing in the principles of infidelity, and of despising all laws both sacred and divine? We say it and truth confirms our word. Such is the President, and such his partisans.' The *Independent Chronicle*, supporting Jefferson, merely published the scurrilous article as carrying its own refutation.[1] This was to be the tone of the opposition to the Administration for eight years.

v

On assuming power, Jefferson found not a single Democrat in office. For some years the Jeffersonians, if not persecuted, had been proscribed. Among the jobholders the vast majority were envenomed partisans who could be counted upon at every opportunity to sabotage the new Administration.

Jefferson was in a quandary. The Federalists were pretending to believe that none of the jobholders who had earned their places by their hate of Jefferson would be molested. Robust partisans among the Jeffersonians, heated by victory after years of persecution and proscription, were equally positive that all should be swept away. Jefferson had in mind a middle course. He did not want to rid the public service of all his enemies at one fell swoop. He doubted the effect upon the public service, but he was thinking, too, of the political reaction. The conciliatory tone of his inaugural address, which the Cabots, Sedgwicks, and Pickerings had taken to themselves, had not been meant for them. Jefferson was thinking of the Federalists of the rank and file who had gone over. These he wished to satisfy, to hold, to merge permanently with his own party. All through the spring, and far into the summer, he was trying to clarify his patronage policy in letters to his friends. Three days after his inauguration he was thinking out loud in a letter to Monroe. An olive branch for the Federalist leaders? Not at all. These he had abandoned as 'incurables,' and he would 'never turn an inch out of the way to reconcile them,' but he thought it possible to win over 'the main body of the Federalists.' Monroe would recall the losses the Jeffersonians suffered during the misrepresentations of the X Y Z madness, and how, on the exposure of the plot, so many had returned. Would it not be prudent

[1] November 5, 1801.

'to give time for a perfect consolidation'? Would not the 'deprivation of office, if made on the ground of political principles alone, revolt our new converts'? Certainly no vacancies would be filled with Federalists until a balance between the two parties had been established. Removals for sufficient cause, of course, but 'they must be as few as possible, done gradually, and bottomed on some malversation or inherent disqualification.' [1]

Constantly he struck this note as he scribbled to his friends that spring and summer. 'The Federal leaders cannot be brought over; they are invincibles ... but I really hope their followers may.' This, he declared, is what he had in mind in his much-debated inaugural address when he 'offered a creed and invited to conciliation first.' [2]

But with increasing pressure for the distribution of the loaves and fishes, Jefferson sought to make his position clear to Giles. 'That some ought to be removed from office and that all ought not, all mankind will agree,' he said. 'But where to draw the line perhaps no two will agree.' Definite governing principles, however, could be adopted. Thus, all appointed to office by Adams 'after the event of the election' should be refused commissions. Second, all officials guilty of official misconduct should be removed. Third, all others, to whom only political objections could be made, should be unmolested, except in the case of United States Attorneys and Marshals. 'The Courts, being decidedly Federalist and irremovable,' he wrote, 'it is believed that Republican Attorneys and Marshals, being the door of entrance to the Courts, are indispensably necessary as a shield to the republican part of our fellow citizens.' [3]

To Jefferson this seemed eminently fair. He had no doubt that the 'justice and good sense of the federalists' would concur 'after they have been in possession of all offices from the very first origin of parties ... no republicans admitted.' [4] So satisfied was he with the fairness of his course that he did not hesitate to submit his plans to Henry Knox, his Hamiltonian colleague in the Washington Cabinet.[5] A bit more he lowered his vizor to Elbridge Gerry

---

[1] *Writings of Jefferson*, x, 218.
[2] To John Page, *ibid.*, x, 233.
[3] To Giles, *ibid.*, x, 238.
[4] To Dr. Benjamin Rush, *ibid.*, x, 241.
[5] *Writings of Jefferson*, x, 245.

with the assertion that those who had 'acted well' would have nothing to fear because of political differences in the past, but that unhesitatingly he would remove those 'who have done ill' regardless of the interpretation of his enemies.[1]

These governing principles determined, he set a high standard for his appointees — 'most respectable and unexceptionable.'[2]

VI

But immediately the removals for sufficient cause began, cries of pain and rage greeted him from his foes. Even historians of the anti-Jefferson school, who have found nothing censurable in the long persecution and proscription of the Democrats, have joined in the hue and cry. The end of the first of Jefferson's Administrations found the Federalists in possession of more than half the offices. But with the first removal, the sniping of his enemies began. The cynical Gouverneur Morris, not surprised at 'natural consequences,' was sure the Jeffersonians would hang themselves.[3] Soon Theodore Sedgwick, no longer rejoicing over the uneasiness of the Jeffersonians because of the moderation of the inaugural address, was bitterly complaining because of 'the most violent removals from offices which are lucrative to the Federalist possessors and filling them with furious Democrats.'[4] Troup, the intimate friend of Hamilton, solemnly was informing Rufus King in London that Jefferson was 'pretty generally displacing the Federalists.' He was sure that Burr was setting a trap for Jefferson by encouraging him to 'pursue a violent course.'[5] In August, Cabot was in his habitual distress over the 'intolerance' of Jefferson. 'Our new chief is less wise than we thought him and yet we have been censured for depreciating his wisdom,' he wrote King. Could anything be clearer than Jefferson's determination to 'persecute the Washington sect'?[6] But to John Quincy Adams all this clamor of Federalists with a persecution complex was more amusing than convincing.[7]

[1] *Writings of Jefferson*, x, 251.
[2] To A. Stuart, *ibid.*, x, 255.
[3] Morris, *Diary*, ii, 415.
[4] *King's Corr.*, iii, 456.
[5] *Ibid.*, iii, 495-96.
[6] *Ibid.*, iii, 497.
[7] *Ibid.*, iii, 525.

VII

Meanwhile, the Federalist scribes were going to the extreme limits in 'depreciating' Jefferson's wisdom. The *Connecticut Courant* solemnly declared that the President had no possible right to discharge or substitute subordinates. No, indeed, the postmaster and collector, the attorney and marshal held 'under the people' and had no responsibility to the President. But 'the Jacobins prove by their greediness and cupidity the charge repeatedly made against them — that all their patriotism was love of loaves and fishes.' [1] The *Courant* was curious to know 'how far Mr. Burr has been instrumental in pushing on his chief in the late removals and appointments.' True, the Democrats detested Burr, but 'let them look to it — the little man will eventually destroy them as the little man in France has destroyed their brother Jacobins in that country.' [2]

Taking their cue from these very Jacobins, some of the Federalist papers concentrated an attack on Jefferson for appointing to office 'only the richest men in his party.' 'With what magical facility can Federal editors change poverty and rags into riches and gold lace,' replied the *Independent Chronicle*. 'There is not a Federalist paper in the Union which has not more than once asserted or insinuated that the Democrats are bankrupts who wish to disorganize society.' [3] And Jefferson's intolerance? 'Never was there an instance of moderation, forbearance, and magnanimity on the part of a government toward its open and inveterate enemies as now displayed by Mr. Jefferson in retaining in offices, held at his pleasure, such a great number of characters, who by themselves, by their connections, or by newspapers under their influence, are constantly maligning, misrepresenting, and traducing his private character and public administration.' [4]

Meanwhile, infuriated by the loss of the loaves and fishes, the Federalist press within a few weeks of the inauguration was surpassing in personal abuse anything ever known before. 'No example on record,' said the *Independent Chronicle*, 'of such a pitiful, petulant, fault-finding, carping and malicious opposition.' [5] The *New England Palladium*, favored by Fisher Ames, was soon sneer-

---

[1] August 8, 1801.   [2] *Ibid.*, 17, 1801.   [3] July 9, 1801.
[4] *Independent Chronicle*, December 10, 1801.   [5] August 10, 1801.

ing at the popular impression that Jefferson was the author of the Declaration of Independence.[1] The *New York Evening Post* was publishing doggerel of a scurrilous character.[2] Major Russell, of the *Columbian Centinel*, so shocked even his fellow partisans by the sewerage he poured forth in a New Year's address that he sought to escape responsibility by pretending that he knew nothing of it until the papers were in the street. The *Independent Chronicle* challenged him on his honor as 'a Mason' to deny the authorship, and there was no response.[3] Thus, from the beginning, the opposition adopted a policy of personal abuse.

VIII

Throughout the spring and summer there was much sharp-shooting between the friends and foes of Aaron Burr, who again was figuring in the hopes of the Federalists. Fisher Ames, nursing his spleen in the Dedham farmhouse, had no doubt that Burr was pushing his captain to obnoxious things 'to drive the Federalists to fury in the hope that they, despairing of victory,' would use him to get revenge.[4] Burr's notable popularity with the opposition had measurably diminished his popularity with the Democrats, and not a few Administration papers were attacking him ferociously.

In the meantime, placidly he went his way, apparently not at all concerned. Suave, courtly, elegant, cynical, and smiling, he seemed serenity itself. In New York the gossips buzzed. Having abandoned a lucrative law practice, the gossips of the coffee-houses were sure his salary would not pay the interest on his debts. His distaste for Jefferson was understood, but Hamilton was being quoted among the merchants as certain 'Jefferson was too cunning to be outwitted.' Among his Federalist friends Burr was confiding that he was not being consulted on patronage and policies, and hoped he would not be. The loungers at the coffee-houses and at the Tammany Wigwam were shaking their heads, and, in refutation, were pointing to the appointments of Edward Livingston as United States Attorney, and of John Swartwout, 'notorious as the runner and tool of Burr,' as Marshal.[5]

---

[1] November 20, 1801.   [2] January 1, 1802.   [3] January 4, 1801.
[4] *King's Corr.*, IV, 3.   [5] Troup to King, *King's Corr.*, III, 460.

On the surface, Burr's mind was occupied with lighter things. His idolized Theodosia had just married, and to her home in South Carolina he was sending her a maid who 'from appearances has been used to counting her beads,' and a cook he was sure was good because he had 'tried her for two weeks.'[1] And now that the charming child who so gracefully had presided over the hospitalities of Richmond Hill was gone, he wished to sell it, for he needed the money more.[2]

The curtain was falling on one phase of his life.

That autumn he was presiding over the Constitutional Convention of New York with his customary dignity. But under cover he was demanding the patronage of New York. In truth, he had not been consulted, but he was posing for his Federalist friends when he pretended to indifference. In September, he was peppering Jefferson with letters, and noting, with growing impatience, the tardiness of the replies. At length he received a cold answer that chilled him. 'These letters relating to offices fall within the general rule which even during the first week of my being engaged in the administration obliged me to establish, to wit, that of not answering letters for offices specifically, but leaving the answer to be found in what is done or not done on them' — so ran the letter. And then, to soften the blow, Jefferson added: 'You will readily conceive into what scrape one can get by saying "no" either with or without reasons; by using a softer language which might excite soft hopes, or by saying "yes" prematurely; and to take away all offense for this silent answer, it is necessary to adhere to it in every case rigidly, as well with bosom friends as strangers.'[3] Burr must have smiled at 'bosom friends.' He knew he did not qualify.

Soon, energetically, he was seeking to force the appointment of Matthew L. Davis, an adoring lieutenant, who later was to become his biographer. This cunning politician wished the Naval Office in New York, and through his intimacy with the father-in-law of Gallatin, he found a friend at court. Gallatin thought him 'suited for the office, of strict integrity, untainted reputation, and pure republican principles,' and told Jefferson so. He was sure 'his political principles stand not on the frail basis of persons' — meaning Burr.[1] But Jefferson was not impressed. He had no confidence in Burr's loyalty, and had no thought of using patronage to strengthen Burr's position in New York. He had already determined to cast his lot with the Livingstons and Clintons — a decision which Henry Adams quaintly calls an 'intrigue.' Thus, patronage factions appeared almost immediately in New York; and in Pennsylvania, Duane, of the *Aurora*, was demanding the absolute proscription of all Federalists and the right to supervise the distribution of their places among his clique. The feud grew worse, with Gallatin standing for moderation, Jefferson supporting Gallatin, and trying to conciliate Duane with soft words.

Meanwhile, in Virginia, the notorious Callender, a victim of the sedition law, not satisfied with a pardon and the remission of his fine, was demanding the post-office in Richmond with much beating of tom-toms. To Madison fell the duty of repelling his demand for office, but soon he realized the impossibility of reasoning with a man 'whose imagination and passions have been so fermented.' 'Do you know,' he wrote Monroe, 'that besides his other passions he is under the tyranny of that of love. The object of his flame is in Richmond. I did not ask her name; but presume her to be young and beautiful, in his eyes at least, and in a sphere above him. He has flattered himself into a persuasion that the emoluments and reputation of a post-office would obtain her in marriage. Of these recommendations, however, he is sent back in despair.'[2] Monroe thereupon summoned the irate applicant and 'endeavored to tranquillize his mind,' reminding him of Jefferson's charity, his pardon, the remission of his fine, the dismissal of the Marshal who had packed the jury against him. 'But still he added,' wrote Monroe, 'that some little office would greatly accommodate him, and without one he did not know how he would subsist.'[3]

The little office was refused, and soon Callender was editing the most scurrilous anti-Jefferson paper in the country to the infinite delight of the Federalists of light and leading who exerted themselves to spread its circulation even to the rarefied atmosphere of Beacon Hill.

[1] Henry Adams, *The Writings of Albert Gallatin*, I, 47.
[2] *Writings of Madison*, VI, 420.   [3] *Writings of Monroe*, III, 290.

IX

Thus, with many of his followers intolerant of Jefferson's toleration, the Federalists were attacking him on every dismissal made, and Cabot was bitterly complaining because of the removal of the collector of Marblehead who admittedly had stolen 'four or five thousand dollars.' Had he not been 'appointed by Washington?'[1] At length an act of impertinence gave Jefferson the opportunity to strike back.

A month before his inauguration, Adams had appointed Elizur Goodrich collector at New Haven. He was a partisan of the most offensive type, with all the intolerance of his party and his kind. As a member of Congress he had participated actively in the conspiracy to raise Burr to the Presidency. His hatred of Jefferson, his principles and policies, were notorious, and no one but knew that in office he would remain a conniving politician practicing sabotage on the Administration he abhorred. Jefferson removed him because of his pernicious political activities, and appointed as his successor Samuel Bishop, a distinguished citizen of New Haven. The honors heaped upon him had vividly revealed the high regard of his neighbors of both political persuasions. But he was the father of Abraham Bishop, whose oration at Yale had shocked the Federalists to hysteria.[2] That was more than enough. An aggressive, uncompromising Federalist had been removed, and the father of an equally uncompromising Democrat had been appointed in his place.

The 'merchants of New Haven,' all Federalists, seized upon the opportunity for political propaganda and prepared a 'Remonstrance' to be spread in party newspapers throughout the country. They presumed to lecture the head of the nation on 'proscription.' The Federalist press pounced on its opportunity with such intemperance that even George Cabot sounded a note of warning. 'The language of some of the Federalist newspapers is perhaps a little too violent, though the sentiments are just,' he wrote.[3]

Jefferson was delighted. The situation was made to his purpose. His decision to move with deliberation in patronage

---

[1] *Cabot*, 326.   [2] Claude G. Bowers, *Jefferson and Hamilton*, 146.
[3] To Wolcott, *Cabot*, 221.

matters had 'produced impatience in the republicans and a belief that we meant to do nothing,' as he phrased it. The merchants, more friendly than they thought, had furnished the occasion for a clear exposition of his views.[1] He seized the occasion with devastating effect. Conceding the right of citizens to express their views on public measures, he replied that 'time was taken, information was sought and such obtained to leave no doubt' of the fitness of Bishop for the post. From unimpeachable sources he knew that Bishop's 'understanding was sound, his integrity pure, his character unstained.' The honors showered upon him by his own town and State 'are public evidence of the estimation in which he is held.' His neighbors had thought him fit to be chief justice of the court of common pleas — 'a court of high criminal and civil jurisdiction wherein most cases are decided without the right of appeal or review.' Bishop had been thought reputable, intelligent, and just enough to be 'the sole judge ... wherein he singly decided all questions of wills, settlements of estates.' More: 'He appoints guardians, settles their accounts, and, in fact, has under his jurisdiction and care all the property, real and personal, of persons dying.' A Federalist legislature had but recently appointed him to this post.

'Is it possible,' asked Jefferson, 'that the man to whom the Legislature of Connecticut has so recently committed trusts of such difficulty and magnitude is "unfit to be the collector of the district of New Haven," though acknowledged in the same writing to have obtained all this confidence "by a long life of usefulness"?'

Turning now to the hue and cry about Goodrich's removal he gave short shrift to the merchants, lashing them for their hypocrisy. 'When it is considered that during the last Administration those who were not of a particular sect of politics were excluded from all office; when by a steady pursuit of this measure, nearly the whole of the offices of the United States were monopolized by that sect; when the public sentiment finally declared itself, and burst open the doors of honor and confidence to those whose opinions they more approved, was it to be imagined that

[1] To Lincoln, *Writings of Jefferson*, x, 273.

this monopoly of office was still to be continued in the hands of the minority?'

Equal rights? 'Does it violate their equal rights to assert some rights in the majority also?' Political intolerance? 'Is it political intolerance to claim a proportionate share in the direction of public affairs?'

And then he closed with a question expressive of his own concept of government, which was to dismay the Federalist leaders. 'If the will of the nation, manifested by their various elections, calls for an administration of government according to the opinions of those elected; if for the fulfillment of that will, displacements are necessary, with whom can they so justly begin as with persons appointed in the last moments of an administration, not foɪ its own aid, but to begin a career at the same time with their successors, by whom they have never been approved, and who could scarcely expect from them a cordial co-operation? Mr. Goodrich was one of these.' [1]

Thus did Jefferson pulverize the remonstrators. Alas, wrote the strangely disillusioned Cabot to King, 'Mr. Jefferson's answer ... will show you that the system of displacing is the avowed system of the Government.' [2] Incredible! it seemed to him. To Oliver Wolcott he wrote that the Federalists were 'surprised at the weakness, and provoked extremely at the pernicious principles avowed by Jefferson in his answer.' [3] Unable to refute the reasoning of the reply, the Federalist press consoled itself with illimitable personal abuse. 'If it had not borne the signature it carried,' said the *Columbian Centinel*, 'a critical reader would have readily supposed it to have been the production of Talleyrand, if not of Albert Gallatin.' [4]

But Jefferson was happy. The reaction among his followers was enthusiastic, and he had expressed no sentiment to which the converts could object.[5] Nor was he to be dragooned into extreme measures by abuse. 'I am satisfied,' he wrote, 'that the heaping of abuse on me, personally, has been with the design and hope of provoking me to make a general sweep of all federal-

[1] *Writings of Jefferson*, x, 268.   [2] *King's Corr.*, ɪɪɪ, 495.
[3] *Cabot*, 321.   [4] July 29, 1801.
[5] Jefferson to Lincoln, *Writings of Jefferson*, x, 273.

ists out of office. But as I have carried no passion into the execution of this disagreeable duty, I shall suffer none to be excited. The clamor which has been raised will not provoke me to remove one more, nor deter me from removing one less, than if not a word had been said on the subject.' [1]

The controversy flamed, the Jeffersonian press taking up the fight, and when 'Lucius Junius Brutus' launched a pamphlet attack, 'Tullius Americus' replied with gusto. 'Indeed,' he wrote, 'no one ought to have supposed that Mr. Jefferson would meet with better treatment than Mr. Adams from a party whose friendship, to be had, must be purchased by each succeeding Administration, whether Adams or Jefferson. Point d'Argent, point d'Sniffe.' [2]

The victory was easily with Jefferson.

x

But the wounds inflicted by the reply were to rankle and poison the peace of his foes, who fell into a state of hysteria. President Dwight of Yale soon was a pathological case. Cabot lost all hope for his country and mankind. Fisher Ames, eating his heart out in his farmhouse at Dedham, momentarily was mad as a March hare. Cabot saw 'Robespierres and Marats' rearing their heads even among the good people of New England.[3] 'We have a country governed by blockheads and knaves,' screamed the scholarly president of Yale.[4] Ames, a kindred soul, and quite as light-headed, in writing to Dwight, wondered if anything could be done 'to prevent the subversion of property and rights of every kind.' [5] And again he wrote that 'the next thing will be, as in France, anarchy, then Jacobinism organized with energy enough to plunder and shed blood.' [6] It was at this time that the Federalists, banqueting at Middletown, Connecticut, proposed as a toast to the President of the United States — 'May he receive from his fellow citizens the reward of his merit — a halter.' [7]

[1] Jefferson to Lincoln, *Writings of Jefferson*, x, 273.
[2] 'Strictures on a Pamphlet Entitled, "An Examination of the President's Reply to the New Haven Remonstrance."'
[3] *Cabot*, 318.   [4] Edward Channing, *The Jeffersonian System*, 12.
[5] Seth Ames, *Works of Fisher Ames*, I, 392.   [6] *Ibid.*, 297.
[7] Channing, 18.

In the days of Federalist supremacy this would have meant
a trial by a packed jury charged by a partisan judge, and a cell;
but Jefferson merely smiled. There were no arrests. Times
had changed.

XI

The constant increase of Jefferson's strength even in New
England did not act as a sedative on the inflamed nerves of the
opposition. The fulminations against Jefferson had been futile,
and in that spring and summer the shadow of his growing popularity rested on New England like a cloud. Rhode Island swept
into the Jeffersonian phalanx, and its legislature voted a complimentary address to Jefferson, who was delighted. His supreme
hope had been the capture of New England. 'I hope,' he wrote
on hearing the news, 'it is the beginning of that resurrection of
the genuine spirit of New England which rises for life eternal.
Vermont will emerge next, because, after Rhode Island, least
under the yoke of Hierocracy.' [1] Within six months Vermont
joined the Jeffersonian procession. Even Massachusetts was yield-
ing to the lure of the 'illusion,' and Cabot wrote heart-brokenly
that 'the legislature certainly will be worse than it has been
in many years.' [2] Yes, 'Jacobinism gains ground . . . and threatens
New England,' he wrote later. 'Already I hear many complain
that our systems must be purged of their excessive democratic
characters or we shall be ruined.' [3] Long faces were drawn
in the Boston parlors in those days of the threatened invasion.

If only New England could be held! Fisher Ames thought
that 'if from New Jersey eastward all should look federal . . .
Jefferson will stand in his place a monument of despair — popular without power.' [4] But this fair picture had vanished now.
What could be done? Even in Connecticut the 'Jacobins' had
made alarming progress, and Ames bethought himself of Dwight.
What had caused the Jeffersonian deluge but the Democratic
press? The Federalists should have a press to meet this propaganda. Why not make the *Palladium* the national organ 'like

[1] To Granger, *Writings of Jefferson*, x, 259.
[2] To King, *King's Corr.*, III, 445.
[3] *Ibid.*, III, 457.   [4] *Ames*, I, 295.

the London *Gazette?*' But Connecticut would have to help. 'Could not your clergy, your Legislature, your good men, be impressed with the zeal to diffuse it at once through your State?' he asked Dwight. The Federalists must strike a common note everywhere and the leaders must take up the pen. 'I think I am entitled to call upon you and to ask you to call on the mighty Trumbull who must not slumber like the mighty Achilles in his tent while the camp is in danger,' he wrote. Dutton, editor of the *Palladium*, was a man of 'talents, learning and taste, and what is more essential, he has discretion,' pleaded Ames. Arrangements were being made to furnish every clergyman in Massachusetts, New Hampshire, and Vermont with a year's subscription.[1]

But even Dwight slumbered in his tent, drunk on his vituperation, and soon Ames was 'sounding the tocsin' in the ears of King. 'Democracy rides the high horse ... Bradley is chosen a Vermont Senator ... New Jersey is said to be democratic ... Delaware has chosen a Democratic Governor by the people' — so spluttered the pen at Dedham.[2] And from Cabot the same despairing note: 'Our elections are grown and are growing worse.... Our best men think more justly than ever ... but their influence over public opinion is less than usual.'[3]

So ran the dismal refrain of the Federalist correspondents — all despairing. But the sodden people, not of the lords elect, were blissfully unconscious of an impending tragedy. Had not property gone over to the Democrats in New York City where in the elections the Federalists, led by Hamilton, had 'failed to get a majority of even free-hold votes — a thing that has never happened before'?[4]

And could anything be more disheartening to the Federalist politicians than the increasing prosperity of the country? An ardent Hamiltonian was writing King that New York City was fairly forging ahead. 'Go where you will, you behold nothing but the smiling face of improvements and prosperity,' King read.[5] Even the pessimistic Cabot could not deny the upward trend.

---

[1] *Ames*, I, 295.   [2] *Ibid.*, IV, 3.
[3] Cabot to Wolcott, *Cabot*, 322.
[4] Troup to King, *King's Corr.*, III, 454.   [5] *Ibid.*

'The popular consolation,' he wrote King 'is ... that all goes
well — prosperity smiles on everybody ... wealth increases and
the new men promise to make great savings.' [1] Even the jaundiced
Ames was writing Dwight, 'I have the pleasure to inform you
that I carried my pigs to a good market.' [2] On Jefferson's election some of the more fanatic Federalists sold out their stocks
in expectation of their fall after the inauguration. 'It is suspected,' said the *Independent Chronicle*, 'that some of these
persons, on finding their stocks rise, are desirous to destroy the
public confidence, hoping thereby that the stocks will fall, and
that they may purchase in at a much lower rate than they
sold out.' [3]

Thus the predicted ruin had not befallen, the loss of confidence was nowhere in evidence. Even business men, concerned primarily with their increasing business, were not afraid
that Gallatin would wreck the public credit. To the prophets
of evil nothing could have been more disheartening.

XII

And no one was more disheartened than Alexander Hamilton.

His friends found him 'supremely disgusted,' and maintaining
his opinion that the Jeffersonians 'had not the talents or virtues
sufficient to administer the government well.' He was sure they
would 'ruin our affairs and plunge us into serious commotions.'
Nothing, he said, 'short of a general convulsion' would 'again
tempt him into public life.' [4] He was positive that 'neither
Jefferson nor his friends have sufficient skill and patriotism to
conduct the political vessel in the tempestuous sea of liberty.' [5]

At this time Hamilton had been in private life for some years.
He had not quite recovered from the shock on finding himself
unable to cure his party's infatuation for Burr some months
before. But, aside from politics, he never had had more reason
for satisfaction with his position. He still was the idol of the
financiers and merchants and his word was law with the Chamber
of Commerce. Never had he been so prosperous. As the head

---

[1] Troup to King, *King's Corr.*, iv, 44.   [2] *Ames*, i, 296.
[3] August 13, 1801.   [4] Troup to King, *King's Corr.*, iii, 495.
[5] *Ibid.*, iii, 461.

of the Bar his income was estimated at something between ten thousand [1] and twelve thousand dollars.[2] 'Hamilton is closely pursuing the law,' wrote Troup to King, 'and I have succeeded at length in making him somewhat mercenary. I have known him latterly to dun his clients for money, and in settling an account with me the other day, he reminded me that I had received a fee for him in settling a question referred to him and me jointly. These indications of regard to property give me hopes that we shall not be obliged to raise a subscription to pay for his funeral expenses.' [3]

Then, too, he was on the verge of the realization of his ambition to possess a country home. About eight miles from Bowling Green, he had acquired land on which he was planning the building of 'The Grange,' and his mind was much occupied with carpenters, architects, and landscape gardeners. In the dawning days of the Jeffersonian era, he consoled himself for his political disillusionments by contemplating the cozy domestic scene of the near future in a house of his own, seated amidst the rural scenes he loved. He drew more and more within himself, and his correspondence with his erstwhile friends, who had scorned his protest against the Federalist support of Burr, diminished. He was a realist, and he saw no early prospect of the overthrow of the Jeffersonians, but he had not given up the fight — he never would.

In the gubernatorial campaign in New York that spring he had plunged with feverish activity into the fight to elect Rensselaer over Clinton, who flew the flag of Jefferson. 'We are anxious for New York,' Cabot had written King, 'where Hamilton has made great and brilliant efforts in favor of Rensselaer.' [4] About the same time, Burr had written that 'Hamilton works day and night with the most intemperate and outrageous zeal, but ... wholly without effect.' [5] But notwithstanding his 'outrageous zeal' the Jeffersonians had made such notable gains that for the first time in New York City they had recruited strength from

---

[1] Ames to Gore, *Ames*, i, 303.

[2] Allan Hamilton, *The Intimate Life of Alexander Hamilton*, 337. (Hereafter cited as *Intimate Life*.)

[3] *King's Corr.*, iv, 104.   [4] *Ibid.*, iii, 445.   [5] *Burr*, ii, 149.

among the freeholders, who no longer saw in the mild features of
Jefferson a resemblance to Marat.

But Hamilton had to fight. Always partial to the pen in the
moulding of public opinion, he determined upon the establishment of a newspaper in New York to stem the rising tide of
democracy. He had canvassed the necessity with John Jay.
In the choice of an editor he had no trouble.

Five years before, a young man of thirty, with a slight reputation as a writer in Massachusetts, influenced mightily in his
style by Sterne and Junius, and ruined through speculations,
had appeared in New York with a letter of introduction from
Robert Treat Paine, with whom he had studied law. Soon he
was established with Aaron Burr in the practice, but in a little
while he disassociated himself from Burr to form a partnership
with John Wells, who had many contacts in literary as well as
political circles. Thus he met Hamilton, and fell under the
spell of his personality. It was on Hamilton's recommendation
that he was made clerk of the circuit court. The revolution of
1800 had swept him out of office, and he was unattached when
Hamilton was looking for an editor. In William Coleman he
found a man of robust convictions, with a slashing style that
could be tempered into one of literary charm, with unbounded
courage, both moral and physical, and with a rare capacity for
understanding and discussing political and constitutional questions. Jovial, witty, kindly, and an entertaining conversationalist,
Coleman had become a sort of protégé of the great leader. To
him was offered the editorship of the *New York Evening Post.*

The purpose was to make it the intellectual clearing-house for
the national Federalist press. In November, the first issue was
on the streets; almost immediately the semi-weekly was to be
found on the tables of leading Federalists throughout the East;
and from the beginning, Hamilton, in the shadow, was directing
its policy and dictating many of its editorials. Many times, late
at night, when the streets were deserted, Coleman might have
been seen slinking into the office or the home of Hamilton, where
the disciple, with pen and pad, sat at a table taking the dictation
of the master. Pacing up and down, Hamilton talked, Coleman
wrote, and the editorial the public read the next day was just

what Hamilton said and nothing more. It had required no polishing, for it was perfect.[1] Soon Hamilton was using the *Post* as the medium for his mass attack on the policies of Jefferson.[2] And soon the articles he wrote were being copied into most of the Federalist papers of the land.

It was just as this child of Hamilton's brain was born that his favorite son, Philip, who had quarreled on politics in a theater, quietly slipped from his home one dawn and rowed across the Hudson to Weehawken to fall before the bullet of a duelist. 'Never have I seen a man so completely overwhelmed with grief,' wrote Troup, 'as Hamilton has been. His countenance is strongly marked with grief.' [3] It was a heavy blow, but Hamilton had work to do.

He was now ready, armed, munitioned, eager for the fray against his old foe. The hour was about to strike. For during the spring, summer, and autumn, Jefferson had not been concerned primarily with patronage. Constantly he had been in touch with his advisers, particularly Gallatin, on plans for drastic changes in government in line with his principles and preaching.

He, too, was ready for the fray.

[1] G. S. Hillard, *Memoir and Correspondence of Jeremiah Mason*, 32–33.
[2] George H. Payne, *History of Journalism in the United States*, 192.
[3] *King's Corr.*, IV, 28.

CHAPTER IV

Jefferson Advances; Hamilton Attacks

I

IN THESE dawning days of the new régime numerous notes
were exchanged between Jefferson and Gallatin regarding appointments and the policies determining them. When the latter
found an irregularity or deliberate dishonesty in an official, the
former immediately was informed; and whenever there were extenuating circumstances, it was Jefferson's function to decide. Time
and again he intervened to save an official whose scalp the more
impatient and intolerant of his followers demanded on party
grounds alone. Pinckney, an ardent spoilsman, demanded the
removal of an official because of 'his electioneering influence and
energy.' Gallatin asked Jefferson for instructions, and he replied
that he 'should have great reluctance' at removing the man,
'especially as he promises the same support to this which he gave
the preceding Administration.' At any rate, Jefferson would wait
for 'more information.' [1]

Gallatin, who cared nothing for patronage and was ignorant of
political organization, a statesman and not a politician, was disposed to carry Jefferson's liberality to extremes. In a circular to
collectors, he announced that appointments to positions under
them should be independent entirely of political affiliations, and
based wholly on the fitness of the appointees for the duties to be
performed. He added that the collectors themselves were forbidden to use their official influence to 'restrain or control' their
subordinates in their political actions.

One day Jefferson was in conference with Madison when the
circular was laid before him. The two read it with no little curi-

[1] Jefferson to Gallatin, *Writings of Gallatin*, I, 36.

osity. They agreed that Gallatin's generosity was a bit strained. Jefferson replied that he heartily agreed that officials should be judged by their official actions regardless of their politics, but he reminded Gallatin of a vital part of the Administration policy he had overlooked — 'to require an equilibrium to be first produced by exchanging one half of their subordinates, after which talents and worth alone to be inquired into in the case of vacancies.'[1]

Soon after the inauguration, Jefferson mounted his horse and rode to Monticello to attend to odds and ends, but soon he was back in Washington, where he remained through July. For three weeks in May, the Madisons were his guests until their house could be put in order, and he talked with Madison almost daily. Throughout these three months there were innumerable consultations between the trio, Jefferson, Madison, and Gallatin, who were the sustaining pillars of the new régime. Patronage played but a minor part in the discussions. They had their heads together on the broad policies to be adopted. The Pickerings and Sedgwicks, who were sure there would be no actual change in the methods of administration or the principles behind them, would have been shocked had they been able to listen in on these conferences.

The trio were as one in their determination to enforce economy. 'We must push to the uttermost in economizing,' Jefferson wrote Nathaniel Macon, Speaker of the House.[2]

This was to be accomplished by reducing the estimates, by the suppression of many unnecessary offices created for political purposes, or because of policies to be abandoned. One of Gallatin's first acts was to wipe out nineteen useless inspectorships.[3]

Soon the Federalists would be denouncing this passion for economy as 'avarice.' 'An odious, degrading and sordid passion,' Sedgwick would write.

Disgusting as the promise of economy was to them, the favorable reaction of the public nauseated them even more. 'Every puny prater,' growled Sedgwick, 'who talks much of the interest of the people, the necessity of public economy, and the importance

[1] *Writings of Gallatin*, I, 28–29.   [2] *Writings of Jefferson*, x, 260.
[3] Gallatin to Jefferson, *Writings of Gallatin*, I, 30.

of calculating every public measure on the principle of taking the least portion possible of the fruits of labor from the mouth which earns it, is sure of an affectionate reception from the people.' Was not 'the decrease of public burdens . . . represented as certain from the election of Mr. Jefferson?' Thus, 'every warm and generous and manly sentiment is to be stifled.' [1]

Equally unanimous were the trio on the adoption of a program for the liquidation of the public debt with the greatest practicable rapidity. Without a rigid, definite policy as to the debt, Gallatin could see it 'entailed on the ensuing generations, together with all the systems which support it, and which it supports.' [2]

Along with the liquidation of the debt, all three were agreed upon the importance of a reduction of the taxes, though Gallatin was not at all sure that an immediate repeal of the internal taxes would not interfere with a speeding-up in the payment of the debt. His estimate of the revenue indicated that the double task could be performed, but he was afraid of unforeseen contingencies. Certainly it would be impossible, he told Jefferson, without rigid economy and a drastic reduction in both army and navy expenditures. The monetary demands of every department would have to be cut to the bone, but where 'thousands' could be saved in the others, 'hundreds of thousands' could be saved in the army and navy departments.[3] This was his view in March; it remained his view in November.[4]

Through these months of herculean labor, Gallatin was cruelly torn between his sense of responsibility to the Treasury and his antipathy to internal taxes. He saw the possible danger, but 'on the other hand, if this Administration shall not reduce taxes, they never will be permanently reduced,' he wrote Jefferson.[5] 'I agree most fully with you that pretended tax-preparations, treasury-preparations, and army-preparations against contingent wars tend only to encourage wars.'

It was to be a bitter work that year for Gallatin.

[1] Sedgwick to King, *King's Corr.*, IV, 34.
[2] To Jefferson, *Writings of Gallatin*, I, 69.
[3] *Writings of Gallatin*, I, 24.   [4] *Ibid.*, 69.   [5] *Ibid.*

II

Meticulous in his pursuit of facts, conscientious, and with a keen sense of his responsibility, Gallatin was incapable of sparing himself. He spent himself unstintingly, prying into every crack and crevice of his department, mastering all the innumerable details of the Treasury with all their ramifications. Working all day, and night after night until midnight, he was to remember this year in the far future with something of horror. His excessive labor 'almost brought a pulmonary complaint.' [1]

His was the unpleasant duty of decapitating useless officials; of insisting on the radical reductions of the monetary demands of the heads of departments. Smith of the Navy found him increasingly obnoxious. Constantly he was preparing plans and revising them, sending them to Jefferson and revising them again. It was disheartening to find both Dearborn and Smith adamantine against his pleas for drastic reductions in their demands for the War and Navy offices. In the end, he was forced to raise the War Department figures from the $930,000 he had proposed to $1,420,000, and to increase those for the Navy from the $670,000 he had proposed to $1,100,000.[2] Even so, he had forced the two Ministers down on their original demands.

And yet, despite his inability to enforce such frugality as he would have wished, his own figures convinced Jefferson that the internal revenue safely could be abandoned. This had impressed Jefferson as of paramount political importance, for tax reduction had been promised. It would have been easy to reduce the taxes by not hastening the payments on the debt, or to have hastened the payment of the debt by the continuation of the taxes, but the Administration determined upon both.

III

Gallatin's heart was set on still another reform in the Treasury — that of concentrating responsibility in finance by adopting the policy of specific appropriations. The old system inaugurated by Hamilton and continued by Wolcott had shocked the meticulous soul of the Swiss financier. He was prepared to fight for the curtailment of his own power — a power Hamilton had assumed.[3]

[1] Adams, *Gallatin*, 300.   [2] *Ibid.*, 292.   [3] Channing, 32.

Long before this, by demanding and securing the creation of the Ways and Means Committee, he had ended the Hamiltonian idea that the Treasury should formulate tax laws and hand them down to the House, constitutionally entrusted with that duty. He had thought Hamilton's dealing with money appropriated had been unbusiness-like and dangerous. Not that he had questioned Hamilton's honesty; but he did insist that the system made for a careless and slovenly policy. After all, it was the people's money and it should be used precisely as the people's representatives had appropriated it, and not as the Secretary might wish. He could not justify to himself the notion that money appropriated for one purpose could be used for another. No longer should the Treasury be a mystery if he could prevent it.

Thus, one day Jefferson sat at his desk poring over a plan submitted by Gallatin for the concentration of responsibility in the spending of the public funds. Throughout his brilliant legislative career, Gallatin had been a persistent critic of the Hamiltonian policy of conceding the Secretary of the Treasury arbitrary powers in putting upon appropriation laws any construction he saw fit. He had complained that there was no check upon the expenditures of the War and Navy Departments. No one of ordinary business acumen or caution today would care to deny that the old system had been 'loose,' as Henry Adams says.[1]

The plan that Jefferson was now reading was so obviously sound that it seems incredible that a storm of protest should have been aroused by its submission. It merely called for 'specific appropriations for each object of a distinct nature, and one to embrace for each Department all contingencies, including therein every discretionary expenditure.' Each appropriation was to be for the calendar year, and all not expended within that time was to revert. Warrants would be issued on requisition of the appropriate department to the person for whom intended and not to the head of the department.

Jefferson was in hearty accord, but this perfectly sound, business-like proposal was to enrage the leaders of the old régime, with Hamilton and Wolcott taking it as a personal affront.

[1] Adams, *Gallatin*, 299.

IV

For five months the Jeffersonians were hard at work on ways and means for putting the party policies into operation. Madison, for the moment, had no major problems, but Jefferson advised with him constantly on the general program. Smith and Dearborn were busy battling with Gallatin, who stoutly insisted on greater sacrifices for economy than they cared to make. Gallatin, harder pressed than the others, bent over tables of statistics day by day and far into the night until he grew pale and wan. Finding that 'current business and the more general and important duties of the office do not permit me to learn the lesser details but incidentally and by degrees,' his irritation with his task increased. The general machinery of administration might be in desperate need of reform, but he dare not touch it until he knew, and the paramount problems of policy denied him the opportunity to investigate. He groaned when he found his best clerks deserting him for more lucrative positions in private business.[1] Nor was he made happier by the necessity imposed by the effrontery of the Bey of Tripoli of sending a squadron of frigates into the Mediterranean to protect American commerce. The speedy and successful termination of the expedition had cost money and threatened to cost more.

On the first of August, Jefferson mounted Wildair and rode over the red dirt roads to Monticello to escape the malaria and to spend two months on his loved hilltop, happy with his daughters and their romping children, with his gardens and his fields.

But even here there was little surcease from correspondence, for letters poured in upon him from Gallatin and the politicians, and Madison rode over from his not distant farm to discuss policies and politics under the great trees on the lawn where the breezes brought refreshment. On Jefferson's urging, Gallatin left the miasmic terrors of the swamp-surrounded capital and went to New York, where he continued to work. Smith was in Maryland. Dearborn and Lincoln were in Massachusetts.

In September, Jefferson summoned his Cabinet back to their posts for the last of the month.

[1] To Jefferson, *Writings of Gallatin*, I, 69.

V

Jefferson had very definite ideas of the relations to be maintained with his Cabinet. These were based largely upon the policy of Washington under whom he had served. Letters of business were addressed either to the President or to the heads of departments. Those addressed to Jefferson would be referred to the head of the appropriate department; those sent to a member of the Cabinet, when requiring an answer, were to be sent to Jefferson for his information. The answer proposed would be included. Usually these would be returned without comment, implying approval. Occasionally he might suggest some alteration, or there would be a query in a brief note. Whenever there was doubt, Jefferson would hold the letter for a personal conference. In this way, by making the Presidency a center, Jefferson at all times would be familiar with all proceedings.[1]

Then, too, the general Cabinet conferences, which had been all but abandoned under Adams, would be resumed, with a day and hour definitely fixed for each week. In addition to the general conferences, the President would see each member on his special problems once or twice a week.[2]

In the preparation of his Messages Jefferson followed an undeviating course. After general discussions with his Cabinet, he would write a rough draft and send the whole to each member with a request that he 'make notes on a separate paper, with penciled references at the passage noted on.'[3] The Cabinet was urged to express its opinions freely, and most of them, and especially Gallatin, responded at length and with entire frankness. Occasionally a member would urge the incorporation of a subject not touched upon.

Thus was the first Message prepared, after a full exchange of views in numerous conferences.

It opened with an optimistic outline of international relations. Peace with the major nations had been preserved. There was no cloud on the horizon. Only the impudence of the Bey of Tripoli had called for the use of armed forces, and, in effectively protecting American commerce, an enemy ship, on which there had been

---

[1] Jefferson to the Cabinet, *Writings of Jefferson*, x, 289.
[2] Jefferson to Gallatin, *Writings of Gallatin*, i, 58.　　　　[3] *Ibid.*, i, 62.

'a heavy slaughter of her men without the loss of a single one on our part,' had been captured. But 'unauthorized by the Constitution, without the sanction of Congress to go beyond the line of defense, the vessel being disabled from committing further hostilities, was liberated with its crew.' Thus evidence had been given that 'it is not the want of that virtue [bravery] which makes us seek their peace, but a conscientious desire to direct the energies of our nation to the multiplication of the human race, and not to their destruction.' The relations with the Barbary States were unsatisfactory, and Congress would be able to judge from the papers laid before it 'how far it will be expedient to leave our affairs with them in their present posture.'

Then came the first declaration of war. The financial condition of the nation, 'with an augmentation of revenue arising from consumption, in a ratio far beyond that in population alone,' indicated that 'we may now safely dispense with all internal taxes.' Scarcely less disturbing to the partisans of the old régime was the warning that a 'sensible and at the same time a salutary reduction . . . in our habitual expenditures' would be necessary. Did this not imply a criticism and hint at dismissals? The next paragraph left no doubt. Had there not been a great multiplication of unnecessary offices in view of the fact that the 'States themselves have principal care of our persons, our property and our reputations'? Had not 'offices and officers been multiplied unnecessarily, and sometimes injuriously to the service they were meant to promote'? Among these officers, dependent on executive discretion, a considerable reduction had been made. The diplomatic service had been curtailed. The inspectors of internal revenue had been dismissed. Several agencies created by executive authority had been abolished. But most offices had been created by act of Congress and Congress alone could act on these. The multiplication of offices, the increasing of expense 'to the ultimate term of burden which the citizen can bear' should be discontinued. It should not be true that 'after leaving to labor the smallest portion of its earnings on which it can subsist, government shall itself consume the residue of what it was instituted to guard.'

The Message raised another challenge on the topic dear to

the heart of the conservative business mind of Gallatin, who had urged its incorporation — the recommendation that barriers be multiplied against the dissipation of public contributions 'by appropriating specific sums to every specific purpose susceptible of definition; by disallowing all applications of money varying from the appropriation in object or transcending it in amount; by reducing the undefined field of contingencies and thereby circumscribing discretionary powers over public money; and by concentrating in a single department all accountabilities for money where the examination may be prompt, efficacious, and uniform.'

Then another sensitive nerve of the Federalist was pressed, and there was thunder in the very serenity of the phrasing. The judiciary system would, of course, 'present itself to the contemplation of Congress — especially that portion of it recently erected.' A statement on the business of the federal courts would be submitted that Congress might be able 'to judge of the proportion which the institution bears to the business it has to perform.'

This emphatically was a declaration of war made with the utmost suavity.

And it was followed by another: With the public mind keen with the memory of the scandalous packing of juries in federal courts, the President invited Congress to consider whether the manner of their selection was in conformity with the intentions of the law. 'Their impartial selection . . . essential to their value,' he continued, 'we ought further to consider whether that is sufficiently secured in those States where they are named by a Marshal depending on executive will, or designated by the court or officers dependent on them.'

And there was still another declaration of war. Hatred of the immigrant, then so important to the material development of the nation, which flamed with such heat in the days of the Alien Law, had inspired the passage of a Naturalization Act denying citizenship under fourteen years of residence. 'Shall oppressed humanity find no asylum on this globe?' Jefferson asked.

There was dynamite enough in this calm, courteously worded, suave document which finally bore the stamp of Cabinet approval.

The Message was ready. The issues were drawn. Soon Congress would convene.

VI

On the presentation of the Message, Jefferson again had revolutionary ideas. Never partial to formalities, pomp, and circumstance, he had never been impressed with the imitation of the European custom of a personal reading 'from the throne,' with the 'Reply to the Address.' The spectacle of senators and congressmen strutting in their best bib and tucker through the streets to the President's house to present the Reply in a pompous speech had always amused him. Whatever his explanation, it is safe to assume that his determination to discontinue the plan of reading the Message himself, with the formalities that followed, was motivated by much the same reason which had led him to abandon the presidential levees. It is natural to suspect, too, that his personal horror of speech-making played a part in his decision. In his note of explanation to the President of the Senate he said, 'I have had principal regard to the convenience of the Legislature, to the economy of their time, to their relief from the embarrassment of immediate answers, on subjects not yet fully before them, and to the benefits thus resulting to the public affairs.'[1] But to his friend, Dr. Rush, he wrote: 'I have prevented the bloody conflict to which the making of an answer would have committed them. They consequently were able to set into real business at once, without losing ten or twelve days.'[2] The *Connecticut Courant* emphasized the latter explanation. No doubt a majority would 'white-wash their chief,' but there were men of 'nice honor' who would never 'sacrifice their reputations for propriety and magnanimity to flatter anyone.'[3]

Congress met. The Message was sent. For the first time there was no prolonged debate on the Reply and no comical procession through the streets.

And then the locusts began to swarm.

VII

The Federalist press fairly frothed with fury. What! the judiciary to be 'destroyed'? The nation to be driven to bank-

[1] *Writings of Jefferson*, x, 300.   [2] *Ibid.*, x, 303.   [3] January 4, 1802.

ruptcy? The navy to be wrecked? The gates of the citadel to be thrown open to the Jacobins? The nation's credit to be ruined? The public service to be decimated for an 'avaricious' economy, and — Federalist office-holders to be forced from the public trough? Monstrous!

But the press was no more infuriated than the Federalist politicians. One correspondent of King's was discouraged because of the abandonment of the old custom of the Address and the Reply. 'Would to God that in this manner only his Administration may be distinguished from that of his predecessors.' [1] Writhing in his wrath, the ailing Ames was less reconciled to fate. 'The President's speech is out,' he wrote. 'He calls it a message. The difference is pretended to be important to save time, money, and ceremony. Is not this philosophy, dignity, etc.?' [2] At this moment the unhappy man at Dedham was seeing daggers in the air, for had not Levi Lincoln set up a paper, the *National Aegis*, at Worcester, to support the Administration under the very nose of the Essex Junto? What taste!

Not to be outdone by his Federalist allies, Aaron Burr contributed an amusing sneer. 'One idea contained in this message,' he wrote his son-in-law, 'is much applauded by our ladies. They unite in the opinion that "the energies of man ought to be principally employed in the multiplication of the human race" and in this they promise an ardent and an active co-operation.... I hope the fair of your State will equally testify their applause of this sentiment; and I enjoin you to manifest your patriotism and your attachment to the Administration by "exerting your energies" in the manner indicated.' [3] But Burr was not to be in the chair when the Message was read, his personal and political problems holding him in New York until the middle of January.

Bayard, indignant at the plan to repeal the internal taxes and rely on customs duties and the sale of the public lands for revenue, urged the merchants to 'come forward if they wish the duties lowered upon any article of importation.' [4]

Monroe, his eye on patronage, gave to the Message a unique interpretation. Would not the repeal of the internal taxes, with-

[1] Joseph Hale to King, *King's Corr.*, IV, 38.   [2] *Ibid.*, IV, 41.
[3] *Burr*, II, 162–63.   [4] *Bayard Papers*, II, 145.

out the necessity of recurrence to them, make it possible for Jefferson to remove 'whomsoever you may think of the dependants of the late Administration'? [1]

But more reliable as a barometer of public opinion was John Quincy Adams. 'The measures recommended by the President,' he wrote King, 'are all popular in all parts of the nation. But they are undergoing a scrutiny in the public newspapers more able and more severe than they will probably meet in either house of Congress.' [2]

VIII

The undeniable popularity of Jefferson's recommendations was gall and wormwood to Alexander Hamilton. The repeal of the internal taxes was as a personal affront, since it interfered with his plan for the creation of a more powerful military establishment. The proposed reforms in the system of finance was a reflection on his own methods. The veiled attack on the Judiciary Act, pushed through on the eve of the inauguration for the obvious purpose of strengthening the position of the Federalist Party in the courts, was a center shot at the very heart of the plan to continue Federalist domination in government despite the manifest will of the people.

The popularity of the recommendations was sinister. The Message must be torn to pieces. And who could do it so well as Alexander Hamilton — perhaps the most brilliant master of controversial writing in the country? He had his own newspaper now, and through the secrecy of his connection he could maintain an anonymous position. Soon the genius of the opposition in savage mood was bending over his desk with pen and pad, and soon the *Post* was publishing article after article of ridicule and denunciation — and no one was deceived as to the authorship. 'A writer in the *New York Evening Post,* said to be General Hamilton, has undertaken particularly to point out great and comprehensive errors in the message,' wrote John Quincy Adams, and his doctrines find great approbation among the Federalists and among all who consider themselves as the profound thinkers

[1] Monroe to Jefferson *Writings of Monroe,* III, ¾22.

[2] *King's Corr.,* IV, 59

of the nation.'[1] The first article appeared December 17, and it
was not until April 8 that the last of the series was published.

Hamilton began in his best satirical vein with observations on
the sending of a message instead of the customary delivery of a
speech. 'Whether this proceeded from pride or humility, from
temperate love of reform or from a wild spirit of innovation, is
submitted to the conjectures of the curious,' he wrote. 'A single
observation shall be indulged — since all agree that it is unlike
his predecessors in essential points. It is a mark of consistency to
differ from them in matters of form.'[2]

Then, clearly stung and disgusted by the favorable reaction to
the Message, Hamilton drew again on his deep vein of satire and
sarcasm. 'Whoever considers the temper of the day must be
satisfied that this message is likely to add much to the popularity
of our Chief Magistrate. It conforms as far as would be tolerated
at this early stage of our progress in political perfection to the
bewitching tenets of that illuminated doctrine which promises
man ere long an emancipation from the burdens and restraints of
government; giving a foretaste of that pure felicity which the
apostles of this doctrine have predicted.'[3]

Dropping the facetious mood, Hamilton now lunged savagely
at his adversary. The Message was enough 'to alarm all who are
anxious for the safety of our government, for the responsibility
and welfare of our nation.' Was it not aimed at 'the sacrifice of
constitutional energy, of sound principles and of public interest
to the popularity of one man'?[4]

Turning now to particulars, he pounced on Jefferson's constitutional scruples against waging against Tripoli an aggressive war
without a formal declaration of war by Congress. Had not Tripoli
declared war against us? We had won a fight, and, instead of
pushing our advantage to the utmost, we had abandoned the
victory. Was it possible that when attacked during a congressional recess the President could repel only each individual attack,
and not capture and retain the vessels of the foe?[5]

Hamilton's facile pen soon was assailing the proposed repeal of
the internal taxes. Did not the mere suggestion imply a 'defi-

---

[1] To King, King's Corr., IV, 60.   [2] Henry Cabot Lodge, Works of Hamilton, VII, 200
[3] Ibid.   [4] Ibid., VII, 201.   [5] Ibid., VII, 205.

ciency of intellect' and 'an ignorance of our financial arrangements'? True, Jefferson had said that the internal taxes were not
necessary to meet current obligations or to pay interest on the
debt or to discharge it. But when the internal taxes were laid,
provision was made that a part be used in paying the debt and
that all surplus at the end of the year should go into a sinking
fund. True, Jefferson thought there was 'reasonable ground' to
believe that this could be abandoned, but belief was not enough
— there must be positive knowledge. What assurance was there
that the import taxes would not diminish? And why should these
import duties not be reduced?

And why abandon internal taxes? Granted that the remaining
sources would be sufficient to meet all obligations, would not
more than sufficient make possible a more rapid discharge of the
debt than had been contemplated? Jefferson had accused the
Federalists of wishing to perpetuate the debt. Why had he
changed his tone? [1] And then, in the next article, Hamilton
changed *his* tone. Had he concluded it possible that the more
rapid discharge of the debt was the intent of the Administration?
Had some hint of the purpose reached him? At any rate, in the
next article he had lost his enthusiasm for the speedy discharge
of the debt. This 'might be injurious in many ways,' since it
would 'produce a money-plethora ... injurious to the energies
and especially to the morality and industry of the nation.'
But in the meanwhile, he had thought of other uses to which
the surplus revenue might be put. Why not spend it on naval
and military preparations, on docks and fortifications, on roads,
bridges, and canals? Great rulers had thus spent money. 'Only
the indolent and temporizing rulers, who love to loll in the lap
of epicurean ease, and seem to imagine that to govern well is
to amuse the wondering multitude with sagacious aphorisms
and oracular sayings,' he said with a squint at his foe.

A third time he attacked the repeal of the internal taxes,
finding now that it would be a blow at the public credit, even
though the creditors' claims be met through other sources of
taxation. Had not the import and excise on distilled spirits

---

[1] The more rapid discharge of the debt was the purpose of the Jeffersonians, but no
reference to this was made in the Message.

been positively pledged to the payment of interest on the debt
and the meeting of certain installments on the principal? Had
not this source of revenue been 'mortgaged' to the public creditor? True, Jefferson insisted that other sources of revenue would
meet the obligations, but 'surely neither the purity of the public
faith nor the safety of the creditor will endure the application
of this principle.' Innovations in the method of payment could
not but disturb the serenity of the bondholders.[1]

Having met one challenge, Hamilton hurried on to the meeting of another — the proposed repeal of the Judiciary Act which
in the twilight hour of the previous Administration had created
new courts and new judges. The repeal of this act, he said,
would be a sweeping attack on the whole judicial system. What
had Jefferson meant, if not a reflection on the federal courts,
when he said that the federal judiciary had been 'multiplied
unnecessarily,' since the citizen looked for the protection of
life, property, and reputation mostly to the State courts? Did
not Jefferson's action, in submitting a list of causes tried in
federal courts since the beginning to show that courts existing
at the time of the creation of the new courts were sufficient to
meet all demands, denote a 'pigmy mind'? Why should not
the citizen have his choice between State and federal courts?
Why force them into State courts, so often bad or unreliable? [2]

Again Hamilton's zeal had led him too far, and in his next
article he admitted that Jefferson aimed to abolish merely the
newly created courts filled on the eve of the inauguration. But
in the next line he was warning against a possible purpose to
abolish all United States circuit courts — something never
suggested.

But had Congress the right to abolish these recently created
courts? It created them, possibly it could abolish them. True,
it was 'not easy to maintain that Congress cannot abolish courts
which have been once instituted and found to be inconvenient
and unnecessary.' Yes, the courts could possibly be abolished,
but abolish the judges sitting in these unnecessary courts? Not
without a violation of the Constitution; for did not the Constitution provide that judges should hold office and draw salaries

[1] *Works of Hamilton*, VII, 206–23.   [2] *Ibid.*, VII, 224–29.

during good behavior? Very well, abolish the court, but touch not the cloak or the salary of the unnecessary judge, for his salary must be continued during good behavior throughout his life even though he render no service to the State. How else guarantee the 'independence of the judges'? How else guard 'from invasion one of the most precious provisions of the Constitution'?

It was when he reached Jefferson's proposal for a liberalization of the Naturalization Law that Hamilton found his anonymous position a protection. Born of alien parentage on an alien shore, he did not hesitate to excoriate the foreigner. Here his hatred of the Irish and the Germans of Pennsylvania, who had enlisted with such zest under the Jeffersonian banner, flared. They, and not native Americans, had elected Jefferson. Oh, the curse of the foreigner! Who ruled France? A foreigner. 'Who rules the councils of our ill-fated and unhappy country? A foreigner.'

Thus the alien from the West Indies sneered at the foreign birth of Gallatin, the foreigner from Geneva, and the pot called the kettle black. This is the lowest descent in demagogy in the public utterances of Hamilton.

'The influx of foreigners' was 'corrupting the national spirit.' But in the development of his theme Hamilton really accepted the Jeffersonian intent. 'Under the peculiar circumstances of the X Y Z incident the law compelling a fourteen-year residence for citizenship may have been extreme,' he said; and this was precisely what Jefferson meant. But why admit them at once on their arrival? Hamilton asked; and Jefferson had no such thought. There ought to be a five years' wait, Hamilton concluded.[1]

And Jefferson's 'multiplicity of officers'? Beginning with a blunt denial of the charge, Hamilton through concessions almost immediately admitted the soundness of Jefferson's position. There might, as Jefferson proposed, properly be a reduction in the personnel of the foreign service. Again he conceded that Jefferson was within reason in proposing the abolishment of the naval agencies, created by Hamilton because of our 'rupture with France,' and no longer needed. Still again, the purpose of

[1] *Works of Hamilton*, VII, 241–44.

their creation having been discharged, Jefferson was not unreasonable in insisting that inspectors of revenue might now be dismissed. And still again, 'a change in circumstances may in some instances have rendered a continuance of some of the agents ... unnecessary; and the Chief Magistrate may even be right in discontinuing them.' [1]

But Jefferson's plan 'to multiply barriers against the dissipation of public money by appropriating specific sums to specific purposes'? This cut Hamilton like a sword. He took it to himself, and he baldly denied that there ever had been a shifting of appropriated funds — though a congressional investigation revealed the truth to be upon the other side.

Such was Hamilton's mass attack. It disclosed only a few clear-cut issues on which the two great leaders were divided. The rest was chaff. The real issues raised were these:

Jefferson proposed the repeal of the internal taxes because they were unnecessary to meet the obligations; Hamilton wanted them retained that surplus revenue might be spent on war preparations and public improvements.

Jefferson proposed the abolishing of the newly created federal courts on the ground that they were unnecessary; Hamilton demanded that they be retained for effect if not for use, and, if abolished, that the judges be retained on salaries.

Jefferson insisted on specific appropriations for specific objects and the ending of the shifting of one fund to another; and Hamilton denied the necessity on the ground that this never had been done.

IX

In the midst of these vigorous polemics, Hamilton, more and more cynical of political conditions, was sick at heart. He saw the democratic drift and could see no means of checking it. It was at this time, in the midst of the preparation of the articles, that, writing Gouverneur Morris in the dead of night, he poured forth his frank confession in a letter.

'Mine is an odd destiny,' he wrote. 'Perhaps no man in the United States has done more for the present Constitution than

[1] *Works of Hamilton*, VII, 251-56.

myself; and contrary to all my anticipations of its fate, as you
know from the beginning, I am still laboring to prop the frail
and worthless fabric. Yet I have the murmurs of my friends
no less than the curses of my foes for my reward.'

And then he added: 'What can I do better than withdraw
from the scene? Every day proves to me more and more that
this American world was not meant for me.'

And then, writing the leader of his party in the Senate, he
continued:

'You, friend Morris, are by birth a native of this country,
but by genius an exotic. You mistake if you fancy that you are
more of a favorite than myself, or that you are in any sort upon
a theater suited to you.' [1]

But, among the Federalists, Hamilton had no cause for disappointment over their reaction to his attack on the Message.
Everywhere it was hailed as far and above every other criticism
that had been made. The articles written anonymously behind
the walls of the house on Cedar Street were eagerly reproduced
by the party organs everywhere and read with keen curiosity by
partisans. Nowhere were they read to more purpose than among
the Federalist members of Congress about the fireplaces in the
Washington boarding-houses, and in their seats in House and
Senate. Riding in the tempestuous sea of a rising democracy,
and puzzled as to which way to turn, Hamilton offered them a
compass and a chart. Thus, these articles became the blue-
prints in the congressional discussions on the repeal of the internal
taxes and of the Judiciary Act. No one but knew the author. The
name of Hamilton once more was on the lips of all his partisans.

The leaders had spoken; and the contest now shifted to the
party leaders in House and Senate. With the two armies drawn
up ready for battle, it is well to make a survey of the leaders —
especially of John Randolph of Roanoke, the one genius among
them, brilliant, eloquent, erratic, and troublesome to friend
and foe.

---

[1] Hamilton to Morris, February 27, 1802, *Works of Hamilton*, VIII, 592–93.

CHAPTER V

The Leaders: Portrait of Randolph

I

WHEN the tocsin sounded for the first legislative battle of the Jeffersonian régime, the personnel in Congress was not so impressive, generally, as it had been before, and was to become again. Madison, Gallatin, Harper, Sedgwick were gone. In the House, the Jeffersonians outnumbered their enemies two to one, and on party measures they outnumbered their foes in the Senate by three.[1] In men of brilliance and distinction, however, the opposition had an advantage numerically in both houses. Senator Uriah Tracy of Connecticut, with but a few years to live, was a master parliamentarian, a practical statesman, forceful and resourceful in debate, and industrious and effective in committee. His colleague, James Hillhouse, was strong in common sense and in the depth of his convictions.

But on the Federalist side there was no one in the Senate to compare with Gouverneur Morris, brilliant, eloquent, witty, a gallant of the school of Versailles and Parisian salons, cynical, contemptuous of democracy, skeptical of liberty, snobbish in his idolatry of titles.[2] 'The greatest orator I have ever heard,' wrote Plumer.[3] Hamilton had assured him he was an 'exotic' among Americans, and John Rutledge has illustrated the meaning in the social sense. 'I arrived in the dark and rain at Pomfret,' he wrote, 'where I heard a clattering of French, and upon entering the inn found Gouverneur Morris with his two French valets ... and his hair buckled up into about one hundred papil-

---

[1] Jefferson to Barlow, *Writings of Jefferson*, x, 319.
[2] *Jefferson and Hamilton*, 339–41.   [3] *Plumer*, 258.

liottes.' His wooden leg, papilliottes, French attendants and French conversation, had his host, hostess and their daughters, with the whole family including the hostler and Betty the cook maid, staring most prodigiously and gave me some idea how the natives looked when poor Cook made his entrée at the Friendly Isles.' [1] He was to the manner born in the court circles of Versailles and the boudoirs of frail Parisian beauties, and no rôle in his life became his nature more than that of a conspirator handling the money for bribing Louis XVI out of prison.[2]

He loomed high above all other members of his dying party in Congress.

On the Jeffersonian side there were two senators of conspicuous talents. John Breckinridge of Kentucky, a new member, had a meteoric rise to leadership because of his strength of mind and character.

But the one Jeffersonian capable of matching the eloquence and sarcasm of Morris in debate was Stevens T. Mason of Virginia, an aide on the staff of Washington at Yorktown, who had entered the Senate in his thirty-fourth year. He was now in his forty-first, with but two years to live. Physically he was of commanding presence. Six feet in height, he carried more than his fair share of fat. His abnormally large gray intellectual eyes, his wide mouth with sternly compressed lips, his splendid high and broad forehead would have set him apart in any assembly as a man of mentality and character. The expectations aroused by his appearance were realized when he spoke, for he was eloquent in the true sense, and Morris was to find in this ailing Virginian a match for his sarcasm and satire. Years before, he had shocked the Federalists by breaking the Senate injunction of secrecy to carry a copy of the Jay Treaty to the press. He admitted it, for he was as audacious as he was able. It was he who had ridden to the Vermont jail with gold in his saddlebags to pay the fine of Matthew Lyon, one of the victims of the Sedition Law.[3] Utterly fearless, absolutely honest, perfectly sincere, he had literally worn himself out in the service of the country.

---

[1] S. E. Morison, *Life and Letters of Harrison Gray Otis*, I, 278. (Hereafter cited as *Otis*.)
[2] *Jefferson and Hamilton*, 341.   [3] *Ibid.*, 388.

In the House, the Federalists had a numerical advantage in leaders of talent, though we need concern ourselves only with the two foremost, Roger Griswold and James A. Bayard. The former, an intense partisan and fluent debater, we shall meet more intimately later on.

James Bayard of Delaware had an unusual mind and a rare capacity for speech. Still a young man, in his thirty-fifth year, imposing in height and girth, with the florid complexion of a high liver, he was conspicuous for his fashionable attire. Among his contemporaries he was noted for his devotion to wine, women, and cards, and it was said that he regularly consumed a bottle of wine a day. No one questioned his integrity any more than his ability.[1] He combined the qualities of a polished orator and vigorous debater. His admirers were inclined to fall into hyper-bole in describing his forensic triumphs. 'Never equalled by Fox, Pitt or Chatham,' thought Cutler.[2] No Federalist in the House enjoyed to such a degree the confidence and respect of Hamilton. A few years more, and we shall find much gossip concerning his attempted negotiations to join the Jeffersonians. Soon he will leave the House for the Senate.

On the Jeffersonian side of the House were a number of cap-able leaders without brilliance — men like Nicholson of Mary-land. Two were men of genius. One of these has been absurdly depreciated by partisan historians and others who too blindly have accepted Henry Adams's anti-Virginian interpretation. For to belittle William Branch Giles is to reject the testimony of most of his contemporaries of both political persuasions. He was a robust partisan, a lusty, gusty, and dangerous oppo-nent in debate, as both Federalists and Whigs were to find. Even the choleric Timothy Pickering confessed to a sneaking admira-tion for his talents.[3] He was of striking appearance, with his very dark complexion, his penetrating dark eyes denoting a superior mind, his black hair and commanding form. It requires more than sectional spleen to wipe out the deliberately expressed admiration of Justice Story for his 'clear nervous expression,' his 'well-digested and powerful condensation,' and for his ability

[1] Plumer MSS., quoted in Beveridge, *Life of John Marshall*, iii, 79.
[2] Cutler, ii, 79.   [3] *Pickering*, iv, 156.

to 'sustain his position with penetrating and wary argument.'
Yes, 'a great natural strength of mind,' said Story.[1] He shared
with Bayard, on the other side, a weakness for liquor and cards.

The other Jeffersonian leader in the House was perhaps the
one great genius in either branch, the brilliant, eloquent, witty,
erratic, picturesque, dramatic, and romantic John Randolph of
Roanoke, who, beginning as the dominant leader of his party,
was to be the stormy petrel of the régime. We must study him
under the microscope, for he was a rare specimen.

II

No one looking down from the gallery of the House fails to
be impressed by one startling figure on the floor. At first glance,
the impression conveyed is that of a young boy of premature
growth, but a closer study of the striking features discloses a
faded complexion with the innumerable wrinkles of old age.
His hair, light and glossy, is parted in the middle and tied
behind with black ribbons. His eyes, a dark clear chestnut,
reflecting his varying moods, alone give animation to his face
which Melbourne thought otherwise 'expressionless as a block
of granite.'[2] Seated in his chair, his shoulders raised, his head
depressed, his body bent, he seems of but ordinary height. His
fingers, that are so conspicuous and deadly in debate, are long,
thin, tapering, and weirdly 'wand-like.' Few contemporaries
attempting a description fail to feature the fingers. His utterly
beardless pointed chin, the boyish beautiful mouth, revealing,
in smiles, teeth of ivory whiteness, accentuate the first impression
of extreme youth. It is when he rises that the impression of
youth gives way to one of the frailty and decrepitude of old age.
The boyish figure is almost ghostly in its emaciation[3] — very
tall and spare. No one fails to note the length and delicacy of
his arms and legs, one finding them 'unsightly' and another
thinking them 'slow and graceful in their movements.'[4] The
length of his legs is out of proporiton with the upper part of
his body.

[1] William Story, *Life and Letters of Joseph Story*, I, 159.
[2] W. C. Bruce, *John Randolph of Roanoke*, II, 80.
[3] Plumer to Emery, *Plumer*, 248.   [4] Bruce, II, 77–78.

His garb is as striking as his body. Frequently he appears in a blue riding-coat and buckskin breeches, for he rides to the Capitol beautifully mounted and accompanied by a black servant, and frequently by his dogs. Usually he appears in white top boots, with drab or buckskin short-clothes, and occasionally in gaiters. He cares nothing for conformity.

Such is this brilliant young genius of thirty, an incongruous combination, with something of the frailty and decrepitude of old age, his face pale and 'corrugated with compartments like a bed quilt,' who by common consent is the most fascinating figure in the country-town capital.

Such is John Randolph of Roanoke.

III

Born an aristocrat, he remains an aristocrat throughout his life. Within his veins runs the mingled blood of a notable English family and of Pocahontas, the Indian maiden. His boyhood was by no means that of the average. There was much of the Byronic in his earliest years, though his mother was as much loved as the poet's was feared. He was reared in a lonely solitude on a desolate estate whose 'groves and solitudes' he was to recall with melancholy affection in later life. As a child he was super-sensitive. He had a morbid pride, and was easily stirred by passions, and was restored to calmness with difficulty.[1] Even in maturity he seemed as 'a man without a skin,' [2] and he himself, speaking of his sensitivity, once said that he had observed in himself from earliest recollections a delicacy or effeminacy of complexion that 'but for a spice of the devil in my temper would have consigned me to the distaff or the needle.' [3] Thus his school days away from home were torture, and he was to recall with bitterness, many years later, that he had been 'tyrannized over and tortured by the most peevish and ill-tempered of pedagogues,' who 'excommunicated me body and soul'; and to remember with aristocratic loathing 'the vulgar habiliments and boorish manners' of his schoolmates, who no doubt were average boys.

[1] Bruce, I, 36–37.
[2] B. W. Leigh, quoted in Bruce, *ibid.*   [3] *Ibid.*

JOHN RANDOLPH
From a portrait by Stuart

More to the guidance of his mother than to his pedagogue was he indebted for his early taste in literature. The lonely days on the plantation had been brightened by the English classics. Before he had entered college he had made the language of the Bible and Bunyan his. He once said that 'Shakespeare and Milton and Chaucer and Spenser and Plutarch and the Arabian Nights Entertainment and Don Quixote and Gil Blas and Tom Jones ... have made up more than half of my worldly enjoyment.' Dryden, Beaumont and Fletcher, Otway, Congreve, Pope, Thomson, Gay, Gray, Sheridan, Cowper, Byron were prime favorites, and, at an uncommonly early age, he had read and re-read Smollett's 'Humphrey Clinker' with his mother. But he was never happier than when he hied himself to the closet among the dusty accumulations of the *Spectator*, and pored over the essays of Addison and Steele. He had a retentive memory and all he read was later woven into the fabric of his style. Speaking of those dawning days he once said, 'Never did higher literary ambition burn in human breast.'

To his college training he owed little. His career at William and Mary was cut short by his voluntary withdrawal, following a duel with a young Federalist over politics. At Princeton, where he attended for a short time, he was disgusted with the teaching of elocution and oratory, for he had read Burke and had opinions of his own. He thought the prizes reserved for 'mouthers and ranters,' and he 'despised the awards and umpires in the bottom of [his] heart.' [1] This contempt for prizes and college honors never left him.

Had he been born in England, he probably would have aspired to a literary career; in America he turned to politics. As a very young man he saw the inauguration of Washington and listened to the debates in the First Congress, and then went home speedily to find himself in the way of political preferment because of the brilliancy of his oratory and the ardor of his opinions. Elected to Congress very early, he became conspicuous immediately in the debates, and during the Adams Administration took his place with the foremost in the bitter battles and feuds. Thus, though young, he was a veteran par-

[1] Bruce, I, 85.

liamentarian and orator, when, with the beginning of the Jefferson
Administration, he found himself in the position of leader of
the majority.

IV

The superiority of his oratory was due in part to the natural
ardor of his nature, and in part to a unique art which was inherent in his personality. When he rose, a hush invariably fell
upon the chamber, and every eye was fixed expectantly upon
the tall ghostly figure. With head up and shoulders thrown back,
his figure seemed to expand under the inspiration of his theme.
His voice was unlike almost any other — clear like a clarion,
penetrating and silvery, and his enunciation was perfect. It was
described by Melbourne as 'sweet as a flute and an octave
higher than other men's voices.' One contemporary found it
'of the clearest tone and most flexible modulation' he had ever
heard. 'In his speech,' says this observer, 'not a breath of air
is lost; it is all compressed into round smooth liquid sound;
and its inflections are so sweet, its emphasis so appropriate and
varied that it is a positive pleasure hearing him speak any words
whatever.' [1] 'What a voice!' exclaims Phoebe Morris. 'Clear,
melodious, and penetrating, it fascinates.'[2] 'A voice that resembles the music of the spheres,' thought another. 'Such,
indeed, is the wonderful clearness of his voice and the perfection
of his enunciation that his lowest tones circulate like echoes
through the halls of Congress.' [3] Horace Binney, himself one
of the polished orators of his generation, was delighted with
'the facility and beauty of his enunciation.' [4] Josiah Quincy
found his voice 'silvery in its tones; becoming unpleasantly shrill
only when conveying direct invective.' [5] James Buchanan
thought it 'shrill and penetrating.' Another has described it as
'one of the sources of his power' — ranging from tenor to treble
with no bass notes. But in the passion of battle, in moments
of scorn and indignation, when the orator was moved to sarcasm
or invective, it had the shrillness of a woman's in excitement.

In gesticulation he was restrained, never having lost his con-

[1] Gilmer, quoted in Bruce, II, 77–78.   [2] Bruce, II, 65.

[3] *Ibid.*, II, 72.   [4] *Ibid.*, II, 65.   [5] *Ibid.*, II, 89.

tempt for the ranting and arm-waving that had disgusted him
at Princeton. His few gestures were apt and graceful. Thus
there appeared to be no effort in his delivery. While speaking,
it was his custom to turn from side to side. His most deadly
gestures were reserved for the attack when he pointed his long
trembling finger at the object of his scorn. Buchanan thought
his 'manner confident, proud and imposing.' He was a consummate master of the 'pause,' one observer recording that 'in the
art of pausing he was unrivaled.' [1] Buchanan, who had studied
all the orators of his time at close range, noted that he 'often
paused for an instant as if to select the most appropriate word.' [2]
Sometimes he would launch into a complicated sentence, arousing curiosity as to its conclusion, and then pause, with his head
gracefully elevated as though struggling with the problem of
his terminal facilities, and then complete the sentence with
grace and force. There was artistry in the pause, in the unexpected and infrequent gesture, in the expression of the eye and
features always suited to the thought conveyed.

As with Prentiss, a generation later, his most finished speeches
were those thrown off without special preparation on the impulse
of the moment. He had the rare gift of catching his illustrations
from the air. Such an event 'was as inevitable' — and he paused,
seeking a comparison. Just then a leaf fluttered down before
his face. With his finger he followed it until it reached the
ground — 'as inevitable as the law of gravitation,' he concluded.[3]
In his diction he was fastidious, seeking the word that would
most perfectly convey the precise shade of meaning. He was
distinguished, too, by his pronunciation, and Pickering, not
thus distinguished, found in him 'a servile conformity' to the
'dictates of fashion.' [4]

In the armory of his oratorical genius the weapons most
feared by his victims were those of wit, satire, sarcasm, and
invective. In the use of these no other man in American history
has been so ruthless and devastating. No philippics have approached those of Randolph in the debates on the Yazoo frauds.
In the use of invective he often became inebriated on his own

---

[1] Jeter, quoted in Bruce, II, 91.   [2] Bruce, II, 90.
[3] W. S. Lacey, quoted in Bruce, II, 209.   [4] *Pickering*, IV, 477.

indignation and with his rhetoric he went beyond all reason and justice, but so brilliant and moving was his phrasing that momentarily his extravagance had effect.

His wit was seldom without its stiletto. If he had a sense of humor, he did not use it in his oratory. His Blifil and Black George attack on Clay is classic, but this was not one whit more severe than scores of others. Thus, when Richard Rush was made Comptroller of the Treasury, Randolph said that 'never were abilities so much below mediocrity so well rewarded; no, not when Caligula's horse was made Consul.' Of another whose ambition overlapped his capacity, he said that 'his mind is like the lands of the headwaters of the Monongahela — naturally poor and made still poorer by excessive cultivation.' Apropos of Samuel Dexter's political instability, he called him 'Mr. Ambi-Dexter.' Edmund Randolph, his own relative, was likened to 'a chameleon on the aspen, always trembling, always changing.' Contemptuously referring to Van Buren's secretiveness, he said he 'rowed to his object with muffled oars.' Turning on his friend Thomas Ritchie, of the *Richmond Enquirer*, he said the journalist had seven principles — 'five loaves and two fishes.' Without malice, he described Benjamin Harden, a vigorous but unpolished speaker, as 'a carving knife whetted on a brickbat'; and wishing to demolish two members of the House named Wright and Rea in one fell swoop, he said the House had two anomalies — 'a Wright always wrong and a Rea without light.' [1]

It was the fashion of his victims in his day, and has been of some historians since, to sneer at his speeches. They were not constructed according to rule. They were not geometrical demonstrations. They were not serene and illuminating essays without passion or feeling. In later life they became too discursive, but no method could have been more effective than that of his earlier years. Diction, precise and perfect; rhetoric, polished, brilliant; eloquence invariably thrilling and tremendous when inspired by a sense of wrong. But he did not reach his conclusions by moving slowly step by step, with recapitulations. He went by leaps and bounds, striking only the high places, but he covered the ground completely. No one ever doubted, when he had

[1] Bruce, ii, 200-04.

finished, what he meant, or why he meant it. A contemporary
critic wrote that, 'however he may seem to wander from his
point occasionally, he never fails to return to it with a bound,
illuminating it with flashing wit or the happiest illustrations,'
and that, despite the eccentricity of his conduct in ordinary
affairs, 'there will be found more of what is called common
sense in his speeches than in those of any other man in Congress.'
In oratory the proof of the pudding is in the eating, and he
never failed to make a profound impression or to hold his listeners
in the hollow of his hand.

v

Randolph liked to think of himself as a simon-pure republican.
He was a stout champion of State rights and an inveterate enemy
of centralization. He championed personal liberty and economy
in the public service. He was a strict constitutionalist. In all
this he was a strict Jeffersonian. But whatever he may have
persuaded himself, he was merely an academic democrat. Funda-
mentally and at heart he was an aristocrat, both in training and
natural bias. We find it in him at the age of nine in his contempt
for his schoolmates because of the crudity of their clothes. The
proprietor of more than eight thousand acres, assessed even in
those days at $153,419.12, master of hundreds of slaves, owner
of a stud of blooded horses valued at thirty thousand dollars, he
could have had only an academic interest in the dispossessed.[1]
He had been born to the purple. It is significant that his contemporaries invariably associated him with the aristocracy of
great possessions and of blood. One wrote that he had 'inherited
his name, family connections, his fine plantations, and a thousand
negroes, which have given him more power in this country than
the Duke of Bedford has in England, and more than he would
have were he possessed of the brilliant wit, fine imagination, and
flowing eloquence of that celebrated Virginian.'[2]

His enemies, as well as admirers, could not disassociate the
man from the splendor of his position. Bitterly retaliating on an
attack, the pugnacious Matthew Lyon said that 'it is a long
time since I have observed that the very sight of my plebeian

[1] Bruce, II, 357.   [2] Ibid., II, 63.

face has had an unpleasant effect on the nose' of the gentleman 'nursed in the bosom of opulence, inheriting the life services
of a numerous train of the human species, and extensive fields.'
Certainly the man who set forth as a great cardinal principle
for the guidance of all statesmen, 'never without the strongest
necessity to disturb that which was at rest,' was not a radical.[1]
He had much of the temperament, the vices and virtues of the
great country gentlemen of the England of the eighteenth century. There, more than in the America of his time, he would
have been at home. Had he not been tortured by physical
infirmities and an incapacity for repose, he might easily have
changed places with Fisher Ames.

A profound affection for England followed him all his days.
How he had thrilled in boyhood at the sight of ships from England entering the James River! 'In those days,' he has told us,
'how often have I called England "my country" when the rumors
of war and separation moved me not.' When, many years later
than the period with which we deal, he caught his first glimpse of
the English coast, he shed tears of joy with the exclamation,
'Thank God that I have lived to behold the land of Shakespeare,
of Milton, of my forefathers. May her greatness increase through
all times.' Visitors at his home of Roanoke found 'an English
coach, English harness and saddlery, English plate, English
clothes and boots, English books,' and always on the table an
English newspaper. It was after his English sojourn that some of
his friends felt he should have remained in England where he was
happiest.[2]

He found but one fly in the ointment of his English devotion —
the treatment of Ireland. 'An Irish Tory sir, I never could abide,'
he once said.[3] When with the exquisite courtesy of which that
political rake was capable, Castlereagh was conducting him about
Saint Stephen's, pointing out the political lions, Randolph afterward recalled that 'such was the fascination of his manners, I forgot for the moment that I was speaking to the man who had sold
his country's independence, and his own.' [4] This inherent love for
England we may well bear in mind in the course of this narrative.

[1] Gamaliel Bradford, *Damaged Souls*, 138.
[2] Bruce, II, 213.   [3] *Ibid.*, II, 412.   [4] *Ibid.*, II, 439.

VI

The eccentricities that have made Randolph an interesting figure through the generations were probably due more to his physical suffering than to his genius. Too much has been made of his impotency, for he was an eccentric long before the days when ardently he was wooing the woman he hoped to make his wife. As a child he was irritable, supersensitive, given to surges of fury that, on at least one occasion, carried him off in a swoon.[1] As a youth he was a victim of insomnia when his mind was far from normal and he could be heard pacing his floor in the night muttering, 'Macbeth has murdered sleep, Macbeth has murdered sleep.' At such times he frequently saddled his horse in the dead of night and rode madly over his plantation, with loaded pistols.[2] From childhood he suffered constantly the torment of shattered nerves; for years he was tortured by a derangement of the stomach, and probably the germs of consumption were draining his vitality all the time.[3] Only an iron will and 'a spice of the devil' could have kept him in the midst of the most nerve-racking, vitality-sapping activities. To add to his torment he had been haunted from early youth with a fear of insanity, and at times, before he really became demented in 1818, his mind unquestionably was deranged.[4]

Thus, suffering physically and mentally, old age crept upon him in his youth, and when at thirty he was the great leader of his party in the House, his face was deeply, thickly seamed with the wrinkles of the venerable as he walked like a ghost down the aisles. It was in the very tumult of the fighting of these dramatic years that he complained of the 'torments of the damned' when, stricken with fever, with excruciating pains flying 'like lightning from his head to his stomach and bowels,' he had recourse to opiates.[5] During the period with which we are now concerned, he felt himself suffering 'from a decay of the whole system, racked with pain and up the greater part of the night with disordered stomach and bowels,' while spitting blood from the lungs.[6]

[1] Bruce, III, 35–37.   [2] *Ibid.*, I, 132.
[3] *Ibid.*, II, 310; Bradford, *Damaged Souls*, 128.
[4] Bruce, II, 331; 333; 338.
[5] *Ibid.*, II, 303.   [6] *Ibid.*, II, 304.

VII

One analyst [1] has implied that his infirmities and temper came from his excesses. The record, from childhood, would seem to indicate rather that his excesses and temper sprang from his infirmities. It was not drink nor gambling nor excesses of any sort that made him a pathological subject even as a child scarcely out of his mother's arms. His wild rides, too vigorous for one so frail, were meant to minister to jangled nerves and mental unrest. 'Bodily motion,' he wrote, 'seems to be some relief to mental uneasiness, and I was delighted yesterday morning to hear that the snipes are come.' [2] His almost morbid interest in racing may be similarly explained, for during the season he rode for many miles through the most inclement weather from track to track. It is of record that as a boy he contracted gambling debts in Philadelphia, but it does not appear that his gambling is the explanation of his wild rides to the tracks, for his most exhaustive and authoritative biographer assures us that his interest in racing 'was that of a gentleman, not a gambler.' He loved horses, and the excitement of the contest relieved him of the introspection that he feared; the interminable rides through the rain gave him the 'bodily movement' that relieved his 'mental uneasiness.'

Authorities are divided as to the extent of his drinking and its effect upon his temper. One says that 'he drank far too much for the good of a temperament like his'; [3] another, who knew him in his cups, testifies that instead of making him surly and quarrelsome, drink made him 'more good-humored.' [4] One of his contemporaries says that while 'he drank much in public, he drank still more in private,' [5] while another testifies: 'I never saw him affected by wine — not even to the slightest departure from the habitual and scrupulous decorum of his manners.' [6] We have positive proof that he drank, but the conflicting evidence would imply that he did not drink to such excess as to attract general attention. In his time most men drank, and few had such inducement for seeking surcease from mental and physical suffering as he

[1] Bradford, *Damaged Souls*, 128.   [2] *Ibid.*, 141.   [3] *Ibid.*, 128.
[4] Benjamin W. Leigh, quoted in Bruce, II, 368.
[5] James A. Vouldin, quoted in Bruce, II, 369.
[6] Thomas H. Benton, quoted in Bruce, II, 374.

had. There is not a scintilla of evidence to show that his outbursts of ferocious temper in the House came from an artificial stimulant. His mental uneasiness and physical suffering offer explanation enough.

VIII

Even his most unfriendly critics have not accused him of excesses with women, since they have preferred the theory of his impotency. And yet there is abundant proof that the failure of his one great love affair contributed something to the unhappiness and mental uneasiness that depressed him always. There are vague hints in his letters that in his early youth he was not a stranger to the lure of transient love. 'Rely upon it,' he wrote, 'that to love a woman as a mistress, although a delicious delirium far surpassing that of champagne, is altogether unessential, nay pernicious, in the choice of a wife.' We have a reference in another letter to a woman in Philadelphia, 'beautiful as the morning star, who was in the best society in Philadelphia, but whose mother kept a boarding-house and knew her real character.' This enchantress, the object of the infatuation of a young relative of Randolph's, may have been the cause of the ruin of his one romance. To convince his friend of the lady's falsity and frailty, his biographer hints that he may have compromised himself. A little earlier he appears to have pressed his attentions with serious intent upon Nancy Randolph, who finally closed the episode by announcing her preference for his brother.[1] But the real passion of his life he reserved for another.

For a time he was engaged to Maria Ward, a famous beauty, with a rare personal and intellectual charm. Her portrait reveals a woman of grace and distinction, not without a suggestion of coquetry. She finally broke the engagement to marry a cousin of the rejected. The wanton and stupid destruction of his letters to her, though she preserved them until her death, deprives us of the one opportunity to see into the heart of Randolph. Here and there we get glimpses into the effect of her rejection on the mind and spirits of Randolph. 'Do you remember,' he wrote years later to a friend of his early life, 'the event which some years ago

[1] Nancy Randolph to Randolph, quoted in Bruce, ii, 280.

prostrated all my faculties and made a mere child of me? I am that very child still. I have tried wine, company, business, everything within my reach to divert my mind from this subject.' In other letters we learn that she returned his love, but over the reason for the breaking of the engagement a veil is drawn. Perhaps it was the story of a youthful indiscretion; perhaps the eccentricity of his character caused parental interference. But he never forgot, and never married.

However, the miscarriage of his romance did not make him an enemy of the sex. In the society of women he was ever graceful and deferential, and they repaid the compliment of his homage with their admiration.

IX

Such is the background of the man who, with erratic brilliance and loyalty, was to lead the Administration forces through four years, and then, for four more, to become Jefferson's most virulent critic. The effectiveness of his oratory cannot be denied, the fidelity of his intent during the first Administration cannot be questioned, but perhaps the tradition which makes him one of the two or three greatest parliamentary leaders in American history may be questioned. The House responded readily to his leadership — but only so long as he accepted the leadership of Jefferson. The fact of his inability to control the House after he deserted the Administration camp implies that the compliance of that body during the first four years of Randolph's leadership was due less to his skill than to the devotion of its members to Jefferson, the most consummate of political leaders.

He had many qualities not usually associated with success in the domination of a parliamentary body. He was not a persuader or conciliator. He was not an organizer. He made no appeal to the love or devotion of those he led. He sought to rule by fear — as Thaddeus Stevens years later did. It was not pleasant to invite the lash of his scorpion's tongue, nor comfortable to keep company with his irritation. It was hard to bow to his aristocratic arrogance. One analyst, who concludes that he 'had a singular power of leading and controlling men,' despite his inability to control them when he sought to draw them off from Jefferson, admits that 'the House regarded him alternately with astonishment, dismay, delight, and disgust.' [1] These are not, with one exception, the qualities that normally make for successful leadership any-where. No doubt many who resented his manner bowed to his will to escape the vicious castigation that awaited their defection. No human being ever was a greater master of vituperation, and none ever had a greater vocabulary of acidic words. None ever matched his verbal abuse and his fierce and savage and contemp-tuous manner. In another generation Thad Stevens was to crush the wavering with a meat-axe; but Randolph used rapier and dagger and cut his victims to shreds bit by bit, salting the wounds as he proceeded. This is what Henry Adams calls ruling the House by 'energy and will.' Thomas H. Benton, who served with Randolph, has another explanation of his power — that of one 'appearing as the "planetary plague" which shed, not war and pestilence on nations, but agony and fear on members.' [2]

Even so, he could be a paragon of urbanity. The courtliness and courtesy of his antagonist he could meet in kind, but this did not apply to members of his own party who deviated one hair's-breadth from his view or program. The shrill voice raised in denunciation, the contemptuous expression of the eye and mouth, the dreadful flow of the most deadly and insulting words in the language — these gave him a period of unique power so long as he led in the sunshine of Jefferson's approval. After that the cowed and cringing were to find their voices in retaliation.

x

Unhappily, Randolph temperamentally was unfit to lead a majority. He was a lone wolf by nature and loved best to fight alone. He found little to interest him in the careful process of construction. He was in finest fettle in the work of destruction. His impatience and irritability made him inadequate in explana-tion and persuasion. For the concession and compromise so essential to constructive achievement he had no stomach. He hated the necessity of consulting others and was a nonconformist when consulted.

He resented the overshadowing leadership of Jefferson, though

[1] Bradford, *Damaged Souls*, 125.   [2] Bruce, ii, 77.

for a time only half conscious of it. He did not know how to work in harness without kicking over the traces. Nor did he covet the responsibility that goes with the leadership of a ruling majority. That he became unhappy with his lot, and regretted the blithesome days of irresponsible opposition, there can be no doubt. By nature an extremist, he could only be happy in the opposition. He was not a man of system nor of business. He could point out the weakness of a measure easier than he could perfect one. However, during his leadership he was an assiduous worker, and distasteful as it must have been, was mindful of the details of the legislative machinery. His genius was in denunciation — which goes with opposition — rather than in exposition — which falls to power. All this he realized quite early in the first Administration when he found his wings were clipped and he was in a kind of bondage. When in Richmond, early in the first Jefferson Administration, he read to George Hay and to Tucker, the biographer of Jefferson, a passage from a novel of Godwin's describing the excitement and the triumphs of a leader of the opposition. By the eager, sympathetic manner in which he read it, and from his comments on it, his auditors concluded that even then he missed and regretted the old carefree days. He had been happy as a brilliant, dashing free lance, falling upon marching columns of the Government and putting them in confusion; he was not happy at the head of the column repelling an attack. For four years leader of the Administration, for four years its most caustic and uncompromising critic, he looms throughout as the most colorful, picturesque, brilliant, and erratic figure of his time.

XI

Socially men found him charming. Josiah Quincy comments that he had extraordinary gifts as a talker, 'for it was not oratory ... so much as elevated conversation that he poured forth.' [1] This brings us to his conversational genius. He was more a monologist than a conversationalist. He shone most brightly when the tracks were cleared. A contemporary has left us a picture of this rare man when he was a solo talker. The company was sympathetic and keen to hear. The talker, in consequence, was in gay

[1] Quoted in Bruce, II, 62.

humor and high spirits. He began in the morning and talked all day, brilliantly, picturesquely, on politics and history, on theology and life. Out of his prodigious memory he poured forth quotations from the Latin and the English classics. He talked in a constant stream that sparkled and murmured melodiously. 'If his conversation were printed,' wrote one who heard him that day, 'it would be quite as entertaining, profound and versatile as his speeches during the present session of Congress.' [1]

But even in conversation, he was a lone wolf. In the presence of other good talkers he was likely to be silent. Washington Irving, proud of the prowess of his countryman, accompanying him to a dinner at Sydney Smith's in London, found that in the presence of the London wits he seemed to lose his luster, though he could be as scintillating as the best of them.[2] And yet, about the same time, an Irish member of Parliament was amazed at the brilliancy of his conversation with Maria Edgeworth with whose novels he seemed more familiar than the author herself. 'Spark produced spark, and for three hours they kept up a fire until it ended in a perfect blaze of wit, humor, and repartee.' [3] He could be as fascinating in an easy-chair as on the floor of the House.

Such was the genius to whose management the Jeffersonians looked to pilot their measures through the popular branch of Congress.

And now we must hasten to the battle-field, for the artillery is roaring.

[1] Sparks, quoted in Bruce, II, 61–62.
[2] Bradford, *Damaged Souls*, 153.   [3] Bruce, II, 440.

CHAPTER VI

Jefferson's Steam Roller

I

THE last of November found the boarding-houses of Washington buzzing with the gossip of the politicians foregathered for the congressional fray. The Federalists at first were inclined to a policy of comparative silence, with a simulated co-operation with all in the Administration that might be 'wise and good.' 'You will probably hear little of the Federalists at present,' wrote Cutler. 'It is a matter of notoriety that the Democrats feel much chagrin in not meeting with a virulent opposition.... In every constitutional measure tending to promote the public good they will find in the minority a cheerful concurrence.' [1] But this complacency was to be short-lived. Jefferson was alert, but seemingly aloof, conferring with party leaders, but giving no indication of a determination to dictate to the legislators. The philosopher was not closing his mind to events beyond the realm of politics. Early in the session he was writing his friend Dr. Benjamin Rush of the introduction of vaccination, expressing the hope that the experiment would be pressed, but warning that the medical profession should 'hit upon some mark or rule by which the popular eye may distinguish genuine from spurious virus.' [2] When in early January the politicians were maneuvering for position, he was warmly greeting a delegation of Indian chiefs in a charming address of fraternal feeling.[3]

But the roaming of his adventurous mind over other fields did not imply a dissipation of his energies. He had set forth his pro-

---

[1] Cutler, II, 49–50.   [2] *Writings of Jefferson*, x, 303.

[3] George Tucker, *Life of Thomas Jefferson*, III. 3.

gram for the session in his Message, and he expected it to be carried out. On nothing was he more bent than upon the repeal of the Judiciary Law enacted by a repudiated party on the eve of its forced retirement, to serve the party purposes of the Federalists. 'They have retired into the judiciary as a stronghold,' he wrote John Dickinson on the eve of the battle. 'There the remains of federalism are to be preserved and fed from the treasury, and from that battery all the works of republicanism are to be beaten down and erased. By a fraudulent use of the Constitution, which has made judges irremovable, they have multiplied useless judges merely to strengthen their phalanx.' [1]

No one doubted at the time the political motive behind the creation of the 'midnight judges' and the passage of the Judiciary Bill. The Federalists had been repudiated at the polls. The people had rejected their measures and their men. After the election, with the existing federal courts amply able to meet all requirements, they had created these new courts, and Adams had hastily appointed the judges exclusively from among the members of the rejected party. The annals of the country present few such shameful spectacles as that in the office of John Marshall, Secretary of State, on the night the old régime went out, when, by the light of candles, he, who even then had been named Chief Justice, feverishly peddled out commissions before the striking of the hour when the new régime was due. The federal judiciary long had been an engine of party and partisan malice. John Marshall, who had just been placed at the head of the Supreme Court, was as bitter a partisan as could have been found anywhere. He had played his ignoble part in the making of the 'midnight judges.' The *Washington Federalist*, matching in scurrility the most miserable journals of the time, was understood to be under his direct influence.[2] It was commonly understood that the Chief Justice was not above the actual writing of political articles for this journal, and the most brilliant of his biographers concludes that 'some of the matter appearing in the *Washington Federalist* is characteristic of Marshall's style and opinions.' [3] Such indelicacies were common before Jefferson made what historians

---

[1] *Writings of Jefferson*, x, 301.
[2] Beveridge, II, 332, note.   [3] *Ibid.*, II, 541, note.

quaintly term his 'attack on the Federal Judiciary' to purge it of
its indecencies.

The Federalist leaders were distressed and alarmed. Hamilton,
in the *New York Evening Post*, was making vigorous attacks on the
threatened repeal, and the leaders in the country-town capital
were poring over his articles for points. They were even frightened
and horrified at the introduction of stenographers to report the
congressional debates. Such truckling to the people! Could anything be more Jacobin than an assumption of the right of the
public to information on the proceedings of government? As the
struggle approached, with excitement running high, the Federalists found themselves in a very critical and delicate position. If
they should combat the repeal inch by inch with 'fair reasoning,
the Jeffersonians would 'have an opportunity of displaying themselves in long speeches which they can give to the public under
advantages denied to the other party, who have no Federal stenographers on the floor.' [1] Distasteful though it was to pander to
the people, perhaps it would be best to play the game. And so
they agreed to reduce their speeches to writing, before or after
delivery, for publication in the party press.[2]

Early in January the debate began in the Senate.

II

Not even the debate on Assumption had attracted so much attention. It was to run along through many weeks and to call forth
the supreme exertions of the foremost orators of both parties.
Eager and excited spectators flocked to the two chambers, and
women, dressed as for a social function, crowded the members in
their seats.

On January 8, 1802, Senator Breckinridge, author of the repeal
measure, opened the debate in a speech of moderate tone from
which mere partisan issues were excluded. An excellent lawyer, a
fluent, forceful speaker, with a graceful and conciliating manner,
he based his argument on the useless expenditure of money on
offices not required. The creation of the new courts had been unnecessary and improper. Calling the roll of cases tried in the federal courts from the organization of the Government, he showed

[1] Cutler, II, 62–63.   [2] *Ibid.*, II, 66.

that they had passed on an annual average of about eight hundred suits, and this without congestion or exertion. Instead of the demands on the courts increasing, there was reason to expect a reduction in the number of cases. In the Southern States a great number of suits had been brought by British creditors, and these were almost at an end. In Pennsylvania great numbers of cases had grown out of the Whiskey Rebellion, and this incident now was history. In all the States there had been many cases under the Sedition Law, now happily no longer in existence. Many more grew out of the Excise Act, and this was about to be repealed.

'Can it be necessary, then,' he asked, 'to increase courts when suits are decreasing? Can it be necessary to multiply judges when their duties are diminishing?'

Whence came the absurd idea that all suits of citizens must find their way to federal courts? It was not the intent of the Constitution that the federal courts should take over the functions properly within the jurisdiction of the State courts.

Nowhere was there a judicial system 'so prodigal and extensive' as in the United States. 'In England, whose courts are the boast, and said to be the security of the rights of the nation, every man knows there are but twelve judges and three principal courts. These courts embrace in their original or appellate jurisdiction almost the whole circle of human concerns.'

But had Congress the power to abolish courts once established? The Federalists contended it had not. Why, in their very act creating these new courts they themselves had abolished some courts to create these others! Their contention of the right then was correct, 'and if it be correct, the present inferior courts may be abolished as constitutionally as the last.'

Ah, but the Federalists insist that the judges cannot be separated from their salaries. 'Because the Constitution declares that a judge shall hold his office during good behavior, can it be tortured to mean that he shall hold his office after it is abolished? Can it be that his tenure shall be limited by behaving well in an office which does not exist? Can it mean that an office may exist, though its duties are extinct? Can it mean, in short, that the shadow, to wit, the judge, can remain, when the substance, to wit, the office, is removed?

'It is a principle of our Constitution, as well as of common honesty, that no man shall receive public money but in consideration of public service.'

And then, anticipating the strange doctrine to be advanced by the Federalists with the support of Hamilton, he went on: 'After the law is repealed, they are either judges or they are not. If they are judges, they can be impeached; but for what? For malfeasance in office only. How, I ask, can they be impeached for malfeasance in office when their offices are abolished? They are not officers, and still they are entitled to the emoluments annexed to the office. Although they are judges they cannot be guilty of malfeasance because they have no office. They are only quasi-judges, so far as regards the duties, but real judges as far as regards the salary. It must be the salary, then, and not the duties which constitutes a judge.'

Such was the opening speech of Breckinridge, unassailable in its logic and common sense, and bottomed on ideas to which everyone subscribes today. But historians were to be more impressed with the rhetorical oratory of Gouverneur Morris, who opened for the Federalists.

At this time there was no more finished orator in the Senate. His fine figure, despite his wooden leg, his kindling countenance, his melodious voice, his graceful gesticulation, his mastery of the art of rhetoric, conspired to make him a master of the spoken word. Though contemptuous, not only of the Constitution he in part had phrased, and of the Republic, which he despised, he was profoundly to impress some historians by his ardent 'defence of the Constitution' against the wreckage that would follow the abolishing of the new courts. His cynicism was proverbial, and his wit had been sharpened by many encounters with the ladies and dandies of the Parisian salons and boudoirs. There was charm in his manner.

'This is the first time,' he began, 'I ever heard the utility of courts of justice estimated by the number of suits carried before them. I have read that a celebrated monarch of England, the great Alfred, had enacted such laws, established such tribunals, and organized such a system of police that a purse of gold might be hung up on the highway without danger of being taken. Had the honorable gentleman from Kentucky existed in those days, he would, perhaps, have attempted to convince old Alfred that what he considered the glory of his reign was its greatest evil. For, by taking the unfrequency of crimes as a proof that tribunals were unnecessary, and thus boldly substituting effect for cause, the gentleman might demonstrate the inutility of any institution by a system of reasoning the most fallacious.'

Turning to the issue, the orator plunged into the theme that the judges, being old, should not be forced to travel such extensive circuits. 'Cast an eye over the extent of our country,' he said, 'and a moment's consideration will show that the First Magistrate, in selecting a character for the bench, must seek less the learning of a judge than the agility of a postboy. Can it be possible that men advanced in years — that men educated in a closet — men who, from their habits of life, must have more strength of mind than of body; is it, I say, possible that such men can be running from one end of the continent to the other? Or, if they could, can they find time to hear and decide causes?'

And then the 'violation of the Constitution'! What would be the effect of repeal? 'It will be that the check established by the Constitution, wished for by the people, and necessary in every contemplation of common sense, is destroyed.... I stand to arrest the victory meditated over the Constitution — a victory meditated by those who wish to prostrate the Constitution for the furtherance of their own ambitious views.... These troops that protect the outworks are the first to be dismissed. These posts which present the strongest barriers are first to be taken, and then the Constitution becomes an easy prey.'

And how was this outrage to the Constitution to be accomplished? It was urged that while 'you shall not take the man from the office, you may take the office from the man; you shall not drown him, but you may sink the boat under him; you shall not put him to death, but you may take away his life.' Did not the Constitution say that the judge's office could not be taken from him during good behavior? And 'yet we may destroy the office which we cannot take away.... It is admitted that no power derived from the Constitution can deprive him of the office, and yet it is contended that by the repeal of the law that office may be destroyed.'

And then he flashed an amazing challenge — 'When by your laws you give to an individual any right whatever, can you, by a subsequent law, rightfully take it away? No!'

And why this clamor about the State courts? Breckinridge had said that citizens looked to the State courts for the punishment of most crimes, for robbery, murder, forgery, rape, and for the settlement of estates. Had the people forgotten what State governments meant before the formation of the Union? Could State courts be trusted?

Skimping the issue, sweepingly to assail the democratic trend of events, the orator plunged into his purple patches.

'Look into the records of time, see what has been the ruin of every republic. The vile love of popularity. Why are we here? To save the people from their most dangerous enemy, to save them from themselves. What caused the ruin of the republics of Greece and Rome? Demagogues, who, by flattery, gained the aid of the populace to establish despotism. But if you will shut your eyes to the light of history, and your ears to the voice of experience, see at least what happened in your own time. In 1789 it was no longer a doubt with enlightened statesmen what would be the event of the French Revolution; before the first of January, 1790, the only question was, who would become the despot.'

And yet, what was Congress about to do? 'To violate the Constitution.' And the effect? 'Once touch it with unhallowed hands, sacrifice but one of its provisions, and we are gone. We commit the fate of America to the mercy of time and chance. . . . Can you violate it? If you can, you can throw the Constitution into the flames — it is gone — it is dead.'

Morris sank into his seat, his masterpiece delivered. The Federalist papers compared it to the greatest orations of Cicero and to the disadvantage of the Roman. The *New York Evening Post* thought it 'an elegant specimen of that gentleman's talents,' and characterized it as 'argumentative yet graceful, bold yet respectful, witty yet dignified, resembling in happy quotation and illustrative metaphor, the manner of Burke, without his exuberance.' [1] The orator had laid it down that once Congress by law grants a right to an individual, it never can, by repeal, take that

[1] January 19, 1802.

right away; that the State courts were undependable if not corrupt; that while Congress could create courts when necessary, it
could not abolish them if the necessity passed; and that the repeal
of the act of the midnight judges would be a death-blow to the
Constitution itself. Hamilton, whose articles had covered much
of the same ground, was most pleased, and wrote Morris a glowing
note of congratulation.[1] King heard from Troup that Morris 'is
much celebrated for his eloquence' because of 'one of the grandest
displays ever exhibited in a deliberative assembly.' [2]

Jackson of Georgia momentarily broke the spell with a sharp
comment on judges during the days of the Sedition Law, and
Tracy, in mournful accents, lamented the evident determination
of the Jeffersonians to stab the Constitution to death.[3]

And then rose the man competent to deal with Morris in
eloquence, wit, and sarcasm, and quite his equal in reasoning,
Stevens T. Mason of Virginia. Drawing himself to his imposing
height, he fixed his extraordinary eyes on Morris, and in one fell
swoop exposed the hypocrisy of the whole Federalist contention
that to abolish a court, once established, was to deal a death-blow
to the Constitution.

'I am inclined to think,' he said, 'that these ideas of the extreme
independence of the judges and the limited powers of the legislature are not very old, but that they are of modern origin and have
grown up since the last session of Congress. For in the law passed
last session . . . which it is now proposed to repeal . . . is to be found
a practical exposition in direct hostility to the principle now contended for, which does not betray that sacred regard for the office
of a judge that is on this occasion professed.'

And why? Because 'in that very law will be found a clause
which abolishes two district courts.' Yes, 'the words of the
twenty-fourth section say expressly, "the district courts of Kentucky and Tennessee shall be and hereby are abolished."' Yes, the
Federalists, including Morris, had 'stripped the judges of their
offices and robbed them of their vested rights.'

And then, in sarcastic tones, his great eyes fixed on Morris, he
opened upon him the floodgates of a sarcasm which the biographer
of Marshall was to find an unsurpassed exhibition of the art.[4]

---

[1] *Works of Hamilton*, VIII, 594.   [2] *King's Corr.*, IV, 102–03.
[3] *Annals*, January 12, 1802.   [4] Beveridge, II, 64.

'Where were these guardians of the Constitution — these vigilant sentinels of our liberties — when this law passed? Were they asleep at their posts? Where was the gentleman from New York who has in this debate made such a noble stand in favor of a violated Constitution? Where was the Ajax Telamon of his party, or, to use his own more correct expression, the "faction" to which he belonged? Where was the hero with his sevenfold shield, not of bull's hide but of brass — prepared to prevent or to punish this Trojan rape which he now sees meditated upon the Constitution of his country by a wicked "faction"? Where was Hercules that he did not crush this den of robbers that broke into the sanctuary of the Constitution? Was he forgetful of his duty? Were his nerves unstrung? Or was he the very leader of the band that broke down these constitutional ramparts?'

The Judicial Department independent? the orator asked. 'Yes, but I never have believed that they ought to be independent of the nation itself.'

And then — the great eyes of Mason resting maliciously on Morris:

'They tell us that the judges have a vested right to their offices — a right not now derived from the law, but from the Constitution, and they assimilate their case to that of a public debt; to the right of a corporation; or a turnpike company or a toll bridge. But he who builds a bridge does a public good that entitles him to a growing remuneration forever. But here the good is temporary. The judge is more like the man who collects the toll, and who receives the promise of an annual payment as long as he discharges his duties faithfully. But a flood comes and sweeps the bridge away. Will the toll-gatherer, like the judge, contend that, though the bridge is gone, he shall, notwithstanding, receive his compensation for life, though he cannot continue those services for which his annual stipend was to be the compensation and reward?'

And did Morris complain of the pertinacity and passion with which the repeal was being pushed? Had he forgotten the scenes in which he had participated when the Judiciary Bill was being rushed through Congress under whip and spur, when amendments were refused consideration, when, over vehement protests, the bill was rammed down the throats of members without compunction?

Undignified haste now? 'If there be blame, on whom does it fall? Not on us who respected public opinion when this law was passed, and who still respect it, but on those who, in defiance of public opinion, passed this law after that public opinion had been decisively expressed. The revolution in public opinion had taken place before the introduction of this project; the people had determined to commit their affairs to new agents; already had the confidence of the people been transferred from their then rulers into other hands. . . . If there is error, it is our duty to correct it; and the truth is no law ever was more execrated by the public.' [1]

The Jeffersonians might well have rested their case on Mason's presentation, but the debate dragged on, and on January 15, Aaron Burr for the first time took the chair. He had lingered long in New York on his private affairs. He was to use his opportunities on this measure further to cultivate the Federalists.

A few days later, hoping thereby indefinitely to delay action, Senator Dayton, an intimate of Burr's, and a Federalist, moved that the bill be referred to a committee for alterations. The vote was a tie — and Aaron Burr cast the deciding vote against the Jeffersonians. There was no mistaking the significance of this maneuver.[2]

III

While the debate drones on, it is well to pause for some reflections upon the significance of Burr's position. It has been fashionable to slur over the attitude of Burr toward the Administration from the moment of its induction into office. To admit the hostility of his intentions would be a justification of Jefferson's distrust. The repeal of the Judiciary Act, as its enactment, was a party measure — and Burr secretly was against the repeal.

After he appeared upon the scene, he wrote that 'the constitutional right and power of abolishing one judiciary system and establishing another cannot be doubted. The power thus to deprive judges of their offices and salaries must also be admitted; but whether it would be constitutionally moral . . . and if so whether it

[1] *Annals*, January 13, 1802.   [2] *Ibid.*, 27, 1802.

would be politic or expedient, are questions on which I could
wish to be further advised.' The constitutional grounds of the
opposition were thus brushed aside with the levity he thought they
deserved. But Burr, not always sensitive to the moralities, was
worried about the morals of the thing.[1] The next day, writing his
son-in-law, he reiterated that 'of the constitutionality of repealing
the law I have no doubt, but with the equity and expediency of
depriving the twenty-six judges of office and pay is not quite so
obvious.' [2]

Throughout the winter he was engaged in a rather furious flirtation with the Federalists. In pious mood, he even sent Senator
Tracy a sermon that had moved him.[3] Even so, some of the
Federalists suspected him of other motives than one of morals.
'Depend upon it,' wrote Cutler, 'there is a Bonaparte ready to
hurl Jefferson from his chair and to take the reins of government
into his own hands.' [4] Troup wrote King that Burr had been
'playing a cunning and ridiculous game whilst the repealing of the
Judiciary Act was before the Senate.' [5] Sedgwick thought that he
would have liked frankly to oppose the repeal, 'but he is too
cunning to oppose openly the ardent wishes of his Master.' [6] The
Hamiltonians were not enthusiastic over their convert, but
Charles Biddle, of Philadelphia, was delighted with his vote to refer the bill. 'Every gentleman, and what I am sure you think of
much more consequence, every lady, was much pleased with your
vote on the Judiciary Bill.' [7]

And then, one day, as the Federalists were gathered about the
board at Stelle's, celebrating Washington's Birthday, they were
astonished to find Burr walking into their midst and asking permission to join in the festivity. Though the *Evening Post* [8] carried
an elaborate account of the celebration, out of deference to
Hamilton no mention was made of Burr's presence or his amazing
toast — 'A union of all honest men.' Most of the Federalist press
was coy, but months later the *Columbian Centinel*,[9] ascribing the
Democrats' enmity to Burr to 'his appearance at the Federalist

---

[1] To Barnabas Bidwell, *Burr*, II, 169.   [2] *Burr*, II, 171.
[3] *Ibid.*, II, 192.   [4] Cutler, II, 98.
[5] *King's Corr.*, IV, 103.   [6] Sedgwick to King, *King's Corr.*, IV, 74.
[7] *Burr*, II, 172.   [8] March 1. 1802.   [9] December 11, 1802

banquet in Washington' and to his toast, thought it 'no wonder' since 'Mr. Burr could not have given them a severer cut, for they know it was by the disunion of honest men they slipped into power.'

But Hamilton was more shocked and disgusted than Jefferson could have been. Writing Gouverneur Morris of the report, his fears are evident. 'We are told here that at the close of the birthday feast, a strange apparition, which was taken for the Vice-President, appeared among you and toasted "the union of all honest men,"' he wrote. And then, with some bitterness, 'I often hear at the corner of the streets federal secrets of which I am ignorant. This may be one.' However, Hamilton thought ''tis a good thing if we use it well,' since, 'as an instrument, the person will be an auxiliary of some value,' but 'as a chief he will disgrace and destroy the party.' [1]

Such was Burr's political status at the very beginning of the Administration.

IV

As a result of Burr's vote the bill was referred to a committee composed, in a majority, of its enemies, and it was hoped that there it would remain indefinitely. But in six days Breckinridge moved for the discharge of the committee. How could a committee pass upon a principle to the exclusion of the other members of the Senate? There was no question of modification. The fight was on the main issue of repeal. 'A degree of presumption I have never heard of,' shouted Morris, with simulated astonishment. 'The committee has sat but a short time, too short,' purred Tracy. But when one member of the committee announced that there was no possibility of an agreement, the vote was taken and the committee was released.

But the debate in the Senate was almost over. The next day Breckinridge and Morris both spoke again without even remotely touching on the real issue and the bill was passed. The effect was further to embitter the debate. The House offered another battlefield and there the Federalists had some giants of debate in preparation. The national gaze was now fixed upon the House.

[1] *Works of Hamilton*, VIII, 593.

V

There the debate was to be so ferocious in tone that Senatoɪ
Mitchill sought to disabuse the mind of a woman correspondent
that coffee and pistols before breakfast would follow. 'To be sure,'
he wrote, 'there have been many warm and some violent speeches,
but here we think very little of them; they are not serious things,
nor do they in any way interrupt social intercourse. Gentlemen
who have made these violent speeches often get together and
laugh and amuse themselves about it afterward.' [1]

Each day at an early hour the House and lobbies were packed
uncomfortably, with women predominating. Each day the
Senate met and quickly adjourned, and senators hurried to the
House to increase the congestion. It was observed that 'Vice-
President Burr was remarkably attentive.' [2] There was such tenseness in the atmosphere that an observer was convinced that 'had
some men of high importance charged with treason been standing
at the bar on trial for their lives the solemnity could hardly have
been greater.' [3] At times the air in the ill-ventilated room was so
foul that some sickened, and on one occasion Bayard almost
fainted. [4]

The Federalists rallied under the brilliant leadership of Bayard,
who was ably supported by the cleverest orators in the party, and
while Randolph was to play his part, the most powerful speech
for the Jeffersonians was to be made by Giles. The long struggle
in the Senate, the virulence of the party press, had whipped the
general public into a high state of excitement, and most of the men
and women who trudged through the mud to the Capitol were
militant partisans.

The struggle began when Bayard moved a postponement to
permit the members to feel the public pulse. 'When in Philadelphia,' one member replied, 'we received memorials from ten
thousand citizens, and this was called public opinion; but when the
elections came on, we found it was incorrect. I know of no better
way of ascertaining public opinion than through the gentlemen
who represent the several districts of the country.' And then he
added that, while wishing to consult public opinion, Bayard had

[1] Mitchill's Letters.   [2] Cutler, ɪɪ, 80–81.
[3] Ibid.   [4] Ibid., ɪɪ, 78.

announced that he 'will vote from the dictates of his own mind.'
Why, then, should Bayard hunger for public opinion? [1]

Randolph wanted no delay. The opposition could not agree on
a reason for it — 'reasons so irreconcilable that if one is correct,
the others must be false.' [2] The motion was voted down.

The next day 'public opinion' began to arrive in memorials and
protests from 'sundry merchants and traders of the city of Philadelphia,' and from the Chamber of Commerce in New York.
Morris had urged that Hamilton secure a protest from the New
York Bar Association, and biographers have insisted that Hamilton doubted the propriety of the attempt. Even so the Bar
Association was called together at the instance of Hamilton. It
met at Little's Hotel on Broad Street, and the fact that Troup
was in the chair was evidence enough of the great man's initiative
in summoning the lawyers; and they were summoned to consider
the attitude of the Bar toward the repeal. Hamilton assumed
charge of the meeting. 'It is my opinion,' said Hamilton, 'that
the contemplated repeal, taken in connection with the known and
avowed object of the repeal, is an unequivocable violation of the
Constitution in a most vital part. However, the reception which
the petition from the Pennsylvania Bar has met with does not give
much promise of a successful reception from the New York Bar.'
He was followed by another lawyer (Riker), who declared the
Judiciary Act 'useless and hurtful.' The divergence of opinion
was cue enough, and the meeting adjourned without action.[3]

So energetic had become Hamilton's intervention in political
affairs, with his articles running in the *Post*, that he became
the object of acrimonious controversy again. Commenting on the
time when he had been the oracle of his party, the *Independent
Chronicle* observed that his 'party are beginning to bring him forward again as the Champion of Federalism. Witness the late
New Year's address of a Federalist editor [Major Russell] which
anticipates the time, not far distant, when "Camillus" will be
called from his exile to guide the councils of his country. Witness
also the late New York Bar meeting and the Federalist publica-
tions occasioned by it.' [4] The Jeffersonians went forth to give

[1] *Annals*, February 18, 1802.   [2] *Ibid.*
[3] *New York Evening Post*, February 12, 1802; *Columbian Centinel*, February 20, 1802.
[4] February 25, 1802.

battle, and soon their papers, especially Cheetham's, were attacking Hamilton for his speech in the Constitutional Convention, expressing his partiality for monarchy. Hamilton's own paper, the *Post*, replied with the comment, 'How far this is consistent with the complaint of the editor just before that the proceedings of the Convention are at this moment wrapped in mystery is left for him to show.' [1] Soon Luther Martin, 'the bulldog of Federalism,' and a member of the Convention, rushed to Hamilton's defense with a lawyer's sophistry, denying that Hamilton had offered any plan, but 'in an able and eloquent address did express his general ideas upon the subject of government which would in all human probability be most advantageous for the United States.' [2] However, the speech as outlined by Cheetham was in perfect accord with the report made at the time by Madison and published years afterward; and Hamilton personally made no denial.

No action having been taken by the Bar Association, Hamilton went to the Chamber of Commerce, which was anti-Jeffersonian, and secured a petition there. 'I did what I thought likely to do most good,' he wrote Morris. 'I induced the Chamber of Commerce to send a memorial.' [3]

Two days later, the heavy artillery was unlimbered in the House when Giles made the greatest parliamentary speech of his career in favor of the repeal. Tall, powerfully built and handsome, his brown eyes glowing, his nervous voice ringing clear, he entered the debate with all the impetuosity and dash of a cavalry charge, while his fellow partisans cheered wildly.

What, he asked, was the inspiration of the Judiciary Act it was proposed to repeal? Hastily sketching the unpopular Federalist measures, and reminding the House of 'the general disquietude' which had forewarned the party then in power of its approaching repudiation, he said 'it was natural for them to look for some department of the Government in which they could entrench themselves in the event of an unsuccessful issue in the elections.' Inevitably they had hit upon the judiciary — beyond the reach of the people. And why? 'Because it was already filled with men who had manifested the most indecorous zeal in favor of their

[1] February 19, 1802.   [2] *New York Evening Post*, May 6, 1802.
[3] *Works of Hamilton*, VIII, 590–91.

principles'; because they held office for an indefinite tenure; and because they were 'further removed from any responsibility to the people than either of the other departments.' A bill was introduced for the creation of additional judges, and then, momentarily abandoned lest its passage before the elections 'tend to increase the disquietude.'

With the repudiation in the elections, the bill hastily was resurrected and passed, and now they say it is 'inviolable and irrepealable.' Yes, this law had become 'the sanctuary of the principles of the last Administration, and the tenure of the judges are the horns of the inviolability within that sanctuary.'

'It is some time,' he continued, 'since a member of this House and sundry printers throughout the United States have been imprisoned to appease the vengeance of an unconstitutional sedition act; ... some time since we have seen the judges, who ought to have been independent, converted into political partisans and like executive missionaries pronouncing political harangues throughout the United States; ... some time since we have seen the zealous judge stoop from the bench to look for more victims for judicial vengeance; ... some time since we have seen the same judicial zeal extending the provisions of the sedition law by discovering that it had jurisdiction of the *non scripta* or common law.' All this is history now. 'These noisy declamations and this judicial zeal are hushed into silence by the audible pronunciation of the public will.' Perhaps the hope may be entertained that 'our pulpits will not much longer be converted into political forums.'

Turning now to the issue before the House, he asked if the courts to be abolished had been created by the Constitution. No, they were formed by Congress to whom the Constitution gave the power. Congress could create 'such inferior courts as Congress shall from time to time ordain and establish.' The judges of these courts were to receive 'compensation for their services.'

'To whom are these services to be rendered? To the people, for the benefit of the people. Who is the judge of the necessity or utility of these services? The Constitution has ordained that Congress or the representatives of the people shall be the tribunal. Suppose there should be no services required, none for the judge to perform, and that Congress should so think and determine. Is the judge entitled to compensation? He is not.'

And why the clamor about 'striking down the independence of the judges'? Why the constant reference to the example of England? 'Congress has the power of originating, abolishing, and modifying the courts here; the Parliament in England have the same power there. Congress cannot remove a judicial officer ... so long as the office itself is deemed useful, except by impeachment, two thirds of the Senate being necessary to conviction; in England judges can be removed ... although the offices may be deemed useful, by a majority of the two houses of Parliament. Congress cannot diminish the compensation of judges here during their continuance in office; in England the Parliament may diminish the compensation ... at their discretion during their continuance in office.

'Whence it is, then, that we hear of the independence of the English judiciary, as being the boast and glory of that country, and with justice too, and at the same time hear the cry of the immolation of the independence of the judges of the United States when, under the interpretation of the Constitution by the favorers of the repeal, the judges here are more independent than those in England.'

And whence the conclusion that a judge is not susceptible to the limitations of other men and has no ambition for power? Why, 'very shortly after the establishment of the courts the judges decided they had jurisdiction over the States in their sovereign capacity. Did this in the judges seem unambitious?

'The judges have determined that their jurisdiction extends to the *lex non scripta* ... the common law. Does this in the judges seem unambitious?

'They have sent a mandatory process leading to a mandamus into the Executive Cabinet to examine its concerns. Does this in the judges seem unambitious?'

Asserting the right of repeal, pronouncing the necessity, ridiculing the theory that the judges had a vested right in their offices, slashing vigorously at the false issues raised, he made a profound impression, and he closed amidst a clamor of excitement. Randolph rose to praise the speech, 'looking much like a bird of

wisdom,' a Federalist thought, and to move an adjournment that
'members might retire for reflection while the deep impressions
they must have received were fresh in their minds.' The motion
prevailed, and the spectators swarmed out into the lobbies.[1]

The next day, before a crowded chamber, Bayard, imposing and
impressive, rose to reply. With equal ardor he made his appeal,
describing the repealers as bent on the destruction of the powers of
the Government, sacrificing national to State pride. Nor was he
lacking in audacity.

'Sir, I think a judge should never be a partisan,' he said, as the
Jeffersonians lifted their eyebrows. 'No man would be more ready
to condemn a judge who carried his political prejudices and
antipathies on the bench. But I have yet to learn that such a
charge can be sustained against the judges of the United States.'

The Jeffersonians, with Jay, Ellsworth, Chase in mind, tittered
aloud.

And victims of the Sedition Law? 'Let me turn his [Giles's] view
from the walks of the judges to the present Executive, who is
driving Federalists from office. There are victims! It is here, sir,
that we see the soldier who fought the battles of the Revolution,
who spilt his blood and wasted his strength to establish the independence of his country, deprived of the reward of his services,
and left to pine in penury and wretchedness. It is along this path
that you may see the helpless children crying for bread, and gray
hairs sinking in sorrow to the grave. It is here that no innocence,
no merit, no truth, no services can save the unhappy victim who
does not believe in the creed of those in power.'[2] And how dare
Giles hold the judges responsible for the Sedition Law? 'On this
score the judges are surely innocent.... No innocent man ever
did or could have suffered under the law.'

And what did Giles mean by his reference to the pulpit politicians? 'The ministers of the Gospel have been represented like the
judges, forgetting the duties of their calling and employed in disseminating the heresies of Federalism. Am I to understand that
the churches are to be shut up?'

And why the chatter about the propriety of creating the courts

---

[1] Cutler, II, 77–78.

[2] At this time the great majority of office-holders still were of the minority party.

and judges on the eve of a new and different Administration? 'I
have no hesitation in avowing that I had no confidence in the persons who were to follow us.'

Four hours had not sufficed for the completion of his argument,
and Bayard was faint in the foul air and asked an adjournment
till the morrow. It was granted, and as the House was adjourning
he was on the verge of a collapse.[1] The following day, still ill,
Bayard resumed, and concluded in two and a half hours a speech
pronounced by his admirers beyond the capacity of Fox or Pitt.[2]

Immediately John Randolph rose. 'I call upon this committee
to decide,' he began, 'whether in this day's discussion the gentleman has evinced that purity of heart or that elevation of sentiment
which could justify me in clothing him with the attributes of a
Curtius or of a Decius.'

To what did the arguments of the Federalists lead? 'If the
present majority should incur the suspicion of the people, as soon
as there is any indication of their having forfeited public confidence,
on the signal of dismissal from their present station, they may
make ample and irrepealable provisions for themselves and their
adherents by the creation of an adequate number of judicial
offices. Now, sir, this is the power which we reject, though it is
insisted that we possess it.'

Sarcastically, he recalled strange proceedings in the courts
when under Federalist domination. 'Lay your hands on the
liberties of the people — they are torpid; but affect their peculiar
interest and they are all nerve. They are said to be harmless, un-
aspiring men. Their humble pretensions extend only to a complete exemption from legislative control; to the exercise of in-
quisitorial authority over the Cabinet of the Executive and the
veto of the Roman Triumvirate over all your laws, together with
the establishing any body of laws which they may choose to declare a part of the Constitution.'

A paltry saving the motive for repeal? 'No, sir, it is to strike
the death-blow to the pretensions of rendering the judiciary a
hospital for decayed politicians, to prevent the State courts from
being engulfed by those of the Union; to destroy the monstrous
ambition of arrogating to this House the right of evading all the
prohibitions of the Constitution and holding the nation at bay.'

---

[1] Cutler, ii, 78.   [2] *Ibid.*, ii, 79.

Attacking the judges? 'If they wished the judges, like the tribe of Levi, to have been set apart from other men for the sacred purposes of justice, they should have considered well before they gave to publicans and sinners the privileges of the high priesthood.' [1]

The austere Macon descended from the chair to contribute a thoughtful defense of the measure; the rhetorical Dana of Connecticut argued eloquently in behalf of the Constitution and the courts; and Griswold threatened secession if the measure passed, to be rebuked sharply by Macon.[2] Nicholson spoke at length and ineffectively, and Rutledge made a 'pathetic' appeal for the Constitution. At times the room, reeking with the poison of so many breaths, was well-nigh insufferable, and once the House sat from ten in the morning until midnight, tied to their seats by the rule against standing. 'From eight in the morning when I breakfasted until one the next morning when I dined, I had no refreshment but water,' wrote Cutler.[3]

At length, at midnight, the vote was had, the measure passed. The Jeffersonians cheered in exultation, though the uncannily penetrating eyes of one of their foes was sure he saw 'a solemn gloom strongly marked on many of their countenances.' [4] But the gloomy forebodings of disaster among the Jeffersonians were washed away in the toasts on the night of the celebration at Stelle's, which was 'illuminated for the occasion.'

The *Connecticut Courant* and the *New England Palladium* appeared in mourning. 'It breaks down the only barrier against licentiousness and party tyranny,' said the *Palladium*. 'Our rights prostrate under the arbitrary power of a mere vote.' [5] The *Washington Federalist* fell into verse:

> Who danced at the grave?
> Alas, such a throng
> As would damn any Song
> Danc'd at the grave.[6]

And then it advised lawlessness — that the judges hold on to their jobs regardless of the act of Congress. 'It is their solemn duty to

[1] *Annals,* February 20, 1802.   [2] *Ibid.,* 23, 1802.
[3] Cutler, II, 91.   [4] *Ibid.,* II, 95.
[5] January 26, 1802.   [6] December 10, 1802.

do it; their country, all that is dear and valuable, calls on them to
do it.' And then, significantly enough from a journal close to John
Marshall, it added: 'By the Judges this bill will be declared null
and void.'[1]

The Jeffersonian *Independent Chronicle* commented that 'judges
should be of no party' and 'should at least appear to have no
party feeling on or off the bench.' Otherwise, it continued, the
nation would suffer by 'the most horrible abuse of power.'[2] In
the *New York American-Citizen* appeared a paean of victory over
Hamilton:

> Pray credit your eyes,
> Nor behold with surprise,
> A problem which baffles solution,
> The Federal Bar
> Were too zealous by far,
> In protecting our dear Constitution:
>   This corps was led on
>   By that amorous man,
>   Generalissimo ex-secretary,
>   Who, true to his trade,
>   Many flourishes made
>   In defense of the Judiciary.[3]

At a Federalist meeting at Vilas's Tavern, Harrison Gray Otis,
charging Jefferson with deliberate design to 'destroy the Northern States,' fell into rhetorical fury over the repeal. 'Not only the
door but the windows of the Temple of Justice have been burst
open and the building is filled with banditti,' he shouted. 'Its roof
is falling and its foundations undermined. Waves and billows en-
gulfing the Constitution, internal taxes bobbing up and down like
drowning kittens, the standing army like wharf rats in a high tide
quitting the encampment.'[4]

So ended Jefferson's first 'attack on the Federal judiciary.'

VI

With the celebration of the victory at Stelle's, the Jeffersonians
pressed on to their predetermined tasks. On nothing was Jefferson
more insistent than on the repeal of the internal revenue taxes. It

---

[1] *Independent Chronicle*, quoting, March 18, 1802.   [2] March 25, 1802.
[3] May 24, 1802.   [4] *Independent Chronicle*, April 7 and 19, 1802.

had long been part of his party's program, and even the momentary hesitation of Gallatin did not give him pause. 'It is perfectly
safe,' he wrote Dickinson. 'They are under a million of dollars and
we can economize the government, pay the interest on the public
debt, and discharge the principal in fifteen years.' [1] The gossips
were busy with speculation. It was whispered about that Gallatin
was in doubt; that the purpose was to 'attack the funded debt'
and to 'lay a direct tax upon the people.' Some of the Federalists
scouted the idea of economy,[2] and others were disgusted with the
thought. While an elaborate correspondence proves that Jefferson
had most carefully planned for the future, John Quincy Adams
was quite sure that the taxes would be repealed for the sake of
popularity and that Jefferson would 'leave the future to take care
of themselves.' [3] But Adams had to admit that Gallatin's report
'exhibits a pleasing view of the present state of our finances.' [4] In
truth, it was the first financial report that was intelligible to the
ordinary man. Jefferson had insisted on a report that anyone
could understand. 'I think it an object of great importance,' he
wrote Gallatin, 'to simplify our system of finance and bring it
within the comprehension of every member of Congress. Hamilton set out on a different plan. In order that he might have the
entire government of his machine, he determined so to complicate
it that neither the President nor Congress should be able to understand it or control him.' [5] Gallatin, with rare genius and painstaking care, had conformed perfectly to the specifications.

But the Federalists had determined to combat the repeal of the
taxes. The *Evening Post* suggested that 'Jefferson is a man of too
much sense to suppose the House of Representatives would agree
to abolish the internal taxes.' It was sure he was merely throwing
the idea out to increase his popularity and with foreknowledge of
its defeat.[6] The *New England Palladium* was not surprised that
Gallatin favored the repeal, 'considering his former shameful
opposition to one of these taxes.' [7] Sedgwick was sure Jefferson's
object was to serve the Southern and Western States 'and to
break down all the internal machinery of the Government.' [8] It

[1] Tucker, ii, 119.   [2] Cutler, ii, 64.   [3] *King's Corr.*, iv, 60.
[4] *Ibid.*   [5] *Writings of Jefferson*, x, 306.   [6] January 7, 1802.
[7] The whiskey tax, February 26, 1802.   [8] *King's Corr.*, iv, 73.

was 'a despicable, sordid passion of avarice,' nothing less. Troup, more complacent, thought that as a result of repeal 'all the whiskey-drinkers will be in spirits.' [1] Such was the tone and temper of the opposition.

Again it was Gouverneur Morris who led the attack in the Senate with his usual cleverness and sophistry. Why repeal the taxes? he asked. Would it not work a hardship on the remote regions by drawing money away to the seaports? True, the customs duties were not sufficient to meet all obligations, but the war in Europe had enormously increased consumption, and with peace there would be a decline. And what assurance that the customs taxes could be collected? Had no one heard of smuggling? Our own merchants? — no, no. But what was to prevent the wretched foreigner from engaging in the trade? 'By what principle are they bound to support the credit, maintain the honor, or advance the dignity of the Government?' Would they not come temporarily to 'carry the honey to their own hive?'

And what opportunities for smuggling! Think of the 'unlimited means of illicit trade in possession of small fishing vessels to the eastward.' Did not 'a single glance at our coast from Cape Hatteras to Cape Cod . . . show the superior facility of approach'? Almost enthusiastic grew the orator over the possibilities for smugglers. From the first of May to the middle of August, vessels could ride at anchor in perfect safety. Innumerable inlets for a 'safe retreat.' Could not revenue vessels be resisted there? Would the people of these neighborhoods assist the officers? Would they not, on the contrary, be 'deriving advantage from a concern in that business'? Use a military force? 'You have none.' And even if you have, what could they accomplish with the coast 'clothed with vast forests of pine, which, proud of their sterility, bid defiance to the hand of cultivation'? And those 'impenetrable morasses whose paths are known only to those who inhabit them'! Send troops against the people of these regions? Why, 'they will meet there a race of men bred from infancy to the use of arms — dangerous marksmen.' Such was the best Morris could do.

Mason of Virginia answered indifferently, thus contemptuously treating the speech of Morris. Smuggling? 'I do not think we are

[1] *King's Corr.*, IV, 102–03.

in such danger of it, unless the art should be learned from the gentleman's speech, who has proved that if it is not moral, it is at least venial to smuggle.' These taxes, odious to the people, were unnecessary to the meeting of national obligations. 'They were the darling child of the first Secretary of the Treasury who had declared that excises were forced upon the people of other countries and should go down here.'

Soon Morris's smuggling argument was abandoned, and the Federalists concentrated on the contention that on the enactment of the excise laws it was provided that excise taxes on stills and distilled liquor should go in part to the payment of the public debt and the interest on it. 'The solemnity of the pledge,' said Tracy, 'is worthy of observation. The taxes have been pledged for the redemption of the public debt, and every creditor of the United States has an interest in the pledge which cannot be trifled with.' [1] Yes, 'this debate,' said Ross of Pennsylvania, 'is in the presence of foreign Ministers, and the declaration goes forth to the world that the Government of the United States will revoke its promises.' Why, in this event, said Ross, 'I would not trust a cent to the engagement of such a government.' [2]

Morris, now abandoning his smuggler's argument, toyed lightly with this violated pledge. Was it not unthinkable that the nation's creditors would not resent the substitution of one means of payment for another? 'Do you suppose your creditors will be the dupes of this new-fangled logic?' [3]

'The pledge is nothing more than the declaration that there will always be funds in readiness sufficiently large to meet our engagements,' Nicholas replied languidly. And so by a party vote the measure passed the Senate, and after a dull debate it passed the House, and the Jeffersonian promise had been redeemed.

VII

Meanwhile, Jefferson and Gallatin were ready with a plan for the facilitation of the payment of the public debt. While the politicians raved, Gallatin was in communication with the banking houses of Holland and with the Baring Brothers, and knew that the 'violated pledge' had influenced them not at all. Indeed, they

[1] *Annals.*   [2] *Ibid.*   [3] *Ibid.*

were eager to lend. One section of the bill provided for the negotiation of a loan 'to pay off installments of the public debt.' In a spirit more of obstruction than of conviction, the Federalists had offered an amendment to prevent any portion of the money borrowed from going to the payment of interest on loans thereafter made. Morris mournfully declared that the bankers would turn a deaf ear to any application for a loan. 'You apply to these bankers with this law in your hand, and what will they say? They will tell you they do not understand it, that you have taken away one pledge which they understood and on which they relied.' Who would have faith in a law drawn by a 'foreigner'? asked the friend of Hamilton, aiming at Gallatin.[1] But Gallatin was thoroughly understood and appreciated in Amsterdam and London, and the Barings had the utmost faith both in his integrity and financial genius. The amendment was defeated, the bill was passed, and, having reduced the taxes on the people, the Administration now set itself to a more rapid liquidation of the public debt.

VIII

It had been a rather nasty session. The *Evening Post* did not hesitate to publish a canard that Jefferson would soon resign, 'perceiving that the tempestuous sea of liberty is likely to become more and more boisterous, as Bonaparte's ships approach.' It was understood he would retire to Monticello.[2] Late in the summer the *American Citizen* was protesting against a report, 'smuggled into circulation in this city, that Mr. Jefferson was mortally ill, and had been given over by his four attendant physicians.'[3] Bitter as the session had been, under the consummate and benevolent leadership of Jefferson it had moved irresistibly to the accomplishment of his purposes. Never had any Congress been under such perfect discipline, not that of the club, but of the harmonious intent. In the bitterness of debate the Federalists had emphasized their distrust of the people and their hatred of democracy. When they thought they were dealing their most deadly blows, the Jeffersonians were most pleased. 'The operations of this session, when known to the people, will consolidate them,' Jefferson wrote

[1] *Annals*, April 24, 1802.   [2] March 26, 1802.   [3] August 25, 1802.

Barlow.[1] To Kosciuszko, a month before adjournment, he had written that 'the people are nearly all united; their quondam leaders, infuriated by a sense of their impotence, will soon be seen or heard of only in the newspapers, which serve as chimneys to carry off noxious vapors and smoke.' [2]

It was a happy Jefferson who on the day of adjournment was writing Joel Barlow of the achievements of the session and the prospects for the morrow. 'Another election,' he wrote, 'it will be two to one in the Senate, and it would not be for the public good to have it greater.' With a keen sense of history, he and Madison had been perfecting a plan in which Barlow was included. 'John Marshall is writing the Life of General Washington from his papers,' he said. 'It is intended to come out just in time to influence the next presidential election. It is written, therefore, principally with the view to electioneering purposes.' In the living-rooms at the White House, he and Madison had conceived the idea of bringing Barlow back from Paris to write a history of the United States from the close of the Revolution onward. 'We are rich ourselves in material and can open all the archives to you; but your residence here is essential because a great deal of the knowledge of things is not on paper, but only within ourselves for verbal communication.' And residence in Washington or in the country near would be pleasant. The city had six thousand people and delightful villages were springing up all around. There was 'a most lovely seat adjoining this city on a high hill commanding a most extensive view of the Potomac,' with 'a superb house and garden' and 'thirty or forty acres to be had.' Would Barlow return? [3]

Jefferson was happy. The country was prospering; the people were contented; property had banished its fears of democracy; and despite the dire predictions of the foe, business confidently was pushing forward to greater achievements. Economies had been effected, old wrongs righted, taxes lowered, and plans perfected for a speedier payment of the debt.

In the weeks and months intervening before the next session, we shall find the Federalist leaders taking counsel among themselves on ways and means of saving the people from 'their worst enemy — themselves'; and spreading abuse with a lavish hand over the Chief of the State.

[1] *Writings of Jefferson*, x, 319.   [2] *Ibid.*, x, 309.   [2] *Ibid.*, x, 319.

CHAPTER VII

Paine's Return; Hamilton's Plan

I

WHEN the thundering in Congress against Jefferson ceased, with adjournment, the opposition press increased the virulence of its attacks. With the discovery that Jefferson had invited Thomas Paine to return in a national vessel to the country he so brilliantly had served, it filled the air with poison gas. True, no other pen had approached his in power in Revolutionary days; true, his pamphlets, 'The Crisis' and 'Common Sense,' had been as mighty armies in the field; true, no other being had done so much in reviving the fainting spirits of the patriots, and Washington had ordered his writings tacked on trees about his camp for the invigoration of his soldiers; but he had written 'The Age of Reason,' pronounced an attack on all religions, and he had charged Washington with ingratitude.

Ardently devoted to liberty, he had become a member of the Convention in the French Revolution to the supreme disgust of Gouverneur Morris, then Minister in Paris, who despised democracy and all its works. True, he was not a Jacobin, or an admirer of Robespierre or Marat, but a follower of Brissot and Vergniaud, the leaders of the Girondists, who stood foursquare for a pure republic, but in days of robust party lying this was not to be known through the Federalist press. When Morris was frowning at the mob that would not cheer the Queen, and thinking it heroism, Paine at the peril of his life was pleading in the Convention for the life of the King. Because he was not a Jacobin, it was Robespierre who had him thrown into prison, and but for an accident he would have perished with the noble figures of the Gironde. It was while awaiting his summons to the guillotine

that he devoted himself to the writing of 'The Age of Reason.'
'The people of France were running headlong into atheism,' he
wrote afterward, 'and I had the work translated into their language to stop them in that career, and to fix them to the first
article of every man's creed, who has any creed at all — I believe
in God.' But to the pious leaders of the Federalists he had attacked God Himself.

While awaiting his summons to the guillotine, Morris not only
did not lift a finger to save him, but poisoned the mind of Washington against the man who so zealously had served him and his
cause. Embittered by the apparent indifference of Washington,
and not knowing of Morris's action, Paine had charged Washington with ingratitude, and thus played again into the hands of his
American enemies.

When James Monroe reached Paris, as Morris's successor, he
instantly set to work with zeal to free the man who had done so
much to free the American people. But the Paine who emerged
from the torture chamber of his cell was physically wrecked, and
to ease his pain he fell into the habit of brandy-drinking. In an
age when most men drank stoutly, the Federalists denounced
him as 'a sot.'

Jefferson, learning of Paine's desire to return to America, wrote
him an invitation to return on the *Maryland*, a national ship, and
signed his letter, with 'affectionate attachment.' The Federalists
accepted this as positive proof that Jefferson was an enemy of
religion!

With the report that Paine was on the seas, the poison guns
began to pop. What! exclaimed the *Courant*, 'the President has
publicly, in the light of day, cordially, nay affectionately, invited
the most infamous and depraved character of this or any age to
take refuge in our country.' [1] In the *Columbian Centinel*, 'Verus'
began a series of insulting open letters to the head of the State.
'Was it because he had libeled Washington, insulted our government, blasphemed his God, and fled from punishment that he was
considered peculiarly worthy of this pointed mark of your friendship?' [2] The *New England Palladium* described the author of
'The Crisis' as 'that disgrace and opprobrium of human nature.'

[1] August 16, 1802.   [2] September 15, 1802.

Why, it asked, should Jefferson wish 'to take to his bosom that old battered bellwether of Jacobinism and infidelity?' Why 'insult the sense and virtue of the country by professions of affectionate attachment to a man so offensive to decency, so smitten with the leprosy of scorn, the natural enemy of every virtue?' Why, indeed, if not to 'employ him in the service of democracy.' [1]

Soon the Federalist scribes were printing insulting stories of Paine's movements, describing him as having the 'indubitable marks of a confessed sot,' and yet able to stand and talk after he had 'swallowed a great quantity of brandy.' [2] Soon the pious souls of a small Massachusetts town were hanging and burning him in effigy in the public square after parading the counterfeit figure through the parks, followed by 'a large number of inhabitants.' No one objected to this degradation of the man whose pamphlets were the equal of armies in the Revolution, 'although it was observed by some that he was invited to the country by President Jefferson.' [3] Old Sam Adams, regretting the 'Age of Reason,' could not forget Paine's work in the Revolution, and wrote him that he had 'frequently reflected on your services to my native land.' Paine's 'Common Sense' and 'The Crisis' 'unquestionably awakened the public mind and led the people loudly to call for a declaration of our national independence.' Therefore, Adams had always looked upon him as 'a warm friend of liberty and the lasting welfare of the human race.' [4]

Jefferson and Paine, one a liar, the other a sot, both offenses to God — so barked the Federalist press day after day for months. But Jefferson was not moved, and when, a little later, Paine appeared in Washington, he was invited to dinner by Jefferson to the horror of the devout. Cutler recorded that at Lowell's Hotel Paine 'ate at the public table to the advantage of Lowell,' since many 'feel a curiosity to see the creature,' and even some statesmen were not above this vulgar weakness.[5] Meanwhile, most of the ladies, sisters of those who danced with the redcoats in Philadelphia the winter Washington was suffering at Valley

---

[1] *New England Palladium*, August 17, 1802.
[2] *Columbian Centinel*, November 15, 1802.
[3] *Ibid.*, February 23, 1803.
[4] *Independent Chronicle*, February 10, 1803.
[5] Cutler, II, 110.

Forge, drew their skirts aside to prevent contamination with the author of 'Common Sense.' But the Gallatins had him at their table, and it was there that the scholarly Senator Mitchill was seated beside the ogre, and described him as 'looking as if he had been much hackneyed in the service of the world — his eyes black and lively, his nose somewhat aquiline and pointing downward.' But he found the old man a brilliant talker, rich in anecdote, and the company was immensely entertained when he read a satirical poem on Gouverneur Morris in the Revolution. 'You would have been pleased to hear the old man speak his piece,' he wrote.[1] The good chaplain of Congress wrote a poem of his own describing Paine descending into hell.[2] Plumer was horrified that Jefferson repeatedly invited him to his table along with the Gallatins, and that even Senator Bradley admitted 'that miscreant Paine to his table.'[3]

Such was the homecoming of the greatest and most useful penman of the Revolution; but every blow at Paine was intended for Jefferson. So low had become the abuse of Jefferson that when, that summer, he made a sentimental pilgrimage to Mount Vernon and stood with folded arms before the tomb, the Federalist press spluttered with ridicule and insults.[4]

II

Meanwhile, enemies of the Administration were whispering among themselves about imaginary dissensions in the official fold. Yes, Madison, who did not approve of Jefferson's policies, was about to resign in disgust. Indeed, it was understood, so ran the gossip, that Jefferson would decline re-election.[5]

But Hamilton, the realist, was not so confident. Convinced that public sentiment ran strongly with the Administration, he had been meditating on a plan to combat the popular madness. Only his intimate friends realized how deeply concerned he was over the political situation. John Jay was in such deep retirement that his name was seldom heard, and the gossip was that Hamilton, nauseated with politics, and intensively occupied with his profession, was making money 'faster than ever.'[6] Those who

---

[1] Mitchill's Letters.   [2] *Pickering*, iv, 77.   [3] *Plumer*, 242–43.
[4] *New England Palladium*, August 6, 1802.   [5] Cutler, ii, 101.
[6] Troup to King, *King's Corr.*, iv, 121.

loved him most were anxious about his health. While his mental
strength and quickness had increased, his physical health was
'impairing.' At the Bar he had become a Colossus, according
to 'the common opinion of the Bar,' and lawyers were reconciled
to defeat when he was the opposing counsel unless he clearly was
on the weaker side. 'And yet,' it was observed, 'he is always complaining that he does not get his share of judgments and decrees.'
This irritability was ascribed to physical decline.[1] That summer
found him frequently astride his horse, riding into the country to
supervise the building of his country seat, the Grange. By August
the house was 'fast reaching perfection.' He was also busy with
his garden for flowers and with another for vegetables. Green-
houses likewise entered into his plan, for he wished to grow
tropical and semi-tropical plants. Even his political associates
could scarcely draw him away from his physician, Dr. David
Hosack, who shared his enthusiasm for horticulture and was
constantly taking him cuttings and bulbs.[2] As autumn came, he
was writing Charles Cotesworth Pinckney, of South Carolina, for
seed, 'some of the water and musk melons,' and also for 'three
or four paroquets,' since his daughter was 'very fond of birds.'[3]

But he was not so easy in his mind over the trend of politics as
his friends imagined. He could 'discover no satisfactory symptoms
of a revolution of opinion in the mass.'[4] And Hamilton finally
faced the fact that the mass cannot be ignored. If the Federalist
Party was to live, it would have to change its tactics.

III

Thus, in 1802, Hamilton sat down to the working-out of a plan
of organization and for effective propaganda among the mass of
the people. It was based upon his theory that 'men are rather
reasoning than reasonable animals, for the most part governed
by their passions.' The Federalists had not sufficiently played
on the passions of men, and in consequence had lost. Had they
ever been so successful as when they played upon the passions
during the hysteria of the X Y Z episode? Thus, Hamilton's
plan from the beginning was doomed by a wrong premise. The

---

[1] Troup to King, *King's Corr.*, IV, 135.   [2] *Intimate Life*, 140; 345.
[3] *Ibid.*, 346.   [4] *King's Corr.*, IV, 133.

Jeffersonians had won the masses, not by playing on their passions, but by appeals to their economic and political interests.

The primary object of the organization Hamilton proposed was twofold. First it was aimed at securing 'the support of the Christian religion.' Since the Jeffersonians were composed, in most part, of Christians, and since their party was in no sense opposed to the tenets of Christ, this evidently was intended as an appeal to the passions. No religion had a place in the Constitution. The complete separation of Church and State had been decreed. But Jefferson, who more than any other single man had insisted on the separation of Church and State and had fought a successful battle on the issue in the Virginia Assembly, had been habitually denounced as an anti-Christ by the political preachers of his time. He was still hated in Virginia for breaking the connection, and in the New England States, where the greater part of the ministers were militant Federalists, he was hated with an unholy hate. More false witness had been borne by the ministers of New England and New York against Jefferson than had ever been borne against any other American publicist. In Connecticut, where the ministers were the absolute dictators of the State, it was a vital issue. It was Hamilton's thought to mobilize all these hates of pious men and to alarm the Christian masses with the fear that the triumph of the democratic principles of Jefferson would mean the downfall of the religion of Jesus Christ. History has shown that on no subject can human passions be aroused to such a murderous frenzy as on that of man's relation to his Maker.

The second object of the new Hamilton organization was 'the support of the Constitution of the United States.' When Hamilton had accepted the Constitution as 'better than nothing,' [1] with the admonition that the object of administration should be to 'acquire for the Federal government more consistency than the Constitution seems to promise,' to the end that it 'may triumph altogether' over the States, Jefferson, on the addition of the ten amendments of the Bill of Rights, had pronounced it 'unquestionably the wisest yet presented to men.' [2] Was the organization, then, to support the Constitution against Jefferson's concept of it?

[1] *Works of Hamilton*, I, 417.   [2] *Works of Jefferson*, VIII, 319–24.

This organization was to consist of a council, with a president and twelve members. Four of these, with the president, would constitute a quorum, and thus its policies could be determined by less than a majority. In each State there was to be a sub-directing council, with a vice-president and twelve members, and here again less than a majority could determine policies. In each State there were to be as many branches 'as local circumstances will permit.'

The organization, thus perfected, was to engage in super-propaganda. Information was to be disseminated through newspapers, 'but pamphlets must be largely employed.' This would cost money which would be raised by levying five dollars annually on each member for eight years. Printed matter was to be sent out free. In all communities, where there was a press, clubs were to be formed to meet each week to listen to the reading of newspapers and essays, written and delivered.

Then the organization was to keep up a 'lively correspondence' among its members with the view to nominating and supporting the most competent men for office. It was to enter the field of benevolence, and here, we may be sure, Hamilton learned a lesson from Tammany. In large centers of population particularly, societies for the relief of immigrants should be formed. This was a notable concession. Academies should be established 'with one professor for instructing the different classes of mechanics.' Had not the Jacobins used the clubs in the cities 'to give an impulse to the country'? Thus did Hamilton evoke the example of the Jacobins he pretended to despise.

Such was the framework of the organization Hamilton conceived to save the country from Jeffersonian democracy. Its immediate object should be speedily to adopt measures for bringing the repeal of the Judiciary Act before the Supreme Court presided over by John Marshall. The branch organizations should bring all possible pressure to bear to force State legislatures to instruct their senators to repeal the repealing act. New England should lead the way.[1]

Having completed his plan, Hamilton submitted it to a few leading Federalist politicians, who found it too academic for their

[1] *Works of Hamilton*, VIII, 596–99.

taste. The polite Bayard wrote that the plan 'was marked with great ingenuity, but he was not inclined to think it applicable to the state of things in this country.' [1]

And so the Constitution and the Christian religion were left naked to their enemies.

IV

While Hamilton was planning and Burr was plotting, Jefferson and his Cabinet were plodding along the dull routine of duty. Despite his distaste for the heat of the capital, with its miasmic swamps near by, Jefferson lingered at his post through the middle of July. There was enough to engage his attention in the foreign situation and in studying the returns from the customs houses. But he had his petty annoyances as well, and one of these has engaged the enthusiastic attention of numerous historians. In July, Monroe sent him a copy of the *Richmond Recorder*, a low paper of small circulation, containing the most scurrilous articles against him by James T. Callender, who was enraged by Jefferson's refusal to give him an appointment. The attacks were both political and personal, and the personal attacks were based on the scourings of the gutters of Charlottesville and reflected on his personal morality. Monroe was in doubt if anything in reply should be said at all, but apropos of the insinuations that Jefferson had hired and paid the Scotch master of scurrility to write attacks of a low nature on Washington and Adams, he suggested that he be furnished the facts about certain sums of money given to the adventurer in journalism.[2] Money had been given on three or four occasions. Infamous attacks had been made on Washington and Adams. And had not Jefferson pardoned Callender? True, he had pardoned all the victims of the Sedition Law — but why drag that in? The incident was made for the purpose of the Federalists, who seized their opportunity. Soon Callender's articles were being published at length and with gusto in the *Connecticut Courant*, the *New England Palladium*, the *Columbian Centinel*, and nowhere more than in the *New York Evening Post*, dominated by Hamilton. Commenting on the action of the *Post*,

[1] *Works of Hamilton*, VI, 543.
[2] *Writings of Monroe*, III, 355.

the *Independent Chronicle* unfairly charged that Hamilton had inspired the filthy stories of Callender.[1]

But the most dignified of the Federalist leaders did become peddlers for Callender's garbage wagon, and the obscure paper was given a larger circulation and was scanned by lewdly glowing eyes in some of the most refined drawing-rooms of Boston. All this Jefferson foresaw the moment he heard from Monroe. 'I perceive that the relief which was afforded him on mere motives of charity may be viewed under the aspect of employing him as a writer,' he wrote. And how did it come about? When Callender's 'Political Progress of Britain' appeared in America and was published in the *Bee*, Jefferson had read it. Mentioning it with approval to a friend in Philadelphia, he had been told that the author was in the city, a fugitive from prosecution because of its composition, and in actual want. This was the first Jefferson had heard of the identity of the author. 'I considered him,' wrote Jefferson, 'as a man of science fled from persecution, and assured my friend of my readiness to do anything I could to serve him.' But it was 'long after this' that he first met him. In the meanwhile, he had written the second part of the 'Political Progress,' which Jefferson found 'much inferior to the first,' and his 'History of the United States.' In 1798, Jefferson had been asked by Lieber to 'contribute to his relief.' He gave him a small sum of money. The next year he was asked to make another contribution by Senator Stevens T. Mason, and again he gave a small amount. Later, when Callender fled from Philadelphia in fear of prosecution and took refuge with Senator Mason, he wrote Jefferson soliciting his aid in getting into a counting-house or school in the neighborhood of Jefferson's home. He added that he had gathered material for another book on which he hoped to make enough to sustain him, but that he lacked the means to buy paper. Jefferson, having no wish to see him in the vicinity of his home, authorized Senator Mason to draw on Jefferson's correspondent in Richmond for fifty dollars, and wrote Callender to consider him a subscriber for as many copies of the forthcoming book as that amount would cover. Still later, Callender renewed his solicitations and again was given money on the same terms. It was at a time when the

[1] September 13, 1802.

Jeffersonians were assisting numerous newspapers opposing the Federalist régime and suffering persecution, such as the *Bee* and the *Albany Register.* By this time the importunities of Callender had taken on the color of blackmail. Like many politicians before and since, Jefferson found it more convenient to give money than to invite attacks, and he was to pay the penalty.[1]

With Jefferson's explanation, Monroe wrote that he would 'give such hints as to prevent anything whatever being done at present, or, if anything is, to give so far as in my power the true direction of the affair.' [2] Soon Jefferson's enemies in Virginia had exhausted their supply of the gutter gossip which malice and envy so eagerly turn upon a commanding figure, and Callender, his paper, and his articles sank into obscurity. The sewer ceased to pour its foul-smelling fluid into the drawing-rooms of the elect, and Callender committed suicide.

v

But the incident had not greatly distressed the object of the attack, who was much more interested in the herculean labors of the zealous Gallatin. As the killing heat fell upon the capital, the latter had taken his family to New York and returned to his lonely house and his arduous duties. He worked with Jefferson through the middle of July. When the latter left for Monticello to escape the malaria and heat and ordered Gallatin to leave, he refused to budge. Every day through July and August found him at his desk and low-spirited in his deserted house. 'The servants do as they please; everything goes as it pleases; ... I smoke and sleep, mind nothing, neither chairs, bedsteads or house. ... I grow more indolent and unsocial every day. ... I have been so gloomy this summer that I mean to frolic all next winter with the girls — assemblies, dinners, and parties. ... You, my dear, will stay home to nurse the children and entertain political visitors' — so he wrote his wife.[3] But he was making history. He was in the watch-tower and all was well.

It was within a week of August when Jefferson reached Monticello. He had longed for his daughters and their children on

---

[1] Jefferson to Monroe, *Writings of Jefferson,* x, 330, 333.
[2] *Writings of Monroe,* III, 356.   [3] Adams, *Gallatin,* 304.

his loved hilltop. 'It will be infinitely joyful for me to be with you there,' he had written his younger daughter, 'after the longest separation we have had for years. I count from one meeting to another as we do between port and port at sea.' [1] His health seemed as robust as ever, but to Dr. Rush alone he had confided that he had found a flaw which promised to relieve him of the fear of a helpless old age. 'It will probably give me as many years as I wish and without pain or debility,' he wrote.[2] To the daughters and grandchildren with whom he romped he made no sign. It was a happy summer. Madison was living at Montpelier, not far away, and the two visited frequently and discussed the increasing gloominess of the foreign prospects.

Politically all was serene, and even the mysterious intrigues of Burr caused no alarm. Burr had journeyed into the South on the pretext of visiting Theodosia in South Carolina, and had been received with great warmth by Jefferson's enemies in Richmond. At Savannah he was met outside the town by the Chatham Troop of Light Horse, greeted in town by a discharge of artillery, and in North Carolina he attended a Federalist dinner, where he made derogatory remarks about the repeal of internal taxes.[3] Cheetham in the *American Citizen* commented sharply on the incident.[4] With the *Citizen* savagely smiting Burr hip and thigh, the *Connecticut Courant* was as vigorously defending him. The Democrats, it said, recognized in Burr 'a man superior in talents to any man of their sect,' and during the late session of Congress Burr 'manifested toward the Democratic Party a degree of reserve that bespoke no strong desire for their company.' [5] That Burr was electioneering under cover was the general impression. But Hamilton's friend Troup thought that 'the general opinion is that Jefferson has not a formidable rival in Burr.' The Clintonians were warmly attached to Jefferson in New York and they were 'much more influential than Burr.' Among the Democrats, Burr had completely lost caste. 'At Washington it is understood he played a little cunning and trimming game,' and 'Jefferson and his friends feel that they

---

[1] *Domestic Life*, 285.   [2] *Ibid.*, 287.
[3] *Connecticut Courant*, June 14, 1802.   [4] May 29, 1802.
[5] June 14, 1802.

know him profoundly.' [1] While the prospects for Burr's advancement through the Democrats were dark enough, Hamilton was not so sure he might not rise on the shoulders of the Federalists. He had never quite recovered from the shock of their 'pollution' in supporting him for the Presidency in 1801. 'The Cabal did not terminate there,' he wrote. 'Several men of no inconsiderable importance among them like the enterprising and adventurous character of this man, and hope to soar with him to power. Many others, through hatred of the Chief and through impatience to recover the reins, are linking themselves with the Vice-President almost without perceiving it and professing to have no other object than to make use of him; while he knows he is making use of them.' [2] Thus Burr was more annoying to Hamilton than to Jefferson. We find no reference to him in the correspondence of Jefferson, Madison, and Monroe in 1802; he figured conspicuously in that of most of the Federalist leaders.

That month of August, Gouverneur Morris, incapable of understanding 'this American scene,' was rejoicing in the passing of Jefferson's popularity. Solemnly he was writing Livingston in Paris that Jefferson 'has outlived his popularity and is descending to a condition which I find no decent word to describe.' [3] And yet never had Jefferson been so popular outside the Federalist press and circle of leadership. More reasonable was the thought of some that Hamilton's popularity was increasing. It never had been great among the masses of the people, and seemingly it had diminished pitifully in the last days of the Adams Administration. But one of his friends, scanning the lists of Federalist toasts on July 4, concluded that he was 'regaining the general esteem and confidence which he seemed to have lost'; and, accepting him as the Federalist barometer, the conclusion was reached that the Federalist prospects were 'looking up.' [4] Thus the leaders of the opposition found Jefferson's popularity diminishing, Hamilton's increasing, and Burr was ruined in 'politics as well as in fortune.' [5]

---

[1] *King's Corr.*, iv, 120–21. [2] *Ibid.*, iv, 133–34.
[3] Morris, *Diary*, ii, 426. [4] Troup to King, *King's Corr.*, iv, 161.
[5] *King's Corr.*, iv, 160–61.

VI

But there was little to justify the Federalist optimism. Not only was New England becoming a battle-ground, but even in Connecticut, that Gibraltar of Federalism, the party, long in power, was being put on the defensive. There the Democrats had hit upon a dangerous issue. The State had been governed without a constitution and under a charter granted by Charles II, which was not in accord with the American spirit after the Revolution. Why should not Connecticut have a written constitution? It was easy for Theodore Dwight, the 'pope of Connecticut Federalism,' to answer in an oration before the Society of the Cincinnati. There was a fundamental law, he said, though not in the form of a written constitution, and its continuance was justified by its testing by experience. Had it not withstood every assault 'of royal prerogative, revolution, and faction'? Why bother about a written constitution? The only people worth considering were satisfied. Thus, one of the tenets of Federalism in Connecticut was adherence to the royal charter, unqualified hostility to a written constitution dictated by the opinion of the people.[1]

Quite as dangerous to the 'peace and quiet' of the people was the clamor now being raised for the separation of Church and State in Connecticut. That struck at the very heart of political power. John Leland, a Baptist minister, with great powers as an exhorter, had raised the question: Why should all the people be taxed for the support of one sect? Why should not Connecticut follow the example of other States and disconnect the Church and State? 'The people of Connecticut,' he wrote, 'have never been asked by those in authority what form of government they would choose. For want of a specific Constitution the rulers run without bridle or bit, or anything to draw them up to the ring-bolt. Should the Legislature make a law to perpetuate themselves in office for life, this law would immediately become part of the Constitution, and who could call them to account?'

Dangerous demagogy, of course, agreed the Federalists. And all the more dangerous because the Baptists would see in Demo-

[1] Richard J. Purcell, *Connecticut in Transit*, 243-44.

cratic success alone the hope for the disestablishment they wished. And the Methodists would join the Baptists.

And then, in the spring, 'Hancock' was writing 'incendiary and seditious' matter such as this:

'You exhibit to the world the rare and perhaps unprecedented example of a people peaceably and quietly consenting to be governed without any compact which secures rights in yourselves or delegates power to your rulers. . . . I am ready to admit that you have been influenced by a sacred regard for order and government, otherwise you would not . . . have consented to be governed by a charter given your ancestors by the British King, and which, since your independence separated you from Britain, has been imposed on you by the act of a legislature not authorized to make the imposition.' [1]

Not only had an issue been found — a constitution and religious liberty — but the Jeffersonians broke all precedents in their choice of candidates for office. The list included men of different classes, professions, and religious creeds. 'It was not a Congregationalist lawyer's list, nor restricted to the Connecticut valley towns,' the public was reminded. The people, and especially the farmers, interested in economy in administration were summoned to its support. The Federalists, amazed and shocked by the audacity of such heresies, were forced to extend themselves. In the spring elections there had been an unprecedented vote. Whence came these mysterious voters? There was something sinister in this presumption. Fifty-five Jeffersonians were sent to the legislature after one of the bitterest of campaigns. In the autumn election, the struggle was even harder, and in Hartford the contest seemed so doubtful that the Federalists were forced to stoop to the low Democratic device of soliciting votes.[2]

With such battling in hidebound Connecticut, it was inevitable that in other sections the Jeffersonians would make progress, and so it was. Nowhere did the Administration party lose ground and everywhere they made headway. Jefferson, convinced that the rank and file of the old enemy was coming over, warned

[1] Purcell, 248.
[2] Ibid., 247-48.

Levi Lincoln in Massachusetts against the use of patronage to
effect even the desired result.[1]

There was no need that year for official pressure. Even in
Massachusetts the leaven of democracy was working. No one
knew it better than Fisher Ames, who was almost hysterical over
the prospects. Shut up in the farmhouse at Dedham he fed on
his misgivings and his hates. Having no unreasoning love for
the Union, the late autumn found him urging the Federalists
to entrench themselves in the States. 'Entrench themselves,' he
wrote, 'and make State justice and State power a shelter of
the wise and the good *and the rich*.' [2] And fight! The Federalists
must fight. And the most effective artillery would be that of
the press. Not a multitude of newspapers, as at present, but
one newspaper into whose columns all the talent of the party
could be poured. 'To attempt to supply material to twenty
federal newspapers is absurd and impracticable,' he wrote. A
better plan would be to 'let a combination of the able men
throughout New England be made to supply some gazette with
such material of wit, learning, and good sense as will make
that superior to anything ever known in this country.' [3] Why
not? 'The pen will govern until the resort is to the sword, and
even then ink is of some importance.' And what paper would
serve so well as the *Palladium*? 'Wit and satire would flash
like the electrical fire, but the *Palladium* would be fastidiously
polite and well-bred. It would whip Jacobins as a gentleman
would a chimney sweeper, at arm's length and keeping aloof
from his soot.' Coarse vulgar phrase would be avoided 'to conciliate esteem,' foreign news would be intelligently presented,
books should be reviewed, and even 'agriculture should have a
share.' [4] That Ames was doing his part is indicated in a letter
to Christopher Gore: 'In the *Palladium* you will see an imitation of an ode of Horace ... you will suspect the author from
the notes. He is unsuspected here and is supposed to be from
Connecticut.' [5]

But Ames's plan no more appealed to the party leaders than
that of Hamilton. The disintegration of the once brilliant party

---

[1] *Writings of Jefferson*, x, 238.   [2] To Gore, *Ames*, i, 310.
[3] To Jeremiah Smith, *Ames*, i, 314–16.   [4] *Ibid.*   [5] *Ames*, i, 312.

was maddening to the sick man at Dedham. It held but three of the New England States. Rhode Island, of course, would 'lend the dirty mantle of its infamy to the nakedness of sansculottism.' New Jersey and New York were not yet hopeless, and Delaware and Maryland were slipping, though 'not as yet emptied of federalism as Pennsylvania is.' Even in the Southern States 'Federalism sprouts,' though 'with such a sickly yellow vegetation as the potatoes show in winter in a too warm cellar.' [1]

Thus, in much less than a year the opposition to Jefferson's Administration was crumbling away, with no unification of policy among the Federalist leaders. It was tending toward an army of generals without privates, of ornate guns without ammunition. Bayard was so hopeless and disgusted that in November he contemplated retirement. 'Not that I despair of the Republic,' he wrote, 'but I am persuaded that the people cannot be reasoned out of their folly.' [2]

VII

The first of October found Jefferson astride Wildair, galloping over the red clay roads of Virginia on his way to Washington. On the fourth day of the journey he arrived, sore all over, 'with a ringing in the head and deafness.' [3] A few days later, Gallatin returned from New York, and very soon the entire Cabinet was on hand. There was much to disturb its serenity.

The retrocession of Louisiana to France was now established, and Jefferson had no illusions as to the significance of such a mighty military power planted between the Western country and the outlet to the sea. It could only mean what Talleyrand intended, the building of a French colonial empire in the Western world. The relentless cruelty of the Corsican, the unexampled credulity of Charles IV, and the cupidity and vanity of Maria Luisa, had conspired to make the retrocession possible. Before the previous session of Congress had adjourned, Jefferson had written Livingston in Paris of his reaction to that event. 'It completely reverses all the political relations of the United States and will form a new epoch in our political course. . . . There

---

[1] To Jeremiah Smith, *Ames*, I, 314.
[2] To Andrew Bayard, *Bayard Papers*. [3] *Domestic Life*, 288.

is on the globe one single spot, the possessor of which is our
natural and habitual enemy ... New Orleans, through which
the produce of three eighths of our territory must pass to market'
— so ran the letter. 'France placing herself in that door assumes to us the attitude of defiance. Spain might have retained
it quietly for years.... Not so can it ever be in the hands of
France.... The day that France takes possession of New Orleans
fixes the sentence which is to restrain her forever within her
low-water mark. It seals the union of two nations, who, in
conjunction, can maintain exclusive possession of the ocean.
From that moment we must marry ourselves to the British fleet
and nation.' However, if France considered Louisiana indispens-
able to her views, she might reconcile it to our interests 'by
ceding to us the island of New Orleans and the Floridas.' Nothing
since the Revolutionary War had 'produced more uneasy sensa-
tions through the body of the nation.' [1]

Some swashbuckling historians of the far future were to
picture Jefferson as a cringing coward because he did not immediately declare war on France, or prepare to repel the landing
of French troops. Being an enlightened statesman, and not a
gasconading militarist, he preferred the settlement of a dangerous and difficult problem by peaceful means, if possible. But
all the while he realized that war might be necessary. Before
Congress met, he had written Livingston that 'we stand completely corrected of the error that either the government or the
nation of France has any remains of friendship for us.' [2] But
Napoleon's experiment in imperialism in Santo Domingo was
working badly, and until that was settled there could scarcely be
an attempt to take possession of Louisiana with troops. There
was always the possibility of an early resumption of the war
between France and England. There was no need for precipitate
action; there was time for negotiations, and these Jefferson immediately set on foot.

But there was worse to follow. Scarcely had the Cabinet
reached Washington when a messenger from New Orleans placed
in the hands of Madison an alarming letter. The Spanish Intendant in New Orleans, Don Juan Ventura Morales, had denied

[1] *Writings of Jefferson*, x, 311.   [2] *Ibid.*, x, 334.

to the Americans the right to deposit their merchandise in that city. He had offered no other place of deposit and given no indication of an intent to do so. And 'the season for the cotton from Natchez and other produce from the settlements higher up to come down approaches'![1] A few days later, Madison heard from William C. C. Claiborne at Natchez. The withdrawal of the right had 'excited considerable agitation at Natchez and its vicinity' and had 'inflicted a severe wound on the agricultural and commercial interests' of the territory which 'would prove to be no less injurious to all the Western country.'[2] There could be no doubt of that. The large part of the produce of Kentucky, Tennessee, and Mississippi depended on the Mississippi and the outlet to the sea at New Orleans to reach the markets. To close the port was to bottle up the products of this new country — a country peopled by ardent, fighting men. That policy maintained meant ruin. Ultimately it meant disunion. It certainly meant war.

Happily Congress had not yet met, and there was time for investigation. Yrujo, the Spanish Minister, immediately informed Madison that the order of withdrawal could not have emanated from the Government at Madrid. Soon it was known that the Intendant had acted over the earnest protest of the Spanish Governor. An excess of zeal, thought Yrujo. At any rate, there was no occasion for alarm and he would send a packet boat at once to New Orleans to demand the reason for the action taken. Meanwhile, he would communicate with Madrid. He sent a sizzling letter of rebuke to Morales.

And to Charles Pinckney, the American Minister in Spain, Madison sent instructions, assuming that the act of the Intendant was without instructions from his Government. This opinion had been expressed by the Spanish Ambassador. 'It is favored by private accounts from New Orleans mentioning that the Governor did not concur with the Intendant,' he continued. But whatever the facts, the President 'expects that the Spanish Government will neither lose a moment in countermanding it,

---

[1] W. E. Hulman to Madison, October 18, 1802; *Annals*, Appendix, 7th Cong., 2d Sess., 920.

[2] Claiborne to Madison, *ibid.*, 922.

nor hesitate to repair every damage which may result from it.'
Pinckney would realize, from his knowledge of the Western
people, how charged the situation was with dynamite. In their
resentment they were amply justified. 'The Mississippi is to
them everything. It is the Hudson, the Delaware, the Potomac
and all the navigable streams of the Atlantic States formed into
one stream.' From Kentucky and Mississippi alone the previous
year the produce carried through New Orleans amounted to
$1,622,672, and that year it would probably show an increase
of fifty per cent. The strongest possible representations had
been made to the Spanish Minister in Washington and he 'readily
undertakes to use it with all the effect he can give it.'[1] And
Yrujo did, right loyally.

Even so it required weeks and months in those days to communicate between Washington and Madrid, and in the meanwhile, the hardy pioneers in deerskin caps and buckskin breeches,
carving a civilization by the sweat of their brows out of the
wilderness of the Western country, were straining at their leashes.
It was their very existence that was involved. They were not
given to wordy negotiations. Their impulse always was to
shoulder a musket and march militantly to their desires. Could
these be held in check until the tone and temper of Paris and
Madrid could be tested? It was a ticklish question. And no
one knew it better than the Federalists, the traditional foes of
the Western settlements. Hypocritically assuming now an attitude of belligerent friendship, they eagerly seized their opportunity to cause complications that might lead to war, or divorce
the Western States from Jefferson.

Such was the state of affairs when Congress met.

[1] *Writings of Madison*, vi, 461.

CHAPTER VIII

The Federalists Play With Fire

I

WHEN Congress convened, all the political advantages were with the Jeffersonians. Never had they presented such a solid phalanx to the foe nor shown themselves so pliable to responsible leadership. Never had the country been so prosperous since the foundation of the Republic, and none of the doleful predictions of the opposition during the previous session had been vindicated by events. The midnight judges were abolished, but there had been no congestion in the courts and the 'postboys' of the bench, as Morris called them, had not been overworked. No creditor of the nation had taken alarm at the repeal of the internal taxes, and Morris's legion of smugglers had not appeared upon the coasts to rob the Treasury of its customs duties. Indeed, the import duties Gallatin conservatively had estimated would be $9,500,000 had poured $12,280,000 into the nation's coffers. With this alone, surpassing by $1,200,000 the highest figure ever yet attained both with the customs duties and internal taxes, there was no occasion for panic among our creditors in London and Amsterdam. As a result of the flourishing finances, the Republic within the year had met 'all the regular exigencies of government' and been able to pay from the Treasury 'upward of eight millions of dollars, principal and interest, of the public debt,' which meant the wiping-out of five and a half millions of the principal. With all this accomplished, there remained in the Treasury four and a half millions 'which are in course of application to a further discharge of debt and current demands.' The bankers of London and Amsterdam, whose anticipated mental torture had wrung tears

from the eyes of the opposition leaders, were more than satisfied. Never had the credit of the nation stood higher in the
money marts of the world.[1]

The political effect had been disastrous to the Federalists.
Troup, the friend of Hamilton, wrote Rufus King that 'the
Democratic Party is gaining strength through the Union generally,' with even 'an evident growth of democracy' in Massachusetts, and with the Jeffersonian strength in no wise diminished in the commercial and financial Empire State.[2] 'Jacobinism is full of ardor and is proud of its power,' groaned the morbid
Ames.[3] He reported his friends 'lazy or in despair,' and urged
'with wonderful eagerness the futility of all exertions to retrieve
the public mind from its errors.' And so, 'weary and disgusted,
despairing, as well I may, of any good effect from my single
efforts, I now claim the quiet repose that, like a fool, I have so
long refused.' After all, 'zeal is a bad sleeper, and I will try
opium with the rest of them.'[4] Even in Massachusetts all was
lost. For 'the Jacobin mode of waging war resembles the expedition of Diomed into the Trojan camp. There is to be seen
only a quick destruction that provokes no resistance — the
victims die without waking.'[5]

Politically, when the session opened, Jefferson was riding
gaily on the crest of popularity, but the 'annihilation' of Federalism in Pennsylvania had encouraged a bitter factional fight
among the Democrats, with the aristocratic Kean leading one
element and Duane and Leib the other. With both ardent in
their fealty to Jefferson, it was a delicate situation in which to
intervene. None but a most consummate politician could have
escaped immersion in the broil. It was quite different in New
York, since in the battle between the Clintons and Burr there
could be no doubt where Jefferson's interest lay. Burr 'despises
the littleness and meanness of the Administration,' wrote Senator
Plumer, a Federalist who knew.[6] Thoroughly informed of Burr's
underhand maneuvers, Jefferson was determined to bring him
into the open and to force the fighting. On the day Congress

---

[1] Jefferson's Message.   [2] *King's Corr.*, iv, 182.
[3] To Dwight, *Ames*, i, 317.   [4] To Gore, *Ames*, i, 318–19.
[5] *Ibid.*, i, 320.   [6] To Judge Smith, *Plumer*, 256–57.

convened, Troup was writing Rufus King that 'Burr is a gone man.' [1]

More annoying to Jefferson than the hostility of Burr was the loss of the brilliant and resourceful Giles in the House. Seriously ill, he had been forced to retire, and the election of Eppes, a son-in-law, husband of the beautiful Mary, as his successor, was only a palliative to the pain of the loss of the most skillful debater in either branch of Congress. [2]

II

Infuriated by the complacency with which Jefferson rode the wave of popularity, the Federalists converged on Washington in an ugly mood. The news that the Spanish Intendant had closed the port of New Orleans to the products of the Western country had spread like wildfire. Afar off in Kentucky and Tennessee could be heard the ominous growling of the people, and no one but knew that these hardy pioneers, who lived with a rifle and a knife, were eager to march forthwith and take New Orleans by storm. They wanted war — and war at once! No longer was it a secret that Louisiana had been returned by Spain to France, and that Napoleon, whose shadow rested hauntingly on the world, was preparing to take possession with trained soldiers. And after that — what? No one knew. No one could ascertain. But Napoleon was Napoleon and that promised little for the respect of treaties or for an understanding making possible the continued use of the port of New Orleans. A denial of the old right of deposit, made good, would mean the ruin of the entire Western country. And that meant war or the separation from the Union of the Western States. A war on France long had been a primary object of Federalist policy, and the separation of the Western country from the Union would have been as balm of Gilead to the Federalist leaders in New England. Instantly the strategy of Federalism was clear — to force a war if possible, to furnish the West with a pretext for separation if necessary, and to make impossible by every human means the success of any peaceful negotiations Jefferson might plan.

At this moment Jefferson's plans were being acted upon in

[1] *King's Corr.*, IV, 192.   [2] *Domestic Life*, 291.

Paris and Madrid. A robust protest and a demand for the repudiation of the action of the Intendant at New Orleans had been made to Madrid, backed in all sincerity by Yrujo, the Spanish Minister. Livingston had been instructed to secure from France an immediate assurance that, when in possession, the right of deposit, formerly granted by the Spanish, would be continued by the French, and to open negotiations for the purchase of the island of New Orleans. But all this required time. No messages then could be flashed under or over the sea and the slow sailing boats required weeks for an exchange of letters.

Could Jefferson successfully enjoin patience and confidence on the Westerners and hold Congress in check pending the experiment with negotiations? Not if the Federalists could prevent it! The Message of Jefferson had been irritatingly calm. Not one word concerning the action of the Spanish Intendant, and one brief paragraph on the retrocession of Louisiana with the suggestion that, if carried into effect, it would result in making 'a change in the aspect of our foreign relations.' [1] But not one militant note. Not enough sword-rattling to be heard above the crinkle of the paper as it was read.

The Federalists were furious. 'Coward,' 'trimmer,' 'shyster,' 'betrayer of American rights and dignity' — so ran the charges of almost incoherent rage. Hamilton was a bit puzzled and far more sober than his subordinates. 'You have seen the soft turn given to the message,' he wrote C. C. Pinckney. 'Yet we are told that the President in conversation is very stout.' Hamilton could see Jefferson's 'great embarrassment.' How could he carry on war without taxes? The substitution of economy for taxation would not do now. And what 'a terrible comment on the abandonment of the internal revenue' a war would be! Still how, without war, could Jefferson preserve his popularity with his Western idolators? Could it be planned for the chief 'to hold a bold language and the subalterns to act a feeble part'? And then he added a declaration of faith which set him apart from his New England followers: 'I have always held that the unity of our empire and the best interests of the nation require that we shall annex to the United States all the territory east

[1] *Writings of Jefferson*, III, 342.

THE FEDERALISTS PLAY WITH FIRE 163

of the Mississippi, New Orleans included.'[1] Thus, Jefferson and Hamilton were as one in favoring the acquisition of this territory, but characteristically they differed as to method. Jefferson would acquire it by peaceable negotiations and by purchase if possible; Hamilton would take it by force.

Ames could see nothing in Jefferson's policy but 'forbearance and disgrace.' He was sure we should 'sit down, as Junius says, as a nation infamous and contented.' By preserving peace we should 'lose character.' But Ames, his ears attuned to the rumbling in the West, had hopes. 'Yet Kentucky may possibly break its bridle and rush into business,' and it was the business of the Federalists in Congress to see that she did. Meanwhile, he left 'Mr. Jefferson to write pretty nonsense about peace and universal philanthropy.'[2]

Senator Plumer, breathing the partisan air of the boarding-houses, was all for war. 'Weak and feeble measures!' he snorted. 'The Federalists were for taking immediate possession of New Orleans,' he wrote.[3] Another Federalist was disgusted with a message 'dressed in the most smooth and popular strains, exceedingly guarded and artfully designed to beguile the unthinking multitude.'[4] When the Americans learned that Jefferson was 'weak and timid,' there would be a change in the politics of the Western country.'[5]

Thus there were four prongs to the Federalists' fork. One to force a war with France and Spain, another to encourage dissatisfaction with the Union in the West, a third to wreck the program of economy and the liquidation of the debt as speedily as possible, and fourth, to divorce the Westerners from Jefferson and enlist them under the banner of their enemies.

Meanwhile, in personal conversations, and through his notes to our Ministers in Paris, London, and Madrid, Jefferson was leaving no doubt of his determination to go to battle if negotiations failed.

Two weeks after Congress met, he kept open house on New Year's Day and Federalists and Democrats flocked to the fes-

[1] *Works of Hamilton*, VIII, 605–06.
[2] *Ames*, I, 317.
[3] To Thompson, *Plumer*, 253
[4] Cutler to Terry, Cutler, II, 120.
[5] Cutler, II, 121.

tivity. Within five weeks partisan bitterness would make the mingling of the partisans impossible.

III

The struggle in the House, which began early, was speedily terminated. Early in January, Roger Griswold, the Federalist leader, offered a resolution calling upon the President to lay before Congress all papers and information respecting the retrocession of Louisiana. Two days later, Varnum of Massachusetts, the Jeffersonian, reported from the committee to which the Message had been referred a resolution on the action of the Spanish Intendant, and set forth the position of the Jeffersonian majority:

'Adhering to that humane and wise policy which ought ever to characterize a free people, and by which the United States have always preferred to be governed; willing at the same time to ascribe this breach of contract to the unauthorized misconduct of certain individuals, rather than to a want of good faith on the part of His Catholic Majesty; and relying with perfect confidence on the vigilance and wisdom of the Executive, they will await the issue of such measures as that Department of the Government shall have pursued for asserting the rights and vindicating the injuries of the United States; holding it to be their duty at the same time to maintain the boundaries and the rights of navigation and commerce through the river Mississippi as established by existing treaties.'[1]

Thus, under the guidance of Jefferson and Madison, did a democratic assembly demonstrate its capacity under provocative circumstances to approach the possible resort to war with dignity and fairness.

Instantly the Federalists were on their feet with an amendment. What! express confidence in the 'vigilance and wisdom' of such men as Jefferson and Madison? Never! They proposed to strike out this expression of confidence. Under the careful leadership of Randolph it was a case of short horse soon curried. Without debate Randolph called for the question and the amendment was voted down by a majority of almost two to one. The Varnum resolutions were then adopted by a party vote.[2]

[1] *Annals,* January 7, 1803.   [2] *Ibid.*

When, four days later, Griswold attempted to secure action on his resolution calling for papers, Randolph expressed surprise, since the Federalists had announced by their action their unwillingness to co-operate in maintaining national rights so long 'as the direction of the Government should be retained by those who now possess it.' Had they not refused to support the declaration of a determination to maintain these rights? 'There was a time, sir,' he added, 'when such conduct would have been denounced by a portion of this House as the essence of Jacobinism and disorganization.'

Thus ended the opposition in the House. It was to be taken up with greater passion and intemperance in the Senate.

IV

The Federalists in the Senate had a crowded program of opposition. Morris and Ross soon were to retire to private life under the persuasion of their constituents and full advantage must be taken of their powers of denunciation. Before the attacks began, *en masse*, on Jefferson's Louisiana policy, the opposition took another fling at the repeal of the Judiciary Act. The famous case of Marbury *vs.* Madison was brewing. Some of the midnight judges whose commissions had not been given when the midnight hour put an end to the bizarre scene in Marshall's office had thought, through Marshall and the partisan Supreme Court, to force their delivery. Late in January a motion was made in the Senate that Marbury be furnished with 'an attested copy of the proceedings of the Senate on the 2d and 3d of March, 1801.' Jackson, the pugnacious, shouted that he would oppose it as 'an attack upon the Executive Department.' More convincing was the lawyer-like Breckinridge. The executive journal was kept exclusively for the benefit of the Senate, he said. An express rule forbade the giving out of copies except with the consent of the entire Senate. Under no rule of propriety could exceptions be made in this partisan case. Even then a suit was pending on a mandamus in the Supreme Court and 'the Senate ought not to aid the Judiciary in their invasion of the rights of the Executive.'

Then rose Gouverneur Morris, leaning on his wooden leg. The motion should be granted, he said threateningly, or else 'the court might issue process, compelling the Secretary to appear and bring with him the journal.' If the Secretary should refuse such process there might be a denial of justice in which Morris could not be a party. What! exclaimed Wright — give the Supreme Court the power to pry into the affairs of the Executive? Never! And then Breckinridge rose again to bring the discussion back to legal grounds. Why the necessity for these copies of the executive journal? Were not commissions made out to Marbury and the others? Everyone conceded it. And did not that carry the proof of the confirmation of their nominations? And there was another sufficient ground for opposition to the motion — 'the Senate should not countenance the Judiciary in their attack on the Executive power, which is not, constitutionally, amenable to the judges.'

Morris instantly was on his feet. A strange position, indeed, for the Senate to take, he said. Here was 'the golden chain let down from Jove to bind the earth to vassalage.' How was the dignity of the President involved? James Madison, 'a subordinate,' abuses his trust, violates his duty, is guilty of malpractice, and is arraigned; and because the culprit is convicted and condemned, is the dignity of the Government, therefore, violated? And the President's rights? He has no rights not given by the Constitution, and the Supreme Court would pass on that.

It was then that a young man of imposing presence, with strong, commanding features, took the floor. DeWitt Clinton was a new member, destined soon to desert the Senate to become the dominant figure in New York. What purpose would be served? he asked. There was but one purpose clear — to cast the weight of the Senate into the controversy in litigation. And issue a summons to Madison? 'Such a step would certainly bring things to a crisis.' A great constitutional pretension had been raised carrying an implication of the right of the Judiciary to control the President.

The question was taken; the motion was defeated by a party vote.[1] But the right of deserving Federalists to compensation for offices non-existent was sacred, and immediately a resolution was proposed to the effect that the repeal of the Judiciary Act was le-

[1] *Annals*, January 21, 1803.

gal and constitutional, beyond the capacity of the Senate to determine. The Supreme Court should be called upon to act. Therefore, a resolution instructing Jefferson to cause an information in the nature of a *quo warranto* to be filed by the Attorney-General against Richard Bennett, for the purpose of deciding judicially on their claims.

The handiwork of Gouverneur Morris, he rose to defend it. A question had arisen on the constitutionality of the repeal. The Senate could not interpret its own acts. The Senate, wise and sober, would set forth no such claim. True, the House, 'immediate representatives of the people, may . . . borne on the heady torrent of public opinion . . . usurp all power.' But the question had passed forever from Congress and only the packed judiciary could determine it.

And why, by denying, divide the nation on the verge of war? 'Can you hope for success while discontent sits brooding in the heart of the country? These judges, indeed, are not numerous, but they do not stand alone. They have relatives, friends, adherents, from blood, affection, principles. Why will you wound a class of citizens numerous and respectable?' And then, with a simplicity unbecoming so hardened a cynic, with a suavity better suited to minds less robust than those of the Jeffersonians, he became persuasive:

'Will the judges rudely declare that you have violated the Constitution, unmindful of their duty and regardless of their oath? No. With that decency which becomes the judicial character . . . upholds national dignity and impresses obedience on the public will; that decency, the handmaid of the graces, which more adorn the magistrate than ermine, aye, than royal robes; with that decency which so becomes their state and condition, they will declare what the legislators meant. . . . They will modestly conclude that you did not mean to abolish the offices which the Constitution had forbidden you to abolish; and therefore finding it was not your intention to abolish, they will declare that the offices still exist!'

Miraculously enough, the Jeffersonians were astounded, and thoughtless enough to give no heed. Again the Federalists failed to convince the Congress that the midnight judges, named to

serve a party end, had a vested right in their salaries.[1] But John
Marshall, on the bench, soon was to accomplish more than his
fellow partisans in the Senate.

V

The night John Marshall, by the light of candles, passed out
commissions to repudiated Federalist politicians as judicial
officers, time would not permit of the distribution of them all.
The purpose both of the Judiciary Act of the dying hours of the
Adams Administration and of the last-minute distribution of
the commissions had been to pack the federal bench against the
democratic trend of the times. On Jefferson's orders, the un-
delivered commissions were not sent to the intended beneficiaries.
And thereupon legal action was taken in an effort to force James
Madison to finish the distribution John Marshall had begun.
Thus came the case of Marbury *vs.* Madison.

The very heart of Federalism was its hatred of democracy. It
had lost the confidence of the greater part of the country. It had
lost control of the Congress that made the laws, and of the Executive who enforced them, but the third department was the
Judiciary, packed with Federalist politicians, who were in for life
and beyond the reach of the people. Scarcely had the wave of
popular condemnation passed over them in 1800 when Federalism
determined to make the executive and legislative departments
subordinate to the Judiciary. This accomplished, they felt a way
would be found to defeat the democratic tendency of the times.

At this time John Marshall hated democracy as much as,
and he hated Jefferson more than Hamilton ever had. But he
knew that an order of his to Madison or the President to deliver
the commissions of the midnight judges would have been ignored.
He had no stomach for a direct conflict with Jefferson. Apparently there never was a moment when there was the slightest
possibility that he would issue such an order.

But could the case be twisted to make possible a decision that
the Supreme Court could veto the laws of Congress signed by the
President? That thought, says Marshall's brilliant biographer,
had been in the mind of the Chief Justice a long while. True,

[1] *Annals*, February 3, 1803.

there was not a line in the Constitution hinting at such a power in one department over the other two independent departments that were amenable to the people; true, there was nothing in the discussions of the Constitutional Convention implying the recognition of such power, and Franklin had said emphatically that it would be unthinkable. But John Marshall proposed to claim the power.

Thus, in sitting down to the preparation of his opinion, he determined to accomplish a double task — to escape the embarrassment of issuing an order Jefferson would ignore, and at the same time, in a vital way, to change the then existing concept of American institutions.

In the thirteenth section of a Judiciary Act, written by Oliver Ellsworth, his predecessor as Chief Justice, he found the authority claimed for him by his fellow partisans. He determined to hold this provision unconstitutional and void. The sole purpose of this irregular proceeding was formally, and in the record, to declare the power of one independent co-ordinate branch of the Government to set aside the actions of the other two.

Never before had the Court laid claim to such power, and Marshall's biographer says that but for Marshall's action then 'the power of the Supreme Court to annul acts of Congress probably would not have been insisted upon thereafter.' [1]

And yet, Marshall's unprecedented action scarcely caused a ripple of public interest. The press was silent. Jefferson had won his point as to the commissions, and the law declared unconstitutional did not interest the people in the least. Thus were American institutions modified without a constitutional amendment and without a reference to the people, and the modification meant thereafter a less democratic form.

Jefferson, who saw it, dissented wholly from it and so expressed himself in private correspondence. He knew that should the power claimed be exercised, the Federalists had won a greater victory than during the heyday of their authority. He waited for the exercise of the power — and waited in vain. Time and again measures of his Administration were denounced by Federalists as unconstitutional, but never once was an appeal made to the

[1] Beveridge, III, 131.

Supreme Court, after Marshall's decision, to set these acts aside. Marshall was to remain on the bench for thirty-two years after his decision, but never was he to annul another act of Congress by his action. And not till twenty years after Marshall was mouldering in the grave was the Supreme Court to evoke and act upon his opinion.

Historians have been chary of the fact that this opinion by one man modified American institutions without a constitutional amendment, and made the American Government in the future much less readily responsive to the public will than is the Government of England; or that it was a blow to Jeffersonian democracy. The act of Marshall, while it did not destroy, curtailed the power of the people, and the Government thereafter was to be less of a democracy than that for which Jefferson had contended, and contended successfully before the people.

To the day of his death, Jefferson never gave his adherence to that opinion.

VI

It was now February. Party bitterness had become white-hot, and the old system of the social ostracism of Jeffersonians, so flagrantly offensive in the days when Mrs. Bingham's drawing-room was closed to them, was now renewed. In Salem, Massachusetts, Jacob Crowninshield, a Jeffersonian statesman and merchant of the highest order, was excluded from the Assembly with which he long had been associated. He was stoutly, contemptuously refused the courtesy of an explanation.[1] About the same time the feast of shells was celebrated in Boston by the Essex Junto. There was much enthusiasm for the toast, 'Virginia — when she changes three-fifths of her Ethiopian skin we will respect her as the head of our White family.' This received uproarious applause from the immediate ancestors of the abolitionists, and was followed with music to the tune of 'Go to the Devil and Shake Yourself.'[2] Gouverneur Morris was insulting his host, a member of the Cabinet, with slurring comments on the Administration, and attending White House dinners to gloat over finding Jefferson 'terribly out of spirits.'[3] Soon the Federalist

[1] William Bentley, *Diary*, III, 2.   [2] *Ibid.*, III, 4.   [3] Morris, *Diary*, II, 430.

leaders were seeking an agreement among themselves to snub the
President's dinner invitations, and, unable to find unanimity on
the vulgar plan, made themselves as boorish as possible at Jefferson's board.[1] But the Administration leaders were by no means
crushed. Madison's health was better that winter than ever
before; Gallatin was standing the strain without evidence of
breaking; and Jefferson was able to boast of 'perfect health,'
notwithstanding excruciating headaches on occasions and an
infrequent twinge of rheumatism.[2]

But the nerves of congressmen were not so steady, and early
in the winter, Senator Christopher Ellery of Rhode Island and
John Rutledge engaged in a tavern brawl. Rutledge, the aggressor,
demanded a duel; Ellery proposed submitting the controversy to
a fair and impartial decision. The Federalists denounced Ellery
as a coward; the Jeffersonians pronounced Rutledge a miserable
bully, since he knew that Ellery was very near-sighted.[3] Such was
the hair-trigger condition when the Federalists in the Senate
turned their heaviest artillery on the Louisiana policy of Jefferson.

VII

The Federalists knew of Jefferson's determination to withhold
his fire on Spain until Madrid could repudiate or acknowledge
the action of the Intendant, and to meet the French menace with
negotiations before resorting to the sword. To their distress they
found that the Westerners remained loyal to their idol, and,
though ready and eager to fight at a nod from Jefferson, they were
holding themselves in check. Under the wise leadership of Breckinridge, the Western element in Congress were keeping their
heads, and this was not in accord with Federalist hopes. And
when Jefferson sent to the Senate the nomination of James
Monroe as special envoy for the negotiations in Paris, the very
confidence of the Westerners in his devotion to their interests
infuriated the opposition. It was at this juncture that they began
to make their record on the purchase of Louisiana.

Monroe never had been a favorite with the Federalists. His
uncompromising republicanism was not relieved by special social

[1] Cutler, ii, 132.   [2] Jefferson to Hawkins, *Writings of Jefferson*, x, 360.
[3] *Independent Chronicle*, January 13, 1803.

graces nor by a sense of humor. Sent as Minister to France in the last days of the Terror, his undisguised sympathy with the original democratic purpose of the Revolution had been made the excuse for much abuse. He had been guilty of cultivating the good-will of the people to whom he was accredited when the Federalists wanted nothing so much as war. Thus, when Jefferson sent in his nomination, they rallied to defeat his confirmation, but without success. Alas, wrote a Federalist senator, 'the measures of Washington are to be reviled, his admirers wounded, and a new order of things established.' [1]

Two days after the confirmation, Senator Ross of Pennsylvania, one of the darlings of the Bingham drawing-room, made his inflammatory speech to wreck the plans of Jefferson. His purpose was well known. The stage was set. The women deserted their teas and card-games to flock in their gayest gowns to the Senate, where they mingled with the senators on the floor. Down the broad and muddy Avenue tramped as many of the six thousand inhabitants as could spare the time, to enjoy the drama. The corridors were crowded. The situation was one of the utmost delicacy, and Ross stepped forth with the recklessness of an inebriated incendiary in the hope of fanning passion into a conflagration.

Very suavely, he began. He knew negotiations were in progress, and he would not think of uttering a word to 'thwart negotiations or embarrass the President.' Thenceforth he was to speak with ever-increasing venom in denunciation of Jefferson's peaceable plans.

'This treaty has been wantonly and unprovokedly violated,' he said, 'not only in what related to the Mississippi, but by the most flagrant destructive spoliations of our commerce on every part of the ocean where Spanish armed vessels met the American flag.'

Having thus marshaled all the long-standing grievances against Spain as part of the attack on the act of the Intendant, he boldly charged the withdrawal of the right of deposit at New Orleans, not to the Intendant, but to 'the officers of Spain,' though he knew that the Spanish Governor and the Minister in Washington had repudiated and denounced the act.

[1] Plumer to Gilman, *Plumer*, 249.

Thus did he assist in the negotiations!

Then he plunged into a demagogic appeal to the Westerners. 'What would be the language,' he asked in quivering tones, 'were such an indignity offered to the Atlantic coast?' Why this callous indifference to the vital interests of the West? And what a fate to which the Administration was consigning the Westerners! 'They cannot go to market. They have no resources but the product of their farms. You suffer the Spaniards to lock them up. You tell them that their crops must rot on their hands, and yet they must pay their debts and taxes. Will it be submitted to? Is this justice? . . . You suffer wanton violation of it without making an effort to remove the obstruction, and you tell them that they must pay you.'

As Ross harangued, with this shameless lying, a slow boat was on its way with the repudiation of the action of the Intendant from Madrid, and Livingston already had assurance that in the event of French possession the treaty would be respected.

But Ross, applauded by the Federalists, was seeking to assist Jefferson in his negotiations. 'Why not seize then what is so essential to us as a nation?' he cried. 'Why submit to a tardy uncertain negotiation? . . . When in possession you will negotiate with more advantage.' Were not the Westerners ready to fight? 'Is this a spirit to be repressed or put to sleep by negotiations?' Wait until the French are in possession, armed, garrisoned, would these gallant spirits then be willing to follow the Government to battle? 'No; their confidence in their rulers will be gone.' And France sell? And here the speaker, with clear malice, sought to spike all negotiations in Paris:

'I have seen it stated in newspapers that those who now pretend to claim that country may be persuaded to sell, by giving two millions of dollars to certain influential persons about the Court ——'

'Order!' cried Wright of Maryland. How dare a senator thus betray in public information received in confidence?

The velvety Burr purred his inability to understand that there was anything improper in the insinuation of bribery. Senator Nicholas, with a contemptuous look at Burr, called for the clearing of the galleries.

'I will never speak,' said Ross, 'upon this subject, sir, with closed doors. The moment you shut your doors I cease, and when they are opened, I shall proceed.'

Reluctantly, Burr had to order the clearing of the galleries.[1] The next day the bill providing an appropriation for the purchase was delivered from the House,[2] and on the following day Ross resumed his generous effort to assist in the peaceable negotiations.

'Where,' he demanded, 'is the nation, ancient or modern, that has borne such treatment without resentment or resistance? Where is the nation that will respect another that is passive under such humiliating degradation and disgrace?' And the remedy offered by Jefferson? 'It is a secret. We are not allowed to speak of it here; it was only committed to confidential men in whispers with closed doors; but by and by you will see it operate like enchantment; it is a sovereign balm which will heal your wounded honor; it is a potent spell, or a kind of patent medicine which will extinguish and forever put to rest the devouring spirit which has desolated many nations of Europe.'

Thereupon Ross offered his inflammatory resolution, amounting to a declaration of war, calling out the army and navy to take forceful possession of the island of New Orleans and adjacent territory, and setting aside a war fund.[3]

Instantly the Federalist press and party were cheering boisterously. 'The spirited and well-timed Resolution which the Federalists have brought forward in the Senate cannot fail to excite the applause of every true American,' said Hamilton's organ, the *Evening Post*.[4] A few days more, and it was publishing Ross's speech in full and again pronouncing the resolution the 'Federalist plan.'[5] But Hamilton's organ wanted war and no negotiations. When 'Coriolanus' in the *Morning Chronicle* apologized for his former demand for war, the *Evening Post* could 'see no reason to retract anything.' Far from it. 'War is undoubtedly a calamity, but national degradation is greater, and besides, it is always inevitably followed by war itself.'[6]

[1] *Annals*, February 14, 1803.   [2] *Ibid.*, February 15, 1803.
[3] *Ibid.*, February 16, 1803.   [4] *Ibid.*, February 23. 1803.
[5] *Ibid.*, February 26, 1803.   [6] *Ibid.*, February 8, 1803.

VIII

Never in congressional history a more deliberately mischievous speech. Ross knew that in private Jefferson, thoroughly aroused, was making no secret of his intention to draw the sword if negotiations failed. He knew that Monroe had bluntly told the French Chargé d'Affaires that the failure of negotiations would mean war. He knew that Gallatin openly proclaimed it. The excitement in Washington increased by the day. Card-tables were abandoned, teacups were forgotten, dancing was taboo, that men and women might hear these ominous discussions.

A few days later, Senator Samuel White of Delaware rose to compete with Ross in stirring animal passions. 'Why negotiate when war would serve?' he demanded. And what if Yrujo had repudiated and denounced the action of the Intendant at New Orleans? Was he in charge of New Orleans? Where was his authority? The responsibility was with the Intendant, 'an immediate officer of the Crown and responsible only to the Crown for his conduct.' Indeed, the manly act of Yrujo was maddening to the Federalists who assailed him roundly for taking the American ground. The *Philadelphia Gazette* found Yrujo's repudiation of the Intendant more threatening than promising. Ridiculous idea, it was, that the Intendant had acted without instructions, and 'every day has disclosed additional reasons for believing that it is a concerted attack on our national rights.' [1]

But for the calm confidence of the people in the wisdom of Jefferson, the speeches of Ross and White, spread sensationally in the press throughout the country, would have been enough to plunge the young Republic into war with the greatest military power on earth. It was time for the Administration to speak. And it was Breckinridge, the Westerner, who took the floor. Clearly, concisely, he set forth the facts. The wrong had been committed; the proper protests had been made; negotiations were in progress.

'Has it been the practice of this Government heretofore to break lances on the spot with any nation who injured us or insulted us?' he asked. 'Has not the invariable course been to seek reparations in the first place, by negotiations?'

[1] Quoted in *Evening Post*, February 3, 1803.

He paused and looked around.

'I ask for one example to the contrary.'

There was no reply from the Federalist group.

'Even under the Administration of Washington, so much eulogized by the gentleman last up.'

There was no reply.

'Were not the Detroit and several other forts within our territory held ten or a dozen years by Great Britain in direct violation of a treaty? Were not wanton spoliations committed on your commerce by Great Britain, by France, and by Spain — and all adjusted through the medium of negotiations?'

And now, negotiations pending, it is proposed to take New Orleans by force? 'A Minister is sent to the offending nation with an olive branch for the purpose of an amiable discussion and settlement of differences, and before he has scarcely turned his back we invade the territories of that nation and with an army of fifty thousand men.'

And what an amazing suggestion from Ross and White that the Western States would invade on their own responsibility or separate from the Union. 'I did not expect to hear such language on this floor.'

Thereupon he offered a substitute for the Ross resolution, authorizing the President, 'whenever he shall judge it expedient, to call upon the governors of the various States to put and keep their militias in readiness for action.' He was empowered to accept volunteers for military service. Money was authorized to meet the cost of such preparations. And on that resolution Jefferson took his stand.[1]

Then rose DeWitt Clinton to support Jefferson's plan. The extraordinary language of Ross and White, he said, would justify severity in reply, but the common sense of the Senate did not call for it. No doubt the Court at Madrid would repudiate the action of the irresponsible Intendant, but Ross and White had introduced other grievances wholly disconnected with the incident at New Orleans.

'War unquestionably is his design,' he said. 'Why mask his propositions? Why not furnish the people at once with the real

Annals, 7th Cong., 2d Sess.

and whole object of himself and friends? If it is bottomed on patriotism and dictated by wisdom, it need not shrink from the touch of an investigation.'

And why the evocations of Washington? 'The United States under his Administration and that of his successor have received injuries more deleterious, insults more atrocious, and indignities more pointed than the present — and pacific measures of negotiation were preferred.' [1]

Nothing had rankled with the Jeffersonians so much as the lofty manner in which Ross and White had insisted that no injury was suffered without energetic action by Washington. What of the British outrages and the negotiation of the Jay Treaty? asked Senator Cocke. Did Ross support negotiations and not war then? He did. What about the tributes to the Algerian pirates? Did Ross vote them instead of war? He did. All this was done in Washington's Administration, and 'if this conduct was wise and just with the Barbary Powers, it must be so with Spain.' [2] And 'did not France capture our vessels and imprison our seamen?' demanded Jackson. 'Did Washington appeal to arms? No, sir. Mr. Adams then came into the Administration. Did he appeal to arms? No, sir, he sent a new set of Ministers who were received and who made the memorable treaty which was ratified.' [3]

IX

The two leading orators had reserved their fire until toward the close. Two days before Morris spoke, the Federalists had a partisan pow-wow at Stelle's, attended as usual by all the stout Federalist partisans of the Supreme Court. The Thursday that Morris spoke, the Senate was crowded to its capacity, with women out in force, for not only was the gallant who had crossed swords with Talleyrand on the field of love a favorite, but this was to be his farewell speech. He began with sentimental references to his coming parting with his Federalist associates. With his customary artistry he painted war in darker colors than the spokesmen of the Administration. He pictured 'the misery of plundered towns, the conflagration of defenseless villages, the devastation of cultured fields.' He painted 'the widow weeping as she traces, in the

[1] *Annals*, 7th Cong., 2d Sess.   [2] *Ibid.*   [3] *Ibid.*

pledges of connubial affection, the resemblance of him whom she has lost forever'; the 'aged matron bending over the ashes of her son.' He described the mistress, her lover killed: 'his lip, the ruby harbinger of joy, lies pale and cold, the miserable appendage of a mangled corpse.'

'Hard, hard,' he said, 'must be the heart which can be insensible to scenes like these, and bold the man who dare present to the Almighty Father a conscience crimsoned with the blood of his children.'

Yes, everyone prayed for peace — but how preserve it? By relying on the warmth and benevolence of the heart of Yrujo?

'I cannot commit the interests of my country to the goodness of his heart.'

The facts? The island of New Orleans and Louisiana have been ceded to France. 'Had Spain a right to make this cession without our consent? . . . No nation has a right to give to another a dangerous neighbor without her consent.'

And yet with our Ministers in Paris and Madrid our Government had not been consulted and Jefferson had been 'treated with contempt,' and 'through him our country has been insulted.'

And what is the effect of the cession on other nations? In rapid, vivid phrasing the orator drew a panoramic picture of the state of Europe under the heel of the Corsican. And yet, conqueror of Europe, Napoleon cannot rest on his laurels. 'In his splendid career he must proceed. When he ceases to act, he will cease to reign. Whenever in any plan he fails, that moment he falls. He is condemned to magnificence. . . . Impelled by imperious circumstances he rules in Europe and he will rule here also, unless by vigorous exertions you set a bound to his power.' Never for a moment had France lost sight of Louisiana nor been blind to its importance. And could the United States hope to get it by negotiations?

'Let me ask,' he continued, 'on what ground you intend to treat? Do you expect to persuade? Do you hope to intimidate? If to persuade, what are your means of persuasion? Every gentleman admits the importance to this country. Think you the First Consul, whose capacious mind embraces the globe, is alone ignorant of its value? Is he a child whom you may win by a rattle to comply with your wishes? Will you, like a nurse, sing to him a lullaby? If you have no hope from fondling attentions and soothing sounds, what have you to offer in exchange? Have you anything to give him that he will take? He wants power; you have no power. He wants dominion; you have no dominion... that you can grant. He wants influence in Europe, and have you any influence in Europe? What in the name of Heaven are the means by which you would render this negotiation successful? Is it by some secret spell? Have you any magic power? Or do you rely on the charms of those beautiful girls with whom the gentleman near me says the French Grenadiers are to incorporate? If so why do you not send an embassy of women?'

Thus, having painted the horrors of war most vividly, he sought to sneer away all hopes of negotiations.

'Having,' he concluded, 'endeavored to show that we have no hope from a treaty, it only remains to consider the natural effect of taking an immediate possession.' Thus Morris declared for war.

It was seven-thirty when he concluded and sat down, surrounded by the jubilant Federalists, cheering lustily. The sick Mason of Virginia rose to suggest that since Morris had invited a debate, and he was indisposed at that late hour, he asked the Senate to adjourn until the morrow. No one but knew Mason to be seriously ill, though few suspected that in less than three months he would be in his grave. Never had Federalist chivalry appeared so tarnished. Instantly they clamored against adjournment. A vote was taken. Burr announced a tie and cast his vote with the Federalists and against the motion of the dying Mason. Fixing his eye sternly on Burr, a Jeffersonian asked him if only twelve had voted for adjournment. Only twelve, Burr replied. 'Then I call for a division,' replied the astonished senator. On the division the vote was thirteen for adjournment and twelve against. The Senate adjourned. The dishonest trick of Burr had failed.

Among those voting to accommodate a dying colleague was Senator Plumer, the Federalist. The courtly and chivalrous Morris flamed with indignation. How dare Plumer vote to adjourn when the Federalists were against adjournment! Because, replied

Plumer, Senator Mason was seriously ill and he wished to do by him as he would be done by under similar circumstances.

With flaming face and curling lips, Morris retorted: 'When a man is resolved to act only according to the convictions of his own mind, the party to which he belongs can never depend upon his support, and I shall not be surprised if within a few years you are not more like a Republican than a Federalist.'

'I cannot say what I may do in the future,' said Plumer, 'but I trust I shall never act contrary to my own judgement to support either party.'

'No man in public life can maintain such an independent course,' snapped Morris.

'I shall fail then as a public man and retire to private life,' said Plumer.

Such was the atmosphere of brutal hate in which Jefferson fought for Louisiana without bloodshed.

X

It was a dying man who rose in the Senate on the morrow. Mason knew his condition, his colleagues saw it. Apologizing for the feebleness of his voice he began: 'Feeble as it is, however, I am not daunted; objects and sounds often present themselves to the senses which surprise without exciting our curiosity, and confound without being comprehensible; mountains of sophistry, like mountains of vapor, fade before the simple and inoffensive rays of reason and truth.'

Of the two propositions pending, one went for negotiations, 'the recourse of pacific nations,' in harmony with 'our uniform practice.' The other leads to war. Morris had manfully conceded it. But Ross had insisted, 'It is not war — it is only going and taking peaceable possession of New Orleans.'

And how would Ross go and take peaceable possession? 'Would he march at the head of a posse comitatus? No. He would march at the head of fifty thousand militia, and he would send forth the whole naval and military force, armed and provided with military stores. He would enter their island, set fire to their warehouses, and bombard their city, desolate their farms and plantations, and, having swept all their inhabitants away after wading through streams of blood, he would tell those who had escaped destruction, "We do not come here to make war on you — we are a very moderate, tender-hearted kind of neighbor, and are come here merely to take peaceable possession of your territory." Why, sir, this is too naked not to be an insult to the understanding of a child.'

But from Morris, no such trifling. 'He threw off the mask at once and, in a downright, manly way, fairly told us that he liked war — that it was his favorite mode of negotiating between nations; that war gave dignity to the species — that it draws forth the most noble energies of humanity. He scorned to tell us that he wished to take peaceable possession. No, he could not snivel; his vast genius spurned huckstering; his mighty soul would not bear to be locked up in a petty warehouse in New Orleans; he was for war, terrible, glorious havoc.'

But even Louisiana, New Orleans, and the Floridas were not enough for Morris.

'He would embroil us with Europe ... and sets us to tilting for that phantom, the balance of power.' And in pursuit of the object of precipitating us into the turbulence of Europe, he was not content to discuss the special grievance against the Intendant, but he wanders far afield to call the roll of all the grievances of the years against the Spanish Government. 'And at length the secret comes out — we are told that we must go to war to restrain the overgrown power of France.'

And what liberties had been taken with history in the course of a wild debate! A senator indignantly had said that there had been a time when 'had a single American citizen been oppressed or injured, the national honor would have been aroused and asserted in his defense.' Marvelous discovery! 'Was it when the commander of the British frigate stopped the American citizen, Captain Jessup, at sea, and because he complained of having his men impressed, tied him up and flogged him at his gangway, that the sense of national dignity was displayed?' Why, since the peace of 1788 the wrongs inflicted on the young Republic by the British were more dishonorable and afflicting than that of New Orleans. 'Yet war was not advocated when Britain insulted and wronged us; recourse was had to measures of a pacific and of

a more certain and efficacious nature. Certain commercial propositions were brought forward to counteract and coerce, by her
commercial nerves, the nation that had wronged us — a procedure
very different from the military peace-march to New Orleans.' [1]

Yes, added Senator Cocke, after enumerating the outrages on
America in other days, 'these things happened in the days of
Washington and where was the redress found? In war? Did he
march an army to Montreal or Quebec? Did we even seize upon
our own forts, in our own States, which they held? No. What,
then, did Washington do? Why, sir, he did no more than we
mean to do now with a thousandth part of the provocation and
injury — he negotiated.' [2]

Thus the debate ended, the Ross resolution was voted down
by a strict party vote, and that of Breckinridge was passed
unanimously.[3]

XI

And there was no difficulty in Madrid. The moment news of
the act of the Intendant reached the Spanish Court at Aranjuez,
orders went forth for the immediate re-establishment of the right
of deposit in New Orleans. Yrujo at once informed Madison,
who was delighted that so little damage had been done in the
Western country and because of the 'evidence of respect in the
Government of Spain for our rights and our friendship.' [4] The
day Yrujo wrote, and the press published the Minister's letter
expressing his 'satisfaction of informing you that my first opinion
has been verified and of declaring in the most positive terms that
the proclamation of the Intendant is an act purely personal without the sanction and without even the knowledge of His Catholic
Majesty,' the Federalist press raved like wild animals at the Zoo
on being deprived of food. The *Columbian Centinel* frothed with
fury. How dared Yrujo announce at once his own repudiation of
the Intendant's act! Suppose Spain had pursued a different
course — where would Yrujo have been? And how dared the
Minister make his first repudiation on his own responsibility,
'to influence the measures of our Government'? Yes, against

---

[1] *Annals*, February 25, 1803.   [2] *Ibid.*   [3] *Ibid.*
[4] To Livingston, *Writings of Madison*, VII, 37.

'such unauthorized and irregular conduct, we have a right, nay, it is our duty, to complain.' [1] Hamilton's organ, the *Evening Post*, could see no reason for satisfaction. Madrid merely recognized the treaty — which, however, had expired and not been formally renewed. Clearly the purpose was 'by temporary closing to make some money at our expense.' [2]

But the advantage was clearly with the Jeffersonian press, which made the most of it. 'What will the people think now?' asked the *Independent Chronicle*. 'What would have been the present state of our public and private credit, our funds and our banks, if war had happened? What would have been the values of our navigation, liable as it would have been to arrest and detention in foreign ports? What the amount of our mercantile premiums of insurance? Perhaps no faction has ever been more completely defeated and exposed to infamy, in so short a period.' Yes, and with the enemy confounded, 'the measures of the Administration have succeeded in every instance, our taxes reduced ... credit strengthened, the manufacturers no longer languishing under an oppressive excise ... a bloated judiciary curtailed within a reasonable compass and yet the law invigorated in its operation ... public peace preserved ... our national honor and interests maintained and extended.' [3]

To Hamilton, the success of our diplomatic representations to Madrid was a crushing blow. About the time Yrujo officially announced their success, Hamilton was the speaker at a Federalist meeting in New York to nominate an Assembly ticket. Never had he spoken with more bitterness as he slashed without restraint at every act of the Administration. The *Citizen* reported him as 'vilifying the Executive and Congress for not going to war,' and declaring that, through recourse to negotiations, they had 'destroyed the energies of the country.' At this time Cheetham, of the *Citizen*, habitually was referring to Hamilton as 'the Croaker' and as 'the gallant of Mrs. Reynolds.' [4]

[1] April 27, 1803.   [2] April 2, 1803.
[3] June 20, 1803.   [4] April 22, 1803.

CHAPTER IX

The Triumph of Paris

I

WITH the politicians growling, and Gouverneur Morris writing maliciously to Livingston to sow dissension between the two negotiators, Monroe hastened his preparations for his voyage. The decision of Jefferson to send Monroe was in no sense a reflection upon Livingston, whose ability was of a high order and whose loyalty to the Administration was the stoutest. Nor was there any mystery in the determination to send assistance to the regularly accredited Minister to France. The explanation is clearly revealed in Jefferson's letter to Monroe, requesting him to accept the responsibility. The situation had become critical because of the withdrawal of the right of deposit in New Orleans. The Western country was aflame. The Federalists, notoriously contemptuous of the West, had seized upon the opportunity to pose as militant champions of that section for political effect and to force Jefferson into war, partly with the expectation of making France the object of attack, and partly, as Jefferson thought, to 'derange our finances,' and prematurely end the program of economy. 'Something sensible, therefore, has become necessary,' wrote Jefferson, 'and indeed our object in purchasing New Orleans and the Floridas is a measure liable to assume so many shapes that no instructions could be squared to fit them.' It thus had become imperative that Livingston should be joined by one fresh from conferences in Washington and more intimately familiar with conditions that had arisen since the regular Minister had left.

The choice of Monroe was demanded by the political conditions. 'There could not be two opinions among Republicans as

to the person' to be sent, said Jefferson. He possessed one necessary qualification that others might have shared — 'the unlimited
confidence of the Administration'; and another that few others
had to such a degree — 'the unlimited confidence... of the
Western people.' These Westerners, impulsively bent on war,
and encouraged in that inclination by the demagogues of the
Federalist Party, had agreed to wait on negotiations, but it was
necessary that they have absolute confidence in the negotiator
and in his militant championship of their cause. 'No other man
can be found who does this,' Jefferson continued. 'The measure
has already silenced the Federalists here. Congress will no longer
be agitated by them; and the country will become calm fast as the
information extends over it; and were you to decline, the chagrin
would be universal and would shake under your feet the high
ground on which you stand with the public.'

And then, with his usual prescience, Jefferson added: 'On the
event of this mission depends the future destinies of the Republic.'[1]

In notifying Livingston of Monroe's coming, Jefferson had
made the purpose clear. 'We must know at once whether we can
acquire New Orleans or not,' he wrote. 'We are satisfied nothing
else will secure us against war at no distant period; and we cannot
press this reason without beginning those arrangements which
will be necessary if war is hereafter to result. For this purpose it
was necessary that the negotiators should be fully possessed of
every idea we have on the subject, so as to meet the propositions
of the opposite party, in whatever form they may be offered; and
give them a shape admissible by us without being obliged to await
new instructions hence.'[2]

Monroe hastened to Washington, and in the drab February
days three men of extraordinary significance in American history
might have been seen gathered about the table in Jefferson's
study, with its charts, books, and bird. Jefferson and his two
great disciples bent to the task of finding a formula for every
possible proposition that might be made. For days he was to be
less accessible to everyone who sought his ear. The jeering of the
Federalists in Congress at the ignominy of negotiations, when the
sword was within reach, did not penetrate to the conference room.

[1] *Writings of Jefferson*, x, 343.   [2] *Ibid.*, x, 352.

Monroe was immensely pleased with his mission. 'I am embark-- ing on a new mission which I neither sought nor expected,' he wrote George Clinton, 'but which I undertake with pleasure, as it is to act on an interest I have always had much at heart.' [1] Just before leaving Washington, a notable dinner was given to Monroe at M'Laughlin's Tavern in Georgetown by the majority of the members of Congress, with all the diplomatic corps in attendance. Senator Nicholas was toastmaster, and many toasts were drunk. Speaking for the foreign Ministers, Yrujo proposed: 'May the powers of Europe never be divided from the United States but by the ocean.' Monroe proposed, 'The Union of the States — May political discussion only tend to cement them.' [2]

'At the dinner all the republicans of the House and Senate were present by invitation. Mr. Burr, no longer considered as a republican, was not invited' — reported the *American Citizen*. 'This is not the effect of negligence,' it continued, 'but of mature deliberation. It is a just and awful sentence pronounced upon his past misconduct and was designed to be so understood.' [3]

After the dinner, thoroughly conversant with Jefferson's views and plans, Monroe started for New York. The winter roads, with their frozen ruts, the miserable accommodations on the way, the inclemency of the weather, exacted their toll, and he reached New York so weary and ill that he was forced to bed under the care of a physician. 'In a day or two I shall be well,' he wrote reassuringly to Jefferson. [4]

But the hardships of travel were just begun. For his voyage he was to be denied a frigate in compliance with one of the reforms of the Administration. Pinckney had been denied one and Rufus King had been refused one for his return. 'Mr. Madison's friend- ship and mine for you, being so well known,' wrote Jefferson, 'the public will have an eagle eye to watch if we grant you any indulgence out of the general rule.' [5] Monroe was furnished funds to take a ship cabin by himself on the earliest possible boat, since 'the moment in France is critical,' and only 'St. Domingo delays their taking possession of Louisiana.' Besides, added Jefferson,

[1] *Writings of Monroe*, IV, 3.   [2] *Independent Chronicle*, March 3, 1803.
[3] February 23, 1803.   [4] *Writings of Monroe*, IV, 2.
[5] *Writings of Jefferson*, X, 343.

'they are in the last distress for money for current purposes.'[1]
Proceeding on the most important mission in American history,
he was to have, as compensation, nine thousand dollars a year
from the time of leaving until his return, and 'a quarter salary
for the expenses of your return as prescribed by law.'[2] Madison
graciously assured him that his expenses in going from Havre to
Paris, or anywhere else his duties might require his presence,
would be paid by the Government. And then, in a burst of
generosity, Madison added: 'In addition . . . you will have a right
to charge for postage and couriers should the latter prove necessary.'[3]

Finding that a ship, the *Richmond*, of four hundred tons,
sailing for Hamburg, could drop him off at Havre, Monroe closed
for a cabin. But after his luggage was put on board, he was forced
to delay a day because Madison's instructions had not arrived;
and when these came, a snowstorm and adverse winds delayed the
sailing for another day.[4]

During the delay he had time to meditate alone on the serious-
ness of his mission. The Ross resolution, though conceived as the
last straw of a sinking party, would 'produce a great effect on
the public mind and . . . more especially in the Western country,'
he was sure. If the negotiations were successful, the Federalists
would be 'overwhelmed completely,' and the party of Jefferson
strengthened; but if they failed, the public would be bitterly
disappointed, and the political effect bad. Only 'complete security
for the future' would satisfy. In the event of failure, there would
be no alternative but war, and he felt that ground should be taken
as an 'ultimatum in the negotiations.'[5]

On March 8, the wind shifted, and Monroe, with his wife and
children, boarded the *Richmond* on fighting edge. As the boat
moved out, the brigade company of artillery on the battery fired
a national salute which was answered by the fort on Governor's
Island. 'We entertain not the least doubt of his mission,' said
the *American Citizen*, describing the departure.[6] With him
Monroe carried the instructions just received from Madison.

[1] *Writings of Jefferson*, x, 343.   [2] *Ibid.*
[3] *Writings of Madison*, vii, 30.   [4] To Jefferson, *Writings of Monroe*, iv, 4.
[5] *Ibid.*   [6] March 9, 1803.

There would be ample time, as the March winds tossed the *Richmond*, to study them.

II

Meanwhile, the Federalist press teemed with absurd and malicious stories intended to make the negotiations obnoxious to Americans. Monroe, said the *Columbian Centinel*, 'is directed to purchase Florida, or at least New Orleans, "even should they cost forty millions of dollars."' [1] Soon it was expanding on the theme, and informing its readers that behind closed doors Congress was appropriating 'an immense sum' for diplomatic purposes. It thought that 'with beaucoup d'argent even Mr. Monroe may be able to effect valuable purchases where Citizen Talleyrand has a commanding influence.' [2] Still harping on the theme, the *Centinel* increased the depth of its scorn. 'What can justify the enormous sum of two million dollars secret service money?' it asked. 'What will Bonaparte think of us? He will consider us blockheads who deserved to be gulled, and he will shrug his shoulders at Mr. Monroe and say "Gad, you have come in a lucky time — we want funds — I am your friend and never intended you an injury. I did not expect your millions, but since you have brought them, I gladly receive them as a pledge of the attachment between the two countries. The money is acceptable, it is at this moment necessary to the measures which are pursuing to perpetuate the glory of this great nation. Pay it to my faithful Talleyrand and tender to Mr. Jefferson the homage of my dearest love."' [3]

When, on his arrival at Havre, Monroe was received with a salute and was called upon by staff officers and a guard of honor, the *Centinel* found its own explanation. 'Talleyrand certainly knows that Mr. Monroe is an enemy of the English and certainly two million dollars ought to purchase a great deal of civility.' [4]

III

The instructions Monroe carried with him to Paris merely put in concrete phrasing the conclusions reached as Jefferson, Madi-

---

[1] January 22, 1803.   [2] January 19, 1803.
[3] March 5, 1803.   [4] June 8, 1803.

son, and Monroe sat about the table in the former's study during those gloomy February days. The object of the negotiations was 'to procure by just and satisfactory arrangements a cession to the United States of New Orleans, and of West and East Florida, or as much thereof as the actual proprietor can be prevailed upon to part with.' They were to be conducted on the theory that France preferred our friendship and neutrality to our enmity and opposition, but she must be convinced that friendship and peace with us must be precarious until the Mississippi shall be made the boundary between the United States and Louisiana. The American envoys were to bear in mind the advantages of the moment — 'the instability of peace in Europe, the attitude taken by Great Britain, the languishing state of the French finances, and the necessity of either abandoning the West India islands or of sending thither vast armaments at great expense.' Napoleon must be disillusioned of his probable idea that only the possession of Louisiana by the French could prevent the Atlantic States from forming an alliance with Great Britain.

Then followed the outline of the plan proposed. It provided certain commercial advantages to France in the waters of this territory for a term of years; pledged the speedy incorporation of the inhabitants of the territory into the Union on an equal footing, and provided in consideration for the cession the payment of an undetermined sum of money.

In his observations on the plan, Madison made it clear that should the purchase be found impossible, a portion of the territory would be acceptable; but should no 'considerable portion be attainable,' the envoys were to get 'a jurisdiction over space enough for a large commercial town and its appurtenances' on the bank of the Mississippi. Should even this be found impossible, the last stand of the envoys should be to improve the existing right of deposit by securing the express privilege of holding real estate for commercial purposes, of providing hospitals, and of having a consul on the ground.

Every conceivable contingency had been discussed with Monroe, and he carried with him a flexible authorization to meet almost any situation that might arise. The conversations in Jefferson's closet had given him a far more intimate view of the

Administration's hopes and fears than he found in the formal instructions he read as the *Richmond* plowed the waters.

IV

Meanwhile, events, foreseen by Jefferson, were moving at quick step in France. Bad news continued to flow into Paris from the bloody welter in San Domingo. The peace with England was drawing to a stormy close. Talleyrand, with or without Napoleon's knowledge or consent, had reported the Corsican's reactions to Livingston's memorial on Louisiana. His letter, thickly sprinkled with courtly phrases and expressions of the Consul's appreciation of Livingston's 'friendly solicitude' for France, solemnly declared that France was not in the least embarrassed in its finances. But because of the 'solicitude, perhaps premature, but in reality, plausible and natural,' felt by the United States as a result of the transfer of Louisiana to France, Napoleon had determined to send a Minister to Washington to enter into a new treaty.[1]

A bit flurried by the cold urbanity of the too polite tone of diplomacy, Livingston replied that, while a new treaty would be acceptable, 'it is not a new treaty for which we now press, but a recognition of the old one, by which the United States have acquired rights that no change in the circumstances of the country obliges them to relinquish and which they never will relinquish but with their political existence.'[2]

Soon after this exchange, Livingston witnessed one of the most dramatic incidents of history and one that was to have a permanent effect on American destiny. The scene was Madame Bonaparte's drawing-room. The members of the diplomatic corps were present. Napoleon entered with hurried steps and passed rapidly down the line, addressing remarks appropriate to the occasion to the American Minister. Passing most of the other diplomats by with a mere nod, he came to an abrupt halt in front of Lord Whitworth, the British Minister.

'I find, my lord, that your nation wants war again,' he said sternly.

'No, Sire, we are most desirous of peace.'

[1] *Annals*, February 19, 1803, 7th Cong., 2d Sess., II, 1112.   [2] *Ibid.*, 1117.

'You have just finished a war of fifteen years,' Napoleon continued.

'It is true, Sire, and that was fifteen years too long.'

'But you want another war of fifteen years,' snapped the Consul.

'Pardon me, Sire, we are very desirous of peace.'

At this point the prefect of the palace approached the angry warrior to announce that ladies were in another room and to request that he join them. He made no reply. With a bow to the guests, he hurried to his cabinet, declining to see the women. Whitworth, much disturbed, related the incident to Livingston, ascribing the outburst to the King's Speech to Parliament, just received in Paris, expressing grave distrust of armaments in the French ports. To Livingston, war now seemed inevitable. He was sure Napoleon 'would not commit himself so publicly unless his determination had been reached.' Perhaps France would need money, after all. With a war in prospect with the greatest naval power on the seas, perhaps Louisiana would not seem so easy to hold. Returning to his house, he sent Madison a description of the incident, and added: 'I shall give all my attention to avail myself of circumstances as they arise, in which I hope shortly to receive the assistance of Mr. Monroe.' [1]

To Livingston, the fog began to lift. Had not Addington in London told Rufus King some weeks before that, in the event of war, Britain's first step would be to occupy New Orleans? King had protested that New Orleans in the hands of the British would be as obnoxious as in the hands of France, and Addington had said the best solution would be for it to be in the possession of the United States. [2]

War now was inevitable. Napoleon was wise. He would need money for the terrific struggle. He would be in no position to hold Louisiana against the naval power of Britain. All this had been set forth in Livingston's memorial which Talleyrand had presumed to dismiss as the mistaken, but well-intended, views of a friend of France. But Talleyrand's dream was an empire beyond the sea, and he had sought to divert Napoleon's attention from Europe to the New World. When, with the Treaty of San Ilde-

[1] *Annals*, 1114.   [2] King to Madison, *Annals*, 1124.

fonso, he had acquired Louisiana from Spain in a bargain he knew would not be kept, the game seemed in his hands. But Napoleon had other views. Europe was his stage. He would not waste his genius on a vast wilderness.

Napoleon's mind was made up, and to decide was to act. On Easter Sunday after Mass he summoned Barbé-Marbois, the Minister of Finance, to his presence, and, speaking with a tone of finality, announced that he would renounce Louisiana. At daybreak the next morning he summoned Marbois again, and said:

'I renounce Louisiana. It is not only New Orleans that I cede; it is the whole colony without reserve. . . . I renounce it with great regret; to attempt obstinately to retain it would be folly. I direct you to negotiate the affair. Have an interview this very day with Mr. Livingston.' [1] Livingston afterward recalled one sentence that Marbois neglected to put in his memoirs: 'I need much money for this war, and I shall not wish to begin it with new taxes.' [2]

The very day Napoleon summoned Marbois from his bed, Talleyrand, with a cynical and enigmatic look in his cold eye, calmly asked Livingston if the United States would like to have the whole of Louisiana, and how much it would pay.

That same evening Monroe, travel-weary after his hurried journey from Havre, drove into Paris.

v

Even though Livingston had protested that he looked forward eagerly to the co-operation of Monroe, he secretly resented his colleague's coming as a reflection on his own capacity. He, too, was still dreaming of the Presidency, and with the success of the negotiations he wished the laurels for himself alone. Mischiefmakers were not lacking, and within a day of his arrival, Monroe was hearing that Livingston, mortified by Monroe's appointment, had 'done everything in his power to turn . . . my mission to his account, by pressing the Government on every point with

---

[1] Marbois, *History of Louisiana*, 274.

[2] F. de Peyster, *A Biographical Sketch of Robert Livingston*, 364. (Hereafter cited as *Livingston*.)

the view to show that he had accomplished what was wished without my aid.' [1] Thus the two envoys, distrustful of one another, were to watch each other as closely as they observed Talleyrand.

Livingston was not without some justification for his resentment. He long had been a commanding political figure, the head of a great manorial house in New York. On the committee that framed the Declaration of Independence, he had won Jefferson's confidence and admiration. He had administered the oath to Washington on assuming the Presidency. Jefferson, in expressing regret because of Livingston's refusal of a Cabinet post, had placed his own estimate on the latter's worth when he wrote that 'men possessing minds of the first order do not abound in any country, beyond the wants of the country.' [2] There was some similarity in the two signers of the Declaration — both aristocrats in their mode of living, both democrats in their political creed. Livingston's greatest handicap in negotiations was in his deafness, but his mind was keen, penetrating, robust, his character strong and consistent. In his dress and manner he was as simple and unaffected as Jefferson himself. It was his combination of dignity and simplicity that early attracted the favorable attention of Napoleon.

Monroe, who was to be the roving diplomat of the Jeffersonian years, was quite as simple in taste and dress and as downright in manner as his associate. No more than Livingston was he fitted for the frothy gaiety and the light chaff of affected drawing-room conversation. Quite as much as Livingston, he was inclined to serious talk that the light-headed might call heavy. Neither one nor the other was noted for wit, humor, or grace. These were precisely the men to pit against Talleyrand, since neither could be influenced by his artificial charm or finesse in management.

VI

Monroe found a different Paris from that he had known on his first mission just after the fall of Robespierre. At that time he had not met Talleyrand, who, finding discretion the better part of valor, was enjoying a safe sojourn abroad. Now he was the Foreign

---

[1] Monroe to Madison, *Writings of Monroe*, IV, 9.   [2] *Livingston*, 356.

Minister, the subordinate of Napoleon, whose masterful manner he found distasteful. Scarcely a year before Monroe's arrival, Talleyrand had felt the heavy hand of his master when he had been summoned to Saint-Cloud and ordered either to marry his mistress or send her away. Mysteriously enough, with his customary cynicism, he had given his name to Madame Grand, and in these days of the negotiations he could hardly have been quite at ease. Brilliant, witty, satiric, cynical, polished in manners, mysterious in technique, unscrupulous, unmoral, he long since had attained the reputation that has clung to him through all the generations since, as one of the most consummate liars of his time. Livingston had tested the quality of his veracity before Monroe's arrival. True only to his selfishness, and faithless to every master he ever served and every mistress he ever had, it is not without reason that in a negotiation involving the transfer of an empire and the payment of millions of francs, Napoleon had resorted to Barbé-Marbois, his Minister of Finance, to conduct the bargaining in the place of the hero of the X Y Z episode.

No one in France better disposed toward the United States could have been found than the Marquis de Marbois. He had pleasant memories of the young nation. Many years before, as a youth, he had served as secretary of the French Legation in Philadelphia. He had entered sympathetically into the American life, been attracted to its society, then by no means crude in Philadelphia, and had married an American girl. Out of his contacts with American statesmen had developed sincere friendships. It was in response to his request for information pertaining to Virginia that Jefferson, then in retirement because of his wife's death, prepared his famous 'Notes on Virginia.' His relations with Jefferson, therefore, were most cordial. He knew and admired Madison. He was honest, earnest, capable, sincere, dependable.

These were the four men immediately concerned with the negotiations, and behind them and inspiring them were Napoleon in Paris, then the foremost figure in the world, and Jefferson in Washington, the foremost philosopher in power. Seldom in history, in any event involving but two nations, have men of such permanent distinction been drawn into negotiations; and never in negotiations of such tremendous import.

VII

Throughout the first day Livingston and Monroe were together, they sat over papers in the apartment of the former, and Livingston heard the latest developments and the secret hopes and fears of Jefferson. That night Livingston gave a dinner for his colleague. Through the window, Marbois could be seen pacing up and down in the garden. He was asked to join the company for coffee. Drawing the French Minister aside, Livingston mentioned the mysterious conversation he had had with Talleyrand — the reference to the sale of the whole of Louisiana. Livingston was surprised to observe that Marbois was not. Something had happened, the latter said. Perhaps no time should be lost. Could not Livingston call at Marbois's house after the guests had retired? Monroe was informed at once and agreed to the meeting, though not perhaps without some chagrin. The last of the guests had departed by eleven, and Livingston hurried to the house of the Minister of Finance.

He found Marbois alone and waiting. Would Livingston repeat the conversation he had had with Talleyrand? He did. Then, concluded Marbois, his master, who had spoken to him on the same subject Sunday, evidently was in earnest. But how foolish, Livingston observed, to make such an impossible proposition, since, with war beginning, Britain might seize Louisiana at any moment. That would not be so bad, said Livingston, since Britain 'would readily relinquish it to us.' All that, on the theory that Britain would win the war and be able to hold her possessions, warned Marbois. True, thought Livingston, but in that event it would be in the interest of the United States to 'contribute to render her successful.' Marbois now admitted that Napoleon had thought of this phase and had read in an English paper that fifty thousand men were being raised to take New Orleans.

At length, throwing aside reserve, Marbois quoted Napoleon's instructions to him: 'Well, you have the charge of the treasury; let them give you one hundred million of francs, and pay their own claims, and take the whole country.'

Livingston was staggered by the amount and showed it in his face. Marbois noticed, and hastily added that he, too, thought the sum exorbitant and had told Napoleon so. Where would the

Americans get that amount? he had asked his master. 'Borrow it,' snapped the Conqueror. Livingston seemed skeptical. Then how much did Livingston think America would pay? asked Marbois. The envoy protested lack of authority, the need for consideration. If the proposition to sell were made, he would consult Monroe, his colleague, and then they would make an offer. What did Marbois think? The negotiator for Napoleon, insisting that he had no authority to act, wondered if sixty million francs, including the payment of the American claims against France, would be within reason. Personally he thought it a proper figure, and he would be very glad to urge it on Napoleon. Livingston still simulated astonishment at the amount. Why ask the impossible? — especially at such a critical moment for France. Failure to acquire New Orleans would mean the triumph of the war party in Congress, which would throw America into the arms of England. Did Napoleon want that? All quite possible, said Marbois —

'But you know the temper of a youthful conqueror; everything he does is rapid as lightning; we have only to speak to him as an opportunity presents itself, perhaps in a crowd, when he bears no contradiction. When I am alone with him, I can speak more freely, and he attends; but this opportunity seldom happens and is always accidental. Try, then, if you cannot come on to my mark. Consider the extent of the country, the exclusive navigation of the Mississippi, and the importance of having no neighbors to dispute you, no war to dread.'

Livingston agreed to consult at once with Monroe. At midnight he left the Treasury, and three o'clock in the morning found him feverishly writing a full report to Madison without seeing Monroe. He would score on the special envoy to that extent at least.[1]

VIII

Monroe was informed, but neither knew how serious was the warning against delay. Long afterward, Lucien Bonaparte was to paint the picture of a scene dramatic, and yet absurd, with Napoleon in the bathtub at the Tuileries. Napoleon's intention

[1] Louisiana Correspondence, *Annals*, 7th Cong., 2d Sess., II, 1128.

had leaked, and it is not a harsh hazard that it was Talleyrand who had whispered in the ears of the Consul's brothers. Lucien had played a conspicuous part in securing the cession of Louisiana back to France. He had reason to be proud. And now it was to be thrown away for money to conduct another war. Impossible! Hurrying home to dress for a Talma evening at the theater, he found his brother Joseph waiting for him with the startling news, 'The General wants to sell Louisiana.' Ah, well, said Lucien, after the first shock, he cannot do it without the consent of the Chambers that never will consent. But Napoleon proposed to act without their consent, Joseph replied. It was agreed that the two brothers should descend upon Napoleon with their protests.

The next morning Napoleon is in his bath. The bath highly perfumed. Lucien is announced — admitted. Intimidated by the very presence of the warrior, he talks lightly of other things, awaiting the arrival of Joseph. At length the proposed sale is mentioned by Napoleon and opinions asked. These descend upon him in the bath in an indignant flood. The Chambers — the Constitution — how dare the warrior defy one and violate the other? The Conqueror is amused. Then, amazed at the effrontery of the brothers, the man in the bath becomes satirical, infuriating Joseph with his sarcasms. He laughs merrily at the brothers' simplicity, and, maddened now, Joseph threatens to denounce Napoleon's act from the tribune. He implies that Napoleon has tyrannically sent innocent men into exile — and warns of a similar fate for the Bonapartes. 'You are insolent,' shouts Napoleon, half rising in the tub, and then, throwing himself back violently into the water, deluges the brothers with the scented water of the bath. The soaked state of the brothers momentarily moderates the storm. Laughter for a moment, and then a resumption of the quarrel. 'If I were not your brother, I should be your enemy!' shouts Lucien. Napoleon moves as if to strike him. 'You my enemy! I would break you — look — like this box,' and he smashed his snuffbox on the floor.

There was rebellion against continuing the negotiations even in the clan of the Bonapartes. Talleyrand was not reconciled. France might learn, and France might speak. No time was to be lost. But Monroe and Livingston knew nothing of the drama about Napoleon's bathtub.

IX

Meanwhile, Monroe was pressing Livingston to arrange for his immediate presentation to Talleyrand, without which he could not participate in the negotiations.[1] Toward the close of the month the two envoys met at the lodgings of Monroe at two o'clock in the afternoon. The latter was so ill he was permitted to recline on a sofa near the table at which Livingston and Marbois sat. The latter began the conversation by presenting the proposition he had been authorized to make, providing for the payment of one hundred million francs and the payment of the claims of American citizens against France, amounting to twenty million more. Without waiting for the expected protest, he hurried on to the admission that the sum was too great, and then promised to persuade Napoleon to accept eighty million francs, including the twenty million due Americans.

Livingston demurred to the debts, insisting that these should be considered as a separate proposition. For had not Napoleon acknowledged the indebtedness? But Marbois was stubborn. Without the inclusion of the debt settlement in the treaty, he could not continue the discussions. The Americans were in possession of the ultimatum of the Conqueror.

A day was spent at Monroe's lodgings preparing the counter-proposition, and the next day at the Treasury they proposed fifty million francs and twenty million more to include the debts. Marbois made short shrift of this proposal. Sixty million francs, or he was through. He had persuaded Napoleon to reduce his original demand by forty million francs, and it would be futile to ask him to concede more. Thus the Americans had fair warning. They receded and agreed.

And the inhabitants of Louisiana? They must be incorporated into the American Union at the earliest practicable moment, Marbois insisted. Neither of the envoys but knew the constitutional difficulties here, but they gave assurance that every effort would be made to satisfy Marbois on this score.

Thus matters stood when the meeting adjourned, with the understanding that the proposal would be submitted to Napoleon for his approval on the morrow.[2]

[1] *Writings of Monroe*, IV, 8.   [2] *Ibid.*, IV, 12–19.

x

Meanwhile, in Washington, Jefferson and Madison were nursing their anxiety and patience as tenderly as possible. Paris never had seemed so hopelessly remote. Throughout the country the Federalists, chortling over the certainty of failure, were loud in their expressions of skepticism. But as Jefferson nursed his patience in the budding time of a Washington spring, his determination to have New Orleans and the unrestricted use of the Mississippi intensified. He had little faith in Napoleon and none at all in Talleyrand, and he knew nothing of the employment of Marbois in the business.

Again his mind turned to a combination with Great Britain. The war would be resumed — no doubt of that. In the event of failure in the negotiations, no time could be lost in preparing for the struggle of force. Jefferson and Madison were in earnest conversation, and again the two sat in the room of the singing bird and prepared new instructions for the envoys in Paris. On April 18, five days after Monroe reached Paris, and before there seemed the slightest possibility that anything had been accomplished, they agreed upon a dispatch. 'The reasonable and friendly views' of the Administration justified hopes of a successful negotiation with the French Government, they wrote. But it was quite possible that these views would 'not be reciprocated,' and might be opposed by 'schemes of ambition.' To meet such a contingency, preliminary provisions should be made.

'Among these arrangements,' ran the note, 'the President conceives that a common interest may recommend a candid understanding and a closer connection with Great Britain; and he presumes that the occasion may present itself to the British Government in the same light. He accordingly authorizes you ... in case the prospects of your discussions ... should make it expedient to open confidential communication with the Ministers of the British Government, and to confer freely and fully on the precautions and provisions best adapted to the crisis, and in which that Government may be disposed to concur, transmitting to your own without delay the result of these consultations.' [1]

[1] Writings of Madison, VII, 44.

XI

Having put this plan in motion, Jefferson relieved his impatience by turning to other things. He had no single-track mind. His interests were universal. The day after the dispatch aiming at a possible Anglo-American alliance, he was writing an acknowledgment of a sermon, expressing opinions upon Jesus Christ and the ancient philosophers. 'Though I concur with the author in considering the moral precepts of Jesus as more pure, correct, and sublime than those of the ancient philosophers,' he wrote, 'yet I do not concur with him in the mode of proving it. He thinks it necessary to libel and decry the doctrines of the philosophers; but a man must be blinded, indeed, by prejudice, who can deny them a great degree of merit. I give them their just due and yet maintain that the morality of Jesus, as taught by himself, and freed from the corruption of later times, is far superior.... They extended their care scarcely beyond our kindred and friends individually, and our country in the abstract. Jesus embraced with charity and philanthropy our neighbors, our countrymen, and the whole family of mankind.' [1]

Thus, while awaiting news from Paris, Jefferson was not unmindful of other interests and duties. He was giving the signal for proceedings against Justice Samuel Chase for his partisan harangue from the bench at Baltimore, and he was sending instructions to Meriwether Lewis for his historic expedition of exploration to the Pacific. [2]

XII

Long before the second instructions reached Paris, the success of the negotiations was assured.

On Sunday, the first of May, Monroe and Livingston entered the historic palace of the Louvre for the former's presentation to Napoleon. Livingston introduced his colleague when the Consul, moving with quick steps, reached them in the line.

'You have been in Paris fifteen days?' he asked.

'I have.'

'You speak French?'

---

[1] *Writings of Jefferson*, x, 376.
[2] To Nicholson, *ibid.*, x, 387; to Lewis, *ibid.*, 398.

'A little.'

'You had a good voyage?'

An affirmative answer.

'You came in a frigate?'

'No; in a merchant vessel chartered for the purpose.'

A few bromidic inquiries about the families of the envoys, and the Conqueror passed on, with the casual observation that their affairs should be settled.

That day the envoys dined with Napoleon at the Louvre, and, after rising, the conversation was continued in the salon.

'Does the Federal City grow much?' Napoleon asked.

'It does.'

'How many inhabitants has it?'

Monroe gave the number.

'Well, Mr. Jefferson, how old is he?'

'About sixty.'

'Is he married or single?'

'He is not married.'

'Then he is a garçon?'

'No,' explained Monroe, 'he is a widower.'

'Has he children?'

'Yes, two daughters who are married.'

'Does he reside always in the Federal City?'

'Generally.'

'Are the public buildings there commodious, those for the Congress and the President especially?'

'They are.'

Then, for the first time, Napoleon made an observation that had political significance:

'You, the Americans, did brilliant things in your war with England . . . you will do the same again.'

'We shall, I am persuaded, always behave well when it shall be our lot to be in war,' Monroe replied cautiously.

'You will probably be at war with them again,' persisted the Consul.

Monroe made no reply.

The envoys left the Louvre to meet again at eight-thirty in the house of Marbois, where the terms of the treaty were discussed, and on the following day the sale was completed.[1] The next day the treaty was signed. Then, conscious of the magnitude and tremendous significance of the transaction, the envoys rose and silently shook hands. Marbois had been a good friend of the United States. Livingston, profoundly moved, exclaimed that 'this is the noblest work of our whole lives.' He alone put in words the vision he had caught of the far future when the many new States to be carved from the purchase would become the granary of one of the greatest nations in all the tide of time.[2]

XIII

When Monroe sailed on his mission there had been no thought of the acquisition of the whole of Louisiana. The instructions were confined to New Orleans and the Floridas, and on the completion of his business in France, he was to proceed to Madrid to negotiate for the purchase of Florida. The negotiators in Paris had been forced to move with the rapidity of Napoleon's thought, and the treaty was signed without knowing the precise boundaries of the purchase. All that Monroe and Livingston knew was that they had acquired the territory ceded to France by Spain. In the beginning neither assumed that Louisiana included the Floridas. In his initial conversation with Marbois, Livingston had asked a pledge that France would not seek, or under any circumstances take, possession of Florida, but would give the United States such assistance as she could in the negotiations with Spain for the purchase of that territory. And Marbois made the pledge. It was not until later that Livingston convinced Monroe and the Administration that a portion of the Floridas, including Mobile, were properly included in the Louisiana purchase.

But while Monroe was lingering in Paris dealing with the odds and ends of the claims part of the treaty, a bitter quarrel was brewing behind the scenes. Spain was making the acquaintance of the French policy of Napoleon.

Godoy, who was much more than the lover of Maria Luisa, was almost prostrated by the rumor that Napoleon had sold Louisiana to the United States. The solemn pledge had been

[1] *Writings of Monroe*, IV, 16–17.   [2] *Livingston*, 372.

given, when Spain, under duress, ceded the territory to France,
that it never would be alienated to any other power than Spain.
In the Spanish archives, Godoy had this pledge in writing, or
so he said. Instantly he instructed the Chevalier d'Azara, the
Spanish Minister in Paris, vehemently to protest. The diplomat
in his protest to Talleyrand wrote with all the vigor and indignation the facts warranted. Napoleon replied with a quibble,
for already he considered himself the sovereign master of the
Peninsula.

None of this was so much as suspected by the American envoys,
but soon Monroe was to find that the Napoleonic pledge to urge
on Spain the cession of the Floridas was made in the Pickwickian
sense. Hurrying his plans for his Spanish journey, Monroe wrote
the wily Talleyrand requesting the good offices in the negotiations that had been promised by Marbois. And the answer
was silence.

A day or two later, Monroe was dining with Cambacérès, the
Consul, who had hurried back from a conference at Saint-Cloud
for the dinner.

'You must not go to Spain for the present,' said the Consul
at table.

But why? asked the astonished American.

'It is not the time. You had better defer it,' was the answer.[1]

Soon thereafter Monroe met Le Brun, the third Consul, who
also had attended the conference at Saint-Cloud, and from him
received the identical advice to defer the visit to Spain.[2] Confused by the mystery and the fog, Monroe was not to know the
reason for the insistent advice until later. France had betrayed
Spain in the cession of Louisiana, and was in no position to
urge any further cession on the nation it had wronged. Just
at this juncture some diplomatic business in London demanded
Monroe's attention and he determined to wait awhile before
going to Madrid.

While Monroe was playing hide-and-seek with Talleyrand and
Marbois, and suspiciously watching the moves of Livingston,
Jefferson, turning the pages of a philosophic work by an old

[1] Monroe's Memorandum, *Writings of Monroe*, IV, 12.
[2] Monroe to Madison, *Writings of Monroe*, IV, 44.

French friend, Cabanis, was thinking of another Paris. The author was living at Auteuil in the house of the former Madame Helvétius with some of her friends. Jefferson was glad he was there. 'Auteuil always appeared to me to be a delicious village,' he wrote Cabanis, 'and Madame Helvétius's the most delicious spot in it.' How happy he had been there, with the liberal souls before the Revolution, who were dreaming of self-government! 'In those days how sanguine we were,' he wrote, 'and how soon were the virtuous hopes of every good man blasted... and how many excellent friends have we lost.... But let us draw a veil over the dead and hope the best for the living.' [1]

Monroe found time to browse among the bookshops looking for something that would interest Jefferson. Discreetly he inquired into the character and present standing in France of some of Jefferson's correspondents there — Lacépède, Volney, du Pont de Nemours; and advised that the continuation of the correspondence on literary and scientific subjects would be useful. 'They have the highest respect and attachment for you and are delighted with your attention.' [2]

In moments of leisure he paid visits to Lafayette and Kosciuszko, finding in the former the 'same ardor that he had when began the French Revolution while you were in France.' But he found Lafayette in bed with a broken hip which was being treated by a torturous new surgical machine. One day Monroe found his way out near the barracks of Saint-André, not far from Saint-Antoine, where Kosciuszko lived modestly. He was greeted by the old friend of American independence with water-pots in his hands, for he was tending his garden.[3]

Monroe now was ready to move on to London as soon as he could make his farewell call on Napoleon. The Conqueror was about to start on a tour of inspection preliminary to plunging into the great struggle with Britain. The day before he left, Monroe was informed by Talleyrand that Napoleon would see him at Saint-Cloud on the morrow. Talleyrand went with him. He found the Conqueror in a mellow mood. Jefferson, he said, was 'a virtuous and enlightened man who understood and pursued

---

[1] Jefferson to Cabanis, *Writings of Jefferson*, x, 404.
[2] Monroe to Jefferson, *Writings of Monroe*, iv, 75.   [3] *Ibid.*

the interests of his country, as a friend of liberty and equality.' Solemnly he insisted that he had been moved to the sale of Louisiana by an ardent desire to preserve forever the close relations of the two countries. Monroe was quite as suave. He knew Napoleon had been inspired by a great and enlightened policy rather than by motives of commerce. Yes, said Napoleon, the relations of the two nations were most friendly, and the United States 'must be on its guard not to give the protection of its flag to the British.' Monroe agreed, and suggested that the Consul might contribute to that end by sustaining the principle that 'free ships make free goods.'

All the while Monroe was wondering if Napoleon would mention the Florida pledge. Soon the latter brought it up with rare frankness. 'This is not the time to pursue that object,' he said, because 'the Spanish have complained much of the cession' of Louisiana. But, asked Monroe coyly, 'would it not be better for the United States to have the Floridas than for them to fall into the lap of the British?' Even so, concluded Napoleon, dismissing the subject, the time had not come for negotiations. Later the project could be revived, suggested Monroe, when America 'should expect his good offices in it.' Napoleon made no definite reply, but Monroe thought he 'seemed to assent.' [1]

Thus the two men parted. Monroe was elated with the part he had played in the greatest diplomatic triumph of his country's history. But a struggle was ahead in Washington.

[1] Monroe to Madison, *Writings of Monroe*, IV, 44.

CHAPTER X

The Seed of Treason

I

THE three months intervening between the adjournment of Congress and the announcement of the triumph of Paris was a period of intense anxiety to Jefferson. Of Hamilton's thoughts during these months we have no record. With his wife he was frequently to be seen at the New or Park Theater in New York, and occasionally he attended the meetings of the Philharmonic Society at Snow's Hotel at 69 Broadway. As much time as he could spare away from his professional duties was spent wandering over the grounds at the Grange, fishing in the waters of the Hudson, or sauntering through the woods, a single-barreled fowling piece on his shoulder, in search of game.[1] 'I hear very seldom from our friend Hamilton, whom you know I love exceedingly,' wrote Cabot to King.[2] After three months of waiting, the Federalists, confident of the failure of negotiations, freely and blatantly predicting it, already were indulging in sarcastic scoffing at the expense of 'the philosopher.'

And then, one day in June, an unofficial message from Paris reached Jefferson, speedily followed with authentic information that the negotiations had succeeded beyond the fondest hopes of the Administration. It was eight o'clock on the evening of July 3 that the people of Washington learned that the whole of Louisiana had been acquired, and on the morning of the nation's natal day the news was officially proclaimed. The country-town capital was seething with excitement at an early hour. A discharge of eighteen guns greeted the dawn. The military was assembled and paraded the dusty streets. At eleven an oration

[1] *Intimate Life*, 349.   [2] July 9, 1803; *Cabot*, 332.

was delivered, and at high noon men and women, in animated mood, were making their way to the White House from every quarter. Never before on the anniversary of the Declaration had so many exchanged felicitations with the Chief of State, for as many as fifty women in their gayest gowns crowded into the presidential presence. And never had Jefferson been a gayer host. A great load had been lifted from his mind, the ambition of a generation had been realized, his enemies confounded, his peace policy vindicated. Punch, cakes, wine 'in profusion' were served, and, moving among his guests, Jefferson, sunny with smiles, paid compliments to the ladies and accepted the congratulations of the men.[1]

He was in jubilant mood when he replied to a note of felicitations from General Horatio Gates, anticipating the Federalist attempt to deprive the Administration of credit for foresight. 'The territory acquired,' he wrote, ' ... has more than doubled the area of the United States, and the new part is not inferior to the old in soil, climate, productiveness, and important communications.' He had observed that 'the grumblers' were uneasy lest some credit come to him, and were ascribing the triumph they had said impossible to the accident of war. 'They would be cruelly mortified,' he wrote, 'could they see our files from May, 1801, the first organization of the Administration, but more especially from April, 1802. They would see that, though we could not say when war would arise, yet we said with energy what would take place when it should arise. We did not by our intrigue produce the war; but we availed ourselves of it when it happened.'[2]

The envoys were assured by Madison of the hearty approbation of Jefferson in their action in going beyond their instructions. 'The ample views of the subject carried with him by Mr. Monroe,' he wrote, 'and the confidence felt that your judicious management would make the most of favorable occurrences, lessened the necessity of multiplying provisions for every turn which your negotiations might possibly take.' But what about the eastern boundaries? Jefferson would like 'the pretensions

[1] Mrs. Smith, 38.
[2] *Writings of Jefferson*, x, 402.

and proofs for carrying it to the river Perdido, or for including any lesser portion of West Florida.' [1]

As the news spread that the national boundary had been doubled without the firing of a shot, the enthusiasm of the masses of the people flamed. The Jeffersonians were beside themselves with joy and bonfires blazed, men marched, bands played, and at banquet and bar copious toasts were drunk to the President. Never had he been so popular. Even from hostile Boston came a note asking him for the day of his birth that it might be celebrated with toast and song. He courteously declined to name the day. 'Disapproving myself of transferring the honors and veneration for the birthday of our Republic to any individual, or of dividing them with individuals, I have declined letting my own birthday be known, and have engaged my family not to communicate it,' he wrote. 'This has been the uniform answer to every application of the kind.' [2]

But though more ardent was the loyalty of his friends, his enemies never had been so bitter. They had sneered at the idea of negotiations and clamored for war, and by the scratch of a pen he had won an empire, out of which some of the greatest agricultural States of the Union would be carved. The Federalists were now predicting that the new acquisition would lead to a Western Confederacy, including the waters east and west emptying into the Mississippi, but Jefferson was not afraid. More annoying was their insistence on the unconstitutionality of the purchase. On this he had no wish to quibble. The Constitution made no provision for holding foreign territory and incorporating it into the Union. He admitted it. 'The Executive in seizing the fugitive occurrence,' he wrote, 'which so much advances the good of their country, has done an act beyond the Constitution.' What should the Congress do, then, under the circumstances? They must risk themselves 'like faithful servants, must ratify and pay ... and throw themselves on their country for doing for them unauthorized what we know they would have done for themselves had they been in a situation to do it.' And then he drew on an analogy: 'It is the case of a guardian,

[1] *Writings of Madison*, VII, 60.
[2] Jefferson to Lincoln, *Writings of Jefferson*, X, 415.

investing the money of his ward in purchasing an important
adjacent territory; and saying to him when he came of age,
"I did this for your good; I pretend to no right to bind you;
you may disavow me, and I must get out of the scrape as I can;
I thought it my duty to risk myself for you."' But Jefferson
had no fear of a disavowal. 'We shall not be disavowed by the
nation, and their act of indemnity will confirm and not weaken
the Constitution, by more strongly marking out its lines.' [1]

Even so, he was not comfortable in his mind, and during
August he toyed seriously with the idea of a constitutional
amendment to cover the case. Twice he submitted such an
amendment to his Cabinet, and twice he was voted down.

Meanwhile, with Spain stoutly contending that, under the
Treaty of San Ildefonso by which Louisiana had been transferred
by her to France, Napoleon had no right to sell, delay was dangerous. Gallatin lingering in New York was a bit alarmed. Suppose the Spanish officials in New Orleans should refuse to leave?
Would it not be well to be prepared the moment Pichon received
the order to give possession to be in position to move in by
force? With the military force at Fort Adams, the militia of
Mississippi and the Kentucky boatmen armed would be sufficient to take possession. 'No time should be lost in having a
supply of arms at Natchez.' [2]

Meanwhile, Madison was in receipt of two stiff notes from
Marquis de Casa Yrujo, the Spanish Minister, protesting against
the sale. The French Ambassador in Madrid at the time of the
retrocession had given the secret pledge that Louisiana never
would be alienated to another nation,[3] and France had not
lived up to the conditions on which the retrocession had been
based.[4] She had failed 'to procure the stipulated recognition
of the King of Etruria from Russia and Great Britain.' In
Madrid, the clever Cevallos, Minister of Foreign Affairs, had,
in conversation with our Minister at that court, denied the right
to sell. But, wrote Madison to Livingston, Spain had known
of our desire for New Orleans and a part of Louisiana. We had

[1] To Breckinridge, *Writings of Jefferson*, x, 407.
[2] To Jefferson, September 5, 1803, *Writings of Gallatin*, I, 152.
[3] Note of September 4, 1803.   [4] *Ibid.*, 27, 1803.

applied to her, and the same Cevallos had informed our Minister of the retrocession to France, and actually had advised that the United States 'address themselves to the French Government in order to negotiate the acquisition of the territories which would suit their interest.' Was not this a recognition by Madrid of the right to sell? And why the silence of Spain throughout the negotiations and before? [1]

Thus, when Congress should convene, Jefferson would be in full possession of every point that would be made against the purchase.

II

The Federalist press, dominated by the foremost Federalist leaders, could have left him in no doubt. The *Columbian Centinel* went mad. Vehemently it protested when the word arrived during a recess of Congress that only the announcement of the purchase had been made. 'This is all the intelligence the servants of the people in Washington choose to disclose to their Masters of an event which involves their dearest interests,' it raved.[2] When it learned the price, it was shocked. 'It is nearly all of the gold and silver in the United States,' it complained. As time went on, its fury increased. At length it went beyond all decent bounds. Was it not well known that in the event of war England would seize on Louisiana? Was not that a better way of getting rid of the obnoxious French as neighbors? 'As for the United States, we do not want a foot of the land, but only the use of the river,' it said. And how shameful the purchase! 'Grant millions to the President to buy our own,' it raved. 'Send Mr. Monroe to coax and let Mr. Livingston with his memorial be his rival in a race of ridicule.' [3] Fifteen millions? And for what? 'Wild land!' [4] And what stupidity to have hurried the negotiations! War was declared within a week, and had we waited, England would have taken Louisiana and relieved us of it.[5] Was it not time to rid ourselves of these Virginia leaders who had 'run in debt for Mississippi moonshine fifteen million dollars'? [6]

[1] Madison to Livingston, *Writings of Madison*, VII, 64.

[2] July 13, 1803.   [3] August 13, 1803.   [4] August 24, 1803.

[5] October 1, 1803.   [6] October 19, 1803.

The *Connecticut Courant* printed the first story of the purchase in large type without comment.[1] Dazed at first, it soon recovered and fell ferociously on the 'outrage.' 'What has become of the two million dollars?' it demanded. 'How much of it was given in bribes in Paris? How much of it stuck between the fingers that carried it? How much of it came back to this country to buy votes and pay for democratic seats?'[2] So low had sunk the *Courant*!

Soon 'A Citizen' was assisting. 'Would the eastern and middle States consent?' he asked. Could anyone doubt Jefferson's object? 'He is not blind to the consequences of adding Louisiana to the United States — he sees in it the ultimate depopulation of the eastern country, and the transfer of power, riches, and independence to that favored latitude.' But 'will the States of New Hampshire, Massachusetts and Maine, Rhode Island, Connecticut, Vermont, New York, New Jersey and Pennsylvania, Delaware and Maryland, tax themselves fifteen millions' to carry the plan into effect? Why purchase it at all? 'The United States do not want this tract of country.' Yes, 'remember, citizens of New Jersey, this country must be colonized at the expense of your men and money — it will be made to drain from you this, the vital fluid of your political strength and social advantage.'[3] More astonishing was the position of Hamilton's paper, the *New York Evening Post*. On the arrival of the news it seemed pleased with the triumph. 'At length the business of New Orleans has terminated favorably to this country,' it began. 'Instead of being forced to rely any longer on the forces of treaties, for a place of deposit, the jurisdiction of the territory is now transferred to our hands and in future the navigation of the Mississippi will be ours unmolested.'[4] But in the fall, when Federalist opposition had crystallized, the *Evening Post* sang another song. Soon it was moaning over the grievances of Spain and complaining that 'we have already assumed a bullying attitude.'[5] More amazing still, it bitterly declared that the treaty 'is exactly like the Jay treaty,' which it did not remotely resemble and which the Federalists had

---

[1] July 27, 1803.   [2] August 10, 1803.
[3] *Trenton Federalist*, quoted in *Courant*, August 17, 1803.
[4] July 5, 1803.   [5] October 31, 1803.

supported to a man.[1] Was it not time, it said again, that 'Congress and Congress alone should have the power of framing treaties'? [2]

But the burden of the song of the *Evening Post* was that we had bought something that belonged to someone other than the party to whom we paid the price.[3] It was toward the close of the *Evening Post's* campaign against the treaty that it published a long and brilliant article, signed 'An American,' in which Rufus King took a stout stand for it. 'I approve the general scope and effect of this treaty,' wrote the anonymous King.[4]

And this was the position of Hamilton.

III

At first, Jefferson had no idea that the bitterness of the opposition would find vent in a treasonable conspiracy. Hamilton, with a statesman's vision and free from sectional bias, knew that an enormous public service had been rendered. Gouverneur Morris, no longer in public life, would not stultify himself as a statesman by questioning the wisdom of the acquisition. But he looked upon Louisiana through the eyes of an imperialist. 'As to the cession of Louisiana I should indeed have lost all shame, as well as pretense to understanding, if I did not approve it,' he wrote. But he was against ever admitting its inhabitants into the Union. Better have a thousand bayonets always in control. Better to fortify New Orleans and hold Louisiana as a province.[5]

Fisher Ames was insufferably disgusted. He felt that 'acquiring territory with money is mean and despicable.' To negotiate instead of taking Louisiana by arms was 'deserving of shame and chains.' Could anything better illustrate 'the abject spirit of the Administration' than the manner in which it possessed itself of Louisiana? [6] And how did we dare violate our neutrality in a war between England and France by paying Napoleon money just before the war began? Think of it! When 'Great

---

[1] November 8, 1803.   [2] November 10, 1803.
[3] November 12, 1803.   [4] December 24, 1803.
[5] To Dayton, *Diary*, II, 453, 454.   [6] To Gore, *Ames*, I, 323.

Britain is fighting our battles and the battles of mankind, and
France is combating for the power to enslave and plunder us
and all the world,' we give her fifteen million dollars! [1] True,
Lord Hawkesbury had told Rufus King we should possess
Louisiana and Castlereagh had told Monroe that the purchase
was 'the effect of a masterly policy,' [2] but the extreme Federalists had become more ardent Britons than the British. Senator
Plumer was convinced that the purchase offered ample justification for secession, and that it was now 'optional with the
old States to say whether they would longer remain in the present
confederacy.' [3] Many complained bitterly of paying fifteen million dollars for the territory from which were to be carved Louisiana, Arkansas, Missouri, Oklahoma, Kansas, Nebraska, the two
Dakotas, the greater part of Idaho and Montana, and parts of
Texas, New Mexico, Colorado, and Wyoming. An outrageous
price! Rufus King, in his loftiest mood, was sure that with his
diplomacy it could have been had for much less.[4] They all agreed
it was unconstitutional. But deep down, the resentment of the
extreme New England Federalists was that, with the States
ultimately to be carved from the new territory, the dominance of
their section would be lost. 'The admission of this State into
the Union,' wrote Cutler, reducing the gossip of the boarding-
houses to his diary, 'not only carries the balance of power in
those States further to the Southward, but in all probability
will lay the foundation for a separation of the States.' [5] Stephen
Higginson, the great Federalist merchant of Boston, was too
disgusted to discuss the matter at all. As to the constitutionality of the proceeding, 'the Jacobins despise such niceties.' [6]
Soon it was being retailed about the Federalist boarding-houses
that before making the treaty Napoleon had sold all the land
in Louisiana to European syndicates, so we had bought a title
that carried no land, for fifteen millions.[7] Jefferson had made
a mess of things, naturally.

Among the New England Federalists another Adams had
arisen to annoy them. John Quincy Adams, not yet forty, had

[1] To Dwight, *Ames*, I, 330.   [2] Monroe to Madison, *Writings of Monroe*, IV, 99.
[3] *Plumer*, 265.   [4] Cutler, II, 138.   [5] *Ibid.*, II, 138.
[6] To Pickering, *Pickering*, IV, 79.   [7] Cutler, II, 140.

gone over to the treaty in the Senate. His position was not unlike that of Jefferson and Madison. The territory should be ours, but since the purchase was outside the Constitution, there should be a constitutional amendment, to cover the defect. Eleven days after Congress met, he walked over to Madison's office to discuss the situation. Madison accepted Adams's view, but found it not 'universally' agreed that an amendment was necessary. A definite decision had not been reached. Adams left with the warning that if no one else offered an amendment he would.[1]

Such was the spirit of the Federalists as the time approached for the delivery of the note of transfer and for taking possession.

Meanwhile, Yrujo was protesting, and Pichon, the French Chargé d'Affaires, was 'surprised' and felt 'some irritation' against his Spanish colleague whom he charged with having stirred up the Government in Madrid.[2] Under these circumstances, the Administration was taking every possible precaution. Gallatin might have been seen in the middle of October in earnest conversation with the members of Congress from the Western States, and the outcome was the assurance that within a fortnight Tennessee and Kentucky could march fifteen hundred armed horsemen into Nashville, aside from the regular troops. Thence they could ride to Natchez and be ready for instant action. If necessary, such was the zeal of the Western country, five thousand volunteers could be raised. It was agreed that Kentucky should furnish two thirds and Tennessee one third of the volunteers.[3] Gallatin thought the larger the expedition the better, because of the moral effect.

Such was the background of the congressional battles about to begin.

IV

Because of the emergency, Jefferson summoned Congress for October. Some familiar faces were conspicuously absent. The two foremost orators who had long delighted the ladies were gone, for Gouverneur Morris had been retired by his constituents

---

[1] Adams, *Diary*, i, 267.   [2] *Ibid.*, i, 272.
[3] Gallatin to Jefferson, *Writings of Gallatin*, i, 162.

and Stevens T. Mason of Virginia was dead. Bayard in the House had been defeated. From Massachusetts were two new senators representing the two poles of Federalist thought, John Quincy Adams and Timothy Pickering — two mortal enemies. The latter had been contemptuously hurled from the Cabinet of the former's father for disloyalty.

Samuel Adams, the robust old revolutionist and Jeffersonian, thoroughly hated by the Federalists, had recently died, and John Randolph rose to pay him tribute, since 'it became the House to cherish a sentiment of veneration for such a man — since such men are rare,' and because it was 'the glorious privilege of minds like his to give an impulse to a people and fix the destiny of nations.' [1] When, in the Senate, Breckinridge moved that senators wear mourning for a month, the ten Federalists in the Senate voted against it. [2]

Meanwhile, Jefferson's memorable Message had been read. It fairly sang with triumph. Not without a tone of exultation he recalled the excitement of the previous session over the withdrawal of the privilege of deposits, announced the repudiation of the act by Madrid, and referred to the previously planned negotiations for New Orleans. Concisely and with dignity, he proclaimed the purchase. Certain provisions of the treaty were solely within the powers of Congress. It would naturally act promptly. Provision would be made for taking possession and for the temporary government of the new domain.

Financially, the Government was prospering. Within the year between eleven and twelve millions had poured into the Treasury, far exceeding the sum counted upon as sufficient to meet the nation's obligations. Three million, one hundred thousand had been paid on the principal of the national debt, which meant that within two years more than eight and a half millions had been paid, exclusive of the interest. New obligations had been entailed by the purchase of Louisiana, but it was hoped that means could be found to meet them without the levying of new taxes.

Unhappily, the flames of war again were illuminating Europe. Our duty of neutrality was plain.

[1] *Annals*, October 19, 1803.   [2] Adams, *Diary*, I, 269.

No one could question the finances, nor point to blunders in policy against which warning had been made. Thus the problem of Louisiana loomed large as the one probable subject of controversy. And there could be no doubt of that.

It was to be a memorable winter — a season of rain and snow that occasionally was to interfere with attendance at the Capitol.[1] Never had the gossips fed so sumptuously on juicy fare. It was the season when Mrs. Merry was having her fling at the vulgarities of democracy, and Tom Moore was giving the crude Americans a treat; when poor Tom Paine was being raked over the coals of partisan hate in the name of God; when Jerome Bonaparte and Betsy Patterson, married, were lyingly dissected in their morals and their manners with the knife of malice at dinners, dances, and in the cloakrooms of House and Senate; when rumor had it that Burr was about to fight a duel,[2] and when everyone knew that Hamilton was meditating a challenge to George Clinton.[3] Speculation buzzed about the mysterious movements of Burr, who did not appear in the Senate for six weeks after it convened, and who absented himself again through February. The initial discussion of the Yazoo frauds and the fierce philippics of the irate Randolph even loosened the tongue of reticence, and one winter day the Federalists rolled and rocked with glee because at a Jeffersonian boarding-house one Sunday evening, hard words had been exchanged between Randolph and a colleague, when the Virginia Hotspur had gallantly ushered the ladies from the room to return and throw a glass of wine in his opponent's face, to break the glass upon his head, and to hurl a gin bottle in his direction. Would there be a duel? Had a warrant been sworn out against Randolph? Why were both absent the next morning — had they gone to Bladensburg?[4] And there was gossip about the boorish conduct of Federalist gentlemen at Jefferson's dinners.

And all the while the Federalist leaders, in House and Senate, were putting their heads together, secretly planning treason — the separation of the States — but that did not enter into the gossip then, nor for a long time afterward.

---

[1] Adams, *Diary*, I, 271; 281–85.   [2] Burr, II, 266.
[3] *Works of Hamilton*, VIII, 610.   [4] Cutler, II, 162.

None of this was greatly to disturb Jefferson nor to enter into his correspondence, voluminous as it was. In the midst of the madness of party, he was keeping a firm but gentle hand on his compliant majority, and thinking of the pleasures of Monticello. He could write home of the acquisition from Algiers of 'a pair of beautiful fowls... with fine aigrates.' These, he admonished, should be kept 'clear of a mixture of any kind.' As soon as Congress adjourned, he and Mary would supervise the building of a chicken-house at Pantope.[1] But this was written to his favorite Mary, to amuse and interest her, for he was gravely worried about her health.[2] It was in this atmosphere of levity and laughter that one of the most significant debates in the early Republic was conducted.

v

The debate began in the House. The Senate had ratified the treaty speedily, with little discussion and by a strict party vote. The House debate opened on October 24, when a Federalist (Griswold) offered a resolution calling upon Jefferson to lay before the House a copy of the treaty between Spain and France and the 'deed of cession' whereby Spain returned Louisiana to the French; also correspondence between Madison and Spain showing that we had obtained Spain's consent to the purchase; and any other papers showing that we had in fact 'acquired any title' by our purchase.

At a time when Yrujo was protesting against the sale, the Federalists thus moved in solid phalanx to the side of Spain and against the United States.

Randolph, who was to manage the debate for the Administration with great skill, took the floor. Pale, boyish in appearance, but a master parliamentarian at thirty, he sought to shame the opposition into silence. Had not the treaty been 'hailed by the acclamations of the nation'? Of course it would receive the 'cordial approbation of a triumphant majority in the House.' In view of the enormous benefits to the nation, he was 'lost in astonishment' that Americans should inquire into the details of the negotiations. Did anyone question the conduct of the

---

[1] *Domestic Life*, 296.   [2] *Ibid.*, 298.

negotiators? Had anyone insinuated that American interests
had been betrayed? Then why endanger the treaty by delay?

And then, his small face wrinkling with scorn:

'Shall this refusal to receive the possession proceed from those
who so lately affirmed that we ought to pursue this object at
every national hazard?'

Injustice to Spain? Were not the objectors the very men who
but recently had insisted that we take Louisiana from Spain by
force?

Nicholson was more intolerant. The Treaty of San Ildefonso
was a secret treaty and not in the possession of the Government
to give, he said. And 'deed of sale' — what was meant by that?
Was it expected that a formal deed of bargain and sale had
been executed between two civilized nations who negotiated by
means of ambassadors?

Ah, replied the author of the resolution, but if Spain refuses
consent and remains in possession, 'it may be necessary to resort
to other measures.' If, however, the treaty be constitutionally
made and ratified there would be nothing to do but to carry it
into effect.

'If it be constitutionally made and ratified!' exclaimed Randolph. 'I am too dull to comprehend how a treaty can be constitutionally ratified which is not constitutionally made. . . . And
yet the gentleman wants documents. To prove what? That the
treaty is constitutional? Not at all; not to decide whether we
have a treaty which contravenes the provisions of the Constitution, but to determine whether we have any treaty at all.' [1]

Yes, replied the author of the resolution, but the treaty pro-
vides different treatment for the vessels of France and Spain
in the ports of New Orleans from that in other ports — directly
'against an important article of the Constitution.'

'But,' said Randolph, 'I regard this stipulation as a part
of the price of the territory. It was a condition which the party
ceding had a right to require, and to which we had a right to
assent.' Would he hear that this is a violation of the Treaty of
London? Well, 'the Court of London being apprized of the
transaction and acquiescing in the arrangement, it would ill

[1] *Annals,* October 24, 1803.

become a member of the House to bring forward such a suggestion.'

What had happened? A treaty had been violated which gave us the right of deposit at New Orleans and this had closed the Mississippi to the products of the West. A portion of the House had demanded violent measures; another preferred first seeking an amicable settlement. Suppose the negotiations had failed? 'We should have appealed to arms, and if fortune had been as impartial as our cause was just we should have possessed ourselves of at least a part of this territory. Did anyone dream of denying our right to the forcible possession of New Orleans if necessary to secure the navigation of the Mississippi? Can a nation acquire by force what she cannot acquire by treaty? Must not the eventual right to a country possessed by force be confirmed by treaty?'

One Federalist member was disgusted by the means through which we had acquired Louisiana. But what could have been expected of a cowardly Administration? 'There are but two ways of maintaining our national independence — men or money. Since we did not use the first, we must have recourse to the last.' Of course it was not well to have the French for neighbors. 'Yes, thank God, we have now a treaty, signed by themselves in which they have voluntarily passed away the only means of annoyance which they possessed. But I do not thank the honorable gentleman who is at the head of the Administration.' No, 'the King of England was by far the most able negotiator we had by declaring war.'

'Without attributing to the President the power of prophecy,' replied Elliott, 'I must hazard the opinion that, in common with all "political philosophers," he foresaw that the peace between England and France would not be permanent.' [1] Nicholson then reiterated that the Federalists had demanded war for the possession of New Orleans. Had we fought and won would they have retained the territory? [2]

Randolph closed the debate and the Administration won.

[1] As a matter of record the whole plan of Jefferson was based on the certain resumption of war.

[2] *Annals*, October 25, 1803.

VI

The battle now shifted to the Senate. Here the purpose of the Federalists was to throw doubt on the validity of the title. 'Did not Spain consider herself injured by the treaty?' asked White of Delaware. Might she not refuse to agree to the cession? Yes, added Wells, another Federalist, were there not strong reasons for doubting the validity of the French title? The war hawks of the previous session who had clamored for taking New Orleans by storm had suddenly become sensitive about the wrongs of Spain.

The explosive Jackson, unable to hold his peace longer, broke in: 'Is not the King of Spain's proclamation declaring the cession of Louisiana to France, and his orders to his Governor to deliver it to France, a title?' he roared.

Then Timothy Pickering rose. Even at this moment he was organizing a conspiracy to separate New England from the Union because of the purchase. We had the right, he said, to acquire new territory by conquest or purchase, and the right to rule it as a 'dependant province.' But the right to incorporate it into the Union? Never! And what of our title under the purchase? The King's proclamation and order? It had been given a year before and much had happened since. And had not Godoy declared that his royal master had not ceded Louisiana to France? Alas, he could see nothing but war as the fruit of these negotiations.

Then, in support of the treaty, followed Dayton of New Jersey, Federalist, and a crony of Burr's, soon to have an unsavory association with Louisiana. The King's proclamation was a fact, the order to deliver was a fact, and what if the order should be revoked, 'of what avail would it be against a third party who had in the meantime become a bona fide purchaser'?

Then rose John Taylor of Caroline, one of the profound political thinkers of his time, to defend the right to acquire territory. Whence came this theory that the Union could not acquire and hold territory under the Constitution? 'The means of acquiring and the right of holding territory being both given to the United States and prohibited to each State, it follows that these attributes of sovereignty, once held by each State, are thus trans-

TIMOTHY PICKERING

JAMES A. BAYARD

JOSIAH QUINCY

ferred to the United States; and if the means of acquiring and the right of holding are equivalent to the right of acquiring territory, then this right, merged from the several States to the United States, is indispensably annexed to the treaty-making power . . . or, indeed, is literally given to the general Government by the Constitution.'

The right to acquire, hold, govern, is clear. But what of the stipulation in the treaty that Louisiana shall be erected into a State? The treaty-making power cannot, by treaty, erect a new State. But it may stipulate for it. In the construction of this article it is proper to recollect that the negotiators must be supposed to have understood our Constitution. It becomes very particularly their duty to do so, because in this article itself they recited 'the principles of the Constitution as their guide.'

Is there anything unconstitutional in the article providing that 'the inhabitants of the ceded territory shall be incorporated in the Union of the United States'? Does this provision mean that they must be incorporated into the Union as States? Not at all. The inhabitants of a Territory may be incorporated into the Union without admitting the Territory as a State.

If the treaty meant that the people should immediately be incorporated into the Union as a State, how absurd another provision that they should have 'the immunities of citizens of the United States' as soon as possible, 'according to the principles of the Federal Constitution.' [1]

Taylor was followed by the Federalist leader, Tracy. 'I have no doubt,' he said, 'but that we can attain territory either by conquest or compact, and hold it, even all of Louisiana, and a thousand times more if we please, without violating the Constitution. We can hold territory; but to admit the inhabitants into the Union, to make citizens of them, and States, by treaty, we cannot constitutionally do; and no subsequent act of legislation, or even an ordinary amendment to our Constitution can legalize such measures. If done at all, they must be done by the universal consent of all the States or partners in our political association. And this universal consent I am positive can never

---

[1] *Annals*, November 3, 1803.

be obtained to such a pernicious measure as the admission of
Louisiana, of a world, of such a world, into our Union.'

And then, in a flash, he disclosed the real secret of the bitter
opposition of the Federalists:

'This would be absorbing the Northern States and rendering
them as insignificant to the Union as they ought to be, if, by
their own consent, the measure should be adopted.'

Breckinridge closed for the Administration. How, he said,
the Federalists have changed their cry since the last session!
Then they wanted New Orleans; now they do not. Then they
were anxious to take it by force; now they cringe at the thought
of taking it without bloodshed. Then they were ardent on the
use of the Mississippi, and where now had their ardor gone?

'It seems to me, sir, that the opinions of a certain portion of
the United States with respect to the ill-fated Mississippi have
varied as often as the fashions. . . . But unfortunately for the
gentlemen no two of them can agree on the same set of objections; and what is still more unfortunate, no two of them concur
in any one objection. On only one thing can they agree — to
vote against the bill. The honorable gentleman from Delaware
(White) considers the price to be enormous; the honorable gentleman from Connecticut (Tracy) says he has no objections whatever
to the price, since it is not too much. An honorable gentleman
from Massachusetts (Pickering) says that France acquired no
title from Spain, and therefore our title is bad; the same gentleman
from Connecticut (Tracy) says he has no objections to the title
of France; he thinks it is a good one. The gentleman from
Massachusetts contends that the United States cannot, under
the Constitution, acquire foreign territory; the gentleman from
Connecticut has no doubt but that the United States may acquire
and hold territory, but that Congress alone has the power to
incorporate that territory into the Union. To what weight, therefore, ought all their lesser objections to entitle them?'

The price too great? Would taking it by force with fifty thousand men have cost nothing? Was the opposition sure the god of
battles was enlisted on our side? Are France and Spain under
Bonaparte contemptible adversaries? Incredible seemed the
carping criticism to Breckinridge. 'Why, this transaction, from

its commencement to its close, not only as to the mode in which
it was pursued, but as to the object achieved, is one of the most
splendid which the annals of any nation can produce.'

Less than a year before, the opposition had passionately declared the necessity of taking possession of part of the ceded
territory. 'Did not gentlemen intend, when they urged its seizure,
that the United States if successful should hold it in absolute
sovereignty? Were any constitutional difficulties then in the
way?' [1]

And then John Quincy Adams rose. What meant this talk of
paying our money and getting nothing? When Louisiana is
formally surrendered to us, when all the military posts are in our
hands, when all the troops have been embarked, what possible
adverse possession can there be to contend against ours? And
until these conditions shall be met, no money shall be paid. True,
the negotiators had exceeded their powers; true, certain stipula-
tions had been made that were beyond the Constitution; but
the cause was right and a constitutional amendment to meet
all necessities should be proposed. Propose it, and 'it will be
adopted by the Legislature of every State in the Union.' [2]

The vote now was taken and only five — Hillhouse, Pickering,
Tracy, Wells, and White — voted against taking possession; and
of these, three were at this moment up to their armpits in a
conspiracy of secession.

VII

And now the fight shifted to the bill providing a temporary
government.

Meanwhile, colorful events in New Orleans. The first of December a high functionary of the Court of Spain arrived in New
Orleans formally and impressively to deliver Louisiana to the
French. The Spanish flag fell, that of France arose, and from
the balcony of the city hall the people were informed of their new
allegiance. Three weeks later, another imposing ceremony in
New Orleans, when the French ruler transferred Louisiana to the
United States. The French flag fell; that of the United States
fluttered from the staff.

[1] *Annals*, November 3, 1803.   [2] *Ibid.*

Louisiana was now ours; and no blood had been shed.

But no time could be lost in substituting a new government for the old. Jefferson and Madison had been in close conference for days with Breckinridge on the forming of a temporary government. If one tenth of what the Federalists claimed were true, nothing could have been more suicidal than the immediate establishment of democratic forms, with an immediate election to choose the rulers. The American element was exceedingly small. There were the French in numbers, clearly unhappy in the loss they had sustained. There were great numbers of the Spanish, more resentful still. There, too, were the Mexicans of the adventurous type, and much of the population was turbulent. At the moment of taking possession, a strong, stern hand was imperatively required. Had the Federalists' preference for war prevailed, no one would have conceived the idiotic notion immediately of turning the government over to the people there. Indeed, the Federalist leaders were demanding that Louisiana be held as a province under the shadow of the sword.

Jefferson brushed this view contemptuously aside. He believed in the right of the people to rule themselves; but he was no mere theorist. He faced facts. He favored a short period of preparation and probation to the end that American dominance might be conclusively imposed upon the new possession. To have acquired a mighty empire for a song, without the loss of a drop of blood, and then, in a spasm of idealism, to have squandered it away, would have been a crime. Just what Jefferson thought, and Madison said, concerning the measure, what Breckinridge wrote, we do not know. That all favored a firm hand in the beginning there can be no doubt.

The idea of a constitutional amendment had been reluctantly abandoned. It would have been gambling with an empire as stakes. Time demanded speedy action. When Adams proposed an amendment in the Senate, not even a Federalist could be found to second the motion. It died without being born.

The Government plan provided for in the Breckinridge bill would seem shocking without an appreciation of the circumstances that justified it as a temporary measure. The President was given power as absolute as that of the King of Spain. He was to name

the Governor and all the officers even to the appointing of the
legislative council. The trial by jury temporarily was restricted
to capital offenses, and in civil suits to cases in which more than
twenty dollars were involved. Drolly enough, the Federalists were
shocked; so, too, were not a few of the Democrats; and among the
opponents of the measures were some of the most ardent of
Jefferson's political friends. The measure passed the Senate
after a debate, unhappily lost to posterity. But when it reached
the House, the debate was full and free and public.

Among the opponents of the bill were Michael Leib of Pennsylvania, a Jeffersonian; Macon, the Jeffersonian Speaker; and
George Campbell, soon to supplant Randolph in the leadership
of the Administration forces. It is not of record that any of them
suffered with Jefferson because of the stand they took. Leib
thought the power given the Governor over the legislative council
'a royal power'; Varnum, Jeffersonian from Massachusetts,
denounced the entire scheme, and demanded that the council
be elected from the beginning; Matthew Lyon was sure the plan
made a Napoleon out of Jefferson; and Campbell said it 'establishes a complete despotism.'

But Dr. Eustis, another Jeffersonian from Massachusetts,
faced the hard facts without a quibble. 'The principles of civil
liberty cannot suddenly be engrafted on a people accustomed to
a régime of a directly opposite hue,' he said. Thus, in a sentence,
did he give voice to the prevailing view, and, no doubt, to the
thought of Jefferson. Even John Randolph was flabbergasted, and
when he could not vote for the measure, he did not vote at all.
With no attempt at discipline the House went its way with its
amendments, making the legislative council elective after the
first year, rejecting the provisions on trial by jury, and limiting
the duration of the act to two years. The Senate promptly rejected the amendments, but reduced the duration of the act to one
year, and with this, the House accepted and the bill became the law.

Louisiana was now the territory of the United States.

VIII

But Jefferson was embarrassed in the choice of a Governor.
The ideal choice would have been a strong character of great

political capacity, of ingratiating manners, able to speak both
French and Spanish, but the combination was impossible to find.
'It will not be easy to find a proper Governor for the newly
acquired territory,' wrote Gouverneur Morris.[1] The thought of
Jefferson turned to Monroe, but he declined in deference to his
family who did not wish to break old ties and move to a land of
strangers.[2] At length the choice fell on Governor William C. C.
Claiborne, of Mississippi. Confronted by unprecedented problems, surrounded with intrigue, envy, jealousy, and turbulent
forces, he occasionally made mistakes in judgment for which he
has been unjustly derided by some historians. But he was a figure
worthy of better treatment. He was in his twenty-eighth year
when he took possession in New Orleans, but a notable career and
executive experience in Mississippi offset his youth. A Virginian
by birth, educated at William and Mary, he had won the confidence and regard of Jefferson when, as a youth, he had served
a short time as a clerk of Congress. The demonstration of some
oratorical power had impelled him to study law, and soon he
enjoyed a large criminal practice in Tennessee. He served with
ability in the Constitutional Convention of his adopted State,
and, on the organization of the Government, he had been appointed a judge of the Supreme Court. In his twenty-first year
he was sent to Congress to succeed Andrew Jackson, and, despite
his disqualification because of his age, he served for five years.
In the face of the bitter efforts of the Federalists for Burr, he
had held his State for Jefferson. Soon thereafter Jefferson
made him Governor of Mississippi. He was just twenty-six. Here
he rendered distinguished service in moderating the factional
troubles created by his predecessor, in organizing new counties,
planning measures of public health and education, and in controlling the negroes. Almost every move he made stood the test
of trial.[3] No American then living had had so much experience
in territorial organization and government.

His honesty never was to be questioned, his motives invariably
were honest, his alertness and diligence in the performance of
duties was acknowledged, and his mild disposition and conciliating

[1] Morris, *Diary*, II, 453-54.   [2] *Writings of Monroe*, IV, 477.
[3] *Dictionary of American Biography*, IV, 115.

temperament guarded him against conscious injustice to anyone. It was a young man of handsome appearance who assumed the government in New Orleans.

With the organization of the government, the finishing touch was put on the supreme achievement of the Republic to this day. After more than a century, great States reaching from the Gulf to the Canadian border, embracing the garden spot of the country, pulsating with industry, teeming with herds of sheep and cattle, bear witness to the vision and the wisdom of Thomas Jefferson.

IX

But the Federalists were unhappy, refusing to join in the celebrations that came in the wake of the formal delivery of Louisiana. In early January the festivities were in full swing. The Federalists were scornful. 'It is to begin here and is expected to run like wildfire to all the dark and benighted part of America,' wrote Cutler. Two days of eating, drinking, dancing had been planned for Washington. 'Every pig, goose and duck, far and near, is said to have been long in requisition.' But the Federalists remained sternly aloof from the general rejoicing. 'We poor Feds are quite in the background,' wrote one of them. 'At Stelle's both Jefferson and Burr in attendance, but no Federalists.'[1] That night they danced at Georgetown, a crowded company, but Adams, who attended with his wife, found the arrangements and decorations 'mean beyond anything of the kind I ever saw,'[2] and Cutler, who merely heard about it, was moved to wrath because they had 'affronted the British Minister and his lady whom they had invited.'[3] A Washington correspondent of the *Connecticut Courant* was not so hard to please about the decorations as Adams. The walls were decorated with 'festoons of laurel.' The windows were all brilliantly illuminated and the reflection on the snow made a striking effect. Two hundred women and three hundred men attended, and despite the pressure 'the most perfect order and the highest flow of hilarity were kept up, without any apparent efforts of the management.' The *Courant's* correspondent felt that 'too much credit cannot be given the management.'[4]

---

[1] Cutler, II, 163; Adams, *Diary*, I, 293.   [2] Adams, *Diary*, I, 293.
[3] Cutler, II, 163.   [4] *Connecticut Courant*, February 15, 1804.

But the *Columbian Centinel* and its 'Gallery Spectator' wrote with fury and some license about the banquet. 'At this noble carousal, in the presence of our philosophers, the band of music played "Ça Ira" and "Carmagnole" and other Revolutionary tunes to which the heads of thousands of Frenchmen danced off their shoulders in the murderous days of Marat and Robespierre.' When Jefferson retired, he was given a great ovation, and when Burr left, there would have been another ovation, thought the scribe, 'but for the indecent grumbling of the President's satellites.' When Varnum proposed 'Union to parties,' the scribe heard much grumbling; and when Nicholson proposed 'The tempestuous sea of liberty, may there never be a calm,' the crowd was happy again. So ran the Federalist version of the dinner.[1]

Meanwhile, the treasonable conspiracy of some of the outstanding Federalist leaders was causing Hamilton no little uneasiness, and one January day he sat down with Rufus King and Gouverneur Morris in a secret conference. That the conspiracy was discussed there can be no doubt; that Hamilton denounced it is quite as certain. All we are permitted to know of the conversation is that all agreed that the Constitution was destroyed, and that 'bloody anarchy' would follow in the wake of Jefferson. Morris did not think the Jeffersonians were destroying the fundamental law to raise a monarchy on its ruins, but 'such is the natural effect of their measures,' he wrote.[2]

But at the moment the winds of disunion swept from an opposite direction, for Federalist leaders were planning the destruction of the Republic. Even James Kent, Chancellor of New York, an intimate of Hamilton, was utterly nauseated by the doubling of the national domain. 'A paltry possession!' he wrote, apropos of the celebration in New York. 'About half the churches refused to let their bells ring,' he wrote with jubilation. And 'the judges were all invited to walk in procession, but we all kept in court on business.'[3] Thus did dignity, respectability, and religion draw back their skirts to evade the contamination of the purchase.

And now we shall follow the resulting trail of treason.

[1] *Columbian Centinel*, February 18, 1804.   [2] Morris, *Diary*, II, 454.
[3] William Kent, *Memoirs and Letters of James Kent*, 132.

CHAPTER XI

Disunionists Rear Their Heads

I

WITH the secession taint in the blood of the New England Federalists from the beginning, a revival in intensified form was inevitable with the acquisition of Louisiana. The feeling that the ultimate opening of the new lands would depress the value of the land of New England, the certainty that in time it would comparatively weaken the old section, economically and politically, gave a powerful impulse to the disposition to destroy the Union rather than submit. 'The admission of the province into the Union must throw New England quite into the background,' wrote the Reverend Manasseh Cutler, M.C. 'Her influence in government from the rapid population of the southward and westward is naturally declining, and this must be nearly a finishing stroke.... The moment Louisiana is admitted to the Union the seeds of separation are planted.'

Throughout the winter of 1803–04, the conspiracy of secession was active, and the plot against the Union was to be handed down to history in the personal letters exchanged among the conspirators.

Drolly enough, many historians persist in describing as 'nationalists,' as differentiated from the Jeffersonians, the Federalist leaders who were deep in the plot. All were stout champions of the Constitution, and given to lip praise of Washington. Each was shocked by Jefferson's 'attack on the federal judiciary,' and in the midst of their patriotic protests each was feverishly conspiring to destroy the Federal Union!

The stern, austere, bigoted Timothy Pickering scarcely needs

an introduction.[1] The bitter partisan of the Adams Cabinet who
could reconcile his puritanic conscience to the base betrayal of
his chief, and whose fingers toyed nervously with newspapers
looking for victims of the Sedition Law, had not mellowed since
his entrance to the Senate. Financially honest, unquestionably
sincere in his prejudices and hates, he had moved to the leadership of his party through the very intolerance of his views and his
tireless energy. But, though he speedily pushed to the front rank
of the secessionists of the Jefferson régime, he was acting, apparently, on the initiative of others from Connecticut. We shall find
him embarrassed by his inability to convince the party leaders in
Massachusetts of the timeliness or the practicability of the movement. Others, not so familiar to history, and yet in positions of
leadership, are deserving of a larger place in the story of their
times.

II

At this time a group of high-flying Federalists were living
harmoniously and much to themselves in the intimacy of a Washington boarding-house. Their sole thought was the embarrassment of Jefferson. Among these, most of them able, some eloquent, the one who stood out because of his wit and humor was
Senator Uriah Tracy, of Connecticut. While not yet fifty, he
was not in good health, and had been a sufferer for three years.
Behind him stretched a long period of public service. An able
lawyer, with a logical mind and unusual powers of advocacy,
he had distinguished himself professionally. In the militia, he
had risen from the bottom to the rank of major-general. He had
served continuously in legislative assemblies in Connecticut and
Washington for fifteen years, and had shown marked capacity for
public business. His intimacy with congressional procedure had
won the admiration even of John Quincy Adams. No one better
deserved the description of 'working member' of the Senate, for
he was as painstaking in committee as he was formidable in
debate. Albeit an intense partisan, inclined to a scornful attitude
toward political opponents, he was uniformly courteous and
accommodating in discussion, keeping a close rein on his temper.

[1] *Jefferson and Hamilton*, 326–31.

'There is no quality more useful and important than good humor,' wrote the sour Adams, 'and this quality Tracy possessed in a high degree.' [1] He was a consummate politician and an expert in his estimate of men, as illustrated by the fact that he confided the secession plan to Plumer, while withholding it from Adams. His party leaders throughout the country held him in affectionate esteem. 'How is Tracy's health?' Fisher Ames asked a friend. 'Pray give him my affectionate regards. I hope David will not slay him. It is attempted because Tracy is a Goliath.' [2] This mingled admiration and affection extended to the social qualities of this great leader. At the mess, about the fireplace at the boarding-house, and at the dinner-table everywhere, Tracy scintillated, according to his contemporaries. That he kept a congenial company in an uproar of merriment we are assured by those who took part in the scene. His barbs usually were aimed at Jefferson and the Democrats. He was as honest as he was able, and to those to whom he gave his friendship, he was as lovable as he was admirable.

He despised democracy, and in 1803 in an address to the people of Connecticut, which was pounced upon by the *New Hampshire Gazette*,[3] he set forth the view that democracy had no place in the American form of government. The people could frame a constitution and elect officers, but there their sovereignty ended. They had no right to interfere with the government thus formed. 'In a democracy,' he said, 'the people control the government, and instead of enjoying any true national liberty, they have only the liberty of making themselves pre-eminently miserable; and therefore it is that democracies have ever moved, and ever must move, with an awfully rapid stride to despotism.' [4]

About that time the *American Mercury* published a letter signed by John Allen, Aaron Smith, and James Gould which created a momentary sensation:

'In the month of November, 1799, Mr. Tracy in his own house, and in conversation with his neighbor, General Skinner, and in the presence of his friend, John Allen [one of the signers], expressed himself in substance as follows: "Our Constitution is good for

[1] Adams, *Diary*, I, 377.   [2] *Ames*, I, 336–37.
[3] Quoted in *Independent Chronicle*, November 3, 1803.   [4] *Ibid.*

nothing, it cannot stand and I have told you this before, but I am
a Senator and have sworn to support it. I shall do all I can toward
it, but it cannot be done. The President and Senators must be
hereditary.... It is quite enough for the common people to be
allowed to choose their representatives.'' [1]

Another present on the occasion, Dan Huntington, wrote that
Tracy had expressed approval of the Constitution, but had observed that 'a monarchy would be the consequence of the state of
things which the madness of democracy was fastening upon us.' [2]
The reference to the effect of democracy, it will be noted, was not
out of line with the speech quoted and unquestionably delivered.
Tracy's views were the views of the Essex Junto.

Intimately associated with him in the secession movement was
Senator James Hillhouse, quite a different character. Many
found, both in his manner and his appearance, a striking resemblance to an Indian, and some suspected he had the red man's
blood in his veins. One of his colleagues, whom he had attacked,
protested to the Senate that he 'would not repine at being stricken
down by the thunderbolts of Jove,' [3] but that he would 'not
submit to being mangled by the tomahawk of this son of Alno-
max.' [4] His dark complexion, his immobile features, his erect
carriage, and his alert walk contributed to that impression. He
was about the age of Tracy at this time. He carried himself with
the dignity and solemnity that came from his deep sincerity. He
emitted no sparks. Though a man of strong mentality, he was
without brilliancy. Educated at Yale, he had begun the practice
of law, but had abandoned it for the more lucrative business of
real estate. He was a very practical man. At a much later period,
Justice Story was to find him 'a very fine venerable man, full of
sound sense and plain heartedness' and 'worthy of his seat.' [5]
He had demonstrated his great physical courage at the head of his
company during the Revolution, and had marched with the
utmost serenity to repel the advance of the British on New Haven.
He was an intense Federalist, though he thought so little of the
Constitution, as it came from the Convention, that he was to
propose amendments that would completely have changed the

[1] Quoted in *Connecticut Courant*, December 21, 1803.   [2] *Ibid.*
[3] Morris.   [4] *Plumer*, 257.   [5] *Story*, 158.

character of the government. His speeches, while laboriously wrought, were compounded of common sense.

But the most militant and outspoken of the conspirators, with the possible exception of Pickering, was Roger Griswold, of Connecticut, who at this time was the acknowledged leader and spokesman of the Federalists in the House. More than any other politician in Connecticut, he resembled the members of the Essex Junto in his offensive attitude toward political foes. He had distinguished himself at the bar when he entered public life; and unlike most of the political leaders of his time, he had begun his career in the national House of Representatives, to which he had been elected in his thirty-second year. In the House, almost immediately, he was accorded the highest standing by his party associates. His deliberately insulting manner had embroiled him in the disgraceful brawl with Matthew Lyon on the floor of the House. In debate he was able, incisive, keenly analytic, and at times eloquent, though he was more debater than orator. No one could be more arrogantly dogmatic or more offensively intolerant. His political views were those of the extreme Federalists, bitterly hostile to democracy. He did not confine his attacks on Jefferson to the open and on the floor, but was prone to busy himself in the circulation of whispered gossiping about the mess-table and in the cloak-rooms. It was he, more than any other, who sought to sow dissension among Jefferson's associates in the Cabinet, solemnly assuring Quincy that Jefferson utterly ignored his ministers, and that Madison had cooled toward his chief.[1]

These were the leaders in the conspiracy to destroy the Union, but about them they drew lesser lights, particularly from Connecticut, and including Plumer of New Hampshire, who, a quarter of a century later, was to establish the reality of the conspiracy and to expose the dishonesty of the denials of the surviving conspirators.

III

When, early in the winter of 1803–04, John Quincy Adams was in New York, he heard that the wide circulation of Tracy's speech against the constitutional amendment on the election of President

[1] *Quincy*, 74.

was a preliminary step toward arousing the legislatures in New
England against the Union. This he found verified on reaching
Washington. The conspirators, eager to get copies of the speech
into the hands of members of the various legislatures, agreed
among themselves to send no personal letters or newspapers so
as not to crowd the mails. One member wrote later that 'the part
I have played has fully occupied my time, having had more than
forty letters to write of considerable length.' The purpose, he
added, was 'to furnish the members of the several legislatures,
especially in New England, with one of the speeches previous to
their meeting.' [1] But the activities of the disunionists were not
thus confined. At the messes where these men ate, about the
fireplaces of the boarding-houses where they lived, and on long
walks over the muddy streets of the capital, secession was the
common topic of conversation.

In their plans, England was to play a part. They had not
scrupled to approach Merry, the British Minister, with a proposal
that Britain reject the Boundary Treaty on the ground, plainly
expressed, that this 'would prove to be a great exciting cause to
then go forward rapidly in the steps they have already commenced
toward a separation from the southern part of the Union,' and
'since they naturally look forward to Great Britain for support
and assistance whenever the occasion shall arrive.' [2]

But England was not the sole ally on which they counted. From
the beginning they had in mind the inclusion of Aaron Burr in their
plans. This Mephistophelian politician, financially ruined, politically destroyed, was open to suggestions. Never had he been
gayer; never had he entertained so frequently or lavishly at
dinners, and never had he surrounded himself more calculatingly
with members of the Federalist Party. 'The Vice-President is
giving very pretty dinners,' wrote Senator Mitchill of New York.
'On Sunday I dined with him and Mr. Armstrong, who is villain-
ously maligned in the pamphlet' put out by one of Burr's friends.[3]

It was at one of these 'pretty dinners' that Timothy Pickering,
James Hillhouse, and Plumer sat down one afternoon. The con-
versation was directed to the necessity of secession by Hillhouse.
He was sure the Union would soon be split into two nations. Burr

[1] Cutler, II, 150–51.   [2] Merry to Hawkesbury.   [3] Mitchill's Letters

seemed in complete accord with the prevailing note of the evening. He 'conversed very freely' and left Plumer with the impression 'that he not only thought such an event would take place, but that it was necessary that it should.' And yet, free from the magnetic influence of that remarkable man, one of the party, on returning to his lodgings and going over in his mind the words of Burr, was shocked to find that there was nothing that 'necessarily implied his approbation of Mr. Hillhouse's observations.' It was the conspirator's first discovery of Burr's rare cunning. 'Perhaps no man's language was ever so apparently explicit, and at the same time so covert and indefinite,' wrote the confused conspirator.[1] Picking their way home over the crude sidewalks that night, Hillhouse continued to discuss the theme with emphasis, for Plumer was a recent convert. 'The Eastern States must and will dissolve the Union,' he said with animation, 'and form a separate government of their own; and the sooner they do this, the better.'[2]

Only a little before this Plumer had been shocked at the idea. Pickering had walked with him for two hours about the northern and eastern boundaries of Washington, and by his manner made such an impression on Plumer that he was never to forget it. Pickering had seemed embarrassed and uncertain. Finally he had said the United States was too large and the interests of the States too varied for the Union to continue long, and that New England, New York, and possibly Pennsylvania, 'might and ought to form a separate government.' Having let his secret out, he paused and faced Plumer for his answer. The latter merely asked if disunion was not the one thing that Washington feared mostly. 'Yes,' Pickering replied, none too reverently; 'the fear of it was the ghost that for a long time haunted the imagination of the old gentleman.' But he discontinued the conversation and never again mentioned the matter to Plumer, who nevertheless was soon embroiled.[3]

However, the fears that 'haunted the old gentleman' sleeping at Mount Vernon did not give pause to Pickering. He was beginning his letter-writing campaign among his friends in Massachusetts, and soon after Christmas in 1803, Stephen Higginson,

---

[1] *Plumer,* 294–95.   [2] *Ibid.,* 298–99.   [3] *Ibid.*

in Boston, was reading a letter from the man from Salem. 'Although the end of all our Revolutionary labors and expectations is disappointed,' he read, 'I rather anticipate a new confederacy exempt from the corrupt and corrupting influence and oppression of the aristocratic Democrats of the South. . . . There will be a separation. . . . The British provinces, even with the assent of Britain, will become members of the Northern Confederacy.' [1] At the same sitting Pickering wrote similarly to Richard Peters with scarcely a deviation; but he added that 'a continued tyranny of the present ruling sect will precipitate the event.' [2]

IV

At the time these letters were written, the plan for the secession had been agreed upon. Its weirdest feature was its contemplation of the employment of both Hamilton and Burr in bringing the separation about. The New England States would lead, New York following under the leadership of Burr, in the event of his election as Governor. New Jersey, it was hoped, would trail New York, and possibly eastern Pennsylvania would follow. The conspirators thought this could be brought about without bloodshed; but if a resort to arms were necessary, it was hoped that Hamilton would agree to become the commander-in-chief! The Northern Democrats, tired of the domination of Virginia, would offer no resistance.[3] Tracy and Griswold proposed that the seceding States merely should recall their senators and representatives from Washington, and refuse to recognize the central authority.[4] To assure the participation of New York, it might be necessary to put Burr at the head of the Northern Confederacy, since, in the event of his election as Governor, he would be in a position of power. This would prove embarrassing, because Hamilton refused to share the Federalists' partiality for Burr. But 'if Colonel Burr is elevated in New York, by the voice of federalism, will he not be considered, and must he not in fact, become the head of the Northern Interests?' asked Griswold of Oliver Wolcott. 'His ambition will not suffer him to be second

---

[1] *Cabot*, 422–23.

[2] Henry Adams, *Documents Relating to New England Federalism*, 338. (Hereafter cited as *Doc. N.E. Fed.*)

[3] *King's Corr.*, IV, 357; conversation with Oliver Wolcott.   [4] *Plumer*, 295–96.

and his office will give him a claim to the first rank.' Of course the consent of 'gentlemen in New York' (Hamilton and King) must be secured to the alliance with Burr; and Burr's views on entering into the scheme must first be ascertained. Nothing could be worse than for the Federalists to raise Burr to gubernatorial honors solely that he might use that elevation as a leaping-stone to the Presidency of the existing Union. The disunionists wanted nothing like that. It was a new Confederacy, born of the wreckage of the old Union, that they wished, and nothing less. 'The project which we had formed,' concluded Griswold, 'was to induce, if possible, the legislatures of the three New England States who remain Federalist, to commence measures which shall call for the reunion of the Northern States.' [1]

With Massachusetts, Connecticut, and New Hampshire trailing out of the Union, the other New England States naturally would follow, and with New York in the combination, New Jersey, and possibly eastern Pennsylvania, would join. Such was the secession plan conceived by Pickering, Tracy, Griswold, Hillhouse, and lesser figures as they talked matters over in their boarding-houses during the winter of 1803-04.

v

But this called for speedy action. The Jeffersonians were making gains, even in New England. Procrastination or timidity would be fatal. And so each of the leaders that winter bent over his desk at his boarding-house writing disunion letters to his friends, seeking their co-operation, and urging them to canvass public opinion in their neighborhoods. It was vitally important that Massachusetts should take Bunker Hill and the Old South Church out of the Union, and it fell largely to Pickering to win over the active support of the Essex Junto and their friends throughout the State.

One day in January, 1804, George Cabot, the soundest of the Essex Junto, sat in his library reading a letter from Pickering. It sounded the usual Federalist minor key in the beginning. Life was going on as before, but who was happy? Certainly not the Federalists. And why not? 'Because they see the public morals

[1] *Doc. N.E. Fed.*, 334.

debased by the corrupt and corrupting system of their rulers.'
Under the hypnotism of Jefferson, were not even Federalists
turning to the vile theories of democracy, and even becoming
apostates to the church? Should the noble band of patriotic
Federalists in the Northern States sit twirling their thumbs until
the principles of genuine Federalism should be overwhelmed?
No! Cabot read, it was not necessary, for the 'principles of the
Revolution point to the remedy — a separation.' And this could
be accomplished 'without the shedding of a single drop of blood.'
A combination of the people of the East with those of the crude
West and the corrupt South would ever remain an incongruity.
And the latter even now were beginning 'to rule with an iron
rod.' Had not some people of Connecticut assured the writer that
should the Democrats in their State get the upper hand 'they
should not think themselves safe, either in person or property'?
But 'a Northern Confederacy would unite congenial characters,
and present a fairer prospect of public happiness.'

But how could the secession be brought about? No time should
be lost. A secession proposition would be 'welcome in Connecticut
and New Hampshire.' New York was essential to the scheme;
how bring her in? 'She must be made the center of the Confederacy.' The legislatures of Massachusetts and Connecticut
and New Hampshire would meet in May; let them act. And who
could doubt but that in time, and probably without delay, the
British provinces of Canada would join the Confederacy, even
with the consent of the British? 'Certainly that Government can
feel only disgust with our present rulers and be pleased to see
them crestfallen.' Energetic men were at work on the plan, and
Tracy had written to 'several of his most distinguished friends in
Connecticut.' [1]

Soon the Federalists of Boston were in a huddle over the astonishing invitation to revolution, poring over each other's letters
from the fast-flying pen of Pickering. Cabot was not displeased
with the thought, but doubted the feasibility of the movement
without some 'crisis in events.' And so, a little later, the conspirators in the Washington boarding-houses were in a huddle
reading his opinions. 'It is not practical without the intervention

[1] *Cabot*, 337–41.

of some cause which should be very genuinely felt and distinctly understood,' he wrote, something directly chargeable to 'our Southern masters.' Such 'for example as a war with Great Britain, manifestly provoked by our rulers.' [1]

One day Fisher Ames dragged his enfeebled body from Dedham to Cabot's library, where, before the blazing hearth, he was handed the Pickering letter. The dying genius flamed as he read. Cabot described the scene for the benefit of the conspirators in Washington. Ames 'read with pleasure' and 'a mingled emotion of anger which it was impossible wholly to repress.' But his feelings were similar to those of all the other Federalists in Boston who had been permitted to read the Pickering letter. Parsons and Higginson had been sympathetic to the idea of disunion, 'but on second thought all of us' held the opinion 'you would collect from the desultory letter I wrote as mine.' [2]

But the impressionistic Pickering was not discouraged, and he wrote on and on to his Massachusetts associates. Theodore Lyman too had heard the disunionist call to arms. 'And must we submit to these evils?' he had read. 'Is there not yet remaining in New England virtue and spirit enough to resist the torrent?' The 'most intelligent of the Federalists in Washington had been reflecting upon the subject with deepest concern.' They all agreed that Massachusetts should lead the procession out of the Union. All New England would follow. New York could be won by making her the center of the Confederacy, and New Jersey would trail behind. Even Pennsylvania 'at least to the Susquehannah might be induced.' And those British provinces of Canada — what more natural than for them to enter too with the parting blessing of London? [3]

At length Stephen Higginson sought to moderate the zeal of the conspirators. He had seen the letters to Cabot and Lyman. 'We all agree,' he wrote, 'there can be no doubt of its being desirable; but of the expediency of attempting it, or discussing it at this moment, we very much doubt.' The difficulty was that it was 'impossible to alarm, much less convince, a large portion of the Federal party here of their danger.' Alas, only 'a small part of those called Federal' were 'sound in their opinions' and looked the

<hr>

[1] *Cabot*, 348.   [2] *Doc. N.E. Fed.*, 353.   [3] *Ibid.*, 343.

real situation in the face.[1] And then Lyman sent a discouraging report to the boarding-house headquarters of the disunionists. There were so few of his acquaintances to whom he dared mention the proposition. Perhaps more of these than he knew favored disunion and remained silent because of the 'impression that they are more singular in their opinion than they really are.' But patience and opportunity were required.[2]

Unabashed, unimpressed, the plodding Pickering, replying to Lyman, admitted that Cabot, Parsons, Higginson, and Ames all thought the project not bad, but premature. But the idea was 'extending in Connecticut' and was beginning 'to be entertained' in New York. The character of the Clintonians in New York, and Chancellor Lansing's refusal to run for Governor, would 'vastly aid Burr's pretensions,' and the conspirators at headquarters were convinced by intelligence received that Burr would be elected. And then, wrote the jubilant Pickering, 'this will break the democratic phalanx of that State and prepare the way for the contemplated event.'[3]

The best Pickering had been able to get from Massachusetts was an agreement on the desirability of disunion, with the warning that the time was not ripe. That Cabot's sole objection was to the practicability of the plan shines out in his letter to Rufus King informing him of the movement. 'The thing proposed is obvious and natural, but it would now be thought too bold and would be fatal to the advocates as public men,' he wrote. 'And yet the time may come when it will be demanded by the people of the North and East and then it will unavoidably take place.' But he added a sentence he had not included in his letter to Pickering: 'I am not satisfied that the thing itself is to be desired.'[4]

VI

Meanwhile, the other conspirators were busy writing their associates in their States. 'Tracy has written to several of the most distinguished friends in Connecticut and may soon receive the answers,' Pickering had written Cabot. Nine days later Tracy had received at least one reply from a distinguished friend, Judge

[1] *Doc. N.E. Fed.*, 361.   [2] *Cabot*, 446.   [3] *Ibid.*, 450.
[4] *King's Corr.*, IV, 354.

Tapping Reeve, which was not so reassuring. In compliance with Tracy's request he had been cautiously canvassing his acquaintances, seeing many and hearing from some by mail. All agreed 'that we must separate, and that this is the most favorable moment.' Three had disclosed timidity or alarm over the prospect of such a decisive step. But 'a settled determination that this must be done has taken fast hold of some minds where you would expect more timidity.' The general opinion was that both the legislatures and the disunionists in Washington should act. The latter should 'come out with a bold address to [their] constituents, taking a view of what has been done under the present Administration, with glowing comments on the ruinous tendencies of the measures,' since 'this would produce all the preparedness that is wanted.' Nothing could do more 'to give the death wound to the progress of Democracy in this part of the country.'

But Tracy's distinguished friend was a bit puzzled as to the 'manner this separation is to be accomplished' unless 'the amendment is adopted by three fourths of the legislatures and rejected by Massachusetts, New Hampshire and Connecticut,' and possibly Delaware. In that event a foundation would be laid.[1]

In the meanwhile Senator Plumer was finally persuaded that 'separation was necessary for the security and prosperity of the Eastern States.' Of the missionaries of secession there was none with whom he conferred 'so often, so fully and freely as with Roger Griswold'; and next to him, with Tracy. His wavering ceased only when Tracy informed him that Alexander Hamilton had agreed to attend a conference of the secessionists in Boston in the autumn.[2] The impression conveyed, intentional or not, was that this conference was 'to recommend the measures necessary to form a system of government for the Northern States' and that Hamilton was to participate in framing the system.[3] Thoroughly convinced now, Plumer agreed to write confidential letters to friends in New Hampshire soliciting their co-operation in the scheme.

Thus, on his return to New Hampshire, he made a more intensive canvass among leading Federalists and 'found some in favor of the measure, but a great majority of them decidedly opposed

---

[1] *Doc. N.E. Fed.*, 342.   [2] *Plumer*, 298–300.   [3] *Ibid.*, 289–92.

to the project.' From various sources he had learned that the sentiment in Massachusetts was quite similar.[1] This disturbed Plumer without drawing him away, and he wrote his friends in vigorous advocacy of the plan. 'What do you wish your Senators and Representatives to do here?' he wrote from Washington. 'We have no part in Jefferson and no inheritance in Virginia. Shall we return to our homes, sit under our own vine and fig tree, and be separate from slaveholders? What is your opinion?' [2] To his predecessor in the Senate he wrote in similar vein. 'Will the Western States think of separation? What is your opinion?' [3]

The virus of disunion by this time had permeated his thinking, and soon he was writing in a belligerent tone: 'I feel no affection for the general government. It is Virginia all over; and you may depend upon it, this sentiment daily gains ground in New Hampshire. We feel that we are Virginia's slave now, and that we are to be delivered over to Kentucky and other Western States when our Virginia masters are tired of us.' [4] But, generally, Plumer was disappointed in the replies to his appeals. Some agreed in principle but had no stomach for the act. Now and then he found one as bent on secession as himself. 'I cannot but hope,' wrote the Reverend Jedediah Mason, a clergyman-politician, 'that New Hampshire, Massachusetts and Connecticut will outride the storm that threatens the ruin of the country. If we were peaceably severed from the rest of the United States, with perhaps some other States joined with us, I think we should do much better.' [5]

Discouraging as was the mere approval of the idea without adherence to the plan, the conspirators pressed on in the desperate hope that something could be expected from New York with the aid of Aaron Burr, who was looming larger and larger in their plans.

VII

The strategy of the conspirators in New York was to secure, if possible, the co-operation of Hamilton and Rufus King — along with that of Aaron Burr! The latter, with his customary cunning, had been very wary in his Washington discussions with the conspirators. Just before leaving Washington, Griswold made an

---

[1] *Plumer*, 289–92.   [2] To Oliver Peabody, *ibid.*, 285–86.
[3] To James Sheafe, *ibid.*, 286–87.   [4] *Ibid.*, 288.   [5] *Ibid.*, 288–89.

effort to pin him down to a bargain — the Federalist support for Governor in return for a pledge of assistance to the disunion movement later. He was received with the suavity which was Burr's second nature, and a mysterious manner which raised hopes by pantomime. Burr knew he could not count on Jefferson, for even then he had been refused a federal appointment he had solicited. Just a few days before the Griswold approach, he had sent some of his friends to Jefferson to inquire if he considered Burr a Democrat, and if he would oppose Democratic support to Burr's gubernatorial ambition. The cautious philosopher had given an affirmative answer to the first question, and to the second had answered that in the case of divisions individual members of the party should vote as they pleased. Another emissary (General John Smith) was sent in the hope of a more satisfactory reply. It was even less promising — that if the Federalists supported Burr, the Democrats must vote against him.[1]

Thus when Griswold sought his interview with Burr the latter was in no position to be definite. Assuming a mysterious manner, he replied that he wished 'very much to see and converse' with Griswold, 'but that his situation in this place [Washington] did not admit of it,' though he would be delighted to see him in New York. Under the circumstances, Griswold could 'not see how he could avoid a full explanation with Federal men,' since 'his prospects depend on the union of the Federalists with his friends.' At any rate he would see him in New York.[2] However, would it not be within the power of friends in New York 'to ascertain his views in the meantime'?

Early in April, Griswold, in New York, met Burr quietly and afterwards called on Rufus King and told him of the conversation. Again he found his man warily shy. He would have to go on in the rôle of a Democrat seeking the nomination, but if nominated and elected he could be counted upon 'to administer the Government in a manner that would be satisfactory to the Federalists in respect to the affairs OF THE NATION.' More to the satisfaction of Griswold was Burr's statement that 'the Northern States must be governed by Virginia or must govern Virginia, and there was no middle ground.' Griswold explained that the Federalists to the

[1] *King's Corr.*, IV, 357.   [2] *Doc. N.E. Fed.*, 354; Griswold to Wolcott.

eastward would be anxious to understand the policy in New York, 'that they might be active or passive according to the opinion they should form on that point.'

When Griswold left the King library, King carefully made a memorandum of the conversation with the comment: 'I could not learn that Griswold engaged anything on his side.' [1]

Within three days there was another historic conversation in the King library. John Quincy Adams, who had the instinct of a reporter, stopped in New York and called during the afternoon on Burr. Adams knew nothing and suspected nothing of the flirtation of the disunionists with Burr, and the conversation was confined largely to Burr's prospects in the elections. At that moment Burr thought if the elections could be held within a fortnight he would 'probably succeed.' Nothing could have persuaded him to be a candidate but 'the absolute necessity of interposing to save the country from ruin by these family combinations' — the Livingstons and Clintons.[2]

That evening Adams found his way to the library of King. There he found Timothy Pickering. The saturnine Pickering and the dour Adams, at swords' points over Louisiana, were not a congenial combination, and the former took his leave soon after the latter appeared. The moment the door closed on Pickering, King turned to Adams. 'Colonel Pickering,' he said, 'has been talking to me about a project for the separation of the States and a Northern Confederacy; and he has also been this day talking of it to General Hamilton. Have you heard anything about it in Washington?' Adams replied that he had heard much, though not from Pickering. Then King continued:

'Well, I disapprove entirely of the project; and so, I am happy to tell you, does General Hamilton.'

Adams expressed his pleasure over the attitude of King and Hamilton, and expressed no little concern over the countenance it had received in Boston and Connecticut. He was sure the incentive was the Louisiana Purchase.[3]

Thus the name of Hamilton as a probable head of the military forces in a civil war had been used without his knowledge or consent. He had agreed to attend the conference in Boston in the

---

[1] *King's Corr.*, iv, 357. [2] Adams, *Diary*, i, 313. [3] *Doc. N.E. Fed.*

autumn with the clear intent to combat secession, and had immediately discussed the danger with King. That the proposed alliance of the Federalists with Burr in the campaign was mentioned by the crafty Pickering is not at all probable.

VIII

Whatever the views of Hamilton or King, the fact remains that Burr entered upon his gubernatorial adventure with the support of the major part of the Federalists and with the prayers of the disunionists. For the second time, the impotency of Hamilton in preventing a stampede of the Federalists to Burr was to be tragically disclosed. Jefferson's influence with his party was more effective, for Burr failed to secure the regular Democratic nomination, which went to Morgan Lewis. Burr became an independent candidate, hoping with his personal following and the Federalists' support to win. There was more than mere arrogance in his confidence. He did not underestimate his genius in organization and in intrigue. He knew that Hamilton would exert himself, but in the cunning of manipulation in city politics he knew his enemy was not his match.

In rooms on John Street he opened headquarters, and there the brilliant spider sat weaving his web. As early as February he was telling his idolized daughter that 'Hamilton is intriguing for any candidate who will have a chance of success against A. B. . . . He would doubtless become the advocate even of DeWitt Clinton if he should be the opponent.'[1] Three years before, in a letter to John Rutledge, Hamilton had poured forth his real estimate of Burr. 'In every sense a profligate; a voluptuary in the extreme, with uncommon habits of expense,' he wrote. 'His friends do not insist on his integrity . . . without doubt insolvent.' In office he would be quite capable of a 'bargain and sale with some foreign power.' A dangerous man 'of a temper bold enough to think no enterprise too hazardous, and sanguine enough to think none too difficult,' with 'irregular and inordinate ambition.' A cunning man like Catiline 'indefatigable in courting the young and profligate,' knowing the weak side of human nature. In natural disposition 'the haughtiest of men, he is at the same time the

[1] *Burr*, ii, 277.

most creeping to answer his purpose ... artful and intriguing to an inconceivable degree.' And his ambition? 'He has in view nothing less than the establishment of Supreme Power in his own person.' [1]

In February Burr mustered his friends in Albany who, 'unanimously determined to support the candidacy of Aaron Burr' and the 'Genuine Republicans,' unanimously nominated Morgan Lewis.[2] The next day mysterious reports were spread that Hamilton was actively favoring the Burr candidacy, and his organ entered a denial. 'This is not true,' said the *Evening Post*. 'It may be true that no active opposition will now be made to him since Mr. Lewis is a candidate.' [3] Five days before Burr's nomination, Hamilton had appeared before a meeting of leading Federalists in Albany to renew his attempt of 1801 to turn his party from its disposition to support this 'Catiline.' He rose with a paper in his hand — one carefully prepared — and read, beginning with the reminder that Burr never had affiliated in support of Federalist principles. 'He will certainly not at this time relinquish the ladder of his ambition and espouse the cause and views of the weaker party.' Should the Federalists support him, his election would give the Democrats a 'more adroit, able and daring' leadership; and while 'virtuous Federalists' who, from miscalculation, may support him, would afterward relinquish his standard, a large number, from various motives, would continue attached to it. In New England this would be particularly unfortunate. The grandson of President Edwards of Yale and the son of President Burr would have a certain natural prestige in that section, and this would make it easier for him 'to disorganize New England if so disposed.'

And then, his conversation with Pickering in mind, Hamilton aimed openly at the disunion movement with special emphasis:

'The ill opinion of Jefferson and the jealousy of the ambition of Virginia is no inconsiderable prop of good principles in that country. BUT THESE CAUSES ARE LEADING TO AN OPINION THAT A DISMEMBERMENT OF THE UNION IS EXPEDIENT. It would probably suit Mr. Burr's view to promise this result; to be chief of the

[1] *Intimate Life*, 367-68.   [2] *Evening Post*, February 28, 1804.
[3] *Ibid.*, February 29, 1804.

Northern portion; and placed at the head of the State of New York, no man would be more likely to succeed.' [1]

Hamilton thus went forth in shining armor to combat the pet scheme of the disunionists of his own party.

Even so, the local politicians of the Federalist persuasion continued to find their way to the room on John Street. There they found the wily politician gay and confident. Even the attacks upon him left him smiling, cynical, and he promised Theodosia to send her 'some new and amusing libels against the Vice-President.' [2]

Not least among the mysterious features of the campaign was the ardor with which Coleman, of Hamilton's organ, rushed to the defense of Burr. Charges had been made that in the settlement of the Behrens estate he had acted in a 'corrupt and indefensible manner,' and Hamilton's organ denounced the charge as 'a villainous attempt to destroy Mr. Burr by the barren calumny.' [3] Two days later, the *Evening Post* was warming to his defense. 'There never was a time when it was more necessary for the people to keep in mind this equitable maxim — hear both sides — than at this juncture.' [4] Not once did the *Evening Post* publish an attack on Burr; it was opposing Lewis.

But Hamilton was temperamentally incapable of viewing the situation with such sweet reasonableness. He was busy with his pen, and outspoken on the perfidy of Burr among those he thought his friends. It was just before the election that he and Chancellor Kent spent a Sunday meandering aimlessly over the hills of Harlem. Kent found him 'much mortified by the conduct of the Federalists,' a 'gloomy imagination' conjuring up dire pictures of coming events.[5] It was at about this time that Hamilton invited both Kent and Gouverneur Morris to have dinner and spend the night in the country at the Grange. It was an evening of dreadful storm, the winds blowing almost a hurricane, and the rain falling in torrents. The comfort-loving Morris did not appear, prevented by the 'Jacobin winds.' Never had Kent seen Hamilton in sweeter or sadder mood because 'the impending elections exceedingly disturbed him, and he viewed the temper, disposition and

---

[1] Hamilton, *Works*, vii, 323–26.   [2] *Burr*, ii, 281.
[3] *Evening Post*, April 17, 1804.
[4] *Ibid.*, April 19, 1804.   [5] *Kent*, 132.

passions of the times as portentous of evil, and favorable to the sway of artful and ambitious demagogues.' [1]

Election day found Burr seated in his headquarters in John Street calmly writing an amusing letter to his daughter, while his lieutenants came and went, interrupting him at his pleasant task. 'I am writing in a storm,' he told her, 'an election storm the like of which you have once been a witness. The thing began yesterday and will terminate tomorrow.' [2] Both parties were claiming majorities, but none knew, though Burr was convinced that he would carry the city. In truth, Kent, writing his wife at this time, was certain that Burr had been elected. 'The election is nearly over,' he wrote, 'and the Burrites are sanguine and appear flushed with the laurels of victory,' claiming a decided majority in the city. To bring this about, wrote Kent, 'the Federalists have been generally brought out,' though 'the cold reserve and indignant reproaches of Hamilton may have controlled a few.' In truth, the Federalists had turned their backs on Hamilton to make it a party obligation to vote for Burr. 'Even Judge Benson,' wrote Kent, 'has yielded to the current, and with the generous fidelity of party spirit has declared he will go with his party and has voted for the Burr ticket throughout.' [3] And Kent was but little less disloyal to Hamilton, for with incredible partisan bigotry he refused to vote for Lewis, while confessing to his 'admiration and respect for his character and attainments.' [4] He merely refrained from striking Hamilton in the face; but he refrained as well from going to his rescue in a fight.

Burr, master in city politics, carried the city, only to be overwhelmed by the returns up-State, and he wrote Theodosia that 'the election is lost by a great majority.' [5] Hamilton's protégé of the *Evening Post* was clearly disgusted. 'Democracy it seems is still in the full tide of successful experimentation,' it said; [6] and two days later it sought to explain Burr's defeat. There had been a period, it said, when Burr's election was almost certain. There was a 'sudden change' due to attacks on Burr's private character, to the success of the Jeffersonians in persuading the people that the Burrites were but a 'feeble folk,' and to another reason. 'The

[1] *Kent*, 327–28.   [2] *Burr*, II, 383.   [3] *Kent*, 142–43.
[4] *Ibid.*, 120–21.   [5] *Burr*, II, 285.   [6] May 1, 1804.

state of the roads of the country, made impassable by late heavy rains and the wet weather which prevailed during the three days of election, operated very much against Mr. Burr IN KEEPING MOST FEDERALISTS AT HOME, ON WHOSE VOTES VERY SANGUINE CALCULATIONS HAD BEEN MADE.' [1] Hamilton was deserted even by his protégé and his organ.

Thus the disunionists lost the election that was to pave the way for 'the great event.' Nowhere was Burr's defeat more bitterly lamented than by the Pickerings and the Griswolds, who had again repudiated the wise leadership of Hamilton.

IX

A few days later, Burr was writing his daughter that Jerome Bonaparte and Betsy Patterson, his wife, had been in New York, but had remained at a distance. 'For reasons unknown to me (doubtless some state policy) we are suddenly become strangers.' [2] Inwardly he was embittered, but to the world he presented an unruffled front. Financially he was ruined. His property was hopelessly mortgaged. The beautiful Richmond Hill, where he had entertained so lavishly and lived in such princely style, could not be held for long. A judgment of forty thousand dollars stood against him. He had been cast off by the National Democracy, and that of his own State had refused him a gubernatorial nomination. His alliance with the Federalists had brought him nothing. And as he reviewed the outlook, his bitterness settled more and more on Hamilton, whose attacks upon him had been carried to him by mischief-makers. With cold calculation he determined to call his enemy to account.

The excuse for action was not far to seek. In February, when dining at the home of John Taylor in Albany among guests he thought his friends, Hamilton had not minced words in derogation of the character of Burr. Soon afterward, a member of the company indiscreetly published an account of the conversation at the dinner-table. He wrote that both Hamilton and Kent had pronounced Burr 'a dangerous man' who 'ought not to be entrusted with the reins of government.' The publication of the letter aroused public interest and a controversy in the press.

[1] *New York Evening Post*, May 3, 1804.   [2] *Burr*, II, 287.

Stung by one critic, the author, in a second letter to the press, said
that he 'could detail . . . a still more despicable opinion which Mr.
Hamilton expressed of Mr. Burr.'

It was almost two months after the election when, one June day,
William P. Van Ness, an intimate personal and political associate
of Burr's, entered the law office of Hamilton with a note from his
leader, enclosing the published letters. 'You must perceive, sir,
the necessity of a prompt and unqualified acknowledgement or
denial of the use of any expressions which would warrant the assertions of Dr. Cooper' — author of the letter. Two days later,
Hamilton replied in a fashion that Burr thought evasive. But in
the last sentence was something that almost smacked of bravado:
'I trust on more reflection you will see the matter in the same
light with me; if not, I can only regret the circumstances and must
abide the consequences.' Then followed an exchange of notes in
which Hamilton does not appear at his best, and in the end he
accepted a challenge.

Throughout the preliminary exchanges, Hamilton gave no
outer sign that anything out of the ordinary was pending. In his
home, among his friends, he appeared in a cheerful mood, but he
was haunted by premonitions of a fatal outcome. He and Burr
met one night at a dinner of the Cincinnati, where, in response to a
clamor from friends, Hamilton sang 'The Drum' with spirit. No
one present could have observed in the conduct of either man that
they were approaching the tragic settlement of their quarrel.
Burr was coldly making his preparations, practicing with his
pistol. Ten days before the duel, he sat at Richmond Hill shivering with the cold all through the day, 'though in perfect health.'
At sunset he had ordered a fire made in his library, and he wrote
his daughter that he was 'sitting near it and enjoying it, if that
word is applicable to anything done in solitude.' [1]

The duel was set for the early morning of July 11. The after-
noon and evening before, Hamilton had spent in the home of
Oliver Wolcott with a company of friends, and after the tragedy,
Wolcott recalled that he was 'uncommonly cheerful and gay.' [2]
Mrs. Hamilton and the children were in the country at the Grange,
and Hamilton was staying in his town house at 52 Cedar Street.

[1] *Burr*, ii, 291.   [2] *Intimate Life*, 407.

The fatal morning came. Hamilton and his seconds rowed across the Hudson to the rocky wooded heights of Weehawken, where they found Burr and his party waiting. There was an exchange of salutations. The seconds measured off ten paces. The choice of position and the right to give the signal both fell to Hamilton. The pistols were loaded in the presence of the principals. They took their positions. The word was given, and Hamilton fell, pierced through by the bullet of Burr. Almost instantly the stricken man fell, Burr started toward him with an expression of regret on his face, but his friends intervened and hurried him from the field.

At first, the surgeon thought Hamilton dead, since he gave no sign of life. He was carried through the wood to the bank of the river and was tenderly placed in a boat, which immediately set off. It was only then that the application of spirits of hartshorn to his face, lips, and temples revived him. He was taken to the home of a friend on Greenwich Street, where every possible effort was made to save him, but it was hopeless.

Over the deathbed scene we may well draw the veil — it was heartrending. As the statesman merged into the husband and father, surrounded by his family and friends, Gouverneur Morris, who had hastened to the bedside, found the scene 'too powerful' and was compelled to 'walk in the garden to take breath.' Later he recovered his composure sufficiently to return to the bedside, where he remained until the end.[1]

With the news of Hamilton's death a wave of emotion and resentment swept the town, affecting even the Federalists who had turned their backs upon him two months before to advance the interest of the man who now had killed him.

Burr had hurried back from the dueling ground to shut himself up in his library at Richmond Hill, and there, immediately afterward, a relative from the country, ignorant of the event, found him — calm, serene, suave. It was only after the visitor had gone into the town that he learned of the dismal event.[2] Most of the Federalist papers went into full mourning with their lugubrious black borders and columns, and for many days the *Evening Post*

[1] Morris, *Diary*, II, 455.
[2] James Parton, *The Life and Times of Aaron Burr*, II, 13.

published eulogies on the dead statesman and bitter attacks on
the man to whose defense it had so ardently rushed two months
before.[1] The tenor of its attacks was that Burr had murdered in
cold blood.[2] Gouverneur Morris, chosen to deliver the funeral
oration from the steps of Trinity Church, was not a little worried
over what he should say, and in his diary he wrote a critical estimate which he was not to use. A few days after the delivery of the
oration, Burr, on his travels, heard from a friend that 'the oration
has displeased many Republicans of the first water' and that
'Governor Morgan Lewis speaks of the proceedings openly as disgraceful.' [3] Whatever may have been thought or said in the inner
circles of the Jeffersonians has been lost to history. In the voluminous correspondence of Jefferson the death of Hamilton is merely
mentioned in an enumeration of the distinguished dead of the
year, and Gallatin notes the event without comment. But the
Federalists for the moment revived their idolatry of their greatest
figure, whose views they had ignored for three years. More
memorial services were held in New England than ever had been
held for a native son, and even the conspirators who had planned
for the sake of disunion to place Burr at the head of the Northern
Confederacy over Hamilton mingled their tears with the rest.
When it was reported that the government of Harvard had forbidden students to attend the eulogy on Hamilton, indignation
flamed. It was explained that they had not been invited, but that
they appeared in class wearing badges of mourning.[4] But the
gossip furnished a choice morsel on which to chew for a while.
With Federalists, who for three years had rebuffed the wise counsel of Hamilton, suddenly weeping copiously and wiping their
eyes on the public, it soon became clear that an attempt was being
made to convert Hamilton's death into political advantage.
However, aside from Governor Lewis's observations on 'the disgraceful' proceedings, the only adverse reaction came from the
Independent Chronicle. It began with an editorial protest against
the frankly political character of the eulogies of Morris and Otis[5]
and continued with a series of articles analyzing the political
character and views of the dead statesman.[6] Though the dis-

---

[1] July 18 to August 24.   [2] July 23, 1804.   [3] *Burr*, ii, 329.
[4] *Columbian Centinel*, August 11, 1804.   [5] August 16, 1804.
[6] August 20, 23, 27, 30, 1804.

unionists knew that Hamilton was bitterly hostile to their designs, they posed in public as his special mourners. Five days before his death, talking with Colonel Trumbull, who was leaving for Boston, Hamilton had said with deep feeling: 'You are going to Boston. You will see the principal men there. Tell them from me, as my request, for God's sake to cease these conversations and threatenings about a separation of the Union.' [1] The defeat of Burr, the resulting death of Hamilton, cancelled the Boston conference and momentarily postponed the plan against the Union. From the moment the great genius fell in the sunlight of a tragic July morning, his party, without respectable leadership, without patriotism, became a discredited and disreputable mob of wreckers and obstructionists.

x

And Jefferson? Throughout the whole of the conspiracy he was constantly informed of the proceedings. In the cunning and tireless Granger he had an espionage corps of the first order. Day by day, Granger, who had contact with the disunion camp, reported to the President. Within twenty-four hours after the meeting in King's library, Jefferson knew. He saw the rise of the conspiracy, he followed its course in secrecy, he knew when it received its death-blow. At no time was he gravely concerned. 'It will be found in this, as in all similar cases,' he wrote in the midst of the conspiracy, 'that crooked schemes will end by overwhelming their authors and coadjutors in disgrace.'

With the collapse, he kept his knowledge locked up in his own mind. The conspirators never knew he knew.

But soon the conspirators and the Federalists generally will be found rallying to the fervent and almost indecent defense of Burr, caught in another conspiracy which would have accomplished the results they sought. Meanwhile, the people will pass on Jefferson.

[1] *King's Corr.*, iv, 330.

CHAPTER XII

The People Pass on Jefferson

I

THE State election in New York with its tragic aftermath gave fair warning to the Federalists of what was ahead in the presidential contest. The battle had begun, when, early in the previous congressional session, the Twelfth Amendment to the Constitution was passed on to the States for ratification. The Republic had narrowly escaped wreckage in 1800 under the old system in which electors voted for two men without indicating which was intended for the Presidency. The better the party discipline, the more probable a recurrence of the tie of 1801. No honest man had doubted the intent of the electors to name Jefferson for the Presidency and Burr for the second place, but their equal vote threw the contest into the House, where the Presidency became the pawn of one of the dirtiest games of politics ever played. It was evident to all who respected the nation's institutions that the method of electing Presidents would have to be changed. The amendment offered provided for the clear designation of the man voted for, for both offices. The electors of each State would vote, and should there be a tie, involving the opposing presidential nominees, the contest would be shifted to the House, where each State, regardless of population, would have one vote.

Instantly, the Federalists were touched in their tender spot again — their simulated devotion to the Constitution. True, the Constitution provided for amendments; true, the old system had demonstrated its weakness; but, said these sophists, splitting hairs, the Constitution had been made by the States and not by the people, and it was the clear intent of the founders that each State should have a vote equal to that of any other. Under the old system this was possible; under the amendment, a State with hundreds of thousands of people would have a greater power than a State with a population one tenth as great. And that was bad! It was a sinister assault on the Constitution! Would these Jeffersonians never cease their nibbling at the sacred fundamental law? Would no one stand up and battle for State rights — the right of Rhode Island to as much voice in the choosing of a President as New York? 'We will!' shouted the Federalist patriots in thunderous tones.

And so the debate dragged through, with Senator Tracy voicing the views of the Federalists in a carefully prepared speech. It was intended for distribution among the members of the various legislatures, as we have seen, to prevent ratification. The patriots contributed in accordance with their means to pay the cost of publication and distribution. In the drab cold rooms of the boarding-houses where they lived, these Federalists were bending over tables addressing envelopes, and enclosing Tracy's speech with a long letter urging the defeat of ratification. They pinned their faith on Tracy as their Goliath, and Fisher Ames was immensely pleased to find the speech copied in the party press. 'It will have an effect on the New England legislatures,' he wrote confidently to Dwight.[1] The *Connecticut Courant* pronounced the speech one of the greatest made 'since the formation of the government,' and solemnly declared that the purpose of the amendment was to perpetuate the power of Jefferson and the Virginians. Would it not make it possible for 'two or three large States to share among themselves the few highest offices of its government?'[2] The *Columbian Centinel* could not restrain its wrath. The Jeffersonians 'fear the election of Mr. Burr to the Presidency, or of any of the Federal candidates as Vice-President,' it said. 'They cannot prevent one or the other of these events from taking place if the Constitution remains as it is; and therefore, under the old pretense of amending it, they are determined, if they have the power, to injure it in one of its wisest provisions.'[3] But Massachusetts would stand against it like Horatius at the bridge. 'And when the freemen and slaves of the Southern States shall destroy individual sovereignty; when the taskmasters of

[1] *Ames*, I, 336.   [2] February 22, 1804.   [3] October 15, 1803.

plantations and their wretched negroes shall give laws to our
country and for a while tyrannize until they force a separation;
at this dark hour, which will sink us into contempt with the world
... Massachusetts ... may boldly say, "I am innocent."" [1]

II

But in an office in Cedar Street, New York, had sat a man
pondering the speech and project with a frown. Alexander
Hamilton had found himself at cross-purposes with his party.
They were politicians; he a statesman. They were sectionalist;
he a nationalist. He had written Gouverneur Morris in favor of
such an amendment. 'After mature reflection,' he wrote, 'I am
firmly confirmed in my full impression that it is a true Federalist
policy to promote the adoption of these amendments, because it is
right, and that the people should know whom they are choosing,
and because the present mode gives all possible scope to intrigue
and is dangerous, as we have seen, to the public tranquillity.' [2]
Too clever by far to be deceived by the sudden ardor of his associates for State rights, Hamilton had no doubt that Burr
entered again into their calculations. Never had he forgotten
that bitter hour, when, casting him aside, the Federalists had
moved heaven and earth to elevate Burr to the Presidency. And
now he thought to prevent an impulse in the same direction.
'Colonel Burr without doubt will resist these amendments,' he
wrote Morris later, 'and he may induce some of our friends to
play into his hands.' Of course the idea of Burr's elevation on
the shoulders of Hamilton's party would be inconceivably
appalling, and 'the worst kind of political suicide.' [3]

But Hamilton no longer was the idolized leader of his party.
Lip service they paid him at a distance, but they were found more
frequently cheek by jowl with Burr. With Hamilton's views well
known, again they had turned their backs upon him and fought
the amendment in both Houses to the last ditch. They fought and
fell, and the fight continued in the legislatures, but the States
responded with rare speed, and by September the amendment
was the law. The shameful huckstering of the last election could
not be repeated.

[1] *Columbian Centinel*, February 8, 1804.
[2] *Works of Hamilton*, VIII, 592–93.   [3] *Ibid.*, VIII, 594–96.

III

Jefferson had not been keen for re-election. He was growing old, and controversy disgusted the philosopher who was happier in an atmosphere of friendship and serenity. Excruciating headaches frequently prostrated him, and he looked from the windows of the mansion to the drab landscape of the Potomac and thought how much sweeter was his hilltop home with woods and fields and orchards spread out for miles about. He longed for Monticello. But more compelling on him than the demand of his party were the bitterness and malevolence of the Federalist attacks which would have made retirement seem like defeat. By early spring he had determined to put his popularity to the test. 'I sincerely regret,' he wrote Elbridge Gerry, 'that the unbounded calumnies of the Federal party have obliged me to throw myself on the verdict of my country for trial, my great desire having been to retire at the end of my present term.' But perhaps it was just as well, he thought. 'If we can keep the vessel of state as steadily in her course for another four years, my earthly purposes will be accomplished.' Then he could retire to his family, his farm and books.[1] Four months later he wrote Philip Mazzei to the same effect. 'The immense load of tory calumnies which have been manufactured respecting me, and have filled the European market' made it necessary 'to appeal once more to my country for justification.' [2]

His nomination was inevitable, the desire of his party unanimous, but Burr for the second place with Jefferson was no longer a possibility. His treachery to the Administration was now notorious, and his cultivation of the extreme wing of the opposition had aroused the disgust of Hamilton. The Jeffersonians turned instead to the veteran leader in New York who so frequently had crossed swords with Burr, and in George Clinton they found their candidate.

This vigorous, resourceful, masterful politician, son of an Irish immigrant, had been elected seven times to the governorship, and had been the most effective war governor of the Revolutionary years. His first election had shocked the snobs, and John Jay, whose snobbery was proverbial, had written lugubriously to

Schuyler that 'Clinton's family and connections do not entitle him
to so distinguished a pre-eminence.' But the people on more than
one occasion later were to show that they thought more of
Clinton's executive capacity than of Jay's family.

The Federalists turned to Charles Cotesworth Pinckney for
their presidential nominee. A thorough aristocrat, as contemptuous of democracy and the masses as Hamilton himself, he was
a handsome man of striking presence, elegant in his manners,
accomplished, cultured, but in no sense impressive politically.
He had served with the X Y Z Commission and had been credited
with the famous retort, 'Millions for defense but not one cent for
tribute.' It was to him that Hamilton turned in 1800 for a Federalist with whom to unhorse Adams, and he had made a tour of
New England in his behalf.[1] But in public service and distinction he did not approach Rufus King who was nominated for
the second post. The ticket was upside down. It is not a rash
surmise that Pinckney's nomination was the first made by the
politicians on the comfortable theory that he would be easy to
control.

IV

Incredible as it seems, that the Federalists could have hoped
for the defeat of Jefferson, it must be borne in mind that they had
no contacts with the average man, and that they were inebriated
in their vituperation. No Executive before or since has ever so
completely kept the faith. No longer were citizens dragged from
their beds at midnight and carried into the country through the
rain to be cast into loathsome cells because of criticism of those in
power. The press was free. The Naturalization Law had been
liberalized within reason. Internal taxes had been repealed and
almost twelve million dollars had been paid on the national debt.
The public service had been purged of parasites and pensioners,
and its efficiency increased. Rigid economies had been enforced
in all the departments. Peace had been maintained despite embarrassments with France and England. Tripoli had been
chastened; Algiers and Tunis had heard the thunder of our guns,
and no longer did we pay tribute to the pirates. The national
domain had been doubled, without bloodshed, and without an

[1] *Jefferson and Hamilton*, 459.

increase in taxes to meet the obligations of the purchase. The Military Academy at West Point had been established for the training of officers.

And never had the country been more peaceable or prosperous, more confident. Four years had convinced the timid of the stupidity of the Federalist warnings that a Jeffersonian triumph would mean anarchy. Law and order prevailed everywhere. No longer could the people be persuaded that a Jeffersonian régime would destroy the nation's credit in the marts of the world, for never had the bankers of London and Amsterdam felt more secure in their loans. In all the towns, including Boston, could be heard the hammers of the carpenters.

v

And the Jeffersonians were unafraid. However, the battle began with a leader designated in each State to manage the campaign — the forerunner of the National Committees that were thereafter to enter into the scheme of politics. Each committeeman was to be held to strict account for the results in his State. A great number of newspapers sprang up in unexpected places that were to continue through the campaign and die. With one of these Jefferson was intimately connected, and it was to survive. In Virginia he had powerful enemies; the one newspaper in Richmond supporting his policies had gone down, and the building had been destroyed by fire. With Madison and Giles, he agreed on the necessity of a newspaper to support the Administration policies and the Jeffersonian concept of the State. In Thomas Ritchie, a clever young bookseller, he found an editor, and the militant *Richmond Enquirer* came into existence when, May 9, 1804, the first issue came from the press. Thus there was a force in Richmond to combat the anti-Jeffersonian sentiment of that town.[1] And in New England a contemporary found 'the increase of gazettes excessive'; though he had attempted to count them, 'they had appeared, disappeared, and changed places so often' he could not ascertain the number.[2] On the newspapers and pamphlets the politicians of 1804 relied.

[1] Charles H. Ambler, *Thomas Ritchie: A Study in Virginia Politics*, 18–19.
[2] Bentley, *Diary*, III, 54.

Intensive campaign speaking had not come into practice, but in New England the Federalists could count on the electioneering speeches of many pulpits. Candidates remained at home as a rule, but Charles Cotesworth Pinckney had made a tour of Massachusetts the previous autumn. At Salem he had driven around the picturesque old seaport with his host, General Derby, and the Jeffersonians were reminded of 'Hezekiah's showing the City to the Babylonians.' Harvard, under Federalist control, gave him an honorary degree, a distinction never accorded to the more intellectual Jefferson.[1]

The political map seemed promising to the Jeffersonians. Four years before, the Federalists had carried all New England, New Jersey, Delaware, half of Pennsylvania, Maryland, and North Carolina. They had no chance in any State Jefferson had then carried. And now Pennsylvania clearly was lost to them. New Jersey had caught the Jeffersonian fever. North Carolina gave every indication of slipping away.

And even in New England the arrogant Jeffersonians were fighting every inch of the ground. In New Hampshire, under the stern leadership of John Langdon, they were putting the fear of the Lord into the hearts of the enemy. Much was made of the 'unconstitutional' purchase of Louisiana, but the people were not impressed. It was not that Jefferson had compromised with his principles, or failed to do what formerly he had promised, but that he had confounded his enemies by showing that their warnings were without warrant in the facts.

Thus, on the whole, it was to be a quiet campaign, with no one excited outside the Federalist drawing-rooms and the editorial columns of the party press.

VI

But it was not to be a happy summer for Jefferson. The moment Congress adjourned he hurried to Monticello, profoundly moved by the illness of Mary, his youngest child, the wife of Eppes. A young woman of unusual beauty, she had long been frail, and in the spring her health failed rapidly. On Jefferson's insistence she was borne for miles by men on a litter to the hilltop

[1] Bentley, *Diary*, III, 41.

in the hope that the air would revive her. When the days were fair, she was taken out for rides upon the lawn, drawn in a carriage by men, but her decline was continuous. No longer young, tenderly devoted to the twenty-six-year-old woman he had been forced to mother, Jefferson was doomed to the torture of watching her slip away. Her resignation, her humility, her sympathy for the father's suffering but intensified the pathos of those final days. One day his elder daughter found him on the lawn seeking consolation in the Bible — a shocking thing for the Federalist political preachers of those days to have seen. The agony of waiting was soon over and on the nineteenth of April, Mary Jefferson passed away.[1]

Later, when the warm weather came, Jefferson again returned to the Monticello he loved for its serenity, but the painful scenes through which so recently he had passed there depressed him. While the Federalist papers, politicians, and preachers were sneering, jeering, ridiculing, malevolently and falsely attacking him, one word of sympathy that touched his heart came from a big rambling white frame house in Quincy, near Boston, where John Adams was living in retirement. The wounded pride of the rugged patriot had not permitted him to seek or accept a reconciliation with the old-time friend with whom so recently he had broken over politics, and Abigail, the wife, shared in her husband's quarrels. But in happier days when Jefferson, a widower, was in Paris, as a colleague of Adams, it was Abigail who had taken the little Mary to her heart and mothered her. With the news of her death, the ice melted, and she wrote a note of sympathy and of praise for the dead child. It was the beginning of a glorious reconciliation.

VII

Under Senator Plumer's leadership the Federalists of New Hampshire for the first time organized intensively and canvassed for votes. Newspapers were distributed free to every house and hotel in town and country by post-riders employed for the purpose.[2] Even in hidebound Connecticut, the Jeffersonians were provokingly active and, the Federalists thought, insolent. The

[1] *Domestic Life*, 299.   [2] *Plumer*, 313–14.

Jeffersonians had found a dangerous issue. The Commonwealth, without a written constitution adopted by the people, was living under a royal charter, moderately amended from time to time, that had come down from the days of Charles II. Why a royal charter after years of independence and after fifteen years of the Republic? asked the Jeffersonians. When, in the spring, the Democrats of Hartford celebrated the purchase of Louisiana, Abraham Bishop, who wielded an oratorical meat-axe, had denounced the existing form of government. Soon a convention was called which adopted resolutions demanding the formation of a constitution. Five justices of the peace, including Revolutionary patriots who dared sign the demand for a constitution, were instantly thrown from office for their effrontery.[1] With a general committee conducting a vigorous campaign under the leadership of Pierrepont Edwards, the Federalists found themselves hard pressed.[2]

In Massachusetts, the province of Maine, tired of the arrogant domination of the Essex Junto, was on the march with banners. The Federalist press reeked with abuse. Petty persecution extending to social life was practiced. A courteous request by the Jeffersonians for the use of the church in Salem for their meeting brought a curt refusal, though the Federalists had a politician in its pulpit. 'The republicans are now excluded from the houses in which they worship,' wrote a Jeffersonian minister.[3] But this proscription but served to heat the fighting blood of the proscribed, and on the nation's natal day they took possession of Salem. Circulating a subscription list to get the funds, they brought a band from Lexington. The day was ushered in by the roaring of cannon and the ringing of bells. At ten o'clock the procession moved with five hundred men. A church had been found for the meeting, for a Congregationalist minister was discovered who had faith in Jefferson, and fifteen hundred people filled the seats. Early that morning the women were busy with the decorations. The gallery was festooned, the pillars wreathed with flowers. The arms of the Republic loomed from the front of the pulpit, and below was an engraving of Jefferson. Another was hung on the front gallery. On his right hand was a picture of

---

[1] Purcell, 253–57; 259–60.   [2] *Ibid.*, 254–55.   [3] Bentley, *Diary*, III, 94.

Washington and on his left a symbol of liberty. Photographs of Madison, Gallatin, and General Gates also looked down on the partisans.

The services opened with 'Hail Columbia' — the 124th Psalm was read — the minister thanked God for Jefferson's Administration. Then followed toasts, and the Jeffersonians dispersed into the streets. All day, at intervals, the cannon roared, and in the evening white rockets illumined the sky and the band from Lexington entertained the people on Washington Square. The story of this day's proceedings sent shivers down the spines of the Bostonians who revolved around the Cabots and the Higginsons. Verily the 'Jacobins' were upon them.[1]

In the fall when Rufus King appeared in Boston the Federalists gave him a dinner of two hundred plates and cheered the toast: 'The Administrations of Washington and Adams: The morning and evening stars of our national glory.' [2] The Federalist press intensified its abuse and the élite of Boston began to bestir themselves, though they canvassed only among their own group to save themselves from contamination. They would not degrade themselves by canvassing among the people.

And frightful rumors were spreading even from Vermont, where the leaven of democracy was working.

VIII

It was a battle of pamphlets and the press.

Gideon Granger, an effective pamphleteer, was plying his pen with vigor, and in farmhouse and in country stores and taverns men were listening eagerly while someone read:

> In the two last years of the last Administration the Executive was authorized to borrow nine million, eight hundred thousand dollars; a part of which was actually loaned at eight per cent; for the last two years no loans have been made or authorized.
>
> In the two first years of the last Administration an additional duty of eight cents per bushel on salt, the stamp tax, and the land tax of two millions of dollars were levied; during the present no tax has been levied; the land tax is discontinued; and the stamp tax, with all other internal taxes, have been abolished.
>
> During the last Administration in three years the national debt

[1] Bentley, *Diary*, III, 94–98.   [2] *Columbian Centinel*, October 20, 1804.

was increased three million and ninety-four thousand, three hundred
and seventeen dollars and forty-two cents; since the present, in two
years, the national debt has been reduced seven million, eight hundred and forty-nine thousand and thirty-seven dollars and thirty-
eight cents.

During the last Administration no payments were made on the
deferred debt; on the first of April, 1801, interest first fell due on
these debts, and the present Administration has annually paid
thereon one million, two hundred thousand dollars.

When the last Administration retired there were one million,
seven hundred and ninety-four thousand and forty-four dollars in
the treasury; now in the same treasury there are five million and
twenty thousand, two hundred and thirty dollars and sixty-two
cents.

And what were the other dire predictions of the Federalists?
They had said that the repeal of the Judiciary Act 'would
loosen the bonds of civil society and defeat the operations of
justice.' The fact? 'Peace, order and happiness prevail — the
Constitution retains its youthful energy — the judges of the
Supreme Court have sanctioned the law and justice is fully
administered as heretofore.'

They had said the repeal of the internal taxes would wreck the
nation's credit and deprive the Government of the means of support. The fact? 'By the economical arrangements of the Government the reduction of expenditures exceeds the reduction of
revenue more than two hundred thousand dollars; and the people
are relieved of annual taxes amounting to near a million.'

So ran the argument of Granger, who had a gift for marshaling
figures so the man in the street and in the corn row could understand; and he was dealing only with the first two years.[1]

The average man could understand the figures marched before
him. He could comprehend the significance of the purchase that
had doubled the national domain. He could appreciate his greater
freedom with the Sedition Act swept away. He could be grateful,
too, that the war hawks had temporarily been silenced, and that
no foreign war had summoned him to sacrifice and death. In the
Aurora of Duane, a brilliant review of the Administration's achievements had appeared and been spread into every nook and corner.

[1] *A Vindication of the Measures of the Present Administration,* by Algernon Sidney.

The Federalists found themselves hard put for arguments. They had the clergy as before; they had the greater portion of the press; and they had no scruples. Jefferson was a tool of France, they cried. The Administration wore a red cap, they thought. The judiciary had been ruined because the midnight judges had been deprived of their jobs provided by a grateful party at the public cost. The Administration was tyrannical, for had it not deprived many Federalists of jobs? Virginia was in the saddle and the Northern States in the ditch, they fairly screamed, especially in New England. And what a dreadful man was Jefferson! Had he not invited Tom Paine to the White House? Was he not an anti-Christ? And what a bitter enemy of labor! Had he not rejoiced that America was free of the proletariat of the European cities? And Louisiana! What an outrageous act, unconstitutional, cowardly, and oh, how costly! Fifteen millions for that waste land! Ridiculous! Why, divided among the States in proportion to their congressional representation, what did it mean to New England? Four dollars a head for every man, woman, and child in Massachusetts; thirty dollars for every family in Connecticut; and on the interest alone New Hampshire would pay eighty-seven dollars a day. Ruin — it meant ruin!

But the Federalist press confined itself mostly to abuse and ridicule. When the Federalists held a party pow-wow at a dinner, 'truly dignified' toasts were drunk to John Marshall and Pickering, and the toast to Judge Chase was to 'The man who dares be honest in the worst of times'; because Jefferson had visited Mount Vernon, where Washington had always been glad to see him, they toasted 'the tomb of Washington,' with the hope that it 'may never be profaned by crocodile tears.' [1]

But ridicule became their favorite weapon. They held their sides with laughter because Jefferson reported to Congress that he had been informed there was a mountain of salt in the new territory. 'Jefferson's salt mountain,' jeered the partisans, and Jefferson's gunboats! These boats, built for speed, had been constructed for the Mississippi to prevent any Spanish depredations on our shipping at a time when trouble seemed possible. One of them had been sent to the waters of Savannah, and then one

[1] *Columbian Centinel*, March 14, 1804.

of the most devastating cyclones ever known in the United States
had fallen on that region, leveling houses, forests, smashing ships,
blowing a cannon at Fort Green weighing two tons forty feet; the
water had deluged the land, and when the flood subsided the gun-
boat was stranded in a cornfield. Could anything more conclusively prove the stupidity of gunboats? At the dinner to Rufus
King one of the guests proposed a toast: 'If our gunboats are of
no use upon the water, may they at least be useful upon the land.'

So ran the course of the campaign, in the midst of a prospering
people, and none but the politicians were impressed. The rank and
file of the Federalists surged all too clearly toward the new régime.
The election of Jefferson was certain, but of course the Federalists
would poll as many as forty electoral votes.

IX

The result was stunning to the opposition. New England, even
Massachusetts and Vermont, marched with a jaunty swing into
the Jeffersonian column, and even in Connecticut the Federalists
had a scare. Pennsylvania was unanimous, New Jersey joined the
procession, North Carolina turned her back wholly on the party
to which she had given half her votes before. Even Maryland, an
anti-Jeffersonian State, gave three votes to Jefferson, and only
Delaware and Connecticut were left. It was a landslide. Jefferson
had been vindicated by a majority surpassing the fondest hopes
of his warmest friends. But Massachusetts furnished the sensation of the election, by casting all her electoral votes for Jefferson!
'Many persons offer to be bearers of the news to Washington,'
wrote Bentley.[1]

Trying to make Rufus King understand the new order, John
Quincy Adams wrote the verdict: 'The power of the Administration rests upon the support of a much stronger majority of people
throughout the Union than the former Administrations ever
possessed since the first establishment of the Constitution. Whatever the merits or the demerits of the former Administrations may
have been, there never was a system of measures more completely
and irrevocably abandoned and rejected by the popular voice.'

And then he added: 'It never can and never will be revived.

[1] Bentley, *Diary*, III, 126.

The experiment, such as it was, has failed and to attempt the restoration would be as absurd as to undertake the resurrection of a carcass seven years in its grave.' [1]

With this triumph it seemed, for a moment, that Federalism was dead; it had, in truth, received its death-blow, but it was to stagger on until it died in the treasonable Hartford Convention some years later. In the Senate but seven remained in opposition; in the House but twenty-five out of a hundred and forty-one representatives could be mustered against Jefferson. He had a mandate as clear as ever was given to a statesman by a people; and immediately after the election the work of purging, not 'wrecking,' the federal judiciary, began with the impeachment of Chase.

[1] *King's Corr.*, IV, 176–77.

CHAPTER XIII

Jefferson 'Attacks the Federal Judiciary'

THE Federalist interpreters of history generations ago, taking their cue from the Federalist politicians, coined the deceptive, if not dishonest, phrase, 'Jefferson's attack on the federal judiciary.' What then was the 'federal judiciary' that Jefferson 'attacked'? It was a judiciary packed with partisans of one political school. It did not merely happen that when Jefferson took office there was not one man on the federal bench belonging to the faith to which the people overwhelmingly had subscribed in the revolution of 1800. The first two Chief Justices actively participated in party management, sitting in caucuses, and using their official prestige to pull their party's chestnuts out of the fire. The published correspondence of the jurists of this period fairly reeks with bigoted partisanship. Not content with dragging their ermine among the cuspidors of party caucuses in secret, it had become the custom of these judges to spout extravagant and insulting partisan harangues from the bench under the pretense of delivering charges to grand juries. These tirades, prepared for publication for party reasons, were regularly printed in the party papers for the purpose of intimidation and propaganda. These jurists were enemies of democracy, and even John Marshall had been weaned away from the liberal principles of his revolutionary youth.[1] Politicians of the Federalist persuasion felt at liberty to solicit these judges to institute prosecutions for political articles.[2]

This was the 'federal judiciary' on which Jefferson declared war.

With the federal courts, from judge and United States district

---

[1] Beveridge, III, 109.   [2] Luther Martin in the Callender case.

attorney to clerk and marshal, active and arrogant partisans, it
was not unusual for both grand and trial juries in political cases to
be packed with partisans hostile to the accused, and during the
reign of terror under the Sedition Law more than one miserable
victim went to trial for liberty or life with the jury deliberately
packed against him.[1] Beveridge admits that these officials 'in
many cases' were Federalist politicians.

This was the 'federal judiciary' that Jefferson was determined
to destroy.

Beveridge, no enemy of the courts, and hostile to Jefferson does
not exaggerate when he says: 'So it was that the juries were nothing more than machines that registered the will, opinion, or even
inclinations of the national judges and the United States district
attorneys. In short, in these prosecutions, trial by jury in any real
sense was not to be had.' [2] The spouting of partisan speeches from
the bench would have been quite enough to incur Jefferson's contempt; but when, in the reign of terror, these judges converted
their courts into shambles for anyone who dared to speak or
write for democracy, he became convinced that the purging of
the judiciary was necessary for the preservation of the liberties
of the people, and to the maintenance of the institutions that had
been set up. No one with an elementary sense of common decency
can read in Wharton's 'State Trials' the outrageous miscarriages
of justice with feelings other than those of loathing and disgust.[3]
'In making up juries,' says Beveridge, 'they selected only persons
of the same manner of thinking as that of the marshals and
judges themselves.' [4] Jefferson fared forth *to wreck that kind of
federal judiciary.*

It was to the maintenance of this corps of the defeated and discredited Federalist army that the politicians turned the moment
the people had voted their party out of power. Here, at least, was
a branch of government not dependent on the favor of the people.
It was packed, even then, with robust Federalist politicians who
were in for life. They might continue to spew offensive partisanship from the bench and continue to pack juries. But this was not
enough. These insatiable politicians wanted more. Thus the

---

[1] Beveridge, III, 42.   [2] *Ibid.*, III, 42.
[3] *Jefferson and Hamilton*, 386–405.   [4] Beveridge, III, 42.

creation of many new circuit courts to furnish easy berths for repudiated politicians out of jobs. Thus the shameful scene the night before Jefferson's inauguration, when John Marshall, Secretary of State and even then named Chief Justice, continued to pass out commissions as judges to his political associates, so the party with the mandate of the nation would have no places to fill. This brazen performance intensified the popular distrust of the federal judiciary which Jefferson heartily shared.

They had degraded the federal bench to the low level of a political stump in a cornfield; they had packed juries in political cases; they had approached during the period of the Sedition Law the savagery and tyranny of a Jeffreys; and this was the federal judiciary that Jefferson proposed to purge, and, by ending these vicious abuses, to lift to the dignity of a department worthy of something better than the contempt of honest men.

II

To the real drama there was a curtain-raiser — a mere episode. John Pickering, judge in New Hampshire, had been brought to Jefferson's attention by the collector of customs in his district because of the jurist's unquestionably insane conduct in the case of the ship *Eliza*. It had been seized for violation of the revenue laws and its owner had appealed to the court for the restoration of his property. Pickering gave the order. When the district attorney reminded him that he had heard no witnesses for the Government, Pickering jeeringly replied: 'You may bring forty thousand and they will not alter the decree.' When the Government asked for an appeal, Pickering refused to grant it. Throughout the proceedings the judge was in a state of beastly intoxication, as was his wont even on the bench. Staggering to the bench, raving, cursing, ordering spectators to sit beside him, and threatening them if they refused, he was for three years given to disgraceful exhibitions.

When Jefferson received these reports, accompanied by affidavits, he merely sent the papers to the House with the suggestion that since he had no constitutional power to remove the offender, the remedy lay with that body.[1] Instantly Federalists raised the hue and cry that Jefferson was trying to 'wreck the federal

[1] Beveridge, III, 164.

judiciary.' In Congress they rallied to a man to prevent the expulsion of such a character from the bench. What! Remove a man who merely cursed and raved in insane intoxication and made a mockery of justice and the law? Outrageous! 'A shameful piece of business,' echoes McMaster, the Federalist historian.[1] 'How can an insane man plead?' demanded the Federalist infuriates. 'Let him designate someone to plead for him,' answered the majority, 'or let his friends persuade him to resign.' He was approached, but he conditioned his withdrawal on an appointment as Chief Justice of the Supreme Court of New Hampshire.[2] Tracy fought stubbornly against his removal, and the melodramatic Timothy Pickering, prone always to see daggers in the air, found the Democrats so crazed with power that he expected to see 'bloody victims to their ambition, inexorable malice and revenge.' Yes, 'one or two Marats or Robespierres with half a dozen congenial spirits' would be able to carry the majority into 'a policy of butchery.'[3] Adams, snooping around the cloakrooms, was shocked to find senators and managers of the impeachment sitting about the fire discussing how to get a demented drunkard off the bench.[4]

The trial was held, the charges were easily sustained, the mental incompetency and drunkenness were established, and Pickering was removed. 'Aha!' cried the Federalists, 'Jefferson's attack on the federal judiciary has begun!'

III

Pickering was too much of a minnow, drunk or sober, to have attracted Jefferson's attention but for his menacing conduct in the case of the *Eliza*. There was another judge, more important and significant, who interested him more. This was Samuel Chase.

Born sixty-five years before, Chase had been a militant champion of colonial rights, and had signed the Declaration of Independence. His career in the Continental Congress had been cut short when he was caught red-handed using his information as a member in trying to effect a corner on wheat. So low did he then fall that Alexander Hamilton made him the object of a fierce in-

---

[1] J. B. McMaster, *History of the People of the United States*, III, 172.
[2] Adams, *Diary*, I, 290.   [3] *King's Corr.*, IV, 362.   [4] Adams, *Diary*, I, 302.

vective. 'It is your lot,' wrote Hamilton of Chase, 'to have the
peculiar privilege of being universally despised. ... Were I inclined to make a satire on the species I would attempt a faithful
description of your heart.' [1] Soon afterward his passions for
speculation reduced him to insolvency. Writing over the signature, 'Caution,' he fought the adoption of the Constitution. He
owed his appointment to the bench to the partiality of McHenry,
who assured Washington that Chase was through with his past
errors. Besides, he was a good lawyer and had 'a valuable stock of
political science.' Though erudite in the law, his decisions were to
bear out in many notable cases his theories of political science.

Though coarse, he was impressive because of his height and
corpulence, fed by a Gargantuan appetite. His shoulders were
broad and burly. His huge face was of the reddish brown of bacon.
His head, with its broad brow, was large and shapely, his hair
thick and now white with years. In any crowd he would have
commanded attention, primarily because of his bulk, and then,
despite his coarseness, there was intelligence on his brow, and
something of mingled mentality and malice in his eyes. When he
spoke, his voice was in keeping with the coarseness of his nature,
and in moments of anger he bellowed like a bull.

Socially, Chase's manners were crude and common, more
adapted to the company of a tavern bar than to good society.
Wit and humor he had, but one was bitter and the other broad.
Mrs. Bingham had found him no gentleman at her table.[2] He
could be good-humored, but few upon whose lives and liberty he
sat felt it, nor did many members of the bar. Among lawyers of his
liking, such as the debauched Luther Martin, he had a certain
comradery that appealed. Justice Story thought his manners
coarse and his approach 'formidable,' and was impressed by his
penchant for grumbling and croaking. His character is reflected
in the fact that he could be kind to an equal, while he was contemptuous toward an inferior. 'In person, in manners, in un-
wieldy strength, in severity of reproof, in real tenderness of heart,
and above all in intellect,' said Story, 'he is, I had almost said, the
exact image of Samuel Johnson.' [3] And as fit for a judicial posi-

---

[1] *Works of Hamilton*, I, 199–209.
[2] *Jefferson and Hamilton*, 131.   [3] *Story*, 167.

tion! Essentially a bully, he loved nothing better than insulting
witnesses and lawyers with sarcasm, knowing they dare not reply
in kind. A bitter partisan, he used the bench as a rostrum, and
such was the intolerance of the man's coarse nature that he acted
upon the theory that a political opponent had no rights a Federalist judge was bound to respect.

IV

Such was Samuel Chase, blood-brother of Jeffreys and Clare,
who in his arrogance at Baltimore went beyond all bounds.

About tables in the dining-room of the Evans Tavern one May
morning were grouped members of the bar; in front, before a table
in a large easy-chair, sat Judge Chase reading a charge to the
grand jury; in the rear of the room were numerous spectators.
Occasionally, as he read, Chase pushed his spectacles back upon
his forehead and appeared to be expanding extemporaneously on
his theme. The charge had been carefully prepared for publication, as was the vicious custom of the federal judiciary in handing
down partisan opinions.

A year before, under the known leadership of Jefferson, the
Judiciary Act of 1801 had been repealed. Notoriously it was
an Administration measure. At this time, too, the people of
Maryland had so amended their Constitution as to extend the
suffrage, which formerly had been limited by property quali-
fications, and the legislature had initiated legislation looking
to the reorganization of the courts. All this had been, and was
being, done in a perfectly constitutional manner. But these
measures of the Federal Government and of the sovereign State
were repulsive to the partisan views of the politician on the
bench.

Having discharged the legitimate functions of his charge, Chase
made a direct attack on the repeal of the Judiciary Act, on the
extension of suffrage in Maryland, and on the pending change in
the State judiciary as certain 'to take away all security of property and personal liberty.' Parroting the language of the Essex
Junto, he went on: 'The independence of the national judiciary is
already shaken to its foundations, and the virtue of the people
alone can restore it.' Thus did he plunge into the very heart of a

partisan controversy and aim a direct attack on the Jefferson
Administration from the bench.

Turning to the change in the Maryland Constitution, which was
not the business of a federal judge, he announced that the extension of the suffrage meant that 'our republican constitution will
sink into a mobocracy.' Yes, he continued, 'I only lament that the
main pillar of our State Constitution has already been thrown
down by the establishment of universal suffrage' and that 'the
whole building totters to its base and will crumble into ruins before
many years elapse.'

And then he struck directly at Jefferson: 'The modern doctrines
of our late reformers that all men in a state of society are entitled
to enjoy equal liberty and equal rights have brought this mighty
mischief upon us. I fear it will rapidly progress until peace and
order, freedom and property, shall be destroyed.'

Such was the partisan tirade, as he himself contended. Among
the spectators were some who heard more offensive expressions.
No one had any doubt that the charge was aimed at Jefferson; no
one could have interpreted 'our late reformers' as any other than
the Jeffersonians; no one but knew Congress had been accused
from the bench with having 'shaken the federal judiciary to its
foundations.'

Outraged by this obnoxious harangue, a young Jeffersonian
who heard it published a bitter attack on Chase, demanding his
impeachment, and sent a clipping to Jefferson, who transmitted it
to Nicholson in the House with a brief comment:

'Ought this seditious and official attack on the principles of our
Constitution, and on the proceedings of a State, go unpunished?
And to whom more pointedly than to yourself will the public look
for the necessary measures?'

And that positively is all the records show Jefferson to have
done. It was time, he thought, to end the partisan chatter of the
judiciary. There is nothing of record that he had any thought of
basing impeachment proceedings on any other charge.

v

But the moment proceedings were proposed, members of the
House began prodding their memories for other offenses of the

jurist, strangely subordinating this, the most open and flagrant, to the rest.[1] The public distrust of Chase rested on an ample foundation — on numerous instances of outrageous conduct in political cases. The average man in the street could not so readily grasp the significance of the blow at the American theory of government; it did not make for colorful drama. And the House preferred to impeach on injustices to individuals rather than on principles of government.

It pounced at once on the case of Fries. An ignorant German immigrant had taken part in the rescue of some victims of the Whiskey Rebellion. Arrested and indicted for treason, he had been found guilty and condemned to death, but the discovery that at least one juror had pronounced him guilty before the trial resulted in a new trial, at which Chase presided.

The able lawyers for Fries admitted the facts, and based their defense on the ground that these facts did not come within the definition of treason. At the beginning of the second trial, before the jury had been chosen, but in the presence of the panel, Chase, who had acquainted himself with the issues of the first trial,[2] ostentatiously handed to Fries's attorney a written opinion confining the defense to a disproval of the notorious facts, and denying it the right to contend that these did not come within the law of treason. It amounted to a conviction without a hearing. When this opinion was handed to the Nestor of the Philadelphia Bar, defending, he indignantly flung it from him with the statement: 'I will never permit my hand to be tainted with a prejudged opinion in any case, much less in a capital case.'[3] His associate, another leader of the bar, approved his action, and the two refused to continue in the case. Alarmed by the spirited revolt of two such distinguished and reputable leaders of the bar, Chase beat an ignominious retreat on the following day. He asked the lawyers to continue in their own way, but added that they would do so at the peril of their reputations! The jury, however, was in complete possession of the opinion of the court, and the lawyers declined to continue.

---

[1] Beveridge calls the Baltimore charge the most serious (III, 219); Henry Adams agrees (*History of the United States*, I, 239).

[2] Admitted by Chase and his attorney, Martin.   [3] Testimony of Lewis.

Thus an ignorant immigrant, penniless and without influential friends, went to trial for his life without counsel. He was doomed to death, the scaffold was in process of erection, when the indignation of lawyers and laymen, and John Adams's sense of justice, intervened, and he was pardoned.

Impeach on that case, cried a number of members.

But why not on the case of Callender? asked others.

This disreputable person, indicted under the Sedition Law, along with his distinguished lawyers, had been given short shrift by Chase, who had boasted on the road to Richmond for the trial that he would teach the Virginia lawyers a thing or two. Mysteriously enough, only three Democrats were summoned on the panel, and none were to serve on the jury — which was notoriously packed. When one robust but honest Federalist asked to be excused because he had formed, and expressed, a bitter opinion on the book on which the indictment was based, and the defense attorneys naturally challenged, Chase intervened, set aside the plea of the prospective juror and the objections of the defense, and pronounced him a competent juror on the flimsy ground that he had expressed no opinion on the indictment he had not seen. When the famous John Taylor of Caroline appeared as a witness for the defense, Chase refused him permission to testify until the questions to be asked had been reduced to writing; and then declared him incompetent on the amazing ground that his testimony would not go to the proving of the truth on the whole of one of the Callender charges. In the course of the trial, so indecent were Chase's insults to the counsel that such high-minded lawyers as William Wirt folded their papers and retired in the midst of the argument.

But why not impeach on the Delaware case? demanded still others.

In the days of the Sedition Law terror, the grand jury in Delaware had reported to Chase that no indictments had been found. Refusing to release them then, as customary, Chase observed that he understood there was a 'seditious' paper in Wilmington, and that it was the 'special duty' of the jury to inquire diligently into the matter. He kept them overnight, ordered the files of the paper transmitted to the jury room, and when, the next day, the jurors announced that they had found nothing seditious, he discharged them. But this was in the days when this sort of action from federal judges was so commonplace that it attracted no general attention

All these incidents in the recent history of Chase's adventures were fresh in the minds of members when John Randolph rose to say that he had information justifying a resolution for an inquiry into the official conduct of Chase.

VI

The discussion of the resolution showed that the impeachment had been taken out of the control of Jefferson, since the one ground on which he had asked impeachment was scarcely mentioned by a single speaker. Immediately the case of Fries entered the debate.[1] Roger Griswold admitted that in this case there might have been an 'error in judgment.'[2] As the debate droned on, with the pathetic Fries looming larger and larger, Randolph burst forth: 'Has it come to this — that an unrighteous judge may condemn whom he pleases to an ignominious death, without a hearing, in the teeth of the Constitution and the laws, and that such proceedings shall find advocates here?'[3]

The second day ushered in the case of Callender along with that of Fries, and not a single member mentioned the Baltimore charge! It was the beginning of a fatal blunder.

The inquiry was voted, with Randolph as chairman of the committee. In a month, an impeachment was reported; two weeks more, and the articles, written by Randolph, were submitted. Eight in number, six dealt with questionable legal points, one with the unimportant Delaware case, and the last, on the Baltimore charge, was made to seem something dragged in. The managers were chosen, with Randolph at their head. They had determined to subordinate the one important political issue involving the principles and forms of government, and to make the most of charges of a purely legal character admitting of technical hair-splitting. And yet, among the managers, there was not one outstanding lawyer to face the legal battery of Chase — the most powerful that could be found at the American Bar.

[1] Smilie; *Annals*, January 5, 1804.   [2] *Ibid.*   [3] *Ibid.*

VII

Meanwhile, the Federalist leaders unanimously agreed that nothing could save Chase. They had determined to vote as a body, before hearing a word of evidence, for the acquittal of the intense partisan who so often had served them on the bench. Robert Goodloe Harper approached Bayard, one of the judges in the impeachment, with the proposed plan for the defense of the accused. And Bayard had no qualms of conscience. Thus the judge advised the attorney on the management of the case on which he was to sit. 'I think decidedly,' he wrote Harper, 'whether with a view to personal or general effect, the Judge ought to have no advocate but himself.' For 'if he appears singly against the host of managers his position becomes at once distinguished and interesting,' since 'nothing is more natural than for the public to take the side of the weakest party, especially where the odds are great and the resistance firm and manly.' Certainly, thought the senator who was to sit in judgment on the evidence, it would be a mistake for Chase to appear at the trial surrounded by lawyers of his own political persuasion. 'The individual would be forgotten, and in and out of doors, the sole consideration would be which party would triumph.' At any rate, 'to employ characters who have been known in politics and are obnoxious to the prevalent sentiment would be extremely indiscreet.' However, he thought the impeachment 'already determined.' [1]

Meanwhile, the managers were preparing for the fray, far from harmonious in their concept of an impeachment.

VIII

The spectators who flocked to the spectacle in the Senate Chamber for the opening of the trial found their expectation of the picturesque satisfied by the arrangements in the room. Aaron Burr had been the stage manager. For the first time he had appeared promptly on the opening of the Senate — his first appearance since the killing of Hamilton. Momentarily some Federalists were shocked at his bravado. The *Connecticut Courant* found that 'many are surprised, some astonished,' and concluded that his purpose was 'to browbeat public opinion,' since 'he is perhaps

[1] *Bayard Papers.*

better calculated for this Herculean task than most other men.'[1] Soon the Federalists, satisfied with Burr's conduct, were not even moved by the advertisement appearing regularly through the trial in the Washington press:

Burr and Hamilton
Museum of Wax-Works

Moulthrop and Bishop

Respectfully acquaint the Ladies and Gentlemen of Georgetown that they have opened at the house of Mr. Semms a new collection of wax-figures, superior to any ever exhibited in America, among which are the following characters:

A striking likeness and representation of the late unfortunate duel between Col. Aaron Burr, Vice President of the United States, and Gen. Alexander Hamilton, wherein Gen. Hamilton is supported by his second after receiving the mortal wound, while Colonel Burr is led from the field by his second. A striking representation of the place where the duel was fought, painted upon scenery, which adds much to the interesting representation.[2]

But Burr was pleased with his stage management. The benches facing him were covered with crimson. Boxes were provided on either side for the managers and the defendant and his counsel. Other boxes were installed for the diplomatic corps and for high officers of the army and navy. The permanent gallery was thrown open to the public, but just beneath it a temporary gallery was constructed and furnished with 'peculiar elegance' for the accommodation of the ladies, who were to flock as to a carnival. At the termination of this gallery of beauty, boxes were built for the ladies of the families of public characters.[3]

In the chair sat Burr, immaculate, in severe dignity. At the bar was Chase, fat, white-haired, looking fully as feeble as he may have felt. About him were grouped his lawyers, every one a bitter Federalist politician, despite Bayard's warning. There sat Luther Martin, short, squat, slovenly, the brilliant drunkard of the

[1] February 14, 1805.   [2] *National Intelligencer*, February 27, 1805.
[3] *Annals*, January 3, 1805.

American Bar, a crony of Chase and an inveterate foe of Jefferson.
Beside him sat Robert Goodloe Harper, eloquent, flashy, flamboyant, but able, who in the days of the Sedition Act had insisted that
a member of Congress writing his constituents in denunciation of
Administration measures would be guilty of a crime.[1] There, also,
were Joseph Hopkinson, young and brilliant leader of the Philadelphia Bar, Philip Barton Key, of Maryland, and Charles Lee,
the Attorney-General in the gladsome days when Jeffersonians
were being scourged with the cat-o'-nine-tails of the Sedition Act.
A congenial company and a remarkable battery of legal talent,
thoroughly competent to split legal hairs for the preservation of
their tottering client.

And among the managers but one colorful figure — the one
genius on either side — John Randolph — but verging on a
nervous and physical collapse.

IX

It was inevitable that it should be a political trial. The Federalist senators, sitting as judges, *had caucused on their vote against conviction before the trial began.* However, that paragon of the
judicial temperament, Timothy Pickering, wrote indignantly of
the 'virulence of the party prosecuting' while admitting that some
'light clouds' had been thrown over the judge's character; [2] and
Senator Plumer, conceding that Chase had been guilty of 'intemperance of language and imprudence of conduct, unbecoming a
Judge,' gallantly concluded that, with this full knowledge, he
would not only vote to vindicate, but, were the issue one of confirmation instead of impeachment, he would vote to put Chase
upon the bench for life.[3] But snooping about the cloak-rooms,
John Quincy Adams was shocked to find Giles, one of the judges,
in consultation with John Randolph, though there had been another consultation between Bayard, another judge, and Harper.[4]

Such was the spirit when Randolph opened for the managers.
Circumscribed by the nature of an opening statement, he spoke
with much restraint, but outlined clearly and concisely the case
against the defendant, taking up each article, one by one. He de-

---

[1] *Jefferson and Hamilton*, 378.
[3] *Plumer*, 323–24.
[2] *King's Corr.*, IV, 439.
[4] Adams, *Diary*, I, 318. 323.

nounced the action of Chase in the Fries case, and the forcing of a Federalist, who had admitted forming and expressing an opinion, on the jury in the case of Callender. He made the most of the unprecedented exclusion of the testimony of John Taylor of Caroline, and finally reached the Baltimore charge.

> I ask this honorable court [he said] whether the prostitution of the bench of justice to the purposes of the hustings is to be tolerated. We have nothing to do with the politics of the man. Let him write and speak and publish as he pleases. . . . If he must electioneer and abuse the government . . . I know no law to prevent or punish, provided he seeks the wonted theatre for his exhibition.
>
> But shall a judge declare upon these topics from the seat of justice? Shall he not put off the political partisan when he ascends the tribune; or shall we have the pure stream of justice polluted with the venom of party virulence?

Here, for the first time, he touched upon the real issue that Jefferson had in mind in suggesting an impeachment. And here he clinched his point:

> It appears to me that one great distinction remains yet to be taken. A distinction between a judge, zealous to punish and repress crime generally, and a judge anxious only to enforce a particular law whereby he may recommend himself to power or to his party. It is this hideous feature of the respondent's judicial character on which I would fix your attention. We do not charge him with a general zeal in the discharge of his high office, but with an indecent zeal in particular cases for laws of doubtful and suspicious aspect. Through the whole tenor of his judicial conduct runs the spirit of party.

And this was the heart and soul of Jefferson's 'attack on the federal judiciary,' the nature of his attempt 'to tear it down.'

But Randolph passed this hurriedly by, and, in his peroration, returned to the Fries case in a passage of genuine eloquence:

> The respondent hath closed his defense in an appeal to the Great Searcher of all hearts for the purity of his motives. For his sake I rejoice that by the timely exercise of that mercy which for wise purposes hath been reposed in the Executive, this appeal is not drowned in the blood of an innocent man crying aloud for vengeance; that the mute agony of a widow's despair and the wailing voice of the orphan do not plead to heaven for justice on the oppressor's head. But for that intervention, self-accusation before that dread

tribunal would have been needless. On that awful day, the blood
of a poor, ignorant, friendless, unlettered German, murdered under
the semblance and the color of law, sent without Grace to the
scaffold, would have risen in judgement at the throne of God against
the unhappy man arraigned at your bar. But the President of the
United States by a well timed act, at once of justice and of mercy,
wrested the victim from his grasp and saved him from the countless
horrors of remorse by not suffering the pure ermine of justice to be
dyed in the innocent blood of John Fries.

This speech delivered, the managers began the presentation of
their evidence. Having established the facts as here set forth by
testimony entirely unshaken in cross-examination in the Fries
case,[1] the managers turned to the case of Callender. The forcing of
Bassett, an admittedly hostile man, on the jury, the exclusion
of the testimony of John Taylor of Caroline, the insulting attitude of the judge toward the lawyers for the defense, were established by the testimony of George Hay.[2] John Taylor cor-
roborated.[3] Even the hostile juror, forced on the jury over the
protest of the defense, and called by Chase's lawyers, admitted
that *he had formed and expressed an emphatic opinion before he
was drawn.*

Another day was wasted on the inconsequential Delaware case.

X

When the managers were ready for the Baltimore charge, John
Montgomery was summoned. In the course of his narrative the
witness said that 'to the best of my recollection the Judge stated
that the Administration was weak, relaxed, and inadequate to the
duties devolved upon it.' This was not charged in Article 8 of
the impeachment. Instantly the cunning lawyers for the defense
seized upon this 'recollection,' having nothing to do with the
actual charge in the article, to convey the impression that
the word 'recollection' was the sole objection to the outrageous
exhibition, and prepared to introduce witnesses to disprove the
word 'recollection.' Even historians, apparently unfamiliar with
Article 8, and unmindful of the unpardonable nature of Chase's
exhibition in Evans Tavern have accepted the position then as-

---

[1] Testimony of Lewis, Dallas, and others, *Annals,* February 9–11, 1805.
[2] *Ibid.,* February 11–12, 1805.   [3] *Ibid.,* February 12, 1805.

sumed by the defense. No other witnesses for the managers had any such 'recollection.' None of the managers in argument were to urge it. Nor had Randolph in his opening statement intimated that anything of the sort had been said. But we shall find the lawyers for Chase making a straw man out of the 'recollection' and knocking it down with ease, and then asking in jubilation, 'Where now is your Article 8?' [1]

The sole interesting point raised by the testimony on the Baltimore charge was whether the charge delivered was confined to that written and read. Montgomery, clearly honest, destroyed the effect of his 'recollection' by saying that Chase read from the manuscript — 'the Judge keeping his eye on the paper before him.' John T. Mason, who followed, differed on this point. 'Judge Chase delivered the charge from a written paper which he had before him,' he said. 'He wore his spectacles all the time, and though he turned over leaf by leaf, he occasionally threw up his head and raised his spectacles on his forehead and spoke as if he were making an enlargement on the criminal charge by extemporary observations in addition to what he had written.' [2] Had this been true, Montgomery might easily have been right in his 'recollection,' since Chase could not extemporize temperately on Jefferson's Administration.

This closed the case for the managers.

XI

Harper opened for the defense on the morrow in his best manner. Instantly he measured the insincerity of the defense when, in referring to the case of Fries, he made the astounding statement that Chase 'felt solicitous for the escape of the unfortunate wretch.' Suavely the orator declared, in reference to Bassett's indisposition to serve as juror on the Callender case because of hostile opinions held and expressed, that the juror was merely moved 'by scruples of delicacy.' On the Baltimore charge he announced that he would present witnesses to prove that Chase had not mentioned the 'Administration' or the 'President' by name. Although Chase was impeached on the charge as written and admitted, as indecent and intolerable, and not on expressions attributed to him by one

[1] *Annals*, February 14, 1805.   [2] *Ibid.*

witness, some interpreters of history have found this defense impressive.[1]

XII

Triumphantly the defense began by showing that while Chase had refused the lawyers for Fries the right to argue that the facts admitted did not come within the law of treason, the same prohibition was imposed on the prosecuting attorney.[2] Aha! cried the friends of Chase, does this not prove even-handed justice? Ignoring the fact that Fries went on trial for his life without a lawyer. the defense showed that Chase had benevolently promised to protect his interest and see that 'no improper questions were asked.' [3]

Then appeared William Marshall, clerk of the court at Richmond, and brother of John Marshall, to make good Harper's promise to prove that Chase did not have his heart set on packing the jury with Federalists, after the long-established Federalist custom of the times. Unhappily the witness did not scintillate on cross-examination.

> Randolph: 'Were you acquainted with the gentlemen who served on the petit jury?'
> Marshal: 'Yes, sir.'
> 'Is there any one of them that comes under the description of being of the same political persuasion as Mr. Giles?'
> 'I believe not, sir.'

This cast such grave suspicion on the Chief Justice's brother that Harper sought to soften the bad impression. Were there no Democrats on the panel which was drawn? he asked hopefully. Marshall with difficulty could think of but two. Randolph recalled three, and then forced Marshall to admit that one was not in Richmond, another had received no notice, and the third had been 'excused' through the active intervention of John Marshall.[4] And this in Virginia where Democrats were as plentiful as leaves in autumn!

XIII

There was a rustling in the chamber when John Marshall took the stand. It was a very modest, soft-spoken, and plainly intim-

---

[1] *Annals*, February 15, 1805.   [2] *Ibid.*   [3] *Ibid.*   [4] *Ibid.*

idated Marshall who raised his hand to be sworn. Beveridge says that 'friendly eye-witnesses record that the Chief Justice appeared to be frightened.' [1] More prescient than the rest, he understood that the curtain was falling on the partisan arrogance of federal judges; and he was intelligent enough to know that the conduct of Chase, in some instances, was indefensible. Then, too, he may not have looked forward with glee to the admission he was to make of the part he himself had played in getting the one Democrat off the Callender jury. He was summoned for the defense; he came dangerously near becoming the star witness for the managers.

He explained his part in ridding the jury of the one Democrat. The man had expressed some delicacy about serving since he was convinced of the unconstitutionality of the Sedition Act. The fact that Bassett, the Federalist, had expressed some delicacy about serving on the jury because of his firm and publicly expressed conviction of the defendant's guilt had not deterred the Federalist court machine from forcing him to serve. But the sense of delicacy in a Jeffersonian was more sacred. Marshall had been most willing to assist the Democrat out of his embarrassment. And so he merely had gone to the court and secured his release; and Chase, responding to Marshall's plea, had reluctantly agreed to get along with a jury without one Democrat upon it.

Then Marshall began his damaging admissions under the compulsion of cross-examination. He admitted that the refusal to hear Callender's lawyers on the constitutionality of the Sedition Act was unusual. He admitted he had never known another instance where, as in the case of John Taylor, the questions to be asked the witness had to be reduced to writing.

'I have never known it requested that a question should be reduced to writing in the first instance in the whole course of my practice,' he said.

He admitted that the exclusion of Taylor's testimony on the ground that it did not prove the whole of a particular charge was novel. 'I never did hear that objection made in court except in this particular case,' he said.

He admitted that it was customary to hear counsel on legal points — a custom disregarded by Chase.

[1] Beveridge, III, 192.

'Is it not usual,' asked Randolph, 'when the opinion of the court is not solemnly pronounced, to hear counsel?'

'Yes, sir,' said Marshall.[1]

These answers threw a chill into the Chase camp, and bitter was the grumbling against Marshall, among the defense lawyers and the Federalist politicians among the senators who had caucused on their vote before the trial began.

At length the Baltimore charge was reached, and witnesses were called to deny that Chase had used the word 'Administration' in his denunciation of a leading Administration measure as calculated to destroy the Constitution; or the word 'Jefferson' in his slurring comments on 'our late reformers.' One witness, with a charming simplicity, having testified that nothing had been said to which any supporter of the Administration could take offense, admitted he thought the charge 'indiscreet' because he had noticed a Democrat editor among the spectators.[2]

In rebuttal, the managers introduced one of the grand jurors at Baltimore, who testified that the impression clearly made on him was that the judge was denouncing the policies of the Administration.

XIV

The evidence was closed. The arguments continued a week, before a chamber packed with ladies dressed as for a formal reception. The first two speakers among the managers (Early and Campbell) spoke exclusively and unimpressively on the Fries and Callender cases, with not one reference to the Baltimore charge. Hopkinson led off for the defense, carefully avoiding the charge at Baltimore. With strange temerity, in view of Chase's formal admission, he solemnly declared that his client was entirely unfamiliar with the proceedings in the first trial of Fries; and immediately he was followed by Martin with the admission that Chase 'had the advantage of perusing the notes of Judge Peters in the former trial' and 'thereby was well acquainted with all the points.'

Luther Martin was a diffuse and slovenly speaker, lax in language, and loose-jointed in his reasoning. Much praise has been lavished upon him by anti-Jeffersonian historians because of

---

[1] *Annals*, February 15, 1805.   [2] *Ibid.*, February 20, 1805.

JOHN MARSHALL
From a portrait by Jarvis

his habitual blackguarding of the author of the Declaration of Independence. But Justice Story found him 'most desultory, wandering and inaccurate,' with 'errors in grammar, and indeed unexampled laxity in speech.'[1] Timothy Pickering, writing a friend while Martin was droning on, complained that he threatened to spoil the effect of Harper's speech, on which high hopes were raised.[2] At length, on the second day, Martin closed, and Harper spoke.

He was an orator, brilliant, polished, artful, a master of sophisticated reasoning. Apparently conceding the questionable conduct of Chase on the first day of the Fries trial, he pleaded in extenuation his reversal on the second day as evidence of repentance. Did the managers answer that repentance came too late? 'But, sir, this is not the rule by which we hope to be judged some day.' But it was apropos of the Baltimore charge that he made his most interesting contribution historically — *an admission of the common practice of federal judges of using the charge to grand juries as a channel through which to pour their partisan spleen, and a plea of the custom, in extenuation of the conduct of Chase, which was thus admitted.* Had not party judges made party speeches from the bench for years? Who questioned the practice now?[3]

Nicholson, following, took up the glove with gaiety. 'Have the judges stood aloof during the political tempests which have agitated the country, or have they united in the " Io triumphe " which the votaries and idolators of power have sung to those who were seated in the seat of Government?' he asked. 'Have they made no offerings at the shrine of party? Have they not preached political sermons from the bench?' And then, accurately, he voiced the intent of Jefferson in his 'attack' on the judiciary. 'The managers wish to teach a lesson to future judges that when intoxicated by the spirit of party, they may recollect the scale of power may turn and preserve the scale of justice equal.'[4]

When Nicholson concluded, the House adjourned until the following day, since John Randolph, who was to follow, was spending the day in bed in a state of physical prostration.

[1] *Story*, 163–64. [2] *King's Corr.*, IV, 441.
[3] *Annals*, February 25, 1805. [4] *Ibid.*, February 26, 1805.

XV

Still desperately ill on the morrow, Randolph was late in arriving, and Nicholson was on the point of asking a further delay when the sick man appeared and requested a delay of but thirty minutes.[1] Always delicate and ailing, he was more than usually worn and weak because of the physical aftermath of his nerve-racking philippics on the Yazoo frauds. Barely had he been able to drag his body to the battleground. To his horror, he then discovered that he had lost the notes he had made for his argument. Thus, sick in body and harassed in mind, he was forced to proceed with none of the advantages of voluminous notes from which the others had spoken. The Federalists took a sadist delight in the sufferings of their foe. In their notes and letters they have passed on to posterity through the pages of biased history the most unfair and exaggerated notions of the argument he made, and his manner of making it.

Cutler found the speech 'outrageous, infuriated declamation which might have done honor to a Marat or Robespierre,' and Plumer, equally partisan, thought it 'replete with invective and even vulgarity.' The malevolent Adams said it was 'honeycombed with the most hackneyed commonplaces ... with a few well-expressed ideas ... much distortion of facts and contortion of body, tears, groans, sobs, with occasional pauses for recollection and continual complaint of having lost his notes.' [2] But Beveridge, better lawyer and orator than any of these, reading the speech in cold blood more than a century later, was to pronounce it 'the best argument for the prosecution.' [3] At times Randolph's face and body were contorted with pain, as Adams so joyfully records.

He began by effectively pulverizing the long since exploded theory of the defense that an offense, to be impeachable, must be indictable. He pounced savagely on Harper's admission of his client's violent temper on the bench 'Today haughty, violent, and imperious; tomorrow humble, penitent, and submissive, prostrating the dignity of his awful function at the feet of the advocate over whom but the day before he had attempted to domineer. Is this a character to dispense law and justice in this country?' he asked with scorn. Passing to the case of Fries, the

[1] Adams, *Diary*, I, 359.   [2] Adams, *Diary*.   [3] Beveridge, III, 212–13.

orator pictured 'the unrighteous judge thirsting for his blood,' and 'the President demanding to hear the evidence and extending the arm of his protection to snatch the victim from the oppressor's grasp.' Turning contemptuously upon Martin, who had cited in justification of his client's acts the examples of certain English judges, notorious for their tyranny, he launched into a fine passage:

> I thank God [he said] that I have studied at the feet of far different Gamaliels from the honorable attorney-general of Maryland, or those by whom it would appear he has been brought up; that I have drawn my notions of justice and constitutional law from far different sources — not from the tribunals of Henry VIII, nor the tools and parasites of the House of Stuart, but from the principles, the history and the lives of those illustrious patriots and their decisions, who brought the Star Chamber to ruins, and their abettors to the block.

Denouncing the forcing of a known hostile juror upon the jury in the case of Callender, he referred savagely to Martin's justification. 'And all this is justified by the authority — of Star Chamber and of Lord Chief Justice Keelyng.' Slashing at the exclusion of the testimony of Taylor, he turned defiantly to the defense: 'What said the Chief Justice [Marshall]? He never knew such a case before.'

At length, as though reluctantly, he reached the Baltimore charge and touched upon it with pitiful inadequacy. At this point the loss of the speaker's notes became manifest. He began to retrace his steps, to ramble back to the case of Fries, never again to touch upon the Baltimore charge. But he rallied to his standard of eloquence for a peroration of stately dignity:

> It remains for you to say whether he shall again become the scourge of an exasperated people, or whether he shall stand as a landmark and a beacon to the present generation and a warning to the future, that no talents however great, no age however venerable, no character however sacred, no connection however influential, shall save that man from the justice of his country, who prostituted the best gifts of nature and of God, and the power with which he is invested for the general good, to the low purposes of an electioneering partisan.
>
> We adjure you in behalf of ... all the people of the United States to exorcise from our courts the baleful spirit of party, to give an awful memento to our judges. ... In the name of the Nation, I demand at your hands the award of justice and of law.

The case was closed.

XVI

This was on Wednesday; the Senate was to vote on Friday.
The rôle of Jefferson in the case was complete when he called the
attention of the House to the Baltimore charge — and that alone.
If he intervened once throughout the trial, as partisan historians
without evidence have charged, not one written line has yet been
found to justify the claim. When, disregarding his idea of a concentration on the Baltimore charge to wander far afield into the
debatable ground of legal technicalities, as the managers did, they
took the case from Jefferson. By dragging in a multitude of
questionable offenses, they weakened the one which fundamen-
tally, to Jefferson, was of paramount importance.

During these days, floating about in the partisan gutters, were
the insinuations that Jefferson had sought to bribe Burr — who
had no vote and was hardly worth a purchase. With the organization of the government in Louisiana the stepson and the brother-
in-law of Burr were given minor posts. 'A bribe, of course!' cried
the Federalists.[1] And Wilkinson, 'friend of Burr,' appointed by
Washington, trusted by Adams, head of the army, familiar with
the Western country, was put in command of the military forces
in the new territory. 'A bribe!' cried the spotless politicians.
And the President had invited the retiring Vice-President to a
state dinner. A bribe![2] And Madison, says McMaster, 'became
gracious.' A bribe! A bribe![3] But Burr, with the noble rectitude
of the immaculate martyr, so touchingly described by the anti-
Jefferson school of historians, had accepted the bribes and refused
to stay bought. Noble figure! Degraded Jefferson!

More worthy of respect is the complaint of Adams that during
the trial Giles, one of the judges, frequently saw Randolph. Had
not Adams heard Giles talking about the case with Randolph in
the cloak-room?[4] Had not the prying eyes of Adams observed the

---

[1] McMaster (III, 176), while sure it was a bribe, admits that the positions were not given
until after the trial — Jefferson insisting on paying the bribe despite the refusal of the
bribed to 'deliver the goods.'

[2] McMaster (III, 176), in his hatred of Jefferson, says that he 'overwhelmed' Burr with
invitations.' He invited him to one dinner.

[3] Though Madison was delighted over Chase's acquittal because of the humiliation of
Randolph. Adams, *Diary*, I, 364–65.

[4] Adams, *Diary*, I, 318, 323.

carriage of Giles in front of Randolph's lodgings; and once, during the trial, had not Randolph and Giles left the chamber together?[1] All true, no doubt. But had the censorious Puritan had the all-seeing eyes of God, he might have seen many political conferences on the issues of the trial, with Martin and Harper sitting in, cheek by jowl, with those judges of the Senate, Pickering, Bayard, and Tracy. Had his genius for snooping led him to the letter-box of Harper, he might have suffered shock on finding Bayard's letter advising the course of the defense before a witness had been called.[2]

Pretense and hypocrisy aside, the case was made political, and politicians treated it as such.

The proof came with the vote. The Senate was tense with excitement. The bearing of the bed of Tracy into the chamber gave to the scene a melodramatic touch. The roll was called on each article, and on none were two thirds cast for conviction. The majority voted to convict on three articles: the forcing of Bassett on the jury, the exclusion of the evidence of Taylor, and the Baltimore charge. The highest vote cast for conviction was on the charge at Baltimore, which the managers had barely touched upon. On the Fries case, which had been a favorite with the managers, the Senate voted acquittal by a majority of two. Five and sometimes six Democrats voted with the Federalists, but on no one article did one single Federalist break the party phalanx perfected for the preservation of the most obnoxious of partisan judges. Had the case not been miserably mismanaged, and had the managers concentrated on the Baltimore charge, Chase might have been removed.

But there were other reasons for the failure. Chase was a Revolutionary figure, even though he had sought a corner on wheat. He was old and feeble, and sympathy played its part in response to Harper's appeal for mercy. The arrogance of Randolph, boasting that it was his impeachment, for which he would get the credit, irritated not a few.[3] Others, wishing to soften the party passions, thought a conviction would accentuate the party spirit.[4] The injection of purely legal questions gave all the advantage to the great lawyers representing Chase, for among the managers there was not one to cope with them.

[1] Adams, *Diary*, I, 363.   [2] *Bayard Papers.*   [3] Adams' *Diary*, I, 364–65.   [4] *Ibid.*

XVII

And what was the feeling of Jefferson?

While his enemies among historians have implied that he was 'distressed,' there is nothing of record to indicate his feeling, *although he had won the very point he sought.* He had no personal interest in the punishment of Chase, the man. Henry Adams, no friend of Jefferson, points out that no one really knows the Administration's views on the event.[1] No word came from Gallatin, none from Jefferson; but there is evidence that Madison was pleased because of the humiliation of Randolph, who had become his bitterest enemy. 'I had some conversation on the subject with Mr. Madison,' wrote Adams, 'who appeared much diverted at the petulance of the managers on their disappointment.'[2]

The venerable jurist had been spared the humiliation of removal, but never again was he to deliver a political speech from the bench, and his last days found him a shrinking violet, as in the days following Hamilton's bitter denunciation on the cornering of wheat. Jefferson cared nothing for Chase himself, for the jurist, to him, was scarcely more than an offensive insect. He did care for the purging of the federal judiciary of the bigoted and insolent partisanship that had converted it into a mere instrument of party.

Jefferson had challenged this arrogance and humbled it. Chase's lawyers had pleaded for mercy. Marshall, appearing for the defense, had seemed frightened. Not until the impeachment of Chase had Federalist politicians conceded openly that the prostitution of the judiciary to the purposes of party was even questionable; not until then had one of them admitted that party speeches in the guise of charges to grand juries were improper. But when Jefferson challenged these practices in the impeachment of Chase, the defense had been forced to admit their impropriety, and never again were the Federalists openly to raise their voices in their justification.

The triumph was Jefferson's; for from the day of Chase's impeachment no federal judge has ever dared so to degrade the judiciary. If Jefferson intended to put a period to the criminal packing of juries by the functionaries of the federal courts, he

---

[1] Adams, *Gallatin*, 327.   [2] Adams, *Diary*, I, 364-65.

again triumphed; for no such scandals have besmirched the judiciary from that time.

By making his vigorous 'attack on the judiciary,' such as it was when the attack was made, he purged it of the practices that were anti-American and morally criminal, and lifted it above the hog wallow of politics to the decent dignity it has since maintained.

CHAPTER XIV

Personalities and Politics

I

DEMOCRATIC principles are in the high road of successful experiment, and we seem to be sailing before the wind in the old track toward monarchy, which has ever been the termination of mob government,' wrote Gouverneur Morris, who could not have been annoyed at the trend.[1] The Jeffersonian avalanche in the elections, followed by the notice served on the federal judiciary, through the Chase impeachment, that the courts no longer could be the engines of party, had tended to inflame the hatred of the repudiated. From this hour on, the fighting of the partisans was increasingly personal. Never was the scurrility of the gutter as a gentleman's weapon to approach that of this period. Social ostracism because of politics became customary in its most offensive form. In Boston, where society was overwhelmingly Federalist, gentlemen of family, character, and accomplishment, such as Elbridge Gerry, were excluded from the drawing-rooms of their neighbors; and soon John Quincy Adams found doors closed in his face. The children of the Boston Federalists grew up under the impression that Democrats, or 'Jacobins,' as they were called, were repulsive creatures from a planet quite remote; and when a Democratic uncle from the district of Maine visited Theophilus Parsons, the younger Theophilus and the other children 'examined him attentively as a specimen of a new and strange breed.' [2] Most distinguished Jeffersonians were discriminated against to their embarrassment at the Boston banks.[3] So foul and unmeasured was the vilification of Governor Sullivan by Major Russell, editor of the *Columbian Centinel,*

---

[1] Morris, *Diary,* II, 464.   [2] Morison, I, 227–28.   [3] *Ibid.,* I, 261.

that the son of the slandered man demanded personal satisfaction. 'Temper is rising and party is in a fury,' wrote an observer.[1]
One day a Federalist lawyer published a letter in the *Boston Gazette* calling Benjamin Austin, a Jeffersonian leader of ability and high standing, 'a liar, a villain and a coward.' The next day the nineteen-year-old son of Austin, on the verge of receiving his degree at Harvard, where he had distinguished himself, met the slanderer of his father on State Street. A moment after the meeting, the lawyer drew a pistol and shot the youth in the breast. Young Austin struck at him with a cane and the assailant threw the revolver at his head, wrested the cane from the dying man, from whose mouth blood was gushing, and beat him as he lay insensible upon the pavement. The lawyer was indicted for murder; but despite the prominence of the parties, the Federalist papers scarcely mentioned the crime, since it would have entailed the publication of the coroner's verdict of willful murder.[2]

In Washington, the pettiness of party malevolence all but ended social intercourse between the Jeffersonians and the opposition. 'Our Federal gentlemen generally decline visiting the Republican members, and vice versa,' wrote Senator Plumer. 'I visit my political opponents freely, converse with them, avoid disputes and obtain much useful information from them.'[3] But Plumer was already moving toward the Jeffersonian camp. On New Year's Day in 1805, the Federalists refused to attend the President's levee, and though it was crowded, the only Federalists to be seen were Plumer, Adams, and Taggart. 'I will never yield implicit obedience to the will of any man or party,' wrote the disgusted Plumer.[4]

The biographer of Josiah Quincy, the new Federalist leader in the House, has apologetically explained that his father's call on Jefferson on reaching the capital was purely one of 'ceremony.' In fact, 'the opinion which he held in common with all the Federalists of that celebrated person made him decline receiving any personal attentions from him, or holding any social intercourse with him.'[5]

[1] Bentley, *Diary*, III, 192.
[2] *Independent Chronicle*, April 7 and August 25, 1806.
[3] *Plumer*, 336.   [4] *Ibid.*, 338.   [5] *Quincy*, 87.

The filth, some unprintable today, poured forth in the Federalist press on Jefferson has never yet been approached in American history. The *New York Evening Post* solemnly proclaimed its conviction that Jefferson would have been capable of 'piling together the bodies of Hamilton, Morris, Bayard, Adams, and Tracy to the amount of one or two hundred and burning them on the altar of democracy, and lighting the funeral pyre with the defaced leaves of the Constitution.' [1] Three years later, the Federalist newspapers would be seriously reviewing a 'poem' by Thomas Green Fessenden, a party hack, then called a satirist, which plumbed the depths of filth. It described Gallatin as 'a rogue' deserving the 'gibbet,' and carried several stanzas indecently after the manner of the brothel or the barroom, charging that one of Jefferson's mulatto house servants, who had cared for his young daughters, was his mistress and the mother of his child. Not content with that, the 'satirist' introduced a footnote charging Jefferson with having attempted the seduction of the wife of a friend. This foul pamphlet ran through numerous editions, and Federalist statesmen of light and leading with pious poses carried copies of the masterpiece about on their persons. [2]

II

We are now upon the threshold of the bitterest political struggles of the Jefferson régime when, confronted with the frown of Napoleon on one side and that of England on the other, the very independence of the Republic is at stake; when party opposition will stoop to treason; and when new conspiracies for the destruction of the Union will be afoot.

For the moment Jefferson had nothing to fear politically. Burr was eliminated definitely. The struggle for the redemption of Connecticut continued with unabated fervor through 1805 and 1806. The Jeffersonians had found a telling issue in their demand for a written constitution framed by the people governed. On the nation's natal day they celebrated with banquets and toasts. 'The State of Connecticut: May she, like her sister States, form

---

[1] *New York Evening Post*, August 18, 1802.

[2] *Democracy Unveiled, or Tyranny Stripped of the Garb of Patriotism*, by Christopher Caustic.

constitutional barriers against inordinate power.' . . . 'The Charter of Connecticut: The gift of a King, supported by the same cloth.' . . . 'The State of Connecticut: May she soon acquire a Constitution of too much health and vigor to be shaken by the fever of ambition or the ague of ignorance' — so ran the toasts.[1] More furious than ever ran the attack. 'The Federalists have priests and deacons, judges and justices, sheriffs and surveyors with a host of corporations and privileged orders to aid their elections,' ran one appeal. 'Let it be shown that plain men, without titles or hope of offices, can do better than the mercenary troops of Federalism.'[2]

Thus, far in advance of the time, the Jeffersonians were perfecting party organizations with town and district managers, with canvassers, with polls recording the politics of every voter, along with the doubtful. Those found doubtful were discussed in secret, and the most promising among the Jeffersonians were assigned the task of coaxing them over. And this, so thoroughly approved in modern party organization, was denounced as revolutionary and sinister by the ruling clique. So meticulous was the canvassing that the party leaders' estimate of the vote in the spring elections of 1806 was borne out almost exactly in the election, when the Democrats made great gains.[3] But the popular appeal and the pageantry of politics were not neglected; and when an editor of Litchfield was arrested and jailed by the State courts for libel, the Jeffersonians met, listened to a prayer and an address, and marched in a body to the jail to pay their respects to the victim. He had been tried by a packed jury in the local court, his case heard by a partisan judge; and, refusing to pay the fine, he went to jail to assert the principle of a free press.[4] Even in Connecticut the Jeffersonians were on the march.

And nowhere were they losing ground. The revenue continued to pour in, the debt continued to be paid, and Gallatin was able to report in May, 1805, that Louisiana, which during the first quarter of 1804 brought in a revenue of thirty-four thousand dollars, had contributed more than three hundred thousand dollars in the last three quarters.[5] Business was prospering, the

[1] Purcell, 271.   [2] *Ibid.*, 273.   [3] *Ibid.*, 274.
[4] *Ibid.*, 275.   [5] *Writings of Gallatin*, I, 231.

people were busy, happy, and contented, and there were few clouds upon the political horizon. Even John Randolph, on the verge of his insurgency, was writing Gallatin of his regret because of Jefferson's determination to retire. 'If I were sure Monroe would succeed him, my regret would be very much diminished,' he wrote significantly.[1]

III

But the political sky was not without its flecks of warning. In Pennsylvania, where Federalism was pulverized, a bitter factional fight had developed for control among the Jeffersonians. On one side Governor McKean, able but arrogant and uncompromising; on the other, the fighting element led by Duane, the militant editor of the *Aurora*. Both protested their devotion to Jefferson, but the followers of Duane were bitter against Gallatin because of patronage disputes. Jefferson, refusing to become a partisan in the quarrel, sought to mollify Duane. He knew the inevitable result would be that the Federalists, by offering a coalition to McKean, would seek to regain control by entering the citadel in a wooden horse of Troy. 'There is an enemy somewhere seeking to sow discord among us,' he wrote Duane. 'Instead of listening first, then doubting, and lastly believing tales handed around without an atom of evidence, if my friends will address themselves to me directly, as you have done, they shall be informed with frankness and thankfulness.' Many lies were in circulation. It was said Jefferson had less communication with the Democrats of the East than previously; true, 'but from accidental circumstances, not from design.' It was said there was but one member of the Cabinet not opposed to him; 'there never was a more harmonious, a more cordial Administration.' It was said he had denounced some Democrats as 'Jacobins' — 'every tittle of it false.' [2]

But the feud was to continue, to Jefferson's embarrassment, both elements loudly proclaiming their undying loyalty to him.

Then, too, with a grave crisis in international affairs approaching, through no fault of Jefferson's he had cause for uneasiness in the congressional situation. Breckinridge had left the Senate to

---

[1] Adams, *Gallatin*, 332.   [2] *Writings of Jefferson*, II, 94.

become Attorney-General, and there was no one to take his place. Giles had been seriously injured in a runaway accident in the spring of 1805 and would not appear in the Senate until in December, 1806. 'To our feelings for your personal suffering,' wrote Jefferson, 'were added those for want of you here. For the importance of matters before Congress and some unfortunate circumstances, your presence here would have been, and still is, of incalculable benefit to the nation.' [1]

Bayard, defeated for the House, had been elected to the Senate, where, despite their meager number, the preponderance of talent was with the Federalists; and no one knew it better than Jefferson. He noted that while his own leaders in the Senate were willing, 'Tracy and Bayard are too dextrous for them'; that Tracy had been on most of the committees, and generally the chairman, and had done much damage in the writing of reports; and that 'the seven Federalists in solid phalanx and joined by some discontented Republicans, some oblique ones, some capricious,' had too often made a majority 'to produce very serious embarrassment to the public operations.' In the House, with its enormous Jeffersonian majority, there were numerous Jeffersonians of good ability, but only one of genius or commanding talent. Should Randolph, in temperamental mood, run off the reservation, the party would be hard put for adequate leadership.

And Randolph was wandering, or rather plunging, off the reservation to become the first important insurgent in the history of Congress.

IV

Randolph was a natural leader for an opposition, a caustic critic, and he had not been happy in the responsible leadership of a majority. Convinced that Jefferson had chosen Madison for the succession, he hated the Secretary of State because of his own partiality for Monroe. The first flaring of the insurgent spirit came with the discussions of the Yazoo frauds, one of the blackest incidents in American history. We must pause for a hasty review of this scandal.

In the winter of 1794–95, under the leadership of William Long-

[1] *Giles*, 101.

street, a member of the legislature of Georgia, was engineered through that body by blatantly criminal methods the sale to four land speculating companies of most of what now comprises the States of Alabama and Mississippi. It was accomplished by the most brazen and defiant bribery, in the open. The little town of Augusta was crowded with speculators wishing to be in at the kill; and not least among them was James Wilson, Associate Justice of the Supreme Court of the United States, bearing on his person twenty-five thousand dollars in bank bills. When the crime had been consummated, he was in possession of seven hundred and fifty thousand acres of good land. So flagrant was the crucifixion of the State that the Governor vetoed the measure. There was a hum and growl from the birds of prey, but the measure was revised to meet some of the gubernatorial objections and passed again, to receive the Governor's reluctant signature. Thus thirty-five million acres of the best land on the continent were sold to speculators for half a million dollars. Only two million acres were reserved for the exclusive entry of the citizens of Georgia. The land companies were to form settlements within five years after the Indian titles had been extinguished.

The moment the news of the sacrifice of the State, in a veritable saturnalia of corruption, trickled to the people, they rose in a storm of fury. In every hamlet and at every crossroads the farmers gathered in tumultuous meetings. Senator Gunn, a ringleader among the racketeers, who had swaggered about the muddy streets of Augusta with a loaded whip, threatening physical harm to timid legislators, was hanged in effigy. The debauched legislators, in fear of lynching, no longer found it safe to venture into a crowd, and some, in panic, fled the State. A young country schoolmaster, destined to real greatness in public life, circulated petitions demanding the immediate righting of the wrong, and Georgia first heard the name of William H. Crawford.

In the next election scarcely a candidate was returned who had not pledged himself to the annulment of the grafters' act. Senator Jackson resigned from the National Senate to enter the State Legislature and lead the fight for the wiping out of the law. The new legislature acted promptly. It passed an act declaring the sale law null and declaring the lands sold under the previous act 'the sole property of the State, subject only to the right of treaty of the United States to enable the State to purchase, under its pre-emption right, the Indian title to the same.'

With advance information on the determination of the legislature, the criminal speculators of the land companies entered upon a campaign of frenzied activity to dispose of the lands to innocent investors. In Boston, three of the companies opened an office, and in a hysteria of speculation the people crowded to buy, for the average price was but fourteen cents an acre. Some who bought paid cash; others gave notes that were immediately sold on the market as commercial paper. The greater part of the purchasers were in New England and the Middle States.

At length the investors, some innocent, others with full knowledge, but unsuspecting that the law might be repealed, heard the doleful news. To some it carried the threat of ruin; to all it brought the certainty of loss. In a panic of fear and anger, they organized the New England Mississippi Company to defend their interests by concerted action. They hurried to the law office of Alexander Hamilton, in New York, and were consoled with a written opinion that, regardless of the criminality of the proceedings, a sale consummated under an existing law was protected by the contract feature of the Constitution.

Then began a battle of pamphlets. Abraham Bishop of Connecticut, ardent Jeffersonian leader, wrote a brilliant exposé of the prospectus of the land companies; and Robert Goodloe Harper, famous Federalist leader, who, with Justice Wilson and Robert Morris, had expected to be a beneficiary of the crime, replied in a pamphlet released only after it had been submitted to Hamilton. This did not enter into the rascality of the conspiracy, but followed the line of Hamilton's opinion.

The situation, long confusing, had now become an impossible tangle. Georgia, sparsely settled by people too poor to pay taxes, found its treasury empty. The currency of the State depreciated until it had no value. The Indian titles to the land had not been extinguished, and this could be done only by the United States dealing with the tribes. Georgia and its land had become a major national problem; and because of the wide sale of the land by the speculators, great numbers of innocent investors were facing ruin.

Just before Jefferson's first inauguration, Congress had passed an act authorizing the President to appoint commissioners to work out a solution of all these difficulties, and to secure from Georgia the cession to the United States of the lands claimed by the State. The cession was made for one million two hundred and fifty thousand dollars, provided the nation would extinguish the Indian titles, settle the British and Spanish claims, and reserve five million acres for the satisfaction of all other claims.

Jefferson appointed James Madison, Albert Gallatin, and Levi Lincoln, three members of the Cabinet of impeccable integrity and keen intelligence. At length they submitted their report, which Beveridge properly describes as 'wise, just, and statesman-like.' [1] The one controversial feature was the provision dealing with the innocent purchasers. The commissioners frankly said that the titles of claimants under the purchase could 'not be supported.' Their eyes were wide open to the corruption. But because so many of the purchasers had bought in good faith, since continuing confusion and litigation would be injurious, not only to the claimants but to the nation, they recommended as a matter of public policy the definitive ending of the controversy on terms that would save to the innocent investor at least a part of his investment. 'The interest of the United States, the tranquillity of those who may hereafter occupy that territory, and various equitable considerations which may be urged in favor of some of the claimants, render it expedient to enter into a compromise on reasonable terms,' they said.

v

But John Randolph was in no mood to compromise. He seldom was. It was that which made him a colorful leader for an opposition and a difficult spokesman for a responsible government. At a time when Georgia was seething with rage, when Gunn was being burnt in effigy on crossroads posts, when legislators were slinking from the State hiding their faces from their fellows, he had visited a friend in Georgia. The infamy of the affair had aroused his anger. Compromise with thieves? Never!

When the bill to carry the recommendations of the commis-

[1] Beveridge, III, 574.

sioners into effect was introduced, Randolph plunged with maniacal fury into the opposition. The Jefferson Administration was involved solely in that the two foremost members of the Cabinet had submitted the report. Jefferson himself took no part at any time, and his two sons-in-law in Congress were to vote consistently with Randolph throughout the struggle. The actual author of the report was Gallatin, his friend, to whom he was devoted. But 'when I first read this report,' said Randolph, 'I was filled with unutterable astonishment, finding men in whom I had, and still have, the highest confidence, recommending a measure which all the facts and all the reasons which they had collected opposed and unequivocably condemned.' [1]

As the fight progressed, and Randolph's fury rose to extreme heights, he brushed Gallatin and Lincoln aside to concentrate his rage and hate on Madison. The reason was apparent: he wished to destroy him to clear the way for Monroe's election to the Presidency. Soon he was trying to smear the Administration itself.

Throughout the session of 1805-06, when the nation was grappling at once with Napoleon, Pitt, and Spain, he continued in philippic after philippic, rising to a crescendo of madness, slashing in all directions, like a negro drunk on gin, regardless of friend or foe, and yet manifesting a genius for invective seldom equaled, if ever approached, in congressional history. His excoriation of the criminality of the legislature and of the land companies was eminently just, and Sheridan's invectives in the trial of Hastings were no more brilliant or severe. But in the exuberance of his rhetoric, in the inebriation of his rage, he soon had Madison and Gallatin parties to the crime, and was hurling the epithet of 'corruptionist' indiscriminately over a body of deliberative men. In Gideon Granger, the Postmaster-General, he sought a victim for his wrath. This cunning and resourceful man was found lobbying for the law to back the compromise, and that was quite enough. Had he not lobbied under slightly similar circumstances for the notorious Connecticut Reserve? 'His gigantic grasp embraces with one hand the shores of Lake Erie and stretches with the other to the bay of Mobile. Millions of acres

[1] *Annals*, February 3, 1805.

are easily digested by such stomachs. Goaded by avarice, they buy only to sell, and sell only to buy. The retail trade of fraud and imposture yields too slow and small a profit to gratify their cupidity. They buy and sell corruption in the gross. The deeper they play, the greater their zest for the game; and the stake which is set upon their throw is nothing less than the patrimony of the people.'

And then, throwing discretion and judgment to the winds, he plunged on:

'This agent is the head of an executive department of the Government, subordinate, indeed, in rank and dignity and in the ability required for its superintendence, but inferior to none in the influence attached to it. . . . This officer having an influence which is confined to no quarter of the country . . . with offices in his gift among the most lucrative, and at the same time the least laborious or responsible under the Government — this officer presents himself at your bar, at once a party and an advocate.'

And, indifferent to the implication, he hurried on:

'When I see this tremendous patronage brought to bear upon us, I do confess that it strikes me with consternation and dismay. Is it come to this? Are the heads of executive departments of the Government to be brought into the House, with all the influence and patronage attached to them, to extort from us now what was refused at the last session of Congress?'

Granger, in a letter to Macon, the Speaker, immediately demanded a congressional investigation, but to no avail. The House discounted Randolph, even some who followed in his wake, and there were other things to do.[1] Matthew Lyon, who was assailed, replied roughly but effectively. 'These charges come from a person,' he said, 'whose fortune, leisure, and genius enabled him to obtain a great share of the wisdom of the schools, but who in years, experience, and the knowledge of the world and the ways of man is many, many years behind those he implicates; a person who from his rant in this House seems to have got his mind as full of British contracts and British modes of corruption as ever Don Quixote's was supposed to have been of chivalry, enchantments, and knight-errantry; a person who seems to think no man can

---

[1] *Annals*, February 1, 1805.

be honest and independent unless he has inherited lands and negroes.'[1]

The mortal fear in which most men held Randolph's tongue was broken, and Lyon's was not to be the last, nor the most ferocious, castigation the enraged leader was to receive. Madison had been mortally affronted, Jefferson alienated, and even Gallatin estranged before Randolph definitely deserted the Administration on the Spanish and British policies. He was to postpone action to put the recommendations of the Yazoo Commission into operation, and some years were to elapse before John Marshall in a notable decision placed the stamp of judicial approval on the theory on which the commissioners acted.

The Federalists generally remained mute throughout this con-troversy, torn by conflicting emotions. It pleased them enor-mously to observe a schism in the Jeffersonian ranks, and they took keen pleasure in Randolph's attacks on the Democratic leaders. But on the Yazoo settlement they dared not join in the attack. They laughed joyously when Randolph sneered at the 'sepulchre tone' of one of the Northern Democrats, and said he spoke 'in the language of the common prayer-book, which might be either said or sung,' and at his gibe at Varnum, of Massa-chusetts, as the 'sworn interpreter of Presidential Messages'; they rejoiced mightily in the sneers at Madison, but they could not join in them. The greater part of the 'innocent investors' in the Yazoo lands were of their own tribe. Hamilton was their legal adviser. Harper was their pamphleteer-defender. A justice of the Supreme Court, and of their political faith, was one of the beneficiaries of the 'steal.' Robert Morris was in up to his armpits in the speculation. If politics entered into it at all — and legiti-mately it did not — Yazoo was their own child. Their smiles of satisfaction were too often checked, as when, in speaking of the criminal conspiracy aimed at the corrupting of the legislature, Randolph said that it 'was hatched in Philadelphia and New York, and I believe in Boston,' and 'the funds were furnished by monied capitalists of those towns.'[2] Pickering assured King that the Federalists 'have every day listened to John Randolph with unmixed pleasure in opposition to the mean dastardly democrats

[1] *Annals*, February 1, 1805.   [2] Bruce, I. 193.

of New England,' but this was not true.[1] The part played in the
controversy by the rival candidacies of Madison and Monroe
seemed promising, for if the Jeffersonians divided, the Federalists
might march between them to an easy triumph.[2] But others
doubted if the controversy would reach so far. 'If you ask me
what good is to result from all this,' wrote Benjamin Tallmadge,
'I must say perhaps no lasting good, and it has been uniformly
found to be true that whenever the principles of the party are
attacked, they will immediately unite as in a common cause.' [3]
Indeed, at one juncture there were whisperings of a possible duel
between Randolph and Dana of Connecticut, a leading Federalist.

This grew out of the reading of Granger's letter demanding
an investigation of Randolph's charges and insinuations. When
Varnum moved a reference to a committee with instructions
to report, pandemonium broke loose, and Macon was unable to
restore order. Randolph had made another of his bitter attacks
and Dana had replied with severity. It was observed that Randolph, much excited, was 'often crying.' 'When Dana sat down,
Johnny came immediately around to his chair and was observed
to be crying while he was whispering to him.' It was thought
that Dana had received a challenge, but this proved to be without
foundation.[4]

Meanwhile, the Federalists found Jefferson's conduct discouraging. Instead of losing his temper and plunging in wrathful mood
into the battle involving the clashing ambitions of his two friends,
Madison and Monroe, he stood serenely aloof. On the Yazoo
question his two sons-in-law were voting with Randolph. This
was maddening. 'While these two divisions of Democrats are
thus canvassing for the next President,' wrote Pickering to King,
'the actual President is exploring the wilds of Louisiana — its
salt plains — its rock or mineral salt — its immense prairies — in
which he has discovered the earthly paradise.' [5]

Clearly such a politician was impossible.

VI

Never had there been such a crowded, sensational session of
Congress. Randolph had dramatized public life. With the Yazoo

---

[1] *King's Corr.*, iv, 476.   [2] Pickering to King, *King's Corr.*, iv, 508–09.
[3] Cutler, ii, 326–27.   [4] Cutler, ii, 187–89.   [5] *King's Corr.*, iv, 508–09.

controversy cropping up at frequent intervals and at unexpected moments, a bitter battle was in progress over Jefferson's plan for the purchase of Florida, and the Administration plan to contest Britain's mistreatment of American commerce with a Non-Importation Act was being debated with a bitterness that had reached white heat.

For a moment it seemed that Thomas Mann Randolph, the son-in-law of Jefferson, would face John Randolph on the 'field of honor.' In the debate on the Naval Appropriation Act, the latter had referred to the 'contumely or hostility' which had been 'manifested during the earlier part of the session.' No reflection was intended on anyone, but the bitterness of months of battling had put less irascible men than Thomas Mann Randolph on edge. He imagined the offensive expression applied to him, and springing to his feet he began an attack. 'An immeasurable distance,' he thought, lay between his talents and those of John Randolph, but he had observed that the latter was 'more prudent of speech outside the House than when protected by the shield of its dignity.' He held the same views of personal honor as John Randolph and had always felt that there were times when 'even steel makes a very proper ingredient in serious quarrels.' Scarcely had he resumed his seat when a congressional friend of the challenged party waited on him to inquire if reference was meant to John Randolph. 'It was,' snapped the overwrought Randolph. Then, replied the friend of the man of Roanoke, his principal was ready to meet the challenger on the morrow or that night — preferably that night. Thomas replied that he was ready; but that if John Randolph would say that the insulting words had not been applied to him, he would, as a man of honor, make amends. The man of Roanoke, when thus informed, replied that the course pursued by his kinsman made any declaration on his part impossible. Thomas named his second; the seconds met and talked; that of John Randolph gave assurance that the offended statesman had an entire misconception of what his principal had said. There was much conversation and scurrying about among the friends of the two Randolphs; and cooling down, and calmly reading the offensive statement, Thomas Mann Randolph saw he was in the wrong. He rose in the House and made his explanation, which John Randolph accepted, and for a moment all seemed serene again. But a controversy rose between the seconds as to what actually had occurred, fighting letters were exchanged through the *Richmond Enquirer*, and for a moment it seemed inevitable that blood would be shed.

Jefferson had followed the controversy with the apprehensions of a father, and at this juncture he intervened, in a note to his son-in-law expressing his opinion of the duel. 'It is not inclination in anybody but a fear of the opinion of the world which leads men to the absurd and immoral decision of differences by duel,' he wrote. 'The mass of mankind, and particularly that thinking part whose esteem we value, would condemn in a husband and father of a numerous family everything like forwardness in this barbarous and lawless appeal.' This brought Randolph to his senses and the controversy died.[1]

It was in this atmosphere, charged with electricity, with social contacts broken over politics, with the participants deliberating in wrathful mood, with hate predominant, that Jefferson's plan for the possible acquisition of Florida was thrown into the Capitol. Here we shall find Randolph emerging as an avowed insurgent — the first in congressional history.

[1] Bruce, I, 202–05.

CHAPTER XV

The Spanish Controversy

I

THE controversy with Spain was hurrying to a crisis before Congress met. This controversy grew out of the spoliations on American commerce in a previous war and the increasingly irritating problem of the eastern boundaries of Louisiana. It had been accentuated by the undiplomatic conduct of Charles Pinckney in Madrid and the equally indefensible activities of the Marquis de Casa Yrujo in Washington. The climax came in the failure of Monroe to negotiate a treaty of understanding at Aranjuez the previous summer amidst the studied insults of the suave Cevallos, the Spanish Minister of State, and the defiant offensiveness of Godoy, who bore the double title of Prime Minister and bedfellow to Maria Luisa.

Previous to the acquisition of Louisiana, Pinckney had sought a settlement of the spoliation claims, and, after long negotiations, a treaty had been signed; but just at this juncture came the purchase of Louisiana, and the resentment in Madrid had prevented ratification. The brusque manners of Pinckney and his crude attempts at intimidation had made his continuance at the Court of Spain impossible, and Monroe was ordered to Madrid to assist, not only in the negotiation of a spoliation treaty, but in the settlement definitely of the eastern boundaries of Louisiana. Monroe had elicited from Talleyrand the positive pledge that the influence of the French Government should be exercised to persuade Charles IV of Spain to part with the Floridas. But Spain was infuriated with France because of the sale of Louisiana. Had not Lucien Bonaparte on the occasion of the retrocession to France given a solemn pledge that France would never part with Louisi-

ana except to return it to her ally? Both Napoleon and Talleyrand had urged Monroe to postpone his negotiations until the hot
Spanish blood had cooled.

Monroe was enjoying himself in London when new events made
imperative the immediate commencement of negotiations in
Madrid. The bitterness over Louisiana had not subsided. The
Spanish soldiers and governors of Florida, through constant
interference with the transportation of American products by the
rivers flowing through their territory to the Gulf, were creating a
crisis similar to that caused by the withdrawal of the right of
deposit in New Orleans. Politicians and press were demanding
war, and war was not improbable.

Monroe left London on his mission with high hopes.[1] He paused
in Paris to remind Talleyrand of his promise and to be answered
with an enigmatic smile. With relays of mules, he went plunging
over the roads of Spain and on to Aranjuez, where the Court was
luxuriating in the famous palace with its gorgeous gardens. There
was Pinckney with the sad tale of his troubles. There was the
cynical, sensuous Godoy, who, on more than one occasion, had
manifested a strange friendship for the young Republic. And
there was Don Pedro Cevallos, the Minister of State, a polished
imitation of the courtly diplomats of the previous century, graceful, gracious, suave, smiling, soft-spoken, a master in the arts of
sophistry and procrastination. Allied with powerful France, he
was reasonably confident that he need not greatly concern himself
with the American barbarians. But he would be gracious. He
would write them long and clever notes, interminable, conceding
nothing, wearing them out as a predecessor had worn out the
Prince of Wales and Buckingham in the marriage negotiations of
long before. Don Pedro rather relished the opportunity for an
epistolary practice that need carry no responsibility. Thus began
the graceful battle of notes. Monroe, impatient, sought to pin
his adversary down to the settlement of some one point, and
Cevallos in sweetest phrasing responded with another note.
Patience! At length Monroe served notice of his wish to retire
from the negotiations, from which nothing could be expected.
Don Pedro was pained. He had enjoyed writing these clever notes

[1] Monroe to Jefferson, *Writings of Monroe*, IV, 252.

as a cat enjoys playing with a mouse. Surely, he suggested, all these points had not been adequately discussed — would not Señor Monroe linger a little longer? But Monroe demanded his passports. They were given with a startling celerity and without a word of civility; and scarcely had Monroe departed when the American Chargé d'Affaires, dropping in on Godoy, was greeted with a yawn and the question, 'How go our affairs? Are we to have peace or war?' Meanwhile, Pinckney packed his luggage and hurried home to become Governor of South Carolina; and when the Spanish spoliation of American commerce noticeably increased, the new Minister was ordered to wait in London for instructions from Washington.[1]

It looked like war; Godoy was almost gleeful over the prospect, with the armies of Napoleon to fall back upon. For a moment, Jefferson strongly favored an alliance with Great Britain for war purposes, but when Madison objected that we had no inducement to offer that we could afford to make, his love of peace prevailed. And Gallatin strengthened his resolve. What would war now mean? he asked Jefferson. It would destroy our commercial intercourse with Italy, Spain, France, and Holland; it would minimize our trade with the two Indies, and would dangerously decrease the national revenues. And would not the renewal of negotiations be more in accord with the primary policies of the Administration? By the modification of our demands, should the negotiations fail, our position would be much stronger, and if war could be held off two years, we should be in better position to wage it.[2] A few days later, Gallatin wrote again. 'As far as I am assured by our friends, war would be unpopular,' he reported. They counted on the wisdom of the Administration to prevent hostilities.[3] And a month later Gallatin was harping on the same theme,[3] concluding that the revival of the war in Europe would give as much as a year for negotiations.[4] About the same time Jefferson, realizing, as Monroe had reported, that Spain was completely under the domination of Napoleon, wrote Gallatin: 'Our question now is, in what way to give Spain another oppor-

---

[1] Monroe's 'Notes on the Differences with Spain,' *Writings of Monroe*, IV, 437.

[2] *Writings of Gallatin*, I, 241.

[3] *Ibid.*, I, 255.   [4] *Ibid.*, I, 257.

tunity of arrangement? Is not Paris the place? France the agent? The purchase of Florida the means?' [1]

The sultriness of August drowsed upon the land when Jefferson asked all the members of the Cabinet for a written opinion on the Spanish problem. These opinions were as various as the minds of the men, but all agreed that war should be the last resort. The discussions continued informally throughout the summer and early autumn, and then in November came an amazing letter from Armstrong, the American Minister in Paris.

A mysterious personage, known to be personally attached to the fortunes of Talleyrand, slipped into the Legation in Paris with a memorandum in Talleyrand's handwriting, suggesting a plan for the settlement of the Spanish question. A new note, sufficiently strong to arouse Madrid from its lethargy, should be sent Cevallos, warning of the danger of the course pursued, and proposing the arbitrament of Napoleon. Should an unfavorable reply be received, this should be sent to Talleyrand, requesting the friendly intervention of the great Corsican. If, in response to Napoleon's intervention, Spain agreed to dispose of the Floridas, as Talleyrand had no doubt she would, the terms of France would be as follows: France was to receive such commercial privileges in Florida as had been granted in Louisiana; the western boundary of Louisiana should be the Rio Colorado and a line running northwesterly, including the headwaters of the rivers falling into the Mississippi, with thirty leagues on each side to remain forever unoccupied; the spoliation claims of Spain to be paid with bills upon the Spanish colonies; and ten million dollars to be paid to Spain.

Instantly Armstrong rejected the proposition because of the sacrifices entailed on the United States. The mysterious messenger departed, and then returned. Ten millions too great? Very well — and he proposed a plan which would have meant the payment of but four millions. Armstrong fell back on his lack of instructions and promised to communicate with Washington.

There could be no doubt that Talleyrand had written the memorandum, but whether Napoleon had been consulted remains a mystery. On October 13, Jefferson had suggested Paris as 'the

[1] *Writings of Gallatin*, I, 267.

place,' France as 'the agent,' and the purchase of Florida as 'the means.' And three weeks later, Armstrong's message with Talleyrand's similar suggestion was laid before him. Jefferson required no more. Negotiations it should be. A French job? He cared not whether it were a French, a British, a Russian, or a Prussian job. He wanted Florida, to prevent a war and to round out the Republic on the Gulf. He would pay Spain; and if Spain gave the money to Napoleon, that would be the business of Spain.

II

The duplication of the sensational Louisiana triumph now loomed before him. Secrecy would be as essential now as in the case of the Louisiana Purchase. The action of Spanish soldiers in crossing into American territory, the spoliation of American commerce, the interference with American produce floating down the Mobile to the Gulf, must be sharply and publicly challenged, that the Americans might know that rather than submit we would fight. A spirited challenge in a public Message would tend to strengthen the American envoy's hands in the negotiations.

But there could be no public proclamation of the plans for negotiation, no laying of the cards upon the table face upward before the game in Paris should begin. Thus it was determined that the annual Message should deal with the protest; and that a secret Message to Congress should guardedly set forth as much as possible of the negotiations, that the money necessary might be provided. Thus the two Messages on the Spanish problem.

With his own pen, Jefferson wrote both Messages and the resolutions to carry the recommendations into effect. Again we find Madison and Gallatin scanning their master's manuscript line by line, and Jefferson, with an open mind and no pride of authorship, accepting most of their suggestions.

Seldom had Congress convened in an atmosphere more intense. The press was hysterical with denunciations, clamoring for war; the people in the corn rows, the taverns, the coffee-shops, on the wharves and the highways, were talking with much swagger. The senators and representatives sat on the edge of their chairs to hear the words that would mean peace or war. And the most warlike were content, for the tone and temper were almost belligerent. It was what Jefferson had hoped. Not only was it meant for the irritated Americans; even more was it meant for the Madrid Ministry and the Foreign Office in Paris. There was no moderating of the wrongs we were resenting. Even the Federalists were pleased. It meant war with Spain — even better, it meant war with the 'Jacobins.' No one doubted that the secret Message a few days later would pave the way for a declaration of war.

Promptly the resolutions bearing on the Message, written by Jefferson, criticized by Gallatin, revised by the President, and unanimously approved by the Cabinet, were introduced and passed.[1] These declared the wrongs suffered from Spain intolerable; that the armed forces of no foreign power would be suffered in Louisiana; that a peaceable solution still was possible, but that pending the attempt, an agreement must be reached that neither nation in disputed territory would strengthen its armed forces; and that should Spain proceed in her defiant course, she would be repelled by force. They also proposed that, just as citizens of Spain should continue to be free from imposts and interference on the Mississippi, those of the United States should enjoy the same immunities on the Mobile and its waters. To maintain these propositions, Congress pledged its support.

Then, three days later, Congress sat in secret session to hear the special Message. Surely it would advance us toward the battlefield. Insurance rates went up, merchant ships were armed, the press was beside itself with frenzy. But the secret Message was an anticlimax. It reviewed the course of previous negotiations in Madrid, asked the authority of Congress forcibly to repel the invasion of Spanish soldiers in territory concededly our own, and turned to the possibilities of further negotiations. War need not follow; but warlike measures might strengthen our hands in the discussions. The conditions in Europe justified high hopes of a successful issue. 'But the course to be pursued will require the command of means which it belongs to Congress exclusively to yield or to deny,' it said.

But there was no announcement of a plan of purchase and no specific reference to an appropriation. This had been discussed

---

[1] Original resolutions, *Writings of Gallatin*, I, 277; Gallatin's criticism, *ibid*, 278· Jefferson's revision, *ibid.*, 281.

confidentially with members of Congress. Gallatin had prepared a resolution, and asked Nicholson to introduce it, appropriating two million dollars for the use of the President in international affairs.

There was a pause. That day Gallatin received a note from Jefferson: 'J. Randolph has just called to ask a conversation with me, for which purpose he will be with me tomorrow morning; everything therefore had better be suspended till that is over.' [1]

The next morning the skeleton figure of Randolph dismounted at the White House door, and Jefferson received him in the office where the pet bird sang. The man from Roanoke was in his most arrogant mood, for he had already determined upon his insurgency. Never, he declared, would he vote a penny for the purchase. It had not been asked in the Message and he would not stand to have the responsibility passed on to the House. A militant public Message had stirred the country with high expectations of an armed resistance, and the House was to bear the onus of doing nothing.[2]

With his usual serenity, Jefferson sought to reason with his erstwhile leader, but soon dismissed him as a lost sheep. The battle had begun.

The special Message had been referred to John Randolph's Committee of Ways and Means, packed by Macon with Randolph's friends. The next day the committee sat, Nicholson among them, with Gallatin's resolution in his pocket. It remained there. Barnabas Bidwell, of Massachusetts, the Administration's sole champion, interpreted the document as Jefferson intended. The others shook their heads in hypocritical negation, and Bidwell was voted down. The committee adjourned, having done nothing.

The next day, Randolph mounted his horse and rode away to Baltimore for a week, and nothing was done. On his return, he called on Madison, whom he hated and for whom he was gunning, and he was to emerge from this interview with the story that Madison had said France would not permit Spain to sell the Floridas, because France wanted money. He had twisted the words of Madison for a purpose.

---

[1] *Writings of Gallatin*, I, 282.

[2] Randolph's version, 'Decius,' *Richmond Enquirer*.

III

And it was not a time for procrastination. Events were moving rapidly in Europe, and in the United States grievances against Spain were multiplying. The Marquis de Casa Yrujo was on a rampage now, and likewise gunning for Madison. A polished, courtly, gallant figure, married to the daughter of one of Jefferson's close friends, he had, on more than one occasion, given dignity to diplomacy by smoothing differences and reconciling his own country and our own. He had been continued in his post on the personal request of Jefferson, of whom he was fond, and whose delightful guest he had often been at Monticello. That he was on the warpath now was not without extenuating circumstances. He had sought to reconcile Spain to our acquisition of Louisiana, and had furiously protested against the action of the Intendant at New Orleans. But when the bill was passed which calmly made Mobile, the property of Spain, part of a revenue district of the United States, he not unnaturally lost his temper. Before Jefferson had placed a satisfactory interpretation on the act, Yrujo, with the measure in his hand, in a most offensive manner had descended like a madman on Madison in his office.

Convinced that his country was the victim of misrepresentations, he lost all sense of proportion and turned secretly to the press to counteract the effect of the attacks. Denied access to the Jeffersonian press, he turned to the Federalist newspapers — and before this incident Madison had not infrequently recognized in articles the hand of the Marquis.

Then Yrujo made a fatal blunder. One day the *Columbian Centinel* of Boston prefaced the publication of one of his letters with the damaging words: 'The following letter communicated to the Secretary of State is published at the request of the Marquis Casa de Yrujo.' [1] In his hot zeal, he applied to Major William Jackson, editor of the *Gazette* in Philadelphia, for the support of his views, leaving no doubt in the mind of the editor that a bribe was intended. Resenting the insult, Jackson gave out a public letter to the press, supported by an affidavit, making the charge. [2]

Here the Marquis, so familiar with social usage, was to be

---

[1] *Columbian Centinel*, October 13, 1804.   [2] October 17, 1804.

subjected to the saddest of all humiliations. After making his attempt on the Philadelphia editor, he sallied forth, quite gaily, on a visit to Jefferson at Monticello. Passing Montpelier, the home of Madison, he pointedly snubbed him by passing on without a pause for salutations. It was while he was drinking Jefferson's wine and eating his turkey that the latter learned of the affidavit of the editor. With the exquisite courtesy of the perfect host, Jefferson did not mention it. A few days longer the two men were together, strolling on the lawn, with all the other guests familiar with the Marquis's delicate situation. He alone was ignorant. But all the while Jefferson was in his kindest, mellowest mood, and when business summoned him back to Washington, he particularly instructed Mrs. Randolph that special pains be taken to make the Marquis's sojourn comfortable and enjoyable. A little later the Marquis set forth on his return to the capital in blissful ignorance of the exposure, again snubbing Madison on the way. On reaching Washington and learning that his host had been cognizant of his action, he was all the more enraged because of his humiliation. He wrote a letter to the press giving the lie to the editor, but no one believed him.

After that, he merely ran amuck. With real sorrow — for Jefferson was fond of him and his beautiful wife — Madison was authorized to demand his recall. When the demand was handed to Cevallos, he said Yrujo had asked for leave, and inquired whether it would not be satisfactory for him to depart without the formality of a recall. He would leave as soon as he could embark without subjecting himself to the perils of the winter seas. Jefferson was more than satisfied.

But months passed and the Marquis lingered. It was discovered that he continued to act officially for his Government; and as the opening of Congress approached, it was learned that he planned to resume his post in Washington. Madison wrote a sharp note forbidding his return — and he returned. Not only did he return, but he replied to Madison with supreme arrogance. No one but his royal master had the power to order him out of Washington, he said.[1] Not satisfied with this, he sent copies of his correspondence with Madison to all the members of the

[1] Madison to Chargé d'Affaires, MS. Archives, American Embassy, Madrid.

diplomatic corps in Washington; and not content even with this, he sent his reply to the press for publication before Madison received it.

Thus this session found the Marquis moving with something of a swagger in Federalist circles, receiving their pats of encouragement, and, by them, constantly informed of the secret proceedings of Congress in executive sessions. At length even the *Columbian Centinel* was irked by the Marquis's conduct and protested with vigor. 'We hope the Executive of the United States will adopt spirited measures to resent a line of conduct which, had it been taken by an American Minister at Madrid or Paris, would have precipitated the Inquisition or the Temple,' it said.[1]

But the *Centinel* could see no objection to the betrayal of the secrets of executive sessions to the Spanish Minister by the Federalist leaders in the Senate. Very earnestly, it denounced these 'secret sessions of the Senate on the Spanish matter' in the same article carrying full information on details of the debates.[2] For the relations of Yrujo and the Federalist leaders was close. 'Many members very social with him,' wrote Senator Mitchill, 'and he boasts that he knows all the secrets of debates behind closed doors.'[3] He had insulted Jefferson, denouncing him as a liar; had insulted Madison; and had defied the United States. Meanwhile, he had enlisted the co-operation of General Turreau, the French Minister, the assassin of Vendée, who between the lashings of his spouse found time for intrigue. Fearing that Turreau was creating the impression in Paris that the recall of the Marquis had been inspired by his devotion to French interests, Madison instructed Armstrong in Paris to explain the situation to Talleyrand.[4]

Meanwhile, John Quincy Adams, indignant at the defiance of the Marquis, introduced his bill defining the status of a diplomat in Washington and providing for the deportation of recalled Ministers who refused to leave. Almost immediately Turreau knocked at his door. He hoped Adams would not press the bill; otherwise he might be sent off and fall into the hands of the English. As to the Marquis, of course he should not have given his

---

[1] *Columbian Centinel*, February 5, 1806.   [2] *Ibid.*, February 26, 1806.
[3] Mitchill's Letters.   [4] *Writings of Madison*, VII, 200.

letters to Madison to the press, but something should be forgiven
a servant 'zealous in support of his sovereign.' Adams sharply
suggested that there was no forgiving the sending of letters to the
other diplomats, and the open insulting of the head of the State.
'Does the Marquis imagine,' asked the aroused Adams, 'that he
and the French and the English Ministers or any other here can,
by concert, give us the law?' Ah, sighed the assassin of Vendée, of
course all that was wrong, but there was nothing wrong in the
letter. 'I well know what the rights and independence of Ministers
are,' snapped Adams.[1]

With the superb spirit with which Adams invariably rose above
party where national rights and dignity were concerned, he supported his bill in a speech. 'The freedom which a Spanish Minister,
unreproved, can take today, the French Minister would claim as
a right tomorrow, and a British Minister would exercise without
ceremony on the next day. A diplomatic censorship would be
established over the supreme executive of the nation, and the
President would not dare to exhibit to Congress the statement of
our national concerns, without previously submitting his Message
for approbation to a Cabinet Council of foreign Ministers. . . . Of
the newspaper appeal to the people, I say nothing. The people of
this country are not so dull of understanding or so depraved in
vice as to credit the assertions of a foreigner, bound by no tie of
duty to them, the creature and agent of their adversary, in contradiction to those of their own officers, answerable to them for his
every word and stationed at the post of their highest confidence.'
But no diplomat should be permitted, first to insult the President,
and, on the demand for his recall, to defy the order that he leave
the capital.[2]

But neither Jefferson nor Madison considered such a measure
necessary, and, while appreciating the attitude of Adams, Jefferson was not eager to intensify the feeling in Madrid at the moment
of beginning negotiations. 'Mr. Worthington told me that he
conversed with the President about it [the bill] and the President
was well pleased with it,' wrote Adams. 'My conclusion from this
is that in reality the President has given the word against the
passage of the bill.'[3]

[1] Adams, *Diary*, I, 410–11.   [2] *Annals*, March 3, 1806.   [3] Adams, *Diary*, I, 412.

Content with the effect of Adams's denunciation of the Marˎ quis's action, the measure was not seriously considered. The irate Minister, flattered and fawned upon by the Federalists, continued his defiance for a year, and finally took his departure, leaving behind, despite his amazing indiscretions, born of passion, a memory not without its fragrance. He was to be a witness of the bitter battles of the session, and to inform his Government constantly of the Administration's secret plans. He had numerous secret spies — they embraced a large part of the Federalist membership in Congress.

IV

To get the background of the exasperating interferences with Jefferson's plans for an amicable negotiation, another incident must be painted in. In the autumn of 1805, Francisco Miranda, a native of Caracas, arrived in New York. For years he had been meandering over Europe seeking to enlist some government in his revolutionary enterprise in South America. Even Pitt had not discouraged him, and in America, Hamilton had given such hospitable ear to his plans for combined military action of England and the United States that he had been offered the leadership of the expedition.[1] In the meantime much water had passed over the dam, and Hamilton was dead. Miranda hastened to Washington, called on both Jefferson and Madison, and as was the custom in the case of foreigners of note, was invited to dinner. The American officials were eager enough to learn, first-hand, the nature of Miranda's movement and what encouragement he had received in London. In the interview with Madison he was told that the United States could have nothing to do with such an enterprise, and he was warned that under the laws of the Republic he would be subject to criminal prosecution. It was not a secret that he had talked with Madison, and when he returned to New York he gave the impression to those he sought to enlist in the conspiracy that it had the approval of the Government. Burr had resorted to the same deceptive device. But to Madison the adventurer held out every appearance of a determination to pay due respect 'to the laws of the land.'[2] Having issued the warning,

[1] *Jefferson and Hamilton*, 427.
[2] Madison to the Chevalier de Fernando, MS. Archives. American Embassy, Madrid.

and convinced that Miranda could not fit out an expedition on
American soil without adequate warning to Washington from
'officers of the United States in the several ports,'[1] Miranda was
dismissed from the minds of Jefferson and Madison.

But Miranda was as dependable as Burr — no more. The
moment he reached New York he arranged with Samuel G. Ogden
for the use of his boat, the *Leander*, and began collecting war
material and enlisting men. No warning reached Washington of
these proceedings — because William S. Smith, surveyor of the
port, the ne'er-do-well son-in-law of John Adams, and a Federalist,
had entered heartily into Miranda's plans. Senator Dayton, soon
to join in the Burr conspiracy, was deep in the plot; and John
Swartwout, marshal, on the recommendation of Burr, was in to
the limit. One morning, with the full knowledge of these disloyal
subordinate officials of the United States, the *Leander* sailed from
the harbor with twenty-five or thirty men.[2] It was not from the
officials of New York nor from the Spanish Legation that Jefferson
learned of the departure of the boat; he instantly ordered the
arrest and punishment of Smith and Ogden, and immediately
Smith and Ogden became Federalist martyrs! Had not Jefferson
and Madison seen Miranda? And did it not follow that they had
given consent? And had not the cunning Miranda sent a letter to
Madison on leaving, asking him 'to keep in deepest secret' the
'important matters' the adventurer had laid before him? Some
historians were to make the most of this without giving their
readers the benefit of Madison's notation on the letter that the
'important matters' referred to the action of the British Government.

Into this mess Yrujo plunged with boyish glee, cheered on by the
Federalists, and ardently supported by the assassin of Vendée.
Indeed, Madison was forced to send a note to Armstrong to the
effect that while the American Government would always be glad
to discuss French affairs with Turreau, his agency for Yrujo
would not be tolerated.[3]

The trial was a farce. The *New York Commercial Advertiser* was
saying that the accused were innocent because Miranda clearly

[1] Madison to the Chevalier de Fernando, MS. Archives, American Embassy, Madrid.
[2] *Ibid.*   [3] *Writings of Madison*, VII, 209.

had the approval of Jefferson and Madison, since they had seen him.[1] The jury was packed by Swartwout. The defense sought to try Madison instead of Smith, just as at Richmond the defense were later to seek to substitute Jefferson for Burr in the dock. The members of the Cabinet were to be dragged in whether they had seen Miranda or not, to be subjected to partisan cross-examination to give color, even in Madrid, to the slander that the American Government had backed the Miranda enterprise. In the end the packed jury performed its allotted task and acquitted the culprits; and when Jefferson dismissed Smith and Swartwout, the Federalists wept copiously over the martyrdom of innocent men, crucified to save the wicked Madison.

Jefferson did not grieve over the failure to imprison the son-in-law of Adams. He had quarreled with his Cabinet because, at first, he opposed the dismissal of Smith before the trial; and after the acquittal he wrote to Gallatin that he had 'no wish to see Mr. Smith imprisoned' because 'he has been a man of integrity and honor, led astray by distress.' [2] And Madison was satisfied that the very assaults upon the Government, together with the vigor of the prosecution, was evidence enough to Madrid that the Government had no complicity in the conspiracy.[3] But the Federalists were not satisfied, bent as they were on creating all possible bitterness to defeat the proposed negotiations for the Florida purchase. Thus, at a moment most critical, Josiah Quincy, Federalist leader in the House, became the special pleader of Smith and Ogden on the floor. With calm effrontery he presented a memorial from the culprits setting forth that they had been 'led into error by the conduct of officers of the Executive Government who now intend to bring upon the memorialists the penalties of the laws . . . in expiation of their own errors.'

It was a new wrinkle, thus to summon Congress to interfere in a pending trial, but Quincy did not shirk.

'False . . . a calumny . . . not a word in the petition charging the Administration . . . that is founded in truth,' protested an obscure member.

[1] Quoted in *Columbian Centinel*, August 27, 1806.
[2] *Writings of Gallatin*, I, 308.
[3] To de Fernando, MS. Archives, American Embassy, Madrid.

With the superciliousness which decadent Federalism had adopted as a uniform, Quincy replied with unction: 'I do not say that the information contained in the petition is true,' he said. But 'a high officer of the Government is implicated' and 'justice requires an inquiry.'

Thus, surrounded by dynamite threatening an international explosion, the patriotic Quincy was swinging a torch as in a party procession.

'I regret,' said Jackson, 'that the gentleman has so far forgotten his own dignity and the duty he owes his country.' And then, after a pause, and speaking directly to Quincy, he went on: 'The petitioners say that the expedition has received the applause and the encouragement of the Government, and the gentleman says this is known to the House. I pronounce this false. I say it is a base calumny of which the gentleman has made himself the organ; and I hold myself responsible in any place the gentleman pleases.'

Closely skirting the edge of disloyalty to his country, and conscious of the indefensibility of his conduct, Quincy began to hedge.

'Did I say the whole information contained in the memorial was true?' he asked. 'Gentlemen will bear me witness that I said I did not believe the fact could be proved. . . . I only meant to say there had been an extraordinary equipment and arming in the harbor of New York. I did not mean to pledge myself as to knowledge of the destination or to the other fact, whether there was time for the Administration to have prevented it.'

'The gentleman did say so,' barked the downright Jackson.

'Such is my impression at present, but I am not certain of it,' Quincy went on waveringly. 'Since I rose I have understood that after this information was received an attachment was made by the Executive to stop the vessel. I did not mean to incriminate the Administration. If my words have such a meaning, I withdraw them.' [1]

Thus did the attempt of the Federalists to defeat the President's plan for the peaceable acquisition of Florida reach its climax in the insinuation and the speedy apology of Josiah Quincy. Confronted by the gravest international problems the Republic had yet known, with powerful enemies without, and these served

[1] *Annals*, April 21, 1806.

zealously by party enemies within — such were the difficulties of
Jefferson when John Randolph began his attacks on the Administration.

V

Learning from Nicholson, on his return from Baltimore, of the
Administration's desire for speedy action, Randolph, in angry
mood, without waiting to rest or change his clothes, summoned
his committee — brushed aside the plan of the President — and
framed, instead, a warlike measure for the 'chastisement' of the
Spaniards. On January 3, his resolution was reported and referred
to the Committee of the Whole House.

Three days later, Randolph moved that the galleries be cleared,
and the debate began. For almost a week it continued in executive
session, though Yrujo was boasting that his secret agents among
the Federalists in Congress were keeping him constantly informed.
The Federalist version of the debate was being sent to Madrid,
and, we may be sure, to Paris. And that which Paris and Madrid
heard was not conducive to a successful negotiation.

That debate is lost, and the only report we have is that of
Randolph in the 'Decius' letters. Among his friends outside, the
gossip ran that he had surpassed himself in the brilliancy and
bitterness of his denunciation of Madison and Jefferson. But
Jefferson, likewise informed, was in no wise concerned. With the
consummate dexterity of a masterful leader, he marshaled his
forces, defeated the Randolph resolution, and secured his appropriation.[1]

The moment the measure reached the Senate, it was referred
to the Committee of the Whole, to the distress of the Federalists,
who for the purpose of delay sought, under the leadership of
Tracy, to refer it to a special committee of which Tracy would
have been chairman. Even Adams was chagrined. Did they want
to push it through without discussion?[2] But, as in the House, the
proceedings in executive session were not secret. 'It is called a
secret and so I must treat it,' wrote Bayard, *though it is certainly
known to every foreign agent in the place.*[3] Indeed, at this moment
several Federalist leaders were cheek by jowl with these 'foreign

[1] Bruce, I, 250; Adams, *History*, III, 137–39.
[2] Adams. *Diary*, I, 387.   [3] *Bayard Papers.*

agents,' as Bayard knew too well. He, the ablest of the Federalists, led the opposition, and Adams thought his speech 'one of the most eloquent appeals to the feelings and reason of the Senate' he had ever heard.[1] But in due time the measure passed.

But Randolph was not content. Two months later, he forced the fighting into the open on a motion calling for the publication of the President's secret Message. At that time the Senate was still wrangling over the confirmation of one of the negotiators; the negotiations had not begun; and as much damage could be done now as in the beginning.

Again the galleries were packed and thickly sprinkled with women; for Randolph never failed to draw a crowd, and his dramatic desertion of his friends had made his disaffection sensational. He began his speech with a review and an explanation, and then repeated his version of his conversation with Madison about France's wanting money.

'I considered it a base prostitution of the national character to excite one nation with money to bully another out of its property, and from that moment ... my confidence in the principles of the man entertaining these sentiments died, never to live again.'

Thus, smashing at Madison, he opened the campaign for Monroe.

But why, asked Alston, put obstacles in the way of negotiations about to begin? 'Idle talk,' snapped Randolph. No effect could be produced in Paris except with money. 'They will look at your cash — if it is enough you will have your business done.' And why discuss the success or failure of negotiations? 'The battle of Austerlitz has settled that.'

Stunned by the intemperance of the attack on Madison, there was a pause in the House. Then the venerable Findley of Pennsylvania rose soberly to suggest that if Randolph had a charge to make against that great man he formulate and present it. Randolph sat mute.

Then Eppes, the son-in-law of Jefferson, who had followed Randolph in the Yazoo fight, rose to protest against the insinuation that bribe money was for the influence of France. He had no doubt the money would be used properly in the purchase of

[1] Adams, *Diary*, I, 394.

Florida from its rightful owner. 'That France may ultimately get the money is highly probable, and why? Has not the gentleman from Virginia told us that the sovereignty of Spain is annihilated? But of what importance is it to us what becomes of the money we pay to Spain?'

The Jeffersonians began to close in on Randolph's slanders. It had been said that Jefferson had told Varnum of Massachusetts he wished a resolution contrary to his Message. Varnum rose to pronounce the story utterly, indefensibly false. More important was the denunciation of the falsehood that Gallatin had told a group, including George Clinton, Jr., that Jefferson had asked that the two millions be drawn before the appropriation had been made. And now this story was crushed by Jackson. 'I happened to see the Secretary of the Treasury at the door of the House,' he said, 'and asked him if it were true and he told me it was not.' And then, more sternly, he went on:

'When the main charge against the Secretary of State is so destitute of truth ... it is not necessary that the other should be repelled — that he told his colleague ——'

'I am not the gentleman's colleague,' growled Randolph.

'Very well, that he told John Randolph ——'

'It is not in order to call gentlemen by name,' interposed Randolph's friend in the chair.

'Sir, I know of no more appropriate appellation unless it be the descendant of Powhatan whom he told that France would not permit Spain to settle her differences with us.' [1]

And Randolph was silent.

But Gallatin was not. Outraged by his friend's brazen misrepresentations, he called on Clinton for his version, and the latter remembered nothing of the kind. [2] Meanwhile, under Gallatin's direction, a resolution was introduced making the inquiry of the head of the Treasury, and Gallatin in a letter to the Speaker, Randolph's friend Macon, pronounced the story false. [3]

The Randolph call for the publication of the secret Message was easily voted down, and the Spanish purchase incident was closed in the House. It left Randolph in a position of isolation.

---

[1] *Annals*, April 5, 1806.
[2] *Writings of Gallatin*, I, 295, 297.   [3] *Ibid.*, I, 299.

A few hardy souls, mostly from Virginia, gathered around him. But he had been exposed as a reckless slanderer of the heads of State. He had parted willingly enough with Jefferson, though Ritchie, of the *Richmond Enquirer*, had solemnly warned him against it; and gladly with Madison, but he had driven away his loyal friend Gallatin as well.[1] This was not without its pathos. By declaring 'there is no Cabinet' and in damning Madison and praising Gallatin, he had sought to sow dissensions at Jefferson's council-table. But he had not split the Cabinet; he had merely parted company with them all. Jefferson had carried his point quietly and with serenity, and Adams was lamenting the ease with which he managed Congress.[2] Randolph was rebuked. His party had decided it best to let him go.[3]

But the opposition of Randolph and the Federalists had reduced the possibilities of a successful negotiation. They had managed to delay action when the same celerity as in the case of Louisiana was required. Insults had been heaped on Spain and France, and they had carried these from the secret sessions to Yrujo and to Turreau, who had sent them to Madrid and Paris. The whole plan had been made public property, and even such Federalists as Bayard complacently contemplated the possibilities of a war with Spain, backed by the conquering armies of Napoleon. 'The most of us here are in expectation of a Spanish war,' he wrote cheerfully. 'I think it likely. ... The success of Bonaparte will encourage the Spaniard to go to war, and I shall not be surprised if the next intelligence should proclaim the event.' [4]

The Yazoo case and the Spanish purchase were not enough to satisfy the insensate hates of this unprecedented session; for Jefferson was threatened with a British war, and in the midst of all the other mischief-making, Randolph was flamboyantly bearing the banner of Britain, cheered on lustily by the Federalists, to a man.

---

[1] Adams, *Gallatin*, 344.   [2] Adams, *Diary*, I, 404.
[3] *Independent Chronicle*, April 2, 1806.   [4] *Bayard Papers.*

CHAPTER XVI

Allies of Pitt

I

MEANWHILE, above the rumbling and the roar of the Yazoo and Spanish purchase opposition could be heard the ominous growl of the British lion. The impressment of Americans into the British Navy had continued through the Administrations of Washington and Adams, despite their protests. And now the evil was increasing. Monroe had been sent to London to negotiate a treaty to eliminate the wrong and to protect the commerce of neutral nations. On his return to England from Aranjuez he was greeted with the intelligence that nearly thirty American ships in British waters had been brought in by cruisers, and he remonstrated 'in the strongest terms.' [1] The return of Pitt to power doomed the pending negotiations. He was not a friend of the American democracy, and the contempt for American commerce and the rights of her seamen was more flagrant than ever. Throughout the summer, fall, and winter Monroe was constantly to trail the British Minister and to find him as eel-like as the man at Aranjuez. With painful regularity, he peppered the Minister with protests as the seizures multiplied. Always something made discussions quite impossible, and in the autumn the Minister of Foreign Affairs left London for Bath to attend the dying Pitt. [2]

In the meantime the British raised more pretensions and put them into force. Sir William Scott, whose contempt for America had been disclosed in his insult to Monroe at an official dinner, handed down the remarkable decision in the *Essex* case. Literally

---

[1] Monroe to Armstrong, *Writings of Monroe*, IV, 309.
[2] Monroe to Madison, *ibid.*, IV, 380.

thousands of Americans were being dragged from American ships in British waters and impressed into the service of the British Navy. Orders in Council wiped out neutral rights. The mistress of the seas was uncompromising in her power, for the brilliant victory of Nelson at Trafalgar had left her without a rival on the waters. A rigid observance of the rules laid down would have meant the ruin of the commerce of the young Republic. Never before, nor since, have the English-speaking nations been so close to an alliance, and Britain chose that moment to arouse a more bitter resentment than that which precipitated the Revolution. Such was the Anglo-American statesmanship of Pitt.

This policy of Pitt's was aimed, in part, at the destruction of the rapidly increasing merchant marine of the Republic. American ships were plowing the waters of all the world and were seen in every port; and the policy of Pitt was directed to the destruction of this prestige.

To that end, it was not enough to drag American sailors from American ships in British ports. British armed vessels assumed the right to use the very harbor of New York as a cruising post, and outrages, the most incredible, were committed by these vessels within sight of the Battery. The frigates *Leander* and *Cambrian* undertook the policing of the harbor. 'Every morning at daybreak,' wrote one of their officers, 'we set about arresting the progress of all the vessels we saw, firing off guns to the right and left to make every ship that was running in heave to.' When quite convenient, they boarded these American ships on an arrogant search. Sometimes as many as twenty-four ships were forced to stand and wait throughout the day until it pleased the British crews to subject them to an intolerable indignity.[1] The merchants in all the ports, though not unfriendly to the English, rose in wrath. Mass meetings were called, and there was much talk of war.

The Federalists were in a quandary, with their pro-British politics on one side and their mercantile interests on the other, and in Massachusetts there was no little torment of spirit among the leaders. Excitement was running high. 'The conversation of the day is on the oppressions which our commerce suffers,' wrote

[1] Captain Basil Hall, quoted in Adams, *History*, III, 97.

Bentley. 'The alarm is so great that vessels fitted for sea still lay in port unable to proceed upon such risks as now exist.'[1] In the farmhouse at Dedham, Fisher Ames was sadly tortured. 'I am very willing that Britain should turn out exceedingly in the wrong,' he wrote gingerly. 'If they are not in the wrong I see not the policy nor fitness in hazarding our commerce, peace, and prosperity on an untenable point.' With British frigates policing the port of New York, firing shots across the bows of American vessels, and lining them up like suspects at a police station, Ames was not quite sure that there was any point to the objections of the American Government.[2] When the Boston merchants, mostly Federalists, called a meeting and named a committee to frame a protest, the Essex Junto was humiliated and distressed. 'Our friend Cabot,' Ames wrote Pickering, 'is much mortified that he is one of them. He hates hypocrisy and he respects principles, and he dreads lest popular feeling should impel the committee to deny what he believes to be true.' The flow of feeling was so fiercely against the interference with our commerce and in our ports that Ames hoped 'the Federalists will be very shy, therefore, and cautious lest they come out an avowed apologist of England.'[3] Ames, like Cabot, hated hypocrisy!

Party feeling was running high in Massachusetts. In Salem the Jeffersonians were excluded from the dancing assembly that winter, and they had to organize an assembly of their own.[4] Madison's able and erudite pamphlet in defense of the American position was ridiculed by the Federalists with ribald mirth.[5]

Such was the tenseness of public feeling when Congress listened to Jefferson's Message on the British phase of the national crisis.

II

'Our coasts have been infested and our harbors watched by private armed vessels,' wrote Jefferson in his Message. 'They have captured in the very entrance of our harbors, as well as on the high seas, not only the vessels of our friends coming to trade with us, but our own also. They have carried them off under pre-

---

[1] Bentley, *Diary*, III, 192.   [2] Ames to Quincy, *Ames*, I, 339.
[3] *Ibid.*, I, 344.   [4] Bentley, *Diary*, III, 201.
[5] *Writings of Madison*, VII, 204.

text of legal adjudication, but not daring to approach a court of justice, they have plundered and sunk them on the way; maltreated the crews and abandoned them in boats on the open sea or on desert shores without food or covering.' These private vessels, seemingly beyond the control of their sovereigns, were being hunted down by a force he had equipped for the purpose. But more important were the armed public ships 'hovering on our coasts and harbors under color of seeking enemies,' to 'the great annoyance and oppression of our commerce.' New principles regarding the rights of neutrals had arbitrarily been laid down, 'founded neither in justice nor the usage and acknowledgment of nations.'

Momentarily, the commercial interests were pleased, and the Federalists depressed. 'Spirited and agreeable to the commercial part of the nation,' wrote a citizen of Salem.[1] In London, Monroe was sitting on the doorstep of the Foreign Office pleading for the consideration of American grievances, and in vain. And the debate in the House at Washington began.

The Message had been referred to Randolph's committee, and there it slumbered. With the crisis growing daily more acute, Randolph and his committee did nothing at all. The frail genius, growing more specter-like every day, was too busy with his denunciations of the Administration to consider the British phase. Night after night he tossed sleepless on his couch; day after day he dragged himself to the House, with his dog at his heels, feverishly to continue his assaults. Pitt, stricken by Austerlitz, and not revived by Trafalgar, had sunk into his grave, mourned by the Federalists.[2] Jefferson was pinning his hopes on Fox, consistent champion of American rights, whose accession struck terror to Ames.

But Randolph's committee did nothing.

At length, eight weeks after the reference to his committee, with not one meeting called, the motion to discharge it was made. Resolutions dealing with the crisis had been introduced, referred, ignored. Crowninshield, of Salem, flushed with anger, took the floor. With the Randolph committee refusing to move, what was the situation? 'Our ships are plundered in every sea, our seamen are impressed, three thousand of them in the service of one nation. . . . I am ready to act,' he said. The committee was discharged without opposition, and Randolph did not deign an explanation.[1] And that same day Andrew Gregg presented his famous resolutions.

These forbade the importation of any goods from England, or from any of its colonies, until satisfaction had been accorded the Republic on its grievances. Why — a declaration of war! shouted the Federalists. Bayard thought 'perhaps it would justify, if carried into effect, a declaration of war on the part of Great Britain.' However, he added, 'the doubt is whether it is not a political maneuver or whether the ruling party have courage to commit themselves to the hazardous responsibilities of the measure.' [2]

In truth, the Administration did not approve its extreme provisions. Gallatin, calculating that it meant a loss of five millions in revenue, was instantly in opposition; and Jefferson realized that it would work a hardship on the Southern planters and would deprive the people of goods to be had from no other source. There was a hurrying back and forth of Administration leaders.

Twelve days later, Nicholson in the House, warning of the effect on revenue, offered his own resolutions providing for the exclusion of certain specified articles that could be had from other than British sources.[3] But February dragged through with no serious consideration of either of the resolutions, until Sloan, of New Jersey, all patience gone, took the floor. The committee discharged for two weeks and nothing done, he began. 'Where is the spirit . . . of Seventy-Six?' he asked. 'Has it fled or is it only sleeping? I hope it is the latter and that it will speedily awake, refreshed and invigorated after its long nap.' [4]

More days of silence; then Randolph rose from his bed to demand the immediate consideration of his constitutional amendment on the removal of judges. Why waste time? he asked. Why not now, and thus return the Republic to the principles the Administration had professed when it entered upon power?

---

[1] *Annals,* January 29, 1806.   [2] *Bayard Papers.*
[3] *Annals,* February 10, 1806.   [4] *Ibid.,* February 12, 1806.

Slashing recklessly on every side, he took the House to task for its delays, and the House gasped. Gregg rose.

And who so responsible for the waste of time as Randolph? he demanded. 'Four weeks ago I presented a resolution,' he said, and Randolph's committee in four weeks had refused to move.[1]

It was not until the fourth of March that Gregg could force the consideration of his resolution. Meanwhile, enraged by his defeats and the realization that the scepter of leadership was slipping from his grasp, Randolph was in a mood for furious opposition.

III

It was a cold, bitter day as men and women picked their way over the frozen streets to the Capitol. Gregg would make his opening speech — and what would Randolph say? The gossip about the fireplace in the Senate cloak-room had been that, exasperated by the disposition to deprive him of the leadership, Randolph would go far; and that he would seek to make impossible the election of Madison or the re-election of Jefferson. The Madison-Monroe fight was on.[2]

In fairly moderate language Gregg reviewed the American grievances and described his resolution. 'What does it say?' he asked. 'It addresses Great Britain in this mild and moderate, though manly and firm, language: "You have insulted the dignity of our country by impressing our seamen. . . . You have plundered us of much property. . . . To these injuries, insults, and oppression we will submit no longer. We do not, however, wish to destroy that friendly intercourse that ought to subsist between nations, connected with the ties of common interests. To prevent such interruption and secure against future aggressions, we are now desirous of entering into such arrangements as ought to be deemed satisfactory to both parties. But if you persist in your hostile measures . . . we must slacken these bonds of friendship. . . . You must not expect to find us hereafter in your market."'

Would it be effective? 'It will strike dismay throughout the empire . . . will be felt by every class . . . especially the commercial and manufacturing part of the community,' and 'these are the main pillars of its support.'

[1] *Annals*, February 24, 1806.   [2] Adams, *Diary*, I, 418.

Injurious to the States? Shut out from the British market we should go to other nations, and 'we will resort to domestic manufactures.'

And could it be enforced? What reason can be assigned why it cannot be as well executed as in former times? 'Are we so abject, so degenerate, as to submit to such national indignity rather than forego the pleasure from an indulgence in British luxuries?'

But would it put us at the mercy of Pitt? 'If he attempts to make a general sweep, self-defense will justify reprisals. The debts owing to British subjects, the immense property owned by them in this country, will of course be laid hold of.' Prohibited by the treaty of 1794? 'True; but if one of the contracting parties violates the contract, the other is released from his obligations. If Britain violates nine articles ... who can consider us bound by the tenth?'

The tone and temper of the speech was mild enough. One or two others spoke, and then there was a bustle of expectation as John Randolph rose. He had risen from a sick bed that morning, pale, weak from loss of sleep and blood, and he loomed like the shadow of an attenuated ghost.

IV

The House now was crowded. There were the leaders of the Senate. The galleries were packed. Randolph was in his most arrogant, bullying mood. Conscious that he was the sole genius in the chamber, he swept his colleagues with a contemptuous glance.

This resolution is tantamount to a declaration of war, he began. And who so stupid as to conceive that our armed forces could prevail? True, men who had not gone 'beyond the horn-book of politics' talked glibly of our ability to cope with the British Navy. Was Britain not the mistress of the seas? And yet men talked wildly, 'goaded on by mercantile avarice, straining their feeble strength to excite the nation to war.' Why, declare war and instantly 'Charleston and Boston, the Chesapeake and the Hudson will be invested by British squadrons.' How will you meet them? 'Will you call on the Count de Grasse ... or shall we apply to Admiral de Gravina, or Admiral Villeneuve, to raise the blockade?'

And what was the excitement about? 'The carrying trade. What part of it? The fair, the honest, the useful trade that is engaged in carrying our products to foreign markets and bringing back their productions in exchange? No, sir. It is the carrying trade which covers enemy's property, and carries the coffee, the sugar, and other West Indian products to the mother country.' Was America to be bullied by Salem, Boston, New York, Baltimore, Norfolk, and Charleston? Then say so bluntly, and summon a committee of their merchants to carry on the Government. 'I, for one, will not mortgage my property and my liberty, to carry on this trade.'

'Bend the back to England?' No, sir, but it will be time enough to discuss our English grievances 'when we have resented the violation of the actual territory of the United States by Spain.'

A naval war? What stupidity! 'What, shall this great mammoth of the American forest leave her native element and plunge into the water in a mad contest with the shark? Let them beware that his proboscis is not bitten off in the engagement.' Yes, 'why take to the waters where you can neither fight nor swim? Look at France — see her vessels stealing from port to port on her own coast and remember that she is the first military power on earth, and as a naval people second only to England. . . . Take away the British Navy and France tomorrow is the tyrant of the ocean. . . . The iron scepter of the ocean will pass into the hands of the nation that wears the iron crown of the land.'

Then, turning viciously on the Administration, he went on:

'The first question I asked when I saw the gentleman's resolutions was, "Is this a measure of the Cabinet?" Not of an open, declared Cabinet. . . . I speak of backstairs influence — of men who bring messages to this House, which, although they do not appear on the journals, govern its decisions. Sir, the first question that I asked on the subject of British relations was, "What is the opinion of the Cabinet? What measures will they recommend to Congress?" My answer was from a Cabinet Minister, too — "There is no longer any Cabinet."'

The foes of Jefferson were now on the edge of their chairs. Here was a direct, though shamelessly false, attack on Jefferson, and though no President had ever been so closely advised as Jefferson by Gallatin and Madison, a falsehood would serve the Federalists' purpose, and they were in high glee.

'Why talk of Spain? There is no longer Pyrenees. There exists no such nation, no such beings as a Spanish King or Minister.' And where do we go to negotiate with Spain? 'To Madrid? No, you are not such quacks as not to know where the shoe pinches — to Paris. After shrinking from the Spanish jackal do you presume to bully the British lion?'

Ah, but there was a reason. 'Britain is your rival in trade, and governed as you are by counting-house politicians, you would sacrifice the paramount interests of your country to wound a rival. For Spain and France you are carriers, and from good customers every indignity is to be endured.'

The Federalists now shifted uneasily in their seats.

In making a contemptuous reference to Madison's pamphlet, the orator noticed members scribbling notes. 'Gentlemen may take notes if they please,' he exclaimed irritably, 'but I will never from any motive short of self-defense enter upon a war. I will never be instrumental to the ambitious schemes of Bonaparte.'

And here he painted in a purple patch:

'I should not hesitate between Westminster and a Middlesex jury on the one hand and the wood of Vincennes and a file of grenadiers on the other. That jury trial which walked with Horne Tooke and Hardy through the flames of ministerial persecution is, I confess, more to my taste than the trial of the Duc d'Enghien.'

Swiftly, he shifted back to Jefferson. 'You gave him money to buy Florida and he bought Louisiana. You furnish means; the application of these means rests with him. Let not the master and the mate go below when the ship is in distress, and throw the responsibility on the cook and the cabin-boy.'

And why had Jefferson insisted on keeping the doors of Congress shut? 'Are the people of the United States, the real sovereigns of the country, unworthy of knowing what — there is much reason to believe — has been communicated to the privileged spies of foreign governments?'[1]

Such was one of the most remarkable speeches ever heard in the House, a rambling, unorganized harangue, with a few such purple

[1] *Annals*, March 8, 1806.

patches as the reference to 'Westminster Hall and a Middlesex jury' and 'the wood of Vincennes and a file of grenadiers.' But the orator had not deigned to discuss the resolutions. With shots being fired across the bows of American ships in American waters, with American ships being swept into prize courts, with American seamen being impressed by the thousands into the service of a foreign navy, he found no reason for complaint.

The Federalists were in a state of confusion. Randolph had assailed Jefferson, and they smiled; he sneered at the merchants, and they scowled. He jeered at Madison, and they laughed; he referred to the spies who carried the news of executive sessions to foreign agents, and they trembled. No one had been spared. Adams thought the speech 'a violent philippic against the present Executive,' [1] and he recorded that Turreau had refrained from attending lest he be forced to listen to 'insults to his emperor.' [2] Senator Plumer, who had hurried with other Federalists from the Senate, found Randolph a man of 'great talents and by far the best speaker in the House,' but thought 'his passions strong, his prejudices violent and inveterate,' and noticed that 'he wants that plain common sense which renders a man at once safe and useful to himself and to others.' [3] Ames, unimpressed by Pickering's high expectations from the disaffection, reminded him that Federalists were 'stubborn hopers.' No, thought Ames, nothing would come of it. 'Randolph, no longer the guest at the great man's private board, no longer his earwig, will not be his antagonist,' he warned. 'If he is, he will lose his party and his influence.' [4]

Jefferson heard the reports of the speech with composure. Dryly he remarked that Randolph had not always been so intolerant of the 'back stairs.'

v

On the morrow the venerable John Smilie administered a gentlemanly rebuke. Randolph, he said, had been lacking 'in respect to the House,' and apropos of the sneer at Madison's pamphlet he said it would live 'when the gentleman and I are dead.' Randolph was eager to war on Spain 'because of her weak-

---

[1] Adams, *Diary*, I, 418.   [2] *Ibid.*, I, 419.
[3] *Plumer*, 340–41.   [4] *Ames*, I, 369.

ness' on the pretext that she had entered American territory —
'nothing more than happened the other day at Detroit when
British officers seized a man with the view to carrying him over
the line.' It was to be hoped, the old man said, that 'such trivial
things, the offspring of accident or personal resentment, will never
be considered a cause for war.'

Randolph sprang to his feet again, and senators were hurrying
to the fray. He was not in favor of maintaining the false dignity
of a nation. 'And what is false dignity?' he cried. 'Playing the
part of a Bobadil — bullying England and truckling to Spain.'

He was charged with not supporting the President in firm
measures? 'What would have been a firm measure?' he demanded.
'An embargo! That would have gone to the root of the evil. . . .
But your slippery mercantile eels can slide over and under' the
Non-Importation Act 'and leave the whole burden to fall on the
planter, the farmer, and the real American.' [1]

On the third day, a member expressed amazement that Randolph thought a demand for the release of our seamen and restitu-
tion for unjust captures 'throwing our weight into the scale of
France,' and the aged Findley, of Pennsylvania, an ancient friend
of Randolph's, rebuked him for his demagogic references to secret
sessions. 'The doors are never closed except on foreign affairs, and
even these are not kept secret on account of our own citizens, but
on account of our foreign relations'; and 'the gentleman from Virginia knows it well,' he said. [2]

It was not until the fifth day of the debate that the real spokesman in it of the Administration took the floor. Barnabas Bidwell
had a fine capacity for constructive public service. After grad-
uating from Yale, he practiced law with notable success in Stockbridge, Massachusetts, and he had just entered the House as a
Jeffersonian from that Federalist stronghold. Because he was a
strong, logical speaker of tact and common sense, the Administration staked high hopes on his capacity for leadership. On the
occasion of his maiden speech, Randolph, naturally a bully, had
insulted him. Wearing his tight-fitting leather breeches accen-
tuating his skeleton legs, with top-boots and a blue riding-coat and
thick buckskin gloves, he had settled himself as if to listen. In a

---

[1] *Annals*, March 6, 1806.   [2] *Ibid.*, March 7, 1806.

few moments he rose noisily and slowly tramped down the aisle, loudly striking the gloved hand with his loaded riding-whip, looking contemptuously at the new member as he passed.[1] But Bidwell possessed ability far beyond the average, and when Randolph wrote his 'Decius' letters, Bidwell, signing himself 'Cato,' replied with such devastating effect in the *Independent Chronicle* that Randolph's biographer, commenting on the 'grave, dignified strain of high-minded remonstrance,' conceded that it is impossible to recognize, in the 'stately toga-clad figure which rises before us in the beginning of the reply,' the 'muscle or periwinkle on the strand' described by Randolph.[2]

It was Bidwell's function to bring the debate back to the resolutions. He began with an unemotional recital of the grievances against Britain, and a review of the steps taken by Madison, reading from his instructions to Monroe. He explained the new principles of neutral trade that Britain had advanced. In no wise intimidated by Randolph's sneer at the 'carrying trade,' he traced the history of its development in glowing terms. Step by step he advanced both against the British contention and that of the congressional opposition, buttressing his facts and figures with Gallatin's reports. He explained the new pretensions of Pitt on the ground of a determination to take over the trade of the world, calculating on our local interests and party divisions and a continued opposition to the Government to prevent a unification on any effective countervailing measures. Assuming from the tone of the opposition that Jefferson would not be effectually supported, England had 'taken this first step in her system to ascertain by the experiment how much we will bear.'

And then he turned on Randolph.

'The carrying trade disconnected with agriculture?' he asked. Why, 'the produce of the farm beyond our own consumption must perish on our hands ... if there were no commerce to carry it to foreign markets and to bring us in return the productions of other countries. This is the very end of commerce.'

Dismiss commerce as an interloper in our national economy? Was not the British Navigation Act one of the causes of the Revolution? Why divide the nation on the basis of sectional

[1] Bruce, I, 248.   [2] *Ibid.*, I, 247.

interests? And what true patriot could contemplate without indignation the impressment of our seamen? Surely something should be done, and at once. The President was engaged in negotiations, and to Congress he had passed the task of determining what legislative measures should be taken. Bidwell would not discuss the various resolutions. He only asked that action be not delayed.[1] It was the one sober statesmanlike speech of the debate.

Bidwell had spoken on a Saturday. Over Sunday the Administration made its plan to strike. On Monday, Eppes, the son-in-law of Jefferson, pleaded for unity of action, and declared the House not tied to the Gregg resolutions. 'I am ready to adopt for the present prohibition a list of enumerated articles,' he said. 'I object to this measure because it will be so extremely injurious to the United States in its operations that it ought not be resorted to until milder remedies have failed.' [2] He had pointed clearly to the Nicholson resolutions.

Then Nicholson took the floor to dumbfound his colleagues. With Randolph and Macon, he had formed the Three Musketeers and dominated the House, but all, in varying degrees and from different motives, had fallen away from Jefferson. Though he had introduced his resolutions, Randolph in the meantime had been running amuck. What would Nicholson do now? Bitterly he attacked the Gregg resolutions as a declaration of war; it was a holding forth of an 'olive branch with a dagger in its boughs.' He followed Randolph in assailing the carrying trade — 'a trade totally unconnected with agriculture and enjoyed by a few merchants only.' Yes, the nation 'may bleed at every pore,' but the merchant 'would have his ounce of flesh.' Such the speech of Nicholson, aping Randolph, attacking the Gregg resolutions, and uttering not one word for his own, or any others. Many wondered if he would withdraw his own resolutions.

Then Macon, the third of the trio, descended from the Speaker's seat to repeat the performance. Again the attack of Randolph on the 'carrying trade.' Grievances against Britain? Well, 'have we no complaints against France and Spain?' came the echo from Randolph's speech. And manufacture our own articles? Ridic-

---

[1] *Annals*, March 8, 1806.   [2] *Ibid.*, March 10, 1806.

ulous! So long as 'the industrious citizen' can be 'a landowner
and cultivator of the soil,' who would turn to manufacture? And
the country demanded legislative measures in accordance with
the President's desire? Macon was not so sure. And what if the
President did recommend — was it incumbent upon Congress to
do his bidding?

Not one word of criticism of the seizure of the ships and the impressment of three thousand American seamen![1]

Randolph, Macon, and Nicholson in varying degrees were now
in opposition with the Federalists, and would soon sleep in the beds
of their own making.

The debate droned on, sometimes to almost empty benches, and
the Federalists sat mute. Josiah Quincy, their leader, was silent.
They dared not join in belittling the carrying trade; they could not
defend Jefferson; and they would not criticize Britain. Ames from
his watch-tower at Dedham was not pleased. 'As Randolph is no
Federalist . . . why, I ask, should the Federalist orators be silent?
I have strong doubts whether the Federalists do not carry their
reserve to an extreme.'[2]

Then the Administration determined to force the issue by proposing the substitution of the Nicholson for the Gregg resolutions.
The change was proposed upon the floor; the House was moving
toward it. This would never do, thought the opposition, which
wanted nothing done at all. Why not discharge the Committee of
the Whole from further consideration of the subject? But the
House overwhelmingly decided otherwise.

Up sprang the highly excited Randolph. Why proceed further?
he asked. Had not negotiations begun? Why not wait on these?
'These resolutions are the production of a political hotbed,' he
shrieked. By this time he was all but raving, almost incoherent.
'There is no Cabinet!' he screamed, his tenor voice rising to the
falsetto of an infuriated woman. Dispatches from Monroe had
come and Gallatin had not seen them, he cried. What! Randolph's crowd accused of playing with the Federalists? Had he
failed to denounce every villain among them? No, his insurgent
group were not Federalists; neither did they stand for Burrism.
'Will they say we are the rotten part of the Republican Party —

[1] *Annals,* March 10, 1806.   [2] *Ames,* I, 275.

the tool of any faction?' And Yazooism — 'Are we Yazoo men?'

He sank into his seat exhausted, having failed so much as to touch upon the matter before the House.

Then Nicholson rose to play the parrot to Randolph, since he had lost interest now in his own resolutions. Why not await dispatches from London? he echoed. Never perhaps had the author of a legislative measure been so deeply distressed over the certainty of its adoption.[1]

The House took the bit in its teeth, rejected Gregg's and all other resolutions, and adopted those of Nicholson. Quincy and the Federalists stood shoulder to shoulder with Randolph and his little band of insurgents. Macon remained in the chair, not voting. Randolph stalked out of the House in melodramatic fashion. And Nicholson, in distress, had to vote for his own resolutions.[2]

Nine days later, the bill, based on the resolutions, was submitted, and again Randolph went on a rampage with sneers, jeers, and insults all around. 'What is it?' he screamed. 'A milk-and-water bill, a dose of chicken broth to be taken nine months hence. Disgraceful!' he shouted. 'This is the strong measure; this is the imposing attitude we have taken. You cannot do without the next spring and fall importations, and you tell your adversary so' — referring to the provision that it should go into operation in nine months unless Britain gave satisfaction in the meantime.

It was Barnabas Bidwell who replied with his accustomed common sense. 'To turn the current of trade at once would operate unjustly,' he said, 'and in a manner hardly consistent with good faith to the merchants, who must have made their calculations and given their orders on the existing state of things.'

The roll was called, and the bill passed — with Nicholson voting for it.[3]

Thus, after four months, the measure that should have been acted upon within two weeks was passed. The British Minister had reported to London that the people of the Republic were divided, and the effect of the measure was destroyed.

[1] *Annals*, March 13, 1806.
[2] *Ibid.*, March 17, 1806.
[3] *Ibid.*, March 26, 1806.

VI

Throughout the acrimonious controversy, Jefferson had remained serene. Still clinging to the hope of a successful negotiation he had sent William Pinkney, one of the foremost members of the American Bar, a polished orator and a staunch Federalist, to London to assist Monroe. To personal abuse he long had been accustomed. So low and foul the abuse had been, so plainly prejudiced and unfair the attacks, that the more decent of his enemies began to blush, and wonder if he were not better than his foes. 'The more impartially I examine the character and conduct of Mr. Jefferson,' wrote Senator Plumer, the Federalist, 'the more favorably I think of his integrity.' [1]

The disaffection of Randolph had been discounted by the violence and utter irresponsibility of his hysterical attacks, and by this time his little party was sadly fading. Jefferson had dismissed all thought of his conciliation. During the remaining month of the session, Randolph almost constantly was on his feet shrilly shrieking denunciations, and spewing insulting epithets on all who would not bend their backs to him.

With the utmost ease Jefferson had held his lines, and all the while he was holding forth the olive branch to individuals who had wavered. Nicholson had lost his usefulness in the House, and he was glad to leave when Jefferson offered him a place on the federal bench he was sure to honor. When a cold reply was received to a conciliatory note to Macon, he was abandoned, along with Randolph.

Far more concerned was Jefferson with the effect of the fight on Monroe. Randolph had been bombarding him with letters, playing the Iago on Monroe's presidential aspirations, with attacks on Jefferson. Monroe's reply could not have been satisfactory. 'There are older men,' he wrote, 'whom I have long been accustomed to consider as having higher pretensions to the trust than myself,' and 'the person who seems to be contemplated by others is in that class.' Besides, a contest with Madison would result in 'harrowing up the feelings and tearing up by the roots ancient friendships' among men 'long in the habit of dangerous and laborious co-operation.' [2]

[1] *Plumer*, 342.   [2] *Writings of Monroe*, IV, 460.

About the time he was writing, he was reading a letter from Jefferson. 'The great body of your friends,' he read, 'are among the foremost adherents of the Administration; and in their support of you will suffer Mr. Randolph to have no communication with them.' [1]

With consummate dexterity, Jefferson quietly was reorganizing and strengthening his forces.

VII

But Randolph's outrageous insults and fabrications called for his elimination from the chairmanship of the Ways and Means Committee which carried the leadership of the House. So long as Macon was Speaker, with the power to name committees and their chairmen, this would be impossible. As the session approached its end, the pent-up resentments of the members found expression in the speech and resolutions of Sloan.

'Should any member of this House be permitted to declare that Yazoo principles governed the high court of impeachment . . . in the trial of Judge Chase?' he asked. 'Shall that member's multifarious declamations and groundless accusations . . . go forth without any investigations or contradictions?' No, the people were entitled to a portrait of Randolph 'drawn to the life.' He who had supported a program with zeal in 1803 had astonished the world by his violent denunciations of a similar program in 1806, 'denunciations composed of a compound of insinuations, innuendoes, and positive invectives.' Invited to bring forward an impeachment, he refused, while continuing his 'declamatory accusations.' Was he disappointed because he had received no diplomatic mission, 'that he might have a chance of improving his property as well as his health'? Had he not seemed 'enamored of the insolent tyranny of the commanders of British armed vessels' and poured forth abuse upon the heads of those 'who will not in all cases agree with his eyes, to hear with his ears, to understand with his heart'? Had he not repeatedly invaded the Speaker's chair and shaken his fist at members, ordering them in imperious tones to 'go down the back stairs'? Did the House approve his ridiculing a venerable member as 'mumbling out his words in such a manner that none could

[1] *Writings of Jefferson*, XI, 168.

understand him,' calling him 'an old toothless driveler, super-
annuated, and in his second dotage'? At a moment of grave international crisis, when measures proposed should have been speedily
considered, had he not pocketed the resolutions and forced a delay
of weeks and months? Had he not deliberately lied when he said
Gallatin had told him that he had been asked to draw money from
the Treasury before an appropriation had been made?

He concluded by offering a resolution to be called up at the
opening of the next session providing for the election of the members of the committees and for their selection of their own chairmen. It also provided that all committees should be asked to report
each Monday 'unless dispensed with by the unanimous consent of
the House.' [1]

The majority had turned insurgent against the triumvirate of
Randolph, Macon, and Nicholson. These resolutions announced
their doom.

VIII

So ended the most dramatic and sensational session of the
American Congress. Time and again the opposition had skirted
the edge of treason, sneaking from executive sessions to the
Ministers of Britain, France, and Spain with confidential information destructive of the plans of the President; with members
justifying or extenuating outrageous attacks on the very sovereignty of the nation.

Scarcely had the members reached their homes when the British
frigate, the *Leander*, whose brazen seizure and search of American vessels in the very harbor of New York had failed to call forth
a word of protest from Quincy, Randolph, or Macon, in firing on
an American vessel killed the helmsman of an unoffending American ship. The arrogance of the armed vessels had grown on the
sustenance furnished by the attacks in Congress on the Government. Regardless of party, citizens of New York poured into the
streets, seized some of the sailors of the offending crew, took away
their provisions, and, as the infuriated people were organizing a
solemn procession, the British Consul took flight. In Boston, the
Federalists, though forced to demand energetic measures, were

[1] *Annals*, April 21, 1806.

alarmed and distressed when Jefferson, in a spirited proclamation, interdicted supplies for British ships and ordered the arrest of the captain of the *Leander* if found on American soil. 'They know not how they stand with their friends, the British,' wrote Bentley, 'and are in as much haste to reprobate the consequences of their measures as they ever have been in adopting them.' [1]

Thus, with national dignity and rights involved, confronted on either side by Britain and France, allied with Spain, Jefferson at this hour literally was surrounded with treason. At a moment when the most elemental sense of national loyalty called for national solidarity, national leaders of the opposition were creeping with their betrayals to Merry, Yrujo, and Turreau, who were reporting to their Governments that the disloyalists of the United States had made it safe to insult the American flag.

And in the meanwhile Jefferson was confronted with the treason of Aaron Burr.

[1] Bentley, *Diary*, III, 225–26.

CHAPTER XVII

Before the Storm

I

JEFFERSON was now halfway through his second Administration, and with every reason for satisfaction. Never had the country been so prosperous. In every center of population the community was moving forward by leaps and bounds. Nothing in his domestic policy, so savagely assailed, had tended to retard the natural development of the nation the fraction of an inch. The dire predictions of the ruin to be wrought by the repeal of the internal taxes and the purging of the judiciary of its notorious impurities had been answered by events. The freedom of speech and of the press had been maintained, despite the unprecedented scurrility poured forth on Jefferson. And the spirit of sectionalism in New England was being conquered as the Federalist strongholds fell, one by one, before the persevering attacks of the Democratic hosts.

Industrially and commercially, the nation had grown steadily under the Jeffersonian policies of six years; and under the wise guidance of Gallatin, the financial policies of Jefferson had richly justified themselves. The year 1806 showed the usual increase in revenue. The receipts of the Treasury had mounted to almost fifteen million dollars. After meeting all current expenses Jefferson had been able to pay two million five hundred thousand dollars of the American claims provided for in the purchase of Louisiana. Of the funded debt he had been able to discharge more than three million dollars of the principal and nearly four million dollars of the interest. He had been able to redeem nearly two million dollars of five and a half per cent stock. In four years and a half he had been able to pay off twenty-three million dollars of the funded debt. And there was a surplus of four million dollars in the Treasury.[1]

Never had the credit of the young Republic stood higher in the money marts of the world; not one obligation had been postponed even for a second; and in the absence of some unforeseen international complication, within three years the surplus would be such as to call for some consideration of its future expenditure.

II

With this in mind, Jefferson and Gallatin had been working on a plan for internal improvements of unprecedented magnitude. An historian, frankly loath to credit Jefferson with more than he could avoid, has said that 'nowhere in all the long course of Mr. Jefferson's great career did he appear to better advantage than when in his Message of 1806 he held out to the country and the world that view of his ultimate hopes and aspirations for national development which was, as he then trusted, to be his last bequest to mankind.'[2]

He had asked himself what should be done about the surplus. Should the impost duties be repealed? That would operate to the advantage of foreign over American manufactures, then in their infancy. In time, perhaps, some few of these might properly be dispensed with; but most of the impost duties were on articles of luxuries that the rich, who required them, could well afford to pay. Thus he determined to keep the imposts, and find means for disposing of the surplus. Would it not be better to spend the surplus in the building of proper roads, the draining of rivers to make them navigable, the digging of canals, and on other objects of material value to the nation? 'By these operations,' he thought, 'new channels of communication will be opened between the States; the lines of separation will disappear, their interests will be identified, and their union cemented by new and indissoluble ties.'

And why, he asked himself, should not a portion of the surplus in prospect be expended on the establishment of a great national university? It seemed that only a public institution could supply the sciences which, 'though rarely called for, are yet necessary to

[1] Message of 1806.   [2] Adams, *Gallatin*, 349–50.

complete the circle, all parts of which contribute to the improvement of the country.'

But could this be done under the Constitution? Clearly, all he had in mind could not, since 'the objects now recommended are not among those enumerated in the Constitution.' Well — three years in advance he would recommend that a constitutional amendment be submitted to the States. Here we have Jefferson, the strict constructionist, who would not, however, forever keep the nation in the strait-jacket of the original constitutional restraints. To him, the Constitution was not a fetish to be worshiped and made sacrosanct against change, but an instrument for the service of the nation, to be changed when changed conditions demanded change in the interest of progress.[1]

All this, essential to a consideration of his statesmanship, was doomed to an indefinite postponement, not because of any fault in Jefferson, but because at this very hour George Canning, across the sea, was launching a program for the destruction of the growing maritime power of the young Republic.

III

Meanwhile, Monroe and William Pinkney were negotiating in London. With the death of Pitt, no friend to the Republic, and the elevation of Charles James Fox to the portfolio of Foreign Affairs, a great load was lifted from Jefferson's spirits. The brilliant Liberal orator had been a consistent friend of the Americans from the days of the Revolution. He was impetuous in his love of liberty, and his sympathies were broad enough to embrace all nations suffering injustice and oppression. Years before, when Jefferson was leading the opposition, it had been the custom at all the Democratic barbecues prevalent at the time to head the toasts with 'Charles James Fox and the Liberals of England.' Now, with Fox in office, perhaps an amicable settlement could be reached.

Soon after taking office, Monroe met Fox for the first time at a reception to the diplomatic corps. Notwithstanding his profound admiration and affection for the man, he had carefully refrained from meeting him lest, under the Ministry of Pitt, he injure the

[1] Message of 1806.

cause of his country. It was more than a political opportunity
when Monroe met Fox; it was a personal satisfaction. Leading the
American off to one side, the great Liberal of England engaged
him in close conversation for half an hour. 'He received me with
great kindness and attention,' Monroe reported, 'and in fact put
me more at my ease in that short time than I have ever felt with
any other person in office since I have been in England.' Fox
inquired as to the status of the negotiations under Pitt, and
listened to a rapid survey of the situation with great attention
and 'apparent interest.' In parting, he expressed a disposition
to reach a friendly agreement, and said, with his winsome smile,
'I have been accused of being too friendly to America.' [1]

A month later, having conversed several times with Fox,
Monroe was sanguine of success. He found the Minister 'very
well disposed toward us,' which was something new in his experience in England. The time, however, had been too short to
do more than skim the surface.[2] Then, toward the close of April,
Monroe was crushed with the gossip that he was to be joined by
a special envoy. Is it true, asked Fox, that either Mr. Burr or
Mr. King is to be sent? Monroe disclaimed all knowledge. If
he received official intelligence to that effect, he would notify the
Minister immediately. Fox 'showed no disposition to delay the
business,' and 'his remarks indeed were of a different character.'
But, to Monroe's horror, on returning home he found a letter
from Madison informing him that a special envoy was being sent
to co-operate with him. Of course no definite commitments could
be made until he arrived.[3]

Meanwhile, however, Monroe continued his contacts with the
great friend of the United States. One night, in the latter part of
May, he attended a reception at Fox's house, hoping for an
opportunity for a clarification of the situation, but the house was
packed, the conditions were inauspicious, and Fox, clearly ill,
retired early. But from a subordinate present, Monroe learned
that the delay was not due to Fox. It was from this subordinate
that Monroe first learned that Fox had been embarrassed by the

---

[1] Monroe to Madison, *Writings of Monroe*, IV, 409–10.

[2] Monroe to Armstrong, *ibid.*, IV, 426.

[3] Monroe to Madison, *ibid.*, IV, 432.

passage of the Non-Importation Act.[1] Lord Holland, a spiritual child of the distinguished Minister, had expressed his regret and the opinion that it would be well to 'let the affair die down' before pushing the negotiations. Monroe left Fox's house with 'no reason to change [his] opinion of Mr. Fox's disposition.' While his present reserve was 'unfavorable,' Monroe was rightly persuaded that he had 'experienced more difficulties in the Cabinet than he had expected.'[2]

Early in June, soon after the party at the Minister's, on the King's Birthday, Monroe had seen Fox in his office. He found Fox frankly much concerned over the Non-Importation Act, because of its effect on public opinion in England. 'It has the air of a menace,' he said, 'and it is not agreeable to do things by compulsion.' Monroe assured him that had there been any anticipation of the change in Ministry, the Non-Importation Act would not have been enacted; and he reminded Fox that the United States had long complained of injuries which the British Government had not attempted to justify — the case of Pierce, for illustration. Yes, Fox replied, full information had been asked on that subject, and, if the officers had acted improperly, appropriate action would be taken.[3] Never once was Monroe to doubt the just intentions and the friendly feeling of the great Liberal statesman. 'My own opinion is that in his conversations and promises to me he was always sincere, and found himself checked in the Cabinet,' he wrote Jefferson, the last of June.[4]

IV

It was not until the first of July that William Pinkney reached London. Though formerly a Federalist, he was to serve in responsible positions under Jefferson and Madison, and in the Cabinet of Monroe. Despite his brilliant qualities — and he was the most polished orator appearing before the Supreme Court — he possessed many of the weaknesses of a prima donna. Monroe was determined to maintain cordial relations with him, but it was not always easy. When Lord Holland sent a note addressed to Monroe alone, and the latter sought to soften the blow to Pinkney's pride

---

[1] To Madison, *Writings of Monroe*, IV, 435.   [2] *Writings of Monroe*, IV, 435.
[3] *Ibid.*, IV, 446.   [4] *Ibid.*, IV, 469.

with the suggestion that it was an oversight due to the writer's informality, Pinkney replied that he could not 'help thinking that Lord Holland pushes his informality rather too far.' [1]

But misfortune constantly dogged the footsteps of Monroe in his diplomatic adventures. Scarcely had Pinkney reached London when Fox was stricken with the dropsy, and he retired to the country home he never was to leave. Monroe hoped for a speedy recovery, but the great man sank rapidly to the grave and America lost its greatest friend in England.

Meanwhile, however, Fox had entrusted the negotiations to Lord Holland and Lord Auckland, both men of eminent ability and good will, and after the sad scenes at Chiswick and the interment at Westminster Abbey, they continued the negotiations.

Lord Holland was a replica of Fox himself. The great statesman had superintended the political education of his kinsman from the latter's youth, when Fox had corresponded with him regularly on political principles and policies. There have been few more charming personalities in English history than Lord Holland. The blood of the Foxes flowed in his veins, with all that that meant of natural eloquence, a capacity for righteous wrath, and a robust sense of justice and fair play. He was a master in debate. Few men had a richer vocabulary or a more logical and analytical mind, and even in conversation he loved nothing more than the intellectual exercise of good-natured disputation. His manners were ingratiating, but they sprang from his heart. His wit, his exhilarating sense of justice, his hatred of oppression and hypocrisy, his love of liberty, his sympathy with the oppressed of all nations, endeared him to most of the generous spirits of his time. Monroe was to know the rare charm of the table at Holland House, which, through so many years, scintillated with the conversation of Fox and Sheridan, Erskine and Curran, the painters, poets, statesmen of the liberal school; and pacing with him the beautiful walks of the grounds, happily still preserved in the heart of London, he came to love the man.

Lord Auckland, then in his sixtieth year, with a brilliant career behind him, did not possess the endearing charm of his associate, but his statesmanship and diplomacy had scored him many

[1] *Writings of Monroe*, IV, 494.

triumphs. Once he had been an ardent supporter and a personal friend of Pitt when the latter had courted his daughter. But the two had quarreled, and, when Pitt resigned, Auckland had remained in the Ministry of Addington. Now he was associated with Fox. If not so sentimentally inclined toward oppressed nationalities, he had an unerring sense of justice, and Monroe came to like him almost as much as he did Lord Holland.

Thus the actors in the negotiations had been perfectly chosen; only the setting was bad. For the British shipping interests and the merchants were more interested in crushing the maritime power of the young Republic than in maintaining amicable relations; and when, after the death of Fox, the Government of 'All the Talents' collapsed, and Canning, wearing a bit awkwardly, but no less arrogantly, the mantle of Pitt, became the head of the Government, the possibilities of a successful issue sadly faded. But Holland and Auckland were permitted to continue the negotiations. The promise in their continuation was gravely shadowed by the frankly hostile attitude of Canning. The American envoys recommended, out of deference to Holland and the memory of Fox, that the operation of the Non-Importation Act be indefinitely postponed, and the negotiators were proceeding slowly when Congress met in December.

v

Throughout the summer, the press had teemed with sensational stories of the mad meanderings of Aaron Burr, and Congress listened in tense silence to Jefferson's report of the conspiracy in his Message. The report on the state of the finances was heard with satisfaction by the Jeffersonians and in glum silence by the opposition. The proposed plan for an extensive co-ordinated system of internal improvements aroused no little interest. The demand for the ending of the slave trade promised more of a controversy than developed. There was nothing definite on foreign relations to report.

The usual sneers from the Federalist press greeted Jefferson's Message, and the notable public paper which had disclosed the healthy state of the Treasury, outlined a comprehensive statesmanlike plan of internal improvements, demanded the outlawing of the slave trade, and announced the blazing of a path across the continent to the western sea, only impressed Fisher Ames as 'insipid.' [1] A more moderate critic from Massachusetts thought that, while its moderate tones did not encourage many of the 'common people to read it,' since they felt 'all was safe in his [Jefferson's] hands,' the opposition could only 'fasten general censures, while nothing serious can be found to promote their ungenerous purpose.' [2]

The session was to be strikingly free of the bitter animosities that had so embittered the preceding one. Even John Randolph the lion had turned fox, with only an occasional snarl. He made no savage attacks on the Administration; he even forgot Yazoo; his attitude toward his colleagues was actually courteous, and he ordered no one 'down the back stairs.' Sloan had reintroduced his resolutions, and these hung over his head like the sword of Damocles. The debate on the suppression of the slave trade was singularly serene and Jefferson soon had the pleasure of signing the law. That on the postponement of the Non-Importation Act was mild enough, and the long discussions of fortifications and defense were free from personalities.

But off the floor, on the streets, in the taverns, the boarding-houses, and about the fireplaces in the cloak-rooms, there were hot discussions on the activities of Burr.

VI

At this time a fascinating new member of the Senate was little disposed to join in the discussions, for he had served Burr with his eloquence in a Kentucky courtroom. Henry Clay, not yet thirty, soon to make an indelible impression on the nation by his eloquence, his genius, his rare personal charm, was little more than a youth. Though scarcely known by name in the country-town capital, no one but felt, in his magnetic presence, the extraordinary qualities of the man. But the sober Senate was not his real arena, and his first session was to be devoted less to the problems of the country than to the pursuit of pleasure. Veterans gathered about him in the cloak-room to listen to his delightful conversation about the fire, which was no more warming than his

[1] Ames to Quincy, *Ames*, I, 376.   [2] Bentley, *Diary*, III, 266.

infectious smile. The observant Plumer found him 'a man of pleasures, fond of amusements,' and a 'great favorite with the ladies,' in attendance at 'all parties of pleasure' and 'out almost every evening.' He recorded with some disapproval that he 'reads little' and that he had heard him say that he intended 'this session should be a tour of pleasure.' Talent all agreed he had, and eloquence of a sort, but he was not 'nice or accurate in his distinctions,' and he 'declaims more than he reasons.' And yet a most companionable man, a gentleman, a pleasant associate, a man of honor and integrity.[1] Too young for jaundice, too new for the harboring of grudges, he was to knock at the door of politicians without regard to party and have a hearty welcome. Drinking lustily in the taverns, flirting frankly, lingering far into the night at the card-table, Henry Clay, harbinger of the new generation, made his initial bow to public life. He was the symbol of change. Within a few months William H. Crawford would appear; and in two years an ardent genius, John C. Calhoun, would take his seat in the House; and within four years the great eyes of Daniel Webster would brood upon the scene.

For the old gods were in the twilight, and the new gods were knocking impatiently at the door.

VII

With here and there a rare bright spot, the session socially was to be dull. The Federalists held sternly aloof from the Jeffersonians, who did not appear to mind. Both parties flocked to the wedding feast in Georgetown of the charming Miss Stoddert, daughter of Adams's Secretary of the Navy. But the politicians of opposing parties flocked together, and at most of the Federalist parties and pow-wows were John Marshall and other Federalist politicians of the Supreme Court.[2] Even the members of the Cabinet, overworked and overwrought, were no longer setting the social pace. Dolly Madison was in Philadelphia in the care of a physician, and her husband, who had discontinued the practice of leaving cards at the lodgings of members of Congress, was inviting few to dine with him. Gallatin, engrossed in his brilliant work, was living like a recluse, neither dining others nor dining

[1] *Plumer*, 353.   [2] *Quincy*, 105.

out, without giving 'even a tea party.' Dearborn and Smith, so
hospitable in the beginning, left cards but invited 'few to tea and
scarcely any to dine.' And Clinton, the Vice-President, who had
brought his carriage, a daughter, and a servant, was living in
a boarding-house 'like a common member.' One senator felt that
'these gentlemen do not live in a style suited to the dignity of their
office.' [1]

It was an ugly winter with much snow, rain, slush, and high
winds, and one day the storm blew out the windows of both houses
of Congress, forcing them to adjourn.[2] A winter of bitter cold,
members hovered about the fireplaces and sometimes adjourned
to escape pneumonia. The facilities for getting about in winter
had not improved, and Adams, caught at the Senate in a downpour, and unable to find a hackney-coach, either at the Capitol
or at Stelle's Hotel, was forced to wait until the House adjourned
to find shelter and conveyance in the carriage of the sergeant-at-
arms.[3]

Throughout the session, Madison, never strong, staggering
under almost unbearable burdens, and ferociously assailed and
ridiculed, was ill, but dragged himself daily to his office; and Jefferson day after day was tortured by sick headaches that drove him
to a dark room every morning by nine o'clock.[4] He was now
looking forward ardently to his release from public cares and to
the life he loved among his books, his fields, and his friends at
Monticello.

VIII

About the roaring fire in the cloak-rooms of House and Senate
the members speculated on how the negotiations might be going
in London.

At the White House, Jefferson was avid for news which trickled
slowly across the sea.

In London, Monroe and Pinkney were grappling with their
problems, finding consolation for their labors about the board at
Holland House and at the house of Auckland.

Now that Fox, America's friend, was sleeping in Westminster,

---

[1] *Plumer*, 352–54.   [2] Adams, *Diary*, I, 451.
[3] *Ibid.*, I, 464.   [4] Dolly Madison to her sister, *Memoirs of Dolly Madison*, 64.

and Canning, sword-rattler of the closet, was in power; now that the shipping interests and the merchants were insisting that American commerce be destroyed, their task was well-nigh hopeless. What though Holland and Auckland were just and friendly, they were but as poor relations barely suffered in the house of Canning, and possessed of no actual power. Finally it was clear that under the stiff instructions there could be no treaty at all, and the two isolated Americans determined to disregard them and do the best they could. The two outstanding features of Madison's instructions called for the ending of impressment and of the condemnation of American ships and cargoes. Fox had taken steps to stop the condemnations before he died. Thoroughly convinced that, without the right of impressment, Britain's mastery of the seas was gone, the British negotiators dared not challenge public sentiment with an open disavowal of the right. Holland, true friend of the Republic, was sincerely distressed, torn as he was between his generous inclinations and the inflexible attitude of Canning. Monroe sympathized, perhaps too much, with his friend's predicament, and when the British negotiators offered, as a substitute for a disavowal in the treaty, a separate note promising that the most scrupulous care would be exercised to prevent unjust impressments, the Americans acquiesced.

The instructions, thus violated, ceased to be the governing force in the envoys' actions, and one after another of the instructions was compromised away. The demand for indemnity for the outrages on American commerce in 1805 was relinquished. The compromise accepted on colonial trade was scarcely such as a self-respecting sovereign nation could accept without a blush. Monroe, with the best intentions, nevertheless had substituted for John Jay in the same rôle.

Two days after Christmas in 1806, Monroe and Pinkney, exuberant and happy with the season's spirit, signed a note to Madison. They had 'agreed with the British Commissioners to conclude a treaty on all the points which have formed the object of our negotiations.' A few days, and the agreement would be whipped into form, and then, by special messenger, hurried to Washington before the Congress had adjourned.

Madison read the note as the session was hurrying to its close.

The four men in London completed their task and met to sign the treaty.

Then Monroe and Pinkney had their greatest shock.

They were handed a letter to the effect that if the United States failed to resist Napoleon's Berlin Decree, Britain would reserve the right to disregard the treaty. Inevitably Jefferson would protest the Berlin Decree, but the implications of the letter were plain enough — a British treaty or a French war.

The Americans were stunned. The pen was in their hands. With the mental reservations that they had not accepted the implications of the letter, they affixed their signatures; and immediately a special messenger was on his way to Washington.

IX

Through a cold and stormy February, Jefferson, Madison, friend and foe in House and Senate, anxiously waited for the treaty. The last day of the session dawned. In the afternoon the capital throbbed with the news that a runner had arrived with the treaty at the British Legation.

There, with feverish haste, Erskine, the young Minister, perused it. The son of Lord Erskine, the champion of liberty and the friend of Fox, this young man was a friend of the Republic, zealous for an amicable settlement. And here was the treaty — signed! No time could be lost. A few hours, and Congress would be adjourned. He hurried with the utmost speed to Madison.

It was a tense moment in the office of the Secretary of State. 'And what is done about impressments?' Madison asked before glancing at the document. Erskine had to admit, with a sinking heart, that he had observed no reference to the subject. He did not fail to observe the expression of utter astonishment on the face of Madison and to read its meaning. And when the British Minister was forced to explain about the note concerning the Berlin Decree, he was left in no doubt as to the fate of the treaty. That alone, said Madison, would make ratification utterly impossible.[1]

Erskine was crestfallen when he took his leave, and Madison hastened to the White House. Jefferson had been ill all day, too

[1] Erskine to Howick, quoted in Adams, *History*, III, 430.

ill to go to the Capitol, as was his custom at the end of sessions. His amazement was even greater than Madison's had been. His customary serenity of manner gave way to a burst of indignation. Instructions violated! The main points abandoned! And an insulting note warning of the repudiation of the treaty unless the Republic practically declared war on France! What had possessed Monroe? Away with such a document! Not by him would it be presented to the Senate.

Meanwhile, in the Senate they were waiting with keen curiosity for the treaty. Hours passed and no messenger from Jefferson appeared. It was almost ten o'clock at night. In two hours the Congress would be dead. Puzzled by the silence, a committee was named to wait upon Jefferson to inquire if he had further communications. Headed by Senator Mitchill, the committee jolted over the hard frozen road to the White House. Jefferson, pale and ill, received them instantly, but it was not the serene statesman beaming benevolence who stood before them. Had he any further communications? he was asked. No — none. 'But the treaty,' timidly suggested Mitchill, 'would he submit that?'

'Certainly not!' said Jefferson, his voice ringing with an anger seldom heard from him. 'Certainly not!'

How our envoys could have agreed to such a treaty was beyond his imagination, he said, unless they felt that in the excitement over the Berlin Decree they had thought war certain. No, he would submit no such treaty; he would instruct the envoys to renew their negotiations. Awed by Jefferson's wrath, the committee hastily withdrew.

In the Senate, the committee was surrounded by excited men. The chagrin of the Federalists was great. With the acceptance of the treaty, not then incompatible with their principles, the game would have been in their hands. What a ghastly joke! they could have exclaimed — the very people who had burned Jay in effigy had made a treaty infinitely worse.

Even among some known as Jeffersonians, such as the crafty Senator Samuel Smith, engaged in shipping, there were harsh comments on Jefferson's stout stand. Hurrying to the White House for an explanation, Smith had no difficulty in getting it:

Jefferson would stand for no treaty that ignored impressments. Smith, red-faced and angry, hurried to Madison. Was not Jefferson assuming a heavy responsibility, he asked, in refusing the treaty without a consultation of the Senate? 'But,' replied Madison, 'if he is determined not to accept, even should the Senate advise, why call the Senate together?' Smith could think of no adequate reason.[1]

But the more he thought about it the more excited he became, and he plunged into a mischief-making correspondence with Nicholson, the friend of Randolph, who was sponsoring the presidential candidacy of Monroe. 'By sending it back he is disgracing his Ministers, and Monroe is one,' he wrote. And suppose the depredations continued; would not Jefferson's refusal of the treaty be held responsible? Would not the popular cry be raised that the rejection was inspired by 'jealousy of Monroe' and Jefferson's and Madison's 'antipathy to Great Britain'? The intriguing senator was searching his mind for all the propaganda he could plant, for Jefferson's refusal to send him as Minister to London or Paris had cut the vain man to the heart.[2]

John Quincy Adams, communing with his loved diary, could find no fault with Jefferson's position;[3] but Josiah Quincy, Federalist leader in the House, thought Jefferson's refusal not only 'absurd' but 'impertinent.' The main popular reason for negotiations had been impressments — and they had been ignored; a cool note had warned that Britain could repudiate the treaty if it saw fit. What 'impertinence' to reject it![4]

Instantly Jefferson ordered Madison to prepare fresh instructions and to ask the envoys in London to resume negotiations.

But there was one phase that worried him not a little. What would be the reaction of Monroe? He had a deep affection for the Minister, but it was the consummate politician in him that impelled him to write a friendly letter to Monroe assuring him of his continuing confidence, and warning him against the machinations of the Randolph group.[5]

---

[1] Smith to Nicholson, Nicholson MSS.   [2] *Ibid.*
[3] Adams, *Diary*, I, 466.
[4] *Quincy*, III.
[5] *Writings of Jefferson*, II, 106.

X

Even so, Jefferson had little to worry him politically in 1807. Never had he been so powerful throughout the nation than just before he entered upon the last of his eight years in office. Even New England had swept into the Jeffersonian column, and Connecticut alone stayed out. In Massachusetts, despite Fisher Ames's brilliant fusillade, the Jeffersonians were in possession of every branch of the government, with James Sullivan as Governor. The Essex Junto had fought him, without scruple, with grotesque misrepresentations to which decent men had reacted unfavorably. After all, it was a bit stupid to assail him, one of the most fluent and forceful political writers of his time, as 'unable to write a sentence of English.' [1] The most significant phase of the drift was that the young men were turning their backs on the old autocrats of New England Federalism and were going in droves into the more liberal Democratic ranks. Ah, moaned the old leaders, it is the 'depravity' of the young which impels them to associate with the party of 'lawlessness and irreligion.' [2] Money-lenders and employers among the Federalists, seeking to stem the tide, were resorting frankly to intimidation. A Jeffersonian worker was threatened with the loss of his job. A Jeffersonian debtor was intimidated with the threat of an immediate exaction of the debt to the last farthing. The Jeffersonians, said the *National Aegis*, 'do not appoint spies to watch with eagle eyes over the conduct of poor tenants and debtors at elections. . . . It is a fact that many mechanics are in a state of bondage in regard to electioneering suffrages.' [3]

Throughout New England, the Jeffersonian fight against the political domination of the clergy was pronounced an attack on 'religion' under the direction of the 'anti-Christ' in the White House. When the Jeffersonians of Vermont passed a religious liberty bill, the *Dartmouth Gazette* [4] cited it as 'a striking instance of the pernicious and direful, the infernal consequences to which the leveling spirit of democracy must invariably tend.' Did it not 'disclose at once its great and only object, *viz.* the eradication

---

[1] Bentley, *Diary*, III, 299.

[2] W. A. Robinson, *Jeffersonian Democracy in New England*, 75.

[3] *Ibid.*   [4] November 18, 1807.

of every moral, virtuous, and religious principle from the human heart'? When, in Massachusetts, the Jeffersonians sponsored a religious liberty bill, and another to quiet the titles in the province of Maine, their action was clamorously denounced as 'a war on property and religion.' [1]

But these were the attacks of unprincipled politicians in the pulpit and out, for among those in the pews were many unable to associate the Nazarene with tyranny and oppression. Not a few bold Jeffersonian spirits among the New England clergy girded their loins for combat. John Leland, a Baptist minister who had participated in the fight for disestablishment in Virginia, was now in Massachusetts bearing the torch with a courage that his foes called effrontery. Another minister, Elias Smith, established a religious paper called *The Herald of Gospel Liberty* and vigorously fought for Democracy and against its clerical enemies.   His defense of Jefferson aroused the wrath of his foes. 'His ideas of religion and government,' wrote Smith, 'accord with the laws of the King of Kings. For this, he is hated by the hypocrites and those who wish to stamp the people into dust and ashes, in order to acquire wealth, riches, and reputation by depriving the people of their rights.' [2] Just as Jefferson in the flesh had led the fight for religious freedom and the separation of Church and State in Virginia, so in the spirit, and through his disciples, he was leading the selfsame fight in New England — to ultimate success.

Yes, New England was coming over. It had broken the back of the Essex Junto, which finally would drag its dying body to the Hartford Convention. For 1807 found three Federalists of note tramping into the Jeffersonian camp. John Quincy Adams avowed the principles of Jefferson; Senator Plumer of New Hampshire enlisted as a Democrat; and William Gray, the most distinguished and the richest merchant in New England, joined the Jeffersonians in the never-ending war.

In New York, the Jeffersonians' triumph was complete. The Federalists in the spring of 1807 hoped to profit by the quarrel between the Clintons and Governor Lewis.[3] But when they approached Lewis with covert promises of support, they found him

[1] Robinson, 78.   [2] *Ibid.*, 146.
[3] Troup to King, *King's Corr.*, v, 8–9.

and his friends 'starting from the sight of Federalists as from the sight of monsters opening their mouths to devour them.'[1] Determined, if possible, to win the legislature, the Federalists in New York City presented a legislative ticket of extraordinary dignity. Rufus King was prevailed upon to head it; but so low had the Federalists fallen that King preferred to call his ticket the 'American Ticket,' and Troup wondered if it would not be wise to drop the obnoxious name 'Federalist' altogether.[2]

But even King proved a source of weakness; for some time before, during the Administration of Adams, when Minister to England, he had persuaded the British Government to refuse permission to Thomas Addis Emmet, then in prison for a political offense, to bring a small colony of Irishmen to Pennsylvania. Emmet never forgave him; for had that permission been granted, he would have taken his brother, Robert, with him, and that brilliant youth would not have died upon the gallows.[3] With the announcement of King's candidacy, Emmet took up his pen, and in an address before the Hibernian Society enlisted the Irish in the fight. In a public letter, Emmet opened hostilities by demanding of King whether he proposed 'submitting to the world any explanation of your interference with the British Government respecting the Irish state prisoners in 1798.'[4] Instantly the Irish patriot was deluged with all the mud of the gutter. When he was treated as a low vulgarian of no consequence, Emmet replied in a four-column letter in the *American Citizen*. 'My private character and conduct are, I hope, as fair as yours,' he wrote to King, 'and even in those matters which I consider as trivial, but upon which aristocratic pride is accustomed to stamp a value, I shall not be inclined to shrink from competition. My birth certainly will not humble me by comparison; my paternal fortune was probably much greater than yours; the consideration in which the name I bear was held in my country was as great as yours is ever likely to be.'[5]

To this letter, Cheetham added a slanderous editor's note, to the effect that 'Mr. King when a lad was a servant to and wore the

---

[1] Troup to King, *King's Corr.*, v, 9.   [2] *Ibid.*, v, 31.
[3] *Jefferson and Hamilton*, 376.
[4] *American Citizen*, April 6, 1807.   [5] April 9, 1807.

livery of Sir John Temple, a near relative of Mr. Emmet.'[1]
The *Evening Post* replied with the most savage abuse of Emmet.
The Federalist judges, William Kent and Thompson, put their
heads together in a plan to disbar the Irish patriot, though he
already was a distinguished member of the New York Bar and
one of its foremost advocates. 'Judge Kent and Judge Thompson
are very dissatisfied with his conduct,' smugly wrote Troup to
King.[2] All the smouldering Federalist hate of the Irish flamed
again. 'The impudent interference of Emmet in our elections!'
snorted Christopher Gore from Boston.[3] And from Philadelphia,
C. J. Ingersoll wrote King: 'It would not be your own wish to be
put up and pelted by Irishmen'; and that 'the citizens of New
York deserve to be stung by fostering that viper Emmet, and he
deserves to be damned.'[4] Emmet was a great lawyer and not
a politician, and the throngs that pass St. Paul's on Broadway in
New York, and note near the entrance of the church the lofty
shaft that bears his name, think of him, not as a 'viper,' but as
one of the distinguished leaders of the New York Bar.

But Emmet played a conspicuous part in this election; King
and his American ticket went down to defeat; and King suffered
the humiliation of running third on his ticket, much to the glee
of the Jeffersonian press.[5] Again the Clintons, in alliance with
Jefferson, triumphed over the combined strength of discredited
Federalists and disgruntled Democrats.

In 1807, Jefferson was confident of his strength, and legislatures
were importuning him to break all precedent and accept a third
term.

XI

But nothing was more remote from his thought. The headaches
were increasing in frequency and severity. He had passed his
youth and middle age. No longer could he bear the brunt of
battles, as he once had done, with serene complacency. And he
was hungry for the air and the scenes of his loved hilltop home.

That year, an attempt was made to disturb the relations between Jefferson and Gallatin. The mischief-makers in Pennsyl-

---

[1] *American Citizen*, April 9, 1807.   [2] *King's Corr.*, v, 31.
[3] *Ibid.*, v, 32.   [4] *Ibid.*, v, 36.
[5] *American Citizen*, May 4, 1807.

vania were redoubling their efforts. Gossips were busy with false news. It has been observed that when Jefferson lost one friend he made two, but he seldom lost a friend; and never without a generous effort to retain him. The moment the gossip reached Jefferson, he wrote Gallatin a frank and affectionate letter expressing his confidence and appreciation of invaluable services, both to the nation and himself. Within twenty-four hours the reply was in his hands. 'In minds solely employed in honest efforts to promote the welfare of a free people,' he read, 'there is but little room left for the operation of those passions which engender doubts and jealousies. That you entertained none against me I had the perfect conviction before I received your note of yesterday. Of your candor and indulgence I have experienced repeated proofs; the freedom with which my opinions have been delivered has been always acceptable and approved. But I am none the less sensible of your kindness in repeating at this juncture the expression of your confidence.' [1]

Tragic, indeed, it would have been had the mischief-makers alienated Gallatin; for the schism among Democrats in Congress was nearing its climax, and the disloyalty of Randolph in the crisis with Britain would soon require his repudiation and dismissal from the leadership of the Administration Party.

[1] *Writings of Gallatin,* I, 31.

CHAPTER XVIII

The Trail of Treason

I

ASTOUNDED by the bitter reaction to the killing of Hamilton, Burr, alert, and constantly informed of developments, remained in seclusion in the library at Richmond Hill. A Federalist paper, probably for propaganda purposes, insisted that 'before and after General Hamilton's death, Colonel Burr was seen riding about the streets, with servants behind, with as much apparent cheerfulness and unconcern as if nothing had happened, or as if he had performed a meritorious action, instead of committing a murder.'[1]

Learning of the indictment in New Jersey, he slipped out one night in a rowboat and made his escape. Soon he was writing with callous cynicism to Theodosia from Philadelphia that 'if any male friend of yours should be dying of ennui, recommend him to indulge in a duel and courtship at the same time — prob est.' And then, referring to his love affair — 'Celeste seems more pliant.'[2] To Philadelphians he presented a bold front. One newspaper at the time described him as 'he unblushingly walks through our streets at noonday, obtrudes himself on public notice, and where the slightest previous acquaintance affords him the shadow of a right, he seizes the hand, nay forces himself into the houses of individuals wearing badges of mourning for the man he has murdered.'[3] But fears of extradition to New Jersey interrupted his courtship, and he hurried away to South Carolina, where he

---

[1] *Columbian Centinel*, July 18, 1804.   [2] *Burr*, II, 332.
[3] *Connecticut Courant*, August 8, 1804.

lingered awhile in the home of a friend on St. Simon's Island, and made an excursion on horseback into Florida. Then, in leisurely fashion, he started North for the opening of the Senate over which we have seen him preside. Virginia accorded him every courtesy, and at Petersburg he fell under the spell of Mrs. West, the actress, to whose performances he went attended by twenty admirers.[1] Ostracized from New York, indicted in New Jersey, his house and furniture sold for about twenty-five thousand dollars, with seven or eight thousand in debts outstanding, his position would have crushed the average man. 'The library and the wine remain,' he wrote Alston. And yet never a more blithesome spirit when he reached the capital. 'Mrs. Merry arrived a few days ago and looks extremely well,' he wrote Theodosia. 'Madame Turreau is supposed to be lost or captured.'[2] Outwardly, it was a winter of drama and festivity, wining, dining, and winning laurels by his irreproachable conduct of the impeachment of Chase. But behind the scenes, Burr, so frivolous to all outward seeming, was making his plans for a desperate enterprise.

A favorite of Mrs. Merry, he had been able to tolerate the dull-witted Minister. He knew of Merry's intrigue with the Federalist leaders in the disunion conspiracy. One day, at this time, Burr sat in secret converse with the representative of George III. With his incomparable plausibility, he poured into Merry's eager ears his plan for the separation of Louisiana and the Western States from the Union. The stupid Merry heard that 'the inhabitants of Louisiana seem determined to render themselves independent of the United States,' the execution of their design merely waiting on the co-operation of the eastern section of the country, and on the 'assurance of protection and assistance from some foreign power.' He heard that the Louisianians, while mostly French or Spanish, would much prefer the assistance of Great Britain, 'but if His Majesty's Government would not think proper to listen to the overtures, application will be made to that of France.' She, no doubt, 'would be eager to attend to it in the most effectual manner,' since this would 'afford the French more easy communication with the continent of America.' Would it not be a great commercial triumph for Britain to have a practical

[1] *Burr*, ii, 348.   [2] *Ibid.*, ii, 253.

monopoly of the trade of this extensive territory? The all-too credulous Merry thought it would.[1]

Of course, Burr would require 'two or three frigates and the same number of smaller vessels at the mouth of the Mississippi to prevent its being blockaded by such forces as the United States could send.' As to money, a mere hundred thousand pounds would be enough 'for the immediate purpose of the enterprise.' Quite properly, England would not wish to be known in the transaction, but the remittances could be so arranged that no one would suspect.[2]

Merry agreed to press the scheme on Pitt.

With this assurance, Burr made plans for a Western tour. Nineteen days before Merry was sending his report to London, Burr was writing Theodosia that 'this tour has other objects than mere curiosity.' [3]

II

Desperate enough was the situation of the man who turned his horse's head toward his future empire. 'In New York,' he wrote Alston, 'I am disfranchised and in New Jersey hanged. Having substantial objections to both, I shall not, for the present, hazard either, but shall seek another country.' [4] He lingered awhile in Philadelphia for conferences with his close associates from New York, of whom there was 'a constant succession,' and among them was John Swartwout, United States Marshal in New York, whom Jefferson removed from office in connection with the Miranda affair.[5]

Then, mounting his horse, he turned westward, and at Pittsburgh he found his 'boat and hands ready.' The boat literally was a floating palace, sixty by fourteen feet, with a dining-room, kitchen and fireplace, and two bedrooms. Roofed from stem to stern, a stairway led to the top which could be used for exercise.[6]

Floating down the Ohio in comparative luxury, he reached Blennerhassett's Island, where a cultivated Irish gentleman, of literary tastes, had established his seat. The master was not at

---

[1] Merry to Harrowby, W. F. McCaleb, *The Aaron Burr Conspiracy*, 20–23.
[2] *Ibid.*   [3] *Burr*, II, 359.   [4] *Ibid.*, II, 336.
[5] *Ibid.*, II, 367.   [6] Burr to Theodosia, *ibid.*, II, 368.

home, but his beautiful and charming wife invited Burr to dinner, and, while captivating the woman, as he always could, he made mental note of the possibilities of the master's fortune.

Soon he was in Cincinnati, meeting Jonathan Dayton, former Federalist Senator, and 'several old army acquaintances' at the home of Senator Smith, with whom Burr had been intimate during the recent congressional session; but General Wilkinson, who was expected, did not appear until after Burr had resumed his journey.

Passing through Kentucky, he started overland to Nashville, where he was received with enthusiastic cordiality. 'I have been received with much hospitality and kindness, and could stay a month with pleasure,' he wrote.[1] He was wined and dined and extravagantly praised by the press. Especially cordial was Andrew Jackson, who admired the physical valor of the visitor, and resented the hue and cry raised against him because of the duel. With his keen penetration into character, Burr gave no hint of such a plan as he had outlined to Merry. Instead, he played on Jackson's obsession against the Spanish by promising to drive the dons from America. And of this Jackson heartily approved.

Reluctantly leaving the incense-laden air of Nashville, Burr took to his boat at the mouth of the Cumberland, and on June 6, 1805, he began a four-day conference with General Wilkinson at the military post of Fort Massac, near the mouth of the Ohio. There he was fitted out with 'an elegant barge, sails, colors, and ten oars with a sergeant and ten faithful hands.'[2] Wilkinson, a natural conspirator, was thoroughly familiar with Burr's unlawful and treasonable plans.

Soon thereafter, Burr was at Natchez, charmed with the luxuries and taste of the wealthy planters' houses.[3] Thence he fared forth for New Orleans, delighted to find his passage through 'a settled country' where he could breakfast and dine each day at the home of a gentleman by merely announcing his approach.

III

On June 25, 1805, he reached the seat of his proposed capital. Meanwhile, Wilkinson, in fine fettle over the plans, had hurried

[1] To Theodosia, *Burr*, II, 370.   [2] *Ibid.*, II, 370.   [3] *Ibid.*

to St. Louis to feel out his officers on treason. To some of these he spoke contemptuously of democracy, and his expectations of anarchy and confusion in the Eastern States as a result of it, and hinted at the establishment of a military empire in Louisiana.

In New Orleans the disaffected gave Burr a hearty welcome. Edward Livingston took him into his home, where Burr, with eagle eye for feminine beauty, was fascinated by the charming creole mistress. 'Fair, pale, with jet-black hair and eyes — little sparkling black eyes which seem to be made for other purposes than those of mere vision,' he wrote.[1] There, too, he made a conspirator's contact with the Mexican Association which aimed at the severance of Mexico from Spain. Daniel Clark, a rich merchant, became his confidant. In his conversations here he recurred to the plan he had outlined to Merry — the separation of the Western States from the Union. These indiscretions soon spread to the streets, and Clark, thoroughly alarmed, and with an alibi in mind in case of trouble, wrote Burr a letter expressing amazement over the gossip, and asking Wilkinson also to write. 'Pray do not disturb yourself with such nonsense,' Burr replied.[2]

Early August found the conspirator back in Nashville lounging at the home of Jackson — 'a man of intelligence and one of those prompt, frank, ardent souls which I love to meet.'[3] There he was honored with a public dinner — 'given not to the Vice-President but to A. B.,' he wrote proudly.[4] But so notorious were Burr's indiscretions at the time that Merry, in Philadelphia, became alarmed and wrote his Government that Burr or 'some of his agents have either been indiscreet . . . or have been betrayed; . . . for the object of his journey is now begun to be noticed in the public prints, where it is said a convention is to be called immediately from the States bordering on the Ohio and Mississippi for the purpose of forming a separate Government.' However, Merry consoled himself with the reflection that 'perhaps the business may be so far advanced . . . as to render any further secrecy impossible.'[5]

While Merry was sending this alarm to London, Burr was

---

[1] To Theodosia, *Burr*, ii, 371.   [2] Adams, *History*, ii, 225.
[3] *Burr*, ii, 372.   [4] *Ibid.*
[5] Merry to Mulgrave, Adams, *History*, iii, 226.

lingering in Tennessee and Kentucky. Then he struck off on horseback through Indiana to St. Louis to see Wilkinson. The spirit of that doughty warrior had measurably subsided. He had been rebuffed in his advances to officers and had made no converts to treason. Burr exerted all his eloquence to revive the martial spirit of the General. The Government at Washington was 'imbecile' and 'would moulder to pieces, die a natural death.' The people of the Western country were ripe for revolt. Wilkinson was not impressed — he knew these Westerners better. 'They are bigoted to Jefferson and Democracy,' he replied. After a week with Wilkinson, Burr started East and reached Washington in November.

IV

There he hurried to the home of Merry in high hope of a favorable answer to his proposition to London. But no word had come. Burr made no secret of his disappointment. It was too bad! He had found the Western country and Louisiana 'completely prepared in every quarter for the execution of his plan.' He had promised his impatient followers to return in March and begin operations. All this had been partly predicated on the expectation of Britain's aid. It really was too bad! In the West, 'persons of the greatest property and influence had engaged themselves to contribute very largely,' and in New Orleans he had found the people 'firmly resolved on separating themselves from their union with the United States.' Because of this passion for separation, the operations would begin in New Orleans, 'probably at the end of April or the beginning of May,' provided, of course, the British Government 'should consent to lend her assistance.'

Merry listened sympathetically, and Burr returned to his mutton. All he wished from Pitt was a naval force, and, this time, a hundred and ten thousand pounds. This could be given in the name of John Barclay, of Philadelphia, and Daniel Clark, of New Orleans. But time was pressing, and, if England did not wish France to step in and get the advantage, she should act. Merry was a bit concerned over this possibility. He must inform London at once. Taking Burr's word as sacred, he wrote London that when Burr reached Louisiana 'he had found the inhabitants so impatient under the American Government that they actually had prepared a presentation of their grievances, and it was in agitation to send deputies with it — to Paris.' What a pity that England should hesitate! Had not 'a person of the greatest influence in East and West Florida' approached Burr in New Orleans with the plea that they be included in the new empire? With England at war with Spain, what more desirable? Too bad! The country was prepared. The moment Louisiana and the Western States drew off, 'the Eastern States will separate themselves immediately from the Southern' and the Republic would be smashed. Knowing of Merry's secret intrigues with the Federalists, Burr hoped this would sound convincing.[1] Much impressed, Merry sent a report of all this to London.

Meanwhile, Burr called on Jefferson and was received with a cold politeness. But time was pressing. Money was needed, and after a week, Burr hastened to Philadelphia, where the Marquis de Casa Yrujo, the Spanish Minister, was staying. There he met his confederate, Jonathan Dayton, who had just been retired from the Senate. He, too, had voted to save the 'Constitution' and the federal judiciary, but was now quite willing to destroy the Federal Union. No one was closer to the treasonable conspiracy, as we shall find. The two men discussed means of raising money. Burr would see what could be done with Blennerhassett, and in the meantime plans were made for approaching Yrujo. The plot was worthy of a Dumas or a Sheridan. Dayton would 'betray' Burr for cash for both! Thus, one day, Yrujo found Dayton in his parlor, spinning a fantastic tale.

There was a great conspiracy, Dayton said. The preceding March, Burr had had frequent conferences with the British Minister concerning a plan for taking the Floridas, and adding them to the Western States that were to form part of a new empire. England was to be compensated with decisive preferences in commerce and navigation. Merry had entered fully into the plot, Yrujo was assured, and had recommended it to his Government. Burr had found the Western country ripe for separation, but on condition that 'an expedition against the kingdom of Mexico' would be included in the scheme. All this had been

[1] Merry to Mulgrave, Adams, *History*, III, 229-32.

favorably considered in London, then abandoned, but now 'Mr.
Pitt has again turned his attention to it.' The movement probably
would be launched in March when a British squadron would
appear off the coast of Florida. The Floridas would be taken, and
then, to make the scheme more popular in the Western country,
the march on Mexico would begin. With the aid of the British
fleet, troops would be landed in Tampico and the Spanish possessions would be turned into independent republics. Was not this
information worth forty thousand dollars? Dayton thought so.
Yrujo, more clever than Merry, was not so sure. He would think
it over. Meanwhile he would write Madrid.

More puzzled than impressed with the fantastic tale, he sent
a report of the conversation, expressing surprise that Jefferson,
'although penetrating,' should have had a two-hour conference
with Burr. [1]

V

Stunned by the failure of England to respond, Burr, about this
time, was willing to retire from the business of treason if he could
find a comfortable berth in some foreign mission. Thus the conference that had puzzled Yrujo, in which Burr frankly asked for
an appointment to a foreign court. Jefferson listened coldly and
left his visitor in no doubt that he would receive no foreign mission
nor any other post within the gift of the President. Burr retired,
hating Jefferson more than ever, and turned his talents to treason
again. [2]

VI

Immediately afterward, Dayton resumed his negotiations with
Yrujo. He now confessed that England had not accepted Burr's
invitation, and implied that the brains of the conspiracy was now
prepared to sell himself to Spain. The attack on the Floridas had
been abandoned, but otherwise the plan still held. Burr had made
contact with a great number 'of adventurers, without property,
full of ambition, and ready to unite at once under the standard
of a revolution which promises to better their lot.' This, to Yrujo,
seemed not impossible. He knew the country had many such.
These gradually were to be introduced into Washington, armed

---

[1] Yrujo to Cevallos, MS. Spanish Archives.   [2] *Plumer*, 348.

and disguised. When Burr gave the word they would fall on Jefferson, the Vice-President, and the Speaker of the House and take them into possession. The conspirators then would seize the public funds, steal the money in the banks, and take over the arsenal. This, Burr thought, according to Dayton, would so stun and paralyze the nation that he would have time to negotiate with each State separately. But in the event of failure, Burr would burn the ships in the navy yard, take the money, and go by sea to New Orleans, where he would proclaim the independence of Louisiana and the Western States.[1]

While awaiting the reaction of Madrid, Burr feverishly set to work in Washington in the furtherance of his plans. Living there at the time was General William Eaton, chafing under what he considered an injustice from the Government, and unfriendly to Jefferson. Following his idea of mobilizing the disaffected, Burr turned at once to him, and during the winter met him frequently at the boarding-house of Sergeant-at-Arms Wheaton, where Burr lived and Eaton frequently dined with congressional friends. Burr sought to enlist him in the plan as second in command to Wilkinson. At first the scheme was confined to a military expedition against the Spanish provinces which, Burr implied, would have the sanction of Jefferson. With maps and documents spread on the table in the light of the candles, he sought to convince Eaton of the practicability of the plan. The bitterness with which Burr spoke of the Administration aroused Eaton's suspicions, and, assuming a confidence he did not feel, he hoped to draw forth the entire plot. Soon Burr was admitting his intent 'of revolutionizing the country west of the Alleghanies' and establishing an empire with New Orleans as the capital. He had visited the Western country and 'had secured to his interest and attached to his person ... the most distinguished citizens of Tennessee and Kentucky and the territory of Orleans.' As to funds, he had 'inexhaustible resources.' As to resistance, 'the army of the United States would act with him.' Wilkinson, in on the plot, would control the army and there would be no opposition at New

---

[1] This report to Yrujo outlines precisely the same plan that Eaton outlined as Burr's scheme. Beveridge (III, 304–50) implies that Eaton lied. The fact that the same story was told Yrujo is convincing corroboration of Eaton's story under oath.

Orleans. And to Eaton he outlined the plan, which Yrujo had heard from Dayton, of seizing the President and the funds in the Treasury. And did Eaton know the officers of the Marine Corps? With the support of this military group, Burr would 'turn Congress neck and heels out of doors' and 'throw Jefferson into the Potomac.' [1]

Convinced that treason was in the offing, Eaton, putting his pride in his pocket, and disregarding the advice of two Federalist congressmen to say nothing, called on Jefferson to urge that Burr be sent out of the country on a foreign mission. Otherwise, he warned of insurrection in the Western country within eighteen months. Jefferson listened coldly and impatiently. He would not give Burr a mission of any sort because he suspected his integrity. An insurrection in the West? He had 'too much confidence in the integrity and attachment to the Union of the citizens of that country to admit any apprehensions of that kind.'

But Eaton had not told Jefferson the full details of his conferences with Burr. He merely implied a suspicion of Burr's intent.

That winter, Burr also attempted the seduction of Commodore Truxtun from his allegiance to the Government, for he also had a grievance. Why should Truxtun waste his time on an ungrateful Government and the navy? he was asked. Burr would like to see the Commodore 'unwedded from the navy ... and not to think any more of those men in Washington.' Burr would make him an admiral, for he planned an expedition into Mexico in the event of a war with Spain. Finding the Government was not cognizant of the scheme, Truxtun cooled, and Burr entered into no such intimacies with him as with Eaton. Finding the Commodore a dangerous prospect, Burr proposed that he write a friendly letter to Wilkinson, to be taken, with others, by a courier about to leave. Truxtun could see no occasion for a letter to the General. The clear intent was, through this letter sent by Burr's courier, to bear out the lie to Wilkinson about the co-operation of Truxtun.

Truxtun was dropped.[2] All hope of seducing Commodore Decatur and Captain Preble was abandoned.

---

[1] Eaton's evidence in Burr's trial.
[2] Evidence of Truxtun, Burr's trial.

VII

Meanwhile, Pitt had died, and with him all hope of British co-operation. Unhappily a dispatch from Merry relating the latest conversation with Burr reached London after Charles James Fox had succeeded, and that staunch friend of America read it with amazement, and in a brief chilly note granted the stupid Minister's 'request' for a recall. The diplomat piteously protested that he had not asked for a recall, but nothing came from London to postpone his departure.[1]

But the conspirators were not wholly without results from their treasonable conversations. Dayton had furnished information and, from time to time, Madrid doled out pin-money to him.[2]

England had failed him; Spain had offered nothing; the attempted seduction of army and naval officers had come to nought; but Burr's sublime capacity for lying had suffered no loss. Thus, in April he was writing in joyous mood to Wilkinson, who seemed to be cooling to the plot. The moment for striking had been postponed until December, but 'the association' was 'enlarged'; confidence was 'limited to few'; the delay, while irksome, would enable them 'to move with more certainty and dignity.' The Administration was 'damned' and John Randolph was helping to damn it.[3]

A month later, weary of awaiting results from Dayton's negotiations with Yrujo, Burr determined to try his powers of persuasion. He hoped to convince the Spanish envoy of the possibility of success. All that was required was some pecuniary aid from Spain and France. The matter had not been broached to Turreau, the French Minister, because the conspirators had no confidence in him, and if Madrid saw fit to take the matter up with Paris, it should be with the injunction that nothing be communicated to Turreau.[4] But Yrujo could see no need for haste. He would be in Spain in the spring of 1807 and would discuss the subject then. Meanwhile, he was informed by Burr that some men from Tennessee, Louisiana, and Kentucky would appear in Madrid concerning the plans. These were agreed that

---

[1] Adams, *History*, II, 250.   [2] *Ibid.*, II, 245.

[3] Wilkinson, *Memoirs*, II, Appendix LXXXIII.

[4] Yrujo to Cevallos, MS. Spanish Archives.

'the interests of these countries' were 'united and in conformity with those of Spain and France.' [1]

Finding Yrujo in such indifferent mood, Burr tried another attack. Again Dayton sat in the Minister's study telling him of Burr's latest mood. The death of Pitt, the accession of Fox, had convinced the leader of the treason plot that the British Government would now be more complacent. Already he was preparing an invitation to London to join in the attack on the Spanish possessions. Dayton was trying to postpone this step by urging the propriety of discussing it first in a conference of the leaders of the conspiracy in New Orleans in December, but Burr had brushed this aside. The plan could always be altered, he had said. Of course Dayton would do all he could to prevent the consummation of this plan, but in the meantime Spain might do well to strengthen her garrisons at Pensacola and Mobile.[2]

All this was transmitted to Cevallos, who, if not a genius, was no fool, and he read it with cynical amusement, and wrote Yrujo that Charles IV was not interested.[3]

So ended the dream of Spanish help. The British dream had vanished long before. It was time to leave Washington.

VIII

Burr turned now toward the great adventure, heading to New Orleans, but it was with grave misgivings regarding Wilkinson. He had notably cooled, never having been quite cordial to the scheme after his failure to interest some of his officers. In May, Burr had received a letter from him which has remained a mystery. At the trial Wilkinson was to demand its production, and pronounce Burr a liar when he replied that it had been burned. Whatever it contained, Burr knew that some unusual exertion was required to hold Wilkinson in the conspiracy. Perhaps he could be frightened into staying in.

And so it was that Wilkinson, in his camp one day, was reading a letter from Dayton. 'It is now well ascertained,' he read, 'that you are to be displaced in the next session. Jefferson will affect to yield reluctantly to the public sentiment, but yield he will. Pre-

---

[1] MS. Spanish Archives.   [2] Yrujo to Cevallos, MS. Spanish Archives.
[3] Cevallos to Yrujo, MS. Spanish Archives.

pare yourself, therefore, for it. You know the rest. You are not a man to despair or even despond, especially when such prospects offer in another quarter. Are you ready? Are your numerous associates ready? Wealth and glory; Louisiana and Mexico!' [1] Five days later, Burr proved himself the most fecund liar of his age when he sent Wilkinson the famous cipher letter which holds the secret of the conspiracy. He assured the General that he had 'obtained funds.' The Eastern members of the army would leave for various points and mobilize on the Ohio. Truxtun was leaving for Jamaica 'to arrange with the Admiral on that station.' The fleet would gather in the Mississippi. The English Navy 'are ready to join.' Ah, it would be 'a host of choice spirits.' Wilkinson would be second in command — under Burr. In August, with Theodosia, Burr would start West, to be joined by her husband 'with a corps of worthies' in October. Meanwhile, would Wilkinson send a list of persons west of the mountains 'who would be useful'? And four or five commissions of his officers to be secured under some pretext? These would be returned. 'Burr guarantees the result with his life and honor, with the lives and honor and fortunes of hundreds, the best blood in the country.'

The plan of operations? Burr would move rapidly from the Falls with five hundred or a thousand men in boats, then being constructed. Before the middle of December, he would meet Wilkinson at Natchez to determine whether he should seize Baton Rouge. Meanwhile, Wilkinson could 'draw on Burr for all expenses.' The people, assured of religious freedom and the imposition of no foreign power upon them, would be with the conspirators. And then, the pean sounded by Dayton — 'The gods invite us to glory and fortune; it remains to be seen whether we deserve the boon.' The bearer of this note, Samuel Swartwout,[2] brother of the United States Marshal, was the soul of honor and trustworthy. 'He has imbibed a reverence for your character, and may be embarrassed in your presence; put him at his ease and he will satisfy you.' [3]

---

[1] This letter was placed in evidence at Burr's trial.

[2] Beveridge insists that at this time he was a man of fine character. Later, as Collector of Customs in New York, he was to steal a hundred thousand dollars of the nation's money.

[3] This letter was produced at the Burr trial.

Here was rank treachery toward a co-conspirator, and justification enough for Wilkinson's withdrawal from the conspiracy had he not withdrawn months before.

The end of July found the high-minded Swartwout hurrying with this letter, and with instructions to Senator John Adair, in Kentucky. Erich Bollman, another gallant and noble figure, was carrying a duplicate by sea.

IX

In early August, Burr began his journey. After he had passed the mountains he threw discretion to the winds. One day he paused at Canonsburg to call on Colonel George Morgan and his sons. It was a family of Revolutionary patriots who had settled in this spot when there was not another family between the Alleghanies and the Ohio. They were men of character and force. The Colonel, informed of Burr's intention, sent his two sons seven miles upon the road to meet and accompany him. As the group rode along, Burr volunteered the opinion that the Union could not possibly last, and that the separation would come in four or five years at the latest. Then he inquired about the state of the militia in that section. Passing a husky laborer employed by the Morgans, he expressed a wish for a thousand such fellows.

At dinner Burr reiterated his contempt for the Union and his dire prediction. Why should the Union be tolerated at the expense of the West? he asked. Did not the money realized on the sale of Western land go to the East? Why should the Western country pay heavy taxes for the benefit of the Atlantic States? At length, growing warmer, he said that with two hundred men he could drive both Congress and Jefferson into the Potomac, and that with five hundred he could take possession of New York.[1] 'God forbid!' exclaimed the old patriot; and one of his sons replied, hotly: 'By God, sir, with that force you cannot take our little town of Canonsburg.' 'Confine yourself to this side the mountains,' said Burr soothingly, 'and I will not contradict you.'

Leaving the table soon afterward, Burr nodded to one of the sons to follow him into the hall, where he asked the youth if he

---

[1] Beveridge (III, 310), dismisses this language as 'looks, jocular innuendoes, and mysterious statements.' But the same language was used with Yrujo and with Eaton.

would like to join a military expedition. Not a word about settling
Western lands! When the young man replied that it would depend
upon the object of the expedition, Burr was silent. This impressed
the Morgan boy as strange. Burr's conduct had convinced the
sons that his purpose was sinister, and they warned their father
against his approach.

That night Burr apparently had gone to bed. The old man sat
listening as his wife read, when, at eleven o'clock, the footsteps of
Burr were heard upon the stairs. 'You'll have it now,' warned the
wife. Burr appeared with a candle in his hand. He sat down and
drew a notebook from his pocket. Glancing at it, he asked his
host if he knew a certain man. Morgan replied that he had reason
to know him, and reason to believe he had been engaged in the
English conspiracy of 1788 which he and General Neville had
put down. Then, with special emphasis, the old man said it was
'a nefarious thing' to attempt to separate the States. This ended
the conversation. Burr closed the book and soon afterward
retired.[1] Thus, Burr left without hinting at his plan to settle
land; he had talked wholly of the 'imbecility of the Government'
and the certainty of disunion. He had boasted what he could do
with armed men. So thoroughly convinced were the Morgans of
Burr's treasonable designs that the old man immediately notified
Jefferson.

x

A few days later, Burr crept into the 'Eden' of Blennerhassett
on his island home. Mrs. Blennerhassett had reported enthusiastically on the cleverness and charm of the invader, and the
master of the house was eagerly waiting to give him welcome.

Harman Blennerhassett, an Irishman born in England, educated
at Trinity in Dublin, and trained to the bar, was to give the sordid
conspiracy its one romantic touch, and to inspire a piece of eloquence that belongs to literature. Sentimental, romantic, a lover
of literature, given to meditation, a disciple of Rousseau and
Voltaire, polished, accomplished, interested in art and science, he
belonged to the closet and not the camp. Had conspiring and
fighting been his nature, he would have found the Ireland of that
day perfectly adapted to his taste, and would not have sought a

[1] Testimony of Colonel Morgan and Thomas Morgan at the Burr trial.

sylvan retreat in the Western wilderness of America. Married to a woman of rare charm and beauty, he had bought the island in the Ohio and sunk a good portion of his patrimony in the building and decorating of a home. The ceilings of this house were covered with frescoes, fine pictures adorned the walls, and the rooms were furnished tastefully with the best of London and Paris importations. The drawing-room was in imitation of the finest Parisian salons of the days of the Grand Monarch. We have been given a vision of the splendid mirrors, gay-colored carpets, and elegant curtains that made this mansion in the wilderness an exotic. On the sideboard in the dining-room stood solid silver plate. The library, with thousands of volumes, was Blennerhassett's comfort — that, and a laboratory where he loved to experiment with his crucibles and retorts. Surrounding the mansion was a garden 'that Shenstone might have envied.' [1] With a beautiful wife and lovely children, with his garden, library, laboratory, and music-room, he was happy and contented when Aaron Burr entered into his life to destroy the earthly paradise he had built.

To this unworldly dreamer, Burr outlined his plan in glowing words. He had taken the Bastrop Grant on the Red River for forty thousand dollars, and only five thousand had to be paid in money. The investors would reap fabulous rewards. While a cloud on the title had prevented previous settlement, that could be remedied. Here Burr entered upon the second phase of his tale. Before a year Louisiana would be independent of the United States. A revolution even then was in preparation, supported by Wilkinson and his army, and Burr as the head of the new empire would make the title good.

Thence he launched into the story of the treason. Tennessee was secured. Kentucky and Ohio were a bit doubtful still, but inevitably would follow Tennessee. Jefferson's Government speedily would crumble. A new empire would arise in the West, with Burr as emperor, and Blennerhassett would go as Minister to England.

Blennerhassett was entranced. 'Wealth and glory' again. Mrs. Blennerhassett lost all sense of realities. With the seductive Burr on one side and on the other the captivating Theodosia, who had

[1] From Wirt's speech at the Burr trial.

joined her father, she was completely won. Husband and wife were in fairyland. An emperor beneath their roof; an empress to be; and soon they would be bowing to Their Majesties in London! Blennerhassett made his generous contribution in money, but he was eager to do more. He knew that Burr's plan contemplated the separation of the Western States, and soon the dreamer sat in his library, Burr still beneath his roof, writing a series of disunion essays for the local papers. Just two days after Burr departed, the first of these appeared in the *Ohio Gazette* of Marietta. With Burr in his house and at his elbow, it is absurd to assume that the hypnotized Blennerhassett had either the time or inclination for idle academic exercises; and with the sworn testimony that the author of these articles showed them proudly in manuscript to mere acquaintances, it is a weird notion that Burr was ignorant of their existence.

The day the first of these articles appeared, Burr reached Cincinnati, where he lingered a few days with his confederate, Senator Smith, talking over the plans, jeering at the Administration, and enumerating reasons for the separation of the States. Then he hurried to Nashville to be fêted again under the patronage of Jackson, who still worshiped him as the Nemesis of the Spanish dons. Scarcely had Burr left Nashville for Kentucky when Jackson issued a mysterious proclamation calling upon all brigade commanders to prepare on the briefest notice to march 'when the Government and the constituted authorities of our country should require.' [1]

Meanwhile, the Blennerhassetts were ecstatic over the gorgeous prospects. Proud of his literary prowess, Blennerhassett was reading his disunion articles to friends, praising Burr's brilliancy and tender-heartedness in the extravagant language of an idolator, and declaring that 'if Mr. Jefferson was any way impertinent' Burr 'would tie him neck and heels and throw him into the Potomac.' Yrujo had heard the words; Eaton had heard them; the three Morgans had heard them; and Blennerhassett had heard them — and there were no contacts between these seven men. They were the words of Burr. And Government opposition? 'With three pieces of artillery and three hundred sharpshooters,

[1] Burr told many that he was secretly backed in his Mexican project by the Government.

he could defend any pass in the Alleghany Mountains against any force the Government could send against him.' [1] The man of the closet had become a war-horse champing at the bit. Why wait? Money? He placed the whole of his possessions at the disposal of Burr.

XI

Boats were being built at Marietta; kilns were constructed on the island for the baking of bread; recruiting was proceeding; bullets were being run; and Burr sent an agent to New York and Philadelphia to inform Dayton and the Spanish Minister, and to raise money. In November, Yrujo knew Burr was using the land project as a 'pretext'; that at Cincinnati the conspirators hoped to possess themselves of five thousand stand of Government arms; that Burr would wait at Natchez until the legislature at Orleans summoned him to his coronation; and that he then would enter his capital in triumph. He knew Burr had written a Declaration of Independence ironically patterned on Jefferson's masterpiece. And all this, Yrujo reported to Madrid. [2] A month later the thoroughly puzzled Minister wrote again. An agent of Burr's had called upon him with instructions that he should disregard rumors that he was to attack Mexico. Not at all — his plan was 'limited to the emancipation of the Western States.' Louisiana, Tennessee, and Ohio were ripe for the rebellion, but there was a division in Kentucky where a military force might be necessary to control the disaffected. When the new empire was established, Burr would negotiate with Spain regarding the boundaries. [3]

At this time, Timothy Pickering, Federalist leader in the Senate, who had sought to make common cause with Burr two years before to destroy the Union, was much interested in the gossip of the press. With a chuckle, he wrote Josiah Quincy; 'Does the disclosure awaken no fears of the future politics of the transalpine States? Will not our imperial mistress, Virginia, allow that her chicken, Kentucky, will one day peck her eyes out?' [4]

It was a happy thought for the 'Nationalist.'

[1] Evidence of Alexander Henderson at Burr's trial.
[2] Yrujo to Cevallos, MS. Spanish Archives.
[3] *Ibid.*   [4] *Pickering*, I, 379.

XII

Meanwhile, Jefferson was being warned in a series of letters by J. H. Daveiss, district attorney in Kentucky, a bitter Federalist, hostile to Jefferson, though permitted to remain in office. In January, 1806, when Burr was trying his seductive arts in Washington, Daveiss had written of a conspiracy financed by Spain for the separation of the Union. Receiving no reply, he wrote again in February, touching more specifically on the activities of Burr. Why Burr's Western trip? To see the country? 'No, he did not see it. He came to Lexington in haste, not in a hurry went on to New Orleans ... by water; at Fort Massac he stopped and for five days was closeted with Wilkinson "to help him arrange his new government"; went on down to Orleans, turned, and galloped back to Nashville, across the great wilderness of Indiana to St. Louis to see Wilkinson again.'

All this was true and easily checked — but where was the proof of a conspiracy? After the third letter complaining of no replies, Daveiss heard from Jefferson that all his letters had been received and shown to Madison and Gallatin, and that Dearborn had been informed 'because the person named by you is under his observation.' Jefferson added that the information was so important it was his duty 'to request a full communication of everything known or heard by you relating to it, and particularly of the names of all persons whether engaged in the combination, or witnesses to any part of it.' [1] Daveiss replied at length, and hearing nothing in answer, wrote indignantly to Madison, who sent a letter from Jefferson saying that the letters had not called for an answer, and that their acknowledgment had been postponed 'to avoid the suspicions of which you seemed to be aware.' Meanwhile, the letters would be kept among Jefferson's private papers.[2]

About this time, the district attorney heard from a leading Federalist that Burr was out to form acquaintances, since the Federalists planned to run him for President in the next election. He wanted nothing to do with such a plan. He knew that Burr was building boats, collecting stores of food, and attempting to engage men for six months. He wrote Madison that 'Burr's accomplices are very busy in disseminating the idea of disunion as

[1] Daveiss pamphlet.   [2] *Ibid.*

well as sentiments of Mr. Burr's greatness, virtue and martyrdom.' [1]

XIII

Within Daveiss's jurisdiction, Burr was lingering through
October, 1806. There had been delays. He had been forced to
wait for Blennerhassett's money. But the boats were being built
and men were being enlisted for the war. Unhappily, the too-
exuberant Blennerhassett was causing trouble with his disunion
articles in the papers. The press was beginning to comment on the
warlike activities. The people near the island were in an ugly
mood, and Mrs. Blennerhassett, thoroughly alarmed, sent her
gardener to Senator Smith in Cincinnati for the address of Burr,
that he might be warned. The Senator, growing nervous, at first
was wary, but finally furnished the information, and the gardener
rode to Lexington, where he gave the warning to Burr, and added
that if he returned 'our people will shoot you.' [2]

This was discouraging. Smith found his courage oozing, and,
like Clark, bethought himself of preparing his defense in writing.
He wrote Burr of the rumors and asked an explanation, and Burr
was too much the lawyer not to avail himself of the opportunity.
'I am greatly surprised and hurt,' he wrote. 'If there exists any
design to separate the Western States from the Eastern, I am
totally ignorant of it.' And then this colossal liar added, 'I never
have harbored or expressed any such intention to anyone' — but
Merry and Yrujo were over the mountains and not likely to talk.

The preparations for the defense were begun none too soon. In
the district court at Frankfort, Daveiss, acting on his own volition,
made complaint against Burr, charging him with planning an
expedition against Mexico and the separation of the States. A
brilliant young lawyer noted for his eloquence, named Henry Clay,
appeared for the accused. The impetuous Daveiss had not taken
time to collect his evidence, and Burr was dismissed in triumph.

Two weeks before this, Jefferson summoned his Cabinet and
laid before it the information in his possession. He knew that the
preceding winter Burr had talked disunion plans with Eaton, and,
apropos of the Western journey, he had been informed that these
plans were being pushed. What action should be taken?

[1] Daveiss pamphlet.   [2] Peter Taylor's evidence in Burr's trial.

The Cabinet unanimously decided to warn the Governors of the
Western States and of Mississippi and Orleans in confidential
letters, and to instruct the district attorneys of the affected section
'on Burr's committing an overt act to have him arrested and tried
for treason.' Meanwhile, gunboats would be ordered to Fort Adams
to stop the passage of any suspicious persons going down in force.
Just what to do about Wilkinson was also discussed. 'Suspicions
of fidelity in Wilkinson having now become very general,' and he
having been charged with complicity with Burr, what should be
done? Such suspicions of Wilkinson had been common since
the formation of the Republic. They had been voiced during the
Administrations of Washington and Adams and nothing had been
done, nothing established. A vainglorious man and a good
soldier, he was the object of envy in military circles, and it was not
unusual for men of the greatest probity to be charged in those days
with infamies. It was decided by the Cabinet to await 'further
information.' The conference was resumed the next day, and it
was decided that Captain Preble and Commodore Decatur should
proceed to New Orleans by land and sea to take command of the
sea forces. Seven gunboats were to be ordered to New Orleans,
unless Gallatin, and Smith, of the Navy Department, found there
was no available appropriation. And John Graham, of the State
Department, should be sent forthwith to trail Burr, 'with discretionary powers to consult confidentially with the Governors,
and to arrest Burr, if he made himself liable.'[1] Unhappily, Gallatin reported that their hands were tied by the acts of Congress;
and the Western mail the next day contained no reference to Burr.
The decision to send Preble and Decatur and the gunboats to
New Orleans was rescinded. But Graham went forth on the trail
of Burr.[2]

With his usual facility in lying and his genius for deception,
Burr, playing easily on the credulity of Blennerhassett, had convinced him that Graham was a friend and in the plot. Hence he
was received by the unfortunate dreamer with rapturous cordiality, and Jefferson's agent listened with amazement as his host laid
bare the plans and hopes of his idol. Graham prepared to act.

Meanwhile, in Kentucky, Daveiss renewed his complaint in

---

[1] Jefferson's Cabinet memorandum.   [2] *Ibid.*

court, and again tall, slender Henry Clay, the light of genius in his
eyes, stood beside the accused. But there had been a scene in
the wings, due to Clay's increasing uneasiness about his client.
In real earnest, Clay demanded a definite denial of treasonable intent, and, with the solemnity of a bishop, the assurance was given.
Thoroughly caught by Burr's manner, Clay did not hesitate in
court to pledge his 'own innocence and honor' on that of his
client. Again Daveiss, in his partisan anxiety to embarrass Jefferson, had been precipitate. His witnesses were not on hand. Senator Smith sprang to horse and disappeared in the woods, and
Senator Adair found it more comfortable to stay away. Again
Burr was discharged while the country courthouse rang with applause over the triumph of innocence. The good people of Frankfort gave him a ball for the delectation of the ladies. Tickets were
taken about town for the ball at Colonel Taylor's, but Burr, who
was not impressed, did not appear until supper-time 'when the
dancing people were a little down in the mouth.' Daveiss was
indignant at the conduct of the snobs, and with some other 'true
Americans,' a supper was arranged, attended by thirty ladies, and
a ball was announced 'in honor of the Union.' Among the women
who appeared at the ball were many who had refused to meet Burr
or to go to his party. The Governor, the Secretary of State, the
President of the Senate and the Speaker of the House, with numerous members of the legislature, attended; and at the supper
toasts were drunk to 'the patriotic ladies of Frankfort' and to the
'damnation of all conspirators.' [1]

But in the meantime Graham had hurried with Blennerhassett's
confession to the capital of Ohio, where he secured the passage of
a law authorizing the Governor to employ the militia against
the conspirators. The Governor made immediate preparations to
seize Burr's boats and provisions at Blennerhassett's Island, where
bullets were being run, guards were mounted, strangers approaching were challenged, and recruits with arms were stationed.[2] The
militia of Wood County, disdaining a special act of the legislature,
were about to descend on the island. Learning of this turn, the
little band of conspirators, with Blennerhassett in their midst,

[1] *American Citizen*, January 12, 1807.
[2] Testimony of numerous eye-witnesses at Burr's trial.

slunk into the boats at midnight and floated down the river, leaving the disillusioned mistress of the mansion standing on the banks.

XIV

Just before this event, one of Wilkinson's officers appeared in Jefferson's study with a letter detailing the General's experiences with Swartwout, who had reached New Orleans with the cipher letter from Burr. The arrival of the officer attracted some attention. 'He killed several horses, it is said, by hard riding,' recorded the *Columbian Centinel*. 'What the matter is now we cannot learn.' [1] The report removed all doubt from Jefferson's mind of the lawless nature of the enterprise. Wilkinson had been approached. Just when that doughty warrior, for thirty years on the pay-roll of the Spanish King, and unquestionably involved with Burr in the earlier stages of the conspiracy, changed front does not appear. His failure to seduce his officers, his certainty that Burr vastly misjudged the disaffection of the Western country, his knowledge that the conspiracy must fail, were quite enough. He told Jefferson the truth as far as Burr was concerned, and it was enough to justify decisive action.

That day, Jefferson again was surrounded by his Cabinet. The issuance of a proclamation was agreed upon. To the members of the Cabinet were assigned separate tasks in communicating here and there with federal officials. Orders went forth to stop all armed vessels on the Mississippi. Wilkinson was instructed to concentrate his forces for the protection of New Orleans if an arrangement with the Spaniards would permit him thus to act. He was to arrest anyone entering his camp proposing such an enterprise or acting as a propagandist for such a cause.[2]

The proclamation, without mentioning names, declared that sundry persons were violating the law by conspiring against Spain, and warned the conspirators to abandon the project. It directed both civil and military officers to seize and hold the persons concerned and such property as was being put to the purpose. This proclamation broke the back of the conspiracy, and instantly divorced from the scheme those to whom Burr had given the assurance that it had the secret approval of the Government.

[1] January 10, 1807.   [2] Jefferson's Cabinet memorandum.

Meanwhile, with Graham persuading Kentucky to follow the example of Ohio, Burr hurried to Tennessee and to the river front where his boats were being built. Thither also hurried Andrew Jackson, no little embarrassed by the reports that were reaching him. Taking a witness with him, he demanded from Burr a disavowal of any designs against the Union. With the nonchalant serenity of a practiced liar, Burr denied any such intention, and Jackson, like Clay, succumbed to the plausibility of the consummate actor.

That Jackson was in great confusion at the time is shown by documentary evidence. Only a few weeks before he had been so convinced that treason was in the air and planned to strike at New Orleans that he had written Governor Claiborne a fervent warning to be on the lookout for 'an attack from quarters you do not at present suspect.' 'Beware of an attack from your own country.' 'You have enemies within your own city that may try to subvert your government and try to separate it from the Union.' And this: 'Keep a watchful eye upon your General.' [1]

About this time, Jackson issued an address to 'Friends and Fellow Soldiers.' He summoned them to preparation. He accepted Jefferson's proclamation as 'sufficient evidence to us that the repose of our country is about to be interrupted; that an illegal enterprise has been set on foot by disappointed, unprincipled, ambitious, and misguided individuals, and that they are about to be carried on against the Government of Spain, contrary to the faith of treaties.' He also said that it was understood that the conspirators 'had assembled at the mouth of the Cumberland River, in considerable force and hostile array; that they had for their object a separation of the Western from the Eastern part of the United States, and that an attack would be made in the first place at New Orleans.' Because of all this, Jackson had issued orders 'to the end that twelve companies of volunteer corps might be prepared to march.' [2]

Such was the position of Jackson at this stage.

Soon Burr was warned, mysteriously, that Tennessee might be forced to act, and he stood not on the order of his going, but he went at once. Graham was on his way thither. Abandoning all but

[1] Submitted at the trial of Burr.   [2] *National Intelligencer*, February 6, 1807.

two of the boats built for him on the Cumberland, leaving his note for five hundred dollars for Jackson to pay, he fled. The proclamation of Jefferson had reached Nashville two days before, but it had not mentioned Burr. As he floated down the river, John Adair was pushing his horse through the wilderness en route to New Orleans. At the mouth of the Cumberland, Burr found Blennerhassett waiting, with the boats that had evaded the militia.

As he approached Fort Massac, neither the proclamation nor the military orders had reached Captain Bissel, or so he claimed. Burr paused here, declined invitations to breakfast and dinner, made contact with Sergeant Dunbaugh, to whom he persuaded the captain to give a twenty-day furlough, when that worthy was inveigled into joining the expedition, and the flotilla floated on. Five days later, Bissel received instructions from Andrew Jackson to prevent the passage.

xv

The day Jackson was sending these belated instructions, Jefferson was writing Wilkinson to guard the cipher letter of Burr and the letters from Dayton and to send them by trusted messengers to Washington to the end that 'all important testimony ... be brought to one center in order that the guilty may be convicted and the innocent left untroubled.' [1] Whatever may have been Wilkinson's guilty knowledge of Burr's plans, he now acted with characteristic vigor. Erich Bollman also had reached New Orleans, and when the young foreigner thought him still in the conspiracy, he had a confidential conversation with Wilkinson. Instantly, Wilkinson determined on martial law, the practical abdication of Claiborne, and the drastic methods of military procedure.

The month before, that noble youth Swartwout had appeared with the cipher letter in his camp.[2] From him, the General had learned that some time before, Burr, in a little house in Philadelphia, was busily engaged seeing visitors, who came singly. He was told that 'Burr was about to levy an armed force of seven

---

[1] *Writings of Jefferson*, II, 127.

[2] Allen Johnson (in *Jefferson and his Colleagues*, 113) refers to him as the notorious Swartwout attached to Burr as a 'gangster.'

thousand men and would descend the river to New Orleans. There some seizing would be necessary, and the Western country would be revolutionized. The army then would proceed to Vera Cruz, where it would land and march upon the City of Mexico.

It was about this time that Erich Bollman arrived by sea with the duplicate letters. More daring than Swartwout, he was more insistent in demanding the part Wilkinson proposed to play, and earnest in explaining that Burr would not retreat since he had 'gone too far to retract,' and 'numerous and powerful friends in the United States stood ready to support him with their fortunes.' [1] While playing the cat-and-mouse act with this equally noble youth, the latter received another letter from Burr and hastened to inform Wilkinson of the contents. Burr would reach Natchez about December 20 with two thousand men, to be followed by four thousand more. It was at this juncture that Wilkinson announced that if Burr attempted to enter New Orleans, he would oppose him with his troops. Embarrassed by this disclosure, Bollman asked if Wilkinson could not make a merely perfunctory defense. Wilkinson thought not. [2]

It was just at this time that Judge Prevost, stepson of Burr, congratulated a friend on the street upon the arrival of General John Adair as second in command to Burr in New Orleans. Wilkinson was informed. A printer told Commodore Shaw that in traveling from Washington he had 'seen a number of men under arms at the mouth of the Cumberland,' and gunboats being built for Burr. Shaw notified Wilkinson. The commander of a packet brought the report that he had passed a fleet flying British colors, cruising off the mouth of the Mississippi. [3] New Orleans was in a state of panic, and Wilkinson, assuming arbitrary power, began making arrests. Bollman was arrested; Swartwout and Ogden were taken; arrests of suspects followed. When Claiborne urged the excited general to yield to the courts, he refused, on the ground that at least one of the judges was in on the conspiracy. Judge Workman was a member of the Mexican Association with whom, historians agree, Burr had entered into close relations. Ignoring the courts, brushing the Governor aside, threatening

[1] Wilkinson's testimony at Burr's trial.　　　　[2] *Ibid.*
[3] Testimony of Commodore Shaw in Burr's trial.

prominent citizens, embargoing the city's shipping, and putting all the people to work on the defenses, Wilkinson created a state of terror, without the slightest authorization from Washington.

XVI

In the meanwhile, Burr with his little flotilla had left Fort Massac and was floating down the Mississippi in utter ignorance of the excitement in New Orleans. He tarried a bit at a military post at Chickasaw Bluffs which had not received the instructions from Washington. When within a short distance of the Bluffs, Burr, with Dunbaugh and a dozen men, took a small boat and floated down in advance of the flotilla, reaching the Bluffs about midnight. He received the hospitality of the garrison, and the next morning he asked Dunbaugh to persuade a dozen men in the garrison to desert. The sergeant was afraid to try; but Burr bribed a lieutenant to organize a company for him and follow down the river. While tarrying here, Burr employed a man to run off six hundred musket balls, and he distributed thirty-six tomahawks among his men.[1]

The boats moved on. Early in January, at the mouth of Bayou Pierre, about thirty miles above Natchez, the flotilla tied up, and Burr went ashore. There in the home of his host he received a shock when, in a newspaper, he read the cipher letter he had written Wilkinson. Only Wilkinson could be responsible for that. Wilkinson had turned against him!

All the gasconading spirit of Burr oozed out, and instantly his mind was intent on methods of escape. The Governor of Mississippi had ordered out the militia to take him. Down the river he would fall into the hands of Wilkinson, which might mean speedy execution. Hemmed in, his empire crumbled. The desperate Blennerhassett, whose entire fortune had been sunk, urged armed resistance to arrest, and though Burr, in a letter, had threatened the Governor with 'civil war,' he had no stomach for such madness. He preferred to surrender — on his own terms.

The intermediary in the negotiations was the promising twenty-eight-year-old attorney-general, George Poindexter, destined to a

---

[1] Testimony of Dunbaugh. The records fail to show that the great lawyers for the defense were able to shake his testimony in the least.

distinguished career. On the western bank of the river the two men met. Burr bore himself with the dignity and hauteur of the proud head of a sovereign state overtaken by ill-fortune. Reading the Governor's letter given him by the attorney-general, he sneeringly disclaimed any intention of injuring 'the citizens of the United States.' Then, Wilkinson's desertion rankling in his heart, he burst forth: 'As to any projects or plans which may have been formed between General Wilkinson and myself, they are now completely frustrated by the perfidious conduct of Wilkinson, and the world must pronounce him a villain.'

Assured by Poindexter that he would be unmolested by the militia if he would peaceably surrender to the civil authorities, Burr agreed to meet the Governor on the following day in the house of a citizen close to where the militia was camping. There he agreed to surrender to the court at Washington in Mississippi, reiterating his distaste for falling into the hands of Wilkinson. Poindexter advised that there was no evidence on which to convict Burr of any offense in the Mississippi Territory, and that the Supreme Court there had no original jurisdiction. He proposed that Burr be sent to Washington, D.C., where the Supreme Court, then in session, could determine from the evidence the district in which he should be tried.[1] The Governor thought otherwise. A grand jury was summoned. It refused to indict, and instead the civil authorities were condemned for interfering with the plans of Burr!

Meanwhile, a negro boy, arousing suspicion, was searched, and from the cape of his coat was drawn a letter in Burr's handwriting to two of his officers who had not deserted their men:

'If you are yet together, keep together and I will join you tomorrow night. In the meantime put all your arms in perfect order. Ask the bearer no questions, but tell him all you think I wish to know. He does not know that this is from me nor where I am.'[2]

Having sent this solemn promise to the victims of his ambition, Burr mounted his horse and spurred it into the Mississippi wilderness.

The American Napoleon did not wait for Waterloo.

---

[1] Henry Adams (*History*, II, 326) is in error in saying that Poindexter tried to get an indictment.

[2] Testimony of Poindexter at Burr's trial.

XVII

By this time the entire country knew of the conspiracy. The Federalists of the disunion school felt no resentment. Burr had failed where Pickering had failed before him. But they cared less for his apprehension. 'No one here seems to care a cent about Burr's plans,' Fisher Ames wrote Quincy two days after the disillusioned hero had fled, leaving his followers to shift for themselves. 'They think him desperate and profligate; but they concern themselves very little about his managing his own affairs in his own way without too much of Mr. Jefferson's regulations.' [1] The same day, Ames wrote Pickering at greater length. He was not surprised, since he had no doubt that Burr's 'desperate situation would urge him into open desperate measures.' His sole surprise was that Burr should have seen any prospect of success. He had thought Burr 'shrewd and intelligent' and incapable of confusing 'peevish discontents among the Western people for deep disaffection.' And then he added the disunion note: 'However, nobody cares for Burr or his conspiracy. . . . Curiosity is hungry, but our patriotism seems unconcerned.' And then, the reason for the indifference of the Eastern disunionists: 'The separation of the Western country has not appeared to me as a probable event.' [2] The separation of the Eastern States was much more plausible.

XVIII

On the very aay Poindexter was treating with Burr on the banks of the Mississippi, John Randolph rose in the House with a resolution calling on Jefferson for facts and papers explanatory of the conspiracy. Burr was still in Mississippi when Jefferson responded at length, setting forth the facts as they had reached him. From time to time he had received a mass of correspondence on the conspiracy, but little had been given under the sanction of an oath 'so as to constitute legal evidence.' The letters dealt with 'rumors, conjectures, and suspicions,' and it had been difficult 'to sift out the real facts.' In September he had 'received intimations' of the designs, and that 'the prime mover in these was Aaron Burr.' Only in October could 'the objects of the conspiracy' begin to be perceived, but it was still 'so blended and involved in mystery that

[1] *Ames,* I, 393.   [2] *Ibid.,* I, 394–95.

nothing distinct could be singled out for dispute.' Under these
circumstances, he had sent a secret agent to the scene of the plot
and the plotters, with instructions to investigate and with power to
confer with governors and military officials and secure their aid
'on the spot.' By this time it was known that boats were being
built, provisions were being collected, and that there was 'an unusual number of suspicious characters in motion on the Ohio and
its waters.' Wilkinson had been instructed 'to hasten an accommodation with the Spanish commander on the Sabine . . . and fall
back to the hinter bank of the Mississippi.' On November 29,
Jefferson had been informed by Wilkinson that he had been approached by the agent of Burr with a communication, partly in
cipher, 'explaining the designs, exaggerating his resources, and
making such offers of emolument and command, to engage him and
the army in his unlawful enterprise.' Thereafter, Burr's general
designs became clearer. He proposed the 'severance of the Union
of these States by the Alleghany Mountains, an attack on Mexico,
the precedence to be determined by conditions and events.' The
other alleged design was the purchase of a tract of land, but this
'was to serve as a pretext for all his preparations, an allurement
for such followers as really wished to acquire settlements in that
country, and a cover under which to retreat in the event of final
discomfiture of both branches of his real design.' [1] Finding, however, that the Western people could not be seduced, and that the
disunion program could not be carried out with the consent of the
people, Burr planned to effect it by force. He proposed to seize
New Orleans, plunder the bank, get possession of the naval and
military stores, and proceed with his expedition to Mexico. To
this end he assembled 'all the ardent, restless, desperate, and disaffected persons who were ready for any enterprise.' Through
misrepresentations, he had enlisted some good men in the
cause.

Such had been the picture when the proclamation was issued.
Jefferson went on to trace the steps taken by the Government and
to praise Ohio for its prompt action. He concluded that there was
'no serious danger to the city of New Orleans,' and that no foreign
nation was involved in the scheme. Two of Burr's emissaries,

---

[1] Yrujo also had called it a 'pretext.'

taken in New Orleans, were being sent to Washington, 'partly on the consideration that an impartial trial could not be expected during the present agitation in New Orleans, and that that city is not as yet a safe place of confinement.'

The House could not complain that it was not in possession of the story, or of what was in Jefferson's mind. It knew, and the public knew, that he thought Aaron Burr guilty.

XIX

Soon Swartwout and Bollman, those noble youths, reached Washington under military escort from Annapolis, where the vessels bearing them from New Orleans arrived, and they were confined at the Marine Barracks.[1] The legal representatives of the Government applied to the district court for a warrant on the charge of treason. It was promptly given; an immediate appeal was taken, and John Marshall entered the case of Burr. Attempts have been made to picture these notoriously involved men as victims of the malevolence of Jefferson, bearing themselves with great dignity and composure. Beveridge criticizes Jefferson for securing an affidavit from Eaton to strengthen the possibility of holding them for trial. There is no evidence whatever that Jefferson did anything of the sort; it may reasonably be assumed that the law officer of the Government did his work; but if convinced as he was of the plot against the Union, and in possession of information essential to the prosecution, it would have been infamous had Jefferson not transmitted it to the law officers of the Republic.

Marshall dismissed the noble youths on the ground that a case of treason had not been made out; but in this opinion he said: '*If a body of men be actually assembled for the purpose of effecting by force a treasonable purpose, all those who perform any part, however minute, or however remote from the scene of the action, and who are actually leagued in the general conspiracy, are to be considered as traitors.*'

This would have sounded the death-knell of Burr; but within a few weeks, John Marshall, by reversing this presumably matured opinion, was to save him.

[1] *National Intelligencer*, January 26, 1807.

XX

Meanwhile, Burr, disguised in the plebeian clothes of a Mississippi boatman, was riding feverishly through the Mississippi wilderness trying to escape. He was lost to the world; irretrievably lost to the faithful followers he had assured he would join on the day following his precipitate flight. He was making for the Spanish frontier.

He was near the border and freedom when he was recognized; the commander of Fort Stoddert was notified, and he was arrested and confined for three weeks in the fort. Then his captors started with him on horseback for Richmond. The callous indifference of these soldiers of the Republic to his sensibilities was to shock some partisans at that time and some historians to this day. The *Columbian Centinel* protested bitterly that the persecuted Burr was being 'hunted by Jefferson and his ragamuffins' (the soldiers) like 'a mad dog ... arrested by a guard of these ragamuffins ... dragged through the country like a horse thief.' [1]   In truth, the rain came down in torrents on the soldiers doing their duty, as well as on Burr — and Burr had no mackintosh! Passing through Chester, South Carolina, he sprang from his horse in the midst of a small crowd, clamoring for a rescue. No one moved — no one but one officer who picked him up and threw him back upon his horse like a sack of meal. It was not until the latter part of March that he was delivered to the constituted authorities in Richmond.

Thus the empire of Aaron the First had crumbled into ruins, bearing with it not a few reputations and the fortunes and the happiness of poor Blennerhassett.

[1] *Columbian Centinel,* April 18, 1807.

CHAPTER XIX

The Trial of Burr

I

IT WAS not until Burr had been turned over to the civil authorities at Richmond that Jefferson's most venomous critics charged him with the persecution of the accused. For almost two years the warnings pouring in upon him concerning Burr's activities had failed to move him to action. Eaton's story had not aroused him. The story of the Morgans did not stir him, and the anonymous letters accusing Burr of a treasonable intent did no more than arouse his mild curiosity. Yrujo was amazed at his toleration and inactivity, and Daveiss, brother-in-law of Marshall, was so infuriated by Jefferson's failure to act that he was persuaded that there was a secret understanding between Jefferson and Burr.[1] After many years, Henry Adams was bitterly to arraign Jefferson for inexcusable lassitude and indifference in failing to strike months before he did.[2] It was only when the evidence was overwhelming that Burr actually was recruiting men and building boats and collecting arms, and when Wilkinson turned on Burr with his letter to Jefferson exposing the attempt to corrupt the army in Louisiana, that the proclamation was issued. And even then the name of Burr was not mentioned. It was intended primarily as a warning to the deceived that the project on foot did not have the sanction of the Government. Nor was the special Message, in which Burr was mentioned in a detailed story of his movements, rushed to the Congress on Jefferson's initiative. It was wrung from him by a resolution in the House, pressed by his most virulent enemy, John Randolph. It was opposed by some of the outstanding spokesmen of the Administration, and Eppes,

[1] Daveiss pamphlet.   [2] Adams, *History.*

the President's son-in-law, discounting the stories afloat as probably chimerical, voted for the resolution solely because he felt Congress was 'entitled to the papers.' Convinced, at last, that Burr's designs, if not treasonable, were calculated to embroil the nation with a friendly Power, Jefferson ordered the arrest of the principals.

This was the part played by Jefferson up to the moment of the trial.

But as soon as Burr reached Richmond, the Federalists raised the hue and cry that, because of jealousy and fear, Jefferson had prostituted his position to the persecution of an innocent man. The moment Burr was turned over to the authorities, the Federalist Party determined that Jefferson should be tried instead of Burr. Quite soon the *New York Evening Post* gave the party strategy away. Let Burr 'but once appear as a persecuted man and his acquittal is certain,' it said.[1] 'It seems probable that before the trial is over, the Government and the criminal will appear to have exchanged situations.' For did not Burr already occupy 'high ground'? What 'high ground'? Why, 'he accuses the President and the Administration with persecuting him in a manner which the laws will not warrant.'[2]

When Burr gathered about him for his defense a numerous, brilliant, and powerful array of lawyers, unsurpassed at the American Bar, and Jefferson authorized the lone United States Attorney to engage two men to assist him, the partisans pounced upon the act as proof of a persecuting spirit.

The fact that John Marshall was to preside inevitably gave the trial a political coloring. No man in America hated Jefferson and his democracy more bitterly. In cases having no political significance, Marshall was the fairest and wisest of jurists, but in causes of a political nature the politician on the bench — and he was a constant and consummate politician — was glaringly revealed. Suave, almost unctuous, wearing a mask of impartial benevolence, he could not keep the mask from slipping, and it was to slip conspicuously more than once in the course of the trial at Richmond, revealing a partisan as malevolent as any that Jefferson ever faced.

[1] *New York Evening Post*, June 6, 1807. [2] *Ibid.*, June 8, 1807.

II

The initial hearing began in the Eagle Tavern and was continued in the House of Delegates in the classic building Jefferson had designed. The Government asked for a commitment on the charge of treason, and presented the affidavits of Wilkinson and Eaton. Wickham, of the defense, declared this was not conclusive proof, and that the worst that could be charged was a plan to attack Mexico, which was not only 'innocent but meritorious.' This description of a crime as 'innocent and meritorious' was not rebuked by the Chief Justice of the United States! In his carefully meditated opinion, Marshall severely criticized the Government for not having all its evidence on hand, and dwelt with much solemnity on the importance of protecting men accused of treason when 'the hand of malignity may grasp any individual against whom its hate may be directed.' Holding the evidence insufficient to hold Burr on the treason charge, he committed him for misdemeanor.

Thus, at the first opportunity, Marshall contributed his bit toward the Burr and Federalist propaganda to create the impression that Jefferson was persecuting an innocent man because of personal hate.

The mask had slipped.

But the reaction was not good. With the indignation aroused by this unnecessary insult to the head of the State, Marshall became suddenly as timid as in the Chase impeachment. Hurriedly summoning the reporters, he declared that the offensive passage 'had no allusion to the conduct of the Government in the case.' Unhappily, no reporter believed him then, and his most brilliant biographer insists, after more than a century, that the disavowal was utterly insincere.[1] Jefferson certainly was not deceived, if deception was the intent.

Burr was released on bail furnished by prominent Federalists.

The reaction of Jefferson was instantaneous. 'The fact is,' he wrote James Bowdoin, 'that the Federalists make Burr's cause their own, and exert their whole influence to protect him from punishment.'[2] And necessary, as Marshall contended, that to hold Burr on a treason charge, the Government should have all the

---

[1] Beveridge, III, 377.   [2] *Writings of Jefferson*, II, 183.

evidence on hand? This, manifestly, was physically impossible, and Jefferson had asked Rodney, the Attorney-General, to say as much to Marshall. The latter had said that 'more than five weeks have elapsed since the opinion of the Supreme Court has declared the necessity of proving the overt acts, if they exist.' And in his most offensive manner he had asked: 'Why are they not proved?' This outraged Jefferson's sense of common fairness. 'In what terms of decency can we speak of this?' he wrote Giles. 'As if an express could go to Natchez, or the mouth of the Cumberland, and return in five weeks, to do which has never taken less than twelve.' And if possible to have collected all the evidence in that time, where should it have been lodged? 'At Frankfort? At Cincinnati? At Nashville? At St. Louis? Natchez? New Orleans? These were the probable places of apprehension and examination. It was not known at Washington until the twenty-sixth of March that Burr would escape from the Western tribunals, be retaken and brought to an Eastern one; and in five days after (not five months or five weeks, as the Judge calculated) he says "it is impossible to suppose the affidavits could not have been obtained." Where? At Richmond he certainly meant, or intended only to throw dust in the eyes of his audience.'

And then he added a paragraph which discloses the intensity of his indignation. 'If there ever had been an instance . . . of federal judges so applying principles of law as to condemn a federal or acquit a republican offender, I should have judged them in the present case with more charity.' [1]

III

So Burr, held under bond for misdemeanor, had three weeks of freedom. They were to be the most pleasant of his life. Richmond was a small town, but it prided itself on its fashionable set and this was mostly Federalist. The sycophancy and snobbery of this society in its adulation of Burr sickened the robust Ritchie, of the *Richmond Enquirer*. The Federalists took the man who had ended the life of Hamilton to their bosoms as a great martyr. Society women flocked around the most notorious libertine of his time with an idolatrous sympathy. The best of the fashionable houses

[1] *Writings of Jefferson*, II, 187.

were thrown open for his entertainment. At dinners and receptions he was the magnet that drew them all.

Among all the dinners featuring Burr as the guest of honor, the one most notoriously intended for propaganda was that given by John Wickham, who, next to Martin, was the most brilliant of Burr's lawyers. To this dinner he had the wretched taste to invite the judge who was to preside at the trial. Marshall's biographer, lamely falling back 'on a story told more than a century after the incident,' implies that the Chief Justice did not know he was to assist in paying homage to a man charged with treason.[1] Judge Tucker, a Virginian living at the time, and more considerate of the character of Wickham, assures us that 'it is proper to add that this gentleman informed the Chief Justice in the course of the morning that he expected Colonel Burr at the dinner.'[2] In a town so small as Richmond, in the case of Wickham, so intimate socially and politically with Marshall, it is incredible that Marshall did not knowingly accept the invitation of the chief strategist of Burr's defense to a dinner in Burr's honor. What though the wines were choice, the food delicious, the juleps fragrant as Marshall's great biographer insists, there were certain fundamental decencies to be observed in a jurist who was to sit in judgment on the guest of honor. Even had he been ungraciously trapped into the acceptance of the invitation, the wonder grows that when he found himself confronted by Burr in Wickham's house, his own sense of propriety did not impel him indignantly to rebuke his host and take his instant departure. Roger Taney would have made his resentment felt.

But Marshall remained with the choice wines, the delicious food, the fragrant juleps, and Burr, during the evening.

Naturally the incident shocked not a few, and the *Richmond Enquirer* denounced Marshall's conduct as 'grossly indecent,' and asked whether it was to be ascribed 'to charity, hypocrisy, or federalism.' The *Virginia Argus* at the time said all that perhaps need be said:

'We acknowledge that the rites of hospitality ought not to be refused to this unfortunate gentleman by those who believe him innocent; but confess our astonishment that men whose intellects

[1] Beveridge, III, 396.   [2] Tucker, II, 254.

are so penetrating as those of Mr. Wickham and Mr. Marshall did not perceive the extreme indelicacy and impropriety of such respect being paid him by the judge who is to preside hereafter on his trial.' [1]

And so the three weeks of festivities and celebrations passed rapidly, with Burr writing cynically to Theodosia of his idolatrous reception, with the fashionable bending the pregnant hinges of the knee as though he already were an emperor in his palace in New Orleans.

IV

Beginning May 22, 1807, the grand jury was busy hearing evidence. With malice toward Jefferson, Marshall had made John Randolph foreman of the jury. The little town was thronged with a conglomerate mass of visiting humanity, army and navy officers, frontiersmen and politicians, architects like Latrobe, and representatives of the press. Young Washington Irving was there, and historians were to quote his pro-Burr comments with gusto, without explaining that he was a paid propagandist sent from New York by Burr's friends to write partisan articles. 'He went,' writes his nephew and biographer, 'on an informal retainer from one of the friends of Colonel Burr. His client had little belief in his legal erudition, and did not look to any approach to a professional début, but thought he might, in some way or other, be of service with his pen.' [2]

By this time Burr had gathered all his legal gladiators about him. Foremost among them was the slovenly Luther Martin, who, even in his cups — and he was seldom out — was a foeman worthy of the steel of the best. He had rushed to the defense of his 'honorable friend,' partly because of admiration for Burr, partly because of his senile infatuation for the youthful Theodosia, but mostly because of his hatred of Jefferson. Throughout the trial, we shall see him, as Blennerhassett so often saw him, drinking brandy from a pint tumbler in public and private, 'fancy denied to his mind, grace to his person or habits . . . gross and incapable of restraint, even upon the most solemn occasions'; and shall hear

[1] Quoted in *American Citizen*, April 16, 1807.
[2] R. M. Irving, *Life and Letters of Washington Irving*, I, 141.

him delivering his invectives, 'rather coarse than pointed,' his eulogies of his persecuted friend, 'more fulsome than pathetic.' [1]

Less picturesque and more gentlemanly, and quite his equal in legal erudition, and far more concise and systematic in his arguments, was John Wickham, leader of the Richmond Bar. He was an aristocrat, noted for the grace and conviviality of his dinners, and, while a staunch Federalist, his services in the British army during the Revolution had closed upon him the door of political preferment. He hated Thomas Jefferson and his democratic philosophy.

More statuesque and imposing than either was the ponderously dignified Edmund Randolph. He had aged, without mellowing, since he had left the Cabinet of Washington under a cloud. He was a bitter Federalist, and hatred of Jefferson was his ruling passion.

The last of Burr's quartet was Benjamin Botts, a young man of much promise, exceedingly clever and daring. He, too, was a Federalist — and he hated Jefferson.

George Hay, the district attorney, was young and incapable of coping in the finesse of legal hair-splitting with Martin and Wickham. He was far from being the rather pathetic and incompetent figure pictured by Marshall's biographer, but he had no spark of genius, no flair for eloquence, no gift for sophistry. He was a sincere, plodding practitioner.

But in genius, in the gifts of fancy, in eloquence, even Burr's galaxy had no match for the young and scintillating William Wirt, then at the dawn of a notable professional career. In legal erudition, he was almost the equal of Martin. Endowed with literary genius, his alone, among all the utterances of this famous trial, were to ring down the century that followed.

Alexander MacRae, a fighting, stubborn Scotchman, was an able lawyer and a merciless opponent in debate. Where Wirt used the rapier, MacRae used the meat-axe. He was a master of sarcasm and invective, and he feared no man, on or off the bench.

These lawyers for the Government were all Democrats, and followers of Jefferson.

Thus, with Burr deluged with Federalist adulation, with his

[1] Blennerhassett, *Diary*.

lawyers bitter Federalists, with the presiding judge a consummate
Federalist politician, and with the attorneys for the Government
Democrats, the stage was set from the beginning for a party
controversy in the court.

V

Scarcely had the hearing of evidence begun when the defense
demanded the presence of Wilkinson, who was on his way. Though
he had been trusted by Washington and Adams, he had become
the pet abomination of the Federalists, and he had been such a
consistent scoffer at Jefferson politically, that he was roundly denounced by the *Evening Post* as 'this gray-haired apostate from
federalism.' [1] Wickham sounded the keynote of the defense when
he assailed Jefferson by innuendo in referring to Wilkinson as 'the
instrument of the Government bound to a blind obedience.'

Wirt eagerly seized the opportunity to speak bluntly to the
court. 'The gentleman is understood, sir,' he said, addressing
Marshall. 'He would divert public attention from Aaron Burr to
another quarter. . . . The gentleman would convert this judicial
inquiry into a political question between Thomas Jefferson and
Aaron Burr.'

Why was Wilkinson not there? 'Because it was impossible in
the nature of things for him to be here at this time.' And then, to
Marshall: 'It was on the first of April that you decided on the
commitment of Aaron Burr; until that decision was known, the
necessity of summoning witnesses could not be ascertained.'
Washington could not have known of the commitment before the
sixth of April. Were Wilkinson ordered to Richmond that moment,
and were the order sent by the mail a hundred miles a day through
a frequent change of horses, it would have been impossible to have
reached New Orleans before the twenty-fifth. Since that time
thirty days have elapsed. Could any human being of the age and
bulk of Wilkinson possibly make the journey of sixteen hundred
miles in thirty days?

It was during this interval of waiting that Burr himself demanded that Jefferson be ordered to deliver the letter from Wilkinson of October 21, 1806, together with all naval and military

[1] September 24, 1807.

orders relating to Burr. It was Burr's contention that the orders commanded the destruction of his boats — *and person!*

Now rose Martin to begin the personal attacks on Jefferson which Marshall, by his toleration, was to encourage throughout the trial. 'We intend to show,' said Martin, 'that these orders were contrary to the Constitution and the law, and that they entitled Colonel Burr to the right of resistance. We intend to show that his person and property were to be destroyed. . . . By these tyrannical orders the life and property of an innocent man were to be exposed to destruction.' The defense had asked for copies of these orders and 'they were refused under presidential influence.' And then, with Marshall complacent, benevolent, and silent, Martin continued:

'He [Jefferson] has assumed to himself the knowledge of the Supreme Being Himself and pretended to search the heart of my highly respected friend. He has proclaimed him a traitor in the face of that country which has rewarded him. He has let slip the dogs of war, the hell-hounds of persecution, to hunt down my friend.' [1]

And Marshall sat in silence.

Instantly Wirt was on his feet exposing Martin's lie about orders to destroy Burr's life. 'The orders,' he said, 'are simply orders to apprehend Aaron Burr, and, if it shall become necessary for that purpose, to destroy his boats. These are the bloody orders which have been so often mentioned with looks of such tragic and mysterious import.'

And unconstitutional for Jefferson to issue such orders? 'He is bound by his oath of office' and 'by the particular act of Congress which prescribes the punishment for misdemeanor charged on the prisoner. The President is required to call the naval and military forces of the country to defeat the enterprise,' and 'we are told that Aaron Burr was to judge whether he would obey or not. If this is so, there is an end of government.' [2]

And then, pausing a moment, and looking Marshall in the eye, he went on:

---

[1] Davis Robertson, *Reports of the Trial of Aaron Burr for Treason*, I, 128. (Hereafter cited as *Burr's Trial.*)

[2] *Ibid.*, I, 139–40.

'I cannot take my seat, sir, without expressing my deep and sincere sorrow at the policy which the gentlemen for the defense have thought it necessary to adopt. Before Mr. Martin came to Richmond, this policy was settled, and on every question incidentally brought before the court we are stunned with invectives against the Administration.'

Holding the eye of Marshall, he continued: 'I appeal to your recollection, sir, whether this policy was not manifested even as early as those new, and, until now, unheard-of challenges to the grand jury for favor. Whether that policy was not followed up with increased spirit in the speeches of Mr. Botts and Mr. Wickham — whether they have not seized with avidity every subsequent occasion, and on every question of abstract law before the court, to fly off at a tangent from the subject to launch into declarations against the Government, exhibiting the prisoner continually as a persecuted patriot, a Russell or a Sydney, bleeding under the scourge of a despot and dying for virtue's sake.'

Another pause — the orator's eye looking steadily at Marshall.

'I beg to know what gentlemen can intend, expect, or hope from these perpetual philippics against the Government.'

Another pause, and then a challenge as gallant as any ever thrown at the foot of a bench by a Curran or an Erskine:

'*Do they flatter themselves that this court feels political prejudices which will supply the place of argument and innocence on the part of the prisoner? Their conduct amounts to an insinuation of that sort.*' [1]

Marshall cringed under this lash. The mask had slipped again. He began to hear the rumble from outside. That evening he was forced to take note of Wirt's direct challenge to him. Weakly addressing lawyers and spectators, he said he had not interfered with the flagrant and gross attacks upon the President spoken 'in the heat of debate,' though he had not approved of them. He hoped that hereafter gentlemen would confine themselves on every occasion to the point really before the court.

But the utter insincerity of this admonition was speedily to appear.

[1] *Burr's Trial*, I, 144.

VI

The very next day this insincerity was disclosed. Edmund
Randolph, still harping on the absent Wilkinson, was crassly impudent.

'But is General Wilkinson,' he said, 'the child of the President?
Are the hearts of Mr. Jefferson and General Wilkinson connected
by the same tender ties as those of father and son?' [1]

And Marshall sat in smug silence!

The Federalist lawyers for Burr knew the man upon the bench
too well to fear a serious rebuke. There was not even a 'gentle
admonition.' The following day, the disgraceful performance was
continued to the evident satisfaction of the Chief Justice. Martin,
coarser than the others, because always in his cups, repeated the
offense.[2] Hay sharply called attention to the continued attacks on
the President, but Marshall uttered not a word.[3]

The next day, Marshall read his opinion on the motion to issue
a subpoena *duces tecum* directed to the President of the United
States. It was precisely what Burr demanded.[4] But in the phrasing of the opinion the mask slipped again. With clear malice afore-
thought, for Marshall wrote his opinions in this trial with the
utmost care, he implied that the Government wished Burr condemned regardless of the merits of the case. The plain implication
was that the prosecution was inspired by personal or political hate.

The moment he ceased reading, MacRae was on his feet, his cold
eye fixed indignantly upon the judge. Again Marshall was to receive, and take, a lashing from a lawyer worthy of the high tradi-
tions of his profession.

'I hope, sir,' he began, 'that I misunderstood an expression
which has just escaped from your honor; but the opinion of the
gentlemen who are with me completely confirms my own concep-
tion. Your honor has declared that if the present prosecution
terminates as it is wished on the part of the United States. I hope,
sir, that nothing has appeared in my conduct to produce such a
conviction in the breast of the court. I trust that it has rather
accidentally fallen from the pen of your honor' — with sarcastic
intent — 'than that it is your deliberate opinion.'

---

[1] *Burr's Trial*, I, 158.   [2] *Ibid.*, I, 167.   [3] *Ibid.*, I, 170.
[4] *Ibid.*, I, 177.

Marshall was considerably confused, but stumbled awkwardly into an explanation. The Government's representatives had so often shown in their opinion that Burr was guilty, he had assumed they wished his conviction.

Again the indomitable Scotchman was on his feet, sharply pointing out to the court 'a considerable difference between the opinions and the wishes of the prosecution'; that from the testimony examined the prosecution thought it extremely probable that Aaron Burr was guilty, 'but this is very different from wishing to find him guilty, or to convict him at all events.' [1]

Again Marshall cringed. That evening he sought again to explain away his offensive reflection on the Government and expressed a wish to strike the insulting phrase from the record.[2]

VII

Hay immediately informed Jefferson of Marshall's action. The President had no disposition to withhold any information or paper necessary to a proper defense of Burr, and he wrote Hay with dignity and fairness. The Wilkinson letter had been turned over to Rodney when he went to Richmond and might be found among the papers delivered to Hay. Otherwise an effort would be made to reach the Attorney-General wherever he might be. If the Wilkinson letter were found, Hay was instructed to use his own discretion in revealing the contents. Only that portion necessary to the legitimate defense of Burr should be given out. But the order for all the instructions of the War and Navy Departments dealing with the Burr conspiracy, Jefferson thought unreasonable. 'It would amount to laying open the whole executive books,' he wrote. However, he would instruct the heads of the two departments to go over their files and see what could be done. Meanwhile, if the defense would indicate the specific papers wanted, it would be much simpler.[3]

Hay read Jefferson's letter to the court, but Burr and Martin were not content. They had sent an express to Washington, they said loftily, with a subpoena to the President, and they would soon know whether Jefferson would defy the court. A day or two later, Burr announced that his messenger had received only a verbal reply from Jefferson, who had bluntly said that personally he would not send the papers. If these were not forthcoming on the morrow, Burr would ask Marshall to crack the whip and drag the President into court.

The following day, Hay read Jefferson's high-toned, dignified, and yet devastating reply to Marshall's threat. Even Marshall's biographer concedes that in this letter Jefferson, the lawyer, shines forth brilliantly. Other historians, not partial to Jefferson, agree that 'the President had the best of the encounter on all scores.'[1]

'As to our personal attendance at Richmond,' Jefferson wrote, 'I am persuaded the court is sensible that paramount duties to the nation at large control the obligations of compliance with the summons in this case, as it would should we receive a similar one to attend the trials of Blennerhassett and others in the Territory of Mississippi, those instituted at St. Louis and other places on the Western waters, or any place other than the seat of government.' The Executive was the one branch of government whose functioning was continuous. 'It could not then intend that it should be withdrawn from its station by any co-ordinate authority.'

And the papers? There was both a public and a private side to these. The former certainly were public property. The latter deal with mere executive proceedings. As to these 'all nations have found it necessary that, for the advantageous conduct of their affairs, some of these proceedings at least should remain known to the executive functionary only. He, of course, from the nature of the case, must be the sole judge of which of them the public interest will permit publication.' And then, with a grave dignity that left the defense gasping, he concluded:

'The respect mutually due between the constituted authorities in their official intercourse, as well as sincere dispositions to do for everyone what is just, will always insure from the Executive, in exercising the duty of discrimination confided to him, the same candor and integrity to which the nation has in like manner trusted in the disposal of its judicial authorities.'

Marshall had been roundly spanked, more in sorrow than in

[1] Edward S. Corwin, *John Marshall and the Constitution*, 98.

anger. 'He had fully earned his rebuff,' concludes an unfriendly critic of Jefferson, 'but that fact did not appreciably sweeten it.' [1]

Having read the letter, Hay turned over to the court the papers from the Navy Department, including the order which had inspired so much bathetic eloquence from Burr and Martin — the one 'to destroy Burr's property and person.' 'You will with your boats take the best position to intercept and to take, and, if necessary, to destroy, the boats descending under the command of Colonel Burr' — so ran the bloody order of the tyrant. Burr had lied again. [2]

Meanwhile, as witnesses filed before the grand jury, and Martin continued his efforts to make Wilkinson the defendant, the defense had another shock. John Randolph, foreman, appeared before Marshall to report that the jury would like the cipher letter from Wilkinson to Burr, presumably in the possession of the accused. Naturally, he said, if this letter would incriminate Burr, the jury had no right to demand it.

Marshall hastened to announce that 'no man can be forced to furnish evidence against himself.'

Burr rose, in the odor of sanctity, to scout the idea that he would ever stoop to divulge the contents of a communication made to him in confidence. No, never! 'It is impossible for me to deliberate on the proposition to deliver up anything which has been confided to my honor.'

Marshall, with his usual suavity, decided that there could be no objection to the grand jury calling before them and examining any man who lay under an indictment. He had overlooked the letter! No, certainly, chimed in Martin, who was not overlooking it. But neither had John Randolph been confused. 'I am afraid,' he said ironically, 'that the object of the grand jury has been misunderstood by the court.' Did not Marshall understand that the grand jury was asking, not for 'the person of Aaron Burr to obtain evidence, but for a certain paper that might be in his possession'? And just then the dour MacRae did not sweeten the session for the defense when, graciously, he said that since Burr's sole objection to delivering the cipher letter was the fear of

---

[1] Corwin, 98.

[2] *Burr's Trial*, i, 256.

'wounding his honor' by the betrayal of Wilkinson's confidence, he had an announcement to make:

'I have seen General Wilkinson, sir,' he said, 'and the General has expressed his wishes to me, and requested me to express these wishes, that the whole of the correspondence between Aaron Burr and himself may be exhibited before the court.' And then, smiling sourly, 'The accused has now, therefore, a fair opportunity of producing the letter; he is absolved from all possible imputation; his honor is perfectly safe.'

And just here it developed that Burr had lied again. Instantly he changed his explanation.

'I have only to say, sir, that this letter will not be produced. The letter is not at this time in my possession, and General Wilkinson knows it.'

Very well, drawled the ironical MacRae, would the court please inform the grand jury of the reply? In the presence of the foreman, Burr had refused the letter on the score of honor; now he admitted he had put it beyond his reach. Stung by the implication, Burr angrily declared that he had put the letter beyond his reach 'with the express view that it should not be used improperly against anyone.'

The spectators and the public without were amazed by this admission. For days Wickham, Burr, and Martin had been trying to have Wilkinson committed, and when the grand jury asked for a cipher letter to Burr from Wilkinson, Burr refused on the ground that he did not wish to hurt Wilkinson. Only in the Richmond drawing-rooms did Burr emerge from this incident in a noble guise.

Marshall silently reduced the substance of these communications to writing and sent them to the jury room.

VIII

The witnesses had been heard, the arguments had been delivered. In the meantine Burr remained the idol of the more select of Richmond society, burdened with dinners. He met his obligations by giving some dinners of his own. Like a Roman demagogue, he was followed by a crowd of partisans to and from the court. Senator Plumer, at the time, recorded the immense popularity of Burr in Federalist circles, but Plumer then was scarcely the unbiased observer Marshall's biographer would have us think. Less than three years before, he, too, was bent on the destruction of the Union, and among the conspirators of 1804 a fellow feeling made them wondrous kind.

But in the midst of these festive scenes, the grand jury returned indictments against Aaron Burr for treason and misdemeanor, and the social idol passed to a cell in the city jail to await his trial.

Within two days, physicians had affirmed that Burr's health would suffer in such unsavory surroundings, and Marshall ordered his removal to the house of Luther Martin, provided the windows were barred and guards were stationed. The Government, however, made other arrangements, and his sojourn in proximity to Martin's flowing bowl was brief. He was sent to the top floor of the new penitentiary, in the hills a little more than a mile from town. There he was ensconced in three large rooms having more than three hundred feet of length. Immediately the jailer was his most obedient servant, a bit too sycophantic to be a good one. 'You would have laughed to have heard our compliments the first evening,' Burr wrote in gay mood to Theodosia. Soon his passion for the pomp and circumstance of power was all but satisfied. 'While I have been writing, different servants have arrived with messages and inquiries, bringing oranges, lemons, pineapples, raspberries, apricots, cream, butter, ice, and some ordinary articles,' he wrote jubilantly to his daughter.[1] The leaders of society beat a pathway to his court — women as well as men. With his jailer proud to be his butler, he was receiving male and female guests who were permitted to visit him 'without interruption, without inquiring their business, and without the presence of a spy.' He thought it well that he had an antechamber for the overflow.[2] To Theodosia, he sent a warm invitation to join him. 'If you come,' he wrote, 'I can give you a bedroom and a parlor on this floor. The bedroom has three large closets and it is much more commodious than you have ever had in your life.'[3]

Blennerhassett was delighted. An emperor at last! 'Burr lives in great style,' he wrote in his diary, 'and sees much company within his gratings, where it is as difficult to get an audience as if he really were an emperor.' Soon the gorgeous Theodosia, radi-

[1] Randall, III, 213.   [2] Ibid.   [3] Ibid.

antly beautiful, brilliant, accomplished, sophisticated beyond her years and time, and only twenty-four, arrived from Charleston.

In these days, before the trial began, the general public had reached certain conclusions. The storm troops of Burr's defense were the Federalists, for Hamilton was sleeping quietly in Trinity churchyard and would not know. The central thought of the partisans of Burr's legal *entourage* was to disregard all decencies in personal attacks on Jefferson. The partisan bias of Marshall, his hate of Jefferson, his toleration of the sneers at the head of the State, were notorious now. The press was reflecting the fighting in the courtroom, for the attempt to mould public opinion was not, as some historians amazingly imply, confined to one party. The barrooms in Richmond continued to buzz with the debate, but in most of the drawing-rooms where Jefferson was hated for his democracy, the sentiment was for Burr. It was from the houses of the 'best people' that the dainties found their way to Burr's court in the penitentiary.

Jefferson had no illusions now about the case. Writing du Pont de Nemours in July, he set forth his personal conviction of Burr's guilt, while describing the conspiracy as 'the most flagitious of which history will ever furnish an example.' And yet, he continued, 'although there is not a man in the United States who is not satisfied of the depth of his guilt, such are the jealous provisions of our laws in favor of the accused that I question if he can be convicted.' [1] To Lafayette, whose rescue Erich Bollman had attempted, he wrote that 'Bollman was Burr's right-hand man in all his guilty schemes' and that 'he communicated to Mr. Madison and myself the whole of the plans, always, however, apologetically for Colonel Burr, as far as they would bear.' [2]

Just what Marshall's thought may have been we can only surmise, though his brilliant biographer has suggested that 'to so excellent a politician as Mr. Marshall, it must have seemed probable that his party friends in New England might be brought before the courts to answer to the same charge as that against Aaron Burr.' [3]

Meanwhile, such evidence as was available had been printed

[1] *Writings of Jefferson*, II, 274.   [2] *Ibid.*, II, 276.
[3] Beveridge, III, 480.

ın pamphlet form, and in every quarter, even the most remote, the people were discussing the conspiracy of Burr.

IX

The air of the House of Delegates was that of an oven, August 3, when the trial for treason began. The Government could not now be criticized for not mobilizing its witnesses. More than a hundred were in Richmond, though quite soon most of these, by an opinion of the court, would be excluded from telling their story.

Immediately it was evident that most of the venire summoned for the jury had formed an opinion. It would have been remarkable, indeed, if the weird activities of the clever Burr, who had shot Alexander Hamilton, had not aroused interest everywhere. The press had teemed with gossip, both for and against the defendant, but Burr was to find that the average normal mind had been convinced of his guilty intent at least. Thus man after man was examined and hastily dropped.

One was sure he was guilty and should be hanged.[1] After this a depressing procession pronounced him guilty. Now and then a prospective juror announced that he had borne arms to put down the Burr conspiracy.[2] The consummate acting of Burr, the simulated amazement of Martin, the scornful expression of Wickham availed nothing to moderate the tone of many of the men of the venire.

Thus, one exclaimed: 'he deserves to be hung.' [3] 'He ought to be hanged,' said another.[4] Another expressed doubt about the overt act. 'Burr,' he said, 'is a man of such deep intrigue as never to jeopardize his own life till thousands fall before him.' [5] The procession lengthens. 'Guilty,' says another. 'My opinion has been strengthened by what I have heard from the lips of Colonel Burr in this court,' he explains.[6] 'Hanging is too good for him,' shouts another.[7] 'Worthy of death,' cries another.[8]

'What opinion have you formed of me?' Burr asks.

'A very bad one,' snaps the man of the venire.[9]

---

[1] Bucky; *Burr's Trial*, I, 371.   [2] Beeson and Prince; *ibid.*, I, 372.
[3] Buckner; *ibid.*, I, 372.   [4] Creel; *ibid.*   [5] Stanard; *ibid.*, I, 377
[6] Goode; *ibid.*   [7] White; *ibid.*, I, 379.   [8] Chamberlain; *ibiu.*
[9] Baker; *ibid.*, I, 380.

'I have said he deserves to be hung,' growls the next man.[1] Hamilton Morrison, a suspended prospect, is recalled. 'I am surprised that they should be in such terror of me,' he says. 'Perhaps my name may be a terror, for my first name is Hamilton.' [2]

'That remark,' snaps Burr, 'is sufficient cause for rejecting him.'

So shocking are the replies of the veniremen that Burr's lawyers, in consternation, can think of nothing better for overcoming the impression than attacking the Government and its legal representatives. 'They wish to hang him as soon as possible to gratify themselves and the Government,' bursts from the alcoholic lips of Martin.

'That is a most unprincipled and most unfounded assertion,' shouts MacRae, on his feet in an instant.[3]

'We wish to proceed without hearing ourselves grossly insulted,' adds Hay.

Marshall, who all these weeks never rebukes Burr's lawyers for their gross insults to the Government and the President, bestirs himself a bit.

'The Government ought to be treated with respect,' he drones softly.[4]

Never before had it been, and never after was it to be, treated with less respect than in the courtroom presided over by the Chief Justice.

At length a jury is accepted. Hay begins his opening statement. He commences with a definition of treason in consonance with that recognized for centuries in England. The framers of the Constitution were lawyers and were thinking in terms of English law and precedent. In the case of Fries, this had been specifically declared by Judge Iredell. And then Hay strikes a vicious blow:

'The only purpose for which I have made the reference to the British laws is to show that the decision of the Supreme Court on this subject, in the case of Bollman and Swartwout, is not an innovation, not a new doctrine.'

That decision had been carefully prepared by John Marshall not many months before. He had said with emphasis:

[1] Haskins; *ibid.*, I, 381.   [2] *Ibid.*, I, 383.
[3] *Ibid.*, I, 385.   [4] *Ibid.*, I, 386.

'If a body of men be actually assembled for the purpose of effecting by force a treasonable purpose, *all those who perform any part, however minute, or however remote from the scene of action, and who are actually leagued in the general conspiracy, are to be considered as traitors.*'

On this unequivocal, matured opinion of Marshall, the Government now takes its stand.

Hay continues. Was it contended that 'the arms must be used, that force must be employed, before war shall be said to be levied'? If true, note the absurdity: 'If ten thousand men were to assemble together and march to Washington for the express purpose of sending the President to Monticello, turning Congress out of doors, and usurping the powers of the Government, they would not be guilty of treason because they had not struck a blow. They advance and proceed; they meet no opposition; the members of the Government disperse through fear; and yet this is not treason.'[1]

And would the defense attack Marshall's opinion in the case of Bollman and Swartwout? Would they contend that no man can be pronounced a traitor till, by striking the blow, he be, or conceives himself to be, beyond the reach of the law? Then the Constitution is a dead letter!

And now Hay sets forth the theory of the Government: 'I shall take it for granted that the law is as I have stated it to be, and that the overt act of treason is complete if there was an assemblage of men on Blennerhassett's Island . . . whether they used force or not. It is incumbent on those who prosecute to show, first, that there was a treasonable design, and second, that there was an assemblage of men for the purpose of effectuating that design.'

And now he outlines his evidence to be submitted, and calls as his first witness General William Eaton.

x

It is the fashion of the pro-Burr historians to ridicule Eaton and his testimony. Much is made of his vanity, and the weakness he shared with Martin — a fondness for drink. The absolutely false impression is conveyed that he made himself ridiculous and

[1] *Burr's Trial*, I, 440. [2] *Ibid.*, I, 446.

JEFFERSON IN POWER

that his testimony was discredited. It was not even shaken; all the legal genius that Burr had called about him could not trip him on a single point. The story we already know is the story that he told, and this story remained unpitted by the concentrated artillery of Burr's legal battery.

At length, disgusted by the inability of his lawyers to make a dent in the testimony of Eaton, Burr himself makes the attempt.

'You spoke of a command,' he says.

'You stated,' replies Eaton, 'that you were assured from the arrangements which you had made that an army would be ready to appear when you went to the waters of the Western country. I recollect particularly the name of Ephraim Kibby, who had been a ranger in General Wayne's army. You asked me about his spirit. You gave me to understand that his brigade was ready to join you, and that the people of that country were ready to engage with you in the enterprise. You spoke of your riflemen, your infantry, your cavalry. It was with the same view that you mentioned to me the man [pointing to Wilkinson] who was to have been the first to aid you; and from the same views you have perhaps mentioned me.'

'You spoke of my revolutionizing the Western States,' Burr continues. 'How did you understand that the Union was to be separated?'

'Your principal line was to be drawn at the Alleghany Mountains,' Eaton replied, unruffled. 'You were persuaded that you had secured to you the most considerable citizens of Kentucky and Tennessee; but expressed some doubt about Ohio. I well recollect that on account of the reason you gave — that they were too much of a plodding, industrious people to engage in your enterprise.'

'How was the business to be effected?' Burr asks.

'I understood your agents were in the Western country; that the army and the commander-in-chief were ready to act at your signal; and that these, with the adventurers that would join you, would compel the States to agree to a separation. Indeed, you seemed to consider New Orleans as already yours, and that from this point you would send expeditions into the other provinces, make conquests and consolidate your empire.'[1]

[1] *Burr's Trial,* I. 483.

Such is the straightforward story that Eaton tells, looking Burr in the eye as he speaks; such is the effect of all attempts of the cleverest lawyers in the country to trip him. Burr drops the witness.

And now other witnesses follow — Peter Taylor, the gardener of Blennerhassett; the three Morgans; witnesses to the events on the island; *and not one shaken in the telling of the story we now know.* More than a hundred witnesses are waiting.

Burr's lawyers now ask Marshall to exclude all further testimony, on the ground that no overt act involving Burr's personal presence on the island has been shown. The effect, of course, would be to end the trial.

And now begins a brilliant ten days' debate. MacRae leads off, resting his argument on the ancient English law which never before had been questioned in an American court, and on which, but a few weeks before, Marshall himself had based his interpretation of treason.

'The prisoner accessory before the fact?' he asks. Why, 'he is the first mover of the plot; he planned it, he matured it, he contrived the doing of the overt acts which others have done. He was the Alpha and Omega of this treasonable scheme, the very body and soul, the very life of this treason.... We regard him as principal and chief mover in the whole plan.' [1]

And now William Wirt, young, handsome, brilliant, rises to take us to the peak of the debate. Erudite and eloquent, he has also shown that he is indifferent to Marshall's frown or benevolence.

Why so sensitive about the word treason? he asks. Is this a court of justice in which a man is being tried for treason, or a Richmond drawing-room in which the delicate sensibilities of the defendant are of primary consideration? And why had Wickham in his argument been so chary of American precedents and carried his hearers back in English history, 'resurging by a kind of intellectual magic to the middle of the sixteenth century, complaining most bitterly of my Lord Coke's bowels' ?

And now Wirt answers his question:

'I will tell you what it was. *It was, sir, the decision of the Supreme Court in the case of Bollman and Swartwout.* It was the

[1] *Burr's Trial*, ii, 39.

judicial exposition of the Constitution by the highest court in
the nation upon the very point which the gentleman was considering, which made him take his flight to England; because it stared
him in the face and contradicted his position.' Yes, that decision
of John Marshall's was directly on the point under consideration.
Had it been favorable to the position of the defense, Wickham
would have 'seized it with avidity.' He would have illustrated it.
He would have adorned it. 'You would have seen it under the
action of his genius appear with all the varying grandeur of our
mountains in the morning sun. He would not have relinquished it
for the common law, nor have deserted a rock so broad and solid
to walk upon the waves of the Atlantic.' But he knew Marshall's
well-matured, carefully prepared opinion in the case of Bollman
and Swartwout 'closed against him completely the very point
which he was laboring.'

And so sweeps on the captivating orator. 'Let us bring it from
the obscurity into the face of day. . . . The inquiry is whether
presence at the overt act be necessary to make a man a traitor.
And what says John Marshall and the Supreme Court? "Those
who perform any part, however minute, or however remote from
the scene of action, and who are actually leagued in the general
conspiracy, are to be considered as traitors."'

It is a rough moment for the Chief Justice, who already knows,
before the conclusion of the argument, that he is going to reverse,
not only the traditional interpretation of treason, but a notable
opinion of his own on which the ink is scarcely dry.

But Wirt sweeps on. Poor Blennerhassett a principal in the
treason and Burr spotless as a star? And now the orator gives to
literature one of its finest passages of eloquence, which will live
much more than a century.

'Who is Blennerhassett?' he asks. In classic language he traces
the story of his paradise on his once-loved island, where he 'rears
a palace and decorates it with every romantic embellishment of
art . . . a shrubbery that Shenstone might have envied . . . music
that might have charmed Calypso and her nymphs'; the library,
the laboratory, and, 'to crown the enchantment of the scene,
a wife, who is said to be lovely beyond her sex, and graced
with every accomplishment that can render it irresistible, had

blessed him with her love and made him the father of several children.'

And now the destroyer enters to 'change this paradise into a hell.' He 'soon finds his way into their hearts by the dignity and elegance of his demeanor, the light and beauty of his conversation, and the seductive and fascinating power of his address.' In a little while, Blennerhassett is changed. 'No more he enjoys the tranquil scene; it has become flat and insipid to his taste. His books are abandoned. His retort and crucible are thrown aside. His shrubbery blooms and breathes its fragrance on the air in vain; he likes it not. His ear no longer drinks the rich melody of music; he longs for the trumpet's clangor and the cannon's roar.' Yes, 'his enchanted island is destined soon to relapse into a wilderness; and in a few months we find the beautiful and tender partner of his bosom, whom he lately permitted not the winds of summer to visit too roughly, we find her shivering at midnight on the winter banks of the Ohio and mingling her tears with its waters that froze as they fell.'

Blennerhassett is listening; so, too, is Burr.

'Yet this unfortunate man ... this man, thus ruined and undone and made to play a subordinate part in this grand drama of guilt and treason, this man is to be called the principal offender, while he, by whom he was thus plunged in misery, is comparatively innocent, a mere accessory.'

He pauses, his bright features suffused with a glow of indignation.

'Is this reason?' he thunders. 'Is it law? Is it humanity? Sir, neither the human heart nor the human understanding will bear a perversion so monstrous and absurd. So shocking to the soul. So revolting to the reason. Let Aaron Burr then not shrink from the high destination which he has courted, and, having ruined Blennerhassett in fortune and character and happiness forever, let him not attempt to finish the tragedy by thrusting this ill-fated man between himself and punishment.'

Nothing finer had ever been heard in an American courtroom, and soon even the enemies of Jefferson, rallied about Burr, were paying tribute to the orator's genius. Even the *New York Evening Post* published the passage with the comment that 'those familiar with the eloquence of the late Lord Chancellor [Erskine], and still more with that of the celebrated Curran, will immediately recognize the resemblance, and may possibly think, with us, that the American barrister does not suffer in the comparison with either.' [1]

The argument for the defense is now closed by Martin, who has been winning laurels in the barrooms through his well-nigh unlimited capacity for the cup. He has been drinking more heavily than usual on the eve of his argument. The maudlin sentimentality about his 'honorable friend' may be the emanation of an alcoholic heart, but his condition in no wise diminishes his rare gift for sophistry. Again Jefferson is clamoring for Burr's blood. Burr had not been personally present on Blennerhassett's Island. No overt act involving his 'honorable friend' had been committed there. Therefore, the court should exclude all further evidence. More than a hundred witnesses were waiting — send them home! Marshall's opinion, too fresh yet for publication in the books? An absurd opinion!

Thus the ten days' debate ends.

XI

Never was Marshall to appear to less advantage than in his labored effort to reverse his own opinion, still all but wet with ink, and to save Aaron Burr from its consequences. Following very closely the reasoning of Burr's lawyers, he reached a conclusion in complete harmony with the necessities of the defense. His occasional deviations from their position in no wise interfered with their primary plan — to shut off further evidence.

When the opinion was heard, Hay rose gravely to announce that in view of the decision he had nothing more to offer the jury in the way of evidence or argument. Let the jury have the case.

In a short while the jury filed back into the courtroom with its verdict:

'We the jury say that Aaron Burr is not proved guilty under this indictment *by any evidence submitted to us.* We therefore find him not guilty.'

Burr sprang to his feet, along with Martin and Wickham,

[1] October 3, 1807.

protesting that the form of the verdict was irregular. It was —
and was so intended to be. It was the clear intent of the jury to
express the opinion that the proceedings which excluded a great
body of witnesses were a bit irregular. 'Of course the verdict must
be corrected,' shouted Martin. 'Did the jury mean to censure the
court?' Unquestionably such was the clear intent. Not caring to
press the embarrassing question further, Marshall suavely instructed the clerk to change the jury's verdict and make it read
'Not guilty.'

That night was one of gay rejoicing in the drawing-rooms of
Richmond, and in his house Luther Martin, drunker than usual,
held his guests almost to dawn about the flowing bowl. Martin
drank brandy only.

XII

But the general reaction, even in Richmond, was not that of
the fashionable set. Marshall was denounced openly. William
Thompson, a young man of brilliant promise, cut off by an un-
timely death, wrote a series of letters to the Chief Justice, bitter
in denunciation. Ritchie, of the *Richmond Enquirer*, attacked the
decision and the general conduct of Marshall throughout the trial
with vigor and in plain language. In his paper appeared a 'Portrait of the Chief Justice' which was copied throughout the
country.

Most historians refrain from an opinion, but one, antipathetic
to Jefferson, and generally sympathetic toward Marshall, has
concluded that 'Marshall's conduct of Burr's trial is the one
serious blemish in his judicial record.'[1] Among the lawyers of
that time there was no such commendation of Marshall's action
as in later times. Thirty years afterward, when called upon to
find a perfect judicial definition of treason, Justice Story, for
years an intimate of Marshall's, passed this decision by, to accept that of Marshall in the case of Bollman and Swartwout for
which the Government contended. Within a few months, John
Quincy Adams, in preparing the Senate report on Senator Smith,
one of Burr's confederates, makes his adverse opinion plain. The
fact that a new definition of treason had been furnished which shut

[1] Corwin, III, 2.

off evidence; that this definition was in direct contradiction to one handed down by Marshall a few weeks before; that Marshall attended a dinner in honor of the defendant before the trial and after the indictment, and was a political intimate of the attorneys for the defense; that he hated Jefferson and repeatedly permitted his hate to burst forth in such fashion as to force him to explanations and apologies during the trial — all this must enter into an opinion on his conduct in this case.

XIII

The trial for misdemeanor followed on instructions from Jefferson when Hay, disgusted, proposed to dismiss the case. Again Burr and Martin sought to force Marshall to enforce his subpoena on Jefferson, but nothing came of it. Nothing could. It would have brought a crisis, for Jefferson would have challenged the right of the Judiciary to order the Executive about in such fashion. The famous letter from Wilkinson expressed his suspicions of a number of citizens in New Orleans, and this, in common justice, Jefferson was determined not to make public. Burr, Martin, and Marshall all knew the reason. The exclusion of evidence brought the misdemeanor trial to a speedy termination. The *Evening Post*, a bit stricken by the jubilation over Burr's 'vindication,' mildly suggested that many thought '*there had been no acquittal, for there has been no trial, no evidence having been given.*' [1] Apropos of its reference to Burr's bitter attack on Jefferson, the *New York American Citizen* said, 'there is no doubt that Burr would make a speech bitterly severe against the President, and that Chief Justice Marshall would listen to it with pleasure, but I venture that there are not ten men in the nation, out of the circle of that foul conspiracy, to whom the exultation will be acceptable.' [2]

Burr finally was committed on a charge of treason in Ohio and gave bail. He went with his confederates and lawyers to Baltimore to continue the celebration with Luther Martin. But the people there were in ugly mood and poured into the streets, intent on the use of tar and feathers. Burr and that noble youth, Swartwout, were spirited to a stage-coach, and rumbled away to Philadelphia. Blennerhassett hid, shivering, in a garret of a tavern. Martin remained secluded in his own house with his bottle, while police guarded him against attack. The mob contented itself by burning Burr, Marshall, and Martin in effigy.

Soon Burr, in Philadelphia, was surrounded by Blennerhassett, Bollman, Swartwout, and Ogden, 'in frequent consultation' and 'occasionally in some bustle.' [1] But soon he was hounded by creditors, and, jumping his bail, he took flight to Europe.

XIV

There was to be no more glamour to his life. His friends in Richmond had given him his last touch of grandeur. Beveridge, who insists on his innocence and on his plan for a settlement on the Red River, says that on his acquittal Burr turned again 'to the execution of his one great plan as though the interruption of it had never happened.' [2]

To what plan did he turn? The record fails to show that he ever again thought of his 'little band of settlers.' Blennerhassett had sunk his all, but his idol showed no disposition to take possession of the land again. In London, he was soon intriguing for financial aid for his Mexican project. If that was his 'one great plan,' he had been guilty of planning an attack on Mexico — the misdemeanor charged. But England soon tired of him and sent him away.

Soon he was in Paris, and here we get another view of his 'one great plan.' Through the intermediation of a young deputy, he sought the aid of Napoleon to carry out his plan of treason. This cannot be a 'Jefferson trick' — the evidence is in the memorandum prepared by Burr which anyone may read today in the Archives Nationales in Paris. These papers were carried by young Mr. Roux from the sordid little room of the conspirator in the Rue Petit St. Augustine to the Tuileries. Here, in these papers, he proposes again the separation of Louisiana from the United States — the same proposition of treason for which he was indicted. In a second memorandum he proposed to Napoleon, if backed by France, to stir up a war between the United States and England so France could take possession of Canada. Clearly 'he started

---

[1] *National Intelligencer*, November 18, 1807.   [2] Beveridge, III, 529.

anew upon the execution of his one great plan as though the interruption of it had never happened.' And the plan was treason! But Napoleon was not impressed. After more than four years of sordid misery in Europe, Burr returned to New York, resuming the practice of law and of his amours; but it was only the ghost of the Burr of 1800 who died alone on Staten Island more than twenty years after the trial.

xv

Meanwhile, with the Federalists seeking to separate New England from the Union, and with Burr trying to separate the Western from the Eastern States, Jefferson had launched a memorable scientific expedition through the wilderness to the western sea to blaze a path for the spreading of American trade, civilization, and institutions from Boston to the Pacific. He conceived it, planned it, trained Meriwether Lewis, his secretary, to lead it; and, after many months of heroic battling among the savages and against more savage nature, this gallant band of nationalists had reached the sunset sea. Lost to their friends for many months, shut in by winter snows, challenged by mountains and an unbroken wilderness, stricken with disease and death, existing at times on herbs, on dogs and horses, they had finally emerged with a scientific report on plant and animal life, on the nature of the country and its people, on the possibilities of trade; and they had blazed a trail over which multitudes would march, planting the flag on the way, and making inevitable the extension of the Union from sea to sea.

There was general rejoicing, but not among the disunionists of Federalism who had sneered at Jefferson's 'philosophical expedition' and gleefully predicted its failure. The disunion conspiracy of the Federalist politicians of 1804 was momentarily defeated; the conspiracy of Burr was crushed; but as young Lewis sat quietly in the courtroom in Richmond on his return, events were moving toward the revival of their treasonable designs.

For the attack on the *Chesapeake* and resulting events would furnish the disloyalists with another opportunity.

CHAPTER XX

The Chesapeake: Treason Mobilizes

I

IN THE midst of the Burr trial the nation was shaken to its foundations, as never before since the battle of Lexington. The frigate *Chesapeake*, fitted out for Mediterranean service, had floated down the Potomac to Norfolk, preparatory to her voyage. Before her departure from Washington, rumors were afloat that deserters from British vessels were enlisted in her crew. The Government investigated and found that the 'deserters' were American citizens.

Thereupon, with a gasconading gesture, Berkeley, commander of the British fleet in American waters, determined on summary action. All British ships under his command were ordered to stop and search the *Chesapeake* wherever found upon the sea. This contemptuous order was borne to the British ships by the *Leopard* the very day the *Chesapeake* reached Hampton Roads.

The American frigate, unprepared for trouble, set sail on the morrow under the command of Commodore Barron, and at the same moment the *Leopard* turned to sea. As the vessels approached each other, the *Leopard* fired a gun, and on being hailed announced that she bore dispatches. Her officers boarded the *Chesapeake* with an arrogant note from her commander charging that there were British deserters on board. Barron read the note and courteously replied that he knew of no such deserters, and that he could not permit the mustering of the crew by any but their own officers. He hoped the incident was closed.

It was only when the British left his ship that Barron noted, with uneasiness, that the guns of the *Leopard* were prepared for action; his own were not. Then he was accosted, through a trumpet, with the warning that 'the orders of the admiral must be obeyed.' He thought to gain time by parley to permit the making of preparations for defense. But almost immediately a cannon shot screamed across the bow of his vessel; then another; then a broadside; and then, for fifteen minutes, the *Chesapeake* was subjected to a raking fire. She was not prepared to reply. When twenty-two shots had been poured into her hull, killing American sailors, one member of the *Chesapeake* crew, bearing a live coal for the purpose, managed to fire one shot. The continuance of the unequal struggle could result only in the sinking of the ship, and the American flag was hauled down.

The British officers boarded the ship, mustered the crew, and pointed out, as deserters, three Americans — all negroes! One real deserter, whose presence was unknown to Barron, was found hidden in an out-of-the-way hole. The prisoners were taken from the ship and the *Leopard* returned to American waters, thus adding insult to injury. Not until the next morning did the crippled *Chesapeake* manage to creep back to Hampton Roads.

The news spread like wildfire, and instantly the entire nation was aflame. In scores of mass meetings the outrage was denounced, and from corn row, wharf, counting-room, and bank went forth a passionate demand for war.

The news reached Jefferson in Washington. The Cabinet was scattered. At once he summoned the Cabinet to the capital. The ailing Madison dragged himself to his post. The summons found Gallatin, also ill, at Havre de Grace, in Maryland. 'I am sorry to be obliged to hasten your return,' Jefferson wrote him, 'and pray it may be without a moment's unavoidable delay.' The returning courier carried the reply: 'I am so much fatigued that I cannot ride all night by the mail; but I will be with you on Wednesday about two or three o'clock in the afternoon.' Jefferson hurried another courier to Gallatin. 'It will save a day in the measures we may determine to take if I can see you soon after your arrival,' wrote Jefferson. 'If you arrive before half past three, come and take a family dinner with me that I may put you in possession of what is under contemplation, so that you may reflect upon it till tomorrow.'[1] Erskine, the friendly British Minister, in New York at the time of the attack, hastened as fast as horses could be pushed to Washington,[2] and on his arrival disavowed the conduct of the British ship, announced that it was unauthorized by his Government, and that he was preparing dispatches ordering the squadron to depart immediately.[3]

Within twenty-four hours, Jefferson had determined on his course. He would not commit the young Republic to the arbitrament of the sword without scrupulously observing the usages of civilized nations by speeding a demand to London for an apology and reparations. In the meantime, he would not summon Congress to deliberate in a moment of national frenzy. He would issue a proclamation forbidding the provisioning of British ships in American waters, and would make all possible provisions for defense along the coast and put the State and national military forces in preparation.

In a day or two, the Cabinet gravely surrounded Jefferson's council table and listened to his proposed proclamation, setting forth with scrupulous fidelity the lengthening list of offenses against American rights, closing the ports to the armed ships of Britain, ordering those in American waters out, refusing admittance to all others unless bearing dispatches, and forbidding citizens to supply food and water to their crews.

The Cabinet approved; couriers that day were speeding their horses in all directions, and soon the proclamation was looming in all the newspapers. Then the Cabinet turned to defense measures, and very soon New York, Charleston, and New Orleans were being put in a state of defense. The militia of Virginia was effectually shutting off communication between the British fleet in the Chesapeake and the shore, and Commodore Decatur had orders to attack at Norfolk if the British fleet attempted to enter the Elizabeth River.

When intelligence reached Jefferson that there was tampering with the Indians in the Northwest, he ordered the Governors of Michigan, Indiana, and Ohio instantly to fall upon the tribes that

---

[1] *Writings of Gallatin*, I, 336–37.
[2] *Columbian Centinel*, July 11, 1807.   [3] *Ibid.*, July 15, 1807.

donned warpaint. 'In war they will kill some of us; we will destroy all of them,' he wrote William Henry Harrison.

With the war hawks howling for an immediate call of Congress, Jefferson consulted his Cabinet. Smith wanted an immediate call, and Gallatin an early one.[1] But here Jefferson was adamant. Not until the last of October, he announced, and no public suggestion of that call until in August. The equilibrium of the public temper must be restored before deliberation.

In the meantime, Madison in Jefferson's closet was working out instructions to Monroe in London. He was admonished that 'this enormity is not a subject for discussion.' He was to remind the British Government that 'the immunity of a national ship of war from every species and purpose of search on the high seas has never been contested by any nation.' He was to say that the British commander had been informed that the objects of his search were American citizens on an American ship, and that two of the three had previously been impressed into the British service in violation of all law. He was to warn of the aroused state of public sentiment, and to say that 'the indignity offered to the sovereignty and flag of the nation, and the blood of citizens so wantonly and wickedly shed, demands in the loudest tone an honorable reparation.' He was to demand a formal disavowal of the deed and the restoration of the seamen to their ship. As a guaranty for the future, he was to demand 'the entire abolishment of impressment from vessels under the flag of the United States.' In the event reparations were denied, he was immediately to return home and warn all American ships in British waters to return at once.[2] These instructions were hurried to London on the *Revenge* as speedily as ocean vessels could then move.

Meanwhile, there had been more insolence from the crew of the *Leopard* and violence in the streets of Norfolk, and the vessel bearing the venerable Vice-President George Clinton and his sick daughter had been fired upon. Off the capes of Virginia the revenue cutter bearing Clinton was fired upon and ordered to stop. The cutter was ordered by her commander to keep on her course regardless of consequences. Launches from the British ships were then armed and dispatched to attack the cutter, into

[1] To Nicholson, *Writings of Gallatin*, I, 338.   [2] *Writings of Madison*, VII, 454.

which they discharged musketry; but finding the men on the
cutter at their posts and ready for action, the launches fell back.[1]
A few days after the sailing of the *Revenge*, Madison wrote again
to Monroe of the new offense, telling him to bring 'these collective
outrages into view.' [2]

III

All this was behind the scenes, but the nation still throbbed
with fury. A spirited call to the citizens of Washington to assemble, in protest, brought out the entire town.[3] Three days later,
the nation's natal day was celebrated with as much frenzy as
fervor. The cannon at the Navy Yard ushered in the day. The
militia paraded before the President's house, wildly cheered by
the spectators. The flags of all nations with whom we were on
terms of friendship were unfurled as usual — all but that of
Britain, which was nowhere to be seen. The President's levee
was crowded, and it was observed that Federalists, hitherto
conspicuously absent from these tributes to the President, 'made
their first appearance and mingled with perfect cordiality with
their republican brethren,' though these were not of the politicians
in Congress. In the East Room, the Marine Band played stirring
patriotic airs. The remainder of the day was given over to
'patriotic hilarity' with numerous parties in different parts of the
town. A banquet was given at Stelle's Hotel, where toasts were
drunk: 'The American People — Ready at a moment's warning
to vindicate the rights, and avenge the wrongs of their country' —
and the hall was in a tumult. 'The President of the United States
— The hand that drafted the Declaration of Independence will
maintain, inviolate, the principles it recognizes' — and the diners
rose and cheered.[4] Young men everywhere were offering their
services in the field; old men were urging war; Gallatin was
consulting bankers and insurance companies; mass meetings were
adopting resolutions to lusty shouts.

In the home of the Essex Junto the first reaction was one of
protest among the Federalists and their press. But it was observed
that the Junto refused permission to the municipal government of

[1] *National Intelligencer*, July 8, 1807.   [2] *Writings of Madison*, VII, 463.
[3] *National Intelligencer*, July 1, 1807.   [4] *Ibid.*, July 8, 1807.

Boston to call a town meeting to pledge support to the National Government in a crisis. When the news of the attack reached Boston, John Quincy Adams rushed about among his Federalist friends urging a town meeting 'in an open, free-hearted manner, setting aside all party feeling,' and pledging their determination 'to support the Government of their country.' He soon learned that the Federalist leaders had put their foot down on the project.[1]

Thereupon, the Jeffersonians proposed to take the initiative, and a meeting was called. A committee of Jeffersonians, with Adams, was named, and spirited resolutions were framed and passed. Thus Boston marched in step with the rest of the nation.

But Cabot, Pickering, Parsons, Higginson, and Ames were enraged at the effrontery of a group of men declaring their country in the right, its adversary guilty of a wrong, and when, on the following day, Adams called at the insurance office, he was told that he 'should have his head taken off for his apostasy to the Federalists.' [2]

With the spotlight thus turned upon them, the Federalists had to act. The apologetic historians who have described their decision to act as inspired by a determination 'not to be outdone' have been more than kind. The Junto neglected to invite Adams to their meeting at Faneuil Hall, but he attended, and again served on the committee. He noted that George Cabot, John Lowell, and Parsons, by their absence conspicuously disassociated themselves from any protest against the attack on the *Chesapeake*. 'They made no pledges,' he observed.

The immediate effect of their coercion into action was manifest in the tone of the Federalist press of Boston, which, within a few days, bitterly was attacking the Government of their own country and blatantly countenancing the action of the British ship. Treason had mounted its horse.

'Many papers in Boston begin to speak more openly their attachment to Great Britain and its measures,' observed a shocked citizen of Salem. 'Nothing American escapes censure.' [3] The Essex Junto had pulled down the American flag, and hoisted the flag of Britain.

---

[1] *Doc. N.E. Fed.*; Adams, *Diary*, I, 468.   [2] Adams, *Diary*, I, 469.
[3] Bentley, *Diary*, III. 314.

Thenceforth, the Federalist leaders of that section were arrayed openly and defiantly against their country.

IV

As the summer advanced, the Federalist papers increased their ardor in defense of Britain's right to search our vessels, to impress our seamen, to do with our merchant marine as she would. On July 26, the *Columbian Centinel* began the publication of a series of articles, signed 'Pacificus,' against war with England, taking the British view of the controversy. When rebuked for giving aid and comfort to the enemy, 'Pacificus' replied that 'it is painful to disclose our country's weakness, but let the mischief rest on the heads of those turbulent and wrong-headed men who by their absurd statements make such a measure necessary.'[1] Major Russell, the editor, was warmly praised for espousing the British cause by 'Philo Veritas' in a letter denouncing 'our unjustifiable conduct' and admitting that 'the attempt here is made to differentiate between the American people and the Administration.'[2]

The average man, however, was waiting on the President until the result of the negotiations could be known.

In the early autumn, David Humphreys, private secretary to Washington, returned from England to inform Jefferson of the spirit there. Just before the attack on the *Chesapeake*, a number of pamphlets had appeared in England urging a rupture in Anglo-American relations. One was titled, 'Concessions to America the Bane of Britain.' Humphreys concluded that war would please certain elements in England. The naval officers would like war; so, too, would the ancient enemies of American independence. And among the former friends of America were not a few who thought war not undesirable. 'Your old friend, John Stockdale, and many others among staunch friends of America in '76 look forward to a war with us as an ... event not very much to be deprecated, at least much less than the loss of the smallest of their naval rights,' he wrote. The frenzy of fear over Napoleon's advance had convinced even these that the slightest challenge to Britain's policy was evidence of hostility to Britain.

---

[1] *Columbian Centinel*, August 22, 1807.   [2] *Ibid.*, October 3, 1807.

Then, added Humphreys, there was another class that resented America's prosperity and the growth of her carrying trade. True, some statesmen realized that war would be injurious to the commercial and industrial interests, but these hoped that somehow access could be found to other markets to make up the loss. Humphreys thought it possible that ultimately merchants and manufacturers might bring the politicians to their senses, but 'how long a period will elapse before their voice can be heard,' he did not know. It was not a comforting report.[1]

One day, Monroe received a deceptive little note from Canning. The latter had heard vaguely of an unpleasant incident in American waters. Did Monroe know anything about it? Writing with Berkeley's full report unquestionably before him, Canning would like so much to learn from Monroe what it was all about. Meanwhile, he could not restrain his 'sincere concern and sorrow at its unfortunate result' — which, after all, he seemed to know about. If the British officer had been culpable, 'the most prompt and effectual reparations will be afforded the Government of the United States.'

The British press had begun to growl ominously before Monroe saw Canning again. He found the Minister posing in the too heavy mantle of the dead Pitt, stiff, unfriendly, admitting nothing, willing to disavow the act of Berkeley, and little more. Monroe bowed himself from the presence and returned to his quarters to prepare a formal note. Canning replied in his most *ex cathedra* manner. Since Monroe's complaint was not based on 'official information,' the British Government was not bound to do more than express a willingness to make reparations — if, indeed, reparations were due. For the moment Canning had abandoned his favorite mood of flippancy for that of pomposity, and, as Monroe thought, spoke in a rather domineering manner. Immediately after this, the London press became increasingly offensive in its bold defense of Berkeley's uncivilized action. There was nothing more to be done until the arrival of the instructions.

Upon the receipt of these, early in September, Monroe saw Canning again. The great man listened with Olympian serenity.

---

[1] F. L. Humphreys, *Life and Times of David Humphreys*, II, 262.

Never had he been so impressive, even patronizing. But when Monroe came to Jefferson's demand for the ending of impressments, he refused to admit this into the discussions.

Monroe hurried back to his quarters to prepare a strong note in line with his instructions. Two weeks passed before there was a reply. Was the President's proclamation authentic? asked Canning, having received it from the American Government at the hands of Monroe. And if so, would it be withdrawn on the disavowal of the act of Berkeley? As to the right of impressment, that was entirely beside the point. That right had been exercised by Britain 'ages previous to the establishment of the United States,' he said. Pleased with the thought, with an amused expression on his handsome face, he asked Monroe if he thought the recognition of independence meant that Britain virtually 'abdicated her own rights as a naval power.' Would not Monroe's instructions permit him to leave the right of impressment out? Monroe replied soberly that they would not. Thus far Monroe got in the negotiations and no farther.

Very soon, Canning lightly dismissed the idea of renewing negotiations on the treaty. However, a special envoy would be sent to Washington on the *Chesapeake* affair. Monroe packed at once for his departure, not without an affectionate farewell with Lord Holland, whom he liked, and with Auckland, whom he admired. The first of November found him bouncing on the winter waves.

v

A few days before he embarked, Congress had convened. The House at length moved into its beautiful quarters in what is now Statuary Hall. The hysteria had died down, as Jefferson had known it would, and, while the air was tense, there was every reason to hope that the lawmakers would proceed to their task with some restraint and moderation. On the opening days, Jefferson was deluged with congressional visitors, day and night. With seven of the eight years of his régime gone, he remained the complete master of the situation.

In the Senate, some familiar faces were missing. Tracy had died in the midst of the *Chesapeake* excitement and was the first to be buried in the new Congressional Cemetery. Henry Clay, who had filled an unexpired term, no longer was paying compliments to ladies or seeing the dawn from the card-table. Bayard remained the outstanding Federalist statesman in the chamber, though Timothy Pickering would speedily pitchfork his way to the leadership of his party. Among the Jeffersonians, the young William H. Crawford appeared upon the threshold of his great career, but Giles, with his genius for debate, was the chief reliance of the President.

In the House, Macon, pulled down by the weight of Randolph, did not even seek re-election to the Speakership, and the Jeffersonians elected Joseph B. Varnum, of Massachusetts, by a large majority. Josiah Quincy thought that 'he was just capable of going through the routine of the office — an automaton ready to move in any direction the magician who pulled the strings jerked him,' [1] but Quincy's estimates of political opponents are without value to history.

With Varnum's election, the plan to elect members of the committees was abandoned, since the elimination of Macon pronounced the doom of Randolph. Jefferson was too consummate a politician to go into battle with his forces led by a personal enemy. Gallatin was sorry to see Randolph displaced because of their personal relations.[2]

It was not difficult to drop Randolph now; his Quids had diminished to less than half a dozen discontents; his friend Macon was relegated to the ranks; his friend Nicholson had taken refuge on the bench. And Varnum appointed George W. Campbell, of Tennessee, to the chairmanship of the Ways and Means Committee. Lacking the erratic genius of Randolph, without his picturesque postures and phrasing, he was nevertheless a man of sound judgment, of good ability, and rich common sense. Madison was to think enough of his capacity to make him Secretary of the Treasury; Tennessee, enough to send him to the Senate; Monroe, enough to send him as Minister to Russia; and Andrew Jackson, enough to make him a member of the commission to settle the French spoliation claims. But Randolph, master of abuse, called him 'the prince of prigs and puppies,' which merely meant that Randolph did not like him.

---

[1] Bruce, I, 306.   [2] To his wife, Adams, *Gallatin*, 363.

It was to be a session of bitterness and personalities. Quincy was to write a reassuring letter to his wife. 'Allow yourself to entertain no apprehensions with regard to me,' he wrote. 'The times are difficult and a tempest is up in the sky, but that is the very moment to be fearless and collected. Fear nothing about my being stung or inflamed by the hornets of the House.'[1] Few men could be so abusive in parliamentary language as Quincy, who appeared regularly, that session, with his hair worked up 'into the most formidable queue at least three inches long and as big as a reasonable Dutch quill,' because his servant, who dressed him in the morning, insisted that hair thus was dressed in New York.[2]

VI

In some heat, Jefferson had written a spirited Message, which Gallatin had found smacking of a manifesto on the eve of war, and he had pleaded for 'caution of language and action which may give us some more time.'[3] Jefferson bowed to the criticism and moderated the tone.' 'I succeeded in getting it neutralized,' Gallatin wrote his wife.[4] Congress listened to the reading in tense silence.

Rapidly outlining the negotiations in London, Jefferson soon reached the *Chesapeake*. 'On this outrage no commentaries are necessary,' he said. 'Its character has been pronounced by the indignant voice of our citizens with an emphasis and unanimity never exceeded.' An armed vessel had been sent to England, Jefferson continued, with instructions to our envoy 'to call on the Government for the satisfaction and security required by the outrage,' and 'a very short interval' should 'bring the answer.' Meanwhile, the aggressions in American waters continued 'in defiance of the authority of the country.' This would necessarily lead 'to the policy either of never admitting an armed vessel into our harbors or of maintaining in every harbor such an armed force as may constrain obedience to the laws, and protect the lives and property of our citizens against their armed guests.'

In the Senate, and without debate, a bill covering all the re-

[1] *Quincy*, 117.   [2] *Ibid.*
[3] Adams, *Gallatin*, 362.   [4] *Ibid.*, 363.

quirements of Jefferson's policy was reported by John Quincy Adams and immediately passed, with Pickering, Goodrich, and Hillhouse alone in opposition.[1] It was quite another story in the House. Josiah Quincy, on mischief bent, and determined to embarrass the American Government in a crisis, opened the attack. He was the most dangerous because the most artful and coolest of the Federalist leaders. Not only was he a masterful debater and an accomplished orator, but he was a close logician and a consummate sophist. He had a genius for covering his real intent with a cloak of disinterestedness, and he could plunge a stiletto into a foe with the innocent expression of a child. In this instance, he solemnly proposed a committee to inquire into 'the circumstances of the attack' on the *Chesapeake*. It was his strategy to avoid the frontal attack, preferred by the Essex Junto, and to fall on the flank of the Administration. He had in mind a provision of the unpopular Jay Treaty that neither nation should resort to retaliation until the offending nation had refused to make reparations, and he interpreted this to mean that there should be no ordinary provisions for a defense in the interval.[2] But his resolution was voted down, four to one.

A few days later, he called for the President's proclamation. How dared the American President interdict British armed vessels from American waters without asking the consent of Congress? Was it not a rule of the British Parliament that this should be the procedure? Several members in amazement asked if it were possible that Quincy had not seen the proclamation in all the papers; but this resolution was adopted, with Eppes, son-in-law of Jefferson, voting for it. But nothing came of it.[3]

Then the Federalists shifted their attack. The Non-Importation Act had just gone into effect, and in the midst of a crisis involving both the honor and the sovereignty of the nation, they began to present petitions praying for repeal. A few days later, the November Orders in Council were announced, though not yet known in the States, and this was the moment chosen by Clay, of Pennsylvania, a friend of Randolph, to present a petition from the Federalist merchants of Philadelphia. It was an insolent party

[1] *Annals*, November 24 and December 1, 1807.
[2] *Ibid.*, November 5, 1807.　　　　[3] *Ibid.*, November 10, 1807.

screed. 'Your memorialists,' it said, 'cannot but view with extreme solicitude the apparent state of the negotiations between their country and Great Britain upon the events of which the safety of their property so materially depends. Their alarm and anxiety is increased by reports, perhaps unfounded, of the nature and extent of the demands made by the Government of the United States and cannot but be great while they are wholly destitute of information from official sources.'

Thus Erskine, the British Minister, sitting in the gallery, heard on the floor a declaration that Jefferson had made unreasonable and unjust demands, but that Congress, by granting the prayer of the petitioners, might intervene to end 'an unyielding adherence to doubtful or unsettled principles.' Canning would have loved the language and the spirit of the memorialists.

Is it possible or decent for Congress to receive such a petition? asked John Rowan, of Kentucky. Smilie, bowed with years, added his protest in quavering tones. 'Nor do I doubt that this memorial was intended to embarrass the operations of the Government and strengthen the British Government in their measures,' he said. Southard, of New Jersey, added his protest against a memorial which contained 'insinuations that the Executive has taken too high ground and demands things that are improper.' 'An insult to the House!' cried Campbell.

And then John Randolph rose to defend the memorialists, and give aid and comfort to the enemy. What! he exclaimed. 'Slap the doors in the petitioners' faces, affecting the airs of an Asiatic monarch?' Ridiculous! However, the House overwhelmingly refused the petition.[1]

But a new method of undermining the American position had been found, and time and again these petitions, denunciatory of the American contention, were presented and read; and time and again the British party, under the leadership of Quincy in the House and of Pickering in the Senate, harped upon the theme that Jefferson had made unfair and unreasonable demands. And in London, Canning read the reports of the support he was receiving and smiled his satisfaction.

[1] *Annals*, November 27, 1807.

VII

Even at this time, the British Government had issued its Orders in Council which literally outlawed American commerce from the seas. Monroe was just returning with the story of his failure. A British envoy was on his way, bearing, not an olive branch, but another insult.

On December 17, 1807, Jefferson learned from Armstrong, in Paris, of Napoleon's determination to enforce the Berlin Decree, and from English papers he learned of the new Orders in Council. Instantly he summoned his Cabinet. It was the unanimous opinion that pending fuller information on the new aggressions, American commerce should be totally suspended. On a used piece of paper on his desk, Jefferson scribbled his Embargo Message, and read it aloud to his councillors. The cautious Madison suggested that, pending official notice, it would be best to eliminate the reference to the Orders in Council. Jefferson drew his pen through the words. Gallatin, having at first given unqualified adherence, wrote Jefferson the same day, proposing that it be limited to a specified time.[1] Numerous notes were exchanged that day. Monroe was due on Sunday, two days later. Should the Message be held up for his arrival for possibly new information? Gallatin could see no reason for it. Very well, said Jefferson, would Gallatin come to the White House before ten-thirty so the Cabinet should be together 'before the Message goes out of our hands'?[2]

Thus the Cabinet again reviewed the document, and, an hour later, both branches of Congress were listening to one of the shortest and most significant of messages. 'The great and increasing danger with which our vessels and seamen and merchandise are threatened from the belligerent Powers of Europe' made it 'of the greatest importance to keep in safety these essential resources.' Therefore, Jefferson recommended 'an inhibition of the departure of our vessels from the ports of the United States.'[3]

Within an hour, the Message was in the hands of a Senate committee, with Adams as chairman, and within three hours it had passed, with the seven Federalists dissenting. In the House, the last word of the Message had scarcely been read when Ran-

---

[1] *Writings of Gallatin*, I, 368.
[2] *Ibid.*, I, 369.   [3] *Annals*, December 18, 1807.

OGRABME, or, The American Snapping-turtle.

The cartoon shows a British ship waiting for a load of tobacco while the turtle — Ograbme is the reverse spelling of Embargo — is preventing the sailor from loading the boat. The figure at the left is probably intended to represent Jefferson.

dolph sprang to his feet with a resolution that 'an embargo be laid on all shipping of the property of citizens of the United States now in port and which shall hereafter arrive.' [1] Had he not in the last session declared for an embargo and denounced Jefferson for not resorting to it? It was agreed to lay the resolution on the table temporarily, and that delay, by some weird process, changed John Randolph from a supporter to an enemy of the embargo and of his own resolution.

The Senate bill having reached the House, Randolph's resolution was shunted aside and the Senate measure taken up. The Federalist amendments to weaken the measure were promptly voted down. An attempt by the Federalists to adjourn was defeated. A vote immediately was forced, and, with Randolph voting against his own resolution, it passed, with the Federalists voting against it to a man. [2] The shameless somersault of Randolph had vindicated Jefferson's determination to have nothing of his leadership.

At first, the drastic measure met with general applause. The legislatures of ten States proclaimed it. Mass meetings cheered it with gusto. When experience soon called for more teeth in the law, Congress voted the supplementary measure. But the Federalists were on the rampage again. Was it not inspired by a desire to serve Napoleon? Soon they would be charging the Jeffersonians with being tools of the French, and a pistol shot at Bladensburg would be the answer. In Dedham, the dying Ames, within fifteen minutes of learning of the law, was writing that his 'heart suffered unusual pangs'; that he 'could not suppress some tears.' But he had no children and 'should not weep or even sigh to see a people carry chains.' Ames's brilliant but unscrupulous articles against the Administration had been suspended by a cold on his lungs, but he had now recovered 'to the state of [his] usual debility,' and would write some more. [3]

Meanwhile, Congress talked about Yazoo, about the wickedness of Wilkinson, and wasted precious days denouncing Washington as a place of residence. And along the coast, shippers were seeking to evade the Embargo Act. In the executive departments preparations for defense were being made.

---

[1] *Annals*, December 18, 1807.   [2] *Ibid.*, December 21, 1807.
[3] *Quincy*, 122.

And in the meantime, Rose, the special envoy from Canning, reached Washington.

VIII

George Henry Rose, son of an excellent father, and father of a distinguished son, was a young man then representing South-ampton in the Commons. His suavity and courtliness scarcely veiled a condescending sense of superiority, and the Americans offered him much amusement from the start. He came, not as an humble bearer of an apology for an indefensible act, but as a master, to impose conditions. That he came to insult rather than conciliate was evident before he landed at Norfolk. From the ship he sent word to Jefferson that he could not land if the procla-mation was to be applied to his vessel. He was informed that the proclamation clearly exempted ships on such a mission. This was not enough for the haughty envoy. Two weeks were lost in a silly exchange of notes.[1] The *Evening Post* in a glowing eulogy made much of his collaboration with Canning in the editing of the *Anti-Jacobin* and of his association, as secretary, with Pitt, and trusted that 'he will meet the reception to which he is on every account entitled.' [2]

It was not until January 14 that Rose reached the capital. When his packet was delayed by an accident below Mount Vernon, the Government dispatched a barge for him and he was taken to the Navy Yard. 'We venture confidently to say that every facility, toward his prompt reception, in the power of the Executive has been rendered,' said the *Independent Chronicle*.[3] The *Columbian Centinel* admitted that he had been graciously received by the Government, and added that 'if the Executive is not too deeply pledged to make common cause with Napoleon,' the mission would 'terminate amicably.' [4] The *Evening Post* sarcastically suggested that it 'must have been a deep policy in our Government to contrive it so that Mr. Rose when he first landed would be surprised and alarmed by the great naval force in this country.' [5] Thus did the Federalist press belittle their own country in a crisis in the face of the foe. It was all very amusing to Mr. Rose.

[1] *Columbian Centinel*, January 13, 1808.   [2] December 10, 1807.
[3] January 15, 1808.   [4] January 30, 1808.   [5] January 19, 1808.

In truth Mr. Rose was both amused and disgusted with Congress too. Swindlers, tailors, weavers, tavern-keepers! he snorted. And, on the very day he was received courteously by Jefferson, he began his pow-wows with Timothy Pickering, who had sternly set his feet in the path of disloyalty. In the charming Peters house in Georgetown, Rose and Pickering met at dinner. Pickering was moved to ecstasy. Rose was so 'placid,' so 'conciliatory' — his views so sound. Had he not spoken with scorn of Jefferson's refusal to submit the Monroe treaty to the Senate? Clearly, thought Pickering, here was a congenial soul. Rose thereafter joined the Federalist coterie.

Madison soon found that he was not on a mission of conciliation when the envoy coolly demanded, as a condition precedent for an apology, a disavowal and the withdrawal of the proclamation. Instead of giving him his passports, Madison proposed that the apology and the withdrawal of the proclamation should be simultaneous. Not content with rejecting this suggestion, Rose, with unfailing suavity, but not without embarrassment, added that among the acts 'required' by Canning as a condition to an apology was the disavowal of Commodore Barron by the United States! Madison listened with amazement. The Republic was asked publicly to proclaim a lie — that Barron had encouraged British sailors to desert. Madison instantly refused to discuss such a proposition, and, on February 14, Rose had his final interview. The little secretary never loomed larger than when he said his country never would make an 'expiatory sacrifice to obtain redress or beg for reparations.' Soon after that, Rose ceased to have any existence with the Administration.

Throughout all this, Rose was receiving all possible encouragement from the Federalists, and was able to inform Canning that the opposition party was strong enough to prevent Jefferson from making any effective opposition to British aggressions. The spirit of treason was rampant, and Pickering was leading the pack as he had in 1803–04.

Soon Pickering was writing confidentially to Rose that 'our best citizens consider the interests of the United States to be interwoven with those of Great Britain and that our safety depends on hers.' More: the opposition would manage to give to the measures of Government 'a direction mutually beneficial to the two nations.' [1] Just after this, and after Pickering and Rose had had their heads together, the former sent the envoy a letter from Rufus King, supporting the British position, with permission to carry the letter back with him to Canning. With gracious condescension, Rose acknowledged the letter and expressed chagrin because of his inability to visit the home of the Essex Junto, 'where for every reason I should find myself the most at home.' [2]

When Pickering was not writing Rose, he was groveling at his feet. In support of the gubernatorial candidacy of Christopher Gore, in Massachusetts, he had written for publication: 'Although Great Britain with her thousand ships of war could have destroyed our commerce, she has really done us no essential injury.' [3] Soon Pickering was calling on Rose with a letter from George Cabot, which was hostile to the Administration's defense of neutral rights. Fearing lest Rose fail to appreciate the significance of the views of the man who was to preside over the Hartford Convention, Pickering wrote that Cabot was a distinguished public man retired to the bosom of his family and 'a select society of friends.' Would not Rose re-read Cabot's letter with this in mind? And another letter had just arrived from Cabot: 'I send it to you for the same reason as the former.'

Pickering had been entranced with the kindly condescension of the cultured Englishman, and now Rose was returning to England. Perhaps a correspondence on Anglo-American affairs could be continued through the crisis. Pickering had a nephew in London. 'Let him, if you please, be the medium of whatever epistolary intercourse may take place between you and me,' he suggested. [4]

Now that Rose was going, he must assure his friend Pickering of his appreciation. 'I set a great price on Mr. Cabot's letter,' he wrote. 'The Essex Junto, such as you have the goodness to describe it to me, must be indeed an honorable fraternity, especially if its brethren are all such as the only one of them I have had the advantage of being personally acquainted with.' Of

---

[1] *Doc. N.E. Fed.*, 266.   [2] *Ibid.*, 368.
[3] *Independent Chronicle*, March 28, 1808.   [4] *Doc. N.E. Fed.*, 308.

course he would gladly avail himself 'of the means you offer me of communicating with you.' [1]

And Timothy Pickering was the father of the Logan law!

Thus Rose returned to advise Canning that Britain need not concern herself over Jefferson's Embargo, since England's partisans in America would prevent its effectual enforcement.

IX

The flattered Pickering now burned his bridges, indifferent whether the flames consumed his country. Bearing the Union Jack as literally as ever it was borne, he plunged into the fray. While living in the house with Quincy, his busy pen scratched paper by the hour in the preparation of a nullification pamphlet. It was a call to Massachusetts and the commercial States to join in refusing the enforcement of the Embargo. Pickering was more than twenty years in advance of Calhoun. 'It was the project of 1804, reproduced by the same individual who had then ineffectually urged Alexander Hamilton . . . to take part in the same design,' wrote John Quincy Adams.[2] When Governor Sullivan refused to receive it, the Federalist papers printed and made the most of it. The disunionists were in ecstasy; the British were delighted. Pickering was flooded with fulsome flattery. 'Impossible,' wrote Cabot, 'that your letter should be read throughout New England without producing great effect.' [3]

Pickering began by enumerating the causes for the laying of the Embargo, dishonestly ignoring the new Orders in Council. It was true that 'a considerable number of vessels were collected in our ports, and many held in suspense; not, however, from any new dangers that appeared, but *from the mysterious conduct of our affairs, after the attack on the Chesapeake.*' Monroe could have reached a settlement regarding the attack, but his instructions were to secure assurances that the impressment of the American seamen would cease; and this demand, Pickering pronounced 'at least of doubtful right.' And why the excitement about impressment? 'It is perfectly well known,' he wrote, that England desires 'to obtain only her own subjects, and that American citizens, impressed by mistake, are delivered up on duly authenticated

[1] *Doc. N.E. Fed.*, 370. [2] *Ibid.* [3] *Pickering*, IV, 129.

proof.' And an insignificant number impressed at worst. And why did Jefferson refuse to send the diplomatic correspondence with France about the Milan Decree? Did they contain the demands of Napoleon? And confidence in the President in a crisis? 'It is that unbounded confidence that is our danger.' And after all, had not Britain 'with her thousand ships' been most considerate, when she could have wiped our commerce from the seas? An astonishing public paper, conceding as a probable right the impressment of American seamen and the seizure of American ships, ignoring the last Orders in Council, deliberately misrepresenting the number of Americans impressed, and insisting that when Americans were taken 'by mistake' they were speedily released. And so difficult to tell an Englishman from an American! exclaimed Pickering. Perhaps the negroes taken from the *Chesapeake* were natives of Surrey! So hard to tell.[1]

The effect intended was the destruction of national solidarity, incitation of men to violations of the law, and to defiance of the National Government. Even the gravest and most dignified of the Federalist leaders busied themselves with the circulation of the seditious screed. Wagner, editor of the *Baltimore North American*, wrote that personally he had sent three hundred copies to the German counties and put them in the hands of the 'right people.'[2] Cabot soon was writing that there had been so many editions that 'I have at last lost my reckoning,' but that at least twenty-five thousand in pamphlet form had been distributed, and more than double that number in the newspapers.[3] Rose, to whom the obsequious Pickering had sent a copy, voiced the British gratitude. 'Your modesty would suffer if you were aware of the sensation produced in this country,' he wrote with unctuous flattery. And then, with the two nations on the verge of war, he glowingly described the thriving conditions in England. 'Our public spirit is high,' he wrote. 'Finances in a state of unexampled prosperity.'[4] Rose hoped to encourage his American correspondent.

From Boston, thousands of copies were sent into Maine. Thousands were printed in Springfield, Northampton, and Boston. A citizen of Salem was sure that hundreds of thousands had been

---

[1] *Columbian Centinel*, March 12, 1808, four columns.
[2] *Pickering*, IV, 133.   [3] *Ibid.*   [4] *Doc. N.E. Fed.*, 371.

distributed throughout New England. 'We have full proof of the zeal,' he wrote. 'We must wait to see the consequences.' But in Salem the pamphlet had no effect, for there the Jeffersonians increased their vote that spring.[1]

John Quincy Adams had read the Pickering pamphlet with rising wrath. Seizing his pen he wrote a scathing reply addressed to Harrison Gray Otis, but before sending it on its travels he submitted it to a friend to see if he had treated his colleague with 'sufficient delicacy.' Immeasurably more brilliant as a writer, he had every intellectual advantage in the contest; but his moral advantage, with his letter predicated on undeniable facts, was even greater. How dared Pickering ignore the Orders in Council as a primary justification for the Embargo! 'Orders once submitted to and carried to the extent of their principles would not have left an inch of American canvas upon the ocean but under British license and British taxation.' And concede the right of impressment? 'Proceeding from a Senator of the United States, specially charged with the maintenance of the nation's rights against foreign Powers, and at a moment extremely critical of pending negotiations, this formal abandonment of the American cause, this summons to unconditional surrender to the pretensions of our antagonist, is to my mind highly alarming.' Turning to Pickering's brazen lie that scarcely any Americans had been impressed, Adams lashed him with the official figures; and replying to Pickering's assertion that when 'mistakes' were made the Americans were speedily released, he easily demonstrated the utter dishonesty of the statement. And in passages of real eloquence he met Pickering's insinuations about the 'mysterious conduct' of the American Government after the attack on the *Chesapeake* with scornful references to the insolent conditions imposed by Canning for an apology — the withdrawal of the proclamation, the disavowal of Barron.[2]

Soon Adams's reply was appearing in the Jeffersonian papers, but it failed to get the circulation the zeal of the nullifiers had given Pickering's.[3] It called down damnation on Adams's head

---

[1] Bentley, *Diary*, III, 359.

[2] *Independent Chronicle*, March 12, 1808, eight columns.

[3] Adams, *Diary*, I, 525.

from the Federalists. He had taken his stand with his country, just as years later he would turn upon his party in defense of Andrew Jackson in an international controversy. It was the Adams way. Soon he would be driven from the Senate.

x

Meanwhile, the bitterness had reached the verge of hysteria. The Federalists more openly were declaring that Jefferson and his supporters were taking orders from Napoleon. At length the climax came in a particularly offensive attack by Gardenier, of New York, a rough, uncouth man, a mere cipher in history, but for the moment the very symbol of his party. Urged on by less courageous allies, he threw all discretion to the winds. In the last days of December, he had gone beyond all decent bounds in an attack described by the *New York Evening Post* as 'one of the severest speeches ever pronounced in Congress against the present executive.' [1] Encouraged by his immunity on this occasion and by the applause of his friends, he soon returned to the attack. Could anyone doubt, he asked, that the Embargo had been laid at the instance of Napoleon? 'Is the nation prepared for this?' he demanded. 'If you wish to try whether they are, tell them at once what is your object — tell them what you mean — tell them that you mean to take part with the Great Pacificator; or else stop your present course. Do not go on forging chains to fasten us to the car of the imperial conqueror.'

Many members were instantly on their feet calling him to order. Varnum calmly hoped the speaker would 'keep within the rules of propriety.' Smiling on his little band of partisans, and now grown cocky, he called Varnum to 'order.' 'It is impossible, sir, for me to speak and keep order in the House at the same time.' Again he was called to order.

Montgomery, of Maryland, immediately rose, pale but coldly calm. Charges of the most infamous character had been made in the House involving the honor of Jefferson and all his party. Would it not be well to adjourn until the morrow when, in a cooler atmosphere, the offense could be considered? 'Let the gentleman from New York establish his charges,' he said. 'If he does so,

[1] December 28, 1807.

those persons under the secret influence must immediately be expelled. If he does not, some other course must be taken in regard to the gentleman.' [1]

The House adjourned in a state of excitement.

The *Evening Post* soon would insinuate that a dueling conspiracy existed, with Campbell, the leader, Montgomery, of Maryland, and Johnson, of Kentucky, as principals. Had they not met in the Speaker's rooms? Were they not all unmarried men? Was not Campbell considered 'one of the best shots in the United States'? [2]

However that may be, on the morrow Johnson rose. 'A base and unprincipled calumny,' he said. 'And what I have said I am glad I did not say until this morning, because it is now deliberately said.'

Campbell then rose, speaking slowly and without excitement. If the charge is true, he said, it should be established that there might be 'a total renovation of the national councils.' If false, 'it ought to consign their authors to disgraceful infamy — an infamy that should mark them out as common calumniators and hold them forth as fit subjects of national contempt.' It was one thing for petty scribblers to circulate lies of French influence, 'but when these charges are borrowed ... and echoed on the floor, it is high time they should be noticed. ... Issue is now joined, and the guilty, whoever they may be, whether the accused or the accuser, must stand forth to receive the sentence of public indignation.'

Montgomery rose. 'Insolent, false, and unfounded!' he said. [3]

The *Evening Post* pronounced these replies 'indecent,' and was sure that whatever the event 'it will be found that our friend is incapable of disgracing himself by shrinking from any responsibility.' [4] Thus the Federalists, more cautious, were quite willing to stand behind Gardenier and see him shot.

Gardenier made no reply on the floor. Instead, he sent Senator White, of Delaware, to Campbell with a challenge. White was referred to Eppes, the son-in-law of Jefferson, and the challenge was accepted. Within two days a group of men might have been

[1] *Annals*, February 20, 1808.   [2] March 17, 1808.
[3] *Annals*, February 28, 1808.   [4] *Ibid.*, February 29, 1808.

seen meeting on a hilltop near Georgetown and walking along the
main road toward Montgomery courthouse, until they passed
the territorial line. But finding themselves surrounded by scores
of men, women, and children spectators, they were forced to defer
the meeting. 'To the utter astonishment of the parties,' wrote
Quincy to his wife, 'they found a hundred and fifty persons . . .
on the spot marked out for the bloody arena, collected with no
desire to prevent, but to share in the pleasures of the spectacle.' [1]
Three days later, the duelists made a more circumspect departure,
jolting over the rough road to Bladensburg. The seconds paced
the distance, loaded the pistols, gave the signal, and Gardenier fell
with a bullet through his body. Campbell immediately returned
to his seat in the House 'as though nothing had happened.' [2]

The stricken man was carried to the nearby home of a bitter
Federalist, and soon Quincy was writing in a different mood. He
had just returned from Bladensburg, whither he had hurried with
Dana, of Connecticut. He found the 'scene heartrending.' That
night Quincy sat through the night with the winged eagle, and the
Federalists took turns at his side until all danger was past. John
Quincy Adams, who had been described by Gardenier a month
before as 'a scoundrel,' [3] dismissed the charge against Jefferson
and his Administration as a lie.

Thereafter the charges of French influence from men in actual
secret communication with British Ministers and agents were
confined to the fireplaces of the Federalist boarding-houses. But
the Federalist 'scribblers' continued their insinuations, and the
Evening Post, after a slurring attack on Montgomery, was forced
to retract.[4] But Gardenier became a hero, and soon merchants
in New York City were giving him a dinner with Rufus King,
Gouverneur Morris, and Harrison Gray Otis among those paying
homage; and a toast was drunk to Timothy Pickering — 'The
modern Cincinnatus: he would have equaled the best of the
Romans in the best days of Rome.' [5] And on July 4, in a New
York village, the Federalists celebrated by burning the author of
the Declaration of Independence in effigy.[6]

[1] *Quincy*, 134–35; *Evening Post*, March 17, 1808.   [2] Adams, *Diary*, I, 517.

[3] Gardenier to King, *King's Corr.*, v, 68.   [4] April 11, 1808.

[5] *Evening Post*, April 22, 1808.   [6] *Ibid.*, July 25, 1808.

XI

For these were the days of raw bones and bloody noses. The hate of the Federalists did not even spare the dead. At the funeral of the excellent Crowninshield at Salem, a relative of Pickering's appeared at the services to insult the mourners.[1] In Washington, General Wilkinson was challenging Randolph, who replied that he would fight only with gentlemen, and the warrior was threatening to placard the town with his opinion of the man of Roanoke. Pike who had scaled the heights that bear his name was making gusty love to unmarried ladies, forgetful of his wife at home, and bearing Wilkinson's challenge to Randolph. Robert Fulton was begging Congress for an opportunity to demonstrate his torpedo, and, under the persuasion of Jefferson, a few attended at Barlow's home in Rock Creek. The friends of Madison and Monroe were at swords' points. The residents of Washington were trembling in their boots as a long debate roared in the Capitol over a proposed removal of the capital from the swamps.[2] In the White House and in the executive offices, preparations and plans for the national defense were being pushed.

As the session neared its close, an unsuccessful effort to repeal the Embargo Act was made, and this attempt, together with the adoption of a resolution authorizing Jefferson to lift the Embargo during the recess if he saw fit, gave the Federalists ample opportunity for propaganda.

But, henceforth, Jefferson's battle for the Embargo was to be 'in the streets,' where disloyalty and lawlessness were in the open. It is time for us to view this scene, and to observe the superb courage and determination with which he fought, to understand the tremendous significance of his policy — for he was seeking a civilized substitute for war.

[1] Bentley, *Diary*, III, 356.   [2] *Annals*, February 2-8, 1808.

CHAPTER XXI

Treason Mounts and Rides Again

I

FROM the watch-tower at the White House, Jefferson surveyed strange scenes, compared with which those of the Whiskey Rebellion and Shays's Rebellion were of utter insignificance, though the same vital principles of nationality were involved. He had not adopted the Embargo with perfect confidence that it would rectify the nation's wrongs. He did not plan it merely to punish the British in their trade. He had come into power at the moment of the complete collapse of all international law. The Napoleonic Wars had pulverized Grotius and Vattel beneath the wheels of the artillery, and anarchy presided over the international relations of nations. Jefferson, with a statesman's vision, was seeking to lay the foundation of a new system, substituting the adjudication of law and reason for the sword. He faced the situation with the unblinking eyes of a realist, and knew that the young Republic had just two alternatives — the Embargo or war.

And Jefferson hated war. He had reduced the taxes; he had paid off an astounding portion of the public debt; with the anticipated accumulation of a surplus in the Treasury, he had formed a majestic program of internal improvements. War would undo much his genius had achieved, piling up more debt, increasing taxes, retarding improvements — and he hated war.

Even so, the Republic dare not submit tamely to the insults heaped upon it, and, unless he followed in the savage bloody footprints of the past, he had to find a new weapon of retaliation. Thus he had adopted the Embargo, pronounced, by one of the few unprejudiced students of the experiment, 'perhaps the most perfect substitute for war up to that time devised.' [1] 'I take it,' Jefferson wrote Madison in March, 'to be the universal opinion that war will become preferable to a continuation of the Embargo after a certain time. Should we not, therefore, avail ourselves of the intervening period to procure a retraction of the obnoxious decrees peaceably if possible?' [2]

It was not the case of a blind, infatuated man assuming the impossible and ridiculous without sound reasons for hoping for success. The fortunes of war had all but shut Britain from European markets. The Embargo would close the American market, the most lucrative of them all. It would cause some distress at home, but it might result in 'starving our enemies.' [3] Jefferson had found the people 'unanimous in their preference of the Embargo to war,' and he expected 'pressure on the throne from the suffering people of England.' [4] Already British merchants, manufacturers, and the most important of publicists were protesting that a commercial war with the United States would mean the ruin of England. 'We have only to shut our ports and remain firm,' wrote J. Barnes, an American living in Italy, in a letter to Jefferson. 'The people of England would do the rest, for British manufacturers being precluded from the continent of Europe, almost entirely their chief resource is the United States. Consequently about one hundred and fifty thousand manufacturers, being thrown out of bread, would rise in mass and compel the Minister to open the ports at any price.' From James Bowdoin, Jefferson had a similar prediction. The Ministry, he thought, would be forced to recall the Orders 'to recover the advantages of our commerce ' since England's 'critical situation with respect to the Continental Powers, the distressed state of her manufacturers at home ... must throw so many embarrassments in the way of her continuing the war without a better understanding with the United States.'

Here was England, engaged in a deadly combat with a mortal foe, excluded from the markets of Europe, which, in normal times, and up to the time of the Embargo, disposed of one third

[1] L. M. Sears, *Jefferson and the Embargo*, 3.   [2] *Writings of Jefferson*, xii, 11.
[3] To Rodney, *ibid.*, xii, 36.   [4] To Thomas Leiper, *ibid.*, xii, 65.

of all she sold in the world to the United States. Jefferson was hopeful that the closing of the American market, if rigidly enforced, would soon drive England to terms without the drawing of the sword.

II

Almost overnight, the extreme Federalists, dominated by the Essex Junto, turned nullificationists, smugglers, if not secessionists and traitors. The Southern and Middle States presented a loyal front. Jefferson was convinced of this when, astride his horse, he rode slowly through Virginia to Monticello, chatting with planters and villagers. 'I have been happy in my journey through the country,' he wrote, 'to find the people unanimous in their preference of the Embargo to war.' [1] Himself a planter, he was suffering with the rest. In the South where the planters were badly hurt, he was to find the most inspiring loyalty throughout. Only in rare, isolated spots did he find exceptions. Fears of insurgency from the politically minded Charles Pinckney, Governor of South Carolina, were baseless. [2] Only at Newberry, South Carolina, where there was a nest of Tories, carrying Pickering's pamphlet in their pockets, was there disloyalty, and a citizen of the town wrote that 'the majority . . . are as loyal subjects to John Bull in their hearts as any about St. James's.' [3] In North Carolina, the rigidity of enforcement by the collector caused resentment, and Gallatin was not unsympathetic toward the protests. [4] Only at New Orleans in the South was there serious laxity, when the collector permitted forty vessels to clear after the Embargo was in effect on the technical ground that he did not have a copy. Gallatin was furious, and in a severe letter of rebuke ordered him to 'enforce the penalties against the owners of every vessel that sailed with knowledge of the law.' [5] In Mississippi, in the infancy of its agricultural and commercial development, the Embargo fell with crushing effect. Every instinct of selfishness cried out against it, but Mississippi stood stoutly with Jefferson amidst the wreckage of its hopes. 'Everyone wishes

[1] To Leiper, *Writings of Jefferson*, XII, 65.   [2] Sears, 80.
[3] Sears, 96-97.   [4] To Jefferson, *Writings of Gallatin*, I, 399.
[5] To Jefferson, *ibid.*, I, 373.

the Embargo raised,' wrote a Mississippian, 'but not until the object for which it was laid is effected, or it is found insufficient to effect it.' [1]

In the Middle States, and especially in Pennsylvania, there was no hue and cry against the law. 'I am much pleased,' wrote Jefferson, 'with the sentiments of the Federalists of Philadelphia as to the Embargo, and that they are not in sentiment with the insurgents of the North.' [2] In truth, the more fluid capital there was able to take full advantage of the compensating possibilities of the measure, and the people thrived.[3] The hostility of the old Tory and aristocratic element did not interest Jefferson at all, but he was puzzled and annoyed by the opposition of the Quakers to a policy seeking a substitute for war.[4]

Thus Jefferson concluded that the opposition was largely sectional. 'While the opposition has in one quarter amounted almost to rebellion and treason,' he wrote, 'it is pleasing to know that all the rest of the nation has approved of the proceedings of the constituted authorities.' [5] But if giving aid and comfort to the enemy, and preaching and practicing the nullification of a law designed to force a hostile nation to reasonable terms be treason, there was swashbuckling, flamboyant treason abroad in the land.

III

Under the inspiration of Rose's secret correspondent, Timothy Pickering, and under the guidance of the Essex Junto, Massachusetts was swept into rebellion as open and defiant as that of Shays. The Boston press teemed with denunciations of the Embargo and justifications of the Orders in Council. Actual mobs were inflamed by demagogues into using violence to prevent enforcement. Loyalists were subjected to foul abuse, persecution, and social ostracism. Villages and towns adopted resolutions prepared and distributed by the Essex Junto.

And Timothy Pickering, the secret correspondent of the British envoy, was acclaimed a hero. Soon after the publication of his pamphlet, he returned to Salem to be received with laurels and

---

[1] Sears, 100.   [2] To Short, *Writings of Jefferson*, XII, 159.
[3] Sears, 62.   [4] Sears, 105.   [5] *Writings of Jefferson*, XII, 190.

homage. A brave show was made by the cavalcade of swaggering young equestrians and Federalist politicians in carriages that escorted him into Salem from his farm. The streets were filled; vessels in Beverly Harbor displayed their flags; a salute was fired from a ship when the Essex drawbridge was reached. A band played him into the stately home of General Derby, and, with Josiah Quincy on the platform, he attacked his country in the face of its foe.[1] But there was bitter resentment, too. 'Who the wretches were who conducted this insult to the Government, I never asked,' wrote Bentley. 'I left the town and spent the day at Nahant.' But he learned that 'the people were with difficulty restrained from violence.' Toward the close of the evening, Pickering was burned in effigy in various parts of the town, but there was no rioting.[2] Even the *Salem Gazette*, a bit concerned by the insolence of the exhibition, announced that the affair was 'rather an act of hospitality than an insult to the Government.' [3] But, with the spreading of the news, rage was by no means confined to Salem. Some time before, Pickering had been hanged and burned in effigy in a suburb of Philadelphia. Notices had invited the public to the hanging and the burning. A gibbet would be erected at the Town Hall in the Northern Liberties, said the notice. Pickering would be hanged in effigy, 'having the British Orders in Council hanging to his neck, and the French decrees to his heels.' Everyone was 'invited to the exit of a traitor,' and Pickering's friends especially were challenged to rescue him if they dared. They did not dare.[4]

IV

At that time there dwelt in Salem the very antithesis of Pickering, one whose self-sacrificing devotion to his country has not had a proper historical recognition. William Gray was one of the richest and most progressive merchants and shipowners of his time. Nine years before, Timothy Pickering had said that 'William Gray is a man of unspotted character, and for mercantile talents and extent of business, the first merchant in the United States.' A man of business vision, with the audacity of business genius, he

---

[1] *Pickering*, IV, 134–36.   [2] Bentley, *Diary*, III, 361.
[3] *Ibid.*, III, 362.   [4] *Pickering*, IV, 159.

had been among the first shipowners to penetrate to the markets of Russia, China, and India. A youthful patriot, he had marched with his company to Lexington. At the time the Embargo was adopted, he was a Federalist member of the State Senate from Salem. As honest and downright in his thinking as he was in business dealings, as kindly as he was rich, he was the foremost citizen of his community. The Gilbert Stuart portrait reveals the rugged honesty, the grim determination, and the underlying kindliness of the man. A Federalist and a friend of Pickering's, respected by the merchants of the Essex Junto, he remained a robust American. That was his offense.

Just after the nullification meeting in Salem, a few friends, gathered at the farm of Speaker Varnum, were discussing the sensational rumor that in Boston, Gray was opposing the resolution denouncing the Embargo.[1] The next day a bomb exploded in the camp of the nullificationists — Gray had opposed the resolution robustly, and vigorously had defended Jefferson! The disloyal board of strategy in Boston had been sitting for two months on his case, when young Stephen Higginson was assigned the task of framing a bitter personal attack for publication in the *Salem Gazette*.[2] When the demand of Gray's friends wrung from the editor the name of the author, young Higginson lamely explained that his information came from Salem. In its utter disregard of truth, it bore the imprint of Pickering's genius in duplicity. Again the disloyalists were in consternation, scurrying about like rats caught in a cage, seeking vainly to hide themselves.[3]

And then, with superb courage and self-respect, Gray himself took up the glove thrown down, in a letter to the *Gazette*. 'I have presumed to think for myself,' he wrote, 'and made the Constitution my guide.' The charge of Jefferson's subserviency to France was absurd. Why was Gray supporting the Embargo? 'I thought it a constitutional measure and I did not think proper to oppose it.' And why did he justify it? Because the Orders in Council and the Milan Decree had made it necessary, unless the Republic was prepared to declare war against the two most powerful nations in the world. 'After these restrictions on our commerce, had not the

---

[1] Bentley, *Diary*, III, 364.   [2] *Ibid.*, III, 375.

[3] *Ibid.*, III, 376.

Embargo been laid, I think a great part of our vessels sent to the
continent of Europe would have been captured and condemned by
the British, and probably the remnant would have fallen into the
hands of the French.' And then? 'The effect on the public mind
would have produced war,' and this, added to the immense loss
due to capture and condemnation, must have been 'a greater evil
than the Embargo.' Why this view of the fate of American
vessels? 'Out of seven vessels which sailed from this district for
the continent of Europe in the month preceding the commencement of the Embargo, *not one ever reached its destination in safety.*'

Then, turning to the vilification part of young Higginson's
screed: 'It is insinuated that I am growing rich, while others are
suffering by the Embargo. I have not reaped any advantage from
it that I know of, in any way whatever; those who know me can
say whether I have benefited others, or taken advantage of their
necessity. So far from reaping profit from the Embargo, my estate
has declined more than ten per cent.' [1]

The disloyalists were beside themselves with rage. How dare a
son of Salem, rich and distinguished, defend the works of Jefferson! Soon the hounds of petty persecution were snapping at his
heels, and, socially 'excluded from all his former associates,' the
foremost citizen of Salem was insulted with impunity.[2] At length
he moved to Boston, and there his loyalty to the American
Government drove him speedily into the party of Jefferson. Never
wavering in his devotion to his country, he loyally supported
Madison in the War of 1812 when his erstwhile friends were in
open treason; and his last public act was to preside over a dinner
at Faneuil Hall in celebration of the election of John Quincy
Adams.

An outstanding patriot of his time, an American of abundant
common sense and impeccable integrity, who placed his country
above his party, he has been shabbily treated by history.

v

But more annoying than the fulminations of Pickering was the
flabbiness or timidity of Governor Sullivan of Massachusetts, one
of Jefferson's own men. He was not a self-effacing politician, and

---

[1] Sears, 172–74.   [2] Bentley, *Diary*, III, 417.

WILLIAM GRAY
From a portrait by Stuart

he was too easily intimidated by the noisy clamor of the disloyalists. Jefferson had adopted a system of licensing merchants for
the importation of flour and other products to provide food for domestic consumption only, and had lodged the licensing power with
the governors, rather than with the collectors, as Gallatin had
preferred.[1] But Gallatin later was to concede that all the governors had been loyal — all but one. That one was Sullivan, of
Massachusetts.

He found it hard to deny appeals for licenses from the merchants and shippers who were his friends.[2] The licenses of Sullivan
soon became a public scandal. Gallatin, poring over his reports,
was utterly amazed at the number of licenses from Sullivan.
'Governor Sullivan dare not refuse flour certificates,' he wrote
Jefferson. 'One mail brought me permits for eleven thousand
barrels.'[3] It was absurd to assume that all Sullivan's flour was intended for consumption in Massachusetts. Thereafter, Sullivan's
reports were scanned with increasing wonder. Two months later,
Gallatin was calling Jefferson's attention to the insatiable appetite
for flour in Sullivan's State. By that time, he had issued certificates for 49,000 barrels of flour, 99,400 bushels of corn, and he had
just issued licenses for more, bringing the whole up to 57,000
barrels of flour and 129,400 bushels of corn. Poring over the
record, Gallatin was enraged to find that Sullivan had given certificates 'for persons resident in Alexandria or Georgetown of whom
he could know nothing.'[4]

Jefferson could see but one possible explanation — the produce
was destined for British consumption. He knew Sullivan's personal
integrity precluded the possibility that he was selling licenses, and
he ascribed his conduct to the timidity of a politician in a hotbed
of opposition. He had been a faithful follower of Jefferson, and
that master of tact so phrased a letter as not to give offense. Calling attention to the extraordinary number of licenses, he said,
blandly, that 'as these supplies, although called for within the
space of two months, will undoubtedly furnish the consumption of
your State for a much longer time, I have thought it advisable to

[1] *Writings of Gallatin*, i, 390.
[2] Thomas Amory, *Life of James Sullivan*, ii, 293.
[3] *Writings of Gallatin*, i, 393.   [4] *Ibid.*, i, 394.

ask the favor of your Excellency ... to discontinue issuing any other certificates, that we may not unnecessarily administer facilities to the evasion of the Embargo Law.'[1] But Sullivan was too penetrating not to feel the force of the blow beneath the velvet glove, and the immediate reaction was one of resentment and rebellion. He had no desire to shoulder the burden of these licenses, he wrote. He had consented only to save the people from actual hunger. Jefferson evidently was oblivious to the fact that, despite these heavy importations, there had been no fall in the price of flour — thus strengthening Jefferson's case against him by the admission. The refusal of more licenses would mean rioting and convulsions, to the mortification of the Administration. And, he added, it was not easy to deal with smuggling in Massachusetts, where the habit had been formed in the days of the Royal Government.[2] However, he would do the best he could.

But two months later it was found that his best was none too good, and Gallatin again was calling Jefferson's attention to the heavy licensing of Sullivan, with the comment that much of the food was intended for exportation. The facilities for smuggling to the British were excellent, with Nova Scotia not far away, and with British vessels hovering in the waters of the State to take the smuggled goods.[3] Another two months, and Jefferson, thoroughly aroused, was ready to break with Sullivan and with Levi Lincoln, the Lieutenant-Governor, who, in Sullivan's absence, was carrying on. 'As we know,' he wrote Lincoln, 'the Sullivan licenses there have overstocked the wants of the Eastern States with flour; the proposal to carry more there is in itself suspicious, and therefore even regular traders ought not to be allowed.' More flour for Nantucket, as Lincoln had requested? There was no need there, unless Nantucket had exported the flour she had received. Did not Lincoln know that Sullivan's permits actually were sold in the markets of Alexandria and elsewhere? No doubt, Sullivan had been actuated by a spirit of kindness, but this had degenerated into unpardonable weakness.[4]

Thus, in the State where the opposition was the most disloyal, Jefferson could not count on the loyalty of his old friends.

[1] *Writings of Jefferson*, xii, 99.   [2] Sears, 81–83.
[3] *Writings of Gallatin*, i, 418.   [4] Sears, 89.

VI

And the enemy there, mounted, booted, and spurred, was riding defiantly over the laws and flaunting constituted authority as brazenly as Shays in his much-denounced rebellion, and with far more cowardice. Even the State courts were presuming to sit on the constitutionality of a national law, and refusing to enforce it against its violators. Gallatin soon found that Sullivan's warning that the loyalty of the State courts could not be counted upon had been moderately phrased.[1]

When officials seized articles found even on board vessels, the courts made the collectors the culprits, until they were threatened with financial ruin. 'Until Congress meets,' advised Gallatin, 'we must depend entirely on force for checking this manner of violating the law.' [2] To reduce law to mockery, the district court at Salem spent several days hearing debates on the constitutionality of the law, for political purposes. 'No ridicule is spared, no insult,' wrote an observer. 'But the people see the design.' [3]

Meanwhile, the Boston Federalist papers were preaching nullification and encouraging violence. The *Boston Gazette* was inflaming the people with attempts to show that Massachusetts would bear the greater part of the burden and suffer irreparable loss.[4]

The *New England Palladium* was extending itself in insulting Jefferson. He had adopted the Embargo on the demand of Napoleon. The people would, and should, defy the law.[5]

Pickering and the Essex Junto feverishly were writing insulting petitions and peddling them out to their tools in villages and towns.[6] So many of these poured in on Gallatin that he discontinued showing them to Jefferson.[7]

Ships were sailing without clearances to unload their cargoes on British vessels nearby, or for conveyance to Nova Scotia or Bermuda.[8]

Under the incitation of demagogues, there was a forcible resistance to the enforcement of the law in Gloucester; and when Gallatin called the crime to the attention of the district attorney, nothing was done.

---

[1] Sears, 84.   [2] To Jefferson, *Writings of Gallatin*, I, 396.
[3] Bentley, *Diary*, III, 388.   [4] Sears, 149.   [5] October 14, 1805.
[6] *Writings of Gallatin*, I, 407.   [7] *Ibid.*, I, 413.   [8] *Ibid.*, I, 336.

At Newburyport, when the collector tried to prevent a ship from sailing without clearance, the worst of the rabble collected on the wharf, and the vessel sailed under the protection of the mob.[1]

Not content with the co-operation of the scourings of the wharves and dives, the disloyalists tried to disaffect the militia, preaching treason even to the armed forces of constituted authority. The Legionary Brigade of Massachusetts denounced the attempt with a public proclamation of its devotion 'to their Country, its Constitution, its Government, and its laws,' and to Jefferson it pledged 'effectual support to such measures as our Government may further adopt.' [2]

Nor, otherwise, was loyalty unique in Massachusetts. The *Independent Chronicle*, of Boston, in a stirring appeal for the Embargo, denounced the Essex Junto with gusto.[3] It pronounced the Federalist faction traitors in the service of England. With them 'even Burr has become a patriot of the first water.' [4]

When the disloyalists of Boston in mass meeting denounced the law, and the loyalists replied with spirit, Jefferson acknowledged their pledge of loyalty. Conceding the debatability of Embargo or war, he regretted 'that overlooking the real source of our sufferings, the British and French edicts, which constitute the actual blockade of our foreign commerce and navigation, they have ... imputed them to laws which have saved them from greater, and have preserved for our own use our vessels, property, and seamen, instead of adding them to the strength of those with whom we might eventually have to contend.' [5] In Plymouth, where the silence of the shipyards was severely felt, the shipbuilders, with the fine spirit of William Gray, assured Jefferson that 'we venerate the laws of our country, we respect its constituted authorities, we will submit to every privation necessary to preserve our just rights and independence as a nation.' [6] At Rochester, in Plymouth County, a mass meeting was called and 'wagons were procured to transport the halt and lame to the meeting,' and one cripple, who missed a conveyance, 'came three miles on crutches.' [7] From

[1] *Writings of Gallatin*, I, 405.   [2] Sears, 129.
[3] December 31, 1807.   [4] January 4, 1808.
[5] *Independent Chronicle*, September 19, 1808.
[6] Sears, 103.   [7] *Independent Chronicle*, September 22, 1808.

Tisbury, Noblesborough, Scarboro, Monmouth, went forth ringing denunciations of the disloyalists, and pledges of support to
Jefferson.[1]

In Marblehead, not a suspicious incident marred the scene, and
in Salem the record was almost as bright, though Pickering was
snooping about, organizing a resistance that would win the contemptuous smile of Rose in London.[2] To the distress of the Essex
Junto, the Massachusetts farmers remained loyal. The misty
eyes of Federalist politicians over the farmer's plight had no
effect. 'Not one murmur ... do we hear from the "poor" farmers,'
said the *Essex Register*. 'Only the merchants of Boston and their
hireling editors, the monied speculators,' were concerned.[3] Even
the *Connecticut Courant* lamented that the farmers of New England were not disloyal to their Government.[4] Nor were the infant
industries of New England found under Pickering's disloyal
banner, since, taking advantage of the opportunities offered by the
Embargo, they were prospering beyond precedent. The Boston
merchants denounced them, and the shoemakers of Lynn replied
with denunciations of their own.[5]

But Massachusetts in large measure was in full rebellion, and
when goods were successfully smuggled to the British across the
border, the Essex Junto shouted with glee — 'So much for
starving the British!'

VII

Along the Canadian border in New York and Vermont, conditions were as bad. In the region of Lake Champlain there was
open and defiant insurrection. Rafts loaded with flour and corn at
the wharves of the lake sailed jauntily to Montreal, guarded by
from fifty to a hundred gunmen, ready to fire into the officers of the
law.[6] Soon pitched battles were being fought, with Pickering's
men shoulder to shoulder with the men from across the border.
'That for starving the British!' shouted the rebels as they sailed
away. The *New York Evening Post* was delighting the disloyalists
at this time with a note from London: 'You will be glad to know

---

[1] *Independent Chronicle*, September 22, 1808.   [2] Bentley, *Diary*, III, 389.
[3] Sears, 180.   [4] *Ibid.*, 181.   [5] *Ibid.*, 166.
[6] *Ibid.*, 187–88.

that our harvest is excellent and well got in, that our exports are immense and increasing rapidly, and that we are getting naval stores from St. Petersburg openly and undisturbedly.' [1] And 'that for starving the British!' laughed the foes of Jefferson. The *Post* had followed this up with another letter from London to the effect that the Embargo actually had served Britain well. Too bad that America was suffering.[2]

Meanwhile, Jefferson's friend, the first John Jacob Astor, was keeping the President informed of the Canadian expectations; [3] and Aaron Burr was doing his bit for Pickering. On taking flight from his own country, he was obliged, by stormy weather, to take refuge at Halifax, where the Governor Provost of Nova Scotia was a relative, through marriage. The *Columbian Centinel* had boasted that he had been received 'as a distinguished citizen,' and the *Independent Chronicle* [4] had replied that it would not be surprised if Pickering should also 'pay a visit to the "only seat" of liberty.' Burr lingered, and was in communication with the disloyalists while there.

In the meantime, convinced that force would be necessary to enforcement on the border, Jefferson urged Governor Tompkins of New York personally to visit the affected region and lead the forces of law and order.[5] And he was ordering naval and military forces to the scene and calling on the governors to put the militia into action.

VIII

Jefferson's proclamation against the rebels in Vermont and upper New York impressed the *Columbian Centinel* as tyrannical and inspired by a fanatic devotion to the Embargo. How could he turn thus upon 'the back settlers of New York and Vermont who have for years been his most ardent supporters'? [6] But the opposition press had thrown temperance to the winds. When a mass meeting of Federalists was held in Washington, the *Centinel* regretted the good old days of Washington and Adams when there was no European war, leaving the impression on the vulgar mind

[1] *New York Evening Post*, October 15, 1808.   [2] November 23, 1808.
[3] To Jefferson, *Writings of Gallatin*, i, 390.   [4] July 25, 1808.
[5] *Writings of Jefferson*, xii, 131.   [6] May 11, 1808.

that Jefferson was responsible for the European struggle.[1] In September, the *Centinel* was running secession letters signed 'Falkland,' purporting to prove that New England and New York could stand alone outside the Union and as a separate nation.[2] This paper's personal attacks were increasingly offensive. Because Campbell, of Tennessee, led in the defense of the Embargo in the House, the *Centinel* described him as 'a wild backwoodsman who perhaps never saw the ocean but on a map, or conceived the taste of it except from a salt-lick.' Nothing, indeed, but 'a duelist and a sharpshooter.'[3] The libels against Madison went beyond all bounds. Was he not implicated in the Yazoo frauds? Had he not said that 'since France wanted money we must furnish it'?[4] And Jefferson! Could anyone doubt that he was bringing suffering on the people because of his orders from Napoleon?

So raved the Federalist press through the summer and autumn of 1808.

IX

But Jefferson, unmindful of the libels, was more than ever convinced of the efficacy of the Embargo, if rigidly enforced, because of its results in England. He knew of the effect there on manufactures; of the distress in the industrial sections; of the rioting in Manchester; of the appalling loss in British trade in the American market. From a correspondent in London he heard that 'so learned an Englishman as Mr. Williams, the friend of Franklin, warned America against a compromise.' Enclosed in the letter was a pamphlet from Alexander Baring, the foremost London banker, denouncing the Orders in Council, and demanding their recall.[5] From Edward Baines, familiar with the commercial and industrial life of Lancaster and the West Riding, Jefferson heard that war, or the loss of the American trade, would be ruinous to that section.[6] He knew that the anti-American policy of the Cabinet had not been carried without ministerial opposition; that powerful protests had been voiced in the Commons; that Lord

[1] *Columbian Centinel*, March 26, 1808.   [2] September 10–14, 1808.
[3] March 23, 1808.   [4] *Columbian Centinel*, July 16, 1808.   [5] Sears, 64–65.
[6] Hirst, 426.

Bathurst, President of the Board of Trade, had sent a protest to
the Prime Minister. He knew that Bathurst had warned that
with the loss of our custom, constituting a third of Britain's
foreign trade, Britain could not continue the war against Napoleon
long.[1] He knew that the *Edinburgh Review*, a powerful organ of
public opinion, was making slashing attacks on the anti-American
policy of Canning, and that the merchants of Liverpool, threatened with ruin, had petitioned Henry Brougham for relief. He
knew that Brougham had assailed the Canning policy with all the
virile eloquence he commanded, and had asked 'why the plunder
of industrious merchants, which is thought disgraceful on land,
should still be accounted honorable at sea.'[2] He had read the
warning of the *Edinburgh Review* of the ruin of Britain's trade and
industry, and of the inevitable development of American industry
to compete with that of Lancaster and Manchester. He knew
that Lord Erskine, an ornament of the British Bar, had brilliantly
sustained the American position in the parliamentary debates.[3]
He knew that merchants and bankers, as powerful on public
opinion as the Barings, had denounced the British policy that had
forced the Embargo as utterly destructive of the business interests
of England.[4]

And he knew that, at a public dinner, Sir Francis Baring had
toasted Thomas Jefferson.[5]

He knew that Lord Holland had sustained the American position and had denounced the British policy as 'an ill-omened sur-
vival of the spirit which caused the Revolution,' and had lamented
that 'any persons were determined to revive that principle . . .
which lost that country forever to Great Britain.'

He had before him the dark picture drawn by Lord Auckland of
the effect of the Embargo in England: 'I am told by the best
customs-house and mercantile authorities that our exports are
almost totally suspended, that our imports are gradually contracting, that orders for manufactures are revoking; and that not only
our European trade is checked and that the demand of goods for
the United States is interrupted.'[6]

He knew that without American cotton, the English mills were

---

[1] Hirst, 434.   [2] *Ibid.*, 436.   [3] Sears, 269.
[4] Hirst, 437.   [5] *Ibid.*   [6] Sears, 277.

crippled; and that while 143,756 bags had been imported in 1807, but 25,426 had been brought in under the Embargo in 1808.[1] The cost of cotton had risen fifty per cent. In 1806, Britain imported to the States to the value of 12,389,488 pounds; and under the Embargo this had shrunken to 5,241,739 pounds.[2] Thus was the Embargo of 'no consequence' to England. In one year the English trade was ruined in the American market which had been taking one third of all Britain's exportations.

But it was the mill workers, reduced to idleness and want, whose groans and growls from Manchester, Liverpool, and London seemed most sinister. Their angry cries of protest were echoed in the parliamentary debates in March. Liverpool was described as threatened with utter ruin, and speakers declared the suffering unprecedented in industrial quarters. Men who had earned a guinea a week were sweeping the streets, or begging for bread. Soon this disfranchised and inarticulate mass was causing grave uneasiness in London, and when ten thousand weavers of Yorkshire cursed the price of bread and demanded work and wages, even the opposition was silenced, lest it incite to revolution.[3] With sixty thousand looms said to be idle, the poor rate in Manchester rose in the Embargo year from four thousand to forty-nine thousand pounds. If other elements entered into the distress, it was the Embargo that wrought the temporary ruin of the cotton industry.[4]

The one historian who has made an intensive study of the Embargo concludes 'that certainly no nation could have anticipated results so gigantic within one year,' and that, 'though conditions in England warranted the continuation of the experiment, America lacked the resolution to pursue it further.'

A part of America, but not all, and certainly not Jefferson.

Never had he been so thoroughly aroused; never had he burned his bridges so completely. Temperamentally opposed to arbitrary power, more given to persuasion than to force, he faced the stern realities of rebellion and acted with vigor and determination. With State authorities he exercised his conciliatory tact, while de-

[1] Sears, 287.   [2] Ibid., 297.   [3] Ibid., 278-79.   [4] Ibid., 280.

manding action. When violations along the Massachusetts coast
became serious, the *Wasp*, the *Argus*, and the *Chesapeake* were
ordered to the troubled waters. Commodore Rodgers was sent to
join the *Revenge*. Gunboats were ordered to Newport, New Bedford, and Barnstable. The *Revenge*, ready for action, plowed the
waters of Martha's Vineyard; the *Wasp* and the *Argus* guarded
the coast between Cape Cod and Portland.[1]

Thus the smuggling to British vessels was stopped; and then
Jefferson and Gallatin concentrated on preventing vessels from
slipping to sea without clearance. They agreed that cruisers only
would serve here, and there were not enough of these.[2]

When dishonest merchants availed themselves of a provision of
the law permitting the sending of ships to bring home property
abroad, Jefferson instructed the collectors to demand the precise
place of the property, the amount, whether in cash or goods, the
kind of goods, and in whose name the goods rested.[3]

When the tricky Smith, Secretary of the Navy, merchant and
shipowner, was inactive, Jefferson lashed him with peremptory
orders. 'Complaints multiply upon us of evasions ... by fraud
and force,' he wrote Smith in Baltimore. 'During the present
summer all the gunboats manned and in commission should be
distributed through as many bays and ports as may be necessary.
... On this subject you will pray consult with Mr. Gallatin, who
will call on you on his passage through Baltimore, and to communicate with him hereafter directly without the delay of consulting me.'[4] Smith ground his teeth and did as he was told.
Before autumn, evasions by sea had been reduced to a minimum.

When, on land, violence opposed itself to the law, Jefferson
turned to the army. When, with his own State in insurrection,
Dearborn wished to retire, Jefferson refused to consider his
resignation. No retirement under fire! The enforcement of the
Embargo now; war, perhaps, tomorrow. And Dearborn stuck to
his post.

A few months more, and the scourings of the Boston streets
were rioting about flour, and violence appeared in other parts of
Massachusetts. Jefferson hurried orders to Dearborn: 'The

---

[1] To Jefferson, *Writings of Gallatin*, I, 402.   [2] *Ibid.*, I, 401.
[3] *Writings of Jefferson*, XII, 12.   [4] *Ibid.*, XII, 93.

Tories of Boston openly threaten insurrection ... the next post will stop it ... on the first symptoms of an open opposition to the law, you will fly to the scene and aid in suppressing any commotion,' he wrote.[1] 'I am not afraid but that there is sound matter enough in Massachusetts to prevent an opposition to the laws by force,' he wrote Crowninshield, the new Secretary of the Navy.[2]

With the approach of autumn, Jefferson and Gallatin were agreeing that war powers should be asked from Congress. Neither was inclined to capitulate to nullification and crime. 'Congress must legalize all means necessary to obtain enforcement,' he wrote Gallatin, 'and I am clearly of opinion that the law ought to be enforced at any expense.'[3] Gallatin agreed. 'Congress must either invest the Executive with the most arbitrary powers and sufficient force to carry the Embargo into effect, or give it up altogether.'[4]

Thus, not for a single second did Jefferson cringe or weaken. Never had he loomed so large as an executive; and never had he worn the armor of a fighting man so admirably. He still had confidence in the efficacy of his plan. There was suffering, and tremendous loss, and some rioting in England; in the United States there were impressive compensations for the loss.

XI

For the suffering in the United States has been grossly exaggerated by historians, accepting Federalist propaganda as a serious source. Sailors were suffering; the fishermen were stricken; but Dr. Channing has sufficiently ridiculed the canard that has passed for 'history' that ships were rotting at the wharves. He has exposed the falsehood that the wharves were deserted during the Embargo by citing the more than ten million dollars in duties collected on these 'deserted' wharves.[5] Four months after the passage of the Embargo Act, the Essex Junto, in furtherance of its theory that starving would result, established soup-houses to catch the eye in Boston; but a canvass by the *Independent Chronicle* revealed that 'the astonishing number of twenty-five daily apply for this excellent refreshment.'[6] The *New York Evening Post* was

---

[1] *Writings of Jefferson*, XII, 119.   [2] *Ibid.*, XII, 121.   [3] *Ibid.*, XII, 121.
[4] *Writings of Gallatin*, I, 395.   [5] Channing, 216–17.   [6] April 28, 1808.

announcing that 'three hundred families in a single town of Salem
... are reduced to the necessity of relying on private charity for
sustenance,' but the *Salem Register* replied that 'we do not know,
nor have we heard on inquiry, of a single family in Salem which
has been reduced by the Embargo to the necessity of relying on
private charity.' [1]

But if commerce was suffering, as in Britain, where manufacturers were chilling their furnace fires, factories were springing up
with startling rapidity in the States. In New England, factories
notably increased despite the difficulty of the capitalists in shifting to manufacture, with their money tied up in shipping and commerce. But in Connecticut, a man in a blue coat with brass but-
tons, and with lace ruffles around his wrist, was wiser than his
neighbors; for David Humphreys, former secretary to Washington
and former Minister to Spain, who had introduced merino sheep
to American pastures, was pushing forward with his woolen mill.
Ignoring the scowls of petty partisans, he saw the opportunity and
took it; and Jefferson, sympathetically following his experiment,
ordered a woolen suit from the Humphreys mill that year.[2] Dr.
Thomas Cooper, the political economist, heard that others in
New England were alive to chance. 'Home manufactures are
increasing to such a degree there,' he wrote, 'that ere long, in
numbers as well as in opulence, that class of the community will
be a full match for the seaport merchants. The latter would separate from the Union and join England if they could.' [3]

But in Pennsylvania, where capital was more fluid, the effect
of the Embargo was magical. Soon the *Philadelphia Price Current*
was creating a sensation by the mere publication of the new mills.
Iron and steel, carpets, cotton bagging, calico, shawls, bedspreads,
earthenware, glassware, soap, sealing wax, bottles and jars, cotton
flannels, and paper — these sprang as by a conjurer's trick upon
the market under the encouragement of the Embargo. The
editor sent a copy of the paper to Jefferson, with the comment
that the record proved that 'by the President's originating partial
deprivations, he has ultimately bestowed on his country immense
and imperishable benefits.' [4]

---

[1] Quoted in *Independent Chronicle*, September 15, 1808.
[2] *Humphreys*, II, 275–78.   [3] Sears, 134–35.   [4] *Ibid.*, 214.

But the Federalists and Tories of Philadelphia were embarrassed. 'Who that walks the streets of Philadelphia,' wrote Charles Jared Ingersoll, one of them, 'and sees, notwithstanding twelve months' stagnation in trade, several hundred substantial and elegant houses building, and the laboring community employed at good wages, who reads at every corner advertisements for workers for factories — who, under such circumstances, that is not too stupid to perceive and too prejudiced to believe when he does perceive, can doubt the solid capital of this country?' What, though the writer was 'too stupid to perceive' that the prosperity was a by-product of Jefferson's Embargo![1] 'You would scarcely recognize Philadelphia, so much has it grown and improved,' wrote young Nicholas Biddle, another partisan of the Embargo year.[2]

That year the Philadelphia Manufacturing Society was announcing the construction of new mill buildings and the installation of machinery to make woolen and cotton cloth by water power; the Premium Society of Pennsylvania Manufacturers was announcing premiums in cash for the best products of various articles,[3] and Charles Thomson, the venerable secretary of the Continental Congress, was writing Jefferson of three new paper mills that had sprung up within a mile of his home. 'No one who does not take pains to keep himself informed ... can have an idea of the rapid strides we are making ... in manufacturing,' he wrote.[4]

But Jefferson had taken pains, and was observing the rapid development of manufacturing with keen delight. 'Our Embargo has produced one very happy permanent effect,' he wrote jubilantly to Lafayette. 'It has set us all on domestic manufactures, and will, I verily believe, reduce our future demands on England fully one half.'[5]

Thus Britain and America were both suffering in commerce; but where England also was suffering in manufacturing, America was moving forward rapidly, and Jefferson was content. It was sheer nonsense that 'ships were rotting at the wharves'; but factory fires were lighting all over the land.

[1] Sears, 217.   [2] Ibid., 218.   [3] Humphreys, ii, 379.
[4] Sears, 135.   [5] Ibid., 137.

XII

But Canning was not alarmed — he counted on Britain's allies in America to break down American resistance and force the defeat of the Embargo.

Neither Jefferson nor Gallatin had any illusions as to that. 'I believe the British Ministry . . . wait for the result of their intrigues and of the exertions of their friends here,' wrote Gallatin to Charles Pinckney.[1] The disloyalists were growing more arrogant and open every day, shouting treason through trumpets. The nephew of Pickering in London was assuring the English that the New England Federalists would force the repeal of the Embargo, while assuring these in America that Britain would cordially receive the returning Northern States! Sullivan was writing Jefferson that 'the old Tories and the old Tory families are resuscitated.'[2] Nor was Sullivan exaggerating. A clergyman from a Connecticut pulpit was urging the separation of the New England States from the Union, and one who heard the seditious utterance assured Jefferson that, while he had not heard treason openly urged before, he had 'for about four years perceived the leading Federalists cautiously beating the pulse of the people to the tune of separation.'[3]

And then a British agent appeared in Boston to hold confidential conversations with the Federalist leaders, but the keen eye of John Quincy Adams observed him, and Jefferson promptly was notified.

John Henry, this British agent, was an Irishman by birth and a low adventurer by nature. Going to America in early youth to live with a relative, he married a French girl who died early, leaving him with two daughters. During Adams's Administration, he was an artillery officer and he held his commission until Jefferson went into power. He then retired to a Vermont farm near the Canadian border, and after five years went to Montreal to study law. Before he entered upon his mission as a spy, an attempt was made to have him appointed to a judgeship, but his application was rejected on the ground that he was 'a mere adventurer,' not even called to the bar. He then ingratiated himself into the good

[1] Adams, *Gallatin*, 375.   [2] Sears, 68–69.

[3] Elisha Tracy; Sears, 103–04.

graces of the confidential adviser of the Governor-General, Sir
James Henry Craig. Thereupon he set forth on a journey through
New England to Boston, and, during his meanderings, he made
contact with the disloyalists, and wrote long letters to his friend,
who gave them to Craig for transmission to Castlereagh in London.

Such was his zeal that Henry was made a British agent with
instructions to make himself the medium of communication between the disloyalists and the British Government. For four
months he was received cordially and confidentially by the
Federalist leaders, conversing with them freely, and transmitting
their opinions, expectations, and desires.[1]

Thus, when the Republic was threatened at once by the greatest military and the greatest naval power on earth, Jefferson was
hampered by disloyalty at home; with Pickering in confidential
correspondence with Rose; with Pickering's nephew encouraging
the British to hold fast to their Orders in Council; with treason
preached openly in pulpits; with a press assailing the American
and defending the British position; and with a British agent sitting
cheek by jowl with disloyalists in Boston and acting as the intermediary of the British Government.

XIII

And Jefferson felt the pressure. The excruciating periodic
headaches with which he had suffered for years were increasing in
frequency and intensity. He had begun to feel the weight of
years. And yet, throughout, he remained steadfastly at his post,
finding time for other things. Riding his horse over the red
clay roads of Virginia on his way to Monticello, his mind was busy
with a plan for the building of a canal at New Orleans.[2] His interest in science never waning, he took time to assemble the bones of
a mammoth, the horns of a mountain ram, and other articles,
for transmission to the National Institute of France. He found
relaxation from his labors by reading four volumes of the Memoirs
of the Agricultural Society of the Seine.[3] At Monticello, his mind
was occupied with the construction of the great western highway,
and he wrote the commissioners regarding the route.[4] When

[1] *Dictionary of American Biography*, vii, 549–50.
[2] *Writings of Jefferson*, xii, 54.
[3] To M. Sylvester, *ibid.*, xii, 88.   [4] *Ibid.*, xii, 117.

Robert Fulton appeared and appealed to him for assistance in preparing a decisive experiment for his torpedo for members of Congress, he wrote Crowninshield, who had rejected the application, ordering that the assistance be granted.[1]

That summer, one of the most brilliant and virulent of his enemies ceased to serve the opposition when the brilliant pen of the dying pamphleteer dropped from the hands of Fisher Ames at Dedham, Massachusetts. Never had he been so feverishly active as in the last year of his life. Small in person, feeble in health, he was, aside from Hamilton, the most brilliant and uncompromising of the Federalists, and during the period of the Embargo his letters to the press were, by odds, the most powerful that appeared against the Administration. His genius with the pen fully equaled his genius as an orator, and he was one of the foremost orators of his time. He died as he had lived — hating democracy and Jefferson.[2]

Ames died at the beginning of the presidential contest that was to determine the succession to Jefferson. The election was to be the test of the popularity of the Administration and its policies. It is time now to follow the contestants into the arena.

[1] To M. Sylvester, *Writings of Jefferson*, xii. 120; 123.
[2] Bentley, *Diary*, iii, 370; *Cabot*, 380.

CHAPTER XXII

Jefferson Vindicated by the People

I

LONG before the end of his second Administration, Jefferson informed his friends of his determination to retire. He had been loaded down with honors, and he was very tired. As early as January, 1807, when he was at the crest of his popularity, when New England was sweeping into his column, when there was not a cloud on his horizon, he wrote Comte de Diodato of his intention. 'At the close of my present term . . . I propose to retire to private life,' he said, 'and to close my days on my patrimony at Monticello and in the bosom of my family. I have hitherto enjoyed uniform health; but the weight of public business begins to be heavy for me, and I long for the enjoyments of rural life. . . . I am entitled to my discharge. . . . I have therefore requested my fellow citizens to think of a successor for me. . . . I have the consolation, too, of having added nothing to my private fortune during my public service, and of retiring with hands as clean as they are empty.' [1]

By the mere nodding of his head, by silence even, he could have been elected for a third term. Legislatures were asking him to reconsider his decision, and friends were importuning him to remain at the helm. 'It is a keen disappointment to me if you persist in your unwillingness to be re-elected,' wrote Pierre du Pont de Nemours. 'I think you are still more useful to your country by remaining at the head of its Government than you were as an instrument in its declaration of independence which may become

[1] *Domestic Life,* 313.

more difficult to maintain than it was to establish. How can you think, in such a situation, of retiring?' [1]

But it was more natural for Jefferson to think of retiring than of breaking the precedent set by Washington. He had strongly regretted the absence of a constitutional prohibition of re-election to the Presidency, fearing that ambitious and unscrupulous men, once entrenched in power, might continue themselves indefinitely; but Washington's voluntary retirement at the end of a second term had reconciled him to the absence of a clause of limitation. 'If the principle of rotation is a sound one, as I conscientiously believe it to be in respect to this office,' he wrote another who had protested against his decision to retire, 'no pretext should ever be permitted to dispense with it. . . . You suppose I am in the prime of life for rule. I am sensible I am not.' [2]

He was adamant to all appeals.

II

His decision wreathed the venerable countenance of George Clinton with a smile of satisfaction. Thus far, the precedents all favored the succession of the Vice-President. And the presidential aspirations of the political boss of New York had budded long before he became the second officer of the Republic. As a consummate politician, he had made common cause with Jefferson in New York politics, but he never had been an ardent admirer of the philosopher, whose methods were more subtle than his own.

By nature, he had been blessed with a robust body, with vigor, supreme courage, with the gift of perseverance, with rare capacity for organization, conciliation, and intrigue. He had been educated in the hard university of experience, where he had specialized in human nature. As a sailor on a privateer in early youth, he had mastered the psychology of the rougher classes. Though he had studied law and practiced with success, without distinction, his flair was for politics.

In his twenty-ninth year he had entered the Provincial Assembly, to find the Revolutionary minority bowing to the leadership of the aristocratic Philip Schuyler, and instantly he challenged his

---

[1] Malone, *Correspondence Between Thomas Jefferson and Pierre S. du Pont,* 96.
[2] To Harry Guest, *Writings of Jefferson,* XII, 224.

senior's domination. With a shock the manorial families soon found they had met their match in a democrat who owed nothing to family or fortune and who depended upon the resources of his own capacious mind. It was the first of many shocks the son of an Irish immigrant was to give the conservatives.

His Irish blood instinctively made him a revolutionist, and he was preaching independence when most of those later reported as pioneers were discussing it as an academic possibility. In the Second Continental Congress he voted for separation; and when the crisis came, he strode from the forum to the field as a brigadier-general of militia to undertake the defense of the Hudson. Though fearless and tireless, he was ignorant of the technique of war, and, realizing his limitations, he resigned his commission with the frank admission of his inefficiency.

Turning at once to civil life, he again shocked the worshipers of wealth and family, when, with scant courtesy, he toppled over the plans of the old-line politicians to make Schuyler Governor and took the place himself. John Jay groaned that 'Clinton's family and connections do not entitle him to so distinguished a pre-eminence.' The rowdy Clintonians replied that it was not the idea of America that 'family and connections' entitle any man to 'pre-eminence' in public life. Six times in succession, the son of the immigrant was to pain the aristocrats by re-elections.

His energy and resourcefulness, his fine fighting qualities, his capacity to inspire men to supreme exertions, his adroitness in public finance, made him, perhaps, the greatest War Governor of the Revolution.

When victory crowned the efforts of the patriots, and most were hoping for a union of the States, Clinton's dream was of New York alone, and as a sovereign nation. The pleas for a union made no appeal to his mind or imagination. He knew and loved New York, and he had the vision to foresee its pre-eminence in commerce and finance; and he could see no advantage in merging with the old colonies into a single state. He frowned on the Constitutional Convention, and he fought the ratification of the fundamental law with a rough eloquence and force, and never ceased his opposition until the fight was over. No American was a more extreme devotee of State sovereignty.

In the modern sense, he was the first real political boss. With sheer force of character and will, he dominated over his party, cheered on by the confidence and affection of the multitude. He was not embarrassed by scruples, and when, in one election, he was actually defeated, he resorted to a subterfuge which had shocked Jefferson. 'To retain the office when it is probable the majority is against him is dishonorable,' Jefferson wrote Monroe.[1] His position, however, was strengthened by the success of his succeeding administrations. And he was a consummate politician of dash and daring. When, in one other election, he narrowly escaped defeat at the hands of an able opponent, he promptly eliminated a potential danger by appointing his opponent to the chief-justiceship of the Supreme Court. And always his keen Irish eyes were surveying the crowd for young men of brilliant promise to attach to his cause. Thus he discovered Aaron Burr, appointed him Attorney-General, transferred him almost immediately to the United States Senate, and, through this protégé, aligned the powerful Livingston clan under his banner. Through the wise use of patronage he built up a political machine which, until then, had never been equaled in the country. He was literally the Boss of New York; and, as such, Jefferson had used him in the elimination of Burr.

But, at once, Clinton was a candidate for the succession to Jefferson. He had little relish and less aptitude for the reward he had received in the second post. Quivering with nervous energy, still vigorous in body, still dominating and domineering by nature, a figure for the arena rather than the forum, he was too bored with presiding over the Senate debating society thoroughly to familiarize himself with the rules of parliamentary procedure. He was an old lion, battle-scarred and untamed, confined in a cage.

Nor was he made any happier by the realization that Jefferson's plans for the succession were not concerned with him. This, however, neither discouraged nor deterred him. As an insurgent, he entered the contest, and so framed his program as to appeal to the Federalists he had fought for more than a generation.

But aside from some Federalists, his candidacy did not appeal. He was then in his sixty-eighth year, and many, who respected his

---

[1] *Writings of Jefferson*, VI. 94.

ability and admired his courage, thought him incapacitated by age. Then, too, he failed in the art of cultivating the politicians of the capital because as a boss he had arbitrarily given orders to inferiors all his life. Senator Mitchill observed that Madison 'gives dinners and makes generous displays to the members,' with the gracious and captivating Dolly giving to his board the warmth and color he lacked; while Clinton 'lives snug in his lodging and keeps aloof from such captivating exhibitions.' And unlike Madison, he had 'nothing of female succor at his side.' [1]

Even so, he figured constantly in the gossip of the politicians throughout the winter. But when Senator Bradley, discussing the congressional caucus with Adams, expressed the hope that 'the old gentleman, Mr. Clinton, would be complimented with a unanimous vote for the Vice-Presidency,' and was asked if Clinton were not to be considered for the Presidency, Adams was told that 'he is too old and we are all witnesses that his faculties are failing.' [2]

Meanwhile, the Federalist leaders, exchanging views, were soon convinced that there was no hope for his election. 'Clinton cannot compete successfully with Madison,' wrote one of King's correspondents.[3] He was sure that Madison would 'find a much more powerful antagonist in Monroe, who is said to have a majority in the Virginia Legislature.' For that reason he continued, 'the Federalists here feel a strong partiality for him.'

Thus, very early, Clinton was eliminated from serious consideration. His aspirations figure in Jefferson's correspondence scarcely at all. 'I already see my old friend Clinton estranging himself from me,' Jefferson wrote Monroe. 'No doubt lies are carried to him, as they will be to the two other candidates.' [4] It was clear that the contest revolved around the conflicting claims and ambitions of Madison and Monroe. As early as 1806, the friends of the latter had launched his candidacy, but from the beginning he was unfortunate in his friends. The stout championship of Randolph and his Quids, the venomous enemies of Jefferson, did infinite harm; and the partiality of the Federalists for him, as against Madison, inexplicable as it was, was not confined to private correspondence, but was openly expressed in the cloak-rooms

---

[1] Mitchill's Letters.

[2] Adams, *Diary*, I, 504.

[3] *King's Corr.*, v, 58.

[4] *Writings of Jefferson*, IX, 177.

and boarding-houses. The best of party men began to frown on
Monroe and to suspect his loyalty to his chief, and, while he never
was disloyal, there was a time when, to outward seeming, he was
no longer the faithful follower of Jefferson. Even Jefferson became uneasy, and about this time wrote Monroe of his ardent
wish to retire from his 'daily drudgery,' and with his rare power
of conciliation, he appealed to the old loyalties:

'But my wish for retirement itself is not stronger than that of
carrying into it the affections of all my friends. I have ever
viewed Mr. Madison and yourself as two principal pillars of my
happiness. Were either to be withdrawn, I should consider it as
among the greatest calamities which could assail my future peace
of mind. I have great confidence that the candor and high understanding of both will guard me against this misfortune, the bare
possibility of which has so far weighed on my mind that I could
not be easy without unburdening it.' [1]

III

Never had Jefferson written with greater sincerity. Madison
and Monroe had been his field marshals from the establishment
of the Republic, and their friendship preceded that. They had
been musketeers during the bitter twelve-year struggle for democracy. Though men of different character and caliber, each fitted
in perfectly with Jefferson's requirements as a party leader. In
more recent years, Monroe's long absence on diplomatic missions
had thrown Madison into more continuous contact. But through
Monroe's prolonged sojourns abroad, the minds of Jefferson and
his disciple had touched intimately in correspondence.

The two chief lieutenants differed. Sometimes even in the midst
of battle, Jefferson had been forced to prod Madison, who disliked
controversy, into action. Because of Monroe's impetuosity and
precipitancy, Jefferson sometimes had been forced to draw reins
on him. Through the twelve years of opposition, organizing,
propagandizing, fighting, now on the charge and now in retreat,
these two men had been Jefferson's most intimate political associates and personal friends.

Their political congeniality was not the sole explanation of

[1] *Domestic Life*, 315.

their intimacy. They were neighbors. Monticello was not far from Madison's charming seat 'Montpelier,' and Monroe had built 'Ashlawn' in the valley within view of Jefferson's hilltop home. It had been constructed during Monroe's absence, and under Jefferson's supervision. Thence, by day, Monroe could look up at the house of the man he proudly proclaimed his leader, and thence, at night, he could see the lights twinkling in the windows of Monticello. Frequently, in the dark and stormy days, the three friends sat under the trees at Monticello planning their political strategy; and in the critical days of the X Y Z hysteria the conference of the trio was held at Ashlawn lest the meeting at Monticello attract too much attention.

The summoning of Madison to Jefferson's council table apparently had met with Monroe's approval, for he then was Governor of Virginia. And Monroe had been paid a supreme compliment by his selection for the most important diplomatic missions of the two Administrations. His success in the negotiations for Louisiana was all that fate allowed him, but his defeat in Spain and England could not have been averted by any living man.

Nevertheless, Monroe was hurt to the heart when William Pinkney was sent to work with him on the British treaty; and the instant rejection of the treaty by Jefferson was bitterly resented by the envoy. Randolph and other mischief-makers sprinkled salt upon the wounds. But the shadow finally was lifted because of Monroe's abiding affection and common sense. He had poured forth his heart in a frank and manly letter to Jefferson, confessing that the sending of Pinkney and the rejection of the treaty had caused him grave concern. He had, however, continued 'to support and advance, to the utmost' of his power, Jefferson's 'personal and political fame,' from 'the high respect [he] entertained for his public services, talents and virtues,' and the conviction that the national interests and Jefferson's 'advancement and fame [were] so intimately connected as to constitute essentially the same cause.' Then, too, he had never forgotten 'the proofs of kindness and friendship' he had received from Jefferson in early life. But his sense of injury had increased on his return, when he was made the object of attacks because of failures impossible to prevent under the circumstances.[1]

[1] *Writings of Monroe*, v. 24.

Jefferson instantly responded with an equally manly letter intended to soothe the wounded feelings of his friend, and Monroe accepted the olive branch with joy. He had feared that 'the friendly feelings which [Jefferson] had so long entertained' for him had 'ceased to exist.' But now he was satisfied that Jefferson's friendship had suffered no change. He felt 'happy that we have had this explanation with each other,' since it had assured him that he had 'misconceived [Jefferson's] feelings and disposition' toward him. Nothing remained now 'but to prevent, as far as possible, all further inquietude.' [1] Naturally, if called to the Presidency he would accept. However, he had done nothing 'to draw the attention of anyone to me in reference to it,' nor should he in the future. No one appreciated Madison's merits more than he, and should he be chosen no one would give a heartier support to his Administration.[2]

A month later, Monroe was trying to cool the ardor of his supporters, forbidding that anything should be said or written in his behalf. Under no circumstances should any attack be made on Madison, which would be 'as impolitick as it is repugnant to our feelings.' Giles's slashing attack on Monroe? It would do no harm, and better by far to treat it with 'silent contempt' — the best answer.[3] In September he was sending Jefferson copies of his letters to Randolph in proof that he had written nothing to conceal.[4] Toward the last of October, he set forth his position on the Presidency in a letter to the brilliant Tazewell, of Virginia. True, on returning from England, he had disassociated himself from the Administration's attitude on the rejected treaty. But he had 'never failed to speak of [the Administration's] perfect integrity in foreign and domestic concerns, of its attachment to free government and the zealous desire to support it, of its great care of the public money, of its attachment to peace.' Nor had he associated himself with 'the republican minority,' since he 'had nothing to do in the part it played.'

As to the prospects? 'With New York there is a good understanding,' he wrote. Clinton had assured one of Monroe's friends that could he be elected, Clinton would decline all support in his

---

[1] *Writings of Monroe*, v, 27.   [2] *Ibid.*, v, 24.
[3] To George Hay, *ibid.*, v, 52.   [4] *Ibid.*, v, 83.

favor. This, Monroe thought, was due to his more favorable status in the New England States. If unable to elect their own candidate, the Federalists, it was thought, 'would prefer me to Mr. Madison.' An arrangement would be possible with them, but was it advisable? The support of the Federalists would put a potent weapon in the hands of 'men like Giles and Nicholson to attack me with,' and it would be feared that his own election would mean a return to the old policies of the Federalist Party.[1]

Thus Monroe remained in the contest, hoping against hope, awaiting the action of the electors. And Jefferson, convinced of Madison's certain election, and thinking it best for Monroe to wait, remained aloof from the struggle.

IV

Madison and Monroe, drawn together by a common love of Jefferson, were antipathetic in temperament. They had crossed swords early over the ratification of the Constitution.

Monroe was uncompromisingly a champion of State rights. Madison favored the unification of the States and a reasonably strong central government.

Madison was a student, a reader, a creature of the closet, ready with his pen, but with little taste for the give-and-take of debate.

Monroe was a man of the arena, always in armor, his blood heated to battle, and prone to lay on with battle-axe and without mercy.

Madison was slow in moving toward decisions; Monroe's chief fault was his precipitancy and impetuosity.

Madison, by taste and instinct, was an aristocrat; Monroe inherently was a democrat with a deep respect for the judgment of the average man.

The contrast of the two may be illustrated by reference to Madison's mansion of Montpelier with its solid dignity, and Monroe's more humble farmhouse of Ashlawn — the difference between the aristocratic planter and the small farmer.

Madison's feelings were not so deep that he could not enjoy social relations with Hamilton and Marshall; Monroe's were so profound and passionate that he would have found their company distasteful.

[1] *Writings of Monroe*, v, 68.

Jefferson had no doubt of Monroe's ability or loyalty to democracy, but he was younger than Madison and could afford to wait.
Then, too, Madison's more intimate identification with Administration policies pointed him out as the logical successor to carry
them on.

v

Meanwhile, the contest actually had been settled as early as in
January, 1808. The practical politician looked to the decision
between the two Virginians in the Old Dominion as determining
the sentiment of the nation. The fight there had been both bitter
and brilliant, with Giles leading for Madison, and Randolph
for Monroe. The contest took on the aspects of a feud, with
insulting letters in the press and with bitter words spoken in
taverns and at the crossroads. The Federalists in New York
were assured that Monroe would have a majority in the legislature, and this speedily was put to the test.

On the morning of January 21, 1808, the little town of Richmond seethed with excitement. The legislators were in session;
the capital was crowded with State politicians assembled to bring
pressure from home on the members. The announcement was
made that the friends of Monroe would meet at the Capitol, and
those of Madison at the Bell Tavern. When the curious in the
streets observed that the greater number were wending their way
to the tavern, little doubt remained as to the event. One hundred
and thirty men crowded into the little tavern, and each cast his
vote for Madison. But sixty appeared at the old Capitol Jefferson
had designed, and this was significant enough, but when ten of
the sixty voted for Madison, the hopes of Randolph were blasted.
Of the one hundred and ninety assembled altogether, one hundred
and forty expressed a preference for Madison and but fifty
for Monroe — a verdict of almost three to one against Monroe.
He was paying the penalty of Randolph's sponsorship. Without
the support of his own State, Monroe's prospects were dark
enough.[1]

The news of the event in Richmond could scarcely have reached
Washington when another blow fell there, in a congressional

[1] Bruce, I, 342.

caucus of the Jeffersonians at the Capitol. There was no more power in the caucus to prevent electors from voting as they wished than there is such power in the modern conventions; but a party system had been established, and without some indication of party sentiment there would be confusion in the minds of the rank and file.

The caucus unquestionably was engineered by Giles, though it was called by Senator Bradley, who had presided over a similar caucus, with the consent of all Democrats, four years before. But, with the issuance of the call, the supporters of Monroe began a stout opposition. What right had the members of Congress to designate a President? The supporters of Monroe would not give their sanction to such an unconstitutional usurpation. Not a few among Madison's supporters determined to remain away as a protest against the method.

Meanwhile, Monroe's friends were busy in the preparation of a protest, and when the attending members filed into the chamber they found pinned to the curtains of the Speaker's desk, alongside the call of Bradley, a denunciation of the caucus written by a member from New York. As many as fifteen of the Jeffersonians remained away, but eighty-nine, an impressive majority, answered to the roll-call. Giles assumed charge; Bradley was called to the chair; the vote was taken, and eighty-three cast their ballots for Madison, with Monroe and Clinton splitting half a dozen votes between them.

Randolph and his insurgents were conspicuously absent, but conspicuously present was John Quincy Adams, who thus in formal manner passed from the ranks of the Federalists to those of the Jeffersonians.[1] The desertion of Adams moved the Federalists to frenzy. 'Would you suppose it possible the scoundrel could summon impudence enough to go to their caucus?' asked Gardenier of King. 'I wish to God the noble house of Braintree had been put in a hole and a deep one twenty years ago.'[2] But Major Russell, of the *Columbian Centinel*, was not so sure about the burial; and, in admitting Adams's attendance at the caucus, he sought to mollify the wrath of his fellow partisans. True, 'the late movements of this gentleman have excited much conversation

[1] Adams, *Diary*, i, 506.   [2] *King's Corr.*, v, 68.

and contemplation among his political friends,' but no doubt he had been moved by a spirit of patriotism and at heart was a Federalist still.[1]

It was just after the caucus that Randolph, without Monroe's knowledge or consent, utterly wrecked the latter's chances by ferociously assailing Madison because of his adherence to the policies of Jefferson. Thus, by his stupid tactics he made a vote for Monroe a vote against Jefferson.

The nomination of Clinton, for second place, did not deter the rugged and determined Clinton from pressing his claims on the first place. And Monroe, despite his setback at Washington and Richmond, remained very much in the field. The issue was now up to the electors.

VI

Aside from Randolph, slashing at both Madison and Jefferson, it was left to the Clintonians to compete with the Federalists in attacks on the two. Cheetham, of the *American Citizen*, of New York, led the pack. He opened fire by publishing numerous letters and extracts from newspapers attacking Madison and praising Clinton.[2] When the *Pittsfield Sun* reported that an alliance was under way between the Clintonians and the Essex Junto, the editor made violent protest. 'We are well satisfied that neither Mr. Clinton nor his friends would stoop to so degrading a measure.' [3] Then followed a declaration that Monroe could have settled the *Chesapeake* incident in London but for the impossible terms laid down by Madison whose sole purpose was to hurt Monroe.[4] Having gone so far, Cheetham made his next appeal to the discontents with a demand for the immediate repeal of the Embargo measure, and vied with the Federalists in its denunciation.[5] Soon he was insisting that 'there is not an enlightened man among the Madisonians who does not in his heart prefer Governor Clinton.' [6] Elect Madison, and 'the Republic is gone and perhaps forever,' since he was committed to 'a ruinous and fatal system.' [7]

[1] *Columbian Centinel*, February 20, 1808.   [2] September 3, 1808.
[3] *American Citizen*, September 10, 1808.   [4] *Ibid.*, September 12, 1808.
[5] *Ibid.*, September 26, 1808.   [6] *Ibid.*, October 7, 1808.
[7] *Ibid.*. October 13. 1808.

Having gone so far, it was a short step to an attack on Jefferson, since Madison was to be elected 'by virtue of the right of the President to nominate his successor — lately added by way of amendment to our Constitution.' [1]

So ran the fight against Jefferson's choice among the disgruntled Democrats.

VII

The Federalist Party had become a shell, without its leaders suspecting it. Dead though it was, it was an animated corpse, making much noise rattling about in its casket. When the decision was reached to renominate Charles Cotesworth Pinckney and Rufus King for President and Vice-President, the *New York Evening Post* was delighted. 'They are blinded by no foreign attachment, biased by no secret influence, nor bewildered by the illusions of political romance,' it sang. Elect them and the nation would be 'extricated from the snares and shackles of Bonaparte and his emissaries,' though the French had no John Henry hobnobbing with the Democratic leaders.[2] The Jeffersonians, considering Pinckney as a mere stalking-horse, gave him little attention and attacked him not at all, though the *Independent Chronicle* of Boston carried one silly slur based on Pinckney's presidency of the Charleston Jockey Club. 'It is a little curious,' it said, 'to see men who profess to revere religion and morality supporting a man for President who is so distinguished for his love of such sports.' [3]

Weirdly enough, the Federalist leaders entertained high hopes of victory. Consorting only with their kind, they found every indication of an insurrection against Jefferson and all his works. Cabot got it from Pickering, and Pickering had heard it from Higginson. They counted on disaffection among the friends of Clinton and Monroe, and more heavily on the Embargo. 'I propose to write a number of short essays to prove that the Embargo will be the means of restoring Federalism, and of course that it is a great blessing,' wrote 'Curtius' in the *Columbian Centinel*.[4] Even Gallatin, who in political judgment was a child

---

[1] *American Citizen*, October 21, 1808.   [2] October 12, 1808.
[3] October 27, 1808.   [4] January 23, 1808.

compared with Jefferson, had the shivers. 'There is almost an
equal chance ... that we will lose the presidential election,' he
had written Jefferson in August. 'I think that at this moment the
Western States, Virginia, South Carolina, and perhaps Georgia,
are the only sound States, and that we will have a doubtful contest in every other.' ¹ Events were to prove Gallatin a poor
prophet.

In September, the *New York Evening Post* was claiming that
Pinckney would get nineteen votes in Massachusetts, nine in
Connecticut, four in Rhode Island, seven in New Hampshire, six
in Vermont, eight in New Jersey, twenty in Pennsylvania, three
in Delaware, six in Maryland, five in North Carolina, and ten in
South Carolina, making a total of ninety-seven votes. The *American Citizen* pounced on the figures, conceding it had no hopes for
Vermont or New Jersey, while ridiculing the claim on Maryland
and North Carolina.² And even the *Citizen* was to find itself
ridiculous.

But in early summer the Essex Junto, sharing Gallatin's
views, organized a committee of correspondence with other States,
together with a Massachusetts committee of twenty members.
Christopher Gore, whose memory lives in the hall that bears his
name at Harvard, was made chairman of the general committee,
and associated with him on the committee were George Cabot,
Harrison Gray Otis, and Senator Lloyd, the mediocre person with
whom they had displaced Adams in the Senate. 'I think the
Federalists never have been more united or more encouraged
than at present,' Gore wrote Rufus King.³

The general committee immediately hurried agents to other
New England States to incite their partisans to action. One
agent reported from New Hampshire that the Federalists would
triumph there. Another agent was speeded to Vermont, and
Harrison Gray Otis sought to animate the partisans in Rhode
Island. Within a month, leading Federalists from throughout the
country were to assemble in New York.

Even so, the stout men of Boston were not so sure of victory,
and they put their heads together to determine where they should

---

¹ *Writings of Gallatin*, ɪ, 401.   ² September 6, 1808.
³ *King's Corr.*, v, 100.

throw their votes to prevent Madison's election. Gore, who sat in the conference, informed King that the Boston Federalists had 'a leaning to Clinton under the idea that he would support and cherish commerce.' [1] But for the bitter enmity between Hamilton and Monroe, they would have preferred to give their votes to the Virginian. [2]

Meanwhile, Jefferson, confident and calm, placed complete reliance on the Middle States, with the exception of Delaware, which had long been attached to the tail of the kite of the Essex Junto. His reports from Pennsylvania were satisfactory, despite the feud, and he was as certain of the Western States as of Virginia. Nor did he have misgivings of any Southern State. Because of the long and intensive fight on the Embargo in New England, he was prepared to see some of those that had enlisted under his banner four years before return to their old allegiance. But he conceded nothing, and urged his supporters in New England to contest every inch of the ground. When, in the spring elections in the hopelessly Federalist State of Connecticut, his party polled its largest vote thus far in history, he was persuaded that a stout fight might save some of the New England States.

Thus, in Massachusetts, the hotbed of opposition, the Jeffersonians stood sternly to their guns. When, in October, Pickering engineered a meeting in Salem for the denunciation of the Embargo, the Tabernacle was packed with ardent partisans on both sides, and a battle royal raged from nine in the morning until the sun went down. William Gray, the rich merchant, led in the debate for the Embargo. He spoke with 'great ease and clearness' in the common-sense exposition of the views of a man of affairs, and, coming from him, the very simplicity and downrightness of his talk had the effect of the most thrilling eloquence. The Jeffersonians cheered wildly; the Federalists furiously hissed the greatest light of commerce in Salem.

Gray was followed by young Joseph Story, whose timid wavering before the storm had deprived him of a renomination for Congress, and whose speech, by its half-hearted tone, was all that the Federalists could wish. After the Federalists made their attack, the vote was taken just as the sun was going down, and

[1] *King's Corr.*, v, 107–08.   [2] Gardenier to King, *ibid.*, v, 58.

in this commercial center of Massachusetts, the Jeffersonians triumphed with a margin of more than a hundred votes. Thus did the Jeffersonians stand to their guns in Massachusetts.[1]

The fight screamed in New England, the press of both parties busy with intemperate charge and counter-charge. Never had the rank and file been so well organized, disciplined, and munitioned, and through the summer and autumn the Jeffersonians gave blow for blow in the enemy's country. It was the home of Timothy Pickering and the Essex Junto, but in the Salem congressional district, the Jeffersonians held Pickering's party to a tie in Salem, held their own in Marblehead and Lynn, and lost the district by a narrow margin because of the disaffection of Cape Ann.[2]

So much for the impression conveyed by some historians that Jefferson was utterly routed in Massachusetts.

VIII

There positively is nothing in the record of that election remotely to justify the conclusion of anti-Jefferson historians that Jefferson was 'put to rout' by the outraged people. The references to his 'rout,' 'defeat,' 'humiliation,' and the 'loss of his popularity' can only mean, to normal minds, that his party was defeated, his candidate overwhelmed. But the facts confront this historical canard.

Jefferson had passed through three years of unprecedented slander of the vilest sort while fighting to maintain the nation's rights without recourse to slaughter, and the Embargo had called for sacrifices that the public felt. He had been harassed by treason and nullification. His foes had been in confidential communication with the foes of their country. In eight years of supreme power he had suffered, as all statesmen must, from the piling-up of resentments and the accumulation of political enemies. He was on the verge of retirement, with no further power to reward his friends or to punish his foes. And yet he triumphed with the most astonishing completeness.

With one hundred and sixty-nine electors, the Federalists 'routed' him by polling but forty-seven votes. He was 'humil-

[1] Bentley, *Diary*, ɪɪ, 391.   [2] *Ibid.*, ɪɪɪ, 395; 397.

iated' because his candidate received almost two thirds of the electoral vote of the nation. Even in New England his enemies were unable to make a sweep, and Vermont, remaining solid as her granite hills, gave her full electoral vote to Jefferson's candidate. The opposition won in Connecticut, where it never had lost; in Delaware, which never had voted for Jefferson; in Massachusetts and in Rhode Island and New Hampshire by narrow margins.

And Jefferson's candidate received every electoral vote of Georgia, Kentucky, New Jersey, Ohio, Pennsylvania, South Carolina, Tennessee, and Virginia. In every instance, where there was a split in the electoral vote of the remaining States, the greater part went to Madison. In Maryland, where the opposition received two votes, the Jeffersonians got nine. In North Carolina, where the Jeffersonians polled eleven votes, the opposition received three. In New York, where the Jeffersonians polled thirteen votes, and the Federalists none, the all-powerful Clinton was able to muster no more than six.

Such was the 'rout' of Jefferson — the sort of rout for which politicians devoutly pray.

Had Jefferson himself consented to a third term he could not have done worse, and he might reasonably have done better. Madison never had been the popular figure that Jefferson had been. The sentimental attachment of thousands for the leader could not be transmitted, by command, to the lieutenant. Most of the friends of Monroe and Clinton, who had resented the congressional caucus, and voted against Madison's electors, would have been loyal to Jefferson. Monroe himself would have been in the front ranks battling for him. By no means of estimating political results known to men with a rudimentary concept of politics can the election of James Madison, with almost two thirds of the electoral vote, be intelligently interpreted as a defeat or humiliation for Thomas Jefferson. His remarkable popularity walked with him through the flames of eight years of Administration and passed with him into private life. Jefferson was both content and happy.

But Congress now convened, and the Embargo fight was on again.

CHAPTER XXIII

Twilight of a Career

I

MEANWHILE, an event in Europe had dealt the Embargo its deadliest blow. The maneuvering of the armies over the plains of Spain had ended in the triumph of the patriots, with the aid of the British, and the Spanish markets again were thrown open to the British merchants and manufacturers. This generously relieved the pressure from the British people on their own Government and greatly reduced the efficacy of the Embargo as an economic weapon against the Ministry in London. Gallatin sensed this instantly as fatal, and Jefferson realized that the effect of the Embargo had been weakened.

At this juncture, too, the Northern Democrats in the commercial States, where the Embargo had reduced their majorities when it had not swept the States back to Federalism, were in a state of panic. What though the Administration had carried two thirds of the electoral votes of the nation, local offices had been lost, and these were important to the local politicians. Politicians of expediency rather than principle, they were eager to abandon the Embargo fight. Still others, not concerned over the local offices, were sincerely intimidated by the rioting and the threats of secession and separation.

But Jefferson stood to his guns, unintimidated and unmindful of expediency. He clung to the belief that, despite the opening of the Spanish markets, the Embargo would ultimately force the British to terms, if rigidly enforced. Where others were retreating, he was advancing. He demanded a stern enforcement act; and with the tide of cowardice running against him, he sought an agreement that the Embargo should run until the following June, with a special congressional session in May to determine the future course.

Having made his position clear, he determined to keep hands off during the brief time he would remain in office. Some historians have ascribed this to every reason but the sane and proper one — an indisposition to commit his successor on the eve of his inauguration. From his day to the present hour, his successors have thought it decent to pursue this policy. Privately, Jefferson still asserted that the only alternative to the Embargo would be war.

In the meantime, the Federalist leaders, with the mobs of the wharves, the smugglers, and racketeers at their back, were more arrogant than ever. The evident timidity of many Democrats increased their temerity. Josiah Quincy, fresh from constant conclaves with the disloyalists of the Essex Junto, had returned to Washington determined to force an immediate repeal. The atmosphere of the capital was heavily charged with the electricity of hate, and there were to be many sinister flashes threatening bloodshed. He entrenched himself in a house remote from the intrusions and turmoil of a boarding-house, and concentrated on the congenial task of injecting the spirit of the Essex Junto into Congress. Easily the most brilliant of the Federalists, he had become the most abusive, and he sallied forth with insults as his weapon, but with the comfortable determination not to hold himself responsible beyond the four walls of the chamber for the personalities in which he proposed to indulge.

Just before this, he had sought the opinion of John Adams, grumbling as usual in the big house in Quincy. The irritable old man wrote him that if the Embargo were continued 'times will be hard,' but the repeal of the Embargo would mean war. 'If you arm our merchant ships there will be war,' he wrote. 'The blood may run too freely for our health and comfort.' And what would Quincy have — war against both France and England? 'Sublime, to be sure,' observed the veteran, 'and if we have a Dutch navy and a Van Tromp to sail the Thames, and a De Ruyter to sail up the Seine, we might gain as much by it as the Dutch did.' [1]

It was not precisely what Quincy sought.

[1] *Quincy*, 145.

The moment Congress convened, the Jeffersonians, with Jefferson's acquiescence rather than with his approval, set themselves to the task of formulating a program on which the party could unite. Out of deference to Madison, Jefferson urged nothing; and Madison took no positive stand. It was Gallatin who sat down with the congressional leaders to find a way. To him was ascribed the task. And the result was the famous Campbell Report, every line of which was written by the head of the Treasury. It reiterated the Jefferson opinion that the one alternative to the continuation of the economic measure was resistance by war — and war with both France and England. Cleverly covering the clear intent to abandon the Embargo, it proposed another Non-Importation Act, aimed at the two great Powers. The question of the actual repeal of the Embargo was left hanging in the air.

Strangely enough, Quincy was convinced that Jefferson had prevailed. In truth, he had not favored the substitution of a Non-Importation Act for the Embargo, but when Madison gave his consent, Jefferson held his peace.

The Report concluded with three resolutions. One to the effect that 'the United States cannot, without a sacrifice of their rights, honor, and independence, submit to the late edicts of Great Britain and France'; another proposing a Non-Importation Act; and a third advising that 'measures ought immediately to be taken for placing the country in a more complete state of defense.' [1] Instantly Quincy was in action with his heavy artillery.

II

The debate opened on the first resolution — that the United States could not submit to the edicts of Great Britain and France. Even so obvious a proposition could not command the support of the Federalists, who were determined to submit, and who were in secret touch with the British to make submission necessary. Quincy was aflame with wrath that such a resolution had been offered in an American Congress.

This, he said, meant the continuance of the Embargo. When he left Boston it had been assumed that it would be repealed. 'With these impressions I arrive in this city. I hear the incantations of

[1] *Writings of Gallatin*, I, 435.

the great enchanter. I feel his spell. I see the legislative machinery begin to move.'

And why continue a law the people of his section would not observe? Expect New England to obey this law? Absurd! 'We have five hundred miles of coast; all furnished with harbors, bays, creeks, rivers, basins — with every variety of invitation to the sea — *with every species of facility to violate such laws as these.*'

Having boasted of the facilities for crime and an indisposition to resist the invitation to lawlessness, he continued. And would Massachusetts, cradle of liberty and independence, submit to privation? 'Our liberty,' he said in one of his exalted flights, 'was not so much a mountain as a sea nymph. She was free as air. She can swim or she can run. The ocean is her cradle. Our fathers met her as she came like the goddess of beauty from the waves. They caught her as she was sporting on the beach. They courted her whilst she was spreading her nets upon the rocks. But an embargoed liberty, a handcuffed liberty, a liberty in fetters, a liberty traversing between the four sides of a prison and beating her head against the walls, is none of our offspring.'

A slur at Jefferson — insults to the members of the House — a threat of insurrection — and a baldly hypocritical expression of a preference for war — and Quincy was through.[1]

The friends of the Administration were infuriated, no less by the threat of insurrection than by the insulting tone. They attacked him savagely, and the gossips of the boarding-houses buzzed with rumors of duels at Bladensburg. 'You may expect to hear that your husband has been abused and pecked at by the whole poultry yard,' Quincy wrote his wife, 'but he keeps up his health and spirits and expects to repay them in time.'[2]

In replying to the attacks a few days later, he injected a provocative reference to slavery which accentuated the sectional prejudices. The fiery Troup, of Georgia, had said that Quincy represented a people engaged in 'a paltry trade in potash and codfish,' and Quincy retorted that these were preferable to 'the growers of cotton and rice and tobacco.' Not only did his constituents deal in these humble articles, 'but they do it with the labor of their own hands — with the sweat of their own brows.'

[1] *Quincy*, 185.   [2] *Ibid.*, 155.

So reckless and intemperate had been his abuse that not a single Federalist dared defend him, and he was rather proud of his isolation. The *Repertory* was reporting that Campbell had threatened to challenge anyone who attacked his Report — a rumor without foundation — and Quincy was writing his wife: 'You may be uneasy, but you know my principles' — which meant that he would resort to abuse, but would refuse to fight.[1]

But the Report was adopted, and the Non-Importation Act was passed. The Embargo was not yet repealed, and the denunciatory and obstructive tactics of the Federalists were intensified. Thus, when the Jeffersonians proposed raising an army of fifty thousand volunteers, Quincy's martial fire was instantly extinguished, and unblushingly he shifted his ground. In truth, his declaration for war had been an oratorical gesture in which his followers refused to join, and, when war finally came, he was found on the side of the Hartford Convention. The Federalists wanted no Embargo; no Non-Importation Act; no war with England. Criticizing everything proposed, they had no constructive substitute to offer, and they stood forth nakedly for submission and surrender. The Jeffersonians stood for the Embargo; and, assuming that war was the sole alternative, they stood for preparations for that grim event. But the moment they proposed to create a volunteer army of fifty thousand men, the Federalists swallowed their gallant words and fought the measure tooth and nail.

Quincy instantly was on his feet opposing the raising of an army, with the insinuation that Jefferson was lying as to its purpose. What! Give Jefferson or Madison, his successor, the power over an army! What assurance it would not be used to crush the Embargo insurrection? Was it replied that 'this excellent man' in the White House would not resort to such a trick? 'Why, sir, this is the very slave's gibberish. What other reason could the cross-legged Turk or the cringing Parisian give for that implicit confidence they yield their sovereigns, except that it is impossible they should abuse their power!'

Running amuck with flagrant personalities, he was constantly interrupted and repaid in kind. A Boston paper reported he had been killed in a duel with Campbell — who had not been the

[1] *Quincy*, 160.

challenger in the duel with Gardenier.[1] And again Quincy reassured his wife, with the reminder that while he would put no
curb upon his tongue, he simply would not fight.[2] Once, only, he
faced the preliminaries of a challenge when he said the actions of
some men 'were natural and inevitable from the situation in which
the gentlemen are placed in relation to the Executive.' Eppes, the
son-in-law of Jefferson, demanded to know if the reference was
to him. Quincy at once disavowed any such thought, and nothing
happened.[3]

However, the volunteer bill was allowed to drop, and the
Jeffersonians concentrated on an enforcement act. It was bitterly
contested by the Federalists, with Quincy leading a filibuster. At
six o'clock in the morning, after nineteen consecutive hours of
ceaseless wrangling, Quincy, utterly exhausted, asked a delay
of twenty-four hours. The request was denied, the vote was
forced, and the act was passed.

III

It was now in January, and the secessionists were playing the
Pied Piper to the water rats of the wharves. In Massachusetts,
the majority in the legislature formally called upon the people to
violate the law and to resist the constituted authority of the nation, the cheaper Jeffersonian politicians there trembling in their
boots.[4] The flag of secession was flying openly.

Meanwhile, Jefferson, refraining from interference with the
policy of his successor, was satisfied with the record. To David
Humphreys he was writing with the keenest satisfaction of the
Embargo's impetus to manufacturing. He had ordered a suit from
Humphreys's mill, and in acknowledging its receipt he had written
that the cloth was 'as good as any man would wish to wear.'
Among the evils of the Embargo he found compensations of an
abiding sort. 'The spring given to manufactures will have durable
effects,' he said. Were peace declared at once, never again would
the States have to import 'one half of the coarse goods' bought
abroad before the Embargo. The coarser goods would continue to
be made in the homes; the finer in the larger factories that had
sprung up in the towns. The commercial element, jealous of the

[1] *Quincy*, 168.   [2] *Ibid.*, 171.   [3] *Ibid.*, 171-72.   [4] Channing, 224-25.

new industry, would complain. But 'my idea is that we should encourage home manufactures,' he wrote. 'I do not think it fair in the shipowners to say that we ought not to make our own axes, nails, etc., here, that they may have the benefit of carrying the iron to Europe and bringing back the nails, etc.' [1]

The next day he was writing that the Federalists wished to sacrifice agriculture and manufactures to commerce and 'to convert this great agricultural country into a city of Amsterdam.' No statesmanship in that, he thought. The true prosperity of a nation, he added, 'depends on a due balance between agriculture, manufactures, and commerce, and not in this protuberant navigation which has kept us in hot water from the commencement of the government, and is now engaging us in war.' [2]

Thus, the last of January, Jefferson, looking back over the path he had followed, was satisfied. 'There never has been a situation in the world before,' he wrote Monroe, 'in which such endeavors as we have made would not have secured our peace.' But should the economic weapon fail, and war come, the nation would again be plunged in debt. 'If we can keep at peace eight years longer,' he said, 'our income, liberated from debt, will be adequate to any war, without new taxes or loans, and our position and increasing strength will put us *hors d'insulte* from any nation.' Five weeks more, and he would pass from power. 'I have no part in affairs beyond the expression of an opinion' because 'I think it fair that my successor should now originate those measures of which he will be charged with the execution and responsibility.'

But, as he wrote, the Northern Democrats were seething with the spirit of rebellion, under the lash of fear. The power to punish or reward had passed from Jefferson, and a panic had seized on some of his followers. They could not wait until June for the repeal of the Embargo. With Joseph Story in the lead, they were rushing pell-mell to the support of Quincy. Jefferson, too wise not to understand the psychology of the situation, listened to the clamor without lifting a finger to silence the malcontents. That was now the business of Madison; and if Madison gave the acquiescence of silence, it was not for Jefferson to intervene.

So the Embargo fight entered its last phase.

[1] *Writings of Jefferson*, XII, 235.　　　　[2] To Leiper, *ibid.*, XII, 235.

IV

Toward the last of January, in a speech opposing the postpone-ment of the repeal, Quincy surpassed himself in abuse of Jefferson and the Administration, and his Federalist followers were de-lighted. 'I had a deputation from Frost's boarding-house, con-sisting of Tallmadge, Upham, and Davenport, and another from the Washington mess consisting of Van Dyke, Lewis, and Van Rensselaer, to thank me,' he wrote with boyish exuberance to his wife.[1] But the reception of the attack in the House was quite different. His assertions were denounced as 'false,' 'malicious,' 'defamatory,' 'cowardly,' and he was described as an 'old Tory' and as 'a friend of Great Britain.' Gardenier, who had paid a penalty for his similar attack, rose to protest that an attempt was being made to force Quincy into a duel. His distaste for fighting, except with his tongue and under the immunity of the House, was known. His friends, therefore, took the weird position that it was unfair to attack him with the only weapon he would use. But who knew what the Democrats might do? One day a friend slipped a brace of pistols into his hands. He declined them, knowing that the duelists of his day were not assassins.[2]

Thus, declaring himself immune from a challenge, he reached the climax of his abuse by proposing an inquiry into Jefferson's official conduct, with the clear thought of an impeachment. The 'conduct' had to do with the collectorship of the port of Boston. Jefferson, having found a political enemy in the post, had refused to remove him because of his Revolutionary services. The old man held on until toward the close of the second Administration, when he re-signed, and Jefferson refused to accept the resignation. Monstrous villainy! It was the charge of Quincy that the place was being held for Dearborn after his retirement from the Cabinet, and some-how the spokesman of the Essex Junto imagined this to be an im-peachable offense. His speech, more than customarily offensive, had been met with a fusillade of insults which he received with all possible complacency. But he had gone to ridiculous lengths and even his friends deserted him. His was the only vote cast for the motion.[3]

[1] *Quincy*, 178.   [2] *Ibid.*, 180.
[3] *Ibid.*, 182.

V

Despite this electric atmosphere, with men toying with pistols. Washington society, such as it was, never had been livelier. There was a surfeit of balls, dinners, teas, card-parties. In the midst of the rapid exchange of insults, the Gallatins gave a ball which turned out to be a jam, notwithstanding a downpour of rain; and Turreau, the French Minister, who had given up lashing his wife to have more time for his anti-American dispatches to Talleyrand, was there 'in all the splendor of gold and diamonds.' [1] While the politicians were draining their reservoirs of vituperation, the ladies were sallying forth in their gay finery to the barracks, delighted with the 'gay appearance of the soldiers,' the 'animation,' and the military music. And, having exhausted the charms of the barracks, they regaled themselves at the Navy Yard, promenading through the vessels; and then on to the new bridge over the Potomac, which was the momentary 'sight' of the town. And then — on with the dance by candlelight.

VI

And the last of January the Democrats of New England and New York were in the full flight of panic over the Embargo. Connecticut now, under the leadership of Governor Trumbull, going beyond the Essex Junto. Trumbull went before the legislature with a ringing nullification message which entitles him to a place in history. Not content with that, the nullification Governor contemptuously brushed aside the request of the Federal Government for the services of the militia.

The Jeffersonians met and denounced this action as 'an enormous stride toward treason and civil war.' Throughout Connecticut, the Jeffersonians, in mass meetings, in dissenting churches and town meetings, took their stand with the Federal Government and pledged their support to Madison.[2] But at the same time Pickering, Cabot, Otis, and Quincy were in correspondence in the preparation of a meeting which foreshadows the Hartford Convention; and John Quincy Adams, in the center of effervescent sedition, was warning Jefferson that secession or separation was in the offing.

[1] Mrs. Smith, 56–57.   [2] Purcell, 280–81.

INTERCOURSE or Impartial Dealings

This Federalist cartoon shows George III, Jefferson and Napoleon.

The English king is threatening Jefferson, 'Well Tommy! I brought you at last to close Quarters, therefore mind what you are about! If you don't behave gently I'll break your limbs and leave you the rest, let me tell you my Boy, keep yourself Cool.'

Jefferson replies, 'Cool? Aye! to be sure! I always keep myself Cool when I get into a Passion, but I must say Lord! have mercy upon us! What an Enormity! to pull my coat on the Highway of all Nations! Lord! What an Inconvenient Restriction.'

Napoleon says, 'Très bien! Mon Oncle Thomas! Dat is very vell! de more you make one Noise, de less dat Jean Boule vill see vat ve are, And and Gloves. N'oubliez pas dat I am de And — I want de Money and must ave it.'

By the middle of February, the panic-stricken Democrats were in open insurrection. Quincy gave them his pontifical blessing. He found 'Jefferson and his friends obstinate,' but was pleased to observe that the Northern Democrats were determined that the Embargo should be raised on March 4. Quincy was fearful that Jefferson would prevail. 'The old enchanter!' 'The Magic Wand!' The politicians plunged into a bitter debate; and even when the motion to postpone repeal until June was overwhelmingly voted down, Quincy was sure the plan to repeal in March would fail. 'Jefferson is a host, and is opposed to it, and if the wand of the magician is not broken, he will yet defeat the attempt,' he wrote.

Then followed a series of secret caucuses, with more and more Democrats running like hares before the hounds, and with Quincy still skeptical of success. The shadow of 'the old magician' cast a chill on all his hopes.

But Jefferson was doing nothing at all. His opinion was known; and the decision reached would affect another's Administration, not his. When, in the end, the Non-Intercourse Act was adopted as a substitute for the Embargo, and the repeal of the latter was fixed for March 4, the inflamed imagination of Quincy assured him that this was but a magician's trick of Jefferson's. But it was not.[1]

If Jefferson felt any sense of outrage or humiliation, he gave no sign. Writing his son-in-law at that moment he said he had 'thought Congress had taken the ground firmly for continuing the embargo until June, and then war,' but that 'a sudden and unaccountable revolution of opinion took place the last week, chiefly among the New England and the New York members, and in a kind of panic they voted the 4th of March for removing the embargo.' It did seem strange that a deliberative body of mature men, who less than a month before had passed the sternest kind of an enforcement act, should so suddenly turn tail and run from their own position. 'And this, too,' wrote Jefferson, 'after we had become satisfied that the Essex Junto had found their expectation desperate of inducing the people there either to separation or forcible opposition.' And that was all.[2]

So ended the first valorous attempt of an American statesman to find, in economic pressure, a substitute for war; and thence on-

[1] *Quincy*, 185.   [2] *Writings of Jefferson*, XII, 248.

ward moved the young Republic toward the second war with England.

VII

Thus, after eight years of unvarying success, Jefferson, within less than a month of his departure, lost his first battle in leadership; and then only after the power to punish and reward had passed from him; and even then, only because he refused to impose any policy on his successor who would have to bear the burden of the battle.

As he sat in meditative mood in the White House in those twilight hours of his power, he could review his eight years of administration with eminent satisfaction.

He had put the young Republic on the democratic tack it was to maintain for years, with liberty, opportunity without privilege, simplicity, with authority and power.

He had brought the vast empire of Louisiana under the flag without the shedding of a drop of blood, and he knew that in time this would become the garden spot of the Republic.

He had launched the first scientific expedition in the nation's history, and had blazed a trail through the western wilderness to the western sea, and turned the eyes of enterprise upon the illimitable possibilities of the vast domain beyond the Mississippi.

Regardless of unprecedented provocation, he had stoutly preserved the liberty of the press, even while it teemed with the vilest lies about his personal and public life; and he had stood four square for the freedom of discussion.

By his quick challenge to Chase, he had purged the federal judiciary of evils that made it abhorrent and tyrannical; had ended definitively the conversion of the bench into a party hustings for the spouting of partisan harangues; and had stopped the criminal practice of packing juries by federal marshals with the knowledge and consent of federal judges.

By abolishing sinecure offices, created for partisan purposes, and by introducing business methods into those remaining, he had greatly reduced the cost of government and rid the nation of its parasites.

He had put the scoffers to shame by the brilliant success of his

financial arrangements. Never in a single year of his two Administrations did the record fail to show an increase in the surplus of
revenue, despite his reduction of the burden of taxation. Even in
the year of the Embargo, he was able to report that on the fifth of
January, 1809, there would be $16,000,000 in the Treasury —
enough to meet the expenses of that year and leave $3,580,000
surplus.[1]

And year by year, after repealing the internal taxes, he had paid
off a portion of the national debt, and when his rule was ended, he
could rejoice in the knowledge that $33,580,000 of the debt had
been wiped out.

In anticipation of the early payment of the debt, he had outlined an ambitious plan of internal improvements of immeasurable
value to the nation, and the fact that he considered this more in
keeping with civilized statesmanship than the waging of destructive wars has been ascribed by some sword-rattlers of the ivory
tower to 'weakness.'

If, without design, his Embargo policy had given a tremendous
impetus to manufacturing, the fact remains that, in his Administration, industry went forward with leaps and bounds.

The record was one of Gargantuan achievement, and the old
man, worn and weary with the toils of state, could reflect upon
it with satisfaction. And, as he sat by candlelight in his study
meditating on the eight years that had passed, he could rejoice in
the realization that he had retained the affections of the people,
and that he had lost no real friends.

His friend Madison had been chosen to succeed him, to carry on
his general policies with the aid of some of his own advisers; and
his friend Monroe felt for him an affectionate admiration and
yielded nothing of his loyalty.

Content, he awaited his release with eagerness. He longed for
the serenity of his hilltop at Monticello.

VIII

When, toward the close of February, the citizens of his home
county expressed a wish to meet him on the road on horseback and
in carriages to give him a neighborly conduct to his home, he re-

[1] Adams, *Gallatin*, 382.

plied that it was impossible to know when he would return. With
the congressional sessions consuming his time, he could not attend
to the winding-up of his affairs until after the inauguration. And
then would come the arrangements of papers for his successor; and
then the packing and closing of his personal affairs. All this would
require an indefinite number of days. 'But it is a sufficient happiness to me,' he wrote, 'to know that my fellow citizens generally
entertain for me the kind sentiments which have prompted this
proposition, without giving to so many the trouble of leaving their
homes to meet a single individual. I shall have opportunities of
taking them individually by the hand at our courthouse and other
public places. . . . Certainly it is the greatest consolation to me to
know that in returning to the bosom of my native county, I shall
again be in the midst of their kind affections, and I can say with
truth that my return to them will make me happier than I have
been since I left them.' [1]

Two days before he relinquished his post, he sat writing to his
old friend Pierre du Pont de Nemours. Soon he would be back
with his 'family, books, and farms.' Never 'did a prisoner released
from his chains feel such relief as I shall on shaking off the shackles
of power,' he wrote. Nature had intended him 'for the tranquil
pursuits of science by rendering these my supreme delight.' But
'the enormities of my times' had forced him to 'take a part in re-
sisting them, and to commit myself to the boisterous ocean of
political passions.' He was happy in the thought that affairs were
to be left in the hands of men capable of taking care of them, 'and
if we are destined to meet misfortunes, it will be because no human
wisdom could avert them.' [2]

The day of his release was bright and crisp. Throngs had poured
into the little capital. The day before, the galleries at the Capitol
were packed with pretty young women from Baltimore and the
surrounding country, who found that politics would serve between
teas and dances. Ten thousand men and women lined the way
from Madison's house to the Capitol. The entire militia from
Georgetown and Alexandria appeared with much éclat to accompany the new chief to his coronation. It had been much simpler at

[1] To T. M. Randolph, *Writings of Jefferson*, xii, 256.
[2] *Domestic Life*, 323.

Jefferson's inaugurations. And when word reached him that a body of cavalry and infantry were on their way to attend him, the old man hurriedly summoned his grandson, and the two mounted and rode away to escape the attention. Down Pennsylvania Avenue they rode, and out from an intersecting street emerged the gay militia. Jefferson lifted his hat in salute, and, putting spurs to his horse, galloped by them. Thus he reached the Capitol alone, as he had wished, and, after tying his horse to the palisades, he entered the building as a private citizen.[1]

Adams thought the scene in the House, where the ceremony was held, 'magnificent,' but noticed that Madison's very brief speech was spoken 'in a tone of voice so low that he could not be heard.' In the crowded chamber sat Jefferson, a smile of satisfaction on his face.[2]

The ceremony over, the crowd pushed through the streets to Madison's house to pay their respects. The street was packed with carriages, and the people had to take their turn in line, and often it required half an hour to reach the door. At the door of the drawing-room stood Madison and Dolly, she 'extremely beautiful, dressed in a plain cambric dress with a very long train ... all dignity, grace, affability.' There Adams again saw Jefferson standing aside, happy in the triumph of his friend.

It was suggested to him that he should return to the White House, since the ladies wished to follow him.

'That is right,' he said, with a smile, 'since I am too old to follow them. I remember in France, when his friends were taking leave of Mr. Franklin, the ladies smothered him with embraces, and on his introducing me as his successor, I told him I wished he would transfer these privileges to me, but he answered, "You are too young a man."'[3]

And follow him they did, though all the servants had been dismissed for the day, and if there were not embraces, there were tears. That night Jefferson accompanied the Madisons to the inaugural ball.

Thus Jefferson passed from power.

[1] *Domestic Life*, 323.
[2] Adams, *Diary*, I, 544.
[3] Mrs. Smith, 62.

IX

He remained in the White House, the Madisons in their home, during the several days required for packing. This constantly was interrupted by visitors and by calls of courtesy on old friends.[1] He was unconcerned with the celebrations all over the country, though most of these were farewell tributes to himself. But the Federalists met at banquets to propose and cheer insulting toasts. That which pleased him most was the resolution of the Virginia Legislature, phrased by the brilliant William Wirt:

'In the principles on which you have administered the government,' it read, 'we see only the continuance and the maturity of the same virtues and abilities which drew upon you in your youth the resentment of Dunmore. From the first brilliant and happy moment of your resistance to foreign tyranny until the present day, we mark with pleasure and with gratitude the same uniform and consistent character — the same warm and devoted attachment to liberty and the Republic — the same Roman love of your country, her rights, her peace, her prosperity. How blessed will be the retirement into which you will go! How deservedly blessed will it be! For you carry with you the richest of all rewards, the recollections of a life well spent in the service of your country, and proofs the most decisive of the love, the gratitude, the veneration of your countrymen.'[2]

At length, the packing was finished. A farewell to Madison, Gallatin, and the rest of the Cabinet, and he rode forth from Washington on his way home.

The roads were miserable, though he had seen worse. The jolting over the frozen ruts finally drove him from his carriage to his horse, and thus for three days he rode steadily over rough roads and through boisterous weather. Anyone meeting him upon the highway then would have seen an old man on horseback, his head bent down because of the blinding snowstorm. But there was a smile on the face of the rider, for he was going home.[3]

At the foot of the mountain where the private road branches off from the main highway and ascends, the rider found his daughter, his grandchildren, and a delirious group of negroes, who marched

[1] *Domestic Life*, 324.   [2] *Ibid.*, 325.
[3] *Ibid.*, 326.

beside him, close to his horse, touching his boots and clothing reverently, and thus was he accompanied to the house.

And Jefferson was home to stay.

x

The farm at Monticello contained more than five thousand acres, and here lived more than a hundred slaves who had no cause to complain of the severity of their master. Seventy miles away was Poplar Forest, with more than four thousand acres, and eighty-five slaves. It was on his hilltop at Monticello that Jefferson was to spend the greater portion of his time during the next seventeen years, but once a year at least found him astride his horse or in his carriage on his way to Poplar Forest for a sojourn of a few weeks. Here it was possible for him to live a simpler life, by escaping the homage of his admirers. The house was comfortable, and on its shelves were his favorite books. And here, safe from the general deluge of mail, he could devote more time to long letters to those he loved. For even at Monticello, he was not permitted the privacy of a retired country gentleman. He was too punctilious and kindly to ignore correspondents who had no claim upon him. He relished the letters from his friends and liked to answer them at length.

When first he returned to Monticello, he enjoyed nothing more than to mount his horse and ride by the hour over his farm, observing the men at work, making suggestions. The estate was sadly in need of supervision, for he had not been happy in his supervisors. But almost immediately the flood of mail kept him at his desk much of the day and in the evening. From every quarter of the world authors sent their books requesting criticism and he felt it his duty to comply. This often meant writing pages of criticism to people of whom he never had heard.

And then the pilgrimages began very soon. Day after day the house was crowded with visitors. Utter strangers would arrive in carriages and on horseback, to remain for two or three days, and they were housed and fed and their horses stabled.

Nor was he ever to find it possible to put behind him the worries and problems of statesmanship, for during the eight years of Madison's Administration his advice constantly was sought, and

during the succeeding eight years of Monroe's régime, it was the
same. Soon he was seeking to conciliate Duane and Gallatin and
thus harmonize the party in Pennsylvania. He grieved over the
early dissensions in the Madison Cabinet, but when, through his
mediation, the ancient friendship of Madison and Monroe was
revived, and the latter entered the Cabinet as Secretary of State,
he was delighted. The ineptitude of Armstrong in the war irked
him, and the burning of public buildings in Washington enraged
him. But when, on the restoration of the Capitol, it was proposed
to place a tablet on the walls with reference to the burning, he
protested strongly that nothing could be gained by an act to perpetuate old misunderstandings. The destruction of the Congressional Library outraged him most of all, and soon he offered
his valuable collection of ten thousand volumes that were to
become the nucleus of the Congressional Library that we know
today.

Madison served his two terms and returned to Montpelier, and
the old neighborly relations of the friends were resumed. Monroe
succeeded, and when at the expiration of his first term he was unanimously re-elected and the old Federalist Party sank into its
grave, Jefferson was convinced that a democratic republic was
assured. And then, in his last days, John Quincy Adams succeeded Monroe, and Jefferson was much pleased because of his
friends at Quincy.

The old bitterness of partisan enmities diminished; the slanders
of the old Federalist Party ceased to make any impression on the
public mind; and soon Daniel Webster, from New England, was
making a sentimental pilgrimage to the shrine of the old philosopher. Even Edward Livingston, with whom he had had a bitter
feud, returned to the fold, and letters of affection and appreciation
passed between them.

But that which pleased the old man most was the reconciliation
with John Adams. The old man at Quincy had become embittered during the fight on his Administration, and, with his defeat
by Jefferson, in 1800, the long-continued social intimacy between
the two great Revolutionary figures had been broken. On the
death of Jefferson's younger daughter, Abigail Adams, as we have
seen, put her resentment aside to write a letter of condolence.

Jefferson replied eagerly, and there was a correspondence which did not touch the embittered Adams. But as the days of his political troubles receded, and old age began to make itself felt, he remembered with a lingering affection his associate of other days. A mutual friend took upon himself the rôle of peace-maker.

At length the old Puritan said:

'I love Thomas Jefferson and I always shall.'

The mutual friend conveyed the remark to Jefferson.

'That is enough for me,' he said.

And thus began the classic correspondence between these two old men which continued without interruption to the end. They wrote at great length on books, on science, on politics past and present, on their common Revolutionary memories, on theories of government, on their philosophy of life. Time and again the irritable patriot at Quincy would become belligerent, and the philosopher of Monticello was ever soothing in reply. In a sense, it was hand in hand that the old men entered the twilight of their heroic days.

From 1819 until the end, Jefferson's keenest interest was in the founding of the University of Virginia, where he hoped that youth would be trained in the ways of ordered liberty and democracy. He busied himself finding professors that met his requirements. And he drew the plans for the buildings — one of his best con-tributions to architecture. So perfectly did he conceive that when, a century later, a new building was necessary, and Stanford White, the greatest living American architect,was summoned to the task, he spent days studying the architectural plans of Jefferson so as not to inject a jarring note into what he considered a symphony in brick and mortar. He could not improve upon it; he thought it vandalism to mar it.

As the buildings were rising, the old man daily sat in the cupola of Monticello looking with delight through his field-glasses on the emergence of one of his life's dreams.

Time passed; the endless pilgrimages continued; and rheuma-tism attacked him, forcing a curtailment of his outdoor activities. No longer could he ride for hours over his farm. A broken wrist made writing painful. And he had his monetary worries. The con-

version of his home into a free national hostelry had helped under-
mine his fortune. He was land poor, and his debts pressed upon
him. At length, toward the end, he asked legal authorization to
sell his beloved home by lottery. But when the news spread, his
countrymen everywhere started subscriptions and enough money
was poured in upon him to meet his obligations, and the lottery
was abandoned.

And then came the visit of Lafayette. Jefferson was very old
and frail, and Lafayette, too, was crippled with age, and only a
little while before he had written Jefferson of the death of Madame
Lafayette, who had shared her husband's affection for the great
American. When the French patriot appeared on the lawn, he
found a feeble old man awaiting him there. They tottered to
each other and embraced. One night Jefferson, with Madison,
attended a dinner in honor of Lafayette at the hotel in Charlottesville, but another read the affectionate address Jefferson was too
feeble to deliver.

So he passed into the deeper twilight. The uninvited guests continued to pour in upon him, and frequently the hall was lined with
the unfamiliar faces of the pilgrims, curiously watching a weak old
man on his way to the dining-room. Sometimes Madison and
Dolly would drive over from Montpelier to sit with their friend
under the trees on the lawn, and Monroe often was there reviewing with him the old battles and the new problems. Jefferson was
conscious of a failing memory, but his mind otherwise was clear
and robust to the end.

One day, toward the close of June, 1826, he was forced to summon a physician. His strength failed rapidly. One night in his
sleep he sat up in bed, his hand and arm moving as though in the
act of writing. He was back in the days of the Revolution. 'The
Committee of Safety— it ought to be warned . . .' he muttered.
In his conscious moments his mind was clear, and he faced the end
with the calm courage of a philosopher. 'I am like an old watch,'
he said, in reply to a friend who sought to encourage him, 'with a
pinion worn out here and a wheel there, until it can go no
longer.'

On the Fourth of July he ceased to breathe and passed to the
immortals.

That day the family had gathered about the deathbed of John Adams in Quincy.

'Thomas Jefferson still lives,' he murmured, with his dying breath.

And Adams spoke for the centuries.

THE END

Books, Manuscripts, Public Documents, Contemporary Pamphlets, and Newspapers Cited and Consulted

BOOKS

ADAMS, HENRY, *Life of Albert Gallatin*, Philadelphia, 1879. (Adams, *Gallatin.*)
    The Writings of Albert Gallatin, 3 vols., Philadelphia, 1878.
    (*Writings of Gallatin.*)
    Documents Relating to New England Federalism, Boston, 1905.
    (*Doc. N.E. Fed.*)
ADAMS, J. Q., *Memoir and Diary*, ed. by C. F. Adams, 12 vols., Philadelphia,
    1876. (Adams, *Diary.*)
AMBLER, CHARLES H., *Thomas Ritchie: A Study in Virginia Politics.*
AMES, FISHER. *See* Ames, Seth.
AMES, SETH, *Works of Fisher Ames*, 3 vols., Boston, 1854. (*Ames.*)
AMORY, THOMAS, *Life of James Sullivan*, 2 vols., Boston, 1859.
ANDERSON, D. P., *William Branch Giles: A Study of Politics in Virginia and the
    Nation.* (*Giles.*)
Annals of Congress, 42 vols. Debates and Proceedings in the Congress of the
    United States, First Congress, First Session, to Eighteenth Congress, First
    Session.
BENTLEY, WILLIAM, *Diary*, 4 vols., Salem, 1911.
BEVERIDGE, ALBERT J., *Life of John Marshall*, 4 vols., Boston, 1917–19.
BOWERS, CLAUDE G., *Jefferson and Hamilton*, Boston, 1925.
BRADFORD, GAMALIEL, *Damaged Souls*, Boston, 1923.
BRUCE, WILLIAM C., *John Randolph of Roanoke*, 2 vols., New York, 1922.
BRYAN, W. B., *A History of the National Capital*, 2 vols., New York, 1914.
BURR, AARON. *See* Bradford, Davis, McCaleb, Robinson.
CABOT, GEORGE. *See* Lodge.
CHANNING, EDWARD, *The Jeffersonian System*, New York, 1906.
CLARK, A. C., *Life and Letters of Dolly Madison*, Washington, 1914. (*Life of
    Dolly Madison.*)
CORWIN, EDWARD S., *John Marshall and the Constitution*, New Haven, 1919.
COUES, ELLIOT, *Lewis and Clark: History of the Expedition*, 4 vols., New York,
    1893.
COXE, TENCH, *Statement of the Arts and Manufactures of the United States.*
CUTLER, MANASSEH, *Life, Journal, and Correspondence*, 2 vols., New York, 1888.
CUTTS, L. B., *Memoirs and Letters of Dolly Madison.* (*Memoirs of Dolly Mad-
    ison.*)
DAVIS, JOHN, *Travels of Four Years and a Half in the United States*, New York,
    1909.
DAVIS, MATTHEW L., *Memoirs of Aaron Burr*, 2 vols., New York, 1852. (*Burr.*)

DODD, WILLIAM E., *Life of Nathaniel Macon*, Raleigh, North Carolina, 1903.

DU PONT. *See* Malone, Dumas.

FORD, P. L., *The Writings of Thomas Jefferson*, 10 vols.

GALLATIN, ALBERT. *See* Adams, Henry.

GAY, SIDNEY, *Life of James Madison*, Boston, 1899.

GILES, WILLIAM BRANCH. *See* Anderson, D. P.

HAMILTON, ALEXANDER. *See* Bowers, Lodge.

HAMILTON, ALLAN MCLANE, *The Intimate Life of Alexander Hamilton*.

HAMILTON, S. M., *The Writings of James Monroe*, 7 vols., 1898–1903.

HART, S. A., ed., *Zebulon Pike's Arkansas Journey*, Denver, 1832.

HIGGINSON, STEPHEN. *See* Higginson, T. W.

HIGGINSON, T. W., *Life and Times of Stephen Higginson*, Boston, 1907.

HILLARD, J. S., *Memoir and Correspondence of Jeremiah Mason*.

HIRST, FRANCIS W., *Life and Times of Thomas Jefferson*, New York, 1926.

HUMPHREYS, F. L., *Life and Times of David Humphreys*, 2 vols., New York, 1917.

HUNT, GAILLARD, *The Writings of James Madison*, 9 vols.

IRVING, P. M., *Life and Letters of Washington Irving*, 4 vols., New York, 1869.

JEFFERSON, THOMAS. *See* Bowers, Channing, Hirst, Johnson, Lipscomb, Malone, Randolph, Robinson, Sears, Tucker.

JOHNSON, ALLEN, *Jefferson and His Colleagues*, New Haven, 1921.

KENT, JAMES. *See* Kent, William.

KENT, WILLIAM, *Memoirs and Letters of James Kent*, Boston, 1898. (*Kent*.)

KING, C. R., *Life and Correspondence of Rufus King*, 10 vols., New York, 1896. (*King's Corr.*)

LEWIS, MERIWETHER. *See* Coues, Elliot, Thwaites, R. G.

LIPSCOMB, ANDREW A., *Writings of Thomas Jefferson*, Washington, 1902.

LIVINGSTON, E. B., *The Livingstons of Livingston Manor*, New York, 1910.

LIVINGSTON, ROBERT. *See* Livingston, E. B., Peyster, F. de.

LODGE, HENRY CABOT, *Alexander Hamilton*, Boston, 1882.
                                  Works of Alexander Hamilton, 10 vols., New York, 1886.
                                  Life and Letters of George Cabot, Boston, 1877. (*Cabot*.)

MACON, NATHANIEL. *See* Dodd.

MADISON, DOLLY. *See* Clark.

MADISON, JAMES. *See* Gay, Hunt, Rives.

MALONE, DUMAS, *Correspondence Between Thomas Jefferson and Pierre S. du Pont*, Boston, 1930.

MARSHALL, JOHN. *See* Beveridge, Corwin.

MCCALEB, W. F., *The Aaron Burr Conspiracy*, New York, 1903.

MCMASTER, J. B., *History of the People of the United States*, 8 vols.

MONROE, JAMES. *See* Hamilton, S. M., Morgan.

MORGAN, GEORGE, *James Monroe*, Boston, 1921.

MORISON, S. E., *Life and Letters of Harrison Gray Otis*, 2 vols., Boston, 1912.

MORRIS, ANN CAREY, *Diary and Letters of Gouverneur Morris*, 2 vols., New York, 1888. (Morris, *Diary*.)

MORRIS, GOUVERNEUR. *See* Morris, Ann Carey.

OTIS, HARRISON GRAY. *See* Morison.

PARTON, JAMES, *The Life and Times of Aaron Burr*.

PAYNE, GEORGE H., *History of Journalism in the United States*, New York, 1920.

PEYSTER, F. DE, *A Biographical Sketch of Robert R. Livingston*, New York, 1876.

BIBLIOGRAPHY

PICKERING, TIMOTHY. *See* Upham.
PLUMER, WILLIAM, JR., *Life of William Plumer*, Boston, 1857. (*Plumer.*)
PURCELL, RICHARD J., *Connecticut in Transit*, Washington, 1918.
QUINCY, EDMUND, *Life of Josiah Quincy*, Boston, 1867. (*Quincy.*)
RANDALL, HENRY S., *Life of Thomas Jefferson*, 3 vols., New York, 1858.
RANDOLPH, JOHN. *See* Bruce.
RANDOLPH, SARAH N., *The Domestic Life of Thomas Jefferson*, New York, 1871. (*Domestic Life.*)
RITCHIE, THOMAS. *See* Ambler.
RIVES, W. C., *History of the Life and Times of James Madison*, 3 vols., Boston, 1868.
ROBERTSON, DAVIS, *Reports of the Trial of Aaron Burr for Treason*, 2 vols., Philadelphia, 1808.
ROBINSON, W. A., *Jeffersonian Democracy in New England*, New Haven, 1916.
ROOSEVELT, THEODORE, *Gouverneur Morris*, Boston, 1888.
SEARS, L. M., *Jefferson and the Embargo*, Durham, North Carolina, 1927.
SMITH, MARGARET BAYARD, *First Forty Years of Washington Society*, New York, 1906. (Mrs. Smith.)
STORY, JOSEPH. *See* Story, William. (*Story.*)
STORY, WILLIAM, *Life and Letters of Joseph Story*, 2 vols., Boston, 1851.
SULLIVAN, JAMES. *See* Amory.
THWAITES, R. G., ed., *Official Journals of Lewis and Clark Expedition*, 7 vols., New York, 1904.
TUCKER, GEORGE, *Life of Thomas Jefferson*, 3 vols.
UPHAM, C. K., *Life of Timothy Pickering*, 4 vols., Boston, 1872. (*Pickering.*)
WHARTON, ANN H., *Social Life of the Early Republic*, Philadelphia, 1816. (*Social Life.*)
WIRT, WILLIAM, *Letters of a British Spy*, New York, 1832.

CONTEMPORARY PAMPHLETS AND LETTERS

Democracy Unveiled, or Tyranny Stripped of the Garb of Patriotism, by Christopher Caustic, LL.B. (Thomas Green Fessenden), New York, 1806.
Papers of James A. Bayard, 1796–1815, ed. by Elizabeth Donnan, *Annual Report* of the American Historical Association for 1913, 2 vols., Washington, 1915.
A Reply to Lucius Junius Brutus's 'Examination of the President's Answer to the New Haven Remonstrance,' by Leonidas, New York, 1801.
Dr. Samuel L. Mitchill's 'Letters from Washington,' *Harper's Magazine*, 1879.
Strictures on a Pamphlet Entitled 'An Examination of the President's Reply to the New Haven Remonstrance' signed 'Lucius Junius Brutus,' by Tullius Americus, Albany, 1801.
A View of the President's Conduct Concerning the Conspiracy of 1806, by J. H. Daveiss, Frankfort, Kentucky, 1807.
A Vindication of the Measures of the Present Administration, by Algernon Sydney (Gideon Granger), Hartford, 1803.

MANUSCRIPT MATERIAL

MSS. Archives, American Embassy, Madrid, 1801–10.
MSS. Yrujo despatches, Spanish Archives, Madrid.

CONTEMPORARY NEWSPAPERS

Albany Register (Jeffersonian).
Aurora, Philadelphia, Pennsylvania (Jeffersonian).
Columbian Centinel, Boston, Massachusetts (Federalist).
Connecticut Courant, Hartford, Connecticut (Federalist).
Independent Chronicle, Boston, Massachusetts (Jeffersonian).
National Intelligencer, Washington, D.C. (Jeffersonian).
New England Palladium, Boston, Massachusetts (Federalist).
New York American Citizen and Advertiser (Independent Jeffersonian).
New York Bee (Jeffersonian).
New York Commercial Advertiser (Federalist).
New York Evening Post (Federalist).
New York Minerva (Federalist).
Ohio Gazette, Marietta, Ohio.
Philadelphia Gazette.
Richmond Enquirer (Jeffersonian),
Virginia Argus.
Washington Federalist, Washington, D.C. (Federalist).

GOVERNMENT DOCUMENTS

Annals of Congress, 1801–09.
Biographical Directory of the American Congress, 1774–1927.
Diplomatic Correspondence, 1801–09.

INDEX

Index

INDEX

case as district attorney, 404, 408–11, 416, 417, 422, 424

Helvétius, Mme., 204

Henderson, Alexander, 383 n.

Henry, John, 472, 473

Higginson, Stephen, 432, 487; disgusted at the Louisiana purchase, 213; letters from Pickering advocating disunion, 235, 236; sympathetic with disunion plan but not convinced of its practicability, 239, 240; his attack on William Gray, 457, 458

Hillard, George S., his *Memoir and Correspondence of Jeremiah Mason.* *See* Mason, Jeremiah

Hillhouse, James, 12, 13, 96, 438; votes against the Louisiana purchase, 223; in a secession conspiracy, 223, 232, 234, 235; sketch of, 232, 233

Hirst, Francis W., his *Life and Times of Thomas Jefferson* cited, 39, 466

Holland, Lord, 357, 435; offends Pinkney, 351, 352; entrusted with the negotiations with Monroe and Pinkney, 352; his personality, 352; a true friend of the United States, 357; supports America on the Embargo, 466

Holland House, 352

Hopkinson, Joseph, as attorney for Judge Chase, 280, 286

Horse-races, 19–21

Hosack, Dr. David, 144

Howick, Charles Grey, Viscount, 358 n.

Huger, Mr. and Mrs. Benjamin, 12

Hulman, W. E., 157 n.

Humboldt, Alexander von, 28; as a guest of Jefferson, 50

Humphreys, David, 433, 434; his merino sheep and woolen mill, 470; Jefferson compliments him on his cloth, 497

Humphreys, F. L., his *Life and Times of David Humphreys* cited, 434, 470, 471

Hunt, G., *Writings of Madison.* *See* Madison, James

Huntington, Dan, 232

Impressment of American seamen by British officers, 328, 329; discussion of preventive measures, 329–42; the *Chesapeake* affair and the resulting discussions, 427–51; Monroe requested to demand the abolishment of, 430; the right upheld by Canning, 435; defended by Pickering, 445, 446; Pickering's views attacked by J. Q. Adams, 447

Independent Chronicle, cited, 61, 64, 65, 74, 127, 134, 142, 148, 171, 183, 186, 231, 252, 295, 327, 442, 444, 447, 462–64, 469, 470, 487; on the success of American diplomacy at Madrid, 183; protests against eulogies of Hamilton, 252; 'Cato' in, 339

Indians, tampering with, 429, 430

Ingersoll, Charles Jared, on Thomas Em-

met, 364; on Philadelphia manufacturing, 471

Internal revenue, Jefferson's proposal to dispense with taxes for, 85, 88–92; the proposal pressed successfully, 133–37

International law, collapse of, 452

Iredell, Judge James, 416

Ireland, John Randolph's feeling for, 106

Irish, the, the Emmets, 363, 364; Federalist hate of, 364

Irving, R. M., his *Life and Letters of Washington Irving* cited, 403

Irving, Washington, with John Randolph in London, 113; sent to the Burr trial by a friend of Burr, 403

Jackson, Andrew, Burr discloses a part of his Louisiana plan to, 369; entertains Burr, 370; Burr's opinion of, 370; after another visit from Burr issues a mysterious proclamation, 382; his state of mind and course of action as Burr's plot develops, 389, 390

Jackson, James, of Georgia, 121, 165; in the Louisiana debates, 177, 220; resigns from the Senate to fight the Yazoo sale in the State Legislature, 300; replies to Quincy in the Miranda discussion, 323; in the debate on Randolph's anti-Spanish resolution, 326

Jackson, Maj. William, editor of the *Philadelphia Gazette*, 316

Jamaica, 378

Jay, John, 76, 131, 143; opposes George Clinton for Governor of New York, 257, 258, 477

Jay Treaty, 177, 438

Jefferson, Martha. *See* Randolph, Martha

Jefferson, Mary. *See* Eppes, Mary

JEFFERSON, THOMAS, 9, 14, 21; attendance at Sunday services, 22–24; and the Bonaparte-Patterson marriage, 27; domestic life in the White House, 30–32; his personal appearance and manners, 32, 33; his daughters, 33–35; his manner of entertaining, 35–38; the Merry incident, 38–46; his dinners, 46–49; his entertainment of Federalists, 46–49; his receptions, 49, 50; Hamilton's enmity, 52, 53; the inaugural address and its effect, 52–56; choosing his Cabinet, 56–60; his patronage policy, 61–71, 78, 79; his increasing strength brings renewed attacks from the Federalists, 71–77; consults with Madison and Gallatin on Administration policies, 78–83; determination to enforce economy, 79–81; adopts Gallatin's policy of specific appropriations, 81, 82, 85, 86; relations with his Cabinet, 84; his course as to Messages, 84; the first Message discusses international affairs, economy in the government, specific appropriations, the judiciary system, and naturalization, and draws important issues, 84–87; his policies attacked by the Federalists, 87–95; alert but not disposed to dictate to Congress, 114; writes to Dr. Rush on vaccination, 114; success of his attack on the Judiciary Act, 133, 134; insistence on repeal of the internal revenue taxes, 134, 135; the measure passes, 137; plans with Gallatin for payment of the public debt, 137, 138; canards concerning, 138; happy over results of the session, 139; invites Thomas Paine from France and entertains him, 140–43; his attitude toward religion, 145; his concept of the Constitution, 145; scurrilous attack by James T. Callender, 147–49; resting at Monticello, 149, 150; seeds of illness, 150; not worried over the intrigues of Burr, 150, 151; and the Louisiana situation, 155–58; on the crest of popularity, 160; never gave his adherence to Marshall's view of the power of the Supreme Court, 169, 170; able to boast of 'perfect health,' 171; appoints James Monroe as special envoy for the Louisiana negotiations in Paris, 171, 184, 185; prepared to make war if negotiations fail, 175; on the importance of the mission to the destinies of the Republic, 185; letters to Robert Livingston, 185; his estimate of Livingston, 193; his 'Notes on Virginia,' 194; awaits with impatience the results of the Louisiana negotiations, 199; authorizes Monroe to confer with the British ministers on the situation, 199; on the moral precepts of Jesus, 200; his French friends and correspondents, 203, 204; Napoleon compliments, 204; his anxiety over the Louisiana negotiations and jubilance at the result, 206–09; submits to the Cabinet an amendment to the Constitution to cover the Louisiana purchase but is voted down, 209; calls Congress for October, 214; his Message announces the purchase, urges prompt action upon it, and emphasizes the duty of neutrality in the coming European war, 215; purchases fowls for Monticello, 217; planning a government for Louisiana, 224, 225; appoints Claiborne its Governor, 225–27; his attitude toward Burr, 243; kept informed of the proceedings of the disunionists but never gravely concerned, 253; not keen for reelection, 257; his renomination inevitable, 257; successes of his first administration, 258, 259; starts the *Richmond Enquirer*, 259; loss of his daughter Mary, 260, 261; reconciliation with John Adams, 261; carries the election of 1804, 266, 267; and the case of Judge John Pickering, 270, 271; Justice Chase's attack upon, 274; refers the matter to Congressman Nicholson, 274; his so-called 'attack on the federal judiciary' only an attack on the partisan

behavior of judges, 281; false charges that he intervened in the Chase trial, 290; the trial an actual triumph for him, 292, 293; foul attacks upon in the Federalist press, 296; embarrassed by factional fights in his party, 298, 299; letter to Giles, 299; aloof from the factional battles of Madison and Monroe, 306; dissuades his son-in-law from a proposed duel, 308; discussing the Spanish problem, 312; determines to adopt Talleyrand's suggestion and open negotiations, 313; his Messages to Congress on the Spanish situation, 313, 314; the break with Randolph, 315, 324–27; his sorrow at Yrujo's behavior, 317; his attitude toward Smith in the Miranda case, 322; his Message to Congress on relations with Great Britain, 330, 331; hears undisturbed of Randolph's attack on him in his speech against Gregg's resolution, 337; sends William Pinkney, a Federalist, to London to assist Monroe, 343; accustomed to personal abuse, 343; Senator Plumer's opinion of his integrity, 343; abandons the disaffected Randolph and Macon, but gives Nicholson a place on the federal bench, 343; a skillful letter to Monroe, 344; the country prospers under his financial policies, 347, 348; his Message of 1806, 348, 349; proposes a national university, 348, 349; his view of the Constitution, 349; demands the outlawing of the slave trade, 353, 354; tortured by sick headaches, 356, 364; refuses to submit Monroe and Pinkney's treaty to the Senate, 359, 360; enters his last year of office with little to worry him politically, 361; his religion attacked and defended, 362; unsuccessful attempt to alienate Gallatin from him, 364, 365; refuses Burr a foreign mission, 373; warned of Burr's treasonous plot but slow to believe in it, 384; takes action against Burr, 385–88; places the facts before Congress, 394–96; charged with persecution of Burr, 398–400; subpœnaed for the Burr trial, he sends a dignified yet devastating reply to Justice Marshall, 409, 410; convinced of Burr's guilt, 414; sends Lewis and Clarke on their expedition to the Pacific, 426; calls the Cabinet after the *Chesapeake* outrage, 428–30; his spirited Message on the situation, 437, 438; his Embargo Message, 440, 441; accused by the Federalists of taking orders from Napoleon, 448; ably defended in Congress, 448, 449; burned in effigy, 450; interested in Fulton's torpedo, 451; regarded the Embargo as the only alternative to war, 452–54; hatred of war, 452; convinced of the support of the Southern and Middle States, 454, 455; his system of licensing merchants for the importation of food, 459, 460; his proclamation against the

534

turn from France, 140, 141; his pamphlets 'The Crisis' and 'Common Sense,' 140–43; his imprisonment by Robespierre, escape from the guillotine, and other experiences in France, 140, 141; his 'Age of Reason,' 141, 142; attacked by the Federalists as a 'battered bellwether of Jacobinism and infidelity,' 141, 142, 216; entertained in Washington, 142, 143

Pamphlets, political, 71

Paris, Burr in, 425

Parsons, Theophilus, the elder, 294, 432; sympathetic with the idea of disunion, but unconvinced of its practicability, 239, 240

Parsons, Theophilus, Jr., 294

Parton, James, his *Life and Times of Aaron Burr* cited, 251

Patterson, Elizabeth, 26–28, 216

Payne, Ann, 5; and Gilbert Stuart, 29

Payne, George H., his *History of Journalism in the United States* cited, 77

Peabody, Oliver, 242 n.

Pederson, Peter, 7, 14

Pennsylvania, factional fight among Jeffersonians in, 298

Pensacola, Fla., 377

'Pentworth,' John Taylor's estate, 19

Perit, Jefferson's steward, 47

Peters, Richard, 236

Peyster, F. de, his *Biographical Sketch of Robert R. Livingston. See* Livingston, Robert R.

Philadelphia, its manufactures in 1808, 471

Philadelphia Gazette, on the Louisiana situation, 175; cited, 316

Philadelphia Manufacturing Society, 471

Philadelphia Price Current and Commercial Advertiser, 471

'Philo Veritas,' 433

Pichon, Louis André, French Chargé d'Affaires at Washington, 14, 39, 209; and Jerome Bonaparte's marriage, 26, 27

Pichon, Mme. Louis André, 7, 14

Pickering, Judge John, 270, 271

Pickering, Timothy, 1, 2, 9, 12, 13, 54, 60, 291, 330, 394, 432, 438, 487, 500; Life by Upham cited, 2, 12, 98, 103, 143, 213, 383, 445, 446, 456; Senator from Massachusetts, 215; his ejection from John Adams's Cabinet, 215; organizing a conspiracy to separate New England from the Union, 220, 223, 229, 230, 234–36; attacks the Louisiana purchase in the Senate, 220; Breckinridge replies to, 222; votes against the purchase, 223; his letters advocating disunion, 235–40; on the case against Judge Pickering, 271; on Judge Samuel Chase, 280; on Martin's defense of Chase, 287; on Randolph's Yazoo speeches, 305, 306 and n.; on Jefferson's aloofness from Democratic clashes, 306; on rumors of Burr's plot, 383; leads the Federalists in

the Senate, 436, 439; his dealings with Rose, the British envoy, 443–45, 473; father of the Logan law, 445; his pamphlet urging nullification of the Embargo, 445–47; 'the modern Cincinnatus,' 450; praise and denunciation of, 455, 456; circulates anti-Embargo petitions and organizes resistance to the Embargo, 461, 463; in the campaign of 1808, 489

Pierce, John, 351

Pike, Capt. Zebulon M., 25, 451

Pinckney, Charles, 186, 454, 472; an ardent spoilsman, 78; as Minister to Spain, 157, 158, 309, 310; goes home to become Governor of South Carolina, 311

Pinckney, Charles Cotesworth, 144, 162; nominated for President by the Federalists, 258; his personality and career, 258; tours Massachusetts, 260; receives an honorary degree from Harvard, 260; renominated for President, 487

Pinkney, William, 349, 481; sent to London to assist Monroe, 343; joins Monroe, 351; his personality, 351; joins Monroe in recommending postponement of operation of Non-Importation Act, 353; unsatisfactory result of his mission, 356–58

Pitt, William, 353, 373; not a friend of American democracy, 328; his policy aimed against the American merchant marine, 329; dies, 331

Pittsburgh, 368

Pittsfield Sun, 486

Plumer, William, 46, 231; on Jefferson's personal appearance, 32; on Thomas Paine, 143; in the Louisiana debate, 179, 180; considers the Louisiana purchase a cause for secession, 213; in the disunion conspiracy of 1803–04, 233–35, 241, 242; Federalists organized under his leadership, 261; his attitude in the Chase case, 280, 288; moving toward Jeffersonianism, 295; on Randolph, 337; his favorable opinion of Jefferson, 343; his estimate of the young Clay, 355; enlists as a Democrat, 362; records Burr's popularity in Federalist circles, 412; not an unbiased observer, 412, 413

Plumer, William, Jr., his *Life of William Plumer* cited, 32, 46, 47, 96, 99, 143, 150, 163, 172, 213, 232, 235, 241, 242, 261, 280, 295, 337, 343, 355, 356, 373

Plumer manuscripts, cited, 98

Plymouth, Mass., 462

Poindexter, George, intermediary in Burr's negotiations for surrender, 392–94

Poplar Forest, 507

Preble, Capt. Edward, 375, 386

Premium Society of Philadelphia Manufacturers, 471

Prevost, Judge John Bartow, 391

Priestley, Joseph, 53

Prince, William, 415 n.

INDEX

535

Privateering, British, 330, 391
Purcell, Richard J., his *Connecticut in Transit* cited, 152, 153, 262, 297, 500
Purviance, Samuel D., M.C. from North Carolina, 12

Quincy, Edmund, his *Life of Josiah Quincy.* See Quincy, Josiah
Quincy, Josiah, 330 n., 341, 342, 354 n., 394, 456; his *Life* cited, 2, 14, 233, 295, 355, 360, 437, 441, 450, 493, 495–97, 499, 501; social life in Washington, 13, 14; on John Randolph's voice, 102; on Randolph's conversation, 112; his call on Jefferson one of ceremony, 295; attacks the Administration on the Miranda affair, 322, 323; declares Jefferson's refusal to submit the Monroe treaty absurd and impertinent, 360; his opinion of Varnum, 436; his estimate of political opponents valueless, 436; writes reassuringly to his wife, 437; his parliamentary abusiveness, 437; his queue, 437; attacks the Government policy in the *Chesapeake* matter, 438, 439; a dangerous opponent, 438; and the Gardenier-Campbell duel, 450; determined to force repeal of the Embargo Act, 493, 494; speaks against the Embargo in Congress, 494, 495; prefers abuse to fighting, 496, 497; opposes raising an army, 496; his unsuccessful filibuster, 497; activities in and out of Congress against Jefferson and the Embargo, 499–501
Quincy, Mrs. Josiah, 13, 14

Randall, H. S., his *Life of Thomas Jefferson* cited, 36, 39, 45, 413
Randolph, Ann, 5
Randolph, Edmund, John Randolph on, 104; one of the defense lawyers in Burr's trial, 404, 408
Randolph, John, 20, 127, 376, 481; a genius, 95; portrait of, 99–113; his leadership in Congress, 110–12; praises Giles's speech on repeal of the Judiciary Act, 130; his speech on repeal, 132, 133; supports Jefferson on the Louisiana crisis, 164, 165; pays a tribute to Samuel Adams, 215; his quarrel with a colleague over the Yazoo frauds, 216; his speeches in the House for the Louisiana purchase, 217–19; refrains from voting on the bill for the government of Louisiana, 225; in the discussion of Samuel Chase's case, 277; heads the managers in the impeachment of Judge Chase, 277, 280; his conduct of the case, 280–84, 286–91; illness during the Chase impeachment trial, 287, 288; regrets Jefferson's determination to retire, 298; partiality for Monroe, 298, 299; his insurgency, 299; happier in opposition than as leader of a majority, 299, 302; violently opposes compromise in the Yazoo matter, 302–06;

quarrel with Thomas Mann Randolph, 307, 308; arrogantly refuses to vote for the purchase of Florida, 315; his ' Decius' letters, 315 n., 324, 339; openly attacks the Administration on the Florida purchase matter, 324–27; introduces an anti-Spanish measure in the House, 324; his resolution defeated, he is left in an isolated situation, 326, 327; he and his committee ignore Jefferson's Message on relations with England and the committee is discharged, 331, 332; demands consideration of his constitutional amendment on the removal of judges, 332; opposes Gregg's resolution and assails Jefferson, 333–37, 341, 342; on the Non-Importation Act, 342; urges presidential aspirations on Monroe, 343; Jefferson seeks to offset his influence on Monroe, 344; resolutions introduced by Sloan eliminate him as leader in the House, 344, 345; grows mild in opposition, 354; calls for facts and papers of Burr's conspiracy, 394, 398; foreman of the jury to try Burr, 403, 411; loses his power in the House, 436; on J. B. Varnum, 436; in the *Chesapeake* crisis, 439–41; favors an embargo but votes against it, 440, 441; declines a duel with Gen. Wilkinson, 451; his championship of Monroe injures the latter, 479, 484–86
Randolph, Martha, Jefferson's elder daughter, 34, 35; her rebuff of Mrs. Merry, 45
Randolph, Nancy, 109
Randolph, Sarah N., her *Domestic Life of Thomas Jefferson* cited, 31, 33, 34, 36, 150, 155, 161, 217, 261, 475, 480, 504–09
Randolph, Thomas Mann, his controversy with John Randolph, 307, 308; letter from Jefferson, 504
Rea, John, 104
Red River, 381, 425
Reeve, Judge Tapping, and the disunion plan, 240, 241
Religion, Jefferson and, 145; in Connecticut, 152
Removals. See Civil service
Rensselaer. See Van Rensselaer, Stephen
Repertory, 496
Revenge, U.S.S., 430, 468
Rhode Island, its legislature votes a complimentary address to Jefferson, 72; Fisher Ames on, 155
Richmond, the ship, 187
Richmond, Va., 397; Burr's trial in, 398–423; scene of a struggle between the supporters of Madison and those of Monroe, 484
Richmond Enquirer, 104, 308, 327; founded to support Jefferson's policies, 259; cited, 315; denounces Marshall's conduct in attending a dinner given to Burr, 402; attacks Marshall's conduct in Burr's trial, 423; 'Portrait of the Chief Justice' in, 423

INDEX

537

SENTRY EDITIONS

(continued on next page)